Practical
Food & Beverage
Cost Control

Second Edition

Join us on the web at

www.hospitality-tourism.delmar.com

Dedication

To Emma, with love

Contents

PART ONE   PURCHASING STANDARDS

Chapter 3   **Introduction to Purchasing** **52**

Chapter 4   **Purchase Specifications** **65**

PART THREE   COST CONTROL STANDARDS

Chapter 14

Staff Planning and Labor Cost Control 278

Foreword

This book brings together the people and steps necessary to make the food and beverage operation of a hotel or stand-alone restaurant a success. It explains in detail, with examples, the process of forecasting, budgeting, menu planning, purchasing, and inventory controls. All of these processes are needed for a profitable outcome.

Many hotels and restaurants do not have a knowledgeable cost controller; they depend on the intuition of many, and believe increased revenues are the only way to increase profit. While this is one way to increase profit, it is not the only way. The same amount saved by a cost control is a 100 percent increase to the bottom line.

With this book, a food and beverage operation with limited management staff will have all the tools needed to control and increase profits.

This book not only emphasizes the checks and balances necessary to achieve and continue to improve profitability, but also stresses the importance of the guests' (customers') perceived value and satisfaction.

Cost control isn't simple; it takes teamwork. Controlling costs in all areas is always the objective, but the truth of the matter is, while you can cut costs in payroll, you must not jeopardize service. Customers will pay more for a meal with great service, and will recommend and return.

The cost of the food and beverage, the proper storage for less waste, and proper menu pricing will lead to a better bottom line. This book takes you through all the procedures to make this happen.

Fran Rizzo,
Hotel and Restaurant Financial Consultant

Preface

This book is designed to share successful cost management strategies and procedures with students and managers who wish to update or renew their cost control knowledge. It includes details on how to plan, assess, and interpret the many cost control aspects of food and beverage operations. It also presents vital financial information so you can learn to meet your company's profit *and* expense objectives. We direct these teachings toward "the manager;" but the truth is that everyone in restaurant management must work together toward the twin financial goals of *minimizing expenses* and *maximizing profit*. You may be a manager, purchaser, controller, analyst, executive chef, food and beverage director, or owner; the common threads of expenses and profits run through all of these roles. The challenge is that your goals may, at times, conflict. This book teaches you how to systematically analyze your operations and determine the best course of action.

This book is markedly distinct from other food and beverage cost control texts, with many inclusions and helpful forms you can use in your business. Some of the important differences are listed here:

- **The author is a full-time practicing controller and a part-time college instructor.** Cost-effective practices are emphasized, and different and improved control techniques are offered for various environments.

- **This is not a strict "theory" book.** The book illustrates, step by step, how to isolate, identify and correct performance, and how to improve your financial position.

- **This book covers critical topics that are often ignored.** Profit improvement, "make or buy" decisions, inventory control tools, and forecasting are included and detailed.

- **This book provides practical information on departmental interaction to help you do your job.** This book addresses the relationships of the controller ("back of the house") with the restaurant manager ("front of the house") and the purchasing department, which are all too often adversarial. Learning to coordinate the efforts of these three areas will have the maximum impact on cost and profitability.

- **This book isolates practical causes and offers solutions.** Many abnormal or changing situations in operational and financial activities require management's action. Part of your job will be to identify these situations quickly and accurately, and respond appropriately.

- **This book highlights how changes in operational statistics affect the company.** The text provides a basis for investigating and interpreting specific changes in data relationships. This information could indicate possible problem situations or undesirable trends. Identifying such trends is crucial to your company's success.

- **This book shows how to view markets and customers.** Such viewpoints will necessarily influence your cost of goods, operational strategies, and pricing.

- **This book contains practical suggestions.** It provides strategies for improving management decision-making in the areas of profitability, financial stability, and staffing issues.

- **This book helps you measure your success**. You will find tools to evaluate your operation, insight into what your numbers mean, practical means to analyze your data, and suggested actions to take.

With today's emphasis on reducing cost, improving quality, and maximizing service, combined with the consumer's ever-increasing quest for value, the information in this book becomes increasingly important. Each chapter in the book provides specific information needed to avoid pitfalls and focus on improving your bottom line. Many examples are included to demonstrate theories and concepts in practice.

It is my hope that by providing an understanding of the principles and practices of food and beverage cost control and profit improvement, *Practical Food and Beverage Cost Control* can capture the discipline's rigor, intellectual richness, challenges, and dynamism for all its readers.

Clement Ojugo

Acknowledgments

A book such as *Practical Food and Beverage Cost Control* is not possible without the synergistic contribution of many people. I am grateful to Keri Culver for her editorial and structural input throughout the text.

Appreciation also goes to the following organizations: Sysco, Costa Fruit and Produce, American Hotel and Motel Association, Software Creation, National Restaurant Association, National Association of Purchasing Management, The Beer Institute and the National Institute on Alcohol Abuse and Alcoholism (NIAAA) for their invaluable knowledge and information on the impact our industry can have both positive and negative.

I wish to express my gratitude to the following industry leaders and colleagues for their endless review of pages and suggestions:

Mary Nelson, Monterey Peninsula College
John Lozano, Asilomar Conference Grounds
Don St. Hilaire, California State University, Pomona
Colin Moody, Monterey Peninsula Country Club
Robert Fried, Author of A Marketing Plan for Life
Paul Lee, Monterey Peninsula College
Amy Spowart, Financial Consultant
Dwight Staffelbach, Marketing Consultant
Lois Nelson, California State Park
Vivian Garcia, Asilomar Conference Ground
Hans Steineger, Delaware North Company

The following people provided me and Delmar Cengage Learning with constructive comments by acting as content reviewers:

Marcel R. Escoffier
Florida International University
North Miami, Florida

Keith H. Mandabach Ed. D
New Mexico State University
Las Cruces, New Mexico

Woojay Poynter
Western Culinary Institute
Portland, Oregon

David L. Tucker
Widener University
Chester, Pennsylvania

Many thanks to Delmar Cengage Learning: Jim Gish and Anne Orgren for the acquisition, development and production of this book. Your support and guidance are greatly appreciated.

Finally, to my family for their constant support and perseverance, I love you all.

About the Author

Clement Ojugo obtained his degree in Accountancy from London School of Accountancy and a fellow of The Association of Costing and Executive Accountants. After many years of practical and teaching experience, he has distinguished himself in the Hospitality and Foodservice Industry. A widely published writer, Clement Ojugo has authored several texts and references for the Hospitality and Foodservice Industry. He is well known by members of the Hospitality Industry through his speaking engagements and journal publications. He is currently the Regional Financial Controller for Delaware North Companies, Parks & Resorts. Clement Ojugo taught at San Francisco State University and Monterey Peninsula College.

Introduction

The restaurant business is very unforgiving when cost management and sales are inadequate, as far as profit and loss statements are concerned. Based on the Restaurant Industry Operations Reports 2007 by Deloitte and Touche, the average profit margins are 5.6 percent for full-service operations and 9 percent for limited-service restaurants. Not only is there little room for financial management missteps, but these problems are also compounded by a lack of understanding and business skills in the following areas:

- Operating expenses too high relative to sales

- Menu items not accurately documented and costed

- Excessive inventory items in relation to sales

- Inaccurate financial reporting

- Inadequate cash flow and absence of well organized operating and financial controls.

Therefore, this book attempts to address these common problems from enlightening angles.

Chapter 1 discusses the roles and functions involved in cost control within the unique context of the food and beverage industry. This responsibility bridges departments, coordinating the functions of accounting, purchasing, storage, issuance, production, and even forecasting.

Chapter 2 offers an introduction to menu planning. This chapter also discusses the importance of front-of-the-house staff in maximizing your sales, and how you can train them to do so. This introduction sets the stage for the next four chapters about Purchasing Standards: Introduction to Purchasing (Chapter 3) Purchase Specifications (Chapter 4), Pricing and Vendors (Chapter 5), and Purchasing Controls (Chapter 6). These four chapters are your start-to-finish guide to sound buying practices, and offer a systematic approach to purchasing. This approach involves identifying and resolving common problems, while also optimizing money-saving opportunities.

The book next turns its focus to beverage standards. Chapter 7 introduces the subject and explains the great variations in beverage manufacturing and pricing. Chapter 8 outlines procedures used to monitor these expensive but stable products to maximize their utilization. In Chapter 9, you will learn about the controls necessary with beverage sales, how to monitor variance between sales and inventory, and what kinds of service procedures maximize your sales.

Chapter 10, Planning for Food Profit and Controls, addresses potential costing techniques and controls, including targeted ideal cost and weighing potential versus actual costs. This chapter also introduces the third part of the book, which deals with controls and calculations you will need to maintain profitability.

Continuing on this theme, Chapter 11 deals with monthly inventory and monthly food cost controls, with detailed procedures for inventory management and costing. This chapter also talks about inventory factors such as employee meals, breakage, spillage, spoilage, promotional expenses, steward sales, and other important issues you will need to control.

Chapter 12 deals with revenue and cash handling control procedures, with sections on what controls are required in outlets and on how to set up your documentation. These steps are vital to any operation's safe maintenance of cash flow. Food and beverage outlets are especially vulnerable to theft and loss in the cash handling process; this book gives you the exact procedures necessary for safety.

Hotels and restaurants now need to focus more than ever on quality service, product variety, and quality. Chapter 13, Menu Analysis and Planning for Sales, discusses menu planning and design as the first step in ensuring profitability and popularity.

This book also includes a far-reaching discussion of staff planning, including how to manage both employee morale *and* labor cost, in Chapter 14. This is an area that requires great creativity and foresight: The success of any operation is dependent on staff training and enthusiasm.

In Chapter 15 you will learn to analyze the relationship between cost, volume, and profit (CVP), and the marginal contribution break-even point(MCB), two functions that will guide your decision making in a precise and calculable way. A variety of options are offered to optimize the decision-making process.

Chapter 16 is about budgeting and controls. Management incentive, as it relates to return on investment (ROI), is covered at length.

The Appendix includes useful checklists, forms, and procedural data for maintaining the viability of cost control in your operation. There is an especially helpful section on weights and measures. You will find that this section is one that you turn to frequently.

SUPPLEMENTS

Online Companion

The tables and forms from "Practical Food & Beverage Cost Control," second edition, may be accessed online at www.delmarlearning.com/companions.

Online Instructor Resources

Instructor resources available online with adoption of this text include:

- A fully updated instructor's manual

- New to this edition: PowerPoint® lecture slides

- New to this edition: A computerized test bank in ExamView® format

NEW TO THE SECOND EDITION OF PRACTICAL FOOD AND BEVERAGE COST CONTROL

Overall

- The new "In Practice" feature opens with a real-world example for students, allowing them to see how the chapter's information and insights apply to the world outside the classroom.

- New In Business boxes provide a glimpse into how real businesses use cost control concepts discussed within the chapter.

- New Quiz boxes and Discussion Exercises are designed to make studying productive and hassle free. It is important for the students to be engaged from start to finish and not to wait until the end-of-chapter questions.

- Case studies have been added to this edition.

- A glossary of terms has been added to the end of each chapter.

Chapter 1: Overview of the Industry and the Manager's Role

- Rewritten with the objective of providing clarity regarding the role of the manager.

- Updated statistics to reflect industry trends for decision-making processes.

- Introduced key performance indicators (KPI) for measuring work and business performance.

- Introduced the Sea Breeze Hotel (SBH)—a case of struggling hotel restaurant operation—to help students relate concepts to the decisions made by working managers.

Chapter 2: Menu Development

- New chapter with the following learning objectives:

- Summarize the importance of understanding customer base when writing a menu.

- Describe how menu selection affects other aspects of the operation.

- Describe the three menu types and their impact on cost control.

- Employ principles of good menu design.

- Understand the concept of barter as it applies to the industry.

Chapter 3: Introduction to Purchasing

- Extensively rewritten to improve the flow and simplify the presentation for students. Introduced EDI and XML technology and why it is vital in today's purchasing practices.

Chapter 4: Purchase Specifications

- Added in-depth coverage of product specification beyond the scope of first edition. The following concepts were introduced as well: yield testing, butcher testing, raw food testing, canned food test/can-cutting testing, staple dry food testing, "blind" taste testing, par levels, purchase orders, inventory on hand, lead time, cost of acquisition, volume pricing, vendor minimum order quantity, safety stock, and perishable and non-perishable products.

Chapter 5: Price and the Vendor

- A new chapter with the the following learning objectives:

- Know how to select a vendor and understand the meaning of price as it relates to purchasing.

- Prepare a market basket report and use a price index to analyze the impact of price and consumption on cost.

- Distinguish between price and value and understand the following types of pricing in purchasing: Firm price, contract price, cost plus price, hedging, consignment purchasing and pricing, and standing order contracts.

Chapter 6: Purchasing Controls

- New, recent examples have been introduced for the following topics:

- Understand how to audit purchasing functions.

- Identify methods of spotting quality problems in receiving.

- Perform proper receiving procedures, using an understanding of tare weight.

Chapter 7: Introduction to Beverages

- Includes a new section on beverage history; updated consumption statistics reflect behavior trends. This provides a contemporary viewpoint on major changes in market preferences and recent developments in the industry.

Chapter 8: Beverage Procedures, from Start to Finish

- Technical discussions have been simplified, material has been reordered from the first edition, and the entire chapter has been carefully retuned to make teaching and learning easier.

Chapter 9: Beverage Controls and Service Procedures

- Introduced a new case regarding secret shoppers as they relate to customer service and business profit objectives. The following new concepts were introduced: bar par stock, color-coded outlet stickers or stamps, waste, breakage, spoilage, and spillage.

Chapter 10: Planning for Food Profit and Controls

- A new case has been introduced to bring real world examples to the classroom. Formulas have been simplified for easy understanding.

Chapter 11: Monthly Physical Inventory and Monthly Food Cost Calculations

- This was Chapter 5 from the first edition. New additions include methods for performing inventory-taking procedures for food and beverage products and cash flow.

Chapter 12: Revenue and Cash Handling Control

- This is an enhanced version of Chapter 7 from the first edition. The following new concepts were introduced:

- Theft in the workplace and procedures to prevent it.

- The economic impact of theft and fraud

Chapter 13: Menu Analysis and Planning for Sales

- Introduced new materials on applying the concept of menu pricing, knowing what causes menu item demand to falter, and devising a response. Incorporated updated statistics and trends for menu profitability and popularity.

Chapter 14: Staff Planning and Labor Cost Control

- This isChapter 8 from the first edition, rewritten with the following new learning objectives:

- Understand fair hiring practices and the differences between salary and wages.

- Apply FLSA rules to payroll processes.

- Calculate overtime pay for hourly employees.

- Use governmental and voluntary deductions in payroll processes.

- Use staff planning to manage employee morale and labor costs.

- Schedule your staff wisely to maximize productivity.

- Create a staffing guide and staffing standards.

- Forecast business volume for adequate staffing.

- Conduct a productivity analysis of sales volume versus labor hours.

- Perform a full-time equivalent (FTE) study.

Chapter 15: Analyzing Cost-Volume-Profit (CVP) Relationships and Marginal Contribution Break-Even (MCB)

- This is Chapter 9 from the first edition, rewritten with the objectives of providing clarity and adding the following topics:

- Sunk cost

- Advantages and disadvantages of break-even analysis

- Discounted value

- Compounded interest

- Discount rate

Chapter 16: Budgeting and Manager ROI

- A new chapter with the following learning objectives:

- Understand both forecasting and budgeting in some depth and utilize their techniques.

- Apply the techniques used for budgeting operational expenses and capital expenditures.

- Explain and utilize the terms *assets* and *liabilities*.

- Apply current ratio and working capital tests to financial results.

- Know how to measure how well the company is doing financially through return on investment (ROI).

With the advent of increasing competition and the declining level of individual disposable income, customers' perception of value is more important than ever. This book reflects this growing influence on your profitability. Understanding the price and value philosophies with which customers make their decisions is the cornerstone to any successful business.

As seafarers looked to the lighthouse for direction along an unfamiliar shore, so too can *Practical Food and Beverage Cost Control* act as a crucial compass for students and managers seeking to master the challenge of running a successful foodservice operation.

I hope you enjoy reading this book as much as I have enjoyed writing it!

Overview of the Industry and the Manager's Role

CHAPTER 1

Learning Objectives

After reading this chapter, you should be able to:

- discuss and understand the general profile of the food and beverage industry;

- understand the variety of cost control measures in the hospitality industry;

- describe the manager's role;

- interpret an income statement;

- explain the differences between budgeting and forecasting, and understand the techniques used for each.

OVERVIEW

The food and beverage industry is incredibly diverse. Think of the differences between a four-star restaurant and a hot dog stand at a football stadium. Or compare a mom-and-pop deli to a chain of upscale urban eateries. These are differences of scale, ambience, menu, and clientele—but all these businesses sell food and beverages to a target market they hope will be satisfied, and they all hope to be profitable. Those who work in the industry are constantly seeking to meet these two goals. Often their most valuable role is controlling costs, and that's what you will learn about in this book. You might be an owner, a manager, a purchaser, or another employee in your company, but whatever your title, if you can decrease costs and increase profit, you will succeed. This book will succeed when you find in it the tools and methods to help you achieve these two goals: profitability and customer satisfaction.

This chapter provides an overview of the nature and scope of the food and beverage industry. In order to understand how to account for costs, and how to control them, several important functions of hospitality accounting are introduced here, including interdepartmental communication, expense control, revenue, and forecasting. We will briefly talk about each of these functions, including their challenges and procedures, in this chapter. While most of these concepts are detailed in later chapters, this introductory chapter builds your understanding of these key concepts and how they interrelate.

The Hospitality Industry at a Glance

In the United States, tourism is the cornerstone of the hospitality industry. Tourism is also the third-largest retail industry, behind automotive sales and food stores. Travel and tourism comprise the nation's largest services export industry and one of its largest employers. In fact, according to the American Hotel and Lodging Association (AHLA), travel and tourism is one of the top three industries, in terms of employment, in 30 states. The tourism industry includes more than 15 interrelated businesses, from lodging establishments, airlines, and restaurants to cruise lines, car-rental agencies, travel agents, and tour operators. According to AHLA's 2008 report, the effects of tourism on the American economy are considerable:

- Domestic and international travelers in the United States spend an average of $1.5 billion a day, $63 million an hour, $1.1 million a minute, and $17,500 a second.

- Tourism generates $552 billion in sales yearly (excluding spending by international travelers on U.S. airlines).

- The tourism industry pays more than $95 billion in federal, state, and local taxes.

- The industry pays more than $159 billion in travel-related wages and salaries and employs 1.7 million hotel property workers.

- Excluding casinos, limited service properties and timeshares, there are 68,875 hotel and motel properties with 15 or more rooms, totaling more than 3 million rooms in the United States and 11.4 million worldwide. Combined 2007 revenues were $106.8 billion, with an average daily rate of $103.64 per available room. Average occupancy rates were 63.2 percent.

The travel industry overlaps with food and beverage to create a major category for the U.S. gross domestic product. Many of us in the industry work in hotels and resorts that have extensive food service offerings. Travelers and visitors account for 20 to 40 percent of sales at full-service restaurants and 15 percent of quick-service sales, according to the 2007 Annual Report of the American Hotel and Lodging Association.

The Food Service Industry

As part of the global hospitality network, the food service industry is considered the foundation of many successful interrelated industries and an integral part of the U.S. economy. According to estimates by the National Restaurant Association (NRA), on a typical day in 2008, the food service industry posted sales of $1.53 billion, for a yearlong total of $558.3 billion. Industry researchers predict that sales will increase 4.4 percent over the prior year, which would constitute more than 4 percent of the U.S. gross domestic product. In addition, for every dollar a consumer spends in a restaurant, another $2.34 is spent in allied restaurant industry sales, such as agriculture, transportation, wholesale trade, and manufacturing, for an overall impact of $1.5 trillion in 2008. The impact of the industry is enormous and growing. Figure 1-1 shows how food service sales have risen dramatically since 1970.

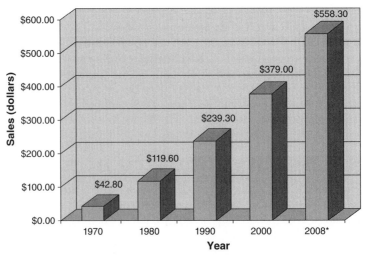

Figure 1-1 Food and Drink Sales. *Courtesy of "Restaurant Industry Operations Report 2007/2008" National Restaurant Association/Deloitte*

These figures represent a progressive trend. In the last year, 48 percent of every dollar Americans spent on food was spent away from home, compared to only 25 percent in 1955. The average annual household expenditure for food away from home in 2008 was $2,676, or $1,070 per person.

More than 70 billion meals and snacks are eaten in restaurants, schools, and work cafeterias each year. Almost half of all adults (47 percent) were restaurant patrons on a typical day during 2008. More than 65 percent of restaurant customers agree that food served at their favorite restaurant provides flavor and taste sensations that they cannot easily duplicate at home.

There were approximately 945,000 locations offering food service in the United States by the end of 2008, an increase of over 85 percent since 1972. The bulk of the industry consists of commercial eating places. Figure 1-2 breaks down restaurant industry sales by category. Figure 1-3 shows the relative number of the various restaurant location types.

It is said that restaurants are the number-one private sector employer. The industry employs around 9 percent of workers in the United States, which translates to over 13.1 million people. More than 40 percent of all adults have worked in the restaurant industry at some time during their lives. Total annual wages and benefits equal $35 billion for full-service restaurants and $29 billion for limited-service (fast-food) establishments. The term *full-service restaurant* refers to more formal, complete table-service operations, while limited-service restaurants are those that are less formal, such as fast-food and take-out eateries. Eating and drinking establishments are extremely labor-intensive; sales per **full-time equivalent (FTE)** were $61,344 in 2006, which is notably lower than other industries. The term *FTE* refers to a measurement equal to one staff person working a full-time work schedule for one year. It is also a way to

full time equivalent (FTE) A way to measure worker productivity in a work schedule.

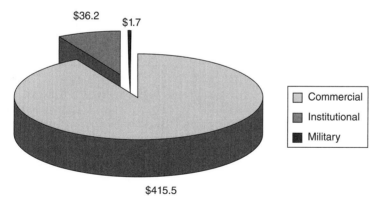

Figure 1-2 Restaurant Industry Sales

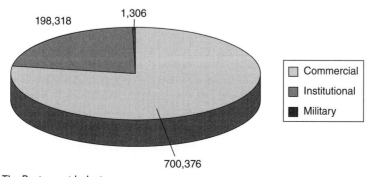

Figure 1-3 The Restaurant Industry

measure an employee's productivity in a project. In this case, a standard full-time workweek of 40 hours is equivalent to 2,080 hours a year (40 hours per week multiplied by 52 weeks).

Restaurants also provide a path to management opportunity: Approximately nine out of ten salaried employees in table-service restaurants started out as hourly employees. Of the 1.4 million managers of food service and lodging establishments in 2008, a higher percentage were of minority origin than in any other industry, and 60 percent have annual incomes higher than $50,000. The magnitude of the food and beverage industry as a whole represents not only incredible opportunity, but also intense competitive challenges. So it is not surprising that many operators (27 percent) say maintaining customer loyalty is a major challenge in 2008, according to an NRA survey. The NRA's annual reports identify other challenges, such as high utility-gas costs, employee retention difficulties, and high insurance costs. The NRA report points out the following trends:

- **Alternative-source ingredients** such as local produce, organics, sustainable seafood, and grass-fed or free-range items are ranking high in full-service restaurants. More than 86 percent of operators said they serve locally sourced items (compared with about three of five family-dining and casual-dining operators). A majority of operators across all full service segments believe locally sourced items will become more popular in the future as opposed to nationally branded item such as Craft or Sysco foods.

- **Specialty alcohol** such as craft beer, signature cocktails, and organic wines are among the top 20 restaurant trends. The NRA operator surveys show that full service restaurants are shaking up their beverage and alcohol options with new offerings.

- **Healthful options.** According to the NRA research, three of four adults—and about the same percentage of teenagers—say they are trying to eat more healthfully in restaurants today. More than eight out of 10 customers say that they see more "healthy" options on restaurant menus than they did two years ago. Nearly one in four adults has used the Internet to research nutrition information for restaurant foods. Quick service operators such as Carl's Jr. and McDonald's said "healthy alternatives" are the number two trend for their segment in 2008.

- **Technology.** Full-service operators continue to attract patrons with improved in-restaurant technology such as wireless Internet access. Though not yet as prevalent, electronic ordering and payment systems at the table will become more popular in the future.

- **Green practices.** Energy conservation practices among restaurants are on the rise. A majority of restaurant operators indicate that they are actively working to cut energy costs.

- **Food safety and security** will continue to be a top public policy issue for the industry into the future.

The Current Outlook for the Food Service Industry

The Consumer Price Index (CPI) for all food increased 4.0 percent between 2006 and 2007—the highest annual increase since 1990. Food-at-home prices, led by eggs, dairy, and poultry, increased 4.2 percent, while food-away-from-home prices rose 3.6 percent in 2007. In 2008, the all-food CPI is projected to increase another 4.5 to 5.5 percent, according to the United States Department of Agriculture (USDA), as retailers continue to pass on higher commodity and energy costs to consumers in the form of higher retail prices.

The main factors behind higher food commodity costs include stronger global demand for food, increased U.S. agricultural exports resulting from stronger demand and a weaker dollar, weather-related production problems in some areas of the world, and the increased use of some food commodities, such as corn, for biofuel uses.

However, prices on foods to eat at home are forecasted to increase 5.0 to 6.0 percent, while prices for food to be eaten away from home are forecast to increase 3.5 to 4.5 percent in 2008. With economic concerns influencing customers' decisions, it is more important than ever to control food and beverage costs in dining establishments. Quality cost control is the main focus of this book.

The Role of the Food and Beverage Manager

In the burgeoning food service industry, the role of the food and beverage manager is to carry out four major activities—communication, cost control, revenue enhancement, and forecasting—to achieve desired financial results for his or her company. **Communication** is the ongoing process of exchanging information between different departments and people both within and outside an organization. **Costs,** also referred to as expenses, describes the sum of all money paid out for goods and services during a given period of time; these are the goods and services used in obtaining revenue. These costs must be managed and accounted for, a process known as **cost (or expense) control**. To control costs, management institutes procedures and monitors feedback to ensure that all parts of the organization are functioning effectively and moving toward overall company goals. Control also means monitoring income, costs, and the flows of products and services, both those internal to and those external to the food service operation. When costs are greater than revenue, the company experiences loss. On the other hand, when revenue beats costs, the company gains a **profit**. This is one of the tools used to measure the effectiveness of managers.

Revenue, a term often used interchangeably with *income* or *sales*, is money received by a business minus returns and discounts in a given period of time. Enhancing revenue is one of the key topics of this book, and it is one of the most important roles of the food and beverage team. **Forecasting** is the process of estimating or predicting future expenses and revenues.

The level of detail and formality involved in the food and beverage manager's four main roles—communication, cost control, revenue enhancement, and forecasting—will depend on the size of the company and the level of management positions, but these essential job functions exist in any food-service establishment. Figure 1-4 is an example of an organizational chart that might be used in a hotel and resort with a food service operation. The four main roles of a food and beverage manager might be split among several people.

In larger establishments or chain operations, many people may be required to carry out these functions. In a smaller restaurant, perhaps just one or two people—the owner and chef, for example—may take on all these roles. In order to fully realize these roles, you must establish and maintain communication throughout your operation, no matter what its size.

Communication

To be effective, communication must be orderly, regular, and dependable. This is a key task of the food and beverage manager. The example that follows illustrates the role of the manager in communicating between departments and demonstrates one of the key challenges and opportunities facing the industry. We will use guest room minibar services as an example to illustrate the depths of these communication challenges.

What Is Guest Room Minibar Service? A guest room minibar is an in-room food and beverage service that many lodging places provide to their guests in an upscale environment. According

communication The ongoing process of exchanging information between different departments and people in an organization.

costs The sum of all money paid out during a given period of time.

expense control refers to managing expenses according to budget.

profit A positive sum after expenses are deducted from revenue or income of a business as shown in an income statement. The opposite of a loss.

revenue is the same as income or sales.

forecasting Estimating future revenue and expense trends.

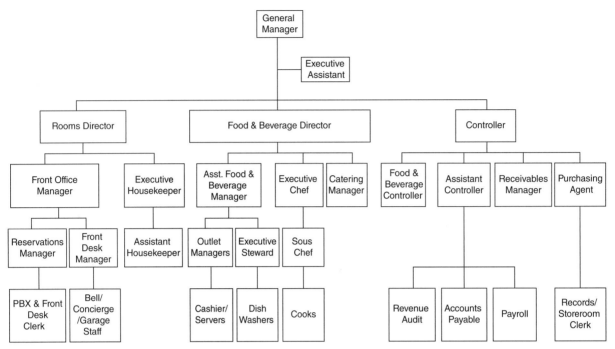

Figure 1-4 Organizational Chart

to the American Hotel and Motel Association, about 35 percent of the 68,875 lodging places in the United States provided guest room minibar services in 2007. For the minibars to be profitable and popular, inventory controls must be in place, the menu item selection must be appropriate, security must be monitored to prevent theft, and the hotel guest must have a positive perception of value and benefit.

The Guest's Perception of Value and Benefits

Most managers make decisions about guest perception of value after compiling and reviewing client surveys over a period of time. Others analyze guest perception based on management experience and judgment. The latter is subjective and thus is prone to individual manager biases and mistakes. However, the objective of any method used is to evaluate the following:

1. *Convenience and effective pricing* to insure guests are provided with an excellent selection of drinks and snacks at the right price and at all times.

2. *Tamper-proof presentation of drinks and snacks* to ensure the quality of the products and to prevent tampered contents. It has been reported in some lodging places that guests refill drink containers with water after use in order to avoid paying for them. As you might imagine, the next guest to find such a beverage is likely to be very dissatisfied.

3. *Accurate and timely posting of guest charges* to prevent the costs of late billing and accounting write-offs when guests dispute their charges. The latter can occur if the minibar inventory was not up to standard before the guest checked in. Late checkouts and DO NOT DISTURB signs can prevent accurate and timely inventory monitoring.

(continues)

(*continued*)

4. *Prompt billing* to ensure the guest is not waiting at the front desk to determine final charge amounts.
5. *Noise reduction and guest privacy* to ensure the system (refrigerator) is noise-free and that there is a minimum of intrusion on guest privacy for restocking.

Some lodging companies simply incorporate a dollar amount into the room rate to cover minibar usage. This amount depends on the level and value of stock items in the guest minibar. This can be a good solution to disputed charges but might raise the room rate significantly, and some guests may decide to stay elsewhere.

Inventory Controls. The manager must be able to account for minibar stock and sales. To do so, sales records must be reconciled with replacement requisitions both to the guest rooms and from the storeroom. Other issues that must be evaluated include adequate stock levels, prevention of spoilage, theft, and labor costs for restocking and stock rotation. Inventory control is covered in more detail in Chapter 11.

Menu Analysis. The objective here is to evaluate sales volume and profitability of stock items. Inventory stock items should be evaluated to determine profitability and popularity with the guests. Menu analysis should be conducted periodically to address issues of slow-moving stock and discontinued stock items. Chapter 13 goes into more detail on this topic.

Security and Preventing Theft. There are two issues here: compliance with laws governing alcohol sales and consumption, and unauthorized minibar access. With the former, you must find an acceptable, legal way to keep minors out of the minibars. Your local or state government should be able to tell you what steps you must take to comply. The latter issue is for you to manage with your own staff. Specialized locks are available to reveal and deter unauthorized entries. Be sure to tell your staff that any theft is grounds for dismissal; stealing even a candy bar is inappropriate in the workplace.

Communication. It is apparent from the above points that a sound dialogue among all departments is required to keep the minibar service running smoothly. Note the following interdepartmental network that must be in place to make minibars work:

1. Housekeeping: to inform the front desk and the minibar attendant of the status of the minibar before releasing the room to the front desk for guest check-in.

2. Bell staff: to inform the front desk if they notice that a guest minibar is unsecured during luggage delivery or guest escort.

3. Front desk: to inform guests about the minibar system and its use.

4. Maintenance: to install reliable and secure locks and to maintain the system for temperature control.

5. Accounting: to answer guest inquiries and track disputed charges and financial reporting.

6. Minibar attendant: to improve guest service, convenience, and satisfaction by choosing products with a minimum of guest disturbance; to follow guest arrival and departure reports for restocking and charging; to contribute to overall profitability; and to present products in a tamper-proof format.

Communication among these different actors is key to making minibar service profitable. Some companies employ automated minibar systems, which can be effective and theft-resistant; one brand name to look for is RoboBar. Companies should review the possible return on investment before making such expenditure, however. Some of the features of an automated system include online, real-time posting of guest charges; minimum level refill options, which add up to labor savings; tamper-proof presentation; automatic stock rotation; electronic locking capabilities; self-diagnostic features that result in prompt resolution of system problems; and a programmable defrost cycle.

As you have seen, communicating about even something as simple as a minibar has numerous challenges. The food and beverage manager—whether this is one person or a team—must face these challenges across a variety of operational components. These challenges increase exponentially as the operation increases in size.

Cost Control

Cost is a term often used interchangeably with *expenses*. Understanding costs and how they behave is critical in the foodservice business. The following example demonstrates the importance of this theme.

Labor Ready, a company based in Tacoma, Washington, was started in 1989 with an investment of about $50,000. The company fills temporary manual labor jobs throughout the United States, Canada, and the United Kingdom. Labor Ready issues over 6 million paychecks each year to more than half a million laborers.

For example, the food vendors at the new Seattle Mariners Safeco Field hire Labor Ready workers to serve soft drinks and food at baseball games. Employers are charged about $11 per hour for these services. Since Labor Ready pays its workers only about $6.50 per hour and offers no fringe benefits and has no national competitors, this business would appear to be a gold mine generating about $4.50 per hour in profit. However, the company must maintain 687 hiring offices, each employing a permanent staff of four to five persons. Those costs, together with payroll taxes, workers' compensation insurance, and other administrative costs, diminish the profit to only about 5%, or a little over 50 cents per hour.

Source: Catie Golding, "Short-Term Work, Long-Term Profits," Washington CEO, January 2000, pp. 10–12

How management controls all costs associated with running a food and beverage business is the focus of this book. In carrying out the control function, managers seek to ensure that the cost control plans and procedures are being followed. Management takes in feedback—from formal periodic reports to anecdotal evidence—to assess whether operations are on track. In a typical food-service operation, this feedback is generally provided by detailed reports of various types. One of these reports, which compares forecasts to actual results, is called a *performance report*. Performance reports suggest where operations are not proceeding as planned and which parts of the organization may require additional attention.

For example, before entering into a contract with the State of California to manage one of the states' premier parks, the concessionaire devises a plan that includes targets for sales volume, profit, and expenses. As the business progresses, periodic reports will be made in which the actual sales volume, profit, and expenses are compared to the targets. If the actual results fall below the targets, top management will be alerted to take appropriate corrective actions. Such action could include changes in procedures, personnel, and equipment.

Many operational factors can affect expenses, including changing labor rates, raw food costs, marketing and advertising costs, or even the type of equipment used. For example, a point of sale (POS) system such as Micros could facilitate all aspects of operation, from guest service to accounting, and result in increased productivity. Similarly, specialized kitchen equipment, such as Alto-Shaam products, can help to reduce cooking losses.

Managers must use make-or-buy decisions (discussed in Chapter 5) to determine whether to buy prepared products to save on labor costs or to purchase less-expensive raw products and prepare them on site. Such decisions will depend on the available in-house resources—labor costs and food costs. In many situations like this you will have to weigh cost factors on a daily basis and determine the optimal action to take.

Take, for example, the experience of Eric Breeze, the owner and general manager of Sea Breeze Hotel (SBH). SBH was a real-estate conglomerate until three years ago, when it was turned into a four-star hotel. Business for SBH is highly seasonal, like that of most hotels and restaurants in the Monterey Bay area. Three years into the business, the hotel still finds it difficult to turn a profit, mainly because its expenses are out of control. In spite of the difficulty, the rooms division reported a profit before taxes of 75 percent; on the other hand, the food and beverage division reported a profit of only 2 percent. The low food and beverage profit was due to high cost. The cost of sales was 38 percent; labor rose to 34 percent; and other expenses (electricity, water, gas, trash, telephone, uniforms, paper supplies, rent, and so on) came to 26 percent.

At a resort like the Sea Breeze, these profit amounts are only part of the larger revenue picture. This is because some departments, such as human resources, security, and accounting, don't generate their own revenue. (In fact, they are sometimes called **non-revenue departments** or **overhead**.) Thus, profits in the revenue-producing departments have to cover the costs of these departments as well. In the organizational chart in Figure 1-4 you can see how these departments relate to one another.

If the rooms division in our example were not so profitable, SBH would be in trouble. "If the food and beverage division were an independent stand-alone restaurant, it would be losing money," said an intern from Monterey Peninsular College. This is because an independent restaurant's **profit and loss statement** has to reflect all expenses involved in supporting the food and beverage revenues, including the expenses of non-revenue departments. Before we continue, it is important to understand the different classifications of costs.

non-revenue departments
Support and service departments that generally do not generate revenue. Examples include Security, Facility, Personnel, Accounting, and Sales.

profit and loss statement
A written document of net revenue and expenses showing the financial gain (profit) or failure (loss) for particular time period.

General Cost Scheme

Costs can be classified in a number of ways, depending on the purpose of the classification. For example, costs are classified one way to determine inventory valuation and cost of goods sold for financial reports, while they are classified in a different way to aid decision-making. A particular cost may be classified in many different ways. This book will teach you the purposes of the various classifications and how to apply them. Common classifications include:

- ***Production costs.*** Costs that are incurred to make a product, like a chicken entrée, are called *production* or *manufacturing costs*. These costs are usually grouped into three main categories: direct materials, direct labor, and production overhead.

- ***Direct materials.*** Direct materials consist of those raw material inputs that become an integral part of a finished product and can be easily traced to it. For example, raw chicken breasts are direct material for making a chicken entrée.

- ***Direct labor.*** Direct labor consists of that portion of labor costs that can be easily traced to a product, such as the cook's hourly payroll cost. Direct labor is sometimes referred to as "touch labor" since it consists of the costs of workers who "touch" the product as it is being made.

- ***Production overhead.*** Production overhead consists of all production costs other than direct materials and direct labor. These costs cannot be easily and conveniently traced to individual products. Examples include equipment maintenance and facility heating costs.

- ***Prime versus conversion costs.*** Prime cost consists of direct materials plus direct labor. Conversion costs consist of direct labor plus production overhead.

- ***Non-production costs.*** Food-service operations incur many other costs in addition to production costs. For financial reporting purposes, most of these other costs are typically classified as selling (marketing) costs and administrative costs. Marketing and administrative costs are incurred in almost all food-service operations.

- ***Marketing Costs.*** These costs include the costs of making sales, taking customer orders, and delivering the product to customers. These costs are also referred to as order-getting and order-filling costs in hotel and resort settings that offer food and beverage services.

- ***Administrative Costs.*** These costs include all executive, organizational, and clerical costs that are not classified as production or marketing costs.

Revenue Enhancement

net income The excess of revenue earned over expenses for the accounting period.

If a business is to succeed or even just survive, revenue must be great enough to pay for the cost of goods sold and other expenses and to provide sufficient **net income**. There are two factors at play here: revenue and expenses. Generally, increasing revenue means consistently delivering the products and services your customer wants at the right price, at the right time. The amounts and trends of revenue are important indicators of a restaurant's progress. Increasing revenue suggests growth, whereas decreasing revenue indicates the possibility of decreased profits and other financial problems in the future. Thus, to detect trends, comparisons are frequently made between net revenues or sales and net incomes for different periods. The *income statement* is a financial statement that summarizes the amount of revenues earned and expenses incurred by a restaurant over a period of time. Managers consider this the most important financial report because its purpose is to measure whether or not the business achieved its primary objective of making an acceptable profit. Take for example Figure 1-5, from the NRA's 2007 annual publication. This report shows the net incomes of restaurant businesses in the United States. For all sales (100 percent), various expenses were deducted from income. The result? Full-service restaurants spend about 96 percent of their gross income on expenses; limited-service restaurants, such as fast-food establishments, spend 93 percent of their gross income on expenses.

Figure 1-5 The Restaurant Industry Dollar. *Courtesy of "Restaurant Industry Operations Report 2007/2008" National Restaurant Association/Deloitte*

The Restaurant Industry Dollar *These Figures are in Percentages*	Full-service Restaurants	Limited Service Restaurants
Where it came from: Food and Beverage Sales	100%	100%
Where it went:		
Cost of Food and Beverage Sales	31.9	30.4
Salaries and Wages, incl. benefits	32.5	28.6
Restaurant Occupancy Costs	6	7
Corporate Overhead	3	4
General and Administrative Expenses	3	2
Other	18	19
Income Before Income Taxes	5.6	9

Two expenses stand out from this independent survey of food service operations across the United States: **food cost** and **labor cost**. Although the percentages vary somewhat from one restaurant to another, the chart offers a benchmark with which to compare profits before tax: 4 percent for full-service restaurants and 7 percent for limited-service restaurants. So, how does the SBH food and beverage division compare? Generally, food and beverage and labor costs are higher in full-service restaurants because both the menus and the skill-set requirements are more complex and costly.

Looking at the Sea Breeze restaurant division's performance, Eric Breeze decided to hire someone with experience in food and beverage management. This could be a chef or any restaurant manager, but it should be someone who has skills to meet the following requirements:

He or she is responsible for developing and implementing policies, procedures, and actions that improve operational efficiency. His or her role will also include maximizing cash flow, increasing profitability, and helping to achieve profit objectives. In carrying out these ongoing tasks, the manager is responsible for analyzing expenses, revenues, and staffing levels, and for implementing cost-effective control procedures. The manager's key job functions lie in cost control, specifically in the following areas:

1. Planning for Labor Productivity Controls (detailed in Chapter 12)

    - developing and communicating plans for improving labor efficiency within budgeted resources and operational goals

    - providing performance feedback to supervisors in order to improve staff scheduling and labor control efforts

    - monitoring productivity statistics to ensure methods are applied and regulated effectively

2. Evaluating and Consulting

    - defining and maintaining historical support documentation that illustrates trends throughout the company

    - analyzing and evaluating deviations from normal and expected business activity, while also exploring causes of deviations

    - identifying and evaluating how internal and external forces affect profitability and operational goals, researching their causes, and recommending appropriate corrective action

    - proposing changes in policy or procedure in the best interests of the operation

3. Financial Reporting

    - gathering and consolidating daily, weekly, monthly, and annual statistics on revenues, expenses, guest counts, and occupancy for reporting purposes

    - preparing and distributing periodic productivity and operating reports

    - verifying billing accuracy and revenue control procedures

4. Protection and Maintenance of Company Assets

    - purchasing and overseeing computer systems (usually point of sale systems and those designed for purchasing, inventory, and menu analysis)

    - ensuring efficient operation and evaluating system effectiveness

    - trouble-shooting minor system problems

    - knowledgeably recommending needed upgrades (in larger companies, staff assistance may be required to accomplish these items)

food cost refers to the cost of food items and ingredients.

labor cost The dollar amount paid to employees.

⑪ **Discussion Topics**

According to the data presented by the NRA, what segment of the restaurant industry achieves the highest percentage profit margin? Why?

⑪ Discussion Topics

Discuss common organizational structures of restaurants, especially the advantages and disadvantages associated with each (from a small local restaurant to a megacorporation). Which functions of the manager are most important?

5. Other Duties

- coordinating and assisting in month-end inventories

- correlating the expense budget with business volumes

- preparing monthly operating reports

- recommending menu pricing

- forecasting costs and revenue contributions

- developing revenue strategies and expense control systems

- establishing and administering the annual profit plan

- developing sanitation standards

- upholding standards of ethical conduct by avoiding actual or apparent conflicts of interest and advising all appropriate parties of any potential conflict

Eric interviewed several promising candidates who matched the role described above before deciding on Myla Thomas. During Myla's job interview, Eric questioned Myla about the steps she would take to implement expense controls.

Eric: As I mentioned earlier, we are going to end 2008 with a very nice profit in the rooms division but not in the food and beverage division. What you may not know is that we had some very big financial problems this year.

Myla: Let me guess. You had problems managing expenses in the first and fourth quarters.

Eric: How did you know?

Myla: Most of your revenues are in the second and third quarter, right?

Eric: Sure, everyone wants to visit Monterey in the spring and summer, but not in the winter months when it is cold.

Myla: So you don't have much revenue in the first and fourth quarter, just like many of your competitors?

Eric: Right.

Myla: And in the second and third quarters, you are busy trying to keep up with heavy demand for rooms and food and beverage services?

Eric: Sure.

Myla: Do you have a system in place for controlling expenses?

Eric: Are you kidding? Of course not. My manager, Robert, has a real-estate background. Hotels, food and beverage, the industry in general is fascinating to him, but he and I are both new to this business.

Myla: Here's my philosophy: Anything I manage I measure. It helps to prevent too much slack and creates disciplined spending. It helps to keep costs in line.

Eric: So what do you think we should do about the situation we have?

Myla: The first step is to work on weekly, monthly, and yearly revenue forecasts that managers can use for staffing and purchasing commitments. The second step is to gain some understanding of inventory management and to develop systems for control. The benefits are lower cost of sales and better control of expenses.

With Eric's full backing, Myla set out to implement cost control initiatives, starting with forecasting and inventory control.

⑪ Notes

This is a good time to invite a food and beverage director to discuss the food service industry as it relates to interdepartmental communication, team effort, cost control challenges, and decision-making processes. Ask the visitor to talk about the process of change in his or her establishment and how it can be difficult at times to make and maintain better controls. Myla, for example, might face resentment in the process of making changes. This vignette is a prelude to many aspects of learning to come.

Cost-effective Initiatives

A key phrase in the food and beverage manager's vocabulary is cost-effective controls. Myla uses cost-effective control alternatives to rectify cost inefficiencies or, in short, to minimize costs while maximizing profits. She believes that controls must be cost-effective and balanced. They must not impact the customer's perceived value; nor may they run afoul of safety laws or lead to financial losses. In controlling costs at the Sea Breeze, Myla will weigh the advantages and disadvantages of alternative methods and select those that will advance the company's objectives. Myla understands that solutions need to be ethical, suitable, and simple to apply. Myla's decisions about cost-effective controls are most crucial in the area of forecasting, inventory management and valuation, and managing the food and beverage **budget**. Each will be covered in greater detail later in this book.

budget A company's plan of operation for a specified period of time that forecasts activity and income, sets limits on expenditures, and establishes any other disposition of company funds.

Forecasting

Business forecasting involves predicting a company's future performance. It is an integral part of the planning process, particularly when the forecast is used as a basis for budget preparation. Myla will also use forecasts to alert management to weaknesses in various areas so that remedial action may be taken in a timely manner to avert the losses SBH is experiencing. The forecasts customarily cover operations issues (such as staffing levels and purchasing) and financial results (such as estimated costs and revenue percentages). Successful forecasting is nothing more than predicting the consequences of a given decision or set of decisions over a specific time period.

There are many approaches to forecasting. In selecting a specific method that suits the circumstances, Myla must consider these important criteria:

- Is the method practical? What resources and data must be available to make it work?

- Are the method's end results useful and reliable?

- Is the method cost-effective?

Forecasting can be accomplished using a statistical method or by estimation; estimation is the most commonly used method in the food service industry. This approach to forecasting, while benefiting from historical data analysis, is relatively subjective. It presumes that the forecaster's experience, knowledge of the restaurant, judgment, and intuition are sufficient bases for developing meaningful and reliable forecasts. To be successful, Myla will need to apply **key performance indicators (KPI)**; this is how companies define and establish a benchmark by which to measure progress. We will be making references to Figure 1-6 (KPI) throughout this chapter.

key performance indicators (KPI) Defined benchmarks by which to measure a company's progress.

In the hotel industry, with both restaurant and catering food and beverage services in one operation, estimated forecasts could be produced using a sales team approach. In this technique, sales and catering managers estimate product sales based on individual client contacts and contracted banquet event orders (BEOs). This estimate then forms the basis for the estimate of room revenues, which in turn is the foundation for food and beverage revenue forecasts and all payroll and other related expenses. This approach is not statistical, but rather integrates judgment factors and experience with situations in which historical data may not be available or applicable. The disadvantage of the sales team approach is that its results are susceptible to the biases of those who are most influential in the group.

A second type of estimation approach is called customer expectation. Here, management collects and judges information from customer surveys to arrive at a forecast; however, this method incorporates customers' expectations of *their* needs and external factors as the basis for forecasting. While it has the advantage of promptly recognizing changes in customer expectations, this technique is difficult to use in markets whose customers are numerous, transient, or not easily identified. For example, surveys conducted by SBH for guest preference of breakfast

Figure 1-6 Food and Beverage KPI

Food and Beverage KPI	Source	Calculation / Definition
Cover count	Point of Sales System (POS)	This is the tally of customers who purchased meals
Cost of Sales	Point of Sales System (POS)	Cost of menu items sold during an accounting period
Cost of Sales percentages	Point of Sales System (POS)	Cost of Goods Sold divided by Sales
Inventory Turns (Current Year vs. Last Year)	Financial System	Cost of Goods Sold divided by Average Inventory
Table Turn	Point of Sales System (POS)	Cover Count divided by Number of Restaurant Seats. It refers to the average number of times during a meal period that a given seat is occupied. This information is used to judge the Effeciency of Seat Capacity
Average Inventory	Purchasing Systems	Beginning plus ending inventory divided by two
Average Age of Inventory	Purchasing Systems	Average inventory divided by cost of sales and multiplied by number of days in a month is used to determine age
Sales Efficiency	POS and Purchasing Systems	Revenue divided by average inventory is used to determine the level of inventory in relation to sales
Average Food Check	Point of Sales System	Food Sales divided by Cover Counts
Average Beverage Check	Point of Sales System	Beverage sales divided by Cover Counts
Average Food and Beverage Check	Point of Sales System	Food and Beverage Sales divided by Cover Counts
Lodging/Room KPI		
Available Rooms	Reservation System	Total physical rooms on property minus rooms "off the market." Off the market means out of room inventory
Average Daily Room Rate	Reservation System	Total occupied Rooms divided by Occupied Rooms
Occupancy %	Reservation System	Total Room Revenue divided by Rooms Available
Revenue per Guest (Per Cap)	Financial System	Revenue divided by Hotel Guest Count
REVPAR	Reservation System	Room Revenue divided by Total Hotel Rooms
Rooms Occupied	Reservation System	"Head on a bed"
Payroll/Labor KPI		
Payroll %	Financial System	Total Payroll per Revenue dollar
Revenue Per Labor Hour	Financial System	Revenue divided by Hourly Employees Labor Hours
Total Payroll Hours	Payroll System	Total Regular plus Overtime Hours
Total Salaries and Hourly Wages	Payroll System	Dollar Amount

buffet over à la carte reveal that 72 percent prefer a buffet. In actuality, however, only 47 percent of guests ordered the buffet, 20 percent ordered room service, and 33 percent selected à la carte items.

A third type of estimated approach is called executive opinion. This method consists of combining and averaging top executives' views. A hotel might bring together executives from areas such as sales, food and beverage, accounting, purchasing, and culinary in order to get the benefit of broad experience and opinion. In a small operation, this might be accomplished by the owner, general manager, or executive chef. In most cases, the purpose of their meeting is to review, analyze, and critique the information from the first and second forecasting approaches. The advantages and disadvantages parallel those of the sales team approach.

The primary disadvantage of forecasting techniques that employ estimates is that they cannot be verified or assessed objectively until after the fact. Further, because the forecast is inherently subjective, poor logic might go undetected, and the results might be entirely unpredictable. As actual results are produced, Myla should analyze them relative to the forecast to identify ways to improve future estimated forecasts.

Revenue Forecast

There are ways, however, to conduct forecasting more scientifically. Figures 1-7 and 1-8 show a food and beverage revenue forecast for the Sea Breeze. Hotel occupancy is added to the forecast because, in a hotel restaurant, guests are the number-one source of food and beverage business. By incorporating the occupancy levels of the whole property and combining this with knowledge of group and catering functions, Myla can assess the number of available guests. Restaurants that are not in hotels will not use the occupancy information columns in Figure 1-7; however, the rest of the chart applies well to most operations. Club establishments might incorporate information about club membership, and stand-alone restaurants can take into account regular customer traffic and local events (such as conventions, festivals, and promotional campaigns) when forecasting. We will discuss Figures 1-7 and 1-8 separately, and then we will combine the charts to show how all this information relates in practice (Figure 1-9).

In Figure 1-7, Column A lists the days and dates of the month, followed by the hotel's forecasted occupancy (Column B) and the associated percentage of potential occupancy (Column C). It is important to understand that the occupancy percentages are the number of occupied rooms divided by the number of available rooms.[1] Columns D, E, and F list available guests per meal period. The term **available guests** refers to registered guests who may dine in a lodging establishment's restaurant. For example, SBH has 1,120 guest rooms. The hotel has several meeting rooms, including banquet spaces that could seat up to 2,000 guests for catering events. Currently, the number of registered guests is 1,500. Half these guests have a previous breakfast engagement in one of the hotel banquet rooms. There are no catering events scheduled for dinner. Therefore, the number of available guests Myla can anticipate is 750 for breakfast, 750 for lunch, and 1,500 for dinner.

available guests The percentage of the total registered guests that may come to dine in a hotel restaurant.

Some of the available guests will choose to dine outside the hotel, and some may order room service. This is where the forecaster's experience comes into play; Myla will have to team up with other managers to gain that knowledge. Myla will have to use historical information to find the relationship between the number of available guests and restaurant cover counts for the groups in-house. When large groups have come to the hotel, she will also check with group leaders to find out if these guests will be using the restaurant for dinner. This data is invaluable in predicting the number of expected guests for breakfast, lunch, and dinner, which in turn will impact purchasing, kitchen staff preparation, and labor cost.

---

[1] The available room quantity, which is not shown on Figure 1-7, is not always equal to total hotel rooms because certain rooms may be out of order. For example, on Day 1, the occupied room count is 560 and the occupancy percentage is 50. Therefore, the available room count on that day should be 1,120. However, on Day 5 the same number of rooms (560) was occupied, but the occupancy percentage was 52.2. This is because only 1,073 rooms were available on Day 5.

Figure 1-7 Department Staff Planning Forecast Model / Revenues and Labor Schedule Summary

K.V.I: Available Guest

Key Volume Indicator = KVI

[A]	[B]	[C]	[D]	[E]	[F]	[G]	[H]	[I]	[J]	[K]	[L]	[M]	[N]	[O]
	Rooms information		Available Guests			Forecast Covers					Forecast Revenues			
Day	Occ	Occ %	Bkfst	Lunch	Dinner	Bkfst	Lunch	Dinner	Other	Total	Food	Bev	Other	Total
1 Mon	560	50.0%	740	740	795	59	52	40	0	151	1,858	427	0	2,285
2 Tue	605	56.4%	795	859	859	64	60	43	0	167	2,029	469	0	2,498
3 Wed	600	56.0%	859	852	852	69	60	43	0	172	2,055	477	0	2,532
4 Thu	565	52.7%	852	802	802	68	56	40	0	164	1,932	451	0	2,382
5 Fri	560	52.2%	802	795	795	64	56	40	0	160	1,912	444	0	2,355
6 Sat	615	57.4%	795	873	1,123	64	61	56	0	181	2,424	541	0	2,965
7 Sun	505	47.1%	873	717	717	70	50	36	0	156	1,780	420	0	2,200
8 Mon	550	51.3%	717	781	781	57	55	39	0	151	1,840	424	0	2,264
9 Tue	605	56.4%	781	859	859	62	60	43	0	165	2,019	465	0	2,485
10 Wed	620	57.8%	859	880	880	69	62	44	0	175	2,099	487	0	2,585
11 Thu	630	58.8%	880	895	895	70	63	45	0	178	2,141	496	0	2,636
12 Fri	635	59.2%	895	902	902	72	62	45	0	179	2,144	497	0	2,641
13 Sat	715	66.7%	902	1,015	1,015	72	71	51	0	194	2,386	549	0	2,935
14 Sun	550	51.3%	1,015	781	531	81	55	27	0	163	1,603	400	0	2,002
15 Mon	515	48.0%	781	731	731	62	51	37	0	150	1,777	414	0	2,190
16 Tue	545	50.8%	731	774	774	58	54	39	0	151	1,837	424	0	2,261
17 Wed	610	56.9%	774	866	866	62	61	43	0	166	2,027	467	0	2,494
18 Thu	625	58.3%	866	888	638	69	62	32	0	163	1,741	421	0	2,162
19 Fri	660	61.6%	638	937	437	51	66	22	0	139	1,381	345	0	1,726

(continues)

(continued)

20	Sat	700	65.3%	437	994	814	35	70	41	0	146	1,895	430	0	2,325
21	Sun	600	56.0%	494	852	352	40	60	18	0	118	1,164	292	0	1,456
22	Mon	550	51.3%	352	781	531	28	55	27	0	110	1,336	310	0	1,646
23	Tue	550	51.3%	531	781	781	42	55	39	0	136	1,764	399	0	2,163
24	Wed	525	49.0%	781	746	746	62	52	37	0	151	1,784	416	0	2,199
25	Thu	545	50.8%	746	774	774	60	54	39	0	153	1,848	427	0	2,275
26	Fri	540	50.4%	774	767	767	62	54	38	0	154	1,828	425	0	2,253
27	Sat	545	50.1%	767	774	774	61	54	39	0	154	1,853	429	0	2,282
28	Sun	475	44.3%	774	675	675	62	47	34	0	143	1,659	389	0	2,048
29	Mon	505	47.1%	675	717	717	54	50	36	0	140	1,700	392	0	2,092
30	Tue	545	50.8%	717	774	774	57	54	39	0	150	1,832	422	0	2,255
31	Wed	505	47.1%	774	717	717	62	50	36	0	148	1,740	406	0	2,146
TOTALS FORECAST:							1,868	1,772	1,188	0	4,828	57,385	13,353	0	70,738
BUDGETED DATA -------->											4,800	57,000	14,000		71,000
% OF FORECAST TO BUDGET -------->											100.6%	100.7%	95.4%		99.6%

Box A

Average Check Statistic

	FOOD	BEV.
Brkfst	$5.03	$1.69
Lunch	$7.11	$2.10
Dinner	$29.79	$5.45
Other	$16.15	$4.07
Other	$9.75	$2.19

Figure 1-8 Hotel and Restaurant

	HOTEL AND RESTAURANT															Month:	5-Jan	
	[P]	[Q]	[R]	[S]	[T]	[U]	[V]	[W]	[X]	[Y]	[Z]	[AA]	[BB]	[CC]	[DD]	Department:		
	$11.50	$6.70	$9.20	$5.40	$4.70	$9.50	$4.50									Authorizing Sign.:		
	FORECAST LABOR HOURS PER STAFFING GUIDE									Labor		Salary		Total Hours	Total Dollars			
				SERVICE LABOR HOURS				Total Svc Hrs	Total Service $	Hours	Dollars	Hours	Dollars			[EE]	[FF]	[GG]
Day	Culinary	Stwrd person	Host/ hostess	Bus person	Food servers	Bar-tender	Cocktail Server	Total Svc Hrs	Total Service $	Hours	Dollars	Hours	Dollars	Total Hours	Total Dollars	Sched Hours	Sched Dollars	Var Hrs to Model
1 Mon	32	6	8	8	8	8	8	40	266	78	$675	8	$90	86	$765	71	631	-15
2 Tue	32	6	0	8	8	8	8	32	193	70	$601	8	$90	78	$691	86	762	8
3 Wed	32	6	0	8	8	8	8	32	193	70	$601	8	$90	78	$691	72	638	-6
4 Thu	32	6	0	8	8	8	8	32	193	70	$601	8	$90	78	$691	170	1506	92
5 Fri	32	6	0	8	8	8	8	32	193	70	$601	8	$90	78	$691	64	567	-14
6 Sat	32	6	8	8	8	8	8	40	266	78	$675	8	$90	86	$765	90	800	4
7 Sun	24	4	0	4	6	8	8	26	162	54	$465	8	$90	62	$555	72	644	10
8 Mon	24	4	8	4	6	8	8	34	235	62	$538	8	$90	70	$628	62	556	-8
9 Tue	32	6	0	8	8	8	8	32	193	70	$601	8	$90	78	$691	78	691	0
10 Wed	32	6	0	8	8	8	8	32	193	70	$601	8	$90	78	$691	78	691	0
11 Thu	32	6	0	8	8	8	8	32	193	70	$601	8	$90	78	$691	80	709	2
12 Fri	32	6	0	8	8	8	8	32	193	70	$601	8	$90	78	$691	82	726	4
13 Sat	32	6	8	8	8	8	8	40	266	78	$675	8	$90	86	$765	90	800	8
14 Sun	24	4	0	4	6	8	8	26	162	54	$465	8	$90	62	$555	70	626	8
15 Mon	24	4	8	4	6	8	8	34	235	62	$538	8	$90	70	$628	72	646	2
16 Tue	24	4	0	4	6	8	8	26	162	54	$465	8	$90	62	$555	62	555	0
17 Wed	32	6	0	8	8	8	8	32	193	70	$601	8	$90	78	$691	76	673	-2
18 Thu	24	4	0	4	6	8	8	26	162	54	$465	8	$90	62	$555	65	581	3
19 Fri	24	4	0	4	6	8	8	26	162	54	$465	8	$90	62	$555	65	581	3
20 Sat	32	6	8	8	8	8	8	40	266	78	$675	8	$90	86	$765	82	729	-4

(continues)

(continued)

21 Sun	24	4	0	4	6	8	8	26	162	54	$465	8	62	$90	62	$555	64	572	2
22 Mon	24	4	8	4	6	8	8	34	235	62	$538	8	70	$90	70	$628	72	646	2
23 Tue	24	4	0	4	6	8	8	26	162	54	$465	8	62	$90	62	$555	59	528	–3
24 Wed	24	4	0	4	6	8	8	26	162	54	$465	8	62	$90	62	$555	62	555	0
25 Thu	24	4	0	4	6	8	8	26	162	54	$465	8	62	$90	62	$555	64	572	2
26 Fri	24	4	0	4	6	8	8	26	162	54	$465	8	62	$90	62	$555	62	555	0
27 Sat	24	4	8	4	6	8	8	34	235	62	$538	8	70	$90	70	$628	72	646	2
28 Sun	24	4	0	4	6	8	8	26	162	54	$465	8	62	$90	62	$555	62	555	0
29 Mon	24	4	8	4	6	8	8	34	235	62	$538	8	70	$90	70	$628	72	646	2
30 Tue	24	4	0	4	6	8	8	26	162	54	$465	8	62	$90	62	$555	64	572	2
31 Wed	24	4	0	4	6	8	8	26	162	54	$465	8	62	$90	62	$555	60	537	–2
	848	150	72	176	212	248	248	956	6,081	1,954	16,838	248	2,202	2,790	2,202	19,628	2,300	20498	98
											16,600			2,800		19,400		19,400	
											101.40%		Standard	99.60%		103.80%		105.70%	

Holiday Allowance: $500

Total Labor Per Standard: $17,338 $20,128

Box B

Staffing Standard

Cover Range		Bartender hours	Cocktail Server hours	Food Server hours	Others Hours	Others hours	Table Busser hours	Kitchen Staff Hours	Steward Hours
From	To								
0	39	8	8	6	0	0	4	24	4
40	59	8	8	8	0	0	8	32	6
60	79	8	8	24	0	0	12	40	8
80	MAX	8	8	32	0	0	16	40	8

Box C

Salaried Labor	Hours	Dollars
Manager	8	90
Culinary	0	0
Total	8	90

Figure 1-9 Combined Figure 1-7 & 1-8

K.VI: Available Guest

Key Volume Indicator = KVI

[A]	[B]	[C]	[D]	[E]	[F]	[G]	[H]	[I]	[J]	[K]	[L]	[M]	[N]	[O]
	Rooms information		Available Guests			Forecast Covers					Forecast Revenues			
Day	Occ	Occ %	Bkfst	Lunch	Dinner	Bkfst	Lunch	Dinner	Other	Total	Food	Bev	Other	Total
1 Mon	560	50.0%	740	740	795	59	52	40	0	151	1,858	427	0	2,285
2 Tue	605	56.4%	795	859	859	64	60	43	0	167	2,029	469	0	2,498
3 Wed	600	56.0%	859	852	852	69	60	43	0	172	2,055	477	0	2,532
4 Thu	565	52.7%	852	802	802	68	56	40	0	164	1,932	451	0	2,382
5 Fri	560	52.2%	802	795	795	64	56	40	0	160	1,912	444	0	2,355
6 Sat	615	57.4%	795	873	1,123	64	61	56	0	181	2,424	541	0	2,965
7 Sun	505	47.1%	873	717	717	70	50	36	0	156	1,780	420	0	2,200
8 Mon	550	51.3%	717	781	781	57	55	39	0	151	1,840	424	0	2,264
9 Tue	605	56.4%	781	859	859	62	60	43	0	165	2,019	465	0	2,485
10 Wed	620	57.8%	859	880	880	69	62	44	0	175	2,099	487	0	2,585
11 Thu	630	58.8%	880	895	895	70	63	45	0	178	2,141	496	0	2,636
12 Fri	635	59.2%	895	902	902	72	62	45	0	179	2,144	497	0	2,641
13 Sat	715	66.7%	902	1,015	1,015	72	71	51	0	194	2,386	549	0	2,935
14 Sun	550	51.3%	1,015	781	531	81	55	27	0	163	1,603	400	0	2,002
15 Mon	515	48.0%	781	731	731	62	51	37	0	150	1,777	414	0	2,190
16 Tue	545	50.8%	731	774	774	58	54	39	0	151	1,837	424	0	2,261
17 Wed	610	56.9%	774	866	866	62	61	43	0	166	2,027	467	0	2,494
18 Thu	625	58.3%	866	888	638	69	62	32	0	163	1,741	421	0	2,162
19 Fri	660	61.6%	638	937	437	51	66	22	0	139	1,381	345	0	1,726

(continues)

(continued)

	Day	Forecast	%													Total
20	Sat	700	65.3%	437	994	814	35	70	41	0	146	1,895	430	0		2,325
21	Sun	600	56.0%	494	852	352	40	60	18	0	118	1,164	292	0		1,456
22	Mon	550	51.3%	352	781	531	28	55	27	0	110	1,336	310	0		1,646
23	Tue	550	51.3%	531	781	781	42	55	39	0	136	1,764	399	0		2,163
24	Wed	525	49.0%	781	746	746	62	52	37	0	151	1,784	416	0		2,199
25	Thu	545	50.8%	746	774	774	60	54	39	0	153	1,848	427	0		2,275
26	Fri	540	50.4%	774	767	767	62	54	38	0	154	1,828	425	0		2,253
27	Sat	545	50.1%	767	774	774	61	54	39	0	154	1,853	429	0		2,282
28	Sun	475	44.3%	774	675	675	62	47	34	0	143	1,659	389	0		2,048
29	Mon	505	47.1%	675	717	717	54	50	36	0	140	1,700	392	0		2,092
30	Tue	545	50.8%	717	774	774	57	54	39	0	150	1,832	422	0		2,255
31	Wed	505	47.1%	774	717	717	62	50	36	0	148	1,740	406	0		2,146
TOTALS FORECAST:							1,868	1,772	1,188	0	4,828	57,385	13,353	0		70,738
BUDGETED DATA-------------------->											4,800	57,000	14,000			71,000
% OF FORECAST TO BUDGET---------->											100.6%	100.7%	95.4%			99.6%

Box A

Average Check Statistic	FOOD	BEV.
Brkfst	$5.03	$1.69
Lunch	$7.11	$2.10
Dinner	$29.79	$5.45
Other	$16.15	$4.07
Other	$9.75	$2.19

HOTEL AND RESTAURANT

Month: **5-Jan**
Department:
Authorizing Sign.:

	[P]	[Q]	[R]	[S]	[T]	[U]	[V]	[W]	[X]	[Y]	[Z]	[AA]	[BB]	[CC]	[DD]	[EE]	[FF]	[GG]
	$11.50	$6.70	$9.20	$5.40	$4.70	$9.50	$4.50											
	FORECAST LABOR HOURS PER STAFFING GUIDE									Labor		Salary						
				SERVICE LABOR HOURS														
Day	Culi-nary	Stwrd person	Host/ hostess	Bus person	Food servers	Bar-tender	Cocktail Server	Total Svc Hrs	Total Service $	Hours	Dollars	Hours	Dollars	Total Hours	Total Dollars	Sched Hours	Sched Dollars	Var Hrs to Model
1 Mon	32	6	8	8	8	8	8	40	266	78	$675	8	$90	86	$765	71	631	−15
2 Tue	32	6	0	8	8	8	8	32	193	70	$601	8	$90	78	$691	86	762	8
3 Wed	32	6	0	8	8	8	8	32	193	70	$601	8	$90	78	$691	72	638	−6
4 Thu	32	6	0	8	8	8	8	32	193	70	$601	8	$90	78	$691	170	1506	92
5 Fri	32	6	0	8	8	8	8	32	193	70	$601	8	$90	78	$691	64	567	−14
6 Sat	32	6	8	8	8	8	8	40	266	78	$675	8	$90	86	$765	90	800	4
7 Sun	24	4	0	4	6	8	8	26	162	54	$465	8	$90	62	$555	72	644	10
8 Mon	24	4	8	4	6	8	8	34	235	62	$538	8	$90	70	$628	62	556	−8
9 Tue	32	6	0	8	8	8	8	32	193	70	$601	8	$90	78	$691	78	691	0
10 Wed	32	6	0	8	8	8	8	32	193	70	$601	8	$90	78	$691	78	691	0
11 Thu	32	6	0	8	8	8	8	32	193	70	$601	8	$90	78	$691	80	709	2
12 Fri	32	6	0	8	8	8	8	32	193	70	$601	8	$90	78	$691	82	726	4
13 Sat	32	6	8	8	8	8	8	40	266	78	$675	8	$90	86	$765	90	800	4
14 Sun	24	4	0	4	6	8	8	26	162	54	$465	8	$90	62	$555	70	626	8
15 Mon	24	4	8	4	6	8	8	34	235	62	$538	8	$90	70	$628	72	646	2
16 Tue	24	4	0	4	6	8	8	26	162	54	$465	8	$90	62	$555	62	555	0
17 Wed	32	6	0	8	8	8	8	32	193	70	$601	8	$90	78	$691	76	673	−2
18 Thu	24	4	0	4	6	8	8	26	162	54	$465	8	$90	62	$555	65	581	3
19 Fri	24	4	0	4	6	8	8	26	162	54	$465	8	$90	62	$555	65	581	3
20 Sat	32	6	8	8	8	8	8	40	266	78	$675	8	$90	86	$765	82	729	−4

(continues)

(continued)

21 Sun	24	4	0	4	6	8	8	26	162	54	$465	8	$90	62	$555	64	572	2
22 Mon	24	4	8	4	6	8	8	34	235	62	$538	8	$90	70	$628	72	646	2
23 Tue	24	4	0	4	6	8	8	26	162	54	$465	8	$90	62	$555	59	528	–3
24 Wed	24	4	0	4	6	8	8	26	162	54	$465	8	$90	62	$555	62	555	0
25 Thu	24	4	0	4	6	8	8	26	162	54	$465	8	$90	62	$555	64	572	2
26 Fri	24	4	0	4	6	8	8	26	162	54	$465	8	$90	62	$555	62	555	0
27 Sat	24	4	8	4	6	8	8	34	235	62	$538	8	$90	70	$628	72	646	2
28 Sun	24	4	0	4	6	8	8	26	162	54	$465	8	$90	62	$555	62	555	0
29 Mon	24	4	8	4	6	8	8	34	235	62	$538	8	$90	70	$628	72	646	2
30 Tue	24	4	0	4	6	8	8	26	162	54	$465	8	$90	62	$555	64	572	2
31 Wed	24	4	0	4	6	8	8	26	162	54	$465	8	$90	62	$555	60	537	–2
	848	150	72	176	212	248	248	956	6,081	1,954	16,838	248	2,790	2,202	19,628	2,300	20498	98
											16,600		2,800		19,400		19,400	
											101.40%		99.60%	Standard	103.80%		105.70%	
												Holiday Allowance:	$500				$500	
												Total Labor Per Standard	$17,338		$2,790		$20,128	

Box B

Staffing Standard

Cover Range		Bar-tender hours	Cocktail Server hours	Food Server hours	Others Hours	Others hours	Others hours	Table Busser hours	Kitchen Staff Hours	Steward Hours
From	To									
0	39	8	8	6	0	0	0	4	24	4
40	59	8	8	8	0	0	0	8	32	6
60	79	8	8	24	0	0	0	12	40	8
80	MAX	8	8	32	0	0	0	16	40	8

Box C

Salaried Labor	Hours	Dollars
Manager	8	90
Culinary	0	0
Total	8	90

Other factors to consider include the percentage of outside customers (people not registered as hotel guests) who may patronize the restaurant on a given day, outside conventions that may increase business, and holidays.

Myla places the forecasts—by meal period and total—in Columns G through J of Figure 1-7. In this example, average check information is contained in Box A beneath the chart. Multiply the average check amounts by the forecasted cover amounts in G through J. These are SBH's forecasted revenues, which will go in Columns L, M, and N.

Labor Cost Forecast

The same process can be applied to labor cost forecasting (Figure 1-8). Note the staffing guide information in Box B below the chart, which we have provided as an example. It works like this: This box lists how many hours Myla will require of each position, based on how busy the restaurant is. For example, if she forecasts 31 covers in the restaurant, she will need 24 hours of kitchen staff, 8 hours of bartending, and 6 hours of food service. (The staffing guide is discussed much more fully in Chapter 14, so you will learn how each of these steps is handled.) Then, in Columns P through V, these positions and hours are listed, along with their rates of pay. Column W totals these hours for service staff, and in Column X these totals are multiplied by their wage rates to reach a total labor cost. Columns Y and Z provide the combined totals for service, stewarding, and kitchen personnel.

In Column AA, salaried labor is counted; this cost is in Column BB. You can see wages for salaried personnel in Box C under the chart. Column CC totals all hours required for that particular day, and DD totals all wages. Column EE lists what Myla has scheduled for the day. On most days, she has more hours scheduled than this staffing guide requires. This could be due to VIPs staying in the hotel or special requests. The staffing guide does not incorporate holiday hours or pay; these are added manually at the bottom ($500). This is an area Myla can fine-tune with more experience in this establishment.

If Myla did use those extra staff hours, the effects appear in the forecasted expenditures in Column FF. The total amount required by the staffing guide plus holiday allowance ($500) is $20,128. The amount scheduled, including holiday pay on July 4, is $20,507. With detailed forecasts like these, Myla can see where extra expenditures are going and act to cut them.

Forecast Review

Myla will have to present her forecast to Eric for his review and approval. Will he accept it as presented? Let's review the information from Figures 1-7 and 1-8.[2]

Summary

Total Average Check: Column O ÷ column K = $70,738 ÷ 4,828 = $14.65. Lower dinner business levels are contributing to a low average check. Hotel occupancy could have an impact. Management needs to introduce menu items that could draw locals with a special menu advertising campaign. (Chapter 15 discusses ways to do this.)

Non-salaried productivity: Column K ÷ (Column EE − Column AA) = 4,828 ÷ 2,052 = 2.35 (covers per total non-salaried scheduled hours). This number is too low. The staffing guide and menu items need to be looked at and revised. (Chapter 14 provides a detailed discussion.)

Non-salaried labor percentage: (Column FF − Column BB) ÷ Column O = $17,717 ÷ $70,738 = 25.05 percent. This number seems high, and may be due to the staffing guide, hourly rate, and menu selections.

---

[2] Myla did not include average daily rate (ADR), rev. par, pace, and on-the-book (OTB), because her responsibilities do not include room revenue. That information is appropriately covered in lodging textbooks.

Any of the above indicators could diminish SBH's opportunity to generate profits. With Eric's full support, Myla needs to work with the management team to address them. As stated earlier, Figure 1-9 is a combined version of Figures 1-7 and 1-8. We discussed them separately to illustrate the different stages of preparing a forecast. Below we have combined them, to show how you would use this chart in practice.

⑪ **Discussion Topic**

How are forecasts generated? What are the advantages of each method?

Inventory Management and Valuation

SBH's inventory-management decisions have significant effects on profit reporting and asset valuations. It is vital that Myla supervise inventory procedures because they directly affect profit, cash flow, production levels, and customer service. Myla must provide input on reorder frequencies, economical order quantities, and the quantities required to meet desired customer service levels. SBH's vendors must be able to assure consistent availability of the products to meet demands.

Myla will have to educate the chef, the manager, and the buyer about how success in inventory management is measured—in terms of available cash flow, decreased theft, reduced cost, and reduced waste. All of these factors could have contributed to the losses SBH is experiencing. Failures can be categorized as misappropriation—buying too much, too little, or incorrect stock—and incorrect valuation, which refers to placing a lower or higher value on inventory than it is actually worth. As an example, a change in menu offerings (or sales mix) may leave material surpluses because product needs have changed. Alternatively, prices may have declined substantially while the inventory value SBH has on the books still has the original high prices.

Proper inventory valuation is required for food and beverage accountancy. A high **inventory turnover ratio**—a figure calculated to show how quickly SBH is using products—may indicate that the company is not buying too much stock. A low ratio means the opposite: The company is buying too much and sinking its cash into that expense. Part of the manager's role is to assist in the management of the inventory, both to turn over stock correctly and to monitor the inventory in a way that helps control costs.

inventory turnover ratio A ratio of sales to inventory, which shows how many times the inventory of a company is sold and replaced during an accounting period.

To be more specific, Myla should also be valuing SBH's inventory, which means using one of a number of methods to count what the company has and match it to a dollar figure. These values are vital to reporting and comparison in order to show where SBH stands, what costs are being incurred, and where waste and inefficiency are damaging the company's profit-making capabilities. If a manager improperly values the inventory, it can distort the important relationships between current inventory and working capital, turnover, and average age of inventory items. These are all ratios and formulas you'll read about in Chapter 11, where inventory methods are discussed in detail.

Inventory Review

Myla examined past inventory policies and practices by reviewing a binder reporting the beginning inventory from January 2006 as $30,000 in goods. During the month of January, food purchases totalled $26,000. At the end of January, the inventory, counted and extended, was valued at $31,000.

Given this information, Myla performed the following calculations:

Cost of sales: **($30,000 + $26,000 − $31,000) = $25,000.**

Cost of sales percentage: $25,000 ÷ $70,738 (revenue from Figure 1-7) = 35.34 percent. This is higher than the cost of sales information in Figure 1-5, which recommends 33 percent for a full-service restaurant.

Other calculations revealed the following:

The average inventory is ($30,000 + $31,000) ÷ 2 = $30,500.

The average age of inventory is ($30,500 ÷ $25,000) × 31 days in January = 37.82 days.

Sales efficiency is $70,738 ÷ $30,500 = 2.32.

After completing the analysis, Myla took the document to Eric and Robert for their review.

Myla: Here are the results of my inventory review. The financial indicators confirm why SBH is losing money. Too much cash is tied in food inventory and cannot be accessed for other important expenses. High inventory is causing spoilage.

Rob: But the chef won't reduce his inventory for fear of running out.

Eric: Well, we'll have to look at that issue. Myla, thank you. I can see from your report that if we don't reduce the level of inventory and improve sales efficiency, the restaurant will continue to drain the profits from the rooms division. Let's schedule a meeting with the chef and the team to address this.

Myla is responsible for reporting to management on the success or failure of an inventory program. These reports should incorporate comments from the restaurant manager or chef regarding the reasons for deficient results, as well as plans for correcting problem areas. In Chapter 11 you will find a detailed set of plans and exercises to help you accomplish inventory goals and objectives.

Summary

Many operations do not have an employee with the title *food and beverage manager* or *cost controller*, but all of the duties described in this chapter are necessary, and someone must to undertake them in any successful operation. This person might be a manager, operator, owner, or other employee who works at controlling costs. Sometimes the tasks are shared by different people in a variety of positions. However it works in an establishment, the person in this role holds a great responsibility for the company. Budgeting, forecasting, inventory control, labor control, and other tasks are very important to the company's profitability. The discussions in this chapter will be detailed further as you continue through this book, with more information and useful forms to help you use the ideas you learn.

CHAPTER QUESTIONS

Critical Thinking Questions

1. What is a forecast?

2. Why is it important to analyze the inventory turnover ratio?

3. If a hotel has 250 rooms, how many room nights are available in a 30-day month?

4. Assuming the data in Question 8, if 5,800 rooms are occupied during this period, what is the occupancy percentage?

Objective Questions

1. Globally, travel and tourism is the world's largest industry. True or False?

2. Successful forecasting is defined as predicting the consequences of a given decision or set of decisions over a given time. True or False?

Multiple Choice Questions

1. In the United States, the food service industry directly supports approximately
   A. 2 million jobs.
   B. 4 million jobs.
   C. 7 million jobs.
   D. 12 million jobs.

2. According to the National Restaurant Association (NRA), on a typical day in 2008, the food service industry is expected to post sales of:
   A. $1.53 billion
   B. $3 billion
   C. $1 billion
   D. $2.5 billion

3. The average annual household expenditure for food away from home in 2008 was:
   A. $4,206
   B. $2,676
   C. $3,000
   D. $1,500

4. The manager's key job functions lie in cost control, specifically in the following areas:
   A. Planning for Labor Productivity Controls
   B. Financial Reporting
   C. Evaluating and Consulting
   D. Protection and Maintenance of Company Assets
   E. Other duties such as developing revenue strategies and expense control systems
   F. All of the above

5. There are many approaches to forecasting. In selecting a specific method that suits the circumstances, consider these important criteria:
   A. Is the method practical? What resources and data must be available to make it work?
   B. Is this method cost-effective?
   C. Are its end results useful and reliable?
   D. All of the above

6. A high inventory turnover ratio—a figure calculated to show how quickly a company is using products—may indicate:
   A. that the unit is buying too much stock
   B. that the unit inventory is exposed to theft
   C. that the unit is not buying too much stock
   D. that the unit revenue is below forecast

7. The bulk of the industry consists of:
   A. institutional eating places
   B. commercial eating places
   C. military eating places
   D. non of the above

8. The term *FTE* refers to:
   A. a measurement equal to one staff person consistently working overtime.
   B. a measurement equal to group of staff persons working a full-time work schedule.
   C. a measurement equal to one staff person working a full-time work schedule for one year.
   D. a measurement equal to two or more staff person working a full-time work schedule for one year.

9. What are the main factors behind higher food commodity costs in the United States?
   A. weather-related production problems
   B. increased use of some food commodities, such as corn, for biofuel uses
   C. stronger global demand for food
   D. all of the above

10. What is the biggest challenge and opportunity the foodservice industry faced in 2008?
    A. maintaining customer loyalty
    B. employee retention
    C. high utility-gas costs
    D. high insurance

CASE STUDY

Note: This case study requires the ability to build on concepts that are introduced only briefly in the text. To some degree, this case anticipates issues that will be covered in more depth in later chapters.

1. Approaches to Forecasting

Fish King Restaurants, a well-known restaurant chain in the Midwest, is in the initial stages of preparing its annual forecast for 2007. Kevin Vieden has recently joined Fish King's accounting staff and wants to learn as much as possible about the company's forecasting processes. During a recent lunch with Scott Bruce, restaurant manager, and Brenda Clement, sales manager, Kevin initiated the following conversation:

Kevin: Since I'm new around here and am going to be involved with the preparation of the annual revenue forecast, I'd be interested to learn how the two of you estimate sales and production numbers.

Brenda: We start out very methodically by looking at recent history and discussing what we know about current accounts, potential customers, and the general state of consumer spending. Then we add that usual dose of intuition to come up with the best forecast we can.

Scott: I usually take the sales projections as the basis for my projections. Of course, we have to make an estimate of what this year's closing inventories will be, which is sometimes difficult.

Kevin: Why does that present a problem? There must have been an estimate of closing inventories in the forecast for the current year.

Scott: Those numbers aren't always reliable, since Brenda makes some adjustments to the sales numbers before passing them on to me.

Kevin: What kinds of adjustments?

Brenda: Well, we don't want to fall short of the sales projections, so we generally give ourselves a little breathing room by lowering the initial sales projection anywhere from 2 to 5 percent.

Scott: So you can see why this year's forecast is not a very reliable starting point. We always have to adjust the projected production rates as the year progresses and, of course, this changes the ending inventory estimates. By the way, we make similar adjustments to expenses by adding at least 10 percent to the estimates; I think everyone around here does the same thing.

Your task:

Kevin, Brenda, and Scott have described the use of what is sometimes called forecasting slack.

1. Explain why Brenda and Scott behave in this manner, and describe the benefits they expect to realize from the use of forecasting slack.

2. Explain how the use of forecasting slack can adversely affect Brenda and Scott.

3. As a management accountant, Kevin Vieden believes that the behavior described by Brenda and Scott may be unethical. Explain why the use of forecasting slack may be unethical.

Learning Objectives

After reading this chapter, you should be able to:

- summarize the importance of understanding the customer base when writing a menu;

- describe how menu selection impacts other aspects of the operation;

- describe the three menu types and their impact on cost control;

- employ principles of good menu design;

- describe the dollar and sense system of menu engineering.

In Practice

Myla Thomas walked into the office of the owner of the Sea Breeze Hotel for her 11 A.M. meeting with the owner, Eric Breeze, and the executive chef, Robert.

"Good morning, Myla, and welcome aboard!" exclaimed Eric as he extended his hand for a handshake. "We are very excited to have you on our team; I have prepared a meeting schedule for you to meet with everyone. Please have a seat," Eric continued, indicating a chair for her.

"Thank you very much," Myla responded, as chef Robert strolled into the room to a corner chair. As soon as Myla and Robert finished exchanging greetings, Eric commented on the work that Robert was doing with the restaurant menu. "It's an excellent example of what is needed." With that opening, Myla asked Robert about the timing of the previous menu overhaul. Robert answered, "It hasn't happened since I have been here, which is a little over two years." Myla politely followed up with another question: "What challenges do you have with the current menu?" For Myla, Robert's answer was very revealing: "The menu is dull, and it doesn't really address our customer complaints. Customers want many choices nowadays, and we need to provide that. My goal is to review and make appropriate changes every season to reflect what is available and affordable. And, of course, cost of sales is an issue, and Eric will be the first person to point that out."

Unexpectedly, Eric turned and handed Myla the menu and said, "Here is the menu Robert is talking about. What do you think?" Myla responded, "I don't see the Sea Breeze identity in the menu. Something else I notice is that it's not easy to read the print font sizes." To his credit, Robert realized some of the errors that had been made. "Yes, you're right. The first version is kind of faulty. The process really has to be corrected."

OVERVIEW

In the food service industry, everything revolves around the menu. Types of menus vary as much as restaurants do. The design and item selections in a fine-dining restaurant's menu are completely different from those of a fast-food or casual restaurant. These differences affect every aspect of the operation—labor cost, food cost, choice of flatware and china, staff training, storage requirements, and restaurant layout and design. In this chapter, we will focus our attention on menu development as it relates to the customer and the menu. Later, after we go into detail about cost control relating to purchasing, recipe costing, inventory and labor, and similar issues, Chapter 13 will cover menu analysis.

As shown in Figure 2-1, menu development and menu analysis differ not only in their user orientation, but also in their emphasis on the future and past performance of the menu. Menu development has a strong future orientation of what the restaurant should represent, based on a predetermined concept. On the other hand, menu analysis is the evaluation of the past—menu cost and/or sales data—for the purpose of identifying customers' needs and perceptions and improving menu performance. When you learn these sets of skills, you will be able to undertake more effective decision making with respect to marketing and operating the menu.

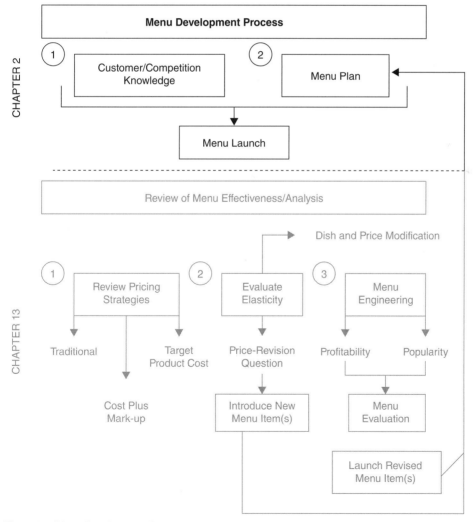

Figure 2-1 Menu Development Process

MENU DEVELOPMENT

The way a menu is developed or adapted is a reflection of how well the restaurant concept or business plan has been defined. Successful menu development depends on two pillars: customer/competition knowledge and menu planning.

Sometimes the menu evolves over time as a restaurant's business plan is refined. In other scenarios, the concept comes first and the menu comes later. In yet other instances, the menu may be the guide that directs the restaurant toward a particular concept. The menu also holds the key to whose responsibility it is to prepare certain dishes, and how those dishes should be served to the customer. The choices that guide your menu call for certain types of advance preparation to help the manager adjust to the workflow. Even if a written menu is not provided to the customer—as in a bed-and-breakfast—some form of menu list in the kitchen and service area is essential for smooth operation of the restaurant. All successful menus start with a good knowledge of the customer base and the competition.

Customer and Competition Knowledge

Designing and preparing a successful menu begins with understanding your customer base and competition. You must assess what customers will want and what they are willing to pay, and you must consider the direct and indirect competition. A good survey is one way to collect focused opinions about your restaurant from current and future customers. This can reveal the demographics of the operation's customers and give insight into what they really think about the restaurant and its competition. A customer survey would contain questions about the following topics:

perceived value The customer's perception of value as it relates to his or her restaurant experience.

- menu selection

- menu pricing and **perceived value** (described below)

- food quality and quantity

- waiting times

- server's knowledge of menu

- cleanliness

- décor

- restaurant location

- promptness of service

- professionalism and friendliness of staff

Designing Your Survey: The Restaurant Minimum Standards Survey

Maximizing sales is tied to how guests respond to your operation, its food, and its service. Many restaurants prepare questionnaires about service levels in order to solicit customer comments. Restaurants use the responses from customers to act upon perceived deficiencies. The customer survey acts as "eyes and ears" for management in the areas of perceived value, cleanliness, service standards, and ambience—the whole restaurant package. How the customer perceives the value of his or her restaurant experience will determine business competitiveness. These quantified questionnaire responses can be measured and charted over time, and they offer an excellent picture of growth and decline.

There are many ways to design a survey. Below are some generally acceptable steps to creating an effective customer survey.

1. Decide what the survey is supposed to elicit. Asking about age group and musical taste can reveal what type of music or entertainment is appropriate for your restaurant. Customers' occupations and education levels will indicate the economic level of the marketplace—including information such as disposable income. Finding out about ethnic and religious orientations can help you formulate food preferences. For example, a Mexican restaurant may not do so well in an Italian community, unless perhaps that community is indeed looking for something different.

2. Identify the audience of the survey and how they will relate to the questions asked. For example, senior citizens and a group of young adults may relate differently to a question about customer parking and access for people with disabilities.

3. Create questions that identify the survey demographic. Experts call these qualifying questions. For example, you can ask "What is your zip code?"

4. Design the questions after deciding on the format of each. Questions can be optional or required, multiple-choice or open-ended. Open-ended questions might be as follows: What is your favorite restaurant? What do you like about its menu?

5. Write the survey. Figures 2-2 and 2-3 are examples of a customer survey based on **restaurant minimum standards**.

6. Conduct a competition survey. This will identify the direct and indirect segments of your competition. **Direct competition** refers to what is called the *homogeneous environment:* for example, all the nearby restaurants that offer the same type of menu that you want to offer. If one such restaurant decides to increase its prices, it may lose sales. **Indirect competition** comes from those restaurants that do not share your restaurant's cuisine but do share your customer base. You want to know if the surrounding population can support another restaurant or menu item like the one you are proposing.

restaurant minimum standards Refers to service, food and beverage offerings, and the entire operation—for instance, cleanliness.

direct competition refers to the homogenous environment: for example, all the restaurants nearby that offer the same type of menu that you want to offer.

indirect competition comes from those restaurants that do not share the same cuisine but do share a customer base.

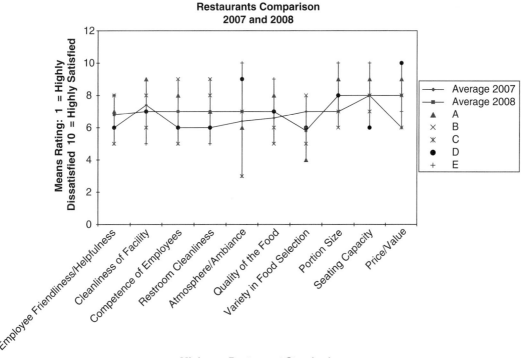

Figure 2-2 Restaurant Comparison

7. Administer a pilot survey with a small sample of people to review the effects.

8. Validate that the results of the pilot survey are meaningful and complete.

9. Make adjustments based on the results of the pilot.

10. Publish the survey and distribute it to your customers and/or potential customers.

11. Collect and tabulate the results.

12. Analyze the results.

Figure 2-3 Example of Restaurant Survey

Restaurant _____ Date _____

Server's Name _____ Host/Hostess Name _____

Items Ordered _____

Were you greeted properly/promptly by host or hostess?

Were you shown to the table and seated properly?

Was the table properly set up?

Were the cushions clean?

Were you properly and promptly greeted by your server?

Did your server offer items from the menu?

Were your questions answered with confidence and poise?

Were dishes served hot or cold, as ordered?

Were the overall appearance and taste of high quality?

Were your water, soda, coffee and/or bread service refilled?

Did your server offer you desserts and coffee?

Were your plates cleared all at once at the end of each course?

Did the server return to the table to inquire if the meal was enjoyable?

Was the menu clean?

Was the lighting level acceptable?

Was the overall cleanliness of the room acceptable?

Was the music volume acceptable?

Was the outdoor volume, if applicable, acceptable?

Was the temperature level acceptable?

Do you feel you received a good value for the price you paid for this meal?

In Denial

Robert Mancuso, gold medalist in the Culinary Olympics, reported, "When I took over at the Sardine Factory in Monterey . . . I got two different pictures from our employees and our customers. While our employees were saying that we were delivering 98 percent customer satisfaction in food quality, our customers thought we were at 60 percent. The irony was, instead of trying to address the customer's complaints, we seemed to think we had to show that we were right and they were wrong." Note the two messages contained in this short quotation. First, make sure you measure the right things. Apparently, the internal measure of food quality that had been used at the Sardine Factory was deficient; it did not capture customer perceptions, which are absolutely crucial. Second, if customers are unhappy, don't tell them they are wrong. Try to figure out why they are unhappy, so you can work to improve that aspect of your operation.

In the example below, we compared five restaurants for two years. The deficiencies noted on the graph clearly show problems that inhibit the effectiveness of menu engineering and up-selling. The performance of these five restaurants shows a bumpy trend. On average, the cleanliness of the facilities is down compared to the previous year. No matter how well waitstaff up-sell, and no matter how well the menu is engineered, if the customers perceive an unclean restaurant, they will not return. These questionnaires reveal where the basics, such as cleanliness, have been neglected. In general, a weekly or monthly evaluation of the guest comments is essential.

Menu Planning

The menu affects every step of a restaurant operation, from planning to everyday functioning. Menu planning involves the following information: menu types, menu nutrition, and menu design. The diagram in Figure 2-4 compares five restaurants to show you how the menu impacts every aspect of their operations. Customers' menu preferences drive equipment needs and procurement cost. For example, a holding cabinet and expensive china and glassware for serving may not be required in a casual bagel shop, but a bagel maker or display case might be required.

Figure 2-4 Restaurant Comparison

	Casual Bagel Shop	Brew Pub-upscale Environment	Elegant Russian Tearoom	Institutional ie. Hospital	Ethnic ie. Thai
Menu Style	Casual and simple a la carte	A la carte or table d'hote	High quality a la carte or semi a la carte	Cycle Menu	A la carte or semi a la carte
Staffing	Not too skilled	Semi skilled	Highly skilled	Skilled in special diets	Skilled in ethnic food
Equipment	Bagel maker, meat slicer	Full range of kitchen equipment	Alto-sham, steamer, sauté, pan, stove, frig.	Full range of equipment. Budget constraint	Suitable equipment for ethnic food
Check average	$5 - $10	$10 - $15	$40 - $80	Set sum. $5 - $12	$10 - 18
Type of service	Fast and casual	Fast not casual	High expectation. Elaborate	Tray service, cafeteria	Not casual
Cost control	Minimum cost control	Minimum cost control	Extensive cost control	High portion control	Extensive cost control
Design atmosphere	Open long counter. Less comfortable, bright lights, square foot (7 to 12)	Casual, square foot per person (11 to 16), comfortable, pleasant	Very comfortable, low dim light, square foot per person (15 to 23), quiet	Open space, self-service	Not casual, square foot per person (10 - 14), pleasant, low music

As you can see, the menu sets the stage for an operation's daily functioning. The choices you make with regards to the menu, staff, style, ambience, price, customers, and equipment will determine the restaurant's profitability.

McDonald's Chic

McDonald's France has been spending lavishly to remodel its restaurants to blend with local architecture and to make their interiors less uniform and sterile. For example, some outlets in the Alps have wood-and-stone interiors similar to those of alpine chalets. The idea is to defuse the negative feelings many French people have toward McDonald's as a symbol of American culture and, perhaps more importantly, to entice customers to linger over their meals and to spend more money. This investment in operating assets has apparently been successful—even though a Big Mac costs about the same in Paris as in New York, the average French customer spends about $9 per visit versus only about $4 in the United States.

Source: Carol Matlack and Pallavi Gogoi, "What's This? The French Love McDonald's?" *BusinessWeek*, January 13, 2003, p. 50.

Menu Type

Once the menu is determined, decisions about purchasing, labor skill levels, and pricing can be made. Menus can stay the same each day (this is called a static or standard menu), change each day, or be a combination of the two. Most of the menus commonly used in the food service industry are either standard or combination. Standard menus are common in chain and ethnic restaurants such as Thai Cuisine. Each type of menu affects the operation's costs in different ways.

Standard Menu

Many bagel shops, diners, and chain restaurants use the standard menuformat. This type of menu offers the same selection of menu items from day to day. Since the same menu items are offered every day, an operation can maintain a record of daily sales for each item. The advantage is that the sales record makes future sales easier to predict. When forecasts are accurate, expenses due to waste from overproduction of a menu item can be minimized. Amounts of food to purchase can be more accurately predicted, resulting in less spoilage and fewer dollars tied up unnecessarily in inventory. Another advantage of the standard menu is that it simplifies culinary processes and employees can be trained on production consistency. A third advantage is that customers know what to expect because they may be returning to their favorite menu item.

A drawback of the standard menu is that it offers little opportunity for use of excess production. If a restaurant prepares too much prime rib, for example, it is difficult to carry over this item for the next day's service. The item will not be the same quality as the first day of service. Some restaurants may use specials either to utilize carryover or to try out new menu items. Also, a standard menu may not be cost effective in a time of rising product cost, since management may not react quickly enough to change the menu to reduce cost. The same is true if management cannot quickly take advantage of inexpensive item that could benefit the business profitably.

Combination Menus

Combination menus offer the manager the flexibility to introduce new menu items through a cycle menu or daily menu and to maintain some amount of signature or standard menu items. These signature items, the ones customers associate specifically with restaurant or operation, constitute a "brand name." Branding is a way for you to make a name in your market by making a unique mark on customers' perceptions.

Combination menus require daily taste testing and training for both kitchen and service staff. They can create imbalances in equipment use and skill-set requirements, depending on the menu of the day. Take, for example, one day's menu item that calls for grilling as opposed to sauté preparation. The chef will depend heavily on the grill and less on the burner during this day. This can change the pattern of operation in the kitchen, affecting different parts of the meal and how quickly meals are served.

Specials

Once a special is determined, it must be communicated to the guest. Attractive boards describing the special can be placed within view of the seated guests. Include a generic *Specials* section in a prime place on the menu, or use a clip-on to advertise the day's specials. Many operators find it cost effective to print pages of specials or even entire menus daily. Durable, attractive menu jackets can be purchased to hold menu inserts. A quality laser printer that prints the appropriate page size is needed.

Specials can be an excellent way to increase profits. Chef's specials can be profitable items that are not on the current menu. They may be left over from different cuts of other menu items, or they can be one of your vendor's best buys for the day. The key to increasing the profit from specials is creativity. Chefs need to be creative with planned daily specials and the use of leftovers, and they should price specials at higher profit margins than regular menu items.

In addition to acknowledging the importance of menu placement, managers find that a significant number of customers accept the suggestions of their servers, who should be trained to offer the specials effectively. You can offer incentives to servers who sell the most specials. Care must be taken to ensure that the plate appearance of a special is particularly pleasing to the guest. The appearance and aroma of the food determine how most people judge a special's acceptability. Even the perceived taste of the food is improved by its visual presentation.

Cycle Menu

Cycle menus are common in schools, hospitals, business cafeterias, conference centers, and lodging facilities that offer room and meal packages. It is favorable and practical in these types of environment that the customers are very frequent and require some variety and choice. Such menus have a set of selections for a period of time, and this set of selections repeats. For example, a four-week menu cycle would start over on week five with the same selections offered on week one. Depending on the previous day's leftovers and on special buys, the chef may introduce new menu items for the day to minimize waste and to improve profitability. The advantages of cycle menus includes those of the standard menu as well as the fact that management can identify customer preferences and make menu changes to enhance customer satisfaction.

Daily Menu

A daily menu is another form of daily special. It also allows the manager to take advantage of special buys and to offer them as daily specials to the customer. With a daily menu, management can quickly react to ever-changing product costs and take advantage of specially priced items to improve profitability. This is a very common practice in upscale and non-ethnic restaurants. Daily menus are generally very profitable if there is no over- or underproduction. If the operation underestimates production and runs out, customers will be dissatisfied. They could also be disappointment if a return customer expects the same item from a previous visit, only to find that their favorite item is not being prepared the same or with the same ingredients. Another disadvantage is that, since the menu changes daily, sales records are more difficult to maintain and to interpret. The main disadvantage of daily menu is planning: purchasing and cooks' training may not be adequate for the daily variation of cuisine.

Menu Nutrition

As the American palate becomes more sophisticated and health-conscious, restaurateurs are aggressively catering to nutrition-minded customers. The trend is toward providing nutrition-conscious customers with ample menu choices. Figure 2-5 provides some of the major food sources for menu consideration. It shows the two major nutrient groups: vitaminsand minerals. Vitamins are chemical compounds that promote good health. They consist of fat-soluble vitamins (A, D, E, and K), and water-soluble vitamins (B and C). Like vitamins, minerals are chemical elements that perform various healthful functions in the body. Minerals comprise about 5 percent of a person's body weight. It is the job of the chef to incorporate all of these elements into the menu.

As little as 15 years ago, healthy menus were something that only hospitals needed to provide for their patients. Now, according to a recent NRA consumer research report, nearly 90 percent of adults prefer more healthful menu choices in order to have greater control of what they eat. In response to the Centers for Disease Control and Prevention's estimate that more than six in ten adults meet the clinical definition of overweight or obesity, restaurants are adding low-fat, low-calorie, and low-carbohydrate items, as well as other healthy selections, to their menus. In addition, virtually all restaurants allow patrons to customize their meals by either substituting foods or altering cooking methods. As the recommended dietary guidelines continue to change, one thing remains the same: Portion control is essential to maintaining a healthy weight. Appropriate portion size depends on the customer's daily caloric requirements, resulting from age, weight, build, and level of physical activity. Experts suggest very limited amounts of fat, oils, and sweets. If you can work with your chefs to design a menu rich in grain products, vegetables, and fruits that are low in fat, saturated fat, and cholesterol—and moderated in sugars, salt, and sodium—it could set your restaurant apart from the rest.

Menu Design

When planning for sales, no tool is more influential than the menu itself. And when designing a menu, generating a profit is a prime consideration. For customers, the menu is the first impression and the most complete representation of a restaurant. The menu describes products and prices these items in order to generate enough sales to make a profit. Studies conducted by the Foodco Corporation indicate that 80 percent of new customers and up to 50 percent of repeat customers don't know what they'll order when they enter a restaurant. Thus the menu plays a large part in determining sales. Menus need to be designed in a way that ensures repeat business, high sales volume, and healthy profit. A good design addresses the menu's layout, physical characteristics, and content.

An effective menu layout entices customers to order the items you want. You achieve that by strategically engineering the layout through graphic design, format, photos, icons, colors, and pricing that, while not the focal point of the menu, should lead to selection of highly profitable items. Everything about the layout should relate to the restaurant and the environment you are creating. You don't want to create an upscale restaurant and then hand customers a cheap, poorly printed menu. If in doubt, hire a professional designer to establish a basic design template. What follows is an account of a not-so-successful restaurant that created a successful experience in a matter of four weeks by improving its menu design.

At Michael's Bistro in downtown Monterey, all menu items were treated the same on the menu, and therefore nothing really caught the customer's eye; nothing was exciting or special. Sales were 45 percent below their seasonal average. The manager learned about menu layout and decided to undertake a new layout for her menu. She learned that most customers don't read menus, but rather scan them, and what they see first and last are the items most likely to remain in their minds longest. It is important, then, to put your most profitable items in places where studies show that customers' eyes are most likely to land.

Figure 2-5 Vitamins. *Courtesy of "The Professional Chef*, 8th Edition*"*: by the Culinary Institute of America. © 2006 by the Culinary Institute of America. Reproduced with permission of John Wiley & Sons Ltd.

Vitamins: Their Function and Common Sources		
Name	**Function**	**Food Source**
WATER-SOLUBLE VITAMINS		
B-complex (thiamin, riboflavin, niacin, folate, biotin, pantothetic acid, B6, B12)	Allow of proper release of energy in the body	Grains; legumes; vegetables; animal protein (B12 only found in animal foods)
Vitamin C (ascorbic acid)	Increases body's absorption of iron, aids in growth and maintenance of body tissue; boosts immune system; contains antioxidant properties	Fruits and vegetables (berries, melons, tomatoes, potatoes, green leafy vegetables)
FAT-SOLUBLE VITAMINS		
Vitamin A	Aids in proper vision, bone growth, reporduction, cell division and differentiation; regulates immune system; maintains surface linings	Animal protein such as liver and eggs; the precursor—beta caroteen—is found in orange, deep yellow and dark green leafy vegetables
Vitamin D	Aids in proper bone formation	Milk; some cereal and breads; fatty fish; egg yolks
Vitamin E	Protects body from damage by free radicals; contains antioxidant properties	Nuts; seeds; seed oils; avocados; sweet potatos; green leafy vegetables
Vitamin K	Aids in proper blood clotting	Dark green leafy vegetables, such as spinach, kale, broccoli
MINERALS		
Calcium (body's most abundant mineral)	Used in the development of bones and teeth; regulates blood pressure; aids in muscle contraction, transmission of nerve impulses, and clotting of the blood	Dairy products (milk, yogurt); broccoli; green leafy vegetables
Phosphorus	Plays a key role in energy-releasing reactions; used in conjunction with calcium for maintaining bones and teeth	Animal protein; nuts; cereals; legumes
Sodium and potassium (electrolytes)	Aids in the regulation of bodily functions; help to maintain the body's normal fluid balance; involved in nerve and muscle functions	Sodium is plentiful in many foods; potassium is found in virtually all fruits and vegetables
Magnesium	Promotes healthy teeth and bones; muscle contractions; nerve transmission; and bowel functions	Green vegetables; nuts; legumes; whole grains
Fluoride	Helps to prevent tooth decay; may help to prevent osteoporosis	Community water; saltwater fish; shellfish; tea
Iodine	Essential for the normal functioning of the thyroid gland; helps to regulate metabolism, cellular oxidation, and growth	Table salt; cod; grains
Iron	Helps to carry oxygen from the lungs to cells; involved in cellular energy metabolism	Liver and red meat; whole grains; legumes; green leafy vegetables; dried fruit

First, the most profitable items in the three-page menu were placed on the inside right page, toward the middle; the manager had learned that this is the menu's "prime real estate." Figures 2-6 through 2-8 identify the best spots on different types of menus, based on the patterns most people's eyes follow when they open a menu. The most profitable items should be placed in these places.

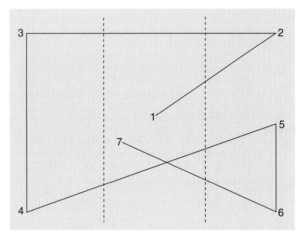

Figure 2-6 Eye Patten for a Three-Page Menu

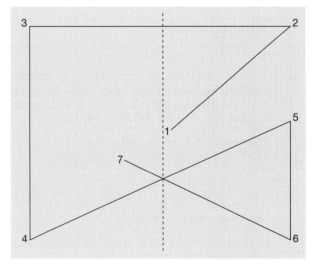

Figure 2-7 Eye Pattern for a Two-Page Menu

Another tactic is to use boxes and icons to sell what you want. Boxes might include specials, or they might simply highlight profitable items. Icons might point out items that are made with a particular fresh ingredient for which your restaurant is famous, or they might indicate heart-healthy items. Figure 2-9 is an example of the use of boxes and icons to sell what you want. According to Dimitri, director of Barneby's Hotels, "You don't have to drop items that are seasonally expensive, but you can minimize their impact" by adjusting their positions in the menu.

Figure 2-8 Eye Pattern for a One-Page Menu

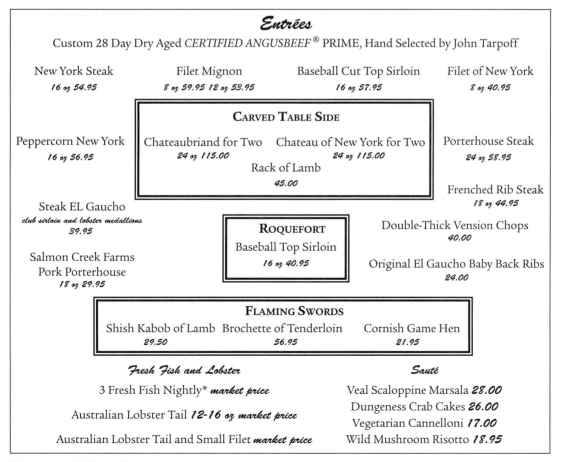

Entrées

Custom 28 Day Dry Aged *CERTIFIED ANGUSBEEF* ® PRIME, Hand Selected by John Tarpoff

New York Steak
16 oz 54.95

Filet Mignon
8 oz 59.95 12 oz 53.95

Baseball Cut Top Sirloin
16 oz 57.95

Filet of New York
8 oz 40.95

CARVED TABLE SIDE

Chateaubriand for Two
24 oz 115.00

Chateau of New York for Two
24 oz 115.00

Rack of Lamb
45.00

Peppercorn New York
16 oz 56.95

Porterhouse Steak
24 oz 58.95

Frenched Rib Steak
18 oz 44.95

Steak EL Gaucho
club sirloin and lobster medallions
39.95

ROQUEFORT

Baseball Top Sirloin
16 oz 40.95

Double-Thick Vension Chops
40.00

Salmon Creek Farms
Pork Porterhouse
18 oz 29.95

Original El Gaucho Baby Back Ribs
24.00

FLAMING SWORDS

Shish Kabob of Lamb
29.50

Brochette of Tenderloin
56.95

Cornish Game Hen
21.95

Fresh Fish and Lobster

3 Fresh Fish Nightly* *market price*

Australian Lobster Tail *12-16 oz market price*

Australian Lobster Tail and Small Filet *market price*

Sauté

Veal Scaloppine Marsala **28.00**

Dungeness Crab Cakes **26.00**

Vegetarian Cannelloni **17.00**

Wild Mushroom Risotto **18.95**

Figure 2-9 Fully-Fleshed Menu

Physical Characteristics

The type of restaurant sometimes dictates the physical characteristics of the menu. For example, in Mexican restaurants, long menus are common because a Mexican menu often offers a tremendous number of items. Italian menus sometimes have colorful Italian art. And because coffee-shop menus wear out quickly due to extensive use, they are typically laminated or in a holder—like a booklet that lets you slide pages in and out. At Michael's Bistro, the manager used the physical size of the menu to grab attention and to affect subtly customers' impression of the menu. The old menu was too large to be handled easily, so the staff changed the size to 8½ by 11 inches. To highlight profitable items, the manager added appropriate eye-catching graphics with color shading. Take a look at Figure 2-10. Which item in the menu draws your eyes first?

The simple graphic pointing to Item Number 2 draws the reader's eye immediately. Another idea is to use photographs of the items you wish to sell. Customers can be persuaded to order an item because they have a visual guarantee that the actual presentation will match the photo on the menu. Managers at Michael's Bistro decided against using photographs because the size of the menu didn't permit pictures of many items, and because customers could reject or judge their meal harshly if its presentation did not resemble its enticing photo closely. Instead they changed the font size to 14 points, which made the text easier to read. They also started using a thick-grained paper with a high-quality feel.

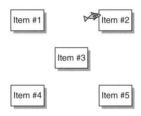

Figure 2-10 Fish Icon Menu

Menu Content

Menu content should appear in the sequence of how the menu items are served: drinks, appetizers, entrées, and then desserts. In Figure 2-11, all elements of good menu description are present. The customer will not wonder what these items are, how they are prepared, or how they are served. They will know what accompanies each dish, and they are reading appetizing descriptive copy to help them decide what to order. Certain words have more selling power than others. For example, "marinated," "roasted" or "cooked in wood-fired oven" have more allure than simply "fried." Also important is the perceived value of the meal and the pricing.

Customer Value Perception

All customers have some idea of price and value when they come to a restaurant to eat. If your prices are above those people expect to pay, your restaurant will have to provide a greater perceived value—better ingredients, friendlier or more efficient service, more creative menu items—to emphasize the value and de-emphasize the price. In Figure 2-11, the menu designers have started by de-emphasizing the price. Notice that the price is not the focal point; it does not stand out when all elements of good menu description are present. The customer should not wonder what menu items are, how they are prepared, or how they are served. They should know what accompanies each dish, and read appetizing descriptive copy to help them decide what to order. Certain words have more selling power than others. For example, *marinated, roasted,* and *cooked in wood-fired oven* have more allure than simply *fried*. Also important is the perceived value of the meal and the pricing.

If customers find menu items that are offered at prices that are somewhat less than they would expect to pay, they perceive them to be of good value and tend to be attracted to those menu items and the operations that offer them. If the customers see prices as too high, either because of their own budgets or because of perceived value, they will avoid an operation in the future.

Small Salads & Soup	*Meat*
PORTABELLA MUSHROOM SOUP Fresh portabella and crèmini mushrooms, caramelized onion, cayenne, fresh leeks, sherry cream 6.95	**BRAISED VEAL SHORT RIBS** Harissa maple glaze, veal stuffed ravioli, fresh herbs, natural jus 18.50
GREEK SALAD Vine ripened tomatoes, cucumbers, kalamata olives, crumbled Feta, toasted pita croutons 6.95	**BISTRO STEAK** Herb chickpea fritters, baby arugula, balsamic ketchup 22.95
CHOP CHOP SALAD Smoked Turkey, wine salami, Provolone, fresh basil, garbanzo beans, Parmesan, crisp romaine, tomatoes, balsamic vinaigrette 8.50	**STEAK FRITES – NEW YORK** Palomino signature steak, herb de Provence butter, red wine shallot topping, pomme frites 33.95
BRAISED LAMB SHANK Chilled romaine, chopped bacon, diced tomato, toasted hazelnuts 7.50	**ROTISERRIE PORK CHOP** Roasted root vegetable and braced pork ragout, wilted swiss chard 18.50
Big Salads	*Pasta*
CHOP CHOP SALAD Smoked Turkey, wine salami, Provolone, fresh basil, garbanzo beans, Parmesan, crisp romaine, tomatoes, balsamic vinaigrette 13.50	**LOBSTER RAVIOLI** Fresh sheets of saffron pasta, lobster and tarragon filling, lobster cream sauce, finished with herb mascarpone 19.95
SPICED PRAWN AND MANGO SALAD Ginger grilled prawns, spiced jumbo cous cous, Fuji apples, mango, bell peppers, cilantro, toasted walnuts 15.95	**RIGATONE BOLOGNESE** Spicy Italian sausage, pear tomato, crushed garlic, oregano, roasted red pepper cream 16.95
CAESAR SALAD With grilled chicken 13.50 With blackened salmon 15.95	**FETTUCINE ALFREDO WITH SEAFOOD** Pan seared prawns, Manila clams, Penn Cove mussels, alfredo cream sauce, Parmesan, cracked black pepper 19.95
GRILLED CHICKEN SALAD WITH WARM PECAN CRUSTED BLUE Baby organic greens, crisp romaine, sliced pear, roasted pecans, maple vinaigrette 15.95	**PENNE GORGONZOLA** Toasted Hazelnuts, black pepper, parsley 13.95

Figure 2-11 Menu Content

On the other hand, if prices are substantially less than customers would expect to pay at a similar restaurant, the customer may question the quality or portion sizes.

Menu Costing

Menu cost is different from menu price. The cost is the money spent by the operation on labor, ingredients, and overhead. In this chapter, menu cost refers to **potential cost**—the expectation of what the food cost *should* be, if you comply with all cost control procedures (discussed in detail in Chapter 9). In other words, it is the standard by which you measure the food cost efficiency of your operation. Using menu recipes, you can easily calculate what each item should cost by adding the cost of each recipe ingredient. You should keep all of this information in your database and update it as prices or menu items change. Before setting menu prices, you should determine what each item costs to prepare. According to the NRA's 2008 survey, only 30 percent of restaurants actually cost out their menu before setting prices. Chain restaurants account for 85 percent of that 30 percent. It's no wonder that the percentage of failed restaurants is so high among other food service operations.

potential cost The expectation of what the cost *should* be, if you comply with all cost control procedures. It is the standard whereby you measure the cost efficiency of your operation.

Menu Pricing

While menu cost is what the operation spends to make an item, **menu pricing** is the establishment of how much a customer is charged for an item. Menu pricing is an integral part of menu content. Pricing methods can help or hinder cost and profit objectives. Pricing can determine sales volume and dramatically affect your bottom line because customers will react to prices so quickly that you often won't get a second chance. Consider your market and your costs to plan what you can—and need to—charge.

menu pricing How much a customer is charged for an item.

Although pricing is often as much an art as a science, your profit margin determines how profitable you are—and you don't want to leave that to chance. Many software programs, such as

Menu Magician from Foodco and Chef Tec, are designed to analyze menu items in order to facilitate maximum guest satisfaction *and* restaurant profit. One way software programs can help is by suggesting an average guest check amount, which can be used as a planning tool. Such programs can also outline sales according to "entrée-only" items so that managers can actually see the sales and profit distribution of all items. This can also be done manually on a simple spreadsheet, but doing so is more time-consuming.

Before we get to detailed menu pricing information in Chapter 13, you will learn about purchasing and costing, which will form the basis of your pricing decisions.

Truth in Menu Content

Truth in menu content is a legal issue as well as a matter of integrity and confidence. The manager must ensure that the menu content is accurate. If you say that your beef is prime or your chicken is free-range, for example, it must be purchased and served that way. Laws limit the substitutions you may make. Often, customers must be told about substitutions so that they can make an informed choice. Think of this as a promise that the manager must keep. Moreover, if you claim certain health or nutritional values associated with any of your menu items, the U.S. Food and Drug Administration (FDA) requires that you substantiate and communicate these facts to your customers. For example, you might make a nutritional or health claim such as "low fat," "organic," or "heart-healthy." Symbols to denote such desired qualities are often printed on a menu. Managers should research how to substantiate such claims—for example, by providing nutritional information upon request—as well as the best ways to ensure consistency in the kitchen. Iis illegal to mislead customers or misrepresent what you serve.

The "Dollars and Sense" of Menu Planning through Staff Training

Menu planning is a powerful tool for realizing objectives of minimizing operating costs and maximizing sales. This can be aided by specific staff training in the area of suggestive selling techniques. Knowing your menu mix percentages is just the first step toward gaining a competitive edge. Menu mix percentages are the number of specific items sold divided by the total number of items sold. Communicate these strategies to your staff members and discuss how they can up-sell or cross-sell items. The knowledge they gain can translate into confidence in dealing with customers.

Here is an example of a manager "sleeping at the wheel":

I led a training workshop for servers at a restaurant that will remain unnamed. By the end of the workshop, I was confident in our servers' abilities to sell, as I witnessed their abilities grow in role play after role play. The room was alive with enthusiasm; I could see them mentally counting their additional tips as they grew more confident in their abilities. As a professional trainer and salesperson, I was satisfied, and I was sure our guests would be, too.

A couple months later, when I found myself sitting in the very restaurant whose servers I had trained, accompanied by the hotel's general manager and our company president, I must admit I was a little smug about what was about to happen.

We were approached by one of the workshop attendees. When the president asked, "How are the crab cakes?" I was ready for her to take the opportunity and run with it. Instead, to my horror, I heard, "Nobody's sent them back yet." I knew the training session was two months ago, but did nothing stick? Although the president was appalled by the response, to add insult to injury, the general manager did not appear to see anything wrong with the server's answer.

(continues)

(continued)

The GM's reaction told me what was wrong, and it had nothing to do with my training techniques.

It was apparent that the server had been "re-educated." Apathy, lack of appreciation, and an obvious lack of confidence in the product had killed the server's enthusiasm before it had a chance to mature into practiced ability. This attitude can run through an organization like a virus and kill any chance of business and personal growth.

Source: Lizz Chambers, CHE, CHA, and Ralph Miller. "Enthusiasm: Have It. Transfer It or Lose It." Hotel News Resource Dec. 6, 2006.

A trained waitperson can confidently suggest the perfect combination of good food and wine if he or she can say, "I've tasted this wine with the pasta special, and it was excellent" or "Have you considered a chardonnay with the salmon you're having?" Perhaps the salmon is one of your slow-moving menu items, and it only needs recognition to achieve the popularity its taste warrants. Many customers are looking for their server's knowledgable opinion. All it takes is familiarity with a few good wines and how they taste with menu items.

Wine can be particularly profitable, and your waitstaff is the key to that profitability. When coaching your staff, ask them to remember this phrase: "Have you decided on a wine with your dinner this evening?" It carries a powerful punch but is so subtle that customers will not feel pressured. The secret is to train employees always to think positively about every order. For example, with customers who request an opinion about the menu, train your staff to suggest the chef's special or the slow-moving but profitable menu item. If customers order three glasses of wine, the staff should thank them and then suggest, "For about the same price, you can have a bottle of the house wine and still have enough left over to top off your glasses later on." This idea is bound to bring an order for the bottle—or at least an appreciation for the interest.

Timing is essential. When the waitperson suggests the second bottle before the entrée but after the first course, he or she has hit upon perfect timing. The customers are going to look at the little bit of wine left in their glasses and think about the good meal yet to come. On the other hand, suggesting the second bottle too soon amounts to pushing the guest. Suggest it after the dinner is served, and the sense of anticipation will be gone; many customers will decline and make do with what they have. And if you or your staff needs some incentives, share with them the chart in Figure 2-12, which assumes an entrée cost of $40.

For the server, the increase in income from two glasses of house wine to two glasses of Chardonnay in 52 weeks is $1,443. The increase from two glasses of house wine to a bottle of Chardonnay in one year is $8,775. From the restaurant's perspective, assuming that fifty covers a night order Chardonnay instead of house wine, the company will gross almost $22,812 more. If every three covers order a bottle of wine, the difference is nearly $119,000. The bottom line is that the staff needs to understand the menu, the wines, and the customer. The staff and the company can both benefit tremendously.

Menu Launch

Once the menu is developed, an effective menu launch becomes the critical step to its success. You launch a menu when you premiere that menu with the public. A menu launch for a new restaurant is far more time-consuming and costly than one for an established restaurant. This is primarily due to name recognition.

You've created a menu that the customer really wants, right? Before attempting a menu launch, make sure that all operational issues (staff training, equipment, and supplies) are taken care of.

Figure 2-12 Wine and Tips Table

	With 2 Glasses of House Wine @ $3.25/ea.	With 2 Glasses of Chardonnay @ $4.50/ea.	With a Bottle of Chardonnay @ $24.00
Wine Charge	$6.50	$9.00	$24.00
Total Dinner	$46.50	$49.00	$64.00
Employee's Tip @ 15%	$6.98	$7.35	$9.60
Tips for five tables	$34.90	$36.75	$48.00
Tips for three turnovers	$104.70	$110.25	$144.00
Tips in five days	$523.50	$551.25	$720.00
Tips in four weeks	$2094.00	$2205.00	$2880.00
Tips in 52 weeks	$27,222.00	$28,665.00	$37,440.00

This will minimize customer dissatisfaction. To maximize your chances for good customer turnout, you may have to spend money on promoting your restaurant through radio, TV, the Internet, magazines, or newspapers. This could be very expensive. Most restaurants barter with other organizations to relieve the expense. There are excellent books on how companies launch new and old products with more ideas than can fit within the scope of this book. We'll limit ourselves to just this very useful one: bartering.

Bartering to Launch a Menu and Boost Sales

bartering Trading goods and services without the exchange of money.

In today's business environment, bartering, one of the oldest forms of trade, has been transformed into a sophisticated way of doing business in the food service industry. **Bartering** is defined as trading goods and services without the exchange of money. Restaurants use bartering as a way to launch new menus and to increase business during slow periods, and magazines or radio stations may barter to fill advertising spaces.

Let's look at an example of how a restaurant might barter to make the difference for their business levels. In 2008, at the urging of friends and family who had tasted his cooking, Carlos Reyes opened a 100-seat restaurant called All-American Cuisine in a tourist area of Los Angeles. The restaurant concept proved an immediate success, first with the locals (who approved of the price and variety) and then with holiday visitors.

After summer was over, restaurant business dropped by 50 percent and Carlos was contemplating closing the restaurant during the winter months. But he was concerned about the cost of reopening the restaurant the following summer: Wouldn't he need to advertise to let people know he was open again? With that in mind, Carlos approached the local radio station with the idea of trading lunches and dinners for airtime, at a rate about equal to his retail prices. The idea was accepted, and both companies entered into a contractual agreement whereby All-American Cuisine would supply lunches and dinners upon request for a total value of $10,000 in return for one hour of airtime every week for the months he planned to be in business.

Three weeks into his summer season, Carlos's business started to pick up, and within six weeks, it was at 95 percent capacity. Now the big question was as follows: How should the restaurant account for its sales from the barter business with the radio station? No money was exchanged, and the cost of the meals served was less than the $10,000 trade value. To begin to answer the revenue recognition question, we must refer to *generally accepted accounting principles* (GAAPs), which require that barter transactions be accounted for at "fair market value." Fair market value in this case is $10,000, and that is what the sales tax payment will be based upon. Without going in-depth into accounting practice, which is beyond the scope of this book, the following journal entry should help clarify the revenue recognition question:

To record contracted rate between All-AmericanCuisine and the radio station (external rate):

	Debit—Balance Sheet	Credit—Balance Sheet
Prepaid Asset—Barter	$10,000	
Deferred Liability—Barter		$10,000

These accounts will be written off to zero as both parties redeem their trade value.

To record actual cost (internal rate): Assume food cost of 30 percent:

	Debit—Profit and Loss	Credit—Profit and Loss
Advertising—Radio	$3,000	
Food Cost		$3,000

This entry effectively recognizes the food cost credit and charges the advertising expense account.

From the above, it is clear that bartering is more than just a fair exchange of goods and services between two businesses. It provides financial bonuses for both companies. In a nutshell, it is a cash-conservation vehicle because paying for business expenses such as advertising with trade dollars leaves more cash available for other, strictly cash expenses.

For more information about barter, contact the International Reciprocal Trade Association: 175 West Jackson Blvd. Chicago, IL 60604.

SUMMARY

When planning for sales, no tool is more important than the menu. Menus need to be structured in order to ensure repeat business, higher sales volume, and increased profitability. To achieve these goals, meeting the customer's needs is critical. Both the content and the appearance of the menu must appeal to the customer.

To maximize profitability, the most profitable items should be emphasized. This may be achieved through strategic placement, highlighting, server suggestions, and appealing descriptive copy. Only by designing and pricing the menu properly can profit be maximized. Once a menu is developed, the staff should be trained fully to sell the most profitable items and to increase check averages. They also must be trained to provide excellent service and to seek feedback from customers about opportunities for improvement, regarding not only the menu, but also all aspects of the operation.

CHAPTER QUESTIONS

Critical Thinking Questions

1. The menu is the primary food service sales tool. True or false?

2. A menu should be laid out to flow in the same order as the items are served in a meal. True or false?

3. Specials should generally be priced at lower-than-average contribution margins to ensure that they will sell. True or false?

4. One advantage of a well-designed menu is that it eliminates the need to train the waitstaff regarding sales techniques. True or false?

5. In maintaining minimum standards, the customers' perception is primary. True or false?

6. What is a market survey, and what are the benefits of giving one?

7. What are the main characteristics of a standard and combination menu?

8. What factors should be considered in creating and designing a menu?

Multiple-Choice Questions

1. In designing a menu, which of the following should be considered?
    A. customers
    B. product availability
    C. skill level of staff
    D. kitchen design
    E. all of the above

2. What is a good way to research your customers' preferences?
    A. Look them up on the Internet
    B. Guess what their preferences will be
    C. Conduct a market survey of past, present and potential customers
    D. Ask your competition what their customers' preferences are

3. Which of the following elements must menu planning include?
    A. Printing the menus from a template
    B. Consulting with your competition
    C. Training your vendors to bring the right ingredients
    D. Considering menu type, menu nutrition, menu design

4. How can you accurately calculate the menu cost of an item on your menu?
    A. Using your menu recipes and the cost and amount of each ingredient
    B. Remembering the cost of similar items at other restaurants where you've worked
    C. Asking your vendors for their opinion of what it should cost
    D. You cannot calculate menu costs because your vendors might change

5. Let's say your menu offers free range chicken and organic beef entrée items on the menu. The vendor couldn't bring either this week. What can you do?

   A. Substitute more economical chicken and beef products

   B. Substitute more expensive chicken and beef products

   C. Inform guests and allow them to decide if they still want the item

   D. Remind guests that free range and organic meats are healthier

6. Wait staff can increase sales by which of the following means?

   A. Presenting the specials using appetizing language

   B. Offering wine pairings to go with the entrées

   C. Making their offers to the customers at the appropriate times during the meal

   D. All of the above

7. Wait staff can also benefit *directly* from increased sales. Why is that?

   A. Good salespeople can work in any industry.

   B. When sales increase, tips generally increase as well.

   C. Customers are more content when they have wine and dessert.

   D. Wait staff enjoy additional training.

8. Which of these is an advantage to using a standard menu?

   A. Standard menus allow for great flexibility from day to day.

   B. You don't need to select items for a standard menu, because these are created by a franchise owner.

   C. Since menu items remain the same, future sales are easier to predict.

   D. Such a menu offers suggestions to your guests, so your servers don't have to do so.

9. When you barter goods and/or services, how are these accounted for in your sales?

   A. Barter transactions should be accounted for at fair market value

   B. Barter transactions are inherently illegal

   C. Barter transactions cost you less, so you should account for them at cost

   D. Barter transactions need not be accounted for, because no money changes hands

10. If your restaurant is very expensive and upscale, your menu must:

    A. Feature organic and vegetarian items

    B. Include a long wine list

    C. Spell out dollar amounts instead of using numerals and dollar signs

    D. Match your image

PART

1

Purchasing Standards

Learning Objectives

After reading this chapter, you should be able to:

- understand the benefits of saving money in the purchasing department;

- understand the role of the purchasing agent in the purchasing process;

- understand basic concepts of ethics and independence in the purchasing department;

- understand the importance of legal contracts;

- understand why technology is vital in today's purchasing practices.

In Practice

Myla Thomas felt optimistic about her future with the Sea Breeze Hotel after her meeting with Eric Breeze and Chef Robert. The meeting gave her a clear insight into how the food and beverage department worked. Her next stop was a meeting with the purchasing manager, Scott Vincent. She arrived at his office for a 10:00 A.M. meeting with him and chef Robert, who both rose from their chairs to exchange warm greetings with Myla.

"People here always seem to be on time for meetings," she commented.

"That's pretty much true. We expect the same from our vendors, too," *responded Scott. "We think it says a lot about how we run our business."*

Myla wanted to know more about that very topic: how Scott and Robert ran this side of the business. She asked, "I want to hear your opinions about something. How do our policies and procedures help or hinder our chances to deal with vendors, or to decide not to deal with a vendor?"

As in Myla's previous meeting with Robert, his answer spoke volumes: "Our policy on ethical conduct keeps us out of trouble. And I hope we can leverage our purchasing power to get better pricing and save money."

"What do you mean by 'keeping us out of trouble'?" Myla asked.

Robert responded, "Our code of conduct keeps everything in perspective. We don't accept gifts because it could imply bribery for business favors."

"Thanks, Robert," responded Myla. But Scott was looking at Robert with a puzzled expression, or so it appeared to Myla. She asked him directly, "Scott, do you have anything to add to that?"

(continues)

> (*continued*)
>
> *"Oh, no, no, Robert is correct," Scott replied, rather hastily.*
>
> *"How about technology in purchasing? Are we up to date?" Myla inquired.*
>
> *"Not quite" Scott answered. "We have a long way to go. We need new computers."*

INTRODUCTION

"Everything is worth what its purchaser will pay for it."

—Publilius Syrus, first century BCE

This statement, over 2,000 years old, is as true today as it was when it first was written. It is particularly true for a restaurant's purchasing agent. Based on our needs, wants, and budget, we all make choices about what to purchase. In doing so, we decide what various goods are worth to us. Just as you learn to make wise choices at home—to maximize your benefits and minimize your costs—so you will learn from this book how to do so for your restaurant or company.

This section on purchasing will lead you through the steps a purchaser takes to make smart choices. You'll notice that these steps are not very different from the steps you take when you do your own shopping. At the store, your grocery list corresponds to the meals you will cook and serve at home. Based on your menu choices and budget considerations, you select a store, particular brands, and cuts of meat in the quantities you want to have on hand. Then, after transporting your purchases home, you store and monitor them based on your needs. For example, you don't put food you plan to use that day in your deep freezer, and you don't leave milk in an unrefrigerated cupboard.

If it seems like these steps are just common sense, you are quite right. And because you've learned common sense as you've made purchases for yourself, you already have the necessary skills to be a professional purchaser, too.

Purchasing for a small "mom-and-pop" establishment differs in scale, and most likely in level of formality, from purchasing for a whole chain of restaurants, but the principles are much the same. By determining needs and then filling them while maximizing value, a purchaser becomes a vital part of an establishment's ultimate success. These principles are equally true for the smallest and the largest establishments, and they are true whether the person in charge of purchasing is the chef, the manager, the owner, or someone whose job is just purchasing the needed goods. The only difference is the nature of the agreement between the purchaser and the vendor, which could be a signed contract in a corporate environment; however, the oral or written *request for price quotation* (RFP), which vendors respond to in the form of a price quote or business proposal (also known as a bid), are the same for large and small operations. The ultimate purpose of requesting bids is to compare vendors' products, profiles, and suitability, in order to gain competitive pricing—the starting point for saving money.

SAVING MONEY

You're worth what you saved, not the million you made.

—John Boyle O'Reilly, Rules of the Road

Your company can increase its profit in two ways: reducing expenses or selling more product. When you sell a dollar more, the contribution to the bottom line is not a dollar; it is much less. You must take into consideration all the expenses that went into selling that additional dollar's worth of food—labor, the cost of the product, and so on. However, when you save on expenses by practicing cost control, you increase your bottom-line profit by that entire dollar. Say, for example, that you save $1,000 by applying effective purchasing techniques—that is, by practicing cost control. That $1,000 is equal to $1,000 more in profit. Then let's assume that you make 30 percent profit on your sales. You'd need to sell $3,333 more in product to bring in $1,000 more in profit. To take the example a step further, if your average guest spends $15, you'd need 222 more guests to bring in $1,000 more in profit. As you can see, competent purchasing and effective cost control give you your best opportunity to increase profits.

Moreover, it is easier to control costs in the purchasing department than anywhere else. Labor costs are often difficult to reduce—you may face a union or minimum-wage laws that keep wages at a set level, or you might experience simple wage competitiveness—if you pay less, you will not maintain a good staff. Overhead costs are often difficult to reduce as well, since the costs of utilities, interest rates, and real-estate or rental prices are not under a company's control. As a purchaser, however, you can control cost efficiency directly, and with impressive and profitable results. In the purchasing section of this book, your tools for maximizing value while making purchasing decisions will be explored and discussed in great detail.

Quiz

If you operate a restaurant with a 5 percent profit margin, saving $1 in purchasing generates as much profit as increasing sales by

A. $5. B. $10.
C. $20. D. $50.

THE RESPONSIBILITIES OF THE PURCHASING AGENT

It is the responsibility of the purchaser to maximize value so that the company gets the most for its money. Purchasing does not consist only of buying the products you need. It is an entire process that includes planning the menu; determining product needs; determining specifications for those needs; selecting vendors; purchasing items; and receiving, storing, and issuing the items. Purchasing even extends into the kitchen, where you will monitor how products are used and served to your customers.

Several competing factors must be evaluated when making purchasing decisions. Overall, the purchaser's job is to evaluate the quality of materials and the services that vendors provide relative to the cost of the products. Cost includes not only the purchase price of the product, but also all the additional costs of putting the resulting food on a customer's plate. These include labor costs, costs from product waste and butchering loss, and costs associated with receiving, storing, distributing, preparing, and serving the food. To sell their products, vendors often provide services beyond just the product. These may include reliability, consistency, and convenient delivery schedules. These factors will need to be considered as well as the specific roles of the purchaser. Below is a detailed description of the purchaser's role.

- *Planning the Menu.* As we discussed in Chapter 2, the menu forms the basis for purchasing goods and services. That is, the choices you make with regards to the establishment's menu, staff, style, ambience, price, customer base, and equipment will determine your purchasing dollars and the restaurant's profitability. It is the responsibility of the purchaser to assist with planning and writing the menu according to your target market.

- *Writing Product Specifications.* **Purchase specifications** are detailed lists of exactly what you will buy and the conditions under which you will buy them. They comprise the company's standards and rules for purchasing goods. These rules are covered in greater detail in Chapter 4. The company's image, menu, prices, and clientele will dictate these standards. Purchase specifications will depend on the market, just as the menu does. For example, while hamburgers are offered on many menus, the quality and size of the burger the operation's purchaser buys will depend upon whether it is for a roadside truck stop or an upscale urban restaurant. For example, the exclusive Pebble Beach Resort offers expensive Angus beef burgers on their menu because their customers expect that level of quality and expect to pay correspondingly high prices. Does your operation have that type of clientele? Your purchasing decisions depend on the market: what are appropriate standards in terms of fat content, price, consistency, shape, and speed of preparation? These standards are referred to as *product identification.*

purchase specifications
Detailed, precise descriptions of items desired to be purchased and under what conditions.

- *Determining the Outlet's Needs According to the Menu and Business Volume.* Purchasing according to the menu and business volume is essential to customer satisfaction and profitability. Purchasing too little can cause product shortages, which may result in customer dissatisfaction and loss of revenue. On the other hand, purchasing too much is a recipe for spoilage, theft, and cash flow issues, all of which can negatively impact profitability.

- *Providing Input about Necessary Changes.* Purchasers must advise management about cross-utilization of products, seasonal products, and difficult-to-get products so that last-minute changes can be made and the menu can be revised.

- *Assessing Potential Suppliers.* Purchasers look for vendors by consulting catalogs, competitors, the Internet, and associates. They also have to evaluate the quality of the vendors they find.

- *Collecting and Reviewing Vendor Bids.* Prices for most perishable products (such as produce, meat, poultry, seafood, and dairy) change weekly. Prices for staples and dry products often change monthly. It is the responsibility of the purchaser to review vendor bid prices before making appropriate purchasing decisions.

- *Negotiating Prices and Conditions with Vendors.* In addition to pricing, conditions that should be discussed with vendors may include early-payment discounts, volume discounts, delivery schedule, and contract pricing. This topic is covered in Chapters 4 and 5.

- *Issuing a Contract or Purchase Order.* Issuing a contract or purchase order after the supplier is selected is a common practice in larger companies, especially those with formal purchasing processes. A **purchase order** usually resembles a purchase requisition. Documentation of items needed is sent to the vendor and submitted to the receiving department. The important contents of this document include the item description, quantity ordered, price, tax, and shipping charges. A copy of the purchase order is also sent to the accounting department to match the signed delivery record with the approved vendor invoice before payment.

purchase order (PO)
An order which includes vendors' prices, products, and agreed arrangements for delivery and payment.

- *Ensuring Proper Delivery.* Proper product delivery is essential for the long-term survival of a vendor-restaurant relationship and for smooth business operations. Proper delivery means using proper equipment to deliver the product on a timely basis. For example, it is often necessary to use refrigerated trucks to deliver perishable products.

- *Receiving, Storing, and Issuing Goods Pragmatically.* Controlling inventory and portion size is critical to the success of any purchasing department. Management should establish **inventory targets** for both the amount to be kept on hand and the **inventory turnover**. An inventory target is the desired level of inventory, while inventory turnover refers to the number of times the inventory of a company is sold and replaced during a given period. The purchaser should highlight slow-moving items, dead stock, and leftover items and bring them to the attention of management. Management should find ways to use these items in the form of employee meals or specials.

inventory target Refers to the desired level of inventory.

inventory turnover A ratio of sales to inventory, which shows how many times the inventory of a company is sold and replaced during an accounting period.

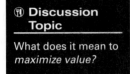

Each of the factors listed must be evaluated from the unique perspective of each food service establishment. These concepts are common sense, and are similar to the factors you weigh when you buy food for your household or choose to dine out. What follows is a detailed examination of how to approach, analyze, and balance these factors in an ethical manner.

Independence and Ethics

The purchaser's role is to represent the company's best interests from start to finish during the purchasing process. All dealings with vendors are the purchaser's responsibility, and they should be standardized, transparent, and ethical. As there is a strong potential for unethical practices that damage the company's reputation, a crucial role of the purchaser is establishing and maintaining ethical practices.

To avoid misunderstanding and confusion, contacts with vendors should be handled through the purchaser. It is the purchaser's responsibility to enforce company policies consistently, so it is best that the purchaser be the direct contact person. This also reduces the possibility of unethical practices by others in your company. Correspondingly, the purchasing department must establish a network of trust with his or her company to earn this independence. This trust is established when a purchaser consistently behaves professionally and ethically. The upper management, then, can trust the purchaser to do his or her job independently and can support the purchaser's decisions.

The professional purchaser must also bring new ideas to the company. When a vendor offers something new or valuable, the purchaser should first introduce the idea to the appropriate staff member, and then arrange a meeting for the vendor and that staff member. Clearly, the purchaser must exercise independent judgment in such matters, and this judgment must be free of any question involving unethical practices.

It is a mistake to deal with vendors who are known to have questionable ethics. If you associate with such a company, you and your company may become "known by the company you keep," meaning you may earn yourself a similar reputation. Such a reputation, whether justified or not, can drive away valuable, reliable, competitive business sources.

In addition, the purchaser can place the company at legal and financial risk. Unethical suppliers might reveal proprietary information to competitors or use it themselves. They might offer a low bid to get your business, only to raise prices at a crucial point in the business season. This is a type of blackmail, as it might be too difficult to change vendors during the high season. Some vendors might also promise a delivery that they know they can't make just to get your order. Or perhaps they may claim to be able to provide a product, but instead "shop" the order to a different company. This could compromise your quality standards or prevent you from getting the products you need. Unscrupulous vendors may even resort to commercial bribery to get your business, even if they haven't earned it. Bribery may take the form of "cash refunds," "gifts," or "samples" to the purchaser. Some vendors have been known to submit or offer blank, incomplete, erroneous, or padded invoices.

Though there may appear to be short-term advantages to special "deals" with unethical vendors, it is poor policy to succumb to the temptation, as your long-term objectives would be jeopardized. In fact, even short-term advantages seldom actually materialize. It is prudent for every company and purchaser to conform to the credo of ethics of the National Association of Purchasing Managers, which requests the following:

The company should take these points into consideration when creating and addressing policy questions in the purchasing department. The purchaser has a leading role in this matter since it involves cost-control responsibilities and possible legal matters. Moreover,

Loyalty to this company
Justice to those with whom he [or she] deals
Faith in his [or her] profession

The following principles form the basis of the National Association of Purchasing Managers Standards of Purchasing Practice:

1. To consider, first, the interests of his [or her] company in all transactions and believe in its established policies.

2. To be receptive to competent counsel from his [or her] colleagues and to be guided by such counsel without impairing the dignity and responsibility of his [or her] office.

3. To buy without prejudice, seeking to obtain the maximum ultimate value for each dollar of expenditure.

4. To strive consistently for knowledge of the materials and processes of manufacture, and to establish practical methods for the conduct of his [or her] office.

5. To subscribe to and work for honesty and truth in buying and selling, and to denounce all forms and manifestations of commercial bribery.

6. To accord a prompt and courteous reception, so far as conditions will permit, to all who call on a legitimate business mission.

7. To respect his [or her] obligations and to require that obligations to him [or her] and to his [or her] concern be respected, consistent with good business practice.

8. To avoid sharp practice. [This term refers to taking advantage of your position for your own personal benefit.]

9. To counsel and assist fellow purchasing managers in the performance of their duties, whenever occasion permits.

10. To cooperate with all organizations and individuals engaged in activities designed to enhance the development and standing of purchasing.

Reprinted with permission from the publisher, the National Association of Purchasing Management, "Principles and Standards of Purchasing Practice."

---

professional handling of these issues establishes a reputation with your company and within the industry. The purchaser's long-term success, and that of the company, depends on following these ethical standards and understanding the legal and contractual consequences described below.

- If an employee cannot be trusted with confidential information relating to product pricing, the manager may be reluctant to share bid pricing with that employee.

- If an employee accepts bribes from suppliers, contracts will tend to go to vendors who pay the highest bribes rather than to the most qualified vendor. Would you like to buy your food from vendors who paid the highest bribe but have a shoddy sanitation record? What could happen to the health and safety of your establishment and customers?

---

⑪ Discussion Topic

A kitchen manager was spotted selling disposable cooking grease to a cosmetic manufacturer on an informal basis. Apparently, this practice started two years ago without anybody's knowledge. She used $2,000 from the $2,500 proceeds for kitchen employees' quarterly picnic events and the rest for personal use.

What arguments are there in favor of a formal salvage program? Do you see any ethical problem with the chef's current practice?

LEGAL ISSUES AND CONTRACTS

A contract is an agreement between two or more parties that is enforceable by law. More specifically, a contract is a set of promises. The law recognizes the performance of these promises as a duty and punishes anyone who breaks them. While a complete discussion of contracts is beyond the scope of this book, the following comments will help you recognize a binding and enforceable contract.

Almost every action you take as a purchaser has some legal significance, and it is imperative that you have a basic grasp of the consequences of entering into a contract. Knowing a bit about the law and purchase orders helps you understand the consequences of your actions, protect your company's interests, and recognize problems requiring expert legal assistance. A good book to read on this topic is *Hotel Restaurant and Travel Law: A Preventive Approach* by Cournoyer, Marshall, and Morris, published by Delmar Cengage Learning.

The Elements of a Contract

Four elements must be present in any contract, whether it is written or spoken, express or implied, when there are two or more parties. A failure or absence of any one of these elements will prevent the creation of an enforceable contract, no matter what the intent of the parties.

1. *Capable Parties.* This means that all parties must be capable of entering a contract. For example, an insane person is not considered capable. In most cases, a minor is not considered capable, either.

2. *Mutual Assent.* This means the contract is voluntary. Force, coercion, and duress prevent the creation of an enforceable contract.

3. *Lawful Objective.* The contract must be free of criminal, immoral, or otherwise illegal objectives, and must in no way be against public policy.

4. *Sufficient Cause to Contract.* This means there is a reason for the contract. It doesn't have to be for money, products, or services, but these causes are the most common. It merely requires *quid pro quo,* a Latin phrase meaning "something for something"—that is, each party expects to receive something as a result of the contract.

Here is an important note to consider: Contracts do not have to be written. Even a verbal commitment that meets the above criteria can be binding. Make sure you discuss these issues with your company to establish the best ways to act in accordance with your contracts and with the law.

TECHNOLOGY IN THE PURCHASING DEPARTMENT

The growing impact of technology in today's food service operation can be found in the NRA's 2004 report: "More than three out of five restaurant operators reported that their operations are more productive than two years ago" because of technology. 80 percent of operators say that personal computers, the Internet, and e-mail have had an impact on efficiency due to online ordering and vendor payment. Widespread use of the Internet is a fairly new phenomenon, and the impact it will eventually have on business is far from settled.

Quick-service restaurants such as McDonald's are beginning to offer self-serve, customer-activated ordering terminals. This could eliminate the order-taker role, as well as the ability to offer alternative menu items when production depletes popular items. The purchasing agent will have to take notice of how these changes impact production and align their systems to address shortages.

Online Ordering

As it has in many other areas of life, the Internet is becoming the great enabler. It allows many users to place purchase orders online, as it has built-in audit trails and is almost universally user-friendly. As an example, the food-service supplier Sysco has created e-Sysco for this purpose. Restaurants that order products from Sysco receive free systems and access to Sysco product catalogs. Orders are placed and confirmations are received online, which eliminates traditional sales and order-processing jobs. Online ordering differs from offline ordering in several important ways:

- *Online ordering eliminates the distance effect.* On the Internet, distance means nothing. When you access a Web site from your desktop computer, it does not matter whether that site is managed on the East Coast or the West Coast. You can place food and beverage orders from anywhere.

- *Automation and timing are transformed.* Purchasing moves faster online. Let's say you find a set of dining-room china and glassware on eBay that would be perfect for your establishment, and you are willing to pay $1,000 for it, but the current bid price is only $150. You could take the long route and sit at your computer, outbidding each new bid until you reach $1,000, but can you devote that much time to such a project? Instead, you can let the system be your automated proxy and do your bidding for you. For this reason and others, ordering online is faster than calling or faxing in your order. It is also less prone to errors.

- *The Internet can be very cost-effective.* Depending on the cost of connection and computer hardware, the Internet may be a relatively small investment. Once you have these basics, however, there are few (if any) additional costs: You can do all of your work without printing a word, except perhaps to print a purchase order confirmation. This type of ordering also saves money for the vendor by reducing necessary staff, a savings that may be passed on to purchasers.

- *Ordering online gives access to a larger—nearly infinite—product database.* Ordering this way enables and facilitates relationships among a great range of businesses and their customers, suppliers, and communities. Such relationships might be more difficult or even impossible to access offline.

- *Unethical vendors have a new way to reach your company.* For all the benefits of access to online resources and vendors, the obvious concern is that the vendor on the other end may have fraudulent intent. It is as important—or more so—to check vendors' reputations when ordering online as when ordering using traditional methods.

- *There is a growing network effect from Internet connectivity.* Steve Case, former CEO of America Online, once said that AOL is in the business of delivering subscribers to one another. The vast stores of information, reviews, resources, and products online are available to anyone with a computer and a connection, with very fast results.

Electronic Invoicing

Today, about 75 percent of companies receive some invoices electronically. Figure 3-1 illustrates the flow of records and products between the purchasing and the accounting departments. The majority of accounting systems rely on purchase orders and invoices to process payment for products received. The manual procurement-to-payment model in Figure 3-1 is being replaced with an electronic procurement-to-payment model in many companies, such as Delaware North Companies (DNC). The important difference between manual and electronic models is that with an electronic model, the roles of the purchaser and accounts-payable representative are being consolidated into one action to process an invoice for payment. This process, called electronic data interchange (EDI), is discussed below. At DNC, however, this

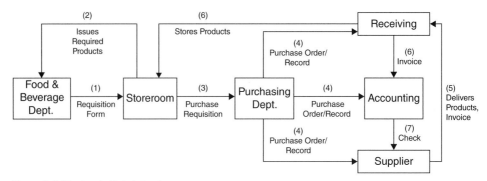

Figure 3-1 Electronic Data Interchange.

Source: William B. Virts, *Purchasing for Hospitality Operations*

reduction of human involvement in processing and filing does not eliminate the need for people altogether. Rather, it shifts their responsibilities from clerical to analytical.

By streamlining the payable and receivable processes in steps 4, 5, 6, and 7 in Figure 3-1, DNC is able to capitalize on fraud detection and prevention and to spend time analyzing and reducing duplicate payments, monitoring legal and regulatory compliance, and updating vendor records.

EDI and XML

The use of electronic invoicing, approval, and payment depend on both EDI and extensible mark-up language (XML). These protocols enable companies to send transactions in the form of a purchase order or invoice via the Internet for electronic review, approval, and payment. Online, people routinely share information that, in the past, would have been considered proprietary and hidden from suppliers. Though keeping this information proprietary has afforded companies leverage over suppliers in the past, today it is possible to use the same information to develop economic ties. This is not to say that proprietary information does not present legitimate implementation costs and security concerns. Most accounts-payable departments are, in fact, understandably leery about transmitting financial information over the Internet. However, encryption technology is becoming increasingly sophisticated and is making security concerns less daunting. In the not-too-distant future online invoicing will be as commonly used as electronic travel and entertainment expense reporting.

EDI and XML work as follows: XML uses codes to tell a Web browser how to display information on the screen. The computer doesn't "know" what the information is; it just displays it. XML provides additional tags that identify the kind of information that is being displayed and exchanged. For example, price data might be coded as <price> $10 <price>. When the computer reads this data and sees the <price> tags surrounding *$10*, the computer will immediately know that this is a price. XML tags can designate many different kinds of information—customer orders, bank statements, product information, and so on—and the tags will indicate to the computer how to display, store, and retrieve the information. Delaware North Companies, Inc., and Office Depot are among early adopters of XML technology, which the companies use to facilitate e-commerce with their major customers.

Before an order is sent out via EDI or in the form of an XML file, the computer draws up a list of electronic purchase orders to vendors. When food products arrive at the company's loading dock, the bar codes that have been applied by the vendor are scanned to update inventory records and to trigger payment for the product. The bar codes are scanned again when the product is requisitioned for use in the kitchen or bar outlet. EDI and XML technology are easy to use. They save labor dollars, provide more accurate data, and save time. The disadvantage is that using them requires computer knowledge to set up and to maintain the systems.

Database Responsibilities

Another enormous technological development in the industry has been the nearly universal use of electronic databases in inventory systems. As a purchaser, you must keep invoicing, requisitioning, and inventory reconciliation up-to-date in such systems. If any information is outdated, the inventory management and valuation processes are worthless. A complete perpetual or periodic inventory and accurate pricing are necessary in order to conduct analytical reviews, write reports, and offer recommendations to management. The purchaser's record-keeping skills are fundamental to achieving these goals. Precise inventory procedures will be discussed in greater detail in subsequent chapters, but it is important to note here the role of technology in maintaining crucial business information.

CHAPTER QUESTIONS

Critical Thinking Questions

1. What ethical standards should a purchasing manager—or any employee—maintain?

2. Why is controlling purchasing expenses far more critical than increasing sales an equal amount?

3. Saving $2,000 on purchases in an operation that averages a 4 percent profit margin is equivalent to increasing sales by how much?

4. What are the four elements of a binding contract, and what do they mean?

5. What is the goal of the purchasing department?

6. Why is controlling the cost of purchases so important to the bottom line?

7. What factors are most important in writing purchase specifications?

Objective Questions

1. Communication between the chef and the purchaser should be one-way, with the chef explaining his product needs and the purchaser procuring them. True or False?

2. Legal and ethical issues are rarely relevant in purchasing decisions. True or False?

3. One of the primary objectives of the purchasing department is to procure the best or highest-quality product available. True or False?

Multiple Choice Questions

1. Which of the following elements is NOT required for a contract to be binding?
   A. capable parties
   B. sufficient cause to contract
   C. mutual assent
   D. fair and equitable exchange

2. What is the *primary* goal of the purchasing department?

    A. Controlling costs and maximizing value
    B. Controlling product usage
    C. Keeping the products locked up and safe from damage
    D. Maintaining a proper inventory at all times

3. Why is it more important to control purchasing expenses than to increase sales an equal amount?

    A. Because the purchaser will get bonuses for saving company funds
    B. Because the budget is increased by whatever amount is successfully controlled
    C. Because all savings through cost control go directly to increase the company's bottom line
    D. Controlling purchasing expenses is not really more critical than increasing sales

4. Saving $2,000 on purchases in an operation that averages a 4 percent profit margin is equivalent to increasing sales by how much?

    A. $8,000
    B. $10,000
    C. $2,000
    D. $20,000

5. Purchasing is an entire *process* that includes several steps. Which of the following is ***not*** one of those steps?

    A. Planning the menu and determining the items needed for that menu
    B. Determining the product specifications for those items
    C. Selecting vendors and purchasing the items
    D. Advertising the menu to potential customers

6. Vendors often provide services beyond just the product. Which of the following is ***not*** something you should look for in your vendors?

    A. Convenient delivery schedules
    B. Free samples for your family to test
    C. Reliably sending you're the items you request
    D. Consistency in the quality of the products

7. Which of the following *is not* one of the four elements of a binding contract?

    A. Capable parties
    B. Mutual assent
    C. Lawful objective
    D. Fair and equitable exchange

8. Which factors are most important for determining how you will write your purchase specifications?

    A. Best prices available
    B. Quality of the goods to be purchased
    C. The company's image, menu, prices, and clientele
    D. Finding the most unique items that are still reasonably priced

9. What are the ***most important*** standards that a purchasing manager should maintain when working with vendors?

    A. All payments should be made to vendors within 14 days of receipt of the items

    B. All dealings should be standardized, transparent and ethical

    C. All deals should be signed off on by the company's owner

    D. Any special bonuses like free items should go to the company's owner

10. Why has technology increased productivity for purchasers?

    A. You have access to an almost infinite database of products

    B. Online ordering eliminates the distance effect

    C. Purchasing databases maintain crucial inventory information

    D. All of the above

11. Receiving and processing invoices electronically does what for a company?

    A. Eliminates the need for employees

    B. Eliminates the need for paper copies of the paperwork

    C. Decreases the need for review of the data in the invoice

    D. Increases the need for technologically-adept staff members

CASE STUDY

Business Ethics

Macrina's Bistro is a publicly owned corporation that owns several restaurants in regions across the country. Matthew Patrick is the president of Macrina's Bistro; Lucille Braun is the purchasing agent; and Kevin Matthew is the executive assistant. All three have been with Macrina's Bistro for about five years. Mary is Macrina's Bistro's controller, and she been with the company for two years.

Matthew: Hi, Mary, come on in. So you say you have a confidential matter to discuss. What's on your mind?

Mary: Matthew, I was reviewing our increased purchases from Sysco last week and wondered why our volume has tripled in the past year. When I discussed this with Lucille, she seemed a bit evasive and tried to dismiss the issue by stating that Sysco can give us one-day delivery on our orders.

Matthew: Well, Lucille is right. You know we have been trying to implement "just-in-time" purchasing and trying to get our inventory assets down.

Mary: We still have to look at the overall cost. Sysco is more of a jobber than a warehouse. After investigating orders placed with them, I found that only 10 percent are delivered from their warehouse and the other 90 percent are drop-shipped from the manufacturers. The average markup by Sysco is 30 percent, which amounted to about $500,000 on our orders for the past year. If we had ordered directly form the manufacturers when Sysco didn't have the item in stock, we could have saved about $450,000 ($500,000 × 90 percent). In addition, some of the orders were late and incomplete.

Matthew: Now look, Mary, we get quick delivery on most items, and who knows how much we are saving by not having to stock this stuff in advance or worry about it becoming obsolete. Is there anything else on your mind?

Mary: Well, Matthew, as a matter of fact, there is. I ordered a Dun & Bradstreet credit report on Sysco and discovered that Bruce Templeton is the principal owner. Isn't he your brother-in-law?

Matthew: Sure he is. But don't worry about Bruce. He has a Harvard MBA, and he understands this just-in-time philosophy. Besides, he's looking out for our interests.

Mary (to herself):   This conversation has been enlightening, but it doesn't really respond to my concerns. Can I legally or ethically ignore this apparent conflict of interests?

Your task:

1.   Would Mary be justified in ignoring this situation, particularly since she is not the purchasing agent? In preparing your answer, consider the Standards of Purchasing Practice.

2.   State the specific steps Mary should follow to resolve this matter.

Purchase Specifications

CHAPTER 4

Learning Objectives

After reading this chapter, you should be able to:

- write product specifications based on product knowledge;

- conduct the following types of product testing:

  - yield test

  - butcher test

  - raw food test

  - canned food test/can-cutting test

  - staple dry food test

  - "blind" taste test

- create the following types of quantity specifications:

  - par level

  - purchase order

  - inventory on hand

  - lead time

  - cost of acquisition

  - volume pricing

  - vendor minimum order quantity

  - safety stock

  - perishable products

  - nonperishable products.

In Practice

Myla Thomas's next appointment with chef Robert and purchasing manager Scott Vincent was a tour of the food and beverage storerooms, walk-in coolers, and refrigerators. "Gentlemen, I am still finding my way around this place. Where do we start?" asked Myla. Chef Robert suggested starting from the loading dock

(continues)

(*continued*)

and walking their way through the storerooms and walk-ins and into the kitchen. The purchaser, Scott, was unenthusiastic, but he walked with them.

Scott led the group onto the loading dock and then to the dry storeroom. Myla couldn't believe her eyes. The shelves in the dry storeroom were overloaded. Products were poorly organized: Identical products had been purchased in different sizes and placed in multiple locations. On the floor lay many cases, some opened, others not. Myla peered toward the back of the shelves and could see dust on products in the back. She asked, "Do we have multiple specs for the same product?"

Scott replied, "Not quite. We are correcting these problems as we go along."

Myla went on to comment, "You seem to have an awful lot of product for a restaurant this size."

"We don't like to run out," Scott exclaimed.

"Do you rotate your product?" Myla asked.

"First in, first out, but obviously we are not following it consistently," Robert responded.

At the first of two walk-in coolers, Robert opened the door and followed Myla in to view the produce. Based on her long experience in the industry, Myla gauged that there was much more product than a restaurant of this size required. The shelving units were packed full of produce, and there were additional cases lying on the floor. Scott grabbed a partial case of rotting tomatoes and three-quarters of a case of spoiled lettuce from the cooler floor. He said, "Let me toss this out. I'll be right back."

When Scott returned, Myla felt the need to address his actions. "Of course, that is going to affect your food cost. I agree with you that we can't run out, but business volume dictates how much to buy."

Scott answered, "Yeah, we probably did order a little more than we needed."

Myla's response to Scott showed how she intended to handle this issue: "Please prepare a spoilage report for my review."

Robert led Myla to the dairy cooler. The products inside were organized much better, but there still seemed to be much more of everything than the restaurant could possibly need. "You won't find any spoilage in here," declared Robert proudly. "I personally supervise this area."

At the locked meat cooler, Robert said he needed to get his keys from his office. When he returned and they entered the cooler, he told Myla, "I am in the process of changing our meat specifications to reflect our new menu, as I mentioned to you in our previous meeting."

"This one appears to be in pretty good shape," Myla commented. "The amount of product seems to be about right, and all products are neatly stored in the shelving units."

INTRODUCTION

purchase specifications
Detailed, precise descriptions of items desired to be purchased and under what conditions.

One cannot think well, love well, sleep well, if one has not dined well.

—Virginia Woolf, *A Room of One's Own*, 1929

When you shop for groceries, you have standards in mind for the products you buy. You have **purchase specifications** of your own, however informal these might be. You might prefer low-fat, organic, or kosher foods; you may choose your menu within a very tight budget; or you might prefer the foods that are easiest to store and prepare, such as prepackaged meals. You choose the types of foods you like, the quantities you like to have on hand, the variety, the brands, and the cuisine, within your own budget. Your standards derive from what you like. If you don't like a product, if it doesn't meet your needs, or if it doesn't give you that feeling of having dined well, you probably won't buy it again. It is much the same for a purchaser—except that you are helping many more people have the experience of dining well.

In Chapter 2, you learned about cuisine, theme, and market. Decisions about these topics are crucial for deciding on a menu—which, in turn, guides all your purchasing decisions. Your menu will impact every step of your operation, from planning to everyday functioning. As the purchaser, you are a crucial component in the team that brings the menu to life, and it is up to you to do so within the quality and cost specifications that best match your restaurant's needs and your target market. To achieve this goal, this chapter will show you how to create these purchase specifications, step by step.

You will need to create purchase specifications in conjunction with all interested parties—meaning all of the restaurant personnel who are affected by the decisions that are made, as well as considering your customers. The chef and customers must be satisfied with the quality of products; the storeroom must be satisfied with the delivery schedule; accounting must approve of the billing procedure; and management must agree with the costs. You will continually review and revise your purchase specifications to meet changing conditions. Each time they are updated, you will need to produce a written version for potential vendors. The vendors can then submit their product samples according to your specifications. This is how they bid for your business.

As the purchaser, you are responsible for making sure you get what you need from vendors—and for making adjustments when what you get doesn't match your company's standards. In creating purchase specifications for your company, you will evaluate the quality, quantity, consistency, reliability, availability, service, safety, and price of the items you need. Each one of these factors will take time and effort to evaluate, but your common sense and consumer experience will help to guide you. What follows are some questions that you and your restaurant team will need to ask yourselves regarding each of these specifications. When you decide on the answers based on your menu, your purchasing decisions will follow.

- *Quality:* What level of quality will your guests expect based on your prices, atmosphere, and image? What level of quality does each vendor offer? When you test a vendor's products, is there a great deal of wasted weight due to poor quality?[1]

- *Quantity:* What quantities will your company require? In what quantities does the vendor offer the products? Do those quantities correspond with your needs? Are there extra charges if you order partial cases or packages? How much storage space do you have?

- *Consistency:* What kind of product consistency can the vendor offer? Is it guaranteed? What are the vendor's policies on substitutions and returns?

- *Reliability:* How reliable is the vendor in terms of delivery schedule and product quality? Does the vendor have references?

- *Availability:* What kinds of seasonal items will you be buying from each vendor? What kinds of price fluctuations can you expect? Is the vendor capable of supplying for your volume?

- *Service:* Does the vendor provide services such as prompt notification of shortages, technical support, reports of your past purchases, good customer service, and effective handling of complaints? What do you need the vendor to do? Can the vendor respond to special orders and delivery requests? How far in advance must an order be placed—two days, six hours, a week? Does the vendor have refrigerated trucks for products that might spoil?

---

[1] A specialized form for use in making in-depth quality decisions is available in the Appendix. This form can be used with vendors to get further detail on how to control waste and to keep product costs down.

- *Safety:* Are the vendor's products processed in accordance with government regulations for food safety? Can you visit their facilities to inspect the conditions for yourself? Do you have any special safety requirements?

- *Price:* Are the vendor's prices consistent with or below those of their competitors? Will the vendor accept lower offers or offer discounts for volume buying? Considering the prices you can charge your target market, can the vendor's prices translate into profit for you?

All of these aspects of a vendor's bid will influence your decisions about what to buy—and from whom—for each product you purchase. If that sounds a little overwhelming—after all, most restaurants have extensive menus—the next section provides you some ways to standardize and organize the information you will need to make your decisions, so that the purchasing process doesn't take all your time.

PRODUCT INFORMATION

It is necessary for a purchaser to have a bank of product information on hand when developing purchase specifications and accepting bids. You can find this information in several trade publications, such as the Meat Buyer's Guide (MBG), the USDA Institutional Meat Purchase Specification (IMPS), and the Seafood Buyer's Guide. There are also local sources that you can use to learn more about a variety of products referred to in this chapter.

Usually, product specifications should include the following:

- The name of the item

- The amount or quantity needed

- The grade, packer brand, USDA number, or other quality information about the item

- The price of the item

- The packaging size and method of delivery

- Other miscellaneous information, such as the item's area or country of origin or the number of days the item (such as beef) should be aged

Figure 4-1 is an example of product specifications for New York steak.

In writing product specifications such as the one in Figure 4-1, details can be eliminated if the purchaser is familiar with commonly used market terms such as *Product # 1180 IMPS* or the grade levels discussed below. The purchaser should be aware that there are different grades for

Figure 4-1 NYS Product Specs

Definition	Description
Product Name & Use	**New York Steak** for lunch and dinner main entrée item
Product #	1180 (IMPS #) denotes - strip loin steaks, boneless, center short cut
Product Yield	From USDA yield grade 3 carcass. Dry aged 14 to 21 days
Product Size	Pre cut – 12 ounce portion sizes
Product packaging	Plastic wrapped in batches. Sixteen portions per batch
Product Delivery	In a refrigerated truck
Country of Origin	USA

each item purchased and different grade categories for different types of items. The following is a description of meat and dairy grades:

All grades are listed from highest quality to lowest:

- Beef: Prime, Choice, Select, Standard, Commercial, and Utility. If one supplier is giving the purchaser a bid on Prime beef and another supplier is bidding on Select beef, the two suppliers are not bidding on the same grade level. Thus, it is important that the purchaser specify the grade that he or she wishes to buy.

- Lamb has the following grades, from highest to lowest: Prime, Choice, Good, and Utility.

- Pork has the following grades, from highest to lowest: No. 1, No. 2, No. 3, No. 4, and Utility.

- Veal has the following grades, from highest to lowest: Prime, Choice, Good, Standard, Utility, and Cull.

- Poultry has the following grades, from highest to lowest: A, B, and C.

- Fish has the following grades, from highest to lowest: A, B, and C.

- Produce has the following grades, from highest grade to lowest: Fancy, No. 1, Commercial, No. 2, Combination, and No. 3.

- Cheeses, have the following grades, from highest to lowest: AA, A, B, and C.

- Eggs have the following grades, from highest to lowest: U.S. Grade AA, U.S. Grade A, and U.S. Grade B.

This chapter is not intended to be a discussion of how products are graded. Rather, it should make you aware that there are different grading systems for different products so that you can make informed decisions about product specifications. You will likely learn more about product grades as you become familiar with the products used in a particular establishment.

Figures 4-2 through 4-7 provide data about different cuts of meat and produce in a useful format. They will help you learn about the product before writing product specifications.

Figures 4-2 through 4-5 list different specifications of fresh meat.

You will need to create a chart of specifications for the items you need for your operation. You can send such a chart to prospective vendors so that they can send you their applicable product prices. All of the information is useful in comparing and analyzing differences in quantity, quality, packaging, and pricing among various vendors. Many vendors carry different brands that you will have to choose from, and they will be packaged differently and have different levels of quality. Since you are setting the specifications and standards for your company's purchases, you will evaluate how the vendors' price quotes and products fit your needs. Figures 4-6 and 4-7 show specifications for produce products.

QUALITY SPECIFICATIONS AND PRODUCT TESTING

In this section we will talk about quality specifications. We use the word *quality* to define a number of parameters for your purchases. Just as at home, how well the product performs—not simply whether it tastes good or whether it costs more—is a measure of how well it meets your needs. In a restaurant, however, you have more opinions to hear. Everyone involved—the vendor, the purchaser, the chef, the restaurant manager, and the guest—views quality differently. Ultimately, all these opinions must figure into the choice of products, and as the purchaser,

FOODSERVICE CUTS OF BEEF

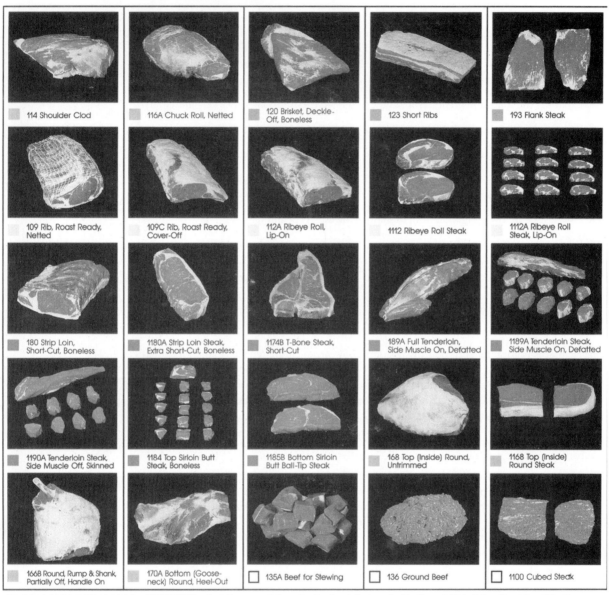

114 Shoulder Clod

116A Chuck Roll, Netted

120 Brisket, Deckle-Off, Boneless

123 Short Ribs

193 Flank Steak

109 Rib, Roast Ready, Netted

109C Rib, Roast Ready, Cover-Off

112A Ribeye Roll, Lip-On

1112 Ribeye Roll Steak

1112A Ribeye Roll Steak, Lip-On

180 Strip Loin, Short-Cut, Boneless

1180A Strip Loin Steak, Extra Short-Cut, Boneless

1174B T-Bone Steak, Short-Cut

189A Full Tenderloin, Side Muscle On, Defatted

1189A Tenderloin Steak, Side Muscle On, Defatted

1190A Tenderloin Steak, Side Muscle Off, Skinned

1184 Top Sirloin Butt Steak, Boneless

1185B Bottom Sirloin Butt Ball-Tip Steak

168 Top (Inside) Round, Untrimmed

1168 Top (Inside) Round Steak

166B Round, Rump & Shank, Partially Off, Handle On

170A Bottom (Gooseneck) Round, Heel-Out

135A Beef for Stewing

136 Ground Beef

1100 Cubed Steak

The above cuts are a partial representation of NAMP/IMPS items. For further representation and explanation of all cuts see *The Meat Buyers Guide* by National Association of Meat Purveyors.

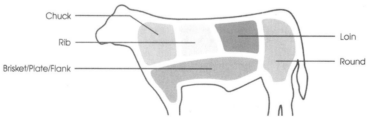

Chuck

Rib

Brisket/Plate/Flank

Loin

Round

Figure 4-2 Beef Specifications. *Courtesy of* "The Meat Buyers Guide: Beef, Lamb, Veal, Pork, and Poultry *by NAMP North American Meat Processors Association.* © 2006. Reproduced with permission of John Wiley & Sons Ltd."

FOODSERVICE CUTS OF LAMB

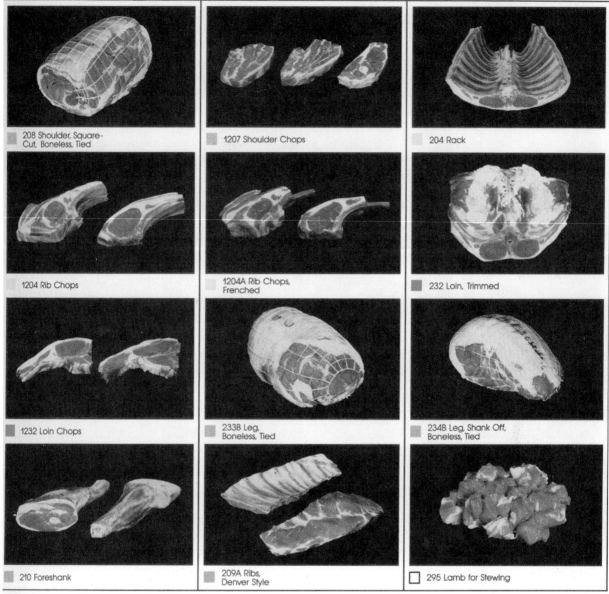

208 Shoulder, Square-Cut, Boneless, Tied

1207 Shoulder Chops

204 Rack

1204 Rib Chops

1204A Rib Chops, Frenched

232 Loin, Trimmed

1232 Loin Chops

233B Leg, Boneless, Tied

234B Leg, Shank Off, Boneless, Tied

210 Foreshank

209A Ribs, Denver Style

295 Lamb for Stewing

The above cuts are a partial representation of NAMP/IMPS items. For further representation and explanation of all cuts see *The Meat Buyers Guide* by National Association of Meat Purveyors.

Shoulder
Rack
Shank/Breast
Loin
Leg

Figure 4-3 Lamb Specifications. *Courtesy of "The Meat Buyers Guide: Beef, Lamb, Veal, Pork, and Poultry by NAMP North American Meat Processors Association. © 2006. Reproduced with permission of John Wiley & Sons Ltd."*

FOODSERVICE CUTS OF PORK

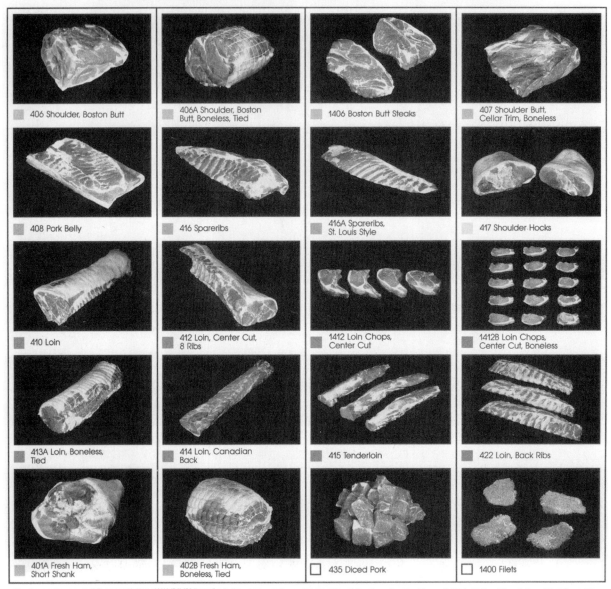

406 Shoulder, Boston Butt	406A Shoulder, Boston Butt, Boneless, Tied	1406 Boston Butt Steaks	407 Shoulder Butt, Cellar Trim, Boneless
408 Pork Belly	416 Spareribs	416A Spareribs, St. Louis Style	417 Shoulder Hocks
410 Loin	412 Loin, Center Cut, 8 Ribs	1412 Loin Chops, Center Cut	1412B Loin Chops, Center Cut, Boneless
413A Loin, Boneless, Tied	414 Loin, Canadian Back	415 Tenderloin	422 Loin, Back Ribs
401A Fresh Ham, Short Shank	402B Fresh Ham, Boneless, Tied	435 Diced Pork	1400 Filets

The above cuts are a partial representation of NAMP/IMPS items. For further representation and explanation of all cuts see *The Meat Buyers Guide* by National Association of Meat Purveyors.

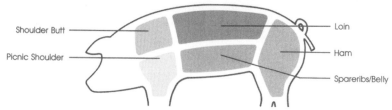

Figure 4-4 Pork Specifications. *Courtesy of "The Meat Buyers Guide: Beef, Lamb, Veal, Pork, and Poultry by NAMP North American Meat Processors Association. © 2006. Reproduced with permission of John Wiley & Sons Ltd."*

FOODSERVICE CUTS OF VEAL

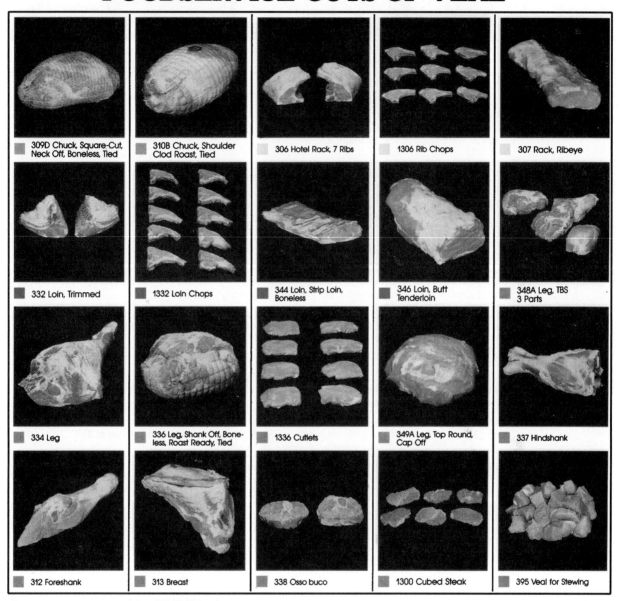

309D Chuck, Square-Cut, Neck Off, Boneless, Tied

310B Chuck, Shoulder Clod Roast, Tied

306 Hotel Rack, 7 Ribs

1306 Rib Chops

307 Rack, Ribeye

332 Loin, Trimmed

1332 Loin Chops

344 Loin, Strip Loin, Boneless

346 Loin, Butt Tenderloin

348A Leg, TBS 3 Parts

334 Leg

336 Leg, Shank Off, Boneless, Roast Ready, Tied

1336 Cutlets

349A Leg, Top Round, Cap Off

337 Hindshank

312 Foreshank

313 Breast

338 Osso buco

1300 Cubed Steak

395 Veal for Stewing

The above cuts are a partial representation of NAMP/IMPS items. For further representation and explanation of all cuts see *The Meat Buyers Guide* by National Association of Meat Purveyors.

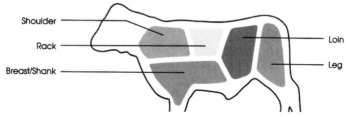

Shoulder

Rack

Breast/Shank

Loin

Leg

Figure 4-5 Veal Specifications. *Courtesy of "The Meat Buyers Guide: Beef, Lamb, Veal, Pork, and Poultry, by NAMP North American Meat Processors Association. © 2007 by North American Meat Processors Association. Reproduced with permission of John Wiley & Sons, Inc.*

Figure 4-6 Fresh Vegetables

Fresh Vegetables—U.S. Grades, Pack Sizes, and Storage Characteristics			
Product	U.S. Grades	Pack Sizes	Storage Characteristics
Artichokes	#1 and #2	Cartons weighing 20 to 25 pounds with counts ranging from 18 to 60.	Store at 38°F (3°C).
Asparagus	#1 and #2	Bunched (approximately 12 bunches of 2 pounds each per crate) or loose (30 pounds per case).	Packed upright in crates with a moist base to preserve quality.
Beans	Fancy, #1, combo, and #2	Cartons or baskets weighing from 26 to 31 pounds.	May be held for short period between 45°F (7°C) and 50°F (10°C).
Broccoli	Fancy, #1, and #2	Half cartons containing 14 to 18 bunches (each weigh 1 1/2 pounds).	Store at 34°F (1°C).
Brussels Sprouts	#1 and #2	Pint containers (12 per tray, or about 9 pounds); 25-pound cartons.	Store at 34°F (1°C).
Cabbage	#1 and Commercial	Cartons or bags weighing 50 to 60 pounds; Savoy cabbage normally packed in 40-pound cartons.	Store at 34°F (1°C).
Carrots	A, B, #1, and Commercial	Varies, most commonly packed as 48 one-pound units and bulk bags weighing 25 to 50 pounds.	Store at 34°F (1°C).
Celery	Extra, #1, and #2	Cartons or wire bound crates of 60 pounds, with counts of 18, 24, 30, 36, or 48 bunches.	Store at 32°F (0°C).
Corn	Fancy, #1, and #2	Wire bound crates of 50 pounds; counts range from 54 to 66.	May be stored at 32°F (0°C) for a short time period.
Cucumbers	Fancy, Extra #1, #1, #1 Small, #1 Large, and #2	Packed in lugs, West Coast lugs, and cartons.	Store at 45°F (7°C).
Iceburg Lettuce	Fancy, #1 Commercial and #2	West—varies in weight per case from 35 to 55 pounds; normally 18, 24, or 30 heads per standard western carton.	All varieties of lettuce may be stored at 34°F (1°C).
Leaf Lettuce	Fancy	Varies, but mostly in 24-quart hampers weighing about 10 pounds.	
Boston Lettuce	#1	Varies, best to purchase by the pound.	
Onion	#1, Combo, #2, and Commercial	Usually packed in 50-pound mesh fiber bags.	Should be stored under dry conditions.
Romaine	#1	Western lettuce cartons holding 24 heads and weighing approximately 40 pounds.	Store at 34°F (1°C).
Sweet Peppers	Fancy, #1, and #2	Bushels with various counts; 80 count is a good size for stuffing.	Store between 46°F (7°C). and 48°F (9°C), with relative humidity of 85%.
Potatoes	Extra #1, #1, and #2	Cartons with counts ranging from 60 to 120 per carton.	Store in cool, dry, dark area. Raw potatoes should not be refrigerated.
Sweet Potatoes	Extra #1, #1, Commercial and #2	Normally packed in bushel baskets of approximately 50 pounds.	Store at 50°F (10°C) with low humidity and use promptly.
Tomatoes	#1, Combo, #2, and #3 (field grading standards; grade identification is lost in repacking)	Sold by the box, which may contain 10, 20, 25, or 30 pounds; weight may vary by 10%.	Bring to full color at 55°F (13°C). Store between 40°F (4°C) and 50°F (10°C) until used.

Source: William B. Virts, *Purchasing for Hospitality Operations* (Lansing, Mich.: American Hotel & Lodging Educational Institute, 1987), pp 256–257

Figure 4-7 Fresh Fruits

Fresh Fruit—U.S. Grades, Pack Sizes, and Storage Characteristics			
Product	**U.S. Grades**	**Pack Sizes**	**Storage Characteristics**
Apples	Extra Fancy, Fancy, #1, and Utility	Loose in cartons weighing 38 to 40 pounds, or tray pack cartons weighing 40 to 45 pounds. Counts range from 48 to 198 per carton	Soften rapidly in warm temperatures. Store at temperatures around 30°F (−1°C).
Apricots	#1 and #2	Lugs weighing 24 to 26 pounds.	Store at temperatures from 32°F (0°C) to 36°F (2°C).
Avocados	#1, Combo, #2, and #3 (grades for Florida only)	California packs—one-layer flats weighing 12 1/2 pounds with counts of 9 to 35 per flat. California and Florida pack double-layer 25 pound lugs with counts of 18 to 96.	Ripen at room temperature, then refrigerate until use.
Bananas	No U.S. grades	Cartons of 40 pounds in assorted sizes; some markets offer a uniform 150 count per carton in petite size.	Bananas should be purchased at the ripeness stage that will hold until anticipated usage.
Blackberries/ Raspberries	#1 and #2	Normally packed in 12-pint flats with overfilled baskets.	Store at 32°F (0°C) with 90% relative humidity.
Blueberries	#1	Shipped in 12-pint flats with overfilled baskets.	Store at 32°F (0°C) with 90% relative humidity.
Cantaloupes	Fancy, #1, Commercial, and #2	Half crates weighing 38 to 41 pounds; 2/3 crates weighing 53 to 55 pounds; and full crates weighing 75 to 85 pounds. Counts range from 12 to 46 depending on container size.	Store at 40°F (4°C).
Cherries	#1 and Commercial	Normally shipped in 20-pound lugs.	Refrigerate at 34°F (1°C).
Coconuts	No U.S. grades	Usually sold by the dozen	Refrigerate at 34°F (1°C).
Cranberries	#1	Typically packed in cartons of 24 one-pound units and 25-pound bulk.	Store at 32°F (0°C) with 90% relative humidity.
Grapefruit	Fancy, #1, Combo, #2, and #3	All areas—7/10 bushel cartons weighing between 38 and 42 pounds with counts ranging from 23 to 64.	Store at 50°F (10°C).
Grapes	Fancy, #1 Table Grapes, and #1 Juice Grapes	Weights vary by shipping area. Normally shipped in flats weighing 17 to 20 pounds and lugs weighing 20 to 26 pounds.	Store near 32°F (0°C) with 90% relative humidity.
Honeydews	#1 Commercial, and #2	Bliss cartons (29 to 32 pounds) or 2/3 cartons (5 to 10 melons with total weight of 30 to 34 pounds).	Honeydews may have to be pre-ripened by letting stand in a warm room for several hours (or days).
Lemons	#1, #1 Export, Combo, and #2	Standard cartons described for grapefruit, weighing between 37 and 40 pounds. Standard counts range from 63 to 235 per carton (115, 145, 165 and 200 counts are most popular).	Store at 50°F (10°C).

(continues)

Figure 4-7 *continued*

Fresh Fruit—U.S. Grades, Pack Sizes, and Storage Characteristics			
Product	**U.S. Grades**	**Pack Sizes**	**Storage Characteristics**
Limes	#1 and Combo	Cartons weighing 10, 20, and 40 pounds. Counts range from 72 to 126 for 20-pound cartons (96 and 108 counts are most popular).	Store at 50°F (10°C).
Nectarines	Fancy, Extra #1, #1, and #2	Generally packed in two-layer lugs of 20 pounds. Counts range from 50 to 84.	Refrigerate at 35°F (2°C).
Oranges	Fancy, #1, Combo, and #2	Standard fruit cartons with counts ranging from 48 to 162 (mandarine orange counts generally 176 or 210).	Refrigerate at 35°F (2°C).
Peaches	Fancy, Extra #1, #1, and #2	Boxes weighing 17 to 18 pounds with counts ranging from 40 to 65; Los Angeles Lub (two-layer) weighing 18 to 23 pounds with counts ranging from 50 to 80.	Peaches ripen rapidly at room temperature. Refrigerate at 32°F (0°C).
Pears	Extra #1, #1, Combo, and #2	Cartons weighing 44 to 45 pounds with counts ranging from 80 to 165; 100 count is a popular eating size.	Store at 40°F (4°C).
Pineapples	Fancy, #1, and #2	Cartons weighing 40 pounds with counts of 8-9-10-12-14-16; 1/2 cartons weighing 20 pounds with counts of 4-5-6-7.	Store at room temperature to ripen, then hold at 45°F (7°C).
Plums	#1	Usually packed in 28-pound lugs with counts ranging from 126 to 225.	Refrigerate at 34°F (1°C).
Strawberries	#1, Combo, and #2	Normally packed in 12-pint flats with baskets heaped.	Store at 32°F (0°C) with 90% relative humidity.
Watermelons	Fancy, #1, and #2	Usually sold individually with a minimum weight specification of 20 pounds recommended.	Store at 65°F (18°C).

Source: William B. Virts, *Purchasing for Hospitality Operations* (Lansing, Mich.: American Hotel & Lodging Educational Institute, 1987), pp 265–266

you must balance people's varying needs. You should do this by testing the products to see how well your specifications are met.

Take, for example, the quality specification for meats. One of the most important measures of quality across the industry is the system of grades given to products of different levels of quality. Figure 4-8 shows a guide to the United States Department of Agriculture (USDA) stamp of approval.

Figure 4-8 U.S. Grade Approval

Your role as a purchaser is to make sure the quality of the products you receive from a vendor matches your specifications, which are based on your menu and market. The tools in this chapter will help you test the products you receive, so that you can determine by hands-on experience whether or not they meet your needs. If you receive products that don't meet your standards, you will have to reject them—and all restaurant staff should be trained to do so as well.

You can avoid many problems by confirming orders with the vendor prior to shipment and checking the confirmation against your order. Correcting discrepancies in advance is much less time-consuming and problematic than dealing with mistaken deliveries after they have arrived at your restaurant. For example, if you ordered extra virgin olive oil but the confirmation reads *vegetable oil,* you can tell the vendor to correct it. If the confirmation explicitly states extra *virgin olive* it is unlikely that the vendor will send you vegetable oil instead. A reliable vendor will not normally confirm an order for which they cannot guarantee a delivery.

Vendors often send sample products, labeled as such and free of charge, to potential customers. With these samples you can test the quality for yourself, as can the chef and the restaurant manager. These tests determine whether the product meets the criteria detailed in your purchasing specifications. You will want to test the product using the same production procedures that will commonly be used. For example, if the product is likely to sit in a steam table for two hours before being served, or to sit in a refrigerator for two days before being used, test it under those conditions. Based on your test results, you can compare quality and cost aspects among vendors. The following discussion of different types of tests gives you a detailed guide on how to carry out each one.

Yield Tests

Yield tests help to determine how much actual, usable product comes out of the raw product a vendor sends you. They help you to differentiate in quality and usable quantity between two or more vendors quoting a price on the same food product. The term **yield** means the net weight or volume of a food item after it has been processed from the as-purchased weight or volume and made ready to eat. The term *as-purchased* refers to the original raw product, which will be processed to **end-product** use (yield).

yield tests determine the amount of usable product available after processing raw items.

yield The net weight or volume of a food item after it has been processed from raw materials and made ready to eat.

Yield may be stated either as a number of portions or as a **yield percentage**. For example, you might get eight 10-ounce steaks from a tenderloin or four servings of red potatoes from a 1-pound bag—the number of portions. You can also calculate the yield percentage, which is the percent of usable product available from the raw product. To find this, divide the usable weight by the as-purchased weight. (Remember that you must use the same units to divide weights—pounds divided by pounds, ounces divided by ounces, and so on.) Then, when you order the same product from the same vendor later, you have a close estimate of the yield you will get from the product.

end product (EP) refers to final yield after processing.

yield percentage is the amount of usable product available from raw materials. To find this, divide the usable weight by the original weight.

As an example of calculating a yield percentage, if your tenderloins usually weigh 11 pounds, and after trimming you get 9.5 usable pounds from the original 11, your yield is 86.4 percent (9.5 pounds of usable weight divided by 11 pounds of original weight.) A 14-pound tenderloin, then, will net 12.1 pounds of usable steaks (14 pounds of original weight multiplied by a yield percentage of 86.4 percent.)

You can further use this yield percentage to calculate the number of portions the product will yield. Multiply the yield percentage by the original weight, and then divide the result by the weight of your portions. If your portion weight for a steak is 8 ounces, or 0.5 pound (again, remember to use equal units when dividing), an 11-pound tenderloin will net 9.5 pounds, or potentially nineteen 8-ounce steaks. A 14-pound tenderloin, multiplied by the yield percentage of 86.4 and then divided by the 0.5-pound portion size, will give you 24 half-pound portions.

end-product price refers to the price of usable product, including the price of wastage.

To continue the example, in some cases the tips of a tenderloin may not conform to steak size and shape specifications, so you won't be able to serve them that way. In that case, your **end-product (EP) price** may be higher than the **as-purchased (AP) price**, because part of

as-purchased price (AP) The original price paid for a product.

the usable meat could not be used as portioned steak. However, you may be able to use the leftovers as ground beef or for other menu items. If you use parts of your product for a less-expensive menu item, the EP price will increase. You will have to judge whether you need to increase your menu prices to reflect the increase in EP price.

EP price is derived as follows:

$$EP = \frac{AP}{Yield\%}$$

As-purchased price simply means the original price you paid for the product.

Quiz

If you purchase a 25-pound case of green beans for $16.00 and it yields 20 pounds of edible beans, what is the end price for a 4-ounce portion of the beans?

Butcher Tests

butcher test A yield test used to determine the actual portion cost of meat, poultry, fish, or seafood after accounting for waste, trim, and cooking losses.

A **butcher test** is one kind of yield test. It is used to determine the actual portion cost of meat, poultry, fish, or seafood after accounting for waste, trim, and cooking losses. Whenever you revise your menu or try out a new vendor, you'll need to conduct a new test. The butcher test is further used to obtain raw and cooked net yield, as well as the correct number and size of standard portions. You will always want to test a representative sample, with at least two pieces, in order to be more accurate by averaging the results. The following steps give you the full test procedure. Figure 4-9 gives an example of a butcher testing chart.

⑪ **Discussion Topic**

Which is more useful: Performing yield testing on samples of the actual product you receive, or referring to published purchasing yield guidelines? Why?

1. Enter all required information into the butcher testing chart. Include the vendor's information, such as the unit prices and purchased weight. These are letters B, C and D on the sample chart (Figure 4-9). We're comparing two vendors, so you'll see two columns on the right with the data for each vendor.

2. Write the name and description of the product being tested at the top of the chart, as we have done with the beef tenderloin. With cuts of meat, be sure to enter all prime and secondary cuts. This accounts for every usable cut you get from a product. For letter A, enter the portion size of the primary cut; in this example, an 8-ounce filet steak.

3. You will often get secondary cuts from meat products, as in the tenderloin example. Fat, plastic wrap, and blood, on the other hand, typically are not used or sold, so do not assign them any value. In our example, ground beef is a secondary cut, but there are no usable bones or stew meat products from the tenderloin.

4. Obtain price quotes from the vendor for per-pound prices on all secondary cuts. Then, in the *Secondary Cuts* box, enter the values and weights of any secondary cuts. Total the weights and values of the secondary cuts and enter them on line E. You'll be using both the weights and the values of these cuts, so be sure to keep them straight by using dollar signs ($) next to the values.

5. Find the primary cut weight by subtracting the weights in line E from those in line D. The result goes in line F.

6. In line G, indicate the number of portions you can get from 1 pound of cleaned product. In this example, each portion weighs 8 ounces; therefore, there are two portions per pound.

7. Line H is very important, as it gives you an accurate **cost per servable pound**. Subtract the secondary cost values (line E) from the full price (line C). Then divide that result by the number of pounds in line F; write the result in line H.

cost per servable pound The cost derived from butcher test results. Calculated by subtracting secondary costs from the purchase price, and dividing by the weight of the primary cut.

Figure 4-9 Raw Beef Test

ITEM: BEEF TENDERLOIN						
	Assumptions				**Vendor 1**	**Vendor 2**
	Quality grade of beef purchased				5# up	6# up
A	Primary Cut per menu item	ounce			8 oz	8 oz
B	Price per pound				$6.21	$6.69
C	Purchase price				$449.60	$484.36
D	Purchase weight	pound			72.4	72.4
	Purchase price per ground beef				$1.38	$1.38

	Butcher Test Results					
			Vendor A	**Vendor B**	**Vendor A**	**Vendor B**
			Weight in pound		Value	
	Blood, Cryovac, & Fat		3.25	5.25	$0.00	$0.00
	Ground Beef at $1.38 per pound		30.86	22.77	$42.59	$31.42
	Beef Bone		0	0	$0.00	$0.00
	Stew Meat		0	0	$0.00	$0.00
E	**Total**		34.11	28.02	$42.59	$31.42

	Calculations of Test Results					
F	Therefore, Primary - Filet Cut *Subtracting weights in line E from weight in line D*	pound			38.29	44.38
G	Portions per pound *pound = 16oz*				2	2
H	Cost per servable pound *derived by (c-e)/f*				$10.63	$10.21
I	Cost Factor per pound *cost factor = h/b*				1.71	1.53
J	Portion Cost Multiplier or Cost Factor (per portion). Derived by (i/g)				$0.86	$0.77
K	Therefore, portion cost *derived by jxb*				$5.34	$5.15
L	Yield percentage (b/h)				58.42%	65.52%
	Notes Line *j* will remain constant until a revision of specification or change of vendors. Line *k* will not remain constant, as long as the vendors change their prices. Meat prices change daily in the US market. The purchaser should monitor line *k* to determine profitability.					

cost per purchased pound Purchase price of a cut of meat divided by the weight in pounds.

8. The cost factor, line I, is the ratio of the cost per servable pound to the **cost per purchased pound**. Divide line H by line B, and enter the results in line I.

9. Line J is simply line I divided by line G; it represents the cost factor made applicable to your portion size.

10. Line K is the actual cost per portion. You derive this by multiplying line J by line B, or by dividing line H by line G. Look back over the chart (Figure 4-9) to see why this is so.

Various meat items are portioned after cooking, including prime rib, London broil, and pork loin. Each of these items must be tested, and the amount of loss during cooking can then be determined. Different grades of meat have different yields and quality characteristics. Higher cooking temperature is another variable, as it tends to increase shrinkage. Studies show a shrinkage loss of 15.8 percent at 325° and 30.4 percent at 500°. In order to increase yields, lower temperatures are recommended for roasting. Lower temperatures also produce a product that is juicier and more evenly browned, an added benefit in the food service business. You will need to determine these variances if they apply to the item you are testing.

cost factor The ratio of the cost per servable pound to the purchase price per pound.

Line I of Figure 4-9 involves a new term: **cost factor**. This is the ratio of the cost per servable pound to the purchase price per pound. This is a very accurate ratio with which to compare vendors. The closer this ration is to 1, the more value (and less waste) you get from what you buy. In our example, Vendor 2's product has more tenderloin filets—and more value—than Vendor 1's product. Once the cost factor has been determined, you can apply it to any current market price and you'll obtain an up-to-date portion cost, as long as the same purchasing and portion standards are applied.

Now you have an accurate price per tenderloin portion: $5.31 for Vendor 1 and $5.11 for Vendor 2 (Figure 4-9). The results from a butcher test can be used in what is called a **make-or-buy decision**: Should you buy the product raw and prepare it yourself, or should you buy it preportioned and save on labor and waste costs? It is true that portion control consistency is often better with preportioned products, unless you have a sufficiently experienced butcher. Preportioned meats also make your inventory easier to calculate because the number of portions a butcher gets from a cut of meat may vary. However, you will have to decide if these benefits justify the added costs.

A butcher test reveals valuable information that was not obvious from the vendors' prices. Had you judged simply from the purchase price per pound, you would have thought Vendor 1 was offering a better price. The results of the butcher test (subtracting the secondary cuts in line E) plus the resulting prices per portion lead to a different and more complete conclusion. In this example, you will be better off selecting Vendor 2 for its higher quality and greater cost effectiveness. This shows the necessity of butcher testing before selecting a vendor. Similar tests should be conducted for all product groups, from meat and fish to produce.

Activities/Assignments

1. Distribute sample butcher yield tests (see Appendix) for an assortment of products. Work in groups of two to calculate the yield percentages.
2. Obtain current produce price sheets from local vendors. Compare the options, select the "best" buys, and justify their decisions.

Raw Food Test

Purchasers perform raw food tests to determine which vendor supplies the best count and weight of fruits and vegetables for specific uses—for example, how many tomatoes come in a case or how many slices you get from one tomato. By performing tests on these items, you will be able to determine yield and waste based on various sizes, types of packaging, and condition of fruits and vegetables—peeled or unpeeled, cleaned and preparation-ready, or uncleaned and requiring preparation. This test allows you to make an informed selection of products and vendors.

Canned Food Test/Can-Cutting Test

Another test used in cost control is the can-cutting test. Whenever large quantities of canned, frozen, or dehydrated items are used, these tests should be performed in order to identify the best buy—how well do the items meet your purchase specifications, including cost?

A canned food test is used to determine the yield of canned goods, either through weighing or counting the drained contents of the container. Use good, scientific-method procedures so that the only variable is the product being tested. For example, use the same size sieve to drain liquids, the same drainage time, and so on. It is always prudent to determine servable weight in this way rather than trusting the printed volume. To determine the end-product price, always perform the calculations using the units as they are sold, whether they are sold by volume, weight, piece, or portion. Read the label, but do not make a judgment until after the test, because a product may contain added air or liquid, or may have a lower density.

"Blind" Taste Test

You can also use your staff members to conduct a taste test of vendors' samples. Using samples from more than one vendor, prepare the products as you would normally prepare them for service. Do not label them in any obvious way; the person who is testing the products should not be able to tell where the product is from. Use several testers, and average the findings to come to a decision about which product tastes best.

QUANTITY SPECIFICATIONS

When we talk about quantity specifications, we are no longer talking about yield. Rather, we are referring to inventory management, including how much to order and how much to keep on hand. There is a great deal to consider in making these decisions wisely for different products: You want a good balance between what you use and what you order. You don't want spoilage, of course, but you do want to take advantage of vendors' volume price discounts, and you want to have stock on hand for unexpected needs. You will need to have a thorough understanding of how quickly your business consumes the products you are ordering, how long it takes your vendor to deliver, and how much safety stock is required. Your experience—both as a consumer and as a professional purchaser—will hone your judgment on when and how much to order.

Although the restaurant manager or chef usually tracks how fast items are consumed (the inventory turnover ratio), the purchaser decides how much to order. The purchaser establishes an inventory schedule—daily, weekly, or more or less frequently—based on the operation's needs. By monitoring usage levels, the purchaser also sets **par levels** for the inventory. These are set amounts that maintain enough stock, but not more than is necessary for your business volume. When the chef or manager sees that something is needed, he or she sends a purchase order, which is a detailed, standardized way to tell the purchaser what is needed. This is how the purchaser knows of a need and begins to fill it. To know how much of a product to order, it is important to consider several contributing factors.

par level Set inventory amounts that maintain enough stock, but not more than is necessary for the business volume.

Inventory on Hand

Inventory on hand is your restaurant's stock of the food and other products you buy and store for use. The stock you have on hand actually costs you money. You lose interest that you

inventory on hand The quantity and value of inventory currently present.

could have earned on what you spent. You spend money to maintain and operate the storage facility. And, of course, spoiled food is pure cost as well. On the other hand, when a guest orders something, you want to have it in stock. Purchasing is a delicate balance between ordering more than you need (and therefore having waste) and ordering less than you need (and therefore running out). Inventory on hand should match what the purchaser's recommended par levels of stock as closely as possible.

Lead Time

lead time The time between the receipt of a purchase order and the receipt of the goods from the vendor.

Lead time is the time between the receipt of a purchase order and the receipt of the goods from the vendor. It should include time to obtain quotation bids, time to place an order, and time for the vendor to make your delivery.

Cost of Acquisition

Many costs can add to the cost of acquisition, including the costs of placing an order, processing an invoice, and delivering the goods. While these expenses are small relative to the value of the food and beverage purchased, they must be weighed when determining the optimum order quantity. Normally, these costs percentages are lower when you order larger quantities less frequently.

Volume Pricing

volume pricing Lower prices when products are purchased in larger quantities.

If the addition of one or more units to an order will result in a lower price for all, you are getting **volume pricing**. Evaluate the various other costs against this lower price—if you purchase too much and it spoils, you will have lost your discount as well.

Vendor Minimum Order Quantity

vendor minimum order quantity Required minimum amounts for orders from a vendor.

If you order from someone who is not your primary vendor, you may be required to order a set minimum amount, the **vendor minimum order quantity**, or pay a premium price. You will have to decide whether making that required minimum order is suitable for your company. Some purchasers buy regularly from more than one vendor, as long as they are competitively priced. Doing so allows you to call on other vendors without a cost penalty when your primary vendor can't deliver.

Safety Stock

safety stock Extra inventory kept on hand to ensure that you will have time to order more before running out.

Safety stock is your cushion; it is an extra amount of product that you keep on hand to ensure that you will have time to order more of that product before you run out. The amount required as a cushion is a judgment made by assessing the restaurant's operations, your suppliers' delivery schedules, and the general economic conditions. Safety stock is important to smooth restaurant operation. If you order too little, the unit cost will usually be higher, shortages may occur, paperwork will increase, and your vendor relationships may suffer. On the other hand, if you order too much, you will have higher inventory costs, greater risk of theft, more spoilage, and less storage space available.

Assessing the amount of safety stock you need is tricky and will probably vary from item to item and from one season to the next. You will want to consult your company's business forecasts plus your own past usage records to decide how much you will need. Note how long each vendor takes to deliver items to you. Based on this analysis, you can estimate a sufficient amount of safety stock to maintain.

How many days' worth of safety stock products do you want to have on hand? How many days' lead time does it take your supplier to deliver products? Finally, what is your average daily use of the item? The following is an example of a formula you can use—the number of days of safety stock desired plus the number of days of lead time, multiplied by the number of units you use each day, determines the appropriate order quantity:

(# of days safety stock + # of days lead time) × average daily use = order quantity

Figure 4-10 provides two examples, with different daily usage and lead times. In each case, assume you'd like a safety stock supply of one day.

Figure 4-10 Daily Usage Charts

Products	Safety Stock in days	Lead time in days	Daily usage
Onions red	1	2	20 pounds
Tomato puree	1	3	3 cans
The order points are computed as follows:			
	(safety stock + lead time)	*x daily usage*	*= order quantity*
Onion	(1+2)	x 20 =	60 pounds
Tomato puree	(1+3)	x 3 =	12 cans

How much you buy will also be affected by whether the products are perishable or nonperishable.

Perishable Products

Perishable products need attention and appropriate handling to avoid spoilage. They also differ from nonperishable products in the following ways:

- they are seasonal.

- they are more frequently purchased.

- their prices are less stable.

Being seasonal or perishable means a product is much more likely to spoil rapidly or to lose freshness or quality. Some examples are fresh fish and seafood, meats, berries, freshly squeezed juices, and some dairy products. These products require great care in handling because they are prone to contamination. It is also important to understand the shelf life of each product.

For these reasons, it is very important for the purchasing manager to pay attention to the **market reports** distributed by vendors. These reports are written by vendors to inform businesses of present and future product conditions, particularly with farm and seafood products, as these constitute the majority of perishable goods. These reports contain information on supply, demand, and prices. Figure 4-11 shows what a market report might look like.

market reports Reports written by vendors to inform businesses of present and future product conditions, particularly with farm and seafood products.

Use market reports to make purchasing decision. For example, if you know that poor weather in California will soon seriously affect your perishable purchases, you can plan ahead. You may even have to revise your menu depending on how severely these issues impact the available supply and prices. Knowing that these products deteriorate quickly, determine the quantity on hand as well as how much you expect to need.

Planning for ordering perishable products should be extensive and systematic. Review your company's business forecast. You'll need to review anticipated banquet functions and special

---

ALLIANT FOODSERVICE
MAY 4, 2008

GENERAL OVERVIEW: All citrus areas are experiencing near-perfect conditions with daytime temperatures in the 60's and 70's. Products from Mexico are in their final week with higher temperatures creating weak quality. We are making the transition to California as product becomes available.

CAULIFLOWER: Expect a significant price increase in the next two weeks as cool temperatures slow down production.

STRAWBERRIES: Supplies are much tighter than ever imagined. Rain caused a bloom drop 10 days ago causing a substantial drop in volume. Supplies increase in one week.

BEST BUYS	GREAT ITEMS FOR MOTHER'S DAY
Spring Greens	Bing Cherries
Asparagus	Vidalia Onions
Strawberries	Long-stem Carnations

Source: ALLIANT FOODSERVICE, May 4, 2005 By Permission

Figure 4-11 Market Reports. *Courtesy of the Alliant Foodservice*

events as well, if your establishment offers such functions. Consider the lead time and how much you will need before placing this order; with a little foresight, you can ensure both quality and timely delivery. For example, fish quality depends on careful handling and freshness, so plan your order to arrive just in time for its use.

You will also want to determine inventory on hand. Record what you have in inventory before placing an order. You will see why this is important as we go through the following case study.

Case Study: Why Experience Matters

Assume it is Thursday afternoon and your restaurant is open every day. The restaurant usually uses between five and six flats of strawberries every three days, or about 1.83 flats per day. Today the banquet chef has submitted a purchase order for two flats of strawberries for a function on Monday. The vendor only delivers on Tuesdays and Thursdays, and you must call by 9:00 A.M. the day before these delivery dates to place an order. Now assume you counted seven flats of strawberries in your storeroom (this is your inventory on hand); you've already received your deliveries for the day and filled your requisitions. Your seven flats will likely be gone before Monday's banquet function, and you can't get a delivery from your vendor either. You will probably have to buy strawberries at the local market, and you should order ten flats. Why ten?

The reason for ordering this amount is demonstrated in Figure 4-12.

Figure 4-12 Order Quantity

Days of safety stock desired	1 day
Lead time	5 days
Average daily use	1.83 flats
So, (5 days +1 day) × 1.83 flats daily use	11 flats
Plus special banquet requisition	2 flats
Plus Wednesday & Thursday	4 flats
Less inventory on hand	7 flats
Therefore, order quantity	10 flats

In this example, notice that Wednesday and Thursday are included in the daily usage calculation. If they are not included for next Tuesday's delivery, you will deplete your stock before the next delivery on Thursday. When purchases are not planned correctly or special needs must be met, you may have to purchase goods from a local market or from an alternate vendor. The prices at markets are often high, and the quality could be low. These are both problems you want to avoid. Look back over this example to see where procedures could be improved. For instance, you might establish a policy of having the banquet chef submit orders earlier. Or, better yet, get a vendor who delivers more often with competitive prices.

Nonperishable Products

Ordering quantities for nonperishable items are determined by usage, storeroom space, cash availability, price, and lead time. The company may have plenty of space, but cash flow could be a problem (or vice versa). You might negotiate a better price package through bulk or volume buying incentives, but storeroom space may limit how much you can buy. Also, because of variations in price levels, delivery schedules, demand, and sales forecasts, the ideal is to place an order to arrive just in time to avoid both running out of product and spoilage. You can do this by using the following formula for nonperishable items:

$$net\ outlet\ demand - stock\ on\ hand + demand\ during\ lead\ time$$
$$+\ safety\ factor = order\ amount$$

Say you usually use one jumbo can of tomato sauce per day. If the demand increases to two jumbo cans per day during the four days' lead time, the above formula helps you account for that urgent need. The formula also includes a safety stock amount, which you will have to determine based on your restaurant's conditions, including storage space, business forecasts, and cash flow. Note, however, what this formula does *not* include: Sometimes a vendor requires that you order a minimum amount, or will give you a better price if you order more. These variables require judgment calls.

You can also establish par levels for nonperishable items. As stated above, these are set amounts—determined by the purchaser—of the minimum and/or maximum of each item to keep on hand. Once these numbers are set, they can easily be adjusted according to the business season or economic conditions. This par level lets you know when to place an order.

If your company's inventory is automated, you can keep your par levels in the computer. What you will want to create is called a **perpetual inventory**, which can also be done manually but is very time consuming without a computer. With this type of inventory you keep a running balance for each item in the storeroom: Purchases are added and requisitions are subtracted from the numbers all month long. Depending on your computer system's degree of sophistication, it may be possible to enter how often you will order products as well as your business volume, and the computer will tell you how much to order! You must check, of course, to see that your actual, physical inventory and the computer-calculated inventory are the same. This is discussed in more detail in Chapter 11, which provides physical inventory and month-end cost procedures.

perpetual inventory A system of accounting for inventory changes, in which beginning and ending inventories are noted along with any sales or purchases.

None of these tools or formulas can replace your judgment as the purchaser, but they do provide guidance in knowing how much to order. Common sense is invaluable in your attempts to keep the right amount of any item on hand. As with the other topics discussed in this section, you can draw on your experience as a consumer to evaluate how much inventory to have on hand and as safety stock, whether volume pricing is worthwhile for you, and how to monitor perishable goods to eliminate spoilage. Monitor how often you run out of an item or end up with spoiled product. Everyday practice and evaluation will help you find the middle ground.

Summary

With the menu and market as a starting point, one of a purchaser's responsibilities is to set purchase specifications for products that will best meet your needs in terms of price, quality, and service. To do this, the purchaser compiles detailed, relevant product information and works with the chef and manager so that their needs are met. The team discusses standards and how different products meet the needs of the target market and your offerings. Together, set product specifications to serve as the backbone of the purchasing process.

Vendors send you products samples, which you and your team can use to test yields, quantity, and even taste. These tests help you determine which vendor's products are right for your operation, and allow you to make an informed decision about the real cost after preparation. At this point you will often have to grapple with make-or-buy decisions, in which you will weigh the relative costs of buying preportioned products versus preparing the products in-house.

Quantity specifications also come into play in setting your purchase specifications. As the purchaser, you evaluate the circumstances at hand (inventory, volume pricing discount offers, business volume levels, storeroom requirements, and lead time, for example) to decide how much product you will want to purchase. When these specifications are then sent to vendors, you will receive bids based on your needs, rather than on what the vendor wants to sell.

Your role is to create an ongoing system for the purchasing process, so that as menus and seasons change, you continue to make good buying decisions for your company.

CHAPTER QUESTIONS

Critical Thinking Questions

1. What is a can-cutting test? How is it conducted?

2. What is accomplished by a butcher test? How is it conducted?

3. How is cost factor calculated?

4. Why might some products have a better value for some food service operators than the same product for another operator?

Objective Questions

For Questions 5–9: You have purchased one 50-pound case of 80 potatoes for $16.00.

5. What is the cost of one potato?

6. What is the cost of 1 pound of potatoes?

7. After cleaning and peeling the potatoes, the case yields an edible weight of 42 pounds. What is the yield percentage?

8. What is the prepared cost per pound?

9. True or false? One of the primary objectives of the purchasing department is to procure the best or highest-quality product available.

For Questions 10–14: Using the butcher test as presented in the chapter, calculate the following for preparing 12-ounce rib-eye steaks from a prime beef rib given these assumptions: purchase weight is 22 pounds; price per pound is $3.85; waste is 3 pounds of blood and fat; secondary cuts bones are 4.8 pounds (value $0.85 per pound); stew meat is 3 pounds (value $2.20 per pound).

10. What is the usable weight of the primary cut?

11. What is the cost per servable pound?

12. What is the cost factor per portion?

13. What is the yield percentage?

14. In a can-cutting test, suppose Vendor A charges $23.00 for a case of 6 #10 cans of corn and Vendor B charges $24.00, and the quality is the same—but one can from Vendor A yields 6 pounds of drained corn and one can from Vendor B yields 6.2 pounds. What is the cost per usable pound for each vendor's product, and which is a better value?

Multiple Choice Questions

1. Assuming a safety stock of one day, a lead time of two days, and a daily usage of five cans, how many cans should the order quantity be?
   A. 15
   B. 12
   C. 20
   D. 10

2. When purchasing, what is the most important thing to consider?
   A. AP price
   B. EP price
   C. EPP price
   D. value

3. The information you need for making product decisions include all of the following *except*:
   A. Menu and ingredient information from the chef
   B. Budget information from the manager
   C. The waitstaff's item preferences
   D. Price and quality information from vendors

4. You are purchasing cans of tomato sauce for your restaurant. Assuming a safety stock of one day, a lead time of two days, and a daily usage of ten cans, how many cans should your order quantity be?
   A. 15
   B. 20
   C. 30
   D. 10

5. When purchasing, what is the most important price consideration?
   A. As-purchased price
   B. Delivery costs
   C. Cost factor
   D. Vendor perks
   You have purchased one 50-pound case of 80 potatoes for $16.00.

6. What is the cost of one potato?

    A. 50 cents

    B. 75 cents

    C. 30 cents

    D. 20 cents

7. What is the cost of one pound of potatoes?

    A. 32 cents

    B. 48 cents

    C. 16 cents

    D. 24 cents

8. After cleaning and peeling the potatoes, the case yields an edible weight of 42 pounds. What is the yield percentage?

    A. 50%

    B. 42%

    C. 84%

    D. 110%

9. What is the end-product price per pound?

    A. 48 cents

    B. 42 cents

    C. 32 cents

    D. 38 cents

These questions are about a butcher test with the following characteristics.

You are preparing 12-ounce rib-eye steaks from a prime beef rib.

The purchase weight is 22 pounds

Price per pound is $3.85

Waste products (blood and fat) come out to 3 pounds

Secondary cuts are 4.8 pounds at $.85 per pound

10. What is the usable weight of the primary cut?

    A. 13.7 pounds

    B. 15.5 pounds

    C. 14.2 pounds

    D. 9.9 pounds

11. What is the cost per servable pound?

    A. $5.96

    B. $4.96

    C. $5.15

    D. $3.85

12. What is the cost factor per portion?

    A. 1.3

    B. 1.8

    C. 2.0

    D. 1.5

Price and the Vendor

Learning Objectives

After reading this chapter, you should be able to:

- understand the meaning of *price* as it relates to purchasing;

- prepare a market basket report;

- use a price index to analyze the impact of price and consumption on cost;

- distinguish between price and value;

- understand the following types of pricing in purchasing:

  - firm price

  - contract price

  - cost plus price

  - hedging

  - consignment purchasing and pricing

  - standing order contracts

- know how to select a vendor, including the following:

  - soliciting bids from prospective vendors

  - finding vendors from many sources

  - deciding to use a vendor or to buy from outside

  - making make-or-buy decisions

- award your business to a vendor by doing the following: reviewing consistency in purchasing and writing a credit memo, determining vendor reliability, determining vendor availability, reviewing vendor supplier services standards, evaluating vendor safety records and health concerns, and following through after a contract is signed.

In Practice

On the way back from their storeroom walk-through with Myla, the purchaser and chef began a conversation about product pricing. Chef Robert suggested to Scott, "You know, we need to do a better job with how we select vendors and establish prices."

(continues)

> *(continued)*
>
> *Scott emphatically replied, "You're damn right about that! My gut tells me that things will be different."*
>
> *The chef wasn't sure about Scott's commitment to do what was really necessary. He answered, "Yes, that's true. What do you think about documenting the vendor selection processes? That would go a long way toward creating transparency and inspiring confidence with Myla."*
>
> *Scott seemed unconvinced. "Sure, sure, but I'm not sure about Myla's intentions. Seems to me she's got a chip on her shoulder."*
>
> *Robert stopped and looked at Scott, surprised. "Her intentions are pretty clear to me. Just look at the last operational audit reports. We flunked. We provided absolutely no evidence of vendor and pricing review before awarding contracts. That's not a chip on her shoulder, that's our faulty practices."*

INTRODUCTION

When you are shopping for yourself, price is always an important consideration, and it helps you determine where to shop. Price is no less important for a professional purchaser. Understanding the functions and recommendations detailed in this chapter will help you reach your goal of saving your company's money when selecting a vendor. In the food and beverage industry, the circumstances and methods of purchasing are unique and somewhat more complex than shopping for home use. In this chapter, you will learn about both the pricing considerations you will encounter and the tools and methods you can use to help make good buying decisions.

For the purposes of purchasing, price simply means the cost at which something is obtained. It is the monetary value set by the vendor for the products and services delivered to the point of use. In addition to the base price, price also includes applicable discounts, the terms of sale, transportation costs, taxes, and insurance.

As the purchaser, you will have to have some idea about the proposed menu prices, probable operating costs, and target customers while designing the menu. If your restaurant is a drive-through diner, caviar and filet mignon will not likely show up on the menu or purchasing specifications; the prices for these items don't match the budgets of a diner's typical customers. The objective of price evaluation, then, is to ensure that the price paid is reasonable in terms of the market, the industry, and the end use of the product to be bought. In addition, understanding of prices is necessary to isolate and eliminate items that carry an unnecessary cost. The price of an item may, at first glance, appear to be very simple to determine, but it can be rather complicated.

market basket analysis compares purchase prices over time and across vendors to build reveal patterns in price fluctuations.

You will need to become familiar with how the vendor prices the needed items. Some vendors may charge you more if you order a partial case or pack size of their product because they have to spend extra money to repackage it for you. You must decide whether to buy an entire case to avoid this high cost or to carry extra inventory that you don't need. It may be cost-effective to buy a few individual cans of 46-ounce tomato juice instead of a case of 6-ounce cans. It all depends on your operation's usage and storage space. Also, you should be familiar with price history, including how and why the price of an item has fluctuated in the past. At times you will have to forecast future prices to advise managers of important changes, particularly if you have a catering department. All of this calls for maintaining a record of price history. The next section discusses **market basket analysis** and price indexing, two methods of keeping such records. Later, we will discuss the pros and cons of various pricing arrangements so that you can make good purchasing decisions.

MARKET BASKET ANALYSIS

Any food-service business experiences price fluctuation. It is up to management to identify the pattern of the fluctuation and act on them. First, the manager should set a particular date, preferably at the beginning of a month. This is called the "base month". The price paid for food and beverage product in the base month can then be compared to future purchase price. The analysis of base month prices and future product prices will reveal the cost impacts of price changes by delineating the difference between vendors.

This type of analysis also provides a statistical monitor of vendors' pricing. Seasonal patterns may reveal plainly the benefits of competitive purchases from different vendors. The chart in Figure 5-1 illustrates a sample market basket analysis of four types of berries from two vendors. We examine purchase prices over a four-month period. Note how the price changes are very different for the two vendors. Assume that the Total Purchased column actually reflects individual items purchased for the four-month period. Note the price changes in purchases from the respective vendors, here called Vendor A and Vendor B.

From Figure 5-1 it is clear that buying from Vendor B is the better choice—as long as we can presume that quality and supplier services are equal, and price is the only variable. In the example, the company has loosened its own standards of buying berries competitively: Though Vendor A's prices have climbed steadily, the purchaser consistently has bought much more product from the vendor with the higher prices. Some purchasers make the opposite mistake—changing vendors every week to take advantage of the lowest prices. The additional costs of this approach may be more than you would save, however. Chapter 4 and 6 discuss some of the associated costs of this kind of buying.

Rebecca Charles, owner of Pearl Oyster Bar in New York, was asked, "How many seafood purveyors do you use?" She answered, "I have about four or five, three just for lobster. In a perfect world, I'd like to have one consistently, but, with the amount we use, I can't afford to pay 50 cents more to one because he's a good guy. I tell them, you're not my friend, you're my fish guy. It's a balancing act between quality and the best price. Getting a good price is important because I price my menu as cheaply as I can to stay competitive. Providing value to the customer is important to me."

Source: Caroline Perkins. "Profiles in Partnership" *National Restaurant News.* April 24, 2006, p. 18.

Survey

The market basket survey is not complete until the percentages of total issues are applied to the average increase of price for each category. This is what was consumed versus what was purchased. If the product has not been consumed, it is not affecting your cost because it is part of your inventory value on hand. You can learn a great deal about usage patterns in this way, and you can monitor the corresponding impact on your costs. In fact, this is a vital part of your record-keeping.

If your system is computerized, this can be simply part of the program. Furthermore, with the aid of the computer you can expand on market basket analysis by introducing an automated inventory and purchasing system that weights your results based on the percentages of total issues as mentioned above. This means the system gives more importance to items when you use more of them. If you use a great deal of an item, such as tenderloin, and the price rises even a small amount, this affects price fluctuation remarkably. On the other hand, if you use less of

Figure 5-1 Market Basket Survey

Market Basket Price Survey					
September thru December					
	Prices per Flat of Berries				
Names of Items	Sept. Price per Flat	Oct. Price per Flat	Nov. Price per Flat	Dec. Price per Flat	Total Purchases from Vendors
Vendor A Strawberries	$12.20	$10.51	$24.88	$34.38	$4,620.74
Vendor B Strawberries	$10.48	$9.14	$32.09	$26.74	$590.98
	Sept.	Oct.	Nov.	Dec.	
Vendor A Blueberries	$22.63	$25.50	$33.53	$44.68	$2,312.23
Vendor B Blueberries	$19.89	$24.88	$24.88	$24.88	$169.09
	Sept.	Oct.	Nov.	Dec.	
Vendor A Blackberries	$22.52	$32.74	$30.45	$26.07	$2,089.13
Vendor B Blackberries	$23.33	$36.25	$31.33	$31.33	$426.32
	Sept.	Oct.	Nov.	Dec.	
Vendor A Raspberries	$12.20	$10.51	$24.88	$30.88	$2,551.07
Vendor B Raspberries	$10.48	$9.14	$32.09	$26.74	$346.22
Total Purchased from vendor A					$11,573.17
Total Purchased from vendor B					$1,532.61

Graph to illustrate the above results

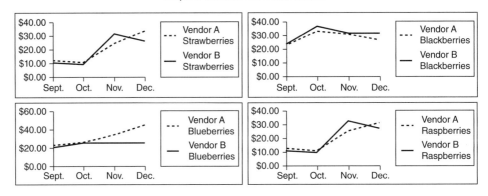

another item, such as a rack of lamb, and the price changes substantially, this will not likely have such an effect on your averages because of the low amount actually purchased and used. In addition, in an automated system, these weighted base-period prices rotate each month (for example, January 2008 is compared to January 2009). Seeing this comparison assists you in making projections, since financial reporting results are most often compared to the budget and to prior-year statistics.

Unit prices are multiplied by the number of units purchased in the present period. The value of the total purchases is compared in present-year and prior-year dollars, and a percent variance is then generated. The advantage of the weighted system can be seen when we make calculations using a traditional method and when we weight the results. Note how the following two examples (Figures 5-2 and 5-3) come out quite differently.

Figure 5-2 Price Comparison

	2008	2009	Variance	% Variance
Tenderloin	$8.10	$7.40	<$.70>	<8.64%>
Lamb Rack	$11.00	$12.10	$1.10	10.00%
Total Meat	$19.10	$19.50	$0.40	2.09%

It appears in Figure 5-2 that the total meat category has suffered a price increase of 2.09 percent. However on the other hand, using the weighted inventory purchasing system method, and therefore weighing the sales mix into the equation, a different conclusion is reached, as shown in Figure 5-3.

Figure 5-3 Price Variance

	2008	2009	Variance	# Lbs. Purchased	2008 Value	2009 Value
Tenderloin	8.10	7.40	<$.70>	1000	8100	7400
Lamb Rack	11.00	12.10	$1.10	300	3300	3630
					$11,400	$11,030

Dollar variance:	Purchases in 2008 dollars	= $11,400
	Purchases in 2009 dollars	= $11,030
	Difference	= -$370
	Percent difference	= −3.25%

The total meat category actually indicates a price decrease of 3.25 percent because the tenderloin activity has a much greater impact than the lamb rack activity (1,000 pounds versus 300 pounds). Menus must be reviewed to accommodate fluctuating prices, and the reviews ought to include this weighting process. This accuracy in price assessment can provide you with a competitive edge in costing and in pricing.

Weighting your averages to achieve this accuracy is a form of what is called a **price index**. This is a set of numbers generated to indicate changes in product prices. The value of the market basket analysis is in developing a price index that will measure the effects of product price changes. This index can be used to compare multiple companies that offer different presentations of the same item. The basic food price index can be calculated yearly, quarterly, or whenever a menu changes. Whatever time period you choose, fix one month as a base month or benchmark; then, when you make comparisons, you can see how the price has changed. The most productive approach is to select fast-moving or high-turnover items in each of the following categories: meat, fish, poultry, fruit, vegetables, grocery, and staples. Choose an item to represent each category; the item you choose should account for over 10 percent of that category's sales. Figure 5-4 illustrates variances in prices.

price index A set of numbers generated via market basket analysis to indicate changes in product prices.

Figure 5-4 shows variance for a selection of items from October to November. Columns A, B, and C are allow you to see exactly how much has been purchased. The price in Column D is the base, or benchmark, price. Column E is the amount the price has changed from the base,

Figure 5-4 Variance Example

VENDOR A Item Description	A Units per Case	B Unit of Measure	C Cases Purchased Nov.	D Base Price Oct	E Variance From Base (e-h)	F Variance Percentage (f/e)	G Unit Price Nov	H Total Purchased Nov
Bakery Section								
Dough Cookie Choc Chunk	21	lbs.	3	$1.48	$0.27	18%	$1.75	$110.25
Dough Cookie Oatmeal Raisin	21	lbs.	5	$1.16	$0.24	21%	$1.40	$147.00
Dough Cookie Sugar	21	lbs.	6	$1.01	$0.54	53%	$1.55	$195.30
Dairy Section								
Cheese Blue Wheel Danish	12	lbs.	1	$1.63	$0.27	17%	$1.90	$22.80
Cheese Boursin Herb	3.75	lbs.	7	$9.14	$1.86	20%	$11.00	$288.75
Grocery Section								
Almond Blanched Sliced	18	lbs.	2	$3.19	$1.06	33%	$4.25	$153.00
Applesauce Fancy	6	#10 cans	6	$2.99	$1.11	37%	$4.10	$147.60
Meat Section								
Bacon Slab 9/13Ct	30	lbs.	24	$2.14	$0.36	17%	$2.50	$1,800.00
Beef Baron	65	lbs.	6	$1.49	$0.16	11%	$1.65	$643.50
Produce Section								
Alfalfa Sprouts Fresh	2	lbs.	48	$1.24	$0.21	17%	$1.45	$139.20
Apple Sliced IQF Granny Smith	30	lbs.	2	$0.67	$0.13	19%	$0.80	$48.00
Seafood Section								
Catfish Fillets	15	lbs.	5	$3.41	$0.59	17%	$4.00	$300.00
Clam Strip Brd Bulk	6	lbs.	3	$2.37	($0.21)	-9%	$2.16	$38.88

while Column F is the variance expressed as a percentage of the base price. Column G is the new price per unit, and Column H shows how much was actually spent in November.

Looking at the seafood section, a price increase of 17 percent occurred in catfish filets between the base month and the current month. The total in purchases of catfish filets was $300, derived by multiplying columns A, C, and G. This simple chart can be used to differentiate between vendor bids and to record price trends. It is somewhat abbreviated, however. To make the chart reflect your variances weighted by how much you actually used the items, you will need to add some columns and data, as shown in Figure 5-5.

List the new calculations across the columns horizontally, list your items vertically along the left side, and complete the data. These in-depth calculations can help you to see how prices have changed while considering how much product was used. This is a more accurate picture of price variation. It gives you a valuable tool for setting or changing menu prices.

Figure 5-5 Menu Pricing

Column/Title	Calculate/Enter
Beginning Period. (Column E in the above example.)	The actual price at the beginning of the period. This is the base or benchmark standard.
Ending Period. (Column H in the above example.)	The actual, or new, price at end of month or period.
Actual Change. (Column F in the above example.)	The actual increase or decrease per item and category. Formula: Beginning Period − Ending Period
Percent Change. (Column G in the above example.)	The actual change as a percentage of the beginning, or base, price. Formula: Actual Change ÷ Beginning Period
Average Percent Change.	Total all Percent Changes in a category. Then, divide that total by the number of items in the category.
% of Total	This is the percentage that a certain category comprises of your total food cost. This information will be generated from the receiving and distribution module of your inventory system, if you are on a computerized purchasing and inventory system.
Average Numeric Change	Total all Actual Changes. Then, divide by the number of items in the category.
Weighted Changes	Multiply "% of total" by Average Change during the period, then divide by 100; this *weights* the variances based on how much was sold from that category.

THE RELATIONSHIP BETWEEN PRICE AND VALUE

Price is the monetary value applied to a product by a vendor, while value is how much the product is worth to the purchaser. Value takes into consideration other things that are valuable to you as the purchaser, such as delivery and service. It is the purchaser's responsibility to obtain the best *total* value; this means that price is only one element. Although price is often the only tangible measure of value, the purchaser must relate this price to the other elements of value. Putting a value on a vendor's services is subjective, but it's important to know exactly what it is about a vendor's service that influences your decision to purchase from them. You might want to include these intangible qualities in future purchase specifications. Think about it from the perspective of your customers: If the vendor consistently delivers high-quality products on time, the customer's experience of your establishment will be affected positively. And it is the customers who will ultimately decide whether or not they are getting value for their money.

TYPES OF PRICING ARRANGEMENTS

To establish a written, binding contract, a definite price should be set forth in the purchase order. This may be either a specific price or a basis for determining a final price. In the case of standard items that have an established market price, such as beverages, even if you don't put a price on the purchase order it is still a binding contract. This means you need to know what you want when you write a purchase order; you don't want misunderstandings with your vendors. The established practice to avoid confusion or even legal problems is to include either a specific price or a basis for determining a final price in the body of the purchase order.

There are several different kinds of price arrangements that you can make with a vendor. You might establish a firm price or a contract price; you might use hedging to establish a price for a period of time; or you may use consignment purchasing or standing order contracts to sell products as they are used. Each of these methods has its uses, as you will see below.

Firm Price

firm price A price the purchaser and the vendor agree to that will not change until the material is delivered and the transaction is completed.

A **firm price** is the most commonly used pricing method in day-to-day purchasing transactions. It means that the price to which the purchaser and the vendor agree will not change until the material is delivered and the transaction is completed. This agreed-upon price may apply to a specific quantity of products, a set time schedule, or even an undetermined quantity within a given time period. Generally speaking, the establishment of a firm price should be the basic goal of the purchaser for each order, unless extenuating circumstances make it advantageous to make other promises, which could result in a lower net final cost.

Contract Price

contract price A commitment to buy a group of items at a certain price.

A **contract price** is a commitment to buy a group of items—whether food and beverage products, chemicals, or office supplies—at a certain price. This type of arrangement is common in an agreement with a primary vendor which receives the bulk of your company's business. Some of your (or your vendor's) specific requirements may not be determined fully when the commitment is made; such laxity is common, if not recommended. The vendor is expected to maintain adequate quantities of these contracted items on hand in order to meet your day-to-day requirements. Vendors selected to participate in these arrangements must satisfy the company's purchase specifications.

When soliciting bids for contract pricing arrangements, you should also provide any necessary special instructions, your annual buying volumes, and the quantities you expect the vendor to have on hand. Plan to negotiate volume discounts during this process, since you are agreeing to buy greater quantities than normal and should be rewarded for it. The **cost-plus** method is one form of contract pricing.

cost-plus Pricing method which involves paying the vendor's actual product cost plus a certain, fixed percentage.

Cost-plus agreements are becoming popular in the food service industry. Under these agreements, your company pays the vendor's actual product cost plus a certain, fixed percentage to cover the vendor's unstable costs. Unstable costs, which should be defined in the contract, include labor, services, delivery, and other overhead items. When there is a high degree of risk involved, making costs difficult to estimate, this type of contract can be very beneficial. When vendors cannot estimate prices, they must add their own cushion (sometimes called *insurance*) to their quotes. They, too, must cover their costs. With the cost-plus contract, you will garner lower bids and pay more only when the vendor pays more.

In accepting a cost-plus contract, you are accepting the risk of price increases. You should only enter into this type of contract with a reputable, ethical vendor, so that you will pay a valid market price for your products. Furthermore, it is difficult to control your costs if prices escalate unexpectedly. Once the agreement is signed, the vendor may not have the incentive to shop cost-effectively because the conditions often stipulate that they have no competition for the duration of the contract. The vendor will be paid its cost plus the percentage, according to the terms of the contract, no matter what that cost is.

You do have one tool to be sure you are getting fair market prices, however. This form of arrangement usually offers you audit privileges of the vendor's cost files. You can check each product's prices against the prices you could get from other vendors in the same time period.

However, reviewing these records takes valuable time, and an unscrupulous vendor could easily falsify those records. If such a contract is deemed wise given your circumstances, choosing an ethical vendor is crucial.

Hedging

Hedging is a contract on a future price. Purchasers use hedging to maintain a fixed price for a product or commodity they will need. The benefit of hedging is that you avoid the risk of increasing prices. Hedging is a common practice. It enables the company to pay a stable contract price for a future product irrespective of future market prices. Hedging is advantageous if you, as the purchaser, can determine how much product will be required based on the product's history, and if you can safely assume that prices will increase.

An example will illustrate the principle of hedging: Assume that a company wishes to lock in the price of a certain grade of beef tenderloin for the next 12 months. Meat prices usually change weekly and are based on supply and demand. The purchaser will review the following information before discussing the options with management:

- The establishment's past, present, and future consumption volumes

- The establishment's cash flow

- Bids from at least three vendors

- The market's price trends (as indicated in Figure 5-6)

- The amount of risk that the prices will not increase as assumed

Note: *The figures used in Figure 5-6 may not be representative of your area. They are only for illustrative purposes.*

You will have to weigh the risks and advantages of hedging before committing your company to such a contract. If the price you agree on is lower than the future market price, you will have saved money for your company. Other advantages include the following:

- Getting a better price without having to purchase a lot of inventory at once

- Protecting inventory values even if the market declines

- Guaranteeing delivery of food and beverage products without storage and other inventory control costs

On the other hand, the drawbacks of hedging include the following:

- The solidity of the commitment you must make, even if your needs change

- The risk of stocking excess product

- Any costs to resell or trade back unused product

- The large volume normally required to enter into such a contract

- The chance that prices may go down rather than up

The vendor also hedges his or her purchase prices by using what is called the *buy hedge*. The following example shows how this works. Assume that on May 1, XYZ Suppliers sells you beef prime ribs for delivery on August 1. The price they charge is the price as of May 1. XYZ Suppliers has three choices in this situation. They can buy the beef in May and hold it until they deliver it to you on August 1. This would establish the price of the beef, but it would incur storing and interest costs, possible quality problems, and an insurance cost on the beef until it is used.

hedging is a contract on a future price, entered into to maintain a fixed price for a product or commodity you will need.

⑪ **Discussion Points**

Let's assume Company A entered into a cost-plus contract: In the first year there was a 9 percent markup on the product, and in the second year the markup was 8 percent. Before purchasing any product at the beginning of the second year, the manager changed the prices for on-hand products to reflect the new 8 percent contract. Now, inventory items are extended with the new markup percentage. Do you see any problem with this practice? Why or why not?

Figure 5-6 Beef Tenderloin 6 UP

Beef Tenderloin Price History Average Index - Price Per Pound													
	Jan	Feb	Mar	Apr	May	Jun	Jul	Aug	Sep	Oct	Nov	Dec	YR AVG.
2006	5.40	5.45	6.00	6.10	5.95	5.75	5.40	5.25	5.30	5.40	5.50	5.20	5.56
2007	5.35	5.30	5.20	5.10	5.05	5.00	4.75	4.55	4.60	4.95	5.20	5.30	5.03
2008	5.50	5.50	5.40	5.30	5.40	5.30	5.90	5.95	5.95	6.10	6.25	6.20	5.73
2009	6.25	6.50	6.95	6.90	7.05	7.25	7.00	7.00	7.25	7.10	6.90	6.80	6.91

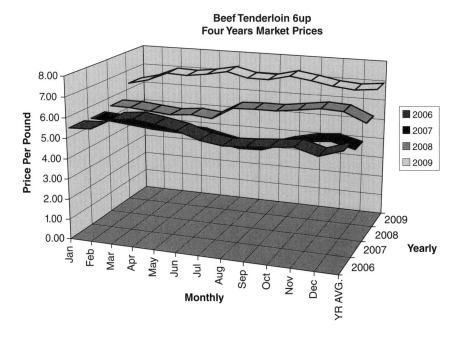

The second alternative is to postpone the beef purchase until just before the delivery date. This involves considerable risk, however, as the price of beef may increase; this could be a considerable loss for XYZ, since they have already established the sale price.

The third alternative is to utilize the buy hedge. In essence, XYZ is doing the same thing you do when you purchase with hedged prices. This will establish the beef cost without risk of price change and without incurring the cost of carrying inventory. In the buy hedge, XYZ purchases futures contracts at the time of the sales contract (May 1), and then sells these futures contracts when they actually buy the beef. Futures prices and cash prices tend to fluctuate together: Any profit or loss due to the change in the cash price of beef between May 1 and August 1 will be offset by a profit or loss in the futures contracts. Therefore, the transaction involved in the buy hedge is a wash; it comes out even.

Cash Market	Futures Market
May 1: Sell 4,000 pounds of beef at $7.05 per pound	May 1: Buy 4,000 pounds of beef of August future at $7.05

Thus, XYZ Suppliers has entered into two contracts of an opposite nature, selling in cash and buying in the future at the same price to avoid the risk of price changes between the time beef is contracted to you (May 1) and the time you will pay for it (August 1).

Consignment Purchasing and Pricing

Consignment is a merchandising technique that promotes resale. Payment for the goods is deferred until they are resold by the buyer. In this system, the vendor will inventory the product on your premises. Your company doesn't own the consigned items until they are used or withdrawn from consignment stock. This type of purchasing is carried out on a very limited scale in the food service industry. However, it is a subject that requires discussion because it can be very helpful in some cases.

The drawbacks of consignment include the difficulty of segregating the stock and the locked-in pricing structure. Storage can also be a concern. An outside or public warehouse may be used to store consigned goods, or the buyer may offer free storage on the company's premises. This may involve extra indirect warehousing and handling costs to the buyer.

However, purchasers have adopted consignment techniques successfully to reduce their companies' inventory investment and to provide immediate access to required items. Care must be taken to minimize consignment of products with high obsolescence or short shelf life.

In order to use consignment purchasing properly, the purchaser must agree to monitor and audit the consignment inventory. One of the principal reasons vendors may not wish to consign stock is their concern that the purchaser will not account for their merchandise properly. In addition to showing the vendor that it will gain more business through consignment, the purchaser must also be able to show the vendor that proper accounting controls will be used. Three principal controls on consigned inventories are identification, segregation, and monitored use. The vendor must identify on the packing list which items are consigned in order to prevent their being mixed with the regular inventory. If consigned inventories become a significant portion of the buyer's inventory, separate colored receiving reports and identification tags may make this process more clear.

The second control involves the physical segregation of consigned inventory. Since the vendor will normally maintain the insurance on consigned inventory, the purchaser must ensure that the merchandise will be stored in a protected space with safeguards against fire, theft, and other hazards.

Third, the purchaser must control the use of the consignment inventory. One of the more frequent abuses of these inventories happens like this: Someone from the kitchen realizes he or she doesn't have enough stock for the dinner period. The purchaser has left for the day, but the kitchen needs the item in a hurry. Someone from the kitchen removes the product from the consignment inventory but fails to write down what he or she took, and the purchaser doesn't even know the item was taken until the vendor checks the inventory and finds the shortage. Unfortunately, this kind of abuse can take place continually unless storeroom access is restricted or monitored. If the vendor consigns product that the buyer cannot reliably account for, the vendor will soon cancel its participation in the arrangement.

The success or failure of consignment depends largely on the accounting controls assigned to it. You must be able to indicate clearly to the vendor the releasing, receiving, disbursing, and reimbursement procedures you will use. All of these procedures should be covered in a written contract with the vendor. Consider these points in your accounting and inventory control procedures:

- Allow the vendor to inspect consigned inventory.

- Establish a schedule for disbursing the consignment inventory.

- Set minimum and maximum inventory levels for consignment items.

- Request an independent inventory-taking service for your company, as well as a periodic audit of controls, and have all findings reported to the vendor.

- Set a date for the maximum amount of time an item may be retained in consignment, keeping in mind shelf-life problems.

consignment purchasing
A merchandising technique in which payment for the goods is deferred until they are resold by the buyer.

- Establish a procedure for handling discontinued or obsolete items so that they are not reordered.

- Establish a product-rotation procedure.

- Reduce vendor invoices by using a disbursement report on items taken from the consignment inventory.

As part of the regular inventory of consignment items, you'll need to prepare a report to serve several purposes. In this report, list all disbursements; this way, the report can be used to pay the vendor. Depending on the terms of the contract, more often than not you will likely also pay for missing stock items.

You can also use this report to reorder items that are falling below the minimum levels. This type of report will also give each product an individual item number. List your beginning inventory, everything you receive, everything you disburse, anything you reject, and your ending inventory. Other important data includes unit prices, par levels, and items you wish to reorder.

Quiz

Committing to a long-term agreement on purchase quantity and a fixed price for goods regardless of market price fluctuations is called

A. firm price.

B. contract price.

C. hedging.

D. none of the above.

Standing Order Contracts

standing order An arrangement made with a vendor to deliver specific goods on a regularly scheduled basis.

The term **standing order** refers to an arrangement made with a vendor to deliver specific goods on a regularly scheduled basis. However, since you are not sending a specific purchase order preceding a delivery, you may easily get products you don't need. Product rotation and credits for obsolete products are normally parts of a standing order agreement; be sure that this condition is respected, so that you do not lose money on spoilage.

first in, first out (FIFO) Method of inventory valuation and management in which cost of goods sold is charged with the cost of raw materials, in-process goods and finished goods purchased first and in which inventory contains the most recently purchased materials.

The person delivering such an order should deliver enough goods to reach a predetermined amount, stock the product using the **first in, first out method**, and immediately write an invoice stating the amounts delivered. Standing orders are convenient, especially if the purchaser knows how much the restaurant will use, as is often the case with daily deliveries of bread or milk. However, there are important disadvantages to standing orders, as follows:

- Storeroom access and security must be more consistently monitored.

- It may be more expensive than other purchasing methods.

- In some cases deliveries are not verified and invoices are not signed before the delivery person leaves the premises.

VENDOR SELECTION

As a consumer, you select a grocery store based on your own needs and criteria, whatever they may be—the availability of organic produce, a convenient location, low prices, delivery service, widest selection, or other qualities. You might check weekly advertisements or visit different stores to evaluate their offerings. You choose a store or stores, and you constantly evaluate whether you are getting the value you want for the services and products you buy. You must also decide whether to buy raw ingredients and make everything from scratch, or to purchase prepared foods that take less time at home. These questions are tied in with pricing, quality, taste, service, and other considerations. This chapter deals with these same questions at the professional level: How do you go about selecting vendors? And how do you make decisions about product choices from those vendors?

Competitive Bids from Vendors

After you identify purchase specifications and completing product testing, competitive bids from vendors come into play. Competitive bids are the price and quantity proposals that vendors present to your company. The purchaser should solicit and select from at least three bidding vendors. There is no harm in entertaining a bid; just be sure to verify the prices periodically to ensure that quoted prices remain within your company guidelines. Use the form in Figure 5-7 to monitor competitive bids.

WEEKLY FOOD BID FORM

Date Received: _____
Prepared By: _____

BID IN EFFECT FROM: _____(DATE)_____ **TO:** _____(DATE)_____

Product Number	Item Description	Pack Size	Brand Name	Unit of Measure	Vendor	Vendor	Vendor	Vendor

Figure 5-7 Weekly Food Bid Form

You may need to find vendors proactively so that you can get the best price available. You can identify vendors through the following means:

- Carrying out a specific investigation involving a supplier and a trial transaction

- Choosing from an established list

- Making a routine selection based on the purchaser's experience

- Using a well-established, well-known company

- Consulting a classified directory

- Reading manufacturers' catalogs and sales literature

- Consulting industry sources such as professional associations

- Interviewing salespeople or other buyers

- Attending trade and product shows

Sometimes the process of selecting a vendor is subject to outside limitations. Some procurement is restricted to domestic sources by the terms of the Buy American Act. If they are legal, reciprocal agreements between countries or companies may narrow the purchaser's choices. The desire to exploit a particular technology or the resources of an affiliate may also be restrictive. Legal factors occasionally restrict the free selection of bidders as well. Warranty requirements, patent rights, license agreements, or other obligations may prevent either buyers or sellers from attempting to purchase or to market products. It is important to understand what boundaries influence the process in your geographic area and in your company.

Once the bids have been received, the purchaser and the manager should review several vendor characteristics to determine compliance with established specifications. Consider having a primary vendor in order to offer a large amount of business to one dependable company. Doing so can lower your prices dramatically. Also consider the following "vendor selection" factors to determine if the vendor is the right choice for your company:

Vendor Selection Criteria

- *Quality needs.* Understanding and communicating your quality needs is essential for a good vendor-purchaser relationship. It is accomplished through adequate and accurate specifications, educating the vendor, and a visit to the vendor's facility.

- *Sales support and other services.* This should be verified based on past performance and on reference checks with current business affiliates.

When Rebecca Charles, owner of Pearl Oyster Bar, was asked, "What do you look for in a distributor?" she responded, "It's all about the relationships. I've followed one saleswoman through three companies. If there is a problem with the cheese they deliver she'll come over and take care of it. She'll even go to the local retail cheese store and buy a replacement if necessary. That's the sign of someone who has been in business for a long time. That's rare in New York."

Source: Caroline Perkins. "Profiles in Partnership," *Nation's Restaurant News.* April 24, 2006. p. 18.

- *Necessary contractual obligations.* These obligations should be reviewed to ensure compliance and to prevent legal restrictions and enforcement.

- *Technical capabilities and support.* This is necessary if the product is of a technical nature.

- *Manufacturing capabilities.* The vendor should, when appropriate, be able to control its own production, thereby reducing problems with its suppliers. The vendor should also be able to provide a realistic production schedule.

- *Management capabilities.* The vendor must have the ability to provide all required supplier services, to ensure back-up inventory on hand, and to offer consistent delivery schedules.

- *Financial strength.* This is crucial in preventing interruption of supply.

- *Labor-to-management relations.* Historically poor relations between a vendor's labor and management often result in erratic delivery performance and inconsistent product quality. Strikes or labor disputes may affect the vendor's service to your company.

- *Past performance.* This provides insight into probable future performance.

- *References.* These are good indicators that establish history with other buyers, yet they are not by themselves a sufficient indicator of a reliable vendor.

- *Pricing structure and incentives.* These should be reviewed in order to ensure that you take maximum advantage of your purchasing power. Find out if the vendor offers incentives for early payment schedules. In turn, increased purchases from the vendor could help free cash-flow constraints.

- *Favorable delivery schedules.*

- *High ethics and no conflicts of interest.* See details about this issue in Chapter 3.

After receiving all bids, purchasers and other decision-makers should make a selection that best satisfies the various interests of the company at that particular time. These can change, and you may find better deals or more valuable services with other vendors. Just make sure you comply with contractual obligations with current vendors. When terms expire, you can renegotiate for better terms or find other vendors.

The Make-or-Buy Decision

As discussed in Chapter 4, many vendors offer products already prepared into portions. You won't incur the labor cost of portioning these items, nor will you pay for waste when you prepare them. These products also cost you more, so you must evaluate whether you can prepare them in-house at a lesser cost. Your yield tests will show you the waste and labor costs of preparing the items; you should measure these costs against the cost of buying the items already prepared. This is called the make-or-buy decision, and it is something you will probably face almost every day in purchasing.

This kind of decision is usually reserved for the most expensive items and for high-volume items. As the purchaser, it is your job to see that all relevant costs are considered, so that you can make an informed decision regarding whether to make or buy the product. To do so, you must evaluate what is called the **prime cost**.

Prime cost factors in the many variable "hidden" expenses that operators incur (whether they realize it or not) when they process products on-site. The term *prime cost* refers to labor, material, and overhead costs incurred in product preparation. Figure 5-8 illustrates the difference in case cost and prime cost to convert bulk celery to diced celery. This example takes you through the stages of produce preparation, adding the costs of each stage to the original case price of the celery. The as-purchased price of $13.50 is only a fraction of the post-preparation, end-product prime cost of $36.22.

prime cost The labor, material, and overhead costs identified in product preparation.

This example is presented to demonstrate the possible impact of a make-or-buy decision involving a food product. There are many hidden costs in preparing products, and you will need to consider which ones affect your cost in each case. Some of these costs include the following:

- *Managing the raw materials:* ordering, receiving, inspecting and storing

- *Utility costs:* water usage, refrigeration, storage, and waste disposal

- *Labor costs:* underutilization of labor capacity, delays and downtime, scheduled and non-scheduled breaks, training, taxes, FICA, insurance, and so on

- *Employee support and training, supervision, and quality control*

- *Workstation preparation, cleanup, and employee hygiene*

- *Additional square footage required for prep and equipment needs*

- *Lost time due to work-related injuries*

- *Value added:* when you purchase preprepped products, you get 100 percent of what you buy; consistency and better inventory controls comprise some of the added value

Use a chart like the one in Figure 5-8 to analyze your make-or-buy decisions, and look out for these and other costs that might be specific to the item or to your company's circumstances.

Figure 5-8 Prime Cost Analysis

PRIME COST ANALYSIS			
Raw material:	**bulk celery**	Finished product:	**Diced**
Raw material gross weight:	**55 pound**	Finished product specification:	**1/4" dice**

1st Prep Stage: Clean, Cut, trim leaves			
Raw material	1 (no. of case) × $13.50/case (cost)	=	$13.50
Direct Labor	20 (min.) × .245 (cost per min.)	=	$4.90
Indirect Labor	4.9 (direct labor cost) × 25% (indirect %)	=	$1.22
Waste	55# (gross wt.) − 36# (yield) = 19 × .07	=	
	(waste cost per #)	=	$1.33
	1st prep stage prime case cost total	=	$20.95

2nd Prep Stage: Hand Dice			
	1st prep stage prime case cost	=	$20.95
Additional direct labor	45 (min.) × 2.45 (cost per min.)	=	$11.02
Indirect labor	11.02 (direct labor cost) x 25% (indirect)	=	$2.75
Waste	36 (1st prep yield) − 34 (2nd prep yield) =	=	
	2 × .07 (waste cost per pound)	=	$0.14
	2nd prep stage prime case cost total	=	$34.86
	34 (2nd prep yield) = 2nd prep cost per #	=	$1.02

3rd Prep Stage: Wash and Dry			
	2nd prep stage prime case cost	=	$34.86
Additional direct labor	4 (min.) × .245 (cost per min.)	=	$0.98
Indirect labor	.98 (direct labor cost) × 25% (indirect %)	=	$0.24
Waste	+34 (2nd prep yield) − 32 (3rd prep yield) =	=	
	2 x .07 (waste cost per pound)	=	$0.14
	3rd prep stage prime case cost total	=	$36.22
	+32 (3rd prep yield) = 3rd prep cost per #	=	1.13*

* Not including materials, cleaning supplies, electricity, water, and overhead expense allocation.

Courtesy of Costa Fruit & Produce.

Considerations Before Awarding Business to a Vendor

Before awarding your business to a vendor, you have a great deal to consider. The vendor must meet or exceed your needs. Remember always that the vendor has to earn your business through ethical behavior, quality products, and service. Your relationships with your vendors are critical for the success of your establishment because your customers expect a great deal from you. For you to be able to provide high-quality service to your customers, the vendor must provide you with some very important guarantees: consistency in quality, reliability of delivery, availability of the products you need, supplier services that are pertinent to your unique needs, and adequate food safety. The following segments detail each of these components, and then describes what to expect after the contract is signed.

Consistency

Restaurant customers rank **consistency** as one of their primary concerns when choosing where to eat. Without consistent products, it is impossible to provide consistent food, and you will lose customers because of it. Consistency in purchasing means that the products purchased remain the same at all times—in line with your written, detailed purchasing specifications. For this to happen, the purchasing manager must insist on consistency in quality and pack size. Deviations should be documented by the receiving clerk and communicated to the purchaser, the chef, and the restaurant manager. Consistency is an important basis for vendor evaluation. The results of such evaluation can tell you whether or not to terminate a purchasing agreement. Figure 5-9 shows one format for judging consistency. If used consistently to evaluate your vendors, this form is a good tool for monitoring and correcting product specification problems.

> **consistency** In purchasing, means that the products purchased remain the same at all times.

The starting point for verifying and monitoring product consistency is at the receiving dock. Receiving meats, poultry, and seafood items, for example, should not be left to an inexperienced receiving clerk. The chef or the butcher should be involved in evaluating a product's quality upon arrival. The receiving clerk can certainly assist with the counting and weighing of the items, as most food products are purchased and invoiced by count or by weight. It is prudent to verify the quality and weight of the product in the presence of the delivery person before signing the delivery invoice.

Discrepancies as a result of quality or quantity (including weight) may be handled by adjusting the invoice or by writing a **credit memo**. (An example of this form, as well as instructions for its use, appears in Chapter 6.) On the other hand, if the quality is not right, the purchaser and the chef may want to send the product back with the delivery person, assuming the operation can function without the product until the next delivery. Consider also the severity of the discrepancy. For example, if you received a delivery of less-aged beef tenderloin such as 5-up instead of highly aged 6-up beef, you may just wish to inform the salesperson and adjust the price accordingly. As long as the mistake is not a habit and the vendor corrects the error quickly, accepting the lower quality may not hurt your business. In either case, when you tell the vendor that you found the error, they will know you are checking closely and are less likely to make this kind of mistake again.

> **credit memo** Used to record a credit due from a supplier when the merchandise received does not conform to what was ordered. The discrepancy could be in terms of quality, quantity, specification, and/ or price.

Consistency will also vary with the seasons. For example, during the winter months strawberries are scarce, and taste and cost are much more variable. You may have to change brands as the seasons change. Prices of off-season strawberries may be so high that you have to raise your menu prices or do without strawberries in the winter season. This holds true for many perishable products, especially produce.

Different supplier sources also affect consistency. Often, a purchaser will buy from different vendors from one week to the next in order to get a better price. These vendors will often differ in pack sizes, brand names, and product taste. Even the same vendor may discontinue

VENDOR EVALUATION FORM

Vendor name: _____ Address: _____ Date: _____

Type of product/services _____

If a rating is poor in any category, document carefully in PERFORMANCE DETAILS section.

CATEGORY		Rating (zone)		
		Excellent	satisfactory	Poor
Quality	Inspection			
	Performance			
	Maintenance			

CATEGORY		Rating (zone)		
		Excellent	satisfactory	Poor
SERVICE	Inspection			
	Performance			
	Maintenance			

CATEGORY		Rating (zone)		
		Excellent	satisfactory	Poor
COST	Price			
	Discout			

Overall appraisal of vendor:
After considering the performance rating

PERFORMANCE DETAILS

Quality _____

Service _____

Costs _____

General
Comment _____

Alternate source: can you recommend a better source. If yes indicate

Vendor name: _____ Address: _____

Prepared by:

Name: _____ Title: _____ Date: _____

Figure 5-9 Vendor Analysis Form

a product or run out of a popular item. Because of this, the purchaser and the chef must consider substitute products from time to time, and the manager will have to respond to any guest concerns about inconsistent quality and presentation. What it all comes down to is that maintaining a consistent product involves a great deal of cost and everyone's effort. Everyone must cooperate to monitor quality while remaining flexible to deal with contingencies. The goals, as always, are to stay in business and to remain profitable.

Reliability

Although it is difficult to gauge overall vendor reliability, this criterion is important because it affects the long-term success of doing business with a particular vendor. In the food service industry, you cannot afford to run out of a menu item on a regular basis because of supplier problems. For example, guests expect that you'll have coffee, tea, and juices at breakfast. You have to be able to depend on the vendor to maintain a steady inventory and timely delivery. On the other hand, reliability goes both ways. For example, the vendor should be able to trust that your company will pay invoices on time and that the purchaser will review their product fairly against other competitors. Vendors go to great lengths to win your business; your part of the bargain is to assure fair and timely treatment. This will go a long way toward building a good relationship with a vendor, and they should respond with equal efforts.

To measure reliability, look at the "vendor selection criteria" list above, and determine whether your vendors have those characteristics. They are excellent gauges of how to select a vendor.

Availability

Availability should be a primary consideration in all purchases. Availability of food products depends on the season, on demand, and on supply. For example, most vegetables and fruits are seasonal, as Figure 5-10 shows.

Berries are often seasonal as well. The disproportionate demand and supply of berries during winter months is mostly to blame for their escalating prices. Without intimate knowledge of a product's history, it is difficult to say why availability fluctuates. However, monitoring availability and planning for shortages are part of the purchaser's job. When selecting a vendor, assess the vendor's history regarding product availability by asking the following questions:

- *Quantity:* Will the vendor be able to meet your company's needs sufficiently at all times? This is important for planning because you don't want supply problems at a critical period in the season.

- *Rate of usage:* At what rate does your company use the product? Use this information to coordinate deliveries. It's important to establish that you want availability but you don't want to have to buy excessive inventory.

- *Lead time:* How long will it take the vendor to get my order to you? This can easily affect your choice of supplier.

- *Long-term commitment:* How long can your company rely on the source of supply? Consideration of long-term availability is important for meeting your continuing needs. For example, you don't want to look for a new milk vendor each week to replace a short supply.

- *Transportation:* How far away is the source of the products? This characteristic can limit availability in some circumstances. If your operation is in a remote area, or if there are few delivery options, you may need to consider transportation carefully.

Figure 5-10 Availability Form

	JAN	FEB	MAR	APR	MAY	JUN	JUL	AUG	SEP	OCT	NOV	DEC
Fruits												
Apricots	x				x	X	x	x				x
Cherries	x	x		x	x	X	X	x				x
Limes	X	x	x	x	x	X	X	X	X	x	X	X
Melons	x	x	x	x	X	X	X	X	X	x	x	x
Tangerines	x	x	x	x	x					x	x	x
Vegetables												
Beets	x	x	x	x	x	x	X	X	X	x	x	x
Cabbage	X	X	X	X	X	X	x	X	X	X	X	X
Eggplant	X	X	X	X	X	X	X	X	X	X	x	x
Herbs, Fresh	x	x	x	x	x	x	x	x	x	x	x	x
Spinach	X	X	x	x	x	X	X	X	x	x	x	x
Specialties												
BabySquash	x	x	x	x	x	X	X	X		x	x	x
Jicama	X	x	x	x	X	X	X	x	x	x	X	X
Shallots	x	x	x	x	x	x	x	x	x	x	x	x
xRegular Availability X Peak Season												
Source: Nobel/Sysco Fruit and Vegetable Availability Chart.												

Supplier Services

Supplier services must be considered in every price evaluation. Just as the quality of a product purchased at a competitive price is a yardstick for measuring the efficiency of procurement, so too is vendor service quality an important yardstick for selecting one vendor over another. Good vendor services can be a true help during your busiest times by helping you to run smoothly, without interruptions in deliveries; by offering technical support; and by keeping good records. Then again, a vendor might not offer anything special to you, or may not even notice how busy you are. You can have either kind of vendor; which would you prefer?

Vendor services generally consist of one or more of the following:

- *Handling of complaints:* A vendor should investigate complaints promptly and thoroughly, report the facts to the purchaser, and take corrective steps. This is a valuable service to the purchaser.

- *Prompt notification:* A good vendor will notify the purchaser if anything is happening or is likely to happen that might affect the purchaser's normal flow of products. Examples include embargoes, strikes, severe weather conditions, and equipment breakdowns.

- *Prompt delivery at all costs:* At times, events beyond anyone's control delay deliveries. Vendors demonstrate good service when they rush that delivery, particularly at their company's expense.

- *Correcting misunderstandings:* A vendor should be willing to make satisfactory adjustments for misunderstandings or clerical errors.

- *Technical support:* Large vendors such as Alliant and Nobel/Sysco sometimes provide electronic purchasing software, user manuals, and even computers to qualifying purchasers. They have invested in technology to enhance the software and to make it more user-friendly. Placing orders through these systems generally averages 25 percent less time than placing orders manually.

- *Reports of purchases:* Most vendors will provide, upon your request, a detailed history of your purchases. This can be a useful planning tool.

- *Customer service:* A good vendor may have a knowledgeable, toll-free customer service line, and you should be able to contact them during your business hours. The local salesperson should be available for product or technical assistance.

- *Miscellaneous services:* Other habits by which vendors are judged include their fulfillment of promises, prompt remittance of credits, and track record backing up their bids.

Safety

As a purchaser, you must be concerned with the suitability and safety of the consumable products offered by your vendors. U.S. Department of Agriculture (USDA) inspections and other federal regulations impose various standards with which you may have to comply. In 1990, Congress passed the Nutritional Labeling and Education Act (NLEA). This law was targeted at the packaged food industry, which was required to have food analyzed by a laboratory in order to substantiate nutritional information scientifically. In May 1994, Congress enacted a similar law to regulate food service operations that made nutrient and health claims on placards, posters, or signs. What all this means is that you must know what you are buying to serve to your customers. It is your responsibility to represent your products and nutritional claims truthfully. Both new and old products must comply with these regulations.

You must also learn about any upgrades and replacements that are needed for your existing equipment and facilities. Any establishment that knowingly or neglectfully serves bad food or beverages could be liable to fines and lawsuits. This is a moral issue as well as a legal one. One of the best ways to verify that the food you receive complies with regulations is to visit the vendor's plant, perhaps even unannounced. On visits, wear the proper attire for sanitary purposes.

Your vendor has a similar responsibility to you, and you should seek a vendor that knows the regulations, follows them to the letter, and helps to keep you informed of changes to your responsibilities and requirements. A vendor earns your business with many services and qualities, and one of these should be its knowledge and attention to the industry and its requirements.

Awarding the Contract

When you do award a a contract, tell the winner promptly so its personnel can make immediate plans to fulfill the purchase contract. Industry practices vary widely in terms of informing losing vendors that they have not succeeded in this competitive bidding process. As a practical matter, it is neither expected nor necessary that unsuccessful vendors be informed on negotiations about minor, repetitive, or low-value purchases. On the other hand, it is good practice to advise losing bidders on major awards. The purchaser should not disclose the successful price to unsuccessful candidates, as all data should be confidential.

After the Contract is Signed

The manager, receiving clerk, and purchaser should continue to track prices on every invoice. They should monitor that all specifications, quality, services, and prices are met. The purpose of watching these specifications is to be sure that the vendor is living up to its end of the contract. In some cases, the contract may allow for periodic review of progress by both parties. This is a good time to resolve variances from established specifications and delivery standards, if any, along with any other unforeseen issues or changes.

SUMMARY

Pricing is a key consideration when selecting a vendor, and it informs many of the other decisions you make as you go through and repeat the ongoing vendor-selection process. To use pricing effectively, it is important to weight the prices based on your usage and to consider this factor seriously when deciding on a vendor. The bidding process helps you to see a cross-section of vendor offerings. You will also want to understand the various pricing arrangements, to be able to evaluate how each will affect your operation and to decide which structures are right for you.

However, vendors also offer other services and other qualities that are very important in your selection process. The vendor needs to work with you to offer the pricing arrangement you want. The vendors need to understand your quality needs, provide sales support and other services, and have the capabilities and financial strength to service your orders. Be sure to check references, and negotiate the best pricing incentives you can based on your business volume. The vendor you select should be of high ethical reputation and standards, so you can establish a trustworthy and dependable operation, free of questions about unethical practices.

Finally, you should evaluate potential vendors on their reliability, consistency, availability, safety, and quality of services. If a vendor fails to attend to your needs in these ways, there are many other vendors who would love to win your contract.

CHAPTER QUESTIONS

Discussion Questions

1. How can you improve the value of the purchase to the food service operator without altering the quality or end product price?

2. If you could buy preprocessed potatoes at $0.75 per pound with 100 percent yield for a 50-pound bag, and you saved $10 in labor costs, by analyzing prime cost, is it a better value to make or to buy the processed potatoes?

3. What vendor services are most valuable, and why?

4. What is the term for a commitment to a long-term agreement on purchase quantity and a fixed price for goods regardless of market price fluctuations?

5. What is the term for a method of procurement, normally used for perishable items, by which a specified amount of product is delivered on a regular basis?

6. When purchasing, what is the most important thing to consider? Please elaborate.

CASE STUDIES

Case Study 1: Make-or-Buy Analysis

"In my opinion, we ought to stop making our dinner rolls and accept that outside supplier's offer," said Mary, managing partner at Wuksachi Restaurant. "At a price of 15 cents per dinner roll, we would be paying 50 cents less than it costs us to bake the bread in-house. Since we use 150,000 rolls a year, that would be an annual cost savings of $75,000." Wuksachi's actual cost to prepare these dinner rolls is shown below (based on 150,000 dinner rolls per year):

Direct material	$20,500
Direct labor	$36,200
Variable overhead	$20,800
Fixed overhead ($2.80 general company overhead, $1.60 depreciation, and $0.75 supervision)	$20,000
Total cost per roll	$0.65

A decision about whether to make or buy the bread is especially important at this time, since the oven used to make the bread is completely worn out and must be replaced. The choices facing the restaurant are as follows:

Alternative 1: Purchase a new baking oven and continue to make the rolls. The oven would cost $18,000; it would have ten years of useful life and no salvage value.

Alternative 2: Purchase the dinner rolls from an outside supplier at 15 cents per roll under a one-year contract.

The new baking oven would be more efficient than the oven that Wuksachi Restaurant has been using and, according to the manufacturer, would reduce direct labor and variable overhead costs by 20 percent. The restaurant would use the space now being used to produce the rolls for storage and an additional refrigerator.

Your task:

1. To assist the director in the making a decision, prepare an analysis showing what the total cost and the cost per dinner roll would be under each of the two alternatives given above. Assume that 150,000 dinner rolls are needed each year. Which course of action would you recommend to the director?

2. Would your recommendation in (1) above be the same if the company's needs were: (a) 200,000 rolls per year or (b) 250,000 rolls per year? Show calculations to support your answer, with cost presented on both a total and a per-unit basis.

3. What other factors would you recommend that the director consider before making a decision?

Case Study 2: Planning Future Purchases

Portobello Restaurant offers fresh orange juice in a 12-ounce glass as part of its breakfast menu. The orange juice costs the restaurant $5 per gallon and is very popular with customers. The average order of orange juice per guest is 1.5 glasses. Below you will see the projected number of customers, by quarter, for 2005 and the first quarter of 2006.

	2005 Quarter				2006 Quarter
	First	**Second**	**Third**	**Fourth**	**First**
Projected Number of Customers	200,000	250,000	300,000	210,000	215,000

Orange juice has become so popular that even customer comments reflect its importance. It has become necessary to carry high inventories as a precaution against stock-outs. For this reason, the inventory of orange juice at the 50 gallons will be on hand to start the first quarter of 2005.

Your task:

Prepare a materials purchases budget for orange juice by quarter and in total for 2005. At the bottom of your budget, show the dollar amount of purchases for each quarter and for the whole year.

Purchasing Controls

Learning Objectives

After reading this chapter, you should be able to:

- understand how to audit purchasing functions;

- understand the importance of receiving controls and be able to create a credit memo and credit invoice;

- identify methods of spotting quality problems in receiving;

- perform proper receiving procedures, using an understanding of tare weight;

- conduct a receiving procedures weekly audit;

- perform the roles and responsibilities of storeroom personnel;

- understand the meaning of first in, first out (FIFO) and last in, first out (LIFO) inventory rotation procedures;

- understand the importance of the following storeroom functions:

  - direct issue and storeroom issue items

  - requirements for different refrigeration temperatures

  - the term *dead stock*

  - storeroom security

  - meat tag system.

In Practice

After the walk-through with Myla, chef Robert decided to take action. "Well, Scott," he said, "let's talk about setting up departmental control evaluations. This will show our efforts to correct any control issues from our last audit." Scott had no time to respond before chef Robert's phone rang and he answered. It was Myla.

"I just wanted to thank you and Scott for the hospitality and warm welcome. I really appreciated it! I wanted to call and give you the heads-up: I just received a letter from our corporate office regarding a visit from our internal auditors," said Myla.

"What a coincidence," Robert replied. "Scott and I were just talking about that. We intend to conduct a self-evaluation of our internal controls."

(continues)

> *(continued)*
>
> *"A self-evaluation? Shouldn't someone independent of your department do that?" Myla asked.*
>
> *"Yes, you're right, of course. But that doesn't absolve us of our responsibility to make sure that the controls are working. In the last audit report, I was reading where it says, 'The primary objective of auditing the purchasing functions is to make sure that the purchaser is carrying out the primary responsibility of the department: obtaining the best value for the establishment, the best quality, and the most appropriate merchandise at the lowest possible price and at the required time. The secondary objective is to verify control of valued merchandise throughout the receiving, storing, and issuing process.'" Robert was taking this responsibility very seriously, and knew he had a vital part to play.*

INTRODUCTION

In your role as a consumer, you don't make purchasing decisions just once. You re-evaluate over time, assess your practices, and make adjustments for various purposes, such as preventing spoilage or obtaining discounts. While your individual buying happens on a smaller scale than restaurant buying, that doesn't mean you want to spend money unnecessarily. One of your roles as a professional purchaser is to control receiving and purchasing functions with an eye toward improving practices. You can make minor improvements that streamline efficiency, cut waste, and provide oversight, thus contributing to the bottom line of your company. To do so, you will have to set and adhere to a schedule of audits, maintain an appropriate and useful database, create receiving controls, and train staff when necessary. You will also need to monitor the storeroom and the issuing procedures and set up requisition systems with the staff of the entire restaurant. These controls are the focus of this chapter.

Audits are usually carried out by an external accountant or, in a large organization, by an internal auditor. Ultimately, responsibility rests with the department manager.

The accountant or auditor should:

- ensure that all price quotations are in writing and accessible at all times, and that vendors adhere to the quoted prices.

- verify price compliance through record reviews and physical inspections of purchase orders and invoices.

- examine merchandise inventories on hand to determine compliance with purchase specifications.

- identify opportunities for revision of food specifications or menu revisions whenever prices rise to an uneconomical level or products go out of season.

- verify that all products are accurately inventoried to establish true asset value.

- verify that orders are placed with the lowest bidder based on set management criteria (any exceptions should be approved by management).

- establish and maintain par levels.

- distribute copies of the vendors' weekly price updates to the receiving clerk and the executive chef (vendors should send you these weekly price updates on products with highly variable prices, such as seafood, meat, produce, and poultry, to help you with price comparisons and to identify "special" buys).

- distribute copies of the weekly audit forms to the receiving clerk and chef as part of conducting, documenting, and monitoring receiving procedures.

- continuously monitor all high-cost items in order to readjust selling prices and/or food recipes if costs get too high.

- ensure that standing orders are not commonly used to purchase products other than milk, eggs, and breads.

RECEIVING CONTROLS

Whoever is receiving deliveries has a unique perspective on a food-service operation, as well as an important responsibility in ensuring that the company is obtaining the quality and quantity of merchandise ordered at the quoted price. He or she helps to provide crucial receiving controls. It may be the purchaser who receives deliveries, or there may be a staff of receiving clerks; in either case, the person in this role is responsible for accurately noting the status of all orders received. We'll use the term *clerk* here, though the person who actually receives shipments may have a different title.

The clerk should verify the supplier, quality, quantity, and price of products delivered before signing any receipt. The receiving clerk needs to ensure that a prenumbered, three-part credit memo is issued. Whenever the weight or product count varies from what was ordered, one copy of the credit memo should be forwarded to the vendor; the second copy should be attached to a daily record of all receipts; and the third copy should be sent to accounts payable. In general, a **credit memo** is used to record a credit due from a supplier when the merchandise received does not conform to what was ordered. The discrepancy could involve quality, quantity, specification, or price. The clerk should also notify the chef or manager immediately when such discrepancies occur, since production needs may be affected right away.

At times a delivery will arrive without an invoice. The receiving clerk should write what is called a **memo invoice** when this happens. A memo invoice is simply a list of all items received. This documentation is critical for accrual and end-of-month cut-off totaling to ensure accuracy of the accrual.

The clerk acts as the eyes and ears of the purchaser. The person receiving deliveries must make sure that all invoices are marked with a receiving stamp that includes when and by whom the order was received. The receiving clerk signs and dates the invoices and verifies quantities, unit prices, and price extensions. Each item must have been ordered using a prenumbered purchase order, and its number must be verified before delivery is accepted. This is the only way to ensure that the items were approved before they were ordered.

The clerk must also bring issues to the attention of the purchasing manager—for example, when a vendor consistently delivers products early or late. The purchaser can then inform the vendor to ensure that it adheres to posted delivery hours. Similarly, the purchaser should be notified when a supplier repeatedly provides merchandise that is substandard in quality or quantity. The clerk should review the product specifications for quality indicators. The following are some examples of quality problems associated with prepared produce products:

- Cauliflower or broccoli with dark spots and wet florets

- Shredded cabbage, diced bell peppers, sliced or diced onions, or carrots that are wet and viscous or have excess liquid in the bottom of the bag

- Sliced radishes that are turning brown or are dry and cracked

- Salad mix or prepared lettuce that is brown or reddish-pink

- Sliced mushrooms that are brown and slimy.

credit memo Used to record a credit due from a supplier when the merchandise received does not conform to what was ordered. The discrepancy could be in terms of quality, quantity, specification, and/or price.

memo invoice A list of all items received.

Auditing the Receiving Function

As the purchaser, you are responsible for proper receiving procedures. Management should also verify that proper receiving procedures are in effect. A random audit of the actual receiving process will help to ensure that all prescribed procedures, as listed below, are followed. This audit should be performed regularly to ensure that all staff members involved are carrying out the functions properly.

tare weight The weight of various empty containers used to determine the net weight of perishables in these containers.

- The quantity of merchandise delivered should be compared to the quantity ordered (weight, volume, and/or unit count).

- All goods purchased by weight must be weighed without wrapping, ice, containers, or packaging materials. The receiving department should keep a record of the weight of various empty containers in order to determine the net weight of perishables in these containers. This is called **tare weight**. If you use a printing scale, receiving clerks won't need to empty any containers, so they won't risk endangering the contents.

- Products bought by count and by containers should be counted individually when received.

- Goods that are purchased in cases should be examined to ascertain that the entire contents of the case are present and of the specified quality.

- In a manual purchasing system, all cases should be marked with price per unit.

- Perishable goods are to be stored promptly and properly using appropriate rotation procedures.

- Clerks should inspect all items for quality, uniformity, and adherence to specifications. The receiving clerk should notify the purchasing manager of discrepancies.

- Perishable goods should be dated and priced on the container, or tagged or labeled if they lack suitable surfaces for direct marking.

- Delivery documents or invoices should be stamped with a receiving stamp and appropriately noted. All food and beverage merchandise is classified as direct or storeroom issue by the purchasing manager or receiving personnel. (See below for a discussion of direct versus storeroom issue items.)

- The accountant should compare the price on the invoice against the price on the purchase order before processing the invoice for payment.

- The accountant should verify that receiving personnel complete credit memos and memo invoices not requiring a specific form when appropriate.

Figure 6-1 is an example of a credit memo.

The credit memo form is used to record a credit due from a supplier. The receiving clerk completes this form when the merchandise received does not conform to what was ordered in terms of quality, quantity, specification, or price. Be sure to train the receiving clerk to have the delivery person sign this form as well. This form may be prepared in triplicate. The original is sent to the vendor to alert them of the discrepancy. The duplicate is sent to the accounts payable department for payable verification. The triplicate is filed in the receiving department.

Random Audit of Receiving Procedures

Use the form in Figure 6-2 to audit the procedures of the receiving department randomly and frequently. In Column 1, describe the item. Note the vendor and the invoice number

Figure 6-1 Credit Memo

CREDIT MEMO				
To:_____		No:_____		Date:_____
Please Issue Your Credit Memo For Items Listed Below				
Quantity	Unit	Item	Unit Cost	Total
Reasons:				
Acct. Department:		Party to whom delivered:		By:
White: Accounting		Yellow: Purchasing		Pink: Vendor

Figure 6-2 Weekly Audit Form

Date: _____			Receiving Personnel: _____				Prepared By: _____	
1	2	3	4	5	6	7	8	9
Item description	Vendor Name	Invoice Number	Does a bid sheet exist for this item?	Is this the lowest bid at the required specification?	Was the item's weight or count checked?	Was the item's quality checked?	Does the quality match what was ordered?	Comments

in Columns 2 and 3. In Columns 4 through 8, write *Yes* or *No* for each question. This audit should be performed while watching receiving personnel in their work; you want to see exactly how they check a product's quality, for example. In this way, you can praise complete work and provide extra coaching if the clerk is not checking the deliveries sufficiently.

Storeroom Functions

The storeroom is an area that requires special security and planning considerations to minimize risks to valuable inventory. You will have to train storeroom personnel to conform to a set of clear requirements that are not to be sacrificed when the establishment is busy or when other pressures exist. The protection of the assets you have purchased is a key to successful cost control. This need for security and accountability must, however, be balanced with the need of your outlets to access the raw materials they are serving your customers. Once procedures are established, however, the operation can be very smooth and consistent.

Storeroom personnel are responsible for controlling how and when merchandise is issued and preventing loss from theft and spoilage. Specific functions include:

- ensuring that storeroom operation hours comply with management standards in order to minimize off-hours entry, as this is a common breach of security.

- maintaining strict control of storeroom keys to ensure security.

- inspecting sanitation in all storage areas and bringing deficiencies to the attention of the purchasing manager.

- verifying that food products are stored in the proper refrigeration units and that proper temperatures are maintained and units are de-iced if necessary, so food quality does not deteriorate and compromise sanitation standards.

- verifying that meat and seafood products in the freezer are wrapped.

- reporting any slow-moving items to the chef and the manager at the end of every month.

- ensuring that all food products have been marked with unit prices and that perishables have been dated and stamped with the vendors' origin.

first in, first out (FIFO)
Method of inventory valuation and management in which cost of goods sold is charged with the cost of raw materials, in-process goods and finished goods purchased first and in which inventory contains the most recently purchased materials.

- practicing either **first in, first out (FIFO)** or **last in, first out (LIFO)** inventory rotation procedures according to your company's policy. FIFO means that you will use the oldest products first. This is advantageous for storeroom purposes and for avoiding spoilage. However, in times of rapid inflation, a FIFO system causes an overvaluation of your inventory. This is because the least expensive (i.e., oldest) inventory item is valued at the new prices. When your inventory is overvalued, you appear to have more profit than you actually do, and you must pay additional taxes.

last in, first out (LIFO)
An inventory costing method that assumes the most recent units purchased are the first units used. The result is that ending inventory consists of the oldest costs and the most recent costs are in the cost of sales.

In inflationary times, you may wish to use a LIFO system to value your ending inventory. In a LIFO storeroom, the most recently purchased products are used and charged, thus reducing current taxes by eliminating inventory profits. However, FIFO should always be used for product rotation in the storeroom, even when an accountant uses LIFO for inventory evaluation.

Issuing Functions

When issuing food to outlets, the objectives are to ensure proper authorization for the release of merchandise and to account properly for daily use. In doing so, issuing personnel must observe the following procedures:

- Correctly record and update all food and beverage issues

- Allocate all direct issue amounts (see below) to the correct outlet each day

- Verify that proper requisition procedures are being followed

Verification of requisition procedures should include both auditing after-hours requisitions and checking who is allowed to take items from the storeroom.

Direct Issue and Storeroom Issue Items

The term **direct issue** means that a purchase is charged directly to a receiving outlet, such as the kitchen. The accounting system presumes that these purchases are consumed on the date of purchase or transferred, so the purchase cost for these items is charged directly to the daily food cost. Direct issue goods are not usually stored in the food storeroom; depending upon space, they are usually delivered to the kitchen outlet that ordered them. The goods most commonly classified as direct issue are bread, dairy products, fruits, vegetables, fish, and meats. Often they are the most perishable products, so leaving them in a storeroom only makes them more likely to spoil before use.

direct issue A purchase charged directly to a receiving outlet.

Storeroom issue items, on the other hand, are food purchases that are sent to the storeroom to be stored and, within a reasonable period of time, issued to the outlet when they are requisitioned. Storing and issuing products can be very secure when you use the procedures outlined in the following sections.

storeroom issue Purchases sent to the storeroom to be stored and issued to the outlet when they are requisitioned.

STOREROOM PROCEDURES

Valuable inventory needs to be protected from theft, spoilage, and waste. Particularly with perishable products, you must follow specific procedures to maintain sanitation and refrigeration. You must also keep and audit records of all products as they enter and leave storage. This is what is called a **perpetual inventory** system—a running tabulation of goods received and issued. A month-end inventory is used as a starting place, and then refigured with each receipt and issuance. At the end of every month, the perpetual inventory should be reconciled to the **physical inventory**, and discrepancies investigated. Discrepancies should be noted as adjustments to the physical inventory in the perpetual inventory report and reported to the manager.

perpetual inventory A system of accounting for inventory changes, in which beginning and ending inventories are noted along with any sales or purchases.

Food products must be kept safe, as defined by federal regulations. This involves storing the goods off of the floor, thereby avoiding problems with insects, rodents, floods, and other sources of contamination. To further ensure safety from rodents and insects, schedule regular exterminator visits.

physical inventory A count of actual inventory items, in order to note quantities and values.

Another important safety measure is to control refrigeration temperatures. Note the temperature guidelines for various products shown in Figure 6-3.

Figure 6-3 Fridge Temp Form

Item	Temperatures
Fresh fruits/vegetables *	42° Fahrenheit/6° Celsius
Dairy products	38° Fahrenheit/4° Celsius
Meat	32–34° Fahrenheit/0–2° Celsius
Fish	32° Fahrenheit/0° Celsius
Freezer items **except bananas, grapefruit, potatoes, and yellow onions, etc. which can be stored at room temperature*	−10° Fahrenheit/−20° Celsius

As soon as perishable products are received, they must be transferred to their respective refrigeration units. In the case of fish and seafood, ice is the best preservative. Ice prolongs the shelf life of these fragile products; be sure to store them so that the water drains off the ice constantly.

The storeroom should be well ventilated, with fans to provide air circulation. In addition to removing smells, this makes the storeroom a more pleasant place to work. Finally, sanitation must be maintained at the highest standard. Spills of any kind must be cleaned and disinfected immediately, and staff should clean all surfaces on a frequent and regular basis. This will mean moving inventory in order to clean underneath packages and shelving, which is crucial to storeroom cleanliness.

The storeroom must be organized logically and in a manner that preserves flavors and shelf lives. Store heavy items that are issued in bulk, such as flour and sugar, closest to the storeroom door. Do so as well with items that are most frequently used. This eases the physical strain on personnel who must lift them. Organize all products by aisle and bin for easy location.

Overall, store different classes of foods according to their special storage requirements. For example:

- Do not store eggs alongside foods with strong odors, such as fish or cheese, since eggshells are porous and can absorb flavors.

- Store tomatoes in the refrigerator to control how quickly they ripen.

- Avoid storing citrus fruits in the same area with vegetables and greens, as this will diminish their shelf lives.

- Do not store mushrooms and berries with potatoes and onions, as they will tend to mold.

- Store meat with the fat side facing up. If you store meat in Cryovac or other plastic, check the packaging to make sure it is not punctured. This helps meat maintain its taste and quality and keeps it from spoiling.

Facilitating storeroom record keeping is much easier with a system for marking or tagging every inventory item. Immediately after receiving items, mark the date and price on perishables with a wax crayon or colored sticker. These should be stored in a way that facilitates FIFO rotation. In practice, the physical rotation of products is far more important than simply dating products. Place new items behind older items. When employees are stressed and busy, they are unlikely to look for the oldest date, and they will simply grab the most convenient product. You want a system that encourages this common-sense rule: Items should be used as soon as possible after receiving, and before newer items of the same type are used.

If you price your goods manually (i.e., without a computerized system), also price all canned goods and staple items with a stamp or crayon before storing them. If you are using an actual cost system (explained in more detail in Chapter 10), storeroom personnel should then calculate the unit cost from the invoice and write the cost on the goods. These cost calculations can be used as a basis for your total cost figures or inventory values.

Storeroom personnel should also keep track of how the inventory moves—or fails to move. The chef must be advised, for example, of any perishables reaching the spoilage stage. These should be used as a restaurant special or for employee meals and should be issued to an outlet as soon as possible via the regular procedures. The storeroom supervisor should perform daily spot-checks of perishables to prevent spoilage from occurring. He or she should also maintain and update a list of **dead stock** items. The term dead stock is used to describe obsolete or discontinued stock items that are no longer in regular use due to menu or service changes. Dead stock items should be kept physically segregated in the storeroom. The value of these items should be updated regularly, and management should consider how to utilize these products as soon as possible.

Monitoring and recording incoming and outgoing products is an important function in the storeroom. Standardize hours of operation, and then post them in a conspicuous place. It is important to impose strict limits on people who enter the storeroom to pick up the items they need for their outlets. Ensure that the staff abides by these hours of operation by proper

dead stock Stock without significant inventory movement in sales due to menu or service changes.

mise en place. Allow after-hours entry only on an exceptional basis, and only in the presence of a manager or security person. Keep a logbook to note the names and departments of people who enter after hours; check this logbook to determine who is using this privilege excessively.

Require that requisitions from outlets be submitted at least 24 hours in advance of needed delivery, in order to allow adequate time to fill the orders. Require greater notice for special-order or limited-delivery items. Schedule staggered delivery times for each outlet or area. This serves two functions: first, the outlet will know when to expect delivery and will plan accordingly; second, you and the issuing staff can plan your day around the deliveries. Each outlet should have a par stock amount, which is a standard amount of each item it should have on hand. These amounts can be based on the chef's and manager's experience, plus an assessment of the outlet's average use. This will help greatly in the requisitioning process. If you serve banquet functions under a separate department, however, banqueting needs should be ordered separately and on the basis of upcoming functions, rather than on a strict par stock basis.

Storeroom security is a vital concern. Stolen goods can be an enormous source of loss for your company if security is not maintained. Take the following measures to minimize the risks of loss from theft:

- Use adequate padlocks or strong locks. Replace locks at least once a year, or change the combination of a combination lock on a weekly basis.

- Issue keys to as few individuals as possible, and let each person know how strictly you expect those keys to be used. Keyholders should never give their keys to anyone, and they should always accompany any storeroom entry. Also, whenever they allow someone into the storeroom after hours, they should enter the visit in the logbook. Keys should be signed out on a daily basis rather than issued indefinitely.

- If you install alarms on coolers and freezers, connect the alarms outside the storeroom to enable other personnel to hear them when the storeroom staff is absent.

Storeroom Requisitions

A storeroom requisition is used to obtain food items from the storeroom. It is prepared in duplicate by the requesting outlet. The original is signed upon issue of the merchandise and is filed in the storeroom; outlet costs are calculated from these issued requisitions. The duplicate copy is retained by the department issuing the requisition.

When writing prices on the requisitions, copy the item price directly from the containers or the weekly price quotation sheet. Alternatively, an automated system can eliminate this step. Direct issue requisitions do not require pricing, as they already have been charged to the receiving outlet. The combination of direct issue items, transfers, and the prices tabulated from requisitions equals the outlet's food cost. This process is known as extension of the price, and it must be carried out consistently in order to measure costs accurately.

After completing the price extensions, food items should be categorized and recorded. When goods are used, they must be accounted for and replaced; the food-item record standardizes this process. The purchaser should then reconcile the record with the physical inventory. This method is used primarily in manual (nonautomated) purchasing systems. The Appendix includes a form called the Daily Storeroom Requisition Recap Form, which can be used for this purpose. You can also design your own form. Simply include the items requisitioned and issued to each outlet.

Meat Tag Systems

meat tag A system for controlling meat by tagging, used for identification and verification of actual use.

When meats are stored centrally and are not issued directly to outlets, storeroom personnel will need to establish a **meat tag** system to identify and price all meat issued. The use of meat tags can ensure an accurate issue price and weight on storeroom requisitions. Further, the system aids in controlling meat waste in the storeroom. One copy of the meat tag is attached to the item or kept in the storeroom until the item is issued. The second copy is sent to the person performing accounting functions so that he or she can reconcile the expense.

As each meat item is received, it is tagged for identification and accurate pricing. You may choose to set up a system in which one meat tag is prepared for each meat item, or one in which a tag is prepared for lots of five or more items. In the case of a banquet order, you might choose to set up the system to tag the entire shipment as a unit. Choose the system that works best for your circumstances, and then prepare the meat tag (shown in Figure 6-4) as follows:

1. Each meat tag has a preprinted number for identification and control purposes.

2. The date is entered on the tag when the item is placed in the storeroom.

3. The vendor or supplier is entered on the tag when the item is received.

4. The meat cut (e.g., strip, loin, prime rib, tenderloin) is entered on the tag.

5. The weight of the item is entered.

6. The unit price of the item is entered, usually on a per-pound basis.

7. The total cost is calculated and shown as an extended price.

When the item is issued and recorded for daily cost purposes, the original meat tag is sent to the person performing accounting and reconciliation functions, where it is stapled to the second copy and filed. If an item is taken without a proper storeroom requisition, it will be easy to identify from the second copy, and the appropriate cost can then be charged. The accounting person should always follow up and determine the cause of any deviation.

Figure 6-4 Meat Tag

MEAT TAG
Serial Number: (pre-printed)
Date:
Vendor:
Cut:
Weight:
Unit Price (per pound):
Extension:

SUMMARY

The value of strict controls in purchasing cannot be overstated. Every dollar saved in purchasing goes directly to profit, and there are many ways to save your company's money. Success in purchasing works for all employees; a profitable company is usually a much better place to work.

About 90 percent of products purchased in the industry are food and beverage products. While similar in many respects, they also have great differences. An endless number of vendors and products makes determining the best buy a great challenge. Throughout the entire process, ethical relationships must be maintained. Additional factors to consider include price, quantity, consistency, reliability, availability, service, and product safety. Often, the factors conflict; for example, the supplier with the best price may not offer the best quality or service. Balancing these factors to optimize purchasing requires a careful analysis of your company's specific objectives. Ultimately, the end user, the consumer, plays a vital role by spending money where he or she intends to get the best value. Each company needs to set appropriate purchasing standards to meet the needs of its target market.

All of your care is for naught, however, if proper receiving, storage, issuing, and inventory controls are not maintained. Proper receiving requires that quality, quantity, and price adhere to standards and are duly recorded. Then the products must be stored securely in the appropriate environment. Depending on cost, frequency of use, and shelf life, some items are issued directly, while others require a requisition and are issued from the storeroom. Use of the products must adhere to recipe and production standards to ensure proper control from purchasing to use. Only by using these control procedures can expenditures for food and beverage procurement be optimized.

CHAPTER QUESTIONS

Critical Thinking Questions

1. What are the primary objectives of receiving? What procedures should be followed to ensure these objectives are met?

2. What are the objectives of auditing the purchasing department?

3. What are the advantages and disadvantages of FIFO and LIFO systems?

4. What are the differences between direct issue and storeroom issue items?

5. Define the following terms: *credit memo*, *memo invoice*, and *tare weight*.

Multiple Choice Questions

1. Proper receiving procedures require checking
    A. the product's quality.
    B. the product's quantity.
    C. the product's price.
    D. all of the above.

2. What common-sense approach in determining how much to purchase is utilized by many food-service operations?
    A. purchase order
    B. stockpiles purchasing
    C. bid sheet
    D. par stock

3. Which of the following is a business form that reduces the amount of the invoice when items are refused or missing in the delivery?
    A. credit memo
    B. transfer memo
    C. pickup memo
    D. invoice addendum

4. Which of the following is a purchase that goes directly into production and is immediately assigned to the outlet that ordered it?

A.   direct purchase

B.   storeroom purchase

C.   seafood

D.   produce

PART

2

Beverage Standards

Introduction to Beverages

Learning Objectives

After reading this chapter, you should be able to:

- define and classify beverages;

- distinguish among various distilled beverages;

- discuss how the history of beverages affects consumption today;

- explain the health and economic impacts of alcoholism, and identify how these issues affect your sales;

- describe moral dilemmas and the law with regard to beverage sales;

- relate your pricing to the clientele and ambience of your establishment;

- calculate the cost of beverage items;

- discuss how availability and price competition affect your business;

- design your own pricing strategies.

In Practice

Two weeks before Myla Thomas was hired, the Sea Breeze Hotel lost its beverage manager. So as one of her first duties, it became Myla's responsibility to recruit and interview a new beverage manager. Myla was pleasantly surprised by the sheer number of interested candidates applying for the position. When she sat down to think about it, she realized she had a strong list of qualifications that she wanted the next manager to have:

- *An in-depth knowledge of the products, from their manufacture to their consumption*

- *Experience making beverage service profitable by implementing cost control procedures in purchasing, storage, and sales*

- *The ability to deliver customer satisfaction*

- *An understanding of the characteristics of beverage products and their consumption trends*

- *An ability to read and interpret profit and loss reports*

Myla knew that consumers could satisfy their needs for beverages in thousands of places; therefore, the next manager's chances of success among so

(continues)

(continued)

much competition would depend largely on his or her knowledge and ability to manage and control costs.

Just before Myla started the first interview, she came across the following statement in the former beverage manager's file:

"Beverages differ significantly from food products in several ways. These differences will affect how you order, receive, store, monitor, and serve beverages, and can impact your cost dramatically. First, beverage packaging is standardized, unlike food packaging. The establishment of just a few packaging styles, rather than the infinite variety found in food packaging, means that storage can be planned around the forms of packaging you know you can expect. Thus, beverage shelf life is generally greater and more consistent than that of food, and the required storage temperatures are less strict. This usually makes beverages easier to order and to stock. Further, beverage costs are normally more stable and predictable, so planning for sales and profitability is fairly straightforward. Access to beverage storage areas is generally limited, so you have greater control. With beverages, you can assume 100 percent yield for what you buy, which is not the case with variable and volatile food products. Staff members are usually the sole cause of yield variances in the beverage system. When you set up strong control procedures, you can build excellent profit in this area. With all these factors making it easier to control beverages, you can do so more accurately, completely, and profitably."

INTRODUCTION

In controlling restaurant costs, you will treat food and beverages quite differently. This section addresses these differences and explains how procedures for beverage control can be employed effectively. You will learn how to approach beverage control in matters such as purchasing, inventory procedures and control, sales, and customer satisfaction. Everyone in your establishment should be asked to cooperate in this effort to ensure the most profitable beverage sales category.

BEVERAGE BASICS

Beverages are both alcoholic and nonalcoholic drinkable liquids. Nonalcoholic beverages include soft drinks, mineral water, and sparkling wines and beers containing no more than 1/2 percent alcohol. Alcoholic beverages, on the other hand, contain **ethanol** and are usually classified as either fermented or distilled spirits. Alcoholic beverages comprise a large portion—in both volume and sales—of the restaurant industry, and their purchase, sale, and consumption will be a chief concern as you work to control costs and maximize profits.

ethanol is alcohol.

Fermented Beverages

We'll start our discussion with a description of the two main categories of alcoholic beverages: fermented and distilled spirits. Fermentation is the action of yeast and grain such as wheat in a solution to form beer, or the action of yeast and grapes to form wine. Simply put, fermented grapes become wine, while wheat becomes beer. This process breaks down sugar from the grain or grapes into two components: alcohol and carbon dioxide gas. The gas escapes into the air, while the liquid alcohol remains behind and forms a fermented beverage. Figure 7-1 illustrates the process of carbon dioxide evaporation. The amount of alcohol left behind depends on the amount of sugar in the grains. Grains with greater sugar content produce a liquid with a higher percentage of alcohol.

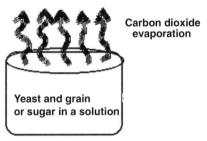

Carbon dioxide evaporation

Yeast and grain or sugar in a solution

Figure 7-1 CO2 Evaporation

The fermentation process produces wine and beer containing varied amounts of alcohol. In a standard beer, alcohol content ranges from 4 to 6 percent, though some specialty imports range as high as 12 or 14 percent. Wines normally range from 12 to 21 percent. Figure 7-2 compares a 10-ounce beer with 4 percent alcohol, a 4-ounce glass of wine with 13 percent alcohol, and a gin and tonic with 1.5 ounces of gin at 45 percent alcohol.

Figure 7-2 Alcohol Content

Product	Alcohol percent	Alcohol volume	Comparison
Ten ounces of beer	4% (as an example)	0.42 ounces	
Four ounces of wine	13% (as an example)	0.52 ounces	30% greater than the beer
1.5 ounces gin	45% (as an example)	0.675 ounces	69% greater than the beer; 30% greater than the wine

The volume of alcohol is directly related to the level of intoxication a person will experience. As a seller of alcohol, it is important that you understand these characteristics of your products. According to a recent national survey of adults conducted by Macchew Greenwald and Associates, only 46 percent of adults surveyed knew that a mixed drink made with 1.5 ounces of 80-proof distilled spirits, a 12-ounce serving of beer, and a 5-ounce serving of wine all contain the same amount of alcohol. This is quite revealing, as you will see from the rest of the chapter.

Beers are manufactured under consistent production standards, particularly by large breweries. However, they are also the most perishable of all alcoholic beverages once they are opened. Further, quality can vary due to improper delivery, storage, or service. Wines, too, can be greatly affected by improper storage and handling, and they can be very inconsistent products. Wine quality must be evaluated constantly because of the instability of the products' manufacture and components.

Distilled Beverages

Distilled spirits are fermented first, then the alcohol is further processed, or distilled, from the fermented liquid. In the distillation process, the liquid is heated in a still (that's where the word *distilled* comes from) to at least 175° Fahrenheit. At this temperature, the alcohol changes from a liquid to a gas and rises. Most of the water solution is left behind because water does not evaporate until it reaches 212° F.[1] The high-alcohol-content gas is channeled off and cooled so that it condenses into a liquid again. The result is what is called a distilled spirit. These spirits are made under rigorous quality control. Because of their resulting stability, distilled spirits, cordials, and liqueurs are considered the most consistent of beverage products. This category includes rum, brandy, and whisky, and its products normally range from 40 to 70 percent alcohol.

Beverage Classification

Which of the beverages you see at a bar are fermented, and which are distilled? Given just these two categories, how can there be so many alcoholic beverages? Figure 7-3 lists the familiar names of alcoholic beverages.

Figure 7-3 Alcoholic Beverages

Fermented		Distilled							
Beers and Ales	Wine	Whiskies	Gins	Vodka	Rum	Tequila	Brandy	Liqueur	others
lager	**table**	*scotch*	*London dry*				*cognac*	*amaretto*	*aquavit*
ale	- white	*Irish*	*Holland*				armagnac	b&b	
draft	- red	*bourbon*					calvados	benedictine	
stout	- rose	*rye*						chartreuse	
light	**aperitif**	*blend*						cointreau	
	- vermouth	*Canadian*						curacao	
	- dubonnet	*light*						drambuie	
	dessert							galliano	
	- sherry							irish mist	
	- port							kahlua	
	- Madeira							pernod	
	- marsalla								
	sparkling								
	- champagne								
	- sparkling burgundy								

The federal government has established standards of identity for various types of distilled spirits, wines, and malt beverages. Figure 7-4 is an example of a label on a bottle of whiskey. This bottle information states certain requirements: what the liquor is made of, how it is made, the type of container it is aged in, and the alcohol content. These rigidly enforced standards

Figure 7-4 Makers Mark Symbol

---

[1]See Appendix 380, *Critical Temperatures for Quality Control,* for details on products and temperatures.

profit margin is determined by subtracting your cost from your sales.

produce a beverage with distinguishable characteristics; federal inspections insure compliance from each manufacturer. Imported products must also meet such standards in order to enter the country. Therefore, everyone will recognize the contents as whiskey.

These standards were developed after the repeal of Prohibition in 1934. The government imposed a strict control system on the new alcoholic beverage industry to avoid the chaos of the Prohibition era. The purpose is twofold: to provide the basis for assessing and collecting federal taxes, and to protect the consumer. Beyond this, the standards can be helpful to you in understanding your products. You will know what you are buying and controlling, as well as the differences between similar products. This gives you a basis with which to analyze your **profit margin**, this chapter's primary focus.

Differences among Distilled Beverages

Distilled beverages are alike in several ways. They are all distilled from a fermented liquid. They all have a high alcohol content. And they are all served primarily before or after meals. Several distinctions are important to the beverage industry, however. Primarily, these are differences of flavor and body, two characteristics of great importance to your customers.

Each type of liquor has a distinct taste or flavor. Within each category, there are further taste differences; for example, bourbon whiskey tastes very different from scotch whiskey, and Irish whiskey tastes different from both. There are also taste differences between brands. Most guests who order these types of drinks know what kind of flavor they are looking for; in the beverage business, you will have to understand their wishes and be prepared to provide them.

proof is the measure of the alcoholic content of a spirit, each degree of proof being ½% alcohol by volume, often written with the degree symbol, as 100°.

Body is another recognizable characteristic. There are full-bodied and light-bodied products within several categories. Three main factors determine both flavor and body:

1. The grains or other ingredients in the original fermented liquid

2. The proof at which the beverage is distilled. **Proof** is the measure of the alcoholic content of a spirit. Each degree of proof is 1/2 percent alcohol by volume, often written with a degree symbol, as 100°.

3. What is done with the spirit after distillation, such as adding flavorings or colored compounds to make the beverage distinctive

These variables make the proliferation of many brand names possible. You'll need to research the types of spirits and the brand differences in order to understand what your customer wants and will pay for. Different vendors can help you with this process, so that you can provide a range of products that is of reasonable size and cost, yet meets your clients' expectations.

THE HISTORY OF BEVERAGES

To understand the beverage industry, there are key moments in U.S. history that explain how laws and practices have evolved. Since the repeal of Prohibition in 1934, consumption trends have changed with the times. Several societal and industry factors have contributed to these changes; some are controllable, and some are not. Figure 7-5 is an example of how consumption has varied with political and social change. It can be read as a chronology of the last several decades.

Overall, alcohol consumption is dropping, but it is decreasing most dramatically in the category of spirits. This information affects you and your beverage outlet directly, and you will need to plan to capitalize on the purchases your customers are still making. A study by the Distilled Spirits Council (DSC) indicates that, as overall consumption drops, the percentage of premium brands consumed has increased. This indicates that people who choose to drink end up drinking lower quantities of distinctly higher-quality beverages. The DSC study confirms the decrease in overall consumption, particularly with regard to distilled spirits (Figure 7-6).

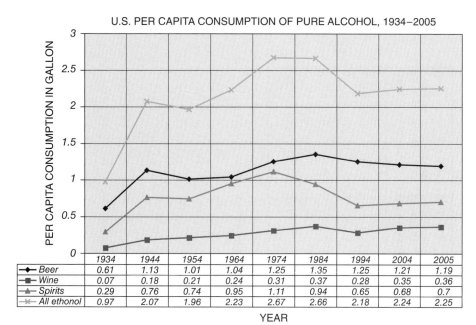

YEAR	1934	1944	1954	1964	1974	1984	1994	2004	2005
◆ Beer	0.61	1.13	1.01	1.04	1.25	1.35	1.25	1.21	1.19
■ Wine	0.07	0.18	0.21	0.24	0.31	0.37	0.28	0.35	0.36
▲ Spirits	0.29	0.76	0.74	0.95	1.11	0.94	0.65	0.68	0.7
✕ All ethonol	0.97	2.07	1.96	2.23	2.67	2.66	2.18	2.24	2.25

Figure 7-5 U.S. alcohol consumption. *Courtesy of U.S. Apparent Consumption of Alcoholic Beverages Based on State Sales, Taxation, or Receipt Data. U.S. Alcohol Epidemiologic Data Reference Manual, Volume 1, Fourth Edition, June 2004, NIH Publication No. 04-5563.*

In Figure 7-6 you can see that per capita consumption by people over 21 was as high as 3.14 gallons in the 1970s, but dropped to only 1.87 gallons in 2007. The decline is in part due to public awareness of the effects of alcohol on health, as well as government interventions such as drinking and driving laws. Other studies conducted by the DSC confirm a proportionate increase in sales of nonalcoholic beverages, such as mineral water and sodas, during these years. A further study, commissioned by the Beer Institute, illustrates another portentous change in beverage demand, as shown in Figure 7-7.

From this study, it is evident that malt beverages such as beer have gained a considerable market share in recent years. When we say malt beverages, we are referring to beverages made from malted grains, usually barley, that are sprouted to about 3/4 inch and then dried. The beer industry's rigorous promotional activities, as well as beer's lower alcohol content, have contributed to its successes. The same is not true with spirits. In fact, the distilled beverage industry has imposed its own restrictions against advertising in the United States; however, these restrictions have been relaxed as the industry's products have lost market share.

The overall distribution of alcohol consumption is illustrated in Figure 7-8.

Why the Changes?

Consumption patterns have changed through the actions of three major forces. Our discussion of these forces will focus on how—and whether—your food and beverage establishment can impact or control these forces while maximizing profitability. The three factors are as follows:

1. Health and economic impacts of alcoholism (uncontrollable)

2. Moral dilemmas and the law (uncontrollable)

3. Pricing and clientele (controllable)

4. The first two of these topics are discussed on the following pages; the third, being controllable, will be discussed in depth later in the chapter.

Apparent Consumption of Distilled Spirits in the United States, License and Control States, 1934 - 2003

Year	License States \a		Control States		Total		Resident Population\b (000)	Adult Population\b (21 & Older) (000)	Per Capita Consumption (Resident) (gal/person)	Per Capita Consumption (21+) (gal/adult)	Number of States
	Wine Gallons (000)	Percentage of Total Consumption	Wine Gallons (000)	Percentage of Total Consumption	Wine Gallons (000)	Percentage Change					
1934	45,892	79.2	12,073	20.8	57,965	---	126,374	77,619	0.46	0.75	28
1944	124,414	74.6	42,265	25.4	166,680	14.5	132,885	85,599	1.25	1.95	46
1954	136,956	72.3	52,515	27.7	189,471	-2.7	161,884	101,910	1.17	1.86	47
1964	209,721	76.0	66,141	24.0	275,862	6.5	191,085	113,261	1.44	2.44	49
1974	314,476	75.4	102,841	24.6	417,317	2.5	213,342	133,110	1.96	3.14	51
1984	324,226	76.0	102,512	24.0	426,738	-1.0	235,825	161,112	1.81	2.65	51
1994	252,286	75.4	82,203	24.6	334,489	-1.9	260,362	181,895	1.28	1.84	51
2003	290,800	75.9	92,582	24.1	383,382	4.6	290,811	205,473	1.32	1.87	51

NOTE: Because of rounding, detail may not add to total.
Beginning with 1992 data, apparent consumption includes low-proof data. Therefore, data before and after 1992 are not entirely consistent.

\a Includes District of Columbia; Alaska, beginning 1959; Oklahoma, beginning 1960; Hawaii, beginning 1965.
\b Population data includes all states for all years except Hawaii & Alaska from 1934-49.
\c Includes Mississippi gallonage from July through December 1966.

SOURCES: Distilled Spirits Council of the United States, Inc.; National Alcohol Beverage Control Association; Bureau of Census, U.S. Department of Commerce.

Figure 7-6 Distilled Beverages

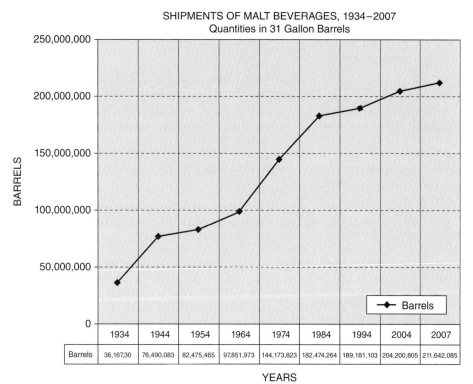

SHIPMENTS OF MALT BEVERAGES, 1934–2007
Quantities in 31 Gallon Barrels

	1934	1944	1954	1964	1974	1984	1994	2004	2007
Barrels	36,167,30	76,490,083	82,475,465	97,851,973	144,173,823	182,474,264	189,181,103	204,200,805	211,642,085

YEARS

Figure 7-7 Malt Beverages Shipments. *Courtesy of the Beer Institute. Note: This chart represents apparent consumption, as it reflects shipments or sales at the wholesale level. This differs from national tax-paid withdrawals plus imports, due to reporting procedures and inventory levels.*

Figure 7-8 Ethanol Beverage Type

Proportional Changes in Kinds of Ethanol by Beverage Types, In Percentages Consumed, 1934–2004								
	1934	**1944**	**1955**	**1964**	**1974**	**1984**	**1994**	**2004**
Beer	63%	55%	52%	47%	47%	51%	57%	53%
Wine	7%	9%	11%	11%	12%	14%	13%	16%
Spirits	30%	37%	38%	43%	42%	35%	30%	31%
All Ethanol	100%	100%	100%	100%	100%	100%	100%	100%

Health and Economic Impacts of Alcoholism

The National Institute on Alcohol Abuse and Alcoholism (NIAAA), a branch of the U.S. Department of Health and Human Resources, as well as other organizations such as Mothers Against Drunk Driving (MADD), have been instrumental in alerting the public to the dangers associated with alcohol abuse. A major study conducted by the NIAAA reveals the following:

- In 2003, 39.9 percent of traffic accident fatalities were alcohol-related. By 2004, the percentage dropped to 39.5 percent, but in 2006 it rose again to about 49 percent. In 2006, alcohol-related crashes killed 16,919 people. Over 1.46 million drivers were arrested in 2006 for driving under the influence of alcohol. This is an arrest rate of 1 for every 139 licensed drivers in the United States.

- Arguably, alcohol abuse and alcoholism have accounted for more economic and social damage than any other public health problem. The cost to society from these disorders is estimated at $90 to $116 billion annually. More than 70 percent of these costs are in the form of productivity losses due to excess morbidity and premature mortality attributed to alcohol use. Less than 13 percent of these funds are spent to treat alcohol disorders or the medical consequences of alcohol consumption.

- Alcohol misuse is involved in approximately 30 percent of all suicides, 50 percent of homicides, 68 percent of cases of manslaughter, 52 percent of rapes and other sexual assaults, 48 percent of robberies, 62 percent of assaults, and 49 percent of all other violent crimes. In addition, approximately 30 percent of all accidental deaths are attributable to alcohol abuse.

- An estimated 20 to 40 percent of persons admitted to urban general hospitals have coexisting alcohol problems and often are undiagnosed alcoholics being treated for consequences of their drinking.

- Liver cirrhosis is the ninth-leading cause of death, with an annual toll of more than 28,000 lives. Persons with alcoholism are also prone to other health problems, including neurological diseases.

- More than 100,000 deaths each year are associated with alcohol-related causes.

- Fetal alcohol syndrome (FAS) is the leading preventable cause of birth defects in the western world. FAS, one of four leading known causes of mental impairment, affects 1 to 3 infants per 1,000 live births. In 2006, the direct cost of treating FAS was about $2.7 billion in the United States.

- Almost 14 million adult Americans meet diagnostic criteria for the medical disorders of alcohol abuse and alcoholism. About 40 percent have direct familial experience with one of these disorders.

Clearly, sufficient reasons exist for due caution in serving alcohol. The alcohol consumer needs to understand the dangers, and your company has to take whatever steps you can to avoid negative impacts. As an outlet for alcoholic beverages, your goals are happy customers and good profits, not problems like those listed above. This brings us to the second force affecting consumption.

Moral Dilemmas and the Law

dram shop law A law requiring that not only must the consumer take responsibility for his or her actions while intoxicated; so too must the provider of the alcohol.

Laws governing alcohol offenses can be very inconsistent. The single exception is that the age at which one can drink has been federally mandated at 21 years. Aside from that, each state treats alcohol-related offenses very differently. In recent years, the term "third-party liability," otherwise referred to as the **dram shop law**, has gained recognition. Under this law, not only must the consumer take responsibility for his or her actions while intoxicated; the provider of the alcohol is considered liable as well. Individuals, hotel and bar personnel, and legislators have grown concerned about the high social cost of alcohol abuse. Bars and restaurants receive money for serving alcohol; third-party liability balances that monetary gain with culpability and prudence. The dram shop law brought about many changes in attitudes and practices within the industry, including the following: encouraging designated driver programs, the sale of mocktails (cocktails without liquor), bartenders' refusal to serve inebriated customers, and bartenders' assisting customers with calling taxis. Manufacturers, too, show respect for the law when they include warning labels on their products or add statements such as "Please drink responsibly" to their advertisements.

Quiz

What is the legal drinking age in the United States? What constitutes intoxication in your state?

In 1980, a tragic event changed the gradual trend toward prudence into a virtual revolution. A drunk driver with five previous arrests killed a 13-year-old in a car accident. The child's mother formed MADD, which has become a formidable body for public awareness. Largely in response to MADD's efforts, legislators introduced laws to reduce drunk driving, often by raising the drinking age and by creating a legal definition of intoxication in terms of blood alcohol content. In Colorado, for example, legal intoxication is measured at .05 percent blood alcohol content and up. In your beverage service, awareness of these laws must be part of how you think about and do business.

Your company policy should include an awareness of these issues and specific policies for staff to follow. Your company and management must support bartenders when they refuse to serve an inebriated customer, and you must actively encourage options like mocktails, designated drivers, cab service, and staff education.

Quiz

Why is an understanding of third-party liability vital to the success of anyone engaged in selling alcoholic beverages?

PRICING AND THE CLIENTELE

Pricing and clientele are areas in which you and your company determine some of the conditions under which alcohol will be consumed in your establishment. Both factors depend largely on the type, location, and patrons of your outlet. Most businesses operate with more enthusiasm than foresight, and they rely solely on advertisement, entertainment, or someone else's successful formula to improve sales. In this section, you will learn how to price your products only after carefully considering cost, availability, competition, and environment. This will not only make you competitive, but also give you a vital edge.

Do Consumers Really Respond to Prices?

Jess Stonestreet Jackson is the founder of Kendall Jackson Winery, which specializes in making popular wines that are good enough to command a premium price. Jackson, who is now a billionaire, prices his wines a few dollars higher than other mainstream wines. For example, if a Clos du Bois chardonnay costs $9 at retail, Jackson will charge $11 for his chardonnay. When chardonnay became the rage in the late 1990s, Jackson tried pushing up his prices by another few dollars over the competition. Unit sales dropped by 18 percent. Jackson rolled back his prices, and the volume recovered.

Source: Tim W. Ferguson, "Harvest Time," Forbes, October 16, 2000, pp. 112–118. Reprinted by permission of Forbes Magazine © 2008 Forbes LLC.

Cost

The cost of a bottle of wine or beer is straightforward; it is also relatively easy to determine the cost of a mixed drink. You simply add the raw costs of the ingredients together. Figure 7-9 is an example of costing a Bloody Mary. We have added commonly used terminology to the worksheet. An explanation of the terms is below the worksheet.

Figure 7-9 One Serving Cost Worksheet

One serving recipe costing worksheet						
1. Item number	M611		2. Is the item active?		YES NO	
3. Item description:	Bloody Mary		4. Revenue group:		Beverage	
5. Prep location:	Lounge Bar		6. Salable?		YES NO	
7. GL Account Number:	01120-130		8. Tracking period:		DAILY MID MAIN	
9. Batch size:	one serving		10. Recipe group:		Beverage	
11. Ingredient item number	12. Ingredient item description	13. Number of recipe units	14. Recipe	15. Unit cost	16. Total cost	17. Percent units cost
87	Vodka Smirnoff 80	1.25	fluid ounce (FZ)	$0.24	$0.30	31.25%
718	juice V-8	5.5	FZ	$0.06	$0.33	34.38%
941	pepper black ground	0.25	WZ	$0.39	$0.09	9.38%
617	spice celery salt	0.5	WZ	$0.13	$0.06	6.25%
197	sauce horseradish	1	FZ	$0.07	$0.07	7.29%
801	sauce Worcestershire	0.25	FZ	$0.21	$0.05	5.21%
555	sauce Tabasco	0.1	FZ	$0.36	$0.03	3.13%
631	lemon fresh	0.167	CT	$0.18	$0.03	3.13%
				TOTALS:	$0.96	100%

18. Potential cost:	$0.96
19. Menu cost:	$5.00
20. Potential percentage:	19.22%
21. Target beverage cost percentage:	20%
22. Targeted menu price:	$4.78

This worksheet is similar to the potential costing worksheet in Chapter 10. We'll list the steps to completing this worksheet here; if you'd like more information, review Chapter 10.

1. *Item number.* This is the menu item number you have assigned. If convenient, you can use the same number as your POS system uses to track the item.

2. *Is the item active?* An active item is one that is being used presently.

3. *Item description.* In this case, it is a Bloody Mary cocktail.

4. *Revenue group.* In this case, the group is "beverage."

5. *Prep location.* This identifies where the recipe is used for companies with multiple locations. This helps new employees, transferred personnel, and others who might not be familiar with the item.

6. *Is it salable?* Salable means that, when this recipe is completed, you'll have a product you can sell. Contrast a recipe for a single Bloody Mary with a recipe for a gallon of Bloody Mary mix for the bar: A single drink is a salable recipe, while a recipe for a mix

that won't be sold until it's further prepared is called a prep recipe. Circle YES or NO to indicate the item's status. This information is used to determine whether this item will be counted when you report sales.

7. *GL account number.* This space lists a general ledger number to which the expenses for this item should be assigned. This is a standard accounting practice. Your department will have several GL account numbers, and you will decide which costs and revenues go to each account. Our number here is just an example; companies use many different formats for these numbers.

8. *Tracking period.* This is used in many operations to state the period of time used when tracking an item's usage. You'll circle DAILY to indicate that the item is tracked every 24-hour period, MID if the item is tracked semimonthly, or MAIN for a standard accounting period, usually one month.

9. *Batch size.* The batch size is the total amount produced by a recipe. In our example, the batch size is one serving. You should practice making the recipe to measure the accuracy of the recipe size.

10. *Recipe group.* Recipes are grouped into categories to control and report what is made and sold. In this case, the category is beverage; you might also have categories such as appetizers, entrées, side dishes, and desserts.

11. *Ingredient item number.* This is the inventory code number, used to identify and track how specific ingredients are utilized.

12. *Ingredient item description.* This is simply the name of the ingredient. It is listed with the generic name first, followed by any specific types. Vodka, juice, and sauce are the generic products, while Smirnoff, V-8, and horseradish specify which ones you should use.

13. *Number of recipe units.* Record here the number of units for each item used in the recipe.

14. *Recipe unit description.* The recipe unit description will be WZ, FZ, CT, or TS depending on whether the inventory item is measured in weighted ounces, fluid ounces, unit counts, or teaspoons, respectively. See Appendix for a detailed listing of units.

15. *Unit cost.* This is the cost per teaspoon, count, weight ounce, or fluid ounce. In the example of vodka, suppose it costs $8.12 per 1-liter bottle (remember that 1 liter equals 33.8 ounces; see Appendix for a conversion table). Divide the price of the liter by the number of ounces to get the price per ounce, or unit cost: $8.12 ÷ 33.8 = $0.24 per ounce. This calculation is performed for all ingredients.

16. *Total cost.* Next, multiply the unit cost (Column 15) by the number of units needed for the recipe (Column 13). For example, 1.25 ounces of vodka is multiplied by its unit cost of $0.24 per ounce, to arrive at $0.30. Once make this calculation for all the ingredients, total all these amounts. The result is the total cost of the serving, or $0.96.

17. *Cost percentage.* The cost percentage is the proportion of the cost of each item to the cost of the whole. Simply divide an item's total cost by the total batch cost to get this percentage. In the case of the vodka, this is $0.30 ÷ $0.96 = 31.25 percent.

18. *Potential cost.* This is the sum of the total costs of all ingredients, or $0.96.

19. *Menu price.* In our example, we set the menu price at $5.00.

20. *Potential percentage.* This is determined by dividing the cost (in our example $0.96) by the selling price, $5.00. This is the percentage cost you will have if you follow all control procedures accurately.

21. *Targeted beverage cost percentage.* We set 20 percent as our target in this example. That's the beverage cost percentage we wanted to achieve for this drink. This compares favorably to the potential percentage in Item 20 and gives us a small cushion in our price to cover errors.

22. *Targeted menu price.* This is derived by dividing the potential cost (Item 18) by the targeted beverage cost percentage (Item 21). It is recommended to set actual price above target price due to cost control issues, which are discussed later in this chapter.

This example lists the ingredient costs of producing a Bloody Mary, but the time and equipment used also must be considered. In these calculations, always use the replacement cost, which is the current cost of replacing the item with one of the same type. Also remember the hidden costs of doing business. While your customers may see only the quality and quantity of the Bloody Mary mix in front of them, you also must consider the costs of storing and creating the recipes. The costs of spillage, spoilage, breakage, ice, payroll, and many other items add to the hidden costs. A customer is unaware of these costs and thus may wonder why a Bloody Mary is so expensive. Managers must, nevertheless, consider these costs when calculating a fair (and profitable) drink price.

Competition and Availability

A customer might pay more for a Bloody Mary at a mountain ski resort than in a state capital, or more in an airport than in the neighboring city, because there is no competition on top of a mountain or in an airport. Competition can influence pricing strategies significantly. Your role will include watching your competition and investigating their pricing structures so that you can make good decisions about how to price your own offerings. You will also want to find out whether what you offer is available in your vicinity. If you're the only establishment offering an extensive wine list, for example, you may be able to take advantage of that lack of competition.

Environment

When customers pay a price for a service or product, they perceive a relationship between price and quality. As you set prices for services, you must keep your target customers' price-quality perceptions in mind. Nowhere is this more evident than in the price of beverages. People who drink wine at home, for instance, are well aware of the actual cost. At your establishment they are paying more money for a bottle of wine. Why? What is it that you offer that makes them willing to pay a premium price, when they could have the same product at home for less? You will have to identify the level of service and quality your target customers expect, which is tied to how much they will be willing to pay. Your pricing strategy can be as easy as understanding your competitors—both the successful ones and those that fail or change strategy. The tricky part, then, is calibrating a good equilibrium for your own outlet or outlets. You will want to consider service levels and ambience with respect to your target audience. If the services and entertainment you provide are extraordinary, your customers might not object to paying more. Always remember that a beverage enterprise is a business, with the goals of maintaining a competitive edge, achieving employee efficiency, and enhancing the owner's investment.

Designing Your Pricing Strategies

Your beverage pricing can affect the number of drinks you sell; therefore, you must put some time and consideration into setting your menu prices. Because of the large variety of products and brands that are found in bar and beverage operations, products are usually categorized to facilitate pricing and control. This eliminates the vast differences among the thousands of different drinks. In general, categories are based on types of drinks and cost.

What Did That Salmon Dish Cost?

Restaurants mark up food costs by an average of 300 percent to cover their overhead and to generate a profit, but the markup is not the same for all items on the menu. Some ingredients—especially prime cuts of beef and exotic seafood such as fresh scallops—are so costly that diners would not tolerate a 300 percent markup. Instead, restaurants make up the difference on the cheap stuff—vegetables, pasta, and salmon. Why salmon? The farmed variety is only $2.50 per pound wholesale—much cheaper than prime restaurant-quality beef. At the Docks Restaurant in New York, a 10-ounce salmon dinner garnished with potatoes and coleslaw has a menu price of $19.50. The actual cost of the ingredients is only $1.90.

To take another example, the ingredients of the best-selling Angus beef tenderloin at the Sunset Grill in Nashville, Tennessee, cost the restaurant $8.42. Applying the average 300 percent markup, the price of the meal would be $33.68. Few diners would order the meal at that price, however, so the restaurant charges just $25. In contrast, the restaurant charges $9 for its grilled vegetable plate, whose ingredients cost only $1.55.

Source: Eileen Daspin, "Entrée Economics," The Wall Street Journal, March 10, 2000, pp. W1 and W4. Reprinted by permission of The Wall Street Journal, Copyright © 2000 Dow Jones & Company, Inc. All Rights Reserved Worldwide. License number 2103290892213.

There is no industry standard for either this categorization or the practice of price markup, but the following list describes recognized categories for beverage service:

- *Well brands.* These are spirits that are poured or served to the guest when the guest does not specify a particular brand. The manager will select these carefully to balance a guest's perception of average quality and an acceptable company cost. Remember that most guests who do not specify a brand either don't have a preference or are price-conscious. Whoever selects your company's well brands will have to determine what the clientele will consider mid-range. A low-quality well liquor may cause guests to complain, while a high-quality product can increase costs dramatically.

- *Call brands.* This refers to brands that a guest requests by name, such as Jack Daniels whiskey or Remy Martin VSOP. They are more expensive, and they represent a guest preference over other brands—and you should price them accordingly.

- *Premium and super premium brands.* These are the high-end examples of call brands; accordingly, they are popular with high-end guests. Louis XIII cognac could be classified as premium or superpremium because of its triple-digit price tag. Prices with these brands are virtually unlimited; you'll have to determine which expensive brands you wish to carry, if any, based on your clientele. You can then rank them as premium or super premium based on their prices.

- *Domestic bottle beer.* These are beers made in the United States, such as Coors, Budweiser, and microbrews like Old Dominion or Fat Tire.

- *Imported bottle beer.* These are beers imported from other countries. Some examples are Dos Equis from Mexico and Guinness Stout from England.

- *Draft beer.* These are keg beers tapped through special instruments; they can be either domestic or imported.

- *Nonalcoholic drinks.* Perrier, root beer, and orange juice are examples.

Example of Wine List

SUGGESTED SELLING PRICES ARE BASED ON THE FOLLOWING MATRIX ----->

(Category c)

< $10 =	33%
< $15 =	35%
< $20 =	37.5%
< $25 =	40%
< $30 =	45%
< $60 =	47.5%

Product Number	Item Description	Case Description	(Category a)		(Category b)					(Category c)
			Case Cost	Bottle Cost	Priced at 40% cost	Priced at 35% Cost	Priced at 30% cost	Priced at 25% cost	Priced at 20% cost	SUGGESTED SELLING PRICE
			SPARKLING WINES							
			DOMESTIC SELECTIONS							
9712	IRON HORSE BRUT	CS=12/750ML	$165.00	$13.75	$34.38	$39.29	$45.83	$55.00	$68.75	$39.29
9764	SPARKLING JORDAN "J" 90	CS=12/750ML	$215.90	$17.99	$44.98	$51.40	$59.97	$71.96	$89.95	$47.97
			SPAIN SECTION							
9707	FREIXENET CORDON NEGRO	CS=12/750ML	$59.93	$4.99	$12.48	$14.26	$16.63	$19.96	$24.95	$15.12
			GERMANY SECTION							
9710	CHAMPAGNE DEINHAD LILA	CS=12/750ML	$59.88	$4.99	$12.48	$14.26	$16.63	$19.96	$24.95	$15.12
			ITALIAN SECTION							
9708	CA DEL BOSCO BRUT	CS=6/750ML	$138.60	$23.10	$57.75	$66.00	$77.00	$92.40	$115.50	$57.75
			FRENCH CHAMPAGNE							
9723	DOM PERIGNON 1.5LT	CS=12/1.5LT	$1,858.00	$154.83	$387.08	$442.37	$516.10	$619.32	$774.15	$325.96
9669	CHAMPAGNE MOET WHITE STAR	CS=24/375ML	$371.99	$15.50	$38.75	$44.29	$51.67	$62.00	$77.50	$41.33
			CHARDONNAY SECTION							
9887	CHARD FORTANT COLLECTOR	CS=12/750ML	$71.90	$5.99	$14.98	$17.11	$19.97	$23.96	$29.95	$18.15
6813	CHARD GRGICH HILLS 94	CS=12/750ML	$287.90	$23.99	$59.98	$68.54	$79.97	$95.96	$119.95	$59.98
			HALF BOTTLE							
9018	CHARD GRIGICH HILLS 93	CS=12/375ML	$155.90	$12.99	$32.48	$37.11	$43.30	$51.96	$64.95	$37.11
9016	CHARD RUTHERFORD HILL 90	CS=12/375ML	$57.50	$4.79	$11.98	$13.69	$15.97	$19.16	$23.95	$14.52

Figure 7-10 Example of Pricing Strategies

- *Wine*. Served by the glass or by the bottle.

- *Cocktails*. Also called mixed drinks, these usually contain distilled spirits mixed with soft drinks, water, or blended mixes like Bloody Mary mix or margarita mix.

- *Highballs*. These are mixtures of a spirit and a carbonated mixer or water. They are served with ice in a highball glass.

Most operators use a similar inventory grouping to determine their pricing strategies. This is very common with bottle wines. The example in Figure 7-10 illustrates how some pricing strategies might work in the bottle wine category. In Column A, fill in your cost, both by case and by bottle. This should always be replacement cost—the cost to replace the bottle at today's prices. (This information, by the way, should always be kept confidential. You will not want to share your data with anyone who is not involved directly with your pricing policies—not even your vendors.)

Then, in Column B, a simple percentage markup is calculated. Actually, in this example, several different percentages have been offered, so that you can select the amount of markup that you deem best. You will be using your judgment and your knowledge of your client base to decide the cost percentages you can safely employ. Profitability is paramount.

Another pricing strategy is illustrated in Column C: a sliding scale. In this strategy, as the cost of an item rises, the cost percentage drops (though the actual amount of markup may still be significant).

Finally, consider the pricing principles of cost, availability, competition, and environment. When considering cost, note also that the costs of inventory maintenance, accounting, storage, personnel, spoilage, and loss of interest on inventory investment—all of which are covered in greater detail in later chapters—must be factored into what you eventually charge your customers. Weigh these factors well, so that your prices will be consistent, fair, competitive, and profitable.

SUMMARY

Beverages differ significantly from food products in several ways. These differences will affect how you order, receive, store, monitor, and serve beverages, and can impact your cost dramatically. Beverages are alcoholic and nonalcoholic drinkable liquids. Since the repeal of Prohibition in 1934, consumption trends have changed with the times. Several societal and industry factors have contributed to these changes; some are controllable, and some are not. The three factors affecting consumption trends are as follows:

- the health and economic impacts of alcoholism (uncontrollable)

- moral dilemmas and the law (uncontrollable)

- pricing and clientele (controllable)

To be successful you need to understand these factors and apply them.

CHAPTER QUESTIONS

Critical Thinking Questions

1. How can the use of a sliding scale strategy help to maximize profitability?

2. What are the factors affecting beverage consumption trends?

3. What are the societal impacts of alcoholism and alcohol abuse?

Objective Questions

1. The most distinctive trend in the consumption of alcoholic beverages has been the decrease in the consumption of distilled spirits over the past decade. True or False?

2. The most important factor in maximizing profitability of the entire beverage operation is maximizing the profit margin on each drink sold. True or False?

3. Because well brands are typically the least expensive of brands available in the house, it is desirable to purchase whatever brand is currently least expensive. True or False?

4. Beer is the most perishable of alcoholic beverages. True or False?

Multiple Choice Questions

1. Which of the following is typically the most consistent?
   A. beer
   B. wine
   C. distilled spirits
   D. fortified wines

2. While overall consumption of alcoholic beverages has decreased,
   A. wine sales have more than doubled in the past decade.
   B. beer sales have more than doubled in the past two decades.
   C. nonalcoholic beverage sales have increased dramatically.
   D. prices for supplies have dropped significantly, thus creating greater profitability.

3. Third-party liquor liability laws are also known as
   A. dram shop laws.
   B. responsible service laws.
   C. driving under the influence laws.
   D. none of the above.

4. If the total potential ingredient cost for one drink is $0.72 and the targeted beverage cost percentage is 18, what is the targeted menu price?
   A. $1
   B. $2
   C. $3
   D. $4

5. If the cost of vodka in a screwdriver is $0.38 and the total cost of the screwdriver is $0.83, what is the cost percentage of the vodka?

    A.   40.2 percent

    B.   45.8 percent

    C.   38 percent

    D.   21.8 percent

6. If a 750-milliliter bottle of vodka costs $8.90, what is the cost per ounce?

    A. $0.35

    B. $0.38

    C. $0.32

    D. $0.40

7. Portion size, portion control, and standardized recipes are essential for

    A.   maintaining consistency.

    B.   controlling costs.

    C.   customer satisfaction.

    D.   all of the above.

CHAPTER 8

Beverage Procedures, from Start to Finish

Learning Objectives

After reading this chapter, you should be able to:

- explain how to purchase beverage products profitably;

- receive beverage products with effective controls;

- store beverage products using proper procedures and knowledge;

- establish and enforce appropriate beverage requisition procedures, such as bottle-for-bottle exchange, back-order guidelines, and proper requisition authorization.

In Practice

Myla began her interview with Dana Miller by asking about her background in cost control. Myla went on to ask Dana about the steps she would take to implement control procedures.

Myla: *In your past experience, how did you balance the pressure to make profit and at the same time maintain high guest satisfaction?*

Dana: *It's simply giving the customers what they want at a fair market price.*

Myla: *Okay! Well, if you're doing everything right, yet your actual cost is excessively higher than your potential cost, what would you do?*

Dana: *There is definitely a flaw in the control procedures.*

Myla: *What do you mean? What type of flaw could it be?*

Dana: *If the potential cost is calculated correctly, then any variance could be traced to employees in purchasing, receiving, storage, and maintaining portion control.*

Myla only wished Dana had been hired sooner. Considering all the irregularities Myla saw in her first visit to the bar (described in Chapter 9), Dana would have her job cut out for her.

INTRODUCTION

When selecting and purchasing beverage products, you will need to make decisions while keeping two complementary goals in mind: your profit goals and your guests' preferences and satisfaction. Let's look at two examples to see how these factors affect your real-world decision-making.

Let's say that Absolut vodka comes in both 750-milliliter and 1-liter bottles. Compare their costs: the 750-milliliter bottle is equal to 25.4 fluid ounces and costs $7.60. Dividing the cost by the number of ounces, we get a cost of $0.29 per ounce. The 1-liter bottle is equal to 33.8 fluid ounces and costs $8.40, with a per-ounce cost of $0.25. That $0.25 per ounce is not a lot of money if your company sells very little Absolut. If your consumption is high, however, the savings can be significant. Over time, your guests' preferences will tell you if the larger or smaller bottles are called for.

Here's another example: An extensive wine list ties up capital in a large inventory that makes no profit until it is sold. But if your guests' preferences lean toward a wide selection, you will have to weigh the extra investment and inventory. If you don't, you may lose market advantage to competitors who do invest in their wine lists. In this process, consider the food and beverage items that complement one another and will generate the desired profit levels with your target market. In this way, you maximize both guest satisfaction and the chances of good profit.

The important concept here is that beverage profit is an achievable goal, not a residue of operations. In fact, many establishments offer beverages as the primary products, and food is secondary. This is because beverages can be quite profitable when control guidelines are followed, while food service carries an array of distinct costs. Use the menu-engineering techniques discussed in this book to evaluate and standardize your beverage profit making.

There is no industry standard for the amount of markup on beverages, so you must set your own standards for success (profit) and failure (loss) for every item you sell. If your percentages of profit are high but you are not selling enough quantity to reach your profit goals, this can easily translate into loss. On the other hand, selling thousands of units of a beverage product that has little or no percentage of profit is equally damaging to the bottom line. Remember, you go to the bank not with percentages, but with the dollar value of your bottom line. According to Paul Lee, director of food and beverage and faculty member of Monterey Peninsular College, "This is the most misunderstood fact in operations: most managers do not understand profitability." It is a challenge to find the middle ground. However, armed with effective purchasing techniques and a clear-cut pricing strategy, you stand every chance of coming out a winner.

In this section we will discuss how to go about purchasing: the policies you set and the procedures you establish; the routines of purchasing, receiving, and issuing beverages; the inventory records and procedures that differ from working with food products; and the use of inventory figures to measure bar cost and purchasing efficiency. The goal of beverage purchasing is the same as that of food purchasing: to provide a steady supply of raw ingredients for the drinks you sell, at minimal cost, to maximize profits. First we will discuss purchasing.

PURCHASING

Just like food products, beverage products are available at several levels of quality. Unlike with food products, however, you cannot simply select a single product to fit your specifications. With beverages, you are likely to have several quality levels in a single establishment—a number of different vodkas, rums, gins, and other beverage types at different levels of quality and price. Customers expect these kinds of choices when they buy beverages. This is as true for wine and beer as it is for spirits. Selecting many varieties that correspond with your customers' wishes, at the most advantageous prices, is an ongoing purchasing challenge.

In addition, you will have to familiarize yourself with your state and county laws and codes regarding beverage purchases. For example, in one county in Colorado, liquor stores are closed on Sundays. Check in your area for regulations that govern how you make and pay for purchases of alcohol.

Deciding what to buy involves two basic factors: the quality of beverages you will pour and the variety of items you will have available. Let's start with quality. Ask yourself (and other restaurant managers) what level of quality your customers will expect and be willing to pay for. It wouldn't be wise to purchase a super premium cognac or expensive wines for a neighborhood sports bar, for example. However, it would be equally unwise not to offer such items in a fine-dining restaurant. As in all other management matters, you must know and understand your client base.

Also bear in mind the quality of your well brands. Well brands are spirits served to guests who do not request a particular brand. The manager and the purchaser should select well liquors carefully, and then stick with them, to establish consistency in drink presentation. Many managers cut costs by using the least-expensive brands, and they assume that the guest cannot tell the difference. This may be true, and it may not: many bars display their bottles, so a guest who dislikes a drink can probably spot the bottle it came from. Other managers may use a premium brand as the well liquor. The manager might make such a decision out of pride, or he or she might justify the decision by saying that the company would be carrying the expensive brand anyway, to respond to customer requests. While this practice means carrying less inventory, it also means charging more money for what guests assume to be a lower-priced drink. Limiting your selection in this way can cost you sales and even customers. You should target an average or middle ground, based on what your establishment's clientele will perceive as average quality. Then you can set prices accordingly.

Another practice to avoid is using very inexpensive liquors while charging premium prices. You cannot fool your customers. They will not return, and they surely will tell others what you charge for low-quality liquor. Richard Hendrie said it very well: "You have to know who you are selling to and how you got them in door. Don't be short-sighted in your strategy. One sale isn't success. Repeat business is success."[1]

Once you decide what to buy, you will have to decide how much to purchase, based on your current and projected sales volume. Unlike most food products, you can sometimes buy partial cases of beverages. Although you will usually have to pay a broken case fee for such a service, it can be cost-effective under certain conditions. Buying partial cases is a common practice, but its advisability will depend largely on the size of your operation and your sales volume. A full case may be too much to carry if you have space constraints, lower sales volume of an item, or cash flow concerns. As with most purchases, in general, the more you can purchase at any one time, the lower your cost will be. Larger purchases allow you to negotiate volume discounts more readily. In the purchasing chapter, this matter is discussed in greater detail.

You must also consider how much liquor to specify in your recipes and to pour in your drinks. Take the Bloody Mary example in the last chapter. This recipe calls for 1.25 ounces of vodka, but perhaps your staff pours only 1 ounce. The guest may notice and become dissatisfied. You may need to set your recipes at a higher amount and adjust the price accordingly. Again, what you're looking for is balance—keeping your customers happy while offering a cost-effective product.

In the two examples below (Figures 8-1 and 8-2), we compare two sets of decisions on quality, quantity, and variety served to show you how your decisions will affect your cost. The same type of chart can also be used with wine, beer, and other beverages. In Appendix you will find a complete list of net unit ounces from different-sized beverage containers, along with a sample worksheet. For these examples we will use two scenarios to show you the difference in profit between two pricing strategies.

Columns A, B, and C of Figure 8-1, under the category *Purchase Data,* list the size, number of ounces, and price for three liquors: well, call, and premium. Well brands, as stated above, are used when a guest does not specify a brand; call is a midrange brand specified by the customer; and premium is a higher-class brand with higher costs (and, therefore, higher prices to the guest). Well, call, and premium categories are listed on the left side of the table. Column D

---

[1] Richard Hendrie, quoted in *The Liaison / UNIQUE VENUES,* Spring 2005.

Figure 8-1 Scenario 1

| Purchase Data | | | | | Sales Data | | | Recipe Cost Information | | | |

	A	B	C	D	E	F	G	H	I	J	K	L
liquor	size	FZ	cost per btl	sale price	# sold mo.	yield %	cost per FZ	pour amt inFZ	pour cost	total cost	total sales	pour cost %
formula							C/B		G×H	I×E	D×E	J/K
well	liter	33.8	$12.00	$2.50	200	100%	$0.36	1.25	$0.45	$90.00	$500	18%
call	liter	33.8	$12.00	$5.00	120	100%	$0.62	1.25	$0.78	$93.60	$600	15.6%
prem.	liter	33.8	$30.00	$8.00	280	100%	$0.89	1.75	$1.56	$436.80	$2240	19.5%
total					600					$620.40	$3340	18.6%

states the price at which the outlet sells drinks made with these liquors, and Column E is the number of items sold in a month. Yield (Column F) in beverage products is always assumed to be 100 percent, unless there is waste or lost beverage, such as happens at times with keg beer. We divide Column C, cost per bottle, by Column B, fluid ounces per bottle, to get the cost per ounce in Column G. Round this to the nearest cent. In Column H we have entered the number of fluid ounces used in a recipe for the drink; Column I, then, is the cost of one pour—Column G (cost per fluid ounce) multiplied by Column H (pour amount in fluid ounces).

Column J, the cost amount for the month, is the result of multiplying Columns I (pour cost) and E (number sold per month). Column K, the total amount of sales in the month, is equal to Column D (sale price) times Column E (number sold per month). Lastly, Column L, cost percentage, is equal to Column J (total cost) divided by Column K (total sales). So, overall, in Scenario 1, you are selling alcoholic beverages at 18 percent cost. This doesn't include any mixers, labor, overhead, or other costs, but we can compare it to a second scenario under the same conditions to see the results of a different pricing strategy (Figure 8-2). The entries that are changed are in boldface type.

Now, let's compare. Scenario 1 represents greater sales, but it also results in a greater cost percentage. This is due to the far greater amount of liquor poured. While Scenario 2 looks better in terms of cost percentages, guests may complain that the drinks they purchased didn't

Figure 8-2 Scenario 2

	C	D	E	F	G	H	I	J	K	L
liquor	cost per btl	sale price	# sold mo.	yield %	cost per FZ	pour amt in FZ	pour cost	total cost	total sales	pour cost %
formula					C/B		G X H	I X E	D X E	J/K
well	$12.00	$2.50	**100**	100%	$0.36	**1.0**	**$0.36**	**$36.00**	**$250**	**14.4%**
call	$21.00	$5.00	120	100%	$0.62	1.25	$0.78	$93.60	$600	15.6%
prem.	$30.00	$8.00	**240**	100%	$0.89	**1.5**	**$1.34**	**$213.60**	**$1920**	**11.1%**
total			**460**					**$343.20**	**$2770**	**12.4%**

contain a fair amount of alcohol for the price: each well drink contains only 1 fluid ounce. Note that the prices of the drinks were the same in both scenarios; this means that the company achieved its lower cost percentage at the expense of the guest's pocketbook and satisfaction. This kind of success may be short-lived.

Remember, you do not take percentages to the bank. The trick in pricing strategy and pour sizes is to balance a higher price (to attain a reasonable cost percentage) and a lower price (to increase sales volume). In the beverage business, sales volume is critical to profitability and success. Keeping your customers coming back and spending more money in such a competitive market is key. The sales volume will also determine your inventory turnover ratio, a topic discussed in detail in Chapter 11.

In brief, your goal is to avoid excess inventory but also to present an image of a reasonable selection. Excess inventory doesn't earn profit; in fact, it is a cost to the operation. There are costs involved in maintaining inventory records, product storage, and capital interest not earned. For many establishments, you will want to limit your choices to popular and well-advertised brand names.

You can implement a product request log, such as the one shown in Figure 8-3, to record guest requests. Guests can make their preferences known to the staff, who then document them. Use common sense when reviewing the log; if you see consistent requests for an item on different occasions, it may be a wise purchase.

Figure 8-3 Beverage Product Request Log

DATE	ITEM REQUESTED	STAFF MEMBER
6-20-05	Coors Light	Nancy M.
6-20-05	Louis XIII	David K.
6-21-05	Coors Light	Henry W.
6-21-05	Absolut Vodka	Jackie S.
6-21-05	Coors Light	Nancy M.
6-22-05	Coors Light	Elaine Y.
6-22-05	Southern Comfort	David K.

In this example, Coors Light is genuinely popular. You should consider making it available. A log like this is much more valid than undocumented reports of requests. When you can see exactly how many people have requested something over a given time period, you can make an informed purchasing decision.

If your guest asks for a brand that you do not carry, you probably will not lose either the sale or the customer if you can offer a well-known brand of comparable quality. However, be sure your staff does offer the substitute—and doesn't give the guest another brand without telling him or her. If the guest calls for a brand, you can be sure he or she knows how it should taste. Any manipulation will cost you trust and clientele.

One of the best ways to limit the number of brands and items stocked is to develop a preprinted menu. When you list what you have, most guests will find something they like. You can change it periodically or even offer drink specials from time to time, but your primary offerings will be laid out for the guest's choosing.

Where you draw the line on brands and items to stock should depend on your storage space, your clientele, your type of business (club, restaurant, hotel, or other type of establishment), your business volume, and your cash flow situation. One way to avoid an overabundance of brands is to follow this policy: Never add a new item of unpredictable sales demand without eliminating a slow-moving item from your menu list. You will have to review your sales history to determine what is needed.

You also need to keep up with new products and to anticipate changes in customer demands. You can do this by reading professional journals and by consulting with your vendors about regional and national trends. Do not, however, let anyone (especially sales representatives) tell you what you should buy. Consider their suggestions, but review your own operational needs before making any decisions.

When choosing the individual items, buying beverages is mostly a matter of brand selection. It's a good idea to taste your own mixed drinks using different brands, and even to solicit customer and staff input. Generic liqueurs, in particular, can taste quite different from one brand to another, but expensive imported brands are not necessarily the best, either.

Purchasing Wine

Buying wine is somewhat more complicated than buying spirits. For house wines you can often buy jug wines if your clients will drink them; they are generally cheaper, and the wine will be consistent from one bottle to the next. However, most operators stay away from jug or gallon wines for serving customers. These wines present many problems, including weight, storage, and negative visual impact. Wines served by the bottle are another matter. They are usually much more expensive, so pouring them by the glass is often not cost-effective. In a high-volume business, however, you could negotiate and establish an inexpensive house wine, maybe with a proprietary label in either a 750-milliliter or 1.5-liter bottle.

Remember, too, that wines are very perishable, and if you do not use them quickly they may spoil. This will affect your cost. In many instances the same wine will vary from one year, or vintage, to another; at times the wine's body and flavor will even change in the bottle during storage. The term **vintage** means the yield of wine or grapes from a vineyard or district during one season. Customer demand for wine is less clear-cut than for beer and spirits. Taste wines before you buy them, and then choose according to what you know of your customers' tastes. It is also important to consider the menu when purchasing wine. Experts will tell you that food tastes different when paired with certain wines, so train your staff to guide the customer to a choice that complements the chosen menu item. Be sure to get as much expert advice as you can. You may find helpful information by asking for the opinions of your staff.

vintage The yield of wine or grapes from a vineyard or district during one season. Wine is usually identified as to year and vineyard or district of origin.

RECEIVING BEVERAGES

Taking delivery of exactly what you have ordered—brands, sizes, and quantities at specified prices in good condition—is the definition of good receiving. This is not different from food receiving, except that food products vary in quality and packaging far more than do beverage products. Thanks to the federal government, liquor manufacturers must maintain consistent quality and packaging standards with all brands and types.

With incoming deliveries, your receiving clerk should inspect the following key areas, using your own purchase order rather than the vendor's invoice:

- Verify the quantity, price, and extension

- Verify the vintage of wines

- Check the expiration dates of beer and soft drinks

- Check the seals and condition of bottles to make sure that none are leaking or broken

- Monitor bottle sizes (it is easy to mistake a 750-milliliter bottle for a 1-liter bottle)

- Check the brand against what was ordered

Discrepancies in any of these areas should be communicated to the manager immediately and should be resolved before the delivery is accepted. Such corrections may require returning defective items and adjusting the invoices accordingly. The delivery person may insist that he or she cannot return any items, such as ones from a partial case; you will have to decide whether to return the entire case or keep the case with the defective items in exchange for credit from the vendor. Your decision will depend on how soon the item will be used and when the next delivery is expected. In Chapter 6 you will find a credit memo and procedures for documenting such discrepancies.

Storage

The storeroom is the setting for the third phase of the purchasing cycle. It performs three functions: physical care to maintain quality, inventory maintenance and record-keeping, and security from theft. Think of the storeroom as an off-limits area; those who work there, such as the storeroom clerk and purchaser, should be the only ones who distribute products. No one should be allowed to enter and take his or her own goods. The storeroom should not be left open and unattended. Door locks should be changed often, particularly if a storeroom employee leaves the company. The keys or combinations should only be available to authorized employees.

Each beverage should have a designated place in a logical arrangement, with similar items grouped on adjacent shelves. Stock must be rotated—that is, new stock is placed at the back and oldest stock is used first. In storing distilled spirits, shelving should be sturdy and well braced because cases of liquor are heavy. Sealed cases should be stacked on low platforms or shelves. The general temperature requirement is from 70° to 80° Fahrenheit.

Store wines on their sides or upside-down in their sealed cases. They are perishable—subject to deterioration via light, warmth, agitation, and old age. Wine needs a cool and dark environment at an air temperature between 50° and 70° Fahrenheit. Most experts recommend a constant 55° to 65°, or cellar, temperature. Move bottles as little as possible and handle them gently. Agitating a wine may upset both its chemistry and its sediment. This makes it unservable until the sediment settles again. Since wines have limited life spans, rotating the stock becomes particularly important. The exceptions to this rule are wines that increase in value with age. Your vendor should be able to give you this information.

Wine corks should be moist to prevent cracks or dryness. Cracks might allow wine to leave the bottle or let oxygen enter. Corks should be inspected for leakage both upon arrival and during storage. If you see leakage before receiving a product, reject it. If you find it later, consider discarding it or giving it to the chef for use in recipes.

Beer has the most limited shelf life. Product rotation is therefore crucial to prevent spoilage and waste. Canned and bottled beer should be stored below 70° Fahrenheit in a dark place. Draft beer and unpasteurized canned or bottled beers should be kept refrigerated. Draft beer should be kept at 36° to 39° and should be used within 30 to 45 days, or as specified on the container.

PROPER BEVERAGE REQUISITION PROCEDURES

If you work in a hotel with several food and beverage outlets, each outlet's bartender should remove all empty liquor bottles from the shelves at a specified time, usually at the end or beginning of a shift. These empty bottles become the basis for, and the physical evidence of, the liquor to be requisitioned. The bartender fills out a **requisition** form, being careful to enter the correct **bin number** (or item number), item description, and quantity required; then she or he sends the empty liquor bottles and the two-part requisition form to the beverage storeroom. In a computerized requisition system, the manual system described above is altered. In such a system, the requisition is entered directly into a computer terminal that is linked to the purchasing system and printer in the storeroom. The purchasing clerk fills out the requisition for either pickup or delivery, depending on your company's policies and procedures. The requisition is then posted or charged to the outlet via the purchasing terminal. In a single-outlet establishment, like a restaurant, the process is the same but on a smaller scale and therefore is a bit simpler.

In both manual and computerized systems, the empty bottles should be sent to the storeroom, where they are checked off by the storeroom clerk to ensure that they are empty, correct, and issued by the company. This is called the bottle-for-bottle exchange system. The clerk further checks that the empty bottles are equal in quantity and brand to the requested bottles. When issuing liquor, the storeroom clerk should ensure that a full bottle is exchanged for a corresponding empty bottle. In this way, the bar's par stock level can be better maintained.

Par stock, or par level as it is sometimes referred to, is the quantity of an item that should be on hand at a given time of the business season. To take this control a step further, attach a point of sale (POS) receipt, from the beginning period when the item was requisitioned to when a requisition is placed, for each item requisitioned. This proves the item was sold and is now being requisitioned to replenish the par stock. The bar should always be stocked with the right number of full, partial, and empty bottles to equal the par levels. Using this system, you can also ensure that no item is replaced if it has not been paid for and recorded in the POS system.

There are some exceptions to bottle-for-bottle exchanges. You may decide to adjust a bar's par levels if consumption volume changes, or you may get a breakage requisition when a bottle is broken. You might also receive an interbar transfer form that accounts for a discrepancy in par levels. These forms, and a description of their use, can be found in Chapter 11.

The storeroom clerk sends the empty bottles for disposal, in the process of which the bottles must be broken. This eliminates the possibility of empty bottles being removed from the trash and used in a subsequent requisition. Standardizing this process guarantees the accuracy and integrity of bar par stock and cost accounting.

Since customers in a hotel may dispose of bottles in their rooms, the requisition of spirits through the room service department should be supported by a sales slip or chit, demonstrating that a full bottle has indeed been sold.

The return of an empty bottle is not required when requisitioning wines, beer, or soft drinks. In these cases, bar par levels are monitored and consistent. For wines, however, it is necessary to submit a POS slip that matches the bin number of the wine being requisitioned. With beer, par stocks should be established by the case. There should be a discernible pattern to the quantities required to restock each type of beer in your bar (or bars, if you have multiple outlets.) In a well managed restaurant or lounge, the outlet's beer requisitions should be matched with sales data from a POS system. While the sales figures may not match exactly the bottles of beer requisitioned, they should be within a minimum variance.

Back-Order Guidelines

If the requested brand of beverage is out of stock, the beverage requisition is marked *out of stock* and is returned to the bar or outlet until the item is received and delivered. The out-of-stock item is recorded in a back-order logbook, and the sales slip is retained by the beverage storeroom clerk. When you see a back order, you should check to see if the par level should be raised. When the item is replenished, the storeroom clerk enters the item into the inventory

requisition Request for food, beverage, supplies, or personnel.

bin number A specific reference number assigned to an inventory item.

par stock Stock levels established by management for individual inventory items in varying outlets.

purchasing system in order to maintain the perpetual inventory. In the accounting for that outlet, the cost of the requisition should be charged to the outlet only when the items are delivered.

Proper Requisition Authorization

The beverage storeroom should have a list of the people who are authorized to requisition beverages. In a larger operation with more than one outlet, establish a time schedule for issuing beverages to each outlet, and stick to it. This confines issuing to times and situations when it can be monitored. In a smaller operation, the manager him- or herself may be the only issuing staff, perhaps reducing the need for a set schedule.

A beverage requisition form should be prepared in duplicate and completed in ink for each and every order. If any changes are required, the first and second copies should be corrected identically and signed by an authorized storeroom staff member. The purchaser and the accountant use the original copy of the requisition for costing. Both copies of the requisition should accompany the merchandise order to the outlet, especially when anyone other than the bartender delivers the requisition. The bartender signs the original after checking that all the merchandise listed on the requisition has been received. The purchasing clerk uses this copy to document the perpetual inventory and a daily record of beverage purchases.

SUMMARY

Following all of the controls in this chapter might seem daunting. Duplicate forms, locked storerooms, empty bottles . . . Is this much control really necessary? Purchasers and others attempting to control costs can testify that, yes, these controls can make or break an establishment. Beverages, as much or more than food, are tempting targets for theft. A fancy bottle of imported rum or an old bottle of wine can be gone in an instant—an expensive instant. You are unlikely ever to find the culprit, but you can initiate controls that help to seal up potential leaks, and you can monitor how your procedures are followed. These are the best bets for your company. In effect, you are trying to create a best-case scenario: How much can your restaurant make under ideal conditions and controls? How far do you vary from those ideals, and why?

CHAPTER QUESTIONS

Critical Thinking Questions

1. What are the primary objectives of beverage receiving? What procedures should be followed to assure objectives are met?

2. For control and customer service, how should a back order be handled?

3. What are the best methods for rotating wine, and why?

4. What impact does customer preference have on actual cost of sales? Please provide data to support your answer.

5. What factors should influence the selection of well brands for a beverage outlet?

6. What are the advantages and disadvantages of automated beverage dispensing systems?

Multiple Choice Questions

1. Portion size and control and standardized recipes are essential for:
   A. maintaining consistency
   B. controlling costs
   C. customer satisfaction
   D. all of the above

2. With incoming deliveries of wine, your receiving clerk should inspect the following key areas, using your own purchase order, rather than the vendor's invoice:
   A. Check the expiration dates of beer and soft drinks
   B. c and d
   C. Check the seals and condition of bottles to make sure that none are leaking or broken.
   D. Check the brand and vintage against what was ordered. Including quantity, price and extension.

3. What is the pour cost percentage?

	B	C	D	E	G	H	I	J	K	L
Liquor	Number Fluid Ounces	Cost per Bottle	Sale Price	Number Sold per Month	Cost per Fluid Ounce	Pour Amount in Fluid Ounces	Pour Cost	Total Cost	Total Sales	Pour Cost %
Formula					C / B		G × H	I × E	D × E	
Well	33.8	$12.00	$2.50	100	$0.36	1.0	$0.36	$36.00	$250	?

   A. 14.4%   B. 15.2%
   C. 14%   D. 14.7%

4. What is the cost per fluid ounce?

	B	C	D	E	G	H	I	J	K	L
Liquor	Number Fluid Ounces	Cost per Bottle	Sale Price	Number Sold per Month	Cost per Fluid Ounce	Pour Amount in Fluid Ounces	Pour Cost	Total Cost	Total Sales	Pour Cost %
Formula							G × H	I × E	D × E	J / K
Call	33.8	$21.00	$5.00	120	?	1.25	$0.78	$93.60	$600	15.6%

   A. $1.00   B. $.62
   C. $.80   D. $.72

5. What is the pour cost?

	B	C	D	E	G	H	I	J	K	L
Liquor	Number Fluid Ounces	Cost per Bottle	Sale Price	Number Sold per Month	Cost per Fluid Ounce	Pour Amount in Fluid Ounces	Pour Cost	Total Cost	Total Sales	Pour Cost %
Formula					C / B			I × E	D × E	J / K
Prem.	33.8	$30.00	$8.00	240	$0.89	1.5	?	$213.60	$1920	11.1%

A. $1.50   B. $1.50
C. $1.34   D. $2.00

6. If the potential cost is calculated correctly, then any variance could be traced to employees in:
   A. accounting and sales
   B. front desk, purchasing, and storage
   C. portion control and accounting
   D. purchasing, receiving, storage, and maintaining portion control.

7. Wine needs a cool and dark environment at an air temperature between _____ Fahrenheit.
   A. 70° and 90°   B. 90° and 110°
   C. 50° and 70°   D. 30° and 50°

8. Draft beer should be kept at _____ and should be used within 30 to 45 days, or as specified on the container.
   A. 36° to 39°   B. 45° to 55°
   C. 55° to 65°   D. 26° to 49°

9. What is the total cost?

	B	C	D	E	G	H	I	J	K
Liquor	Number Fluid Ounces	Cost per Bottle	Sale Price	Number Sold per Month	Cost per Fluid Ounce	Pour Amount in Fluid Ounces	Pour Cost	Total Cost	Total Sales
Formula					C / B		G × H		D × E
Well	33.8	$12.00	$2.50	100	$0.36	1.0	$0.36	?	$250

A. $250   B. $40
C. $12   D. $36

10. What is the total sales?

Liquor	B Number Fluid Ounces	C Cost per Bottle	D Sale Price	E Number Sold per Month	G Cost per Fluid Ounce	H Pour Amount in Fluid Ounces	I Pour Cost	K Total Sales
Formula					C / B		G × H	
Well	33.8	$12.00	$2.50	100	$0.36	1.0	$0.36	?

A. $300   B. $100
C. $250   D. $12

Objective Questions

1. Because well brands are typically the least-expensive brands available in the outlet, it is desirable to purchase whatever brand is currently least expensive. True or False? Explain your answer.

2. The one goal of over riding importance in selecting and purchasing beverage products is your profit goal. True or False?

3. You will achieve maximum success in profitability and customer satisfaction by following industry standards in your mark up on beverage costs. True or False?

4. In choosing the brands of liquor for your well drinks the rule of cheaper is better applies. True or False?

5. Too much focus on profit in marking up your drinks can be counter productive if it sacrifices customer satisfaction.

6. If you don't have the brand a customer requests it is best to supplement a comparable brand serve the drink and see how the customer reacts upon tasting it. True or False?

7. Access to the store room for wines should be left open to the employees so that when the establishment is critically busy filling customers drink requests is not in any way delayed. True or False?

8. Not moving better wines from place to place in the store room improves the effective life and taste of these wines. True or False?

9. When a liquor bottle is empty proper disposal consists of putting the empty in a recycling trash bin to comply with environmental concerns and in some locales regulations. True or False?

10. Expensive bottles of wine or spirits are prime targets of the unscrupulous employee and can when pilfered dramatically affect your operation's profitability. True or False?

11. The goal of beverage purchasing is the same as that of food purchasing: to provide a steady supply of raw ingredients for the drinks you sell, at minimal cost, to maximize profits. True or False?

Beverage Controls and Service Procedures

Learning Objectives

After reading this chapter, you should be able to explain and apply knowledge about:

- beverage control, including portion size control (PSC) and standard drink recipes (SDRs);

- other beverage controls, such as the following:

  - bar par stock

  - color-coded outlet stickers or stamps

  - waste, breakage, spoilage, and spillage

  - interbar transfer

  - control of cash bars

  - control of hosted bars

  - banquet beverage storeroom procedures

- beverage cost variance;

- service procedures regarding wine, liquor, and beer service; guest requests for unusual recipes; and suggestive selling techniques.

In Practice

As soon as Myla Thomas was named manager of the Sea Breeze Hotel in Monterey, she quickly walked over to the hotel bar to observe the operation. So far, only the owner, Eric Breeze, knew that Myla had been named manager, and she preferred it that way! She entered the bar area, walked over to the bar, and sat down. Upon seeing her enter, the bartender walked over and asked, "What can I get for you, Miss?"

"I'll have a glass of your house merlot," Myla replied as she glanced around the room and at the TV screen. There was a basketball game on: LA Lakers playing the Bulls in Chicago.

Myla watched the bartender pour wine into a wine glass up to the top of the glass. She watched him ring $4.50 on the cash register and place the check in front of her.

(continues)

(*continued*)

A waitress approached the servers' station at the side of the bar and yelled out, "Hey, Colin! I need three Bud Lights, a Bombay Sapphire and tonic, a Seven and Seven, and two house merlots!"

Obediently, Colin opened up the Bud tap and stuck a beer glass under it. Myla watched him dispense the beer, which he did rather carelessly. He poured a certain amount of beer down the drain as he attempted to get solid beer to the rim of the glass. As he finished the first glass, he set it down without shutting off the tap and leisurely placed the second glass under the tap. Meanwhile, more beer was going down the drain. He did the same with the third glass.

Having filled three beer glasses and placed them on a tray, Colin took a cocktail glass, filled it with ice, and grabbed the bottle of Bombay Sapphire gin. He filled three-quarters of the glass with gin and the rest with tonic from the dispenser gun, stuck a lime wedge on the side of the glass, and placed the glass on the tray.

Colin grabbed another glass, filled it with ice, grabbed a bottle of Seagram's Seven whiskey, looked at it, and said to the waitress, "I'll be right back, Vivian. I have to get another bottle of Seven Crown." Before leaving, he recorded No Sale on the cash register so he could open it and grab a key from the cash drawer.

A few minutes later, Colin returned with not only a bottle of Seven Crown, but also a bottle of Bacardi rum and another of Grey Goose vodka. After setting the bottles on the bar, he grabbed a glass, filled it with ice, filled the glass halfway with whiskey, topped it out with 7UP from the dispenser gun, dropped in a maraschino cherry, and placed it on the tray.

Finally, Colin took two wine glasses and filled each to the rim with merlot. He took the tray over to the waitress and said, "Here you are, Vivian." Vivian took the tray back into the dining room.

Colin then walked over to the order entry system's printer and casually ripped off a series of chits that had been building up, rolled them into a ball, and tossed them into the trash can.

"Wow!" Myla exclaimed quietly to herself. "Colin did everything wrong that you possibly can! He got his own liquor from the liquor room since he had the key. Half the beer ended up in the drain; the waitress had to walk gingerly so she wouldn't spill the wine or beer; and at least one patron was going to wonder why his drink was so strong. The customer may think he is getting a good value, but the company's liquor costs are going sky-high! Beer and wine costs would also be well above what they could be.

"And I bet some of those drinks weren't recorded in the order entry system," Myla thought. Colin didn't even look at the chits coming off the printer to see what was actually ordered.

Just then, a customer walked up to the bar with an empty beer glass. "Hey, Colin!" he yelled out. "How about a refill?"

"Sure, Bob!" Colin replied, and he started filling the glass with Coors Light in the same careless manner with which he filled the earlier glasses.

As Colin brought over the beer, Bob dropped a dollar on the bar. Colin walked over to the cash register, rang No Sale, and put the dollar bill in the tray.

(*continues*)

(continued)

Myla couldn't believe her eyes. "He just gave away a free beer and commingled his tip money with the company's cash receipts! I bet his cash register always comes up even," she mused.

Myla continued to observe Colin tend bar for about 45 minutes. She set $5 on the bar and indicated that she wanted to pay.

"Could I have a receipt, please?" she asked Colin.

"Sure, Miss," Colin replied. Myla watched Colin as he recorded the transaction on the cash register and placed the $5 inside the till.

"I wonder where the beverage manager is," Myla thought. "Probably at home watching the Lakers game."

INTRODUCTION

Myla played the role of a secret shopper in the story above. A secret shopper measures and compares customer service levels, spots trends, and provides accurate feedback in the form of mystery guest hotel, restaurant, and spa reports. Managers view secret shopping as an independent verification of what is working and what needs fixing. There are several companies on the Web that offer these types of services to hotels and restaurants.

Despite the worst-case scenario painted in this story, your staff can actually play very positive roles in the beverage profitability of your establishment. While you and the management team set up procedures that establish control over your inventory assets, your servers and bartenders are out there on the front line, making sure your guests' needs are heard and answered. Again, you are balancing the needs and preferences of your clients with your profit-making goals. Both control in the back of the house and service in the front of the house can help you achieve these goals.

The starting point in beverage control and sales is the establishment of portion size control (PSC) and standard drink recipes (SDRs). All employees and managers must work to see that these two controls are followed. Without them, you will not be able to evaluate valid data or to control costs. The objectives of these controls are

- to monitor and identify deviations from standard operating procedure (SOP) so that you can quickly correct the situation.

- to aid the manager in compiling cost data, which is used to compare and analyze potential versus actual cost.

- to provide a basis for consistency.

- to set ingredient quantity guidelines.

- to simplify and standardize training information.

- to serve as a continuous source of reference for everyone involved in service.

- to act as a watchdog for combating both internal and external theft.

PORTION SIZE CONTROL (PSC)

Portion size control is the standardization of beverages in order to control both quantity of liquor and quality of the drink. It is vital to create a method for pouring exact portions because you are often dealing with numerous bartenders and possibly high turnover. The point here, as always, is consistency. This is undeniably important to building a client base. New customers expect your Bloody Mary to taste like others they have had, and repeat customers expect it to taste like the last one they ordered from you.

Meeting customer expectations may be even more important for good profit than setting your drink prices correctly. Sales price multiplied by sales volume produces your revenue. You cannot build volume with drinks that do not meet customer wishes consistently. To achieve this, you need portion size control (PSC) for each and every drink. When PSC is in place and followed by the whole staff, the customer will get the same drink no matter who makes it.

Another advantage of consistency is accurate control of the amount of liquor poured. If you control the quantity of liquor, you also control costs. In this way you can maintain your cost-to-sales ratio and protect your profit. To achieve all of this, standardize three elements of each drink: size, recipe, and glass.

Size

There are three common methods of measuring liquor. The first is to use an automated pouring device, with which the major ingredients are measured and dispensed through a handgun or specialized pourer. These shut off at pre-established amounts per drink. A second way is for the bar staff to pour drinks using an established **jigger** size and to fill them only to the line on the jigger. A third method is to free-pour. This is a subjective form of measurement that involves turning the bottle, with a pourer in place, and pouring upside down at full force. The bartender counts in his or her head; to pour an ounce, for example, he or she might count "One, two, three" or "Ten, twenty, thirty." This method is not recommended because it is the least accurate; it is only as consistent as the bartender. Free-pouring varies between bartenders and from day to day.

jigger A measuring device used to serve predetermined quantities of a beverage.

Inconsistency is one of the biggest sources of guest complaints. Mr. Jones might receive a perfect Bloody Mary from one bartender at lunch on Monday; then, on Tuesday at dinner, his drink might be diluted or too strong or too peppery. Even the same bartender will make very different drinks at times. The way to combat this is to implement standardized recipes, discussed later in the chapter.

Computerized dispensing systems are used for portion control, perpetual inventory, standard recipe controls, and accuracy in guest charges. These systems have an electronic control device attached to each bottle to monitor and control the amount of alcohol dispensed. Beverages are poured accurately each time. Some systems have check-processing capabilities that ensure that the guest is charged properly for every drink. Taking control over the pouring of beverages is one of the most critical decisions a manager can make. The following are some of the advantages of using computerized dispensing systems:

- Less time is needed to train bartenders.

- There is less spillage and less breakage.

- Prices are preprogrammed into the machine, so pricing mistakes are eliminated.

- Standard recipe pour amounts are consistent and accurate.

- The system deters dishonest employees from stealing or giving away free drinks.

- Operational control of the bar is improved.

- You have an accurate accounting of the sales and profitability of each item.

- The system produces the sales, inventory, and employee reports you need.

There are several automated dispensing systems on the market; not all of them provide you with every advantage mentioned above. The biggest criticism is that the systems can break down on occasion. The following are some other disadvantages:

- Because of the way beverages must be stored, guests cannot see the bottles or the brand names at the bar. Ambience and brand promotion are lost.

- Most systems cannot mix all possible drinks that are available.

- Most bar operations do not have a contingency plan for use when the computer breaks down. Therefore, a malfunction can literally shut down sales until manual operation is installed.

- A dishonest employee may be able to beat the system by breaking it.

As a manager, you must weigh these advantages and disadvantages in light of your own operation. You should research the available models and try them out, weighing your operation's needs against each system's functions. Whether or not you choose an automated dispensing system, you will still need to establish adequate PSC standards.

STANDARD DRINK RECIPES (SDRs)

A successful standard drink recipe, or SDR, is a carefully calculated relationship of ingredients, with further calculations and standards for the glass, ice, and garnish. This is one area in which the chef's expertise can play an important role; it is advisable to combine the chef's cuisine with a suggested drink that goes well with the food. Many diners are calorie-conscious, however, so chefs may need to keep this in mind when suggesting drinks. Twelve ounces of regular beer contains 150 calories; 5 ounces of wine contains 100 calories; and 1.5 ounces of 80-proof distilled spirits contains 100 calories.

There are many bar books to refer to when planning a drink menu and making recipe calculations. Simply write down the exact recipe for each drink you serve. Then, train the bar staff to follow the recipes consistently; this way, they'll produce a consistent product no matter who tends the bar.

Prepare each drink and take its photograph; compile these photos into a visual presentation manual for your bar staff. The following information should be included:

- The amount of the primary ingredient to be poured (which becomes the jigger size you need to make available to your staff)

- The other ingredients and their amounts or proportions to the major ingredient

- The size of the glass to be used

- The amount of ice in the glass

- The amount of garnish and its arrangement on the glass

The ice in the glass is a key ingredient in any drink made with a carbonated mixer or juice. Its function is to chill the drink and control the proportion of liquor to mixer by taking the place of liquid in the glass. The ice goes into the glass first. The more ice you use, the less mixer goes in the drink.

Experts will tell you that the size and shape of the ice cubes makes a difference. With large, square cubes you have to fill the glass more full with ice, as these cubes have big spaces between them. If you want a strong proportion of mix in relation to liquor, use less ice or a larger glass. If you want a stronger liquor taste, use more ice or a smaller glass. All of these factors must be considered in writing your SDRs and establishing their consistent use.

GETTING SPECIFIC: HOW THE CONTROLS WORK

Your costs will vary widely when different amounts are poured. Review the information in Figure 9-1. From a 33.8-ounce (1-liter) bottle of vodka, you can get 33.8 one-ounce servings, 27 one-and-one-quarter ounce servings, or 22.5 one-and-a-half-ounce servings. Let's assume the bottle price was $12 and you are selling one drink for $3. Watch what happens to your cost when you have three bartenders who use different pours (Figure 9-2).

Figure 9-1 Control for Liter Sized Bottles

Size	Number of Fluid Ounces	Yield in 1-Ounce Drinks	Yield in 1.25-Ounce Drinks	Yield in 1.5-Ounce Drinks
Full Bottle	33.8	33.8 portions	27.0 portions	22.5 portions
Half Bottle	16.9	16.9 portions	13.5 portions	11.3 portions
1/10 Bottle	3.38	3.4 portions	2.7 portions	2.3 portions

Figure 9-2 Sales Variations with Different Pours

Bartender	Portion served	# of Drinks, (per the table above)	Liter Cost	Portion Cost	Selling Price	Total Sales (# of drinks x price)	Cost %
A	1 FZ	33.8	$12.00	$0.36	$3.00	$101.40	11.83
B	1.25 FZ	27	$12.00	$0.44	$3.00	$81.12	14.79
C	1.5 FZ	22.5	$12.00	$0.53	$3.00	$67.59	17.75

You can see that, for just this one item, the cost difference is staggering. The difference between the 1-ounce and the 1.5-ounce servings in terms of cost percentage is 5.92 percent. This is equivalent to Bartender B giving away 6.8 drinks while Bartender C gives away 11.27 drinks.

If this difference were applicable to total sales figures, the impact on your bottom line could be critically significant. If you are not controlling your recipes (with SDRs) and pours (with PSC), you will need to implement such measures right away.

Master Beverage Pour Cost Sheet

You can use Figure 9-3 to determine the ingredient costs for your beverages and to keep them all in one place. The data must be accurate to be relevant. If you have more than one outlet, use a separate form for each, as you may have different pricing strategies from one outlet to another. Use and update these forms for each outlet. The information gives you a ready perspective on costs across your beverage offerings.

🍷 **Exercise**

Use a measuring device (jigger) to pour a certain amount and then try to free-pour the same amount.

Figure 9-3 Master Beverage Pour Cost Sheet

Product Number	Item Name	Size of Item	Portion per Bottle	Portion Cost	Mixers Cost	Total Cost	Selling Price in $	Cost %

Other Beverage Controls

The manager is the custodial authority of the beverage storeroom. He or she will be monitoring the stock of each item at all times. When everything is systematically in place, he or she can easily notice if something is missing. One method to systematize your storeroom is to use **bin cards**, including a unique bin number for each item.

bin cards A manual system for keeping track of inventory items

A typical bin card shows the brand name, bottle size, quantity on hand, and bin or inventory code number. The minimum or maximum stock levels may also be recorded on the cards, as this information makes it easier to determine purchasing needs. The card is then affixed to the appropriate shelf. Bin cards note each entry and exit of a product. They are also very useful in a perpetual inventory system. The amount of stock delivered is added to the quantity on hand, and the amount issued is subtracted. The number of bottles shown on the bin should always agree with the actual number on the shelf. Storeroom personnel will need to spot-check inventory against the bin cards to help keep track of inventory. The information on the card, then, provides reliable rates of inventory use.

Another aspect of beverage control is eliminating the confusion in bottle sizes, spelling of names, and different brands. The purchasing manager should identify every kind of beverage carried in the restaurant or bar by means of a bin number or item number. Each type of beverage is assigned a block of numbers. For example, in a four-digit system, gin might be 1000, rum 2000, tequila 3000, and so on. Then particular brands would fall into those categories—for example, Tanqueray is 1001, Beefeater's is 1002, and so on. This system makes storage, inventory, par stock, and ordering procedures more organized and standardized. Bin or item numbers are used in a beverage control system for the following reasons:

- To simplify and standardize beverage control procedures and forms

- To facilitate purchasing, storing, requisitioning, and recording of physical inventories

- To provide precise numerical product descriptions to be used in inventory and purchasing control systems

The restaurant or bar par stock list is one of the most important procedural controls in a beverage control system. A par (Figure 9-4) is a pre-established limit of an outlet's beverage stock.

A copy of each par stock listing should be located in the outlet itself; there should also be one in the manager's office and one in the beverage storeroom. Each outlet is then issued only enough beverages to meet those par numbers. The purchasing clerk should never issue any beverage product in a quantity greater than the par value without special authorization

Figure 9-4 Example of Par Stock

Item	Number to Always Have on Hand (par stock)
Shotz Beer six-packs	6
Applewood Creme de Menthe 1 liter	1
Reposado Tequila 750 ml	3
Bumblebee Gin 1 liter	2
Haberdash Peach Schnapps 750 ml	1

by the manager. This might be necessary if the par value is being modified because of an increase in the outlet's business activity. For the most part, however, issuing over par will not be necessary, and this control provides a strong basis for beverage cost reckoning. Establishing par levels for each outlet, and sticking to them, can even eliminate the need for monthly inventory. The person in charge of inventories should conduct regular spot checks to be sure that par stock is maintained. If these levels are in place, you need only multiply the par stock by the purchase price to determine inventory value figures. This system also does the following:

- Assures adequate supply

- Minimizes the physical inventory kept in stock, which helps reduce the opportunity for theft and maximize cash flow

- Reduces the number of trips to the storeroom and thus improves the labor productivity of the bartender and purchasing clerk

- Facilitates requisitioning when empty bottles are counted for return

- Provides an immediate inventory accountability by all personnel

- Discourages a bartender from bringing in his or her own bottle and selling its contents; the outlet-coded sticker or stamp system (see below) will also help to prevent this form of pilferage

For a par stock listing to be worthwhile, the par stock should be spot-checked on a random, unannounced basis in each outlet at least once per month (in addition to the inventory process). These spot-audits, however, are no substitute for direct, hands-on involvement by the manager who has supervisory authority over the bartender. Outlet managers should also understand the par stock system and see that it is enforced.

Color-Coded Outlet Stickers or Stamps

Color-coded outlet stickers or stamps should be placed on liquor bottles when they are requisitioned from the beverage storeroom. These stamps will identify all bottles as company issue, and will also indicate to which outlet they were issued to provide a backup check of where the bottles go. This can prevent theft and can also keep staff from trading bottles between outlets without documenting the transfer.

To enact this procedure, the storeroom clerk should mark all the liquor bottles for a given outlet with some type of color-coded outlet sticker or stamp, as established by the purchasing manager. This sticker or stamp should be placed on the back label of the bottle, rather than on the bottom; this facilitates recognition during inventory-taking and spot-checking procedures. The stamps should be impervious to removal. During any random check, every liquor product in an outlet should match its par stock, and all the full, partial, and empty bottles should have that outlet's identifying color sticker or stamp on them.

Waste, Breakage, Spoilage, and Spillage

Waste is a common occurrence in the food and beverage industry. This does not mean it should simply be accepted as tolerable. Your job is to minimize its occurrence and to control procedures when it does occur. Consider the case of breakage. If a bottle is broken or spoiled in storage or at a bar, the manager or bartender should return the broken bottle neck or spoiled product to the person in charge of the inventory. This inventory control person should complete and sign a requisition for the item and return the requisition to the manager or bartender, who will then submit the signed requisition with the daily order. This provides an authorized paper trail of the variances that inevitably occur, so that patterns or problem areas can be tracked.

The requisition, together with the spoiled or empty bottle or the broken bottle neck, is returned to the beverage storeroom for replacement. The broken bottle neck is discarded. The requisition should be clearly marked as breakage. From an accounting perspective, the bar should bear the cost of breakage. If the quantity in question is more than a single bottle (for example, a case falls from a pallet or mechanical lift), the manager should be notified to verify physically that this breakage has occurred.

When a bottle of wine has been sold to the guest and then is judged to have spoiled, the sale of this spoiled product should remain documented through the POS system. It may be channeled to a special spoilage account set up by the manager or simply voided. For purposes of requisition, a record of the void slip will serve as proof.

Spoilage involves either ingredient spoilage or a guest who mentions dissatisfaction with the quality of a drink. Spillage, on the other hand, is what happens when a server spills all or part of a drink. The server may reorder the same drink and process a separate beverage charge through the POS system. The check should then be settled or closed, with all explanatory notes included and signed by the outlet manager as spillage or dissatisfied guest. The bar should bear the cost of spillage; spoilage also should be charged to the outlet if the item could not be returned to the vendor for credit. The manager should complete a breakage, spoilage, and spillage report to justify why actual cost is different from potential cost. (See Chapter 10 for this form.)

Interbar Transfer

In an operation with more than one outlet, interbar transfers are commonly carried out. These transfers need to be included in an outlet's cost. While the transfer of full bottles from one bar to another is discouraged, on those occasions when it is necessary, train your staff to use an interbar transfer form. An example of this form can be found in Appendix. It should be completed and signed by the receiving bartender at the time of the transfer, and each bartender should retain a copy. To make this explanation clear, let's call the receiving bar Bar A and the transferring bar Bar B.

Bar B now has one bottle short of its par stock, having sent a bottle to Bar A; the copy of the interbar transfer form serves as reconciliation when Bar B's par is audited. The form is then used in lieu of the usual empty bottle when Bar B submits its beverage requisition to the beverage storeroom; the bartender should attach the form to the beverage requisition.

Bar A now has one bottle over par, and the interbar transfer form will serve to reconcile the item if the par is audited. This form also explains why, in the case of liquor, there is a bottle with Bar B's stamp in Bar A's stock. Bar A's bartender should not submit the empty bottle to the beverage storeroom as a requisition, thereby increasing the par. If the bartender in this outlet were to forget and try to requisition a replacement bottle, the storeroom clerk should notice that the sticker or stamp is from another outlet and should not fill the requisition without authorization from the manager.

Cash Bar Control

In a cash bar, a guest pays for each drink as it is ordered. This type of service is often used in the case of banquet events like weddings or large parties. Cash bars are often carried out in a remote location, such as a banquet room or an outdoor deck. However, it should operate with the same type of controls as the main bar. Because such remote locations often preclude the use of automated dispensing systems and POS access is unlikely, pouring methods should be established to monitor and account for all revenues collected. One way to account for sales and inventory, and to ensure that there is no missing revenue, is to use a cash bar worksheet as in Figure 9-5.

Figure 9-5 Cash Bar Control Sheet

Smith Wedding Items	Date: April 5ᵗʰ		Location: Restaurant Deck	
	A Beginning Inv.	B Additions	C Ending Inv.	D A + B − C
Vodka Blitski	1	2	1	$1 + 2 - 1 = 2$
Tequila Rodeo	2	0	2	$2 + 0 - 2 = 0$
Gin Parker	3	1	1	$3 + 1 - 1 = 3$

If you multiply the results in Column D of Figure 9-5 (2, 0, and 3) by the selling price for each of those drinks, you should get the amount of the cash that the event hosts paid for the function. If there are differences, the manager should investigate them. One person should be in charge of monitoring the cash bar operation for effectiveness and control, and he or she should use this form to monitor what is used and sold, and at what prices. In Chapter 12, you will find a detailed discussion of how this process works, both for regular POS systems and for special banquet events.

The procedures and policies you develop for cash bar control will help to prevent loss of cash due to theft. In addition, the following controls should be incorporated into cash bar systems:

- *Ticket or guest check control systems.* Some operations have a cashier sell tickets that can be given to the bartender in exchange for a drink. This frees the bartender from handling cash, facilitates better service, and allows tighter controls. The number of drinks consumed should match the drink tickets sold and collected. When there are void transactions where the drink tickets are sold, have the manager authorize them and make the reason for the void clear for reporting purposes.

- *Recording sales.* It may be cost-effective to use a cash register for cash bar events. This saves hours of manual paperwork time, frees employees from memorizing item prices, and facilitates service procedures. The drink prices can easily be preprogrammed into the register.

- *House bank.* The bank is an amount of money with which the employee begins the shift. The size of the bank should depend on the expected amount of business. Servers may carry individual banks, or the bartender may collect all cash received. Choose a method that meets the needs of your operation.

In a hosted bar, the host pays for all items consumed. The price, agreed upon ahead of time, is applied to the amount of services or food and beverage consumed. When the price is per bottle, a special par stock is set up just for that function, and the amount of food or beverage consumed is computed by subtracting the ending inventory from the beginning inventory (par inventory plus any additions during the event). Generally, there is no cash for staff to steal in a hosted event, because payment for services and goods is not made directly to them; however, adequate record controls must still be established for billing and accounting.

BANQUET BEVERAGE STOREROOM PROCEDURES

Banquet beverage use brings up special issues that cannot be reconciled through standard procedures. A banquet beverage storeroom is commonly established for banquet service in large operations, because this type of service is markedly different from any outlet service we have discussed. The banquet manager should restock from the purchasing beverage storeroom as needed by using a requisition form. This form may be preprinted with all the beverage products you carry. The bartender would then only need to enter the quantity needed.

For each individual banquet, a special banquet beverage requisition is completed. Products should be issued from a separate banquet beverage storeroom to the individual service bars. After the function, all unused liquor should be returned to that storeroom. If you have enough banquet business to have standard issues to banquet rooms, these can be entered on a requisition form, and they should be charged by function. A **standard issue** is a repeated restocking of products to par levels, just as in a regular outlet. Every item issued, minus the ending inventory, should be charged to that function. In most cases your company will establish a contract with the banquet client prior to the event. The charges can then be reconciled to that contracted price.

standard issue A repeated restocking of banquet beverage products to par levels, just as in a regular outlet. Every item issued, minus the ending inventory, should be charged to the function.

BEVERAGE COST VARIANCE

When you compare your actual cost to your potential cost, the difference between them is called the variance. This amount will probably vary from month to month, due to the ever-changing nature of the business. Assuming that control procedures are followed and there are no significant changes in the sales mix, the beverage variance percentage should not be more than 1 percent off from the calculated potential cost.

Calculating potential cost for your beverage business is essentially the same as doing so for food. Begin by determining the number of drinks per bottle and multiplying this by the selling price per drink. This is the potential sales per bottle. For example, a 1-liter bottle will yield approximately 27 drinks at 1.25 fluid ounces each. If the drinks are sold at $3.75 each, the potential sales reach $101.25 for one bottle. If your cost for that bottle was $22, you need only divide that cost by the potential sales to reach the potential percentage. In this case it is 21.7 percent.

But perhaps you do not sell all drinks made with a particular liquor at the same price or with the same amount of alcohol. In this case, you will need to determine weighted averages for both drink size and selling price. Let's take a $14 bottle of gin as an example, as shown in Figure 9-6.

The number of ounces used (415.5) divided by the number of drinks sold (315) gives you your average drink size, 1.32 ounces. This number, divided into your bottle size (1 liter or 33.8 ounces), equals the average number of drinks per bottle, 25.6.

Next, find your average selling price by dividing total sales by total number of drinks sold. Your average selling price is $3.18. Multiply this average price by the average number of drinks per bottle. In our example, this is $3.18 × 25.6 for a total of $81.41. This is your potential sales value per bottle. The potential beverage cost is equal to the cost divided by the potential sales, or $14 ÷ $81.41. We get a potential beverage cost percentage of 17.2.

Figure 9-6 Weighted Averages

Name of Drink	FZ of Gin Used	Selling Price (& number sold last month)	Total Sales	Total Ounces
martini	1.5	$3.75 (16)	$60.00	24
gin & tonic	1.25	$3.00 (150)	$450.00	187.5
gin fizz	1.0	$2.75 (39)	$107.25	39
gin on the rocks	1.5	$3.50 (110)	$385.00	165
		Total sold: (315)	Total: $1002.25	Total: 415.50 FZ

Now you need to determine your actual sales revenue. Simply multiply the numbers of each drink sold by the drink's selling price, and total the result. In our example, the total revenue was $1,002.25. Your POS reports should show you the actual number of drinks sold at each selling price and the sales mix of each category.

The next step is to determine the actual beverage cost percentage. The formula for calculating the beverage cost for a specified period is as follows:

Beginning Inventory + Purchases − Ending Inventory = Cost of Product Consumed

In food and beverage operations, which commonly transfer food products such as juices and garnish fruit to the bar, adjustments to the gross cost need to be made. Similar adjustments must be made for any products transferred from the bar to the kitchen, such as wine for cooking. In these cases, the gross beverage cost would be adjusted as follows:

Cost of Product Consumed + Transfers to Bar − Transfers from Bar
= Net Cost of Product Consumed

Using our example, assume the net beverage cost was $180 and the total beverage sales was $1,002.25; the actual beverage cost percentage would be $180 divided by $1,002.25 = 18.0 percent. Now we can compare the potential cost—at 17.2 percent—with the actual 18 percent we calculated.

Compare these two numbers to check for significant variations. When you have added up many items across food and beverage categories, however, it can be hard to see where problems lie. This is made worse if your company has multiple outlets, as we illustrate in the example below. In addition, companies that do not have a perpetual inventory system tabulated by outlet or that have not computed their cost by outlet may find it difficult to identify exact causes of variances because outlets are different and may have varying stock and pricing. So, what do you do? The example in Figure 9-7 shows how to allocate the unexplainable cost variance, so that (for accounting purposes) you can charge a proportionally correct amount to each outlet's costs.

In the example shown in the figure, the calculated potential costs sit at 21.63 percent, while the actual percentage was 22.77. The cost overages on Line 9 are allocated to the outlets proportionally based on their actual revenue. Dividing the actual cost by the potential cost derives the factor of 1.05. The factor could be used also to derive the actual allocated cost on Line 9 by multiplying it by the potential cost. As you can see, there are a lot of small issues—such as losses, waste, and failure to inventory properly—that turn out to be significant when these costs are totaled and compared each month. These are the sorts of issues that can explain a variance. The following list includes many possible reasons to investigate if you are seeing unwarranted variances in your costs.

MONTH __,

LINE #	BEVERAGE OUTLETS	ACTUAL REVENUES	POTENTIAL %	POTENTIAL $	ADJUSTED ACTUAL $	ADJUSTED ACTUAL %
1	BANQUETS	40,360.06	21.50%	8,677.41	9,133.87	22.63%
2	ROOM SERVICE	5,815.18	23.00%	1,337.49	1,407.85	24.21%
3	CAFE	1,222.75	23.40%	286.12	301.17	24.63%
4	FINE DINING	30,545.63	24.00%	7,330.95	7,716.58	25.26%
5	THE BAR	36,249.75	19.50%	7,068.70	7,440.53	20.53%
6	TOTAL	114,193.37	21.63%	24,700.68	26,000.00	22.77%
7	ACTUAL FOOD COST ------------------------------>			26,000.00		
8	FACTOR TO ACTUAL (actual/potential cost)-->			1.0526		
9	THEREFORE, THE AMOUNT TO BE ALLOCATED			1,299.32		

Figure 9-7 Actual versus Potential Cost

Incorrect Charges

- A food requisition has been charged to beverage cost, or vice versa.

- Beverage revenue has been processed as food revenue, or vice versa.

- Sales tax has been mistakenly included in calculating potential beverage cost.

Incorrect Physical Inventory Valuations

- Items have been incorrectly counted or double-counted. (The person who counts the items during inventory-taking can simply turn the label on the bottle to the back when it has been counted, as a reminder not to count the item twice.)

- Inventory extension is incorrect. This occurs most commonly when the database is corrupted. An example might be that an increased purchase price has not been updated in the inventory item files, or a bottle of one size is recorded under a different size.

- An entry or entries are incorrect. For example, one bottle of vodka is entered as one case.

Sales Mix Changes

- More premium label products are sold. Premium labels are usually higher in pour cost than well brands. Refer to the sliding scale pricing strategy, discussed in Chapter 7.

- Bottle beer sales are higher than those of draft beer. Bottle beers are usually higher in cost than draft beer.

- Imported beer sales increase over those of domestic brands. Domestic brands are usually cheaper than imported brands.

- Wine sales increase. Wine cost percentages are usually higher than those of all other categories of beverage products.

Incorrect Drink Pricing

- Pricing is inadequate to cover costs.

- Item entry into the POS system is incorrect due to staff error.

Incorrect Par Stocks

- Par stocks are not being maintained. If you are using par stock figures to extend your inventory, make sure they are correct.

- Missing, spilled, spoiled, or broken merchandise is not accounted for properly.

- Bottles are not marked or coded by outlet.

Overpour, Spillage, and Underpour

- Bartenders may overpour or spill products when preparing drinks. They may not be using pour-top control devices.

- Electronic liquor dispensers are not checked every 30 days and recalibrated as necessary.

- Draft beer dispensers are not properly calibrated to reduce foam.

- Service staff may overpour wine by the glass.

Inadequate Cash Control Procedures

- A transaction was not prechecked on the POS system before preparing the drink.

- The sale amount recorded on the register did not correspond to the number and type of drinks served.

- The guest check was not placed in front of the guest or customer immediately after serving, in order to have evidence of the transaction openly available at all times.

- The *No Sale* key was used during a sale. Major differences among bartenders' sales on the same shift might be an indication of this problem.

- Guest check controls are not enforced.

- Bartenders may be making change from their tip jars.

- Overages or shortages are not investigated. This problem is common when bartenders undercharge guests in order to earn large tips or to please friends. When guests ask for a favorite employee, it could be because that employee favors them with unauthorized discounts.

- The employee may be charging for a drink not served, and the guest unknowingly pays for it. A dishonest bartender could resell that drink and pocket the cash.

Purchasing

- Beverages are not purchased competitively.

Your job is to investigate these areas of possible loss and, when necessary, implement appropriate controls. People are very creative; you may even discover new problems not mentioned in this section.

SERVICE PROCEDURES

You have seen the unique challenges facing the manager in the operation of an outlet and in the sale of beverages. The purpose of the following sections is to set up standard operating procedures (SOPs) to aid you and your employees in training and coaching. No training or staff system is perfect; you may need to refine what is mentioned here to fit your company's needs. Without the consistent and accurate cooperation of your staff, however, all of your controls may be worthless. Be sure to include comprehensive training and ongoing coaching for your staff as an operational goal and necessity. Below we provide information that you can use in training your service staff; it is written in a style that speaks directly to servers and bartenders. Be sure to emphasize that these are the procedures and behaviors that you expect your staff to perform. Cody Plott, president of Pebble Beach Company, phrases it like this: Service should "exceed the expectation of every guest, by providing a once-in-a-lifetime experience . . . *every time.*"

When Guests Arrive

- Greet guests with a welcome as they come into the room. If you're busy, acknowledge them with a word or a smile and establish eye contact. If guests know that they have been recognized, they will not mind a short delay in service. No matter where you are in the room, always keep your eye on the other tables.

- Always face the tables while standing at the bar.

Serving Our Guests

- Always be positive. "May I get you another cocktail?" or "Would you care for another round?" is preferable to "Is that all?"

- Place cocktail napkins in front of the guests with any logo, emblem, or written material facing them.

- If you know the guests, call them by name. If they are regular patrons, remember their favorite brand or cocktail and how they like it.

- Suggest one or two featured beverages to the customer when ordering. Use up-selling techniques to encourage customers to purchase more premium products.

- Serve cocktails as soon as possible.

Pouring Drinks

- Place the pour spout in the bottle in such a way that the label is turned toward guests seated at the bar. This allows guests to see what is being poured.

- Never overfill a glass so that it spills on the bar or on the guests when they attempt to drink the cocktail. Never pick up a glass—clean or dirty—by the rim. Always hold stemmed glasses by the stem.

- Strictly adhere to the company pour policy in accordance with recipes. Use pour control devices on all liquor bottles, except odd-sized liqueurs or cordials.

Presenting a Check to a Bar Guest

- Always process the order through the POS system, if available.

- Always place the guest check in front of the bar guest at the same time the cocktail is served. This is very important!

Service Standards We Expect

- Ensure that the table is maintained well at all times. For example, remove soiled napkins and replace used ashtrays. Used ashtrays should always be replaced with a clean one.

- Be alert for minors. If there is the slightest doubt, ask for identification; if the person can't produce an ID, or if you have reason to distrust the ID he or she provides, you will have to refuse service courteously.

- Never argue with a guest. Call the manager to settle disputes.

- It is every staff member's responsibility to refuse service to an intoxicated person. If there is a problem, call the manager.

- Be alert to the guest's need for another cocktail.

- Talk, but be a good listener. Don't join conversations, and never give the impression of listening in on a conversation. Be attentive without being overly familiar.

- If you make an error with a cocktail, rectify it at once. Make the correction without question, and clearly dispose of the mistaken drink. Notify the manager and give a copy of the spillage report to the accountant.

Collecting Payment

- Do not attempt to collect payment until guests indicate that they are ready to pay or to sign the check. If the guest pays by credit card, note his or her last name and expiration date on the guest ticket. If it is a hotel room charge, have the guest print and sign his or her name and room number; then match the information on the registered guest list to the name and room number on the check.

- Finalize the closed check in the POS system. Immediately return change or a credit card receipt to the guest along with the check stub receipt.

Quiz

If you (as manager) see your best bartender pour a drink and "forget" to ring it up, what should you do?

When Guests Depart

- Express your appreciation and invite guests to return.

- Tables should always be wiped down with a damp cloth. Wipe crumbs from chairs, replace ashtrays, and replenish matches. Tidy the floor if necessary.

Our Restaurant Standards

- Always be courteous and helpful to fellow employees. This will be noticed and appreciated by guests.

- Pay particular attention to personal appearance and grooming, and wear a clean uniform.

- When leaving the floor for any reason, tell the room manager or the bartender first.

SPECIFIC PROCEDURES: BEER SERVICE

For both bottle and draft beer, always serve beverages cold, at approximately 40° Fahrenheit. Certain specialty beers may have other temperature requirements, which your vendor should be able to provide. Use cold glasses when serving beer; a room-temperature glass makes a beer mediocre. Fill the glasses with ice cubes, or put them in the refrigerator—whatever is necessary to serve cold beer in a prechilled glass. Beer temperature rises 2° Fahrenheit in an unchilled, rinsed, thin-shell glass, and it rises 4° to 5° in a rinsed, heavy-shell glass or mug.

Draw or pour beer properly. The size of the head you put on each glass can be controlled by the angle at which you hold the glass at the beginning of the draw. If the glass is held straight and the beer drops into the bottom of the glass, a deep head of foam will result. If the glass is tilted sharply (about 90°) and the beer flows down the side of the glass, the head of foam will be minimized. How much you tilt the glass and when you straighten it to allow the head to form can be determined by a few trial draws. You can also control foam by opening the lever fully. Partial pull of the lever can create too much air.

Keep your beer glasses clean. This is very important, as beer will lose its delicate taste and zest when it is poured into a glass with the slightest film of soap, grease, lipstick, cream, or other substance. A beer glass should be washed each time it is used unless the guest requests that the glass be refilled. Proper cleaning and drying can be accomplished in these simple steps:

1. Empty and rinse used glasses with clear water prior to washing.

2. Wash each glass with a brush in water containing a solution of odor-free and nonfat cleaning compound that will clean the surface of the glass thoroughly and rinse off easily in clean water.

3. After washing the glass, rinse it in clean, cool water. The final rinse should be sanitized. Do not dry glasses with a towel. Stack them on a rack or on a corrugated surface where they can drain freely and air can circulate in them.

4. One of the secrets to serving a perfect glass of beer is to rinse the glass in cold, clean water before filling.

Ring the order through the POS system. Serve beer by placing the glass (serving from the right) in front of the guest. In the case of bottled beer, pour the glass one-third full and place the bottle (with the label facing the guest) next to the glass. Then, thank the guest. Most people will react more positively when they feel appreciated.

SPECIFIC PROCEDURES: WINE SERVICE

Prepare the supplies you will need for wine service: a wine bucket for whites and sparkling wines, a wine opener, a service cloth, and the correct number of the right kind of wine glasses for what you are serving. Set the glasses on the upper right side of the table setting, above the knife. Then, present the bottle so that the host can read the label. (The host, male or female, is the person who orders the wine.) Wait until the host confirms that this is the bottle of wine that he or she ordered.

Remove the foil cap by placing the bottle near the edge of the table and cutting the cap cleanly without twisting the bottle. Move your hand around the bottle; the label should face the host. Use the knife part of the corkscrew to cut the foil 0.5 inch from the top of the bottle. Remove the foil cap and wipe the bottle neck with the service cloth before uncorking.

To uncork the wine, insert the tip of corkscrew into the middle of the cork while keeping the bottle on the table. The corkscrew should enter straight and should not break the cork. Turn the corkscrew until the tip of the screw almost reaches the bottom of the cork. Then, remove the cork by placing the lever on the neck of the bottle. Push the lever down, grasp the lever and cork together, and lift the cork out gently. Unscrew the cork and place it next to the host. Wipe the mouth of the bottle with a cloth again.

When opening champagne, do not pop the cork. Maintain pressure on the champagne cork as it pushes against your hand. Do not hold the champagne bottle by the neck. Your hand will cause the air in the neck to warm up and expand. This may cause an unexpected forceful release of the cork from the bottle. An ideal way is to wrap a towel around the cork and then grasp and wiggle the knob of the cork with a twisting motion. Let the pressure inside the bottle and the twisting of the knob force the cork out.

Serving the host from the right side, pour a minimum of 1 ounce of wine into a glass by holding the bottle in your right hand with the label facing up while pouring. Do not lift the wine glass when pouring, and do not allow the bottle to touch the wine glass. Wait for the host's approval, and then proceed to pour the wine for the other guests. Follow these instructions while pouring the wine:

- Serve ladies first, moving counterclockwise and ending with the host.

- Never overfill a wine glass. White wine glasses should be a maximum of two-thirds full, while red wine glasses should be a maximum of one-half full (5 ounces in either case).

- Old red wines should be treated with care and poured gently. Do not angle them abruptly.

- To avoid drops from running down the bottle neck, twist the bottle a half turn before lifting it away from the glass.

Lastly, in the case of chilled wine, place the bottle in the wine bucket (which should be 6 inches from the edge of the table) near the host. A red wine should simply sit on the table without a bucket. Be sure to enter the order into the POS system and verify the proper sales price (report any discrepancy to the accountant or manager on shift). Retain the wine tag, which is usually the company control number for identifying the type of wine sold and POS receipt. At the end of the day, you will do the following:

- Take all wine tags and complete a wine requisition sheet. Submit this wine requisition sheet, along with the wine tags, to the purchasing department.

- The storeroom should not issue a replacement bottle of wine if a wine tag, wine bin number, and POS receipt are not presented.

SPECIFIC PROCEDURES: GUEST REQUESTS FOR UNUSUAL RECIPES

When a guest orders a drink the bartender is not familiar with, the bartender should be honest with the guest. However, if the guest can provide the recipe, method of preparation, glass to be used, garnish, and so on, the bartender should be pleased to prepare the drink. The bartender should relate the ingredients and portions to a similar drink and charge the guest accordingly. In the event that there is an unstocked liquor or ingredient involved, advise the guest accordingly. Do not make a substitution without the guest's knowledge or suggestion; just politely suggest another drink.

Do not be ashamed to admit not knowing an unusual drink; simply follow the above procedure. For example, in some areas of the country, water is requested with the word *ditch* or *branch*. Ask the guest courteously what he or she means if you do not understand, and later, inform the manager and the accountant so the other staff can be alerted to language that they, too, might hear.

Service Procedures: Suggestive Selling Techniques

Suggestive selling is the creative and enthusiastic merchandising of your products to generate sales and to enhance guest service. To be an effective salesperson, a service staff member must be knowledgeable and must put to use all the selling aids and tools available. These selling aids and tools include the following:

- Food and beverage menus

- Cocktail and wine lists

- Your own knowledge

- Your enthusiasm

- Proper language and manners

- Food and beverage product boards

- Table tents or posters

- Your sincerity

- Your confidence in your products

The key to these selling techniques is suggestion. Servers need to be trained to "read" the customers so that they can suggest something appropriate. They should not say, "Can I get you something to drink?" Servers should guide guests to order something specific.

Techniques to Use

- Be positive. Phrase sentences so it sounds as though the guest is already sold on the idea and they need only tell you the particular item. Here is an example:

  Server: "Good evening. May I take your order?"

  Guest: "I'll have a Budweiser."

  Server: "The shrimp cocktail is excellent. May I order one for you?"

- You can also offer two choices, making it more difficult for a guest to say no. Don't ask if guests want something, but ask *which one* they'll have: "Deep-fried zucchini or onion rings would go great with your Budweiser."

- Understand the ingredients and preparation methods used to help in sales: "Try our deep-fried zucchini."

- Be honest.

- Servers can be salespeople, but they do not have to be pushy to be effective.

- Know the chef's specials before beginning the shift.

SUMMARY

Beverages differ from food in several respects: greater consistency in quality, availability, price, packaging, and yield, as well as looser storage requirements. As a result, control procedures differ significantly. Alcoholic beverages are usually classified as fermented wines and beer on the one hand, and distilled spirits and cordials on the other. Several trends are evident in the beverage market. As health concerns regarding the consumption of distilled spirits have risen, sales have dropped significantly. Concurrently, sales of beer and nonalcoholic beverages have increased, and premium brand sales now account for a greater percentage than they have for decades. In addition, numerous laws have been enacted to curtail alcohol abuse. One that affects beverage operations directly is the legal notion of third-party liability. These kinds of restrictions on the growth of beverage sales mean you must be even more careful with your pricing and sales strategies.

Competition and service levels are key factors in these considerations. When setting prices, consider all costs associated with production, not just product cost. Watching and managing your potential versus actual costs over time can give you an edge in future pricing.

Inventory procedures are distinctly aided by a bin number system, whereby each item has a specific, standard number and location. This helps to simplify control procedures and forms and facilitates purchasing, storing, requisitioning, and recording of physical inventories. One of the most important tools to help control physical inventory is the bar par stock. It is used to assure adequate supply, to minimize inventory stock, to reduce trips to the storeroom, to facilitate requisitioning, to increase inventory accountability, and to reduce theft. Additional methods for improving control include color-coded stickers or stamps, bottle-for-bottle exchange, maintaining a perpetual inventory, and requiring properly authorized requisition forms for issuance of beverage products. It is also important to maintain records of all breakage, spoilage, and spillage, as well as internal transfers, when your establishment has more than one outlet.

Standardized portion sizes and recipes must be followed to control quality and costs. Automated dispensing systems help to achieve this goal, and they should be considered as a possible way to increase control and consistency.

As with food, potential beverage costs must be compared to actual beverage costs to determine any variances so that corrective actions can be taken. Possible causes of variance are incorrect charges, incorrect physical inventory valuation, sales mix changes, incorrect drink pricing, incorrect par stocks, overpour, spillage, underpour, and inadequate cash control procedures. Your job is to monitor and control these possible causes and to use that data to locate the problems when they do occur.

Proper service procedures must be followed regardless of the types of beverages being served. In addition, suggestive selling can increase not only guest satisfaction, but also check averages.

CHAPTER QUESTIONS

Critical Thinking Questions

1. What is a perpetual inventory system, and why is it important?

2. How do standard pour sizes of drinks contribute to your control systems?

3. What are the advantages and disadvantages of using automated beverage dispensing systems?

4. When a guest orders a glass of wine, it is important to fill the glass completely. True or False?

5. List five ways to *mis*manage revenue with use of guest checks, and list controls to prevent them.

6. How would you determine your actual and potential beverage cost percentages? What do you do with this information when you calculate it? Why is it important?

7. Describe inventory-taking procedures.

8. If the menu price of a beverage is $3.95, and the potential cost of the beverage is $0.95, what is the potential beverage cost percentage of the item?

9. If the potential cost of a beverage is $0.85 and the targeted beverage cost is 20 percent, what is a reasonable menu price for the beverage?

10. If the potential cost of a beverage is $0.85 and the targeted beverage cost is 25 percent, what is a reasonable menu price for the beverage?

11. If a case of liquor (12 bottles) is sold in 750-milliliter bottles for $89.90, what is the cost per ounce?

12. If a case of liquor (12 bottles) is sold in 1-liter bottles for $110.90, what is the cost per ounce?

13. Restaurant A buys beer for $18 per case (24 bottles), as does Restaurant B. In order to generate more business, Restaurant A sells this beer for $1.50, but Restaurant B considers this too low a markup and sells its beer for $2.95. What is the potential beverage cost at each restaurant?

14. Using the data above, if Restaurant A sells 10,000 bottles per month, and Restaurant B sells 1,000 bottles, what is the gross profit of each restaurant based on beer sales?

15. If liquor costs $0.33 per ounce, a beverage item's potential cost is $0.60 based on 1 ounce of liquor, and the beverage sells for $2.95—but the bartender pours 1.3 ounces of liquor into the drink—what is the actual cost of the beverage?

16. In the example above, what is the variance in dollars and in percentage?

17. If the beginning beverage inventory is $2,000, purchases are $12,000, the ending inventory is $3,000, and beverage sales are $55,000, what is the actual beverage cost percentage?

CASE STUDY

Case Study: Cheating the Customer

Amy Anderson was hired by Water's Edge Restaurant as a waitress and cashier. Shortly after taking the job, she was shocked to overhear an employee bragging to a coworker about shortchanging customers. She confronted the employee, who then snapped back, "Mind your own business. Besides, everyone does it and the customers never miss the money." Amy didn't know how to respond to this aggressive stance.

Your task:

What would be the practical consequences for the food service industry and for consumers if servers and cashiers shortchanged customers at every opportunity?

PART

3

Cost Control
Standards

Planning for Food Profit and Controls

Learning Objectives

After reading this chapter, you should be able to:

- distinguish targeted, potential, and actual costs of food products and identify the components of each;

- determine your targeted ideal cost;

- know the importance of accurate database information for potential costing;

- differentiate between purchase price and yield price;

- apply yield percentage to potential cost;

- derive potential cost using the following techniques:

  - listing and costing out ingredients

  - batch prep recipe costing

  - accompaniment recipe

  - sales mix recipes

- derive actual food cost results;

- understand the following components of actual food cost:

  - cost of food sold to customers

  - cost of food lost through poor purchasing practices

  - cost of food lost in receiving and storage

  - cost of food lost in production process

  - cost of food lost by the front of the house

- using knowledge about actual food cost, control the cost of entrée items.

In Practice

Myla Thomas, the new manager at the Sea Breeze Hotel, took a walk-through visit to the kitchen of the hotel. She saw the cooks busy at work preparing entrées for patrons. One of the cooks took a chit from the printer, read it, and clipped it on an overhead row of clips. He took out a steak and dropped it on

(continues)

(*continued*)

the grill. Meanwhile, he pulled a steak off the grill, added a baked potato to it, put a ladleful of vegetables on the plate, grabbed a chit from the overhead rack, tore it halfway, and set it next to the plate under the heat lamp. "That's exactly the way it should work," Myla thought to herself.

Myla watched as a waiter walked into the kitchen and said to a young cook, "Hey, Eddy! I need a shrimp and chicken pasta number 2."

"Sure thing!" Eddy replied, "Coming right up." Myla could not believe her eyes. No chit came out of the printer for this order. "It's no wonder food cost is higher than potential," she thought. Nevertheless, Eddy promptly walked over to the refrigerator, grabbed a bag of shrimp and some precooked chicken, and started preparing the meal. Myla realized that no sale was recorded for that transaction. She wonders to herself, "How much of a tip is the waiter getting for pulling off this little trick? Or is she just keeping the money for the meal?"

Myla walked over to the salad station. The young woman working at the salad station was busy filling orders coming off the POS printer. After ten minutes, the woman left for a moment. Meanwhile, the waiter walked into the kitchen, went behind the salad station, and opened a cooler. She grabbed a premade shrimp cocktail, took four additional giant shrimp from a pan, added them to the shrimp cocktail, and walked out of the kitchen. Not only was the shrimp cocktail not recorded on the order entry system, but the portion was 50 percent larger than standard, Myla noted.

Myla went to the dessert station and once again observed a young man filling orders based on chits coming out of the POS printer. He set the orders in front of him and put the chit next to the order. Myla observed that he was not tearing the chits halfway to ensure they could not be reused. Meanwhile, a waiter walked in and said, "Michael, I entered three cheesecakes, but another customer at the table decided she would like one too. Give me a fourth cheesecake, and I'll enter it when I get back to the POS station."

"Sure," Michael replied. He cut a slice from the cheesecake and placed it on the counter for the waiter. "I bet that chit never comes out on the printer!" Myla thought. "And where is the manager? It will be interesting to see the difference between target cost, potential cost, and actual cost."

The concepts of targeted, potential, and actual food costs—and their relationships to one another—are the focus of this chapter. Calculating these costs, analyzing the results, and—most importantly—identifying opportunities for controlling expenses are approached from a pragmatic perspective. You will learn how to use these methods in the most practical and fitting fashion for your establishment.

INTRODUCTION TO FOOD PROFITABILITY

Profit is what remains when you subtract expenses from revenue. As economist Joseph A. Schumpeter said, "Profit is the expression of value of what the entrepreneur contributes to the production." We have covered this fundamental role in earlier chapters. To improve your profit, or bottom line as it is sometimes called, management works to maximize revenue and to minimize expenses. Expenses include food costs, labor costs, rent or mortgage payments, utilities, insurance, license fees, advertising, repairs and maintenance, and administrative or general expenses. The company must create—and act upon—a detailed action plan for each of these expenses.

Management's action plans are directed by what is called the profit objective. This is a specific percentage that the company can reasonably expect to earn in profit. The action plan, then, is a specific set of actions to be performed in order to achieve the profit objective. The restaurant manager, controller, food and beverage manager, purchaser, and owner should be involved in setting the profit percentage and in delineating the steps needed to reach it.

targeted ideal cost The ideal amount your company wants to spend; it is your goal, or what you have budgeted to spend.

potential cost The expectation of what the cost should be, if you comply with all cost control procedures. It is the standard whereby you measure the cost efficiency of your operation.

actual cost What you actually spend on the product. The product cost that appears on the profit and loss statement as expenditures.

In this chapter we will discuss one type of expense, which is very much under your control as purchaser: minimizing food cost. In this context, the profit objective will be related to three cost calculations: targeted ideal cost, potential cost, and actual cost. Many computer systems widely used in the industry, such as Foodco, will calculate these figures quickly and accurately. **Targeted ideal cost** means the ideal amount your company wants to spend; it is your goal, or what you have budgeted to spend. **Potential** (or theoretical) **cost** is the calculated expectation of what the cost should be, assuming you comply with all cost control procedures. Finally, **actual cost** is what you actually spend on the product.

All of these new terms can be explained best by using an example, which is illustrated in Figure 10-1. We'll call it Michael's Bistro, and we'll assign it the following income and expense statement for last year.

Figure 10-1 Michael's Bistro

	Actual Dollars	Percent of Sales
SALES		
Food Sales	$325,110	63%
Beverage Sales	$191,060	37%
Total Sales	$516,170	100%
EXPENSES		
Cost of Food Sales	$94,580	29%
Cost of Beverage Sales	$43,944	23%
Total F&B Cost of Sales	$138,524	27%
LABOR		
Payroll Wages	$190,800	37%
Other Payroll Expenses	$51,400	10%
Total Payroll Cost	$242,200	47%
OTHER EXPENSES		
(includes insurance, utilities, general expenses)	$60,600	12%
TOTAL REVENUE	$516,170	100%
TOTAL EXPENSES	$441,324	85%
NET PROFIT	$74,846	15%

To find the actual percentage Michael spent on cost last year, we divided cost by sales. In our example, you can see that this number is 29 percent for food. Now, we'll use this number to calculate our targeted ideal cost.

TARGETED IDEAL COST

Finding the targeted ideal cost is a balancing act. It must not be unrealistically low; nor can it be so high that your company cannot make a profit. The company must set a percentage amount that the owners want in profit, based on how much is needed to stay in business and how much return is expected for the investment. You are going to use that percentage to monitor and evaluate operations. Targets that are impossible to reach will be an endless source of frustration for management and staff.

At Michael's Bistro, the profit last year was 14.5 percent. Michael is forecasting increased business next year because he is located right next to the new convention center. His goal is a profit of 15.5 percent this year. However, Michael knows that increased sales will not mean more profit unless he cuts his percentage of cost. Therefore, Michael's plan is to reduce food and beverage cost by 1.5 percent. Now we can calculate Michael's targeted ideal cost.

First, consider the total sales amount as 100 percent. Next, subtract the percentages of other business expenses, including labor, from that 100 percent. This leaves a percentage that must be divided between two areas: profit and food cost. Subtract the desired profit percentage from this number, and the remaining percentage will be the percentage that can be spend on food. Review how this works in Figure 10-2.

Figure 10-2 Percentage to be Spent

100%	(total sales dollars)
−47%	Less payroll percentages
−12%	Less other expense percentages
=41%	Equals percentage of revenues remaining
−15.5%	Less desired profits
=25.5%	Equals the targeted ideal food and beverage cost percentage

Are those figures—25.5 percent food and beverage cost and 15.5 percent profit objective—realistic? This question is best answered by individual establishments, and the answer depends on individual operation and cost control measures.

As he makes his plan to save that 1.5 percent cost, Michael will need to consider the following possible problem areas:

- The menu prices may be too low or too high.

- He may be spending too much on purchasing goods.

- The chefs may not be preparing the recipes accurately.

- He may be losing money on products that do not yield much after having been prepared in the kitchen.

- His competitors may have more attractive prices or portion sizes.

Suggested Target Percentages

The target percentages you use will be entirely dependent upon your operation. You will need to weigh two competing factors. On one hand, the customer must be assured of sufficient value to warrant their continued business. On the other hand, the company must be assured of sufficient profit. Perhaps in your establishment, lowering prices may draw more business and therefore actually increase your profit. Figure 10-3 offers some target percentages currently in use; however, remember that you cannot take your own percentages from a chart in a book. You will have to calculate them in each establishment given the unique circumstances you face.

Figure 10-3 Suggested Target Percentages

Suggested Target Percentages					
Appetizers	=	20–30%	Breakfast entree	=	23-30%
Mexican food	=	20–28%	Breakfast side order	=	20–30%
Italian food	=	25–33%	Lunch entree	=	27–30%
Children meal	=	30–50%	Lunch side order	=	25–30%
French fries	=	15–20%	Dinner entrees	=	30–40%
Beverage	=	8–15%	Dinner side order	=	27–40%
Soft ice cream	=	15–25%	Salad bar	=	35–45%
Desserts	=	25–30%	Salads	=	25–35%
High profit special	=	20–25%			

We will assume that Michael's targeted ideal food cost percentage of 15.5 is a reasonable expectation, given his restaurant. This gives us a basis from which to work on calculating his menu items' potential cost.

POTENTIAL COST

A potential cost is the expectation of what the food cost should be, if you comply with all cost control procedures. In other words, it is the standard by which you measure the food cost efficiency of your operation. Using your menu recipes, you can easily calculate what each item should cost by adding the costs of each recipe ingredient. You should keep all of this information in your database and update it as prices or menu items change. The difficulty of potential costing is that it does not take into account possible waste, spoilage, or cooking errors. It is the cost of the menu item if nothing is burned, misused, spoiled, or wasted in any way.

You will need to update your potential cost calculations each time you purchase something new, when your product costs change, or when you create a new menu. These updates are important; menu item pricing, updated recipes, and changing ingredient costs will all affect your results. Each of these factors is discussed in upcoming sections.

To figure potential costs, you will want to prepare some data for the potential costing process. Using a computerized inventory system can simplify these tasks, but it can all be done manually as well. In our discussion, we will introduce some of the features of the Foodco system in order to illustrate the steps you will take.

First, you will need to conduct product tests and document the results. These test procedures are detailed in Chapter 4. For example, in a butcher test you and your staff prepare and portion meat, poultry, and seafood products for sale. Prepare, or prep, the products by cleaning and cutting them to specified sizes. Then, portion the products to determine their costs. With this information you will be able to compare products from different vendors and establish your selling prices. This information will also be used in potential costing.

Figure 10-4 is a worksheet that coordinates your data for potential costing. You will need accurate inventory records to begin. From there, we will explain each part of the worksheet, why it is needed, and how to find the right data to include. You will begin to see the difference between purchase price and end-product price: The former affects your inventory calculation, and the latter is used for potential recipe costing.

Starting inventory # ①		Inventory group ②			GL code ③			
	How you purchased the product from your vendor ⓐ			How you inventory a part of a case ⓑ		Recipe breakdown ⓒ		
①	Inventory item description ④	Full case description (how you purchased from vendor) ⑤	Full case cost $ ⑥	Part of case description for inventory purpose ⑦	Number of parts per case ⑧	Unit desc. ⑨	Units per case ⑩	Prep yield % ⑪
	Beef tenderloin	Case = 1 pound	$6.69	Pound	1	WZ	16	65.50%
3245	Carrots baby	case=1/24ct	$14.70	count	24	ct	24	100.00%
4024	Celery pascal	case=1/24ct	$11.51	count	24	ct	24	100.00%
3223	Onion red	case=1/25#	$11.20	pound	25	wz	400	100.00%
3208	Squash yellow	case=20#	$8.64	pound	20	wz	320	100.00%
3207	Squash zucchini fresh	case=20#	$10.56	pound	20	wz	320	100.00%
3856	Broccoli florrette iceless	case=4/3#	$13.63	count	4	wz	192	100.00%
3218	Cauliflower florette	case=2/3#	$10.66	count	2	wz	96	100.00%
4220	Base vegetarian	case=6/2#	$82.75	count	6	wz	192	100.00%
4227	Tomato puree	case=6/#10can	$16.50	count	6	wz	660	100.00%
4532	Spice thyme ground	case=6/11oz	$33.59	count	6	wz	66	100.00%
4688	Spice basil sweet leaf	case=1/5.5oz	$4.96	count	1	wz	5.5	100.00%
4659	Spice pepper grnd. black	case=1/5#	$28.48	count	1	wz	80	100.00%
4452	Salt bulk	case=1/25#	$3.20	pound	25	wz	400	100.00%

Figure 10-4 Inventory Worksheet

The numbers in Figure 10-4 are only examples; you will soon learn how to conduct your own yield tests and to complete this form on your own. The worksheet contains eleven fields or areas to fill out. We will go through each one and show how this sheet works. Steps 1 through 8, which describe the different phases of recording inventory items, form the foundation for the yield test results in Steps 9 through 11.

1. *Inventory Number (#)*. All inventory items should have a number to identify the items in the inventory and to control their use. The numbers here are just examples; your numbering system will depend on your company.

2. *Inventory Group.* Each item is assigned to a group. In this case, the items are in the food group, since we are dealing with potential costing for food. For beverages this would be classified under the beverage group.

3. *General Ledger Code (GL).* This code provides internal tracking information when you receive a product from a vendor. It is also used in accounting to pay invoices by designating an account number to the group of items. The numbers may be designated for you by your computer system, or you may be able to input codes you have devised.

In Columns 4, 5, and 6, you will use information from your vendors' invoices. This information is included on the worksheet to set the stage for comparing the vendor's raw products with their yield. These three related columns are grouped together as *How you purchased the food from the vendor,* Group A.

4. *Inventory Item Description.* Simply write the product name in this column. In our example, we use beef tenderloin and several produce items. Note that the descriptions begin with the generic name, such as *beef* or *carrots,* and then are followed by more specific descriptions, such as *tenderloin* and *baby.* Always listing them in this way makes it easier to locate and categorize the items correctly.

5. *Full Case Description.* This column describes what a standard full case contains when it comes from the vendor. You may need this number for future calculations. Most entrée items, such as beef, are purchased by the pound. Therefore, the case description in this instance is 1 pound of beef tenderloin.

6. *Full Case Cost ($).* What you pay the vendor for one full case is recorded here. For the beef tenderloin, we show $6.69 per pound.

Columns 7 and 8 describe how to inventory a *partial* case. These two columns comprise the chart's Group B. The information in these columns is used in the inventory, ordering, and receiving phases.

7. *Partial Case Description.* The information in this column describes how you inventory a partial case when taking a physical inventory. This can be done in a number of different ways, as not all vendors have the same packaging sizes on like items. For example, a case could equal four 5-pound blocks or eight 3-pound blocks.

8. *Number of Parts Per Case.* This column lists the number of partial units per case. This information is used to calculate cost breakdown on a part of a case. For instance, in our example a case of 1-pound beef tenderloin costs $6.69. When you record the parts per case, it will record the pound cost at $6.69. This will be different if you are calculating for a case of cans of tomato purée. In our example above, the case costs $16.50 and the number of parts is six; this, then, will record the cost at $2.75 per case part.

The third division of the chart, Group C, deals with your recipe breakdown. This refers to how many recipe units (such as ounces, counts, or teaspoons) you get per case, and how much they cost. As we saw in Chapter 4, you lose some of your product whenever you prepare it. This is unavoidable, but it can be minimized—and you are just the person to make sure this happens.

9. *Recipe Unit Description.* The recipe unit is the measuring unit from your recipe. The following units are typically used in the industry. A more extensive list is included in Appendix.

	Unit	Abbreviation	Examples
A.	weight ounce	(WZ)	meats, onions
B.	fluid ounce	(FZ)	soft drinks, milk
C.	count	(CT)	eggs, napkins
D.	teaspoon	(TS)	spices
E.	portion	(PR)	prep recipes, sales mix

Below are examples of common equivalent amounts. Again, see Appendix for a more complete list.

Common Unit Name	Abbreviation	Equivalent
pound	WZ	16 WZ per pound
gallon	FZ	128 FZ per gallon
#10 can	FZ	105 FZ per #10 can
quart	FZ	32 FZ per quart

10. *Recipe Units Per Full Case.* The number of recipe units per full case tells you exactly how many weight or fluid ounces, teaspoons, or counts of an item come in a case. For example, there are 400 weight ounces of onions in a 25-pound case. This may not be simple for every item. For example, a case of sliced pickles may contain 2,640 slices (CT), or a case of tomato sauce may have 6 #10 cans at 105 FZ per can, giving you a total of 630 FZ for all 6 cans. You may occasionally need to refer to a conversion table or measuring scales in order to determine the number of recipe units per case.

From these recipe units, you can break down the case cost and calculate the potential recipe unit cost. The potential recipe unit cost is also affected by Column 11, as follows:

11. *Prep Yield Percentage.* This last column lists your prep yield percentages for each item. You will find the process for calculating these percentages in Chapter 4. For our purposes here, you simply need to know that this is the yield (how much usable product you end up with after preparation) divided by the total purchase amount. In our example, beef tenderloin has a yield percentage of 65.5. The original, as-purchased price of $6.69, multiplied by this yield percentage, becomes an end-product price of $10.21 per pound.

It is important to note the different uses of the as-purchased price and the end-product or yield price. The as-purchased price is your inventory cost and is not altered by yield percentages. However, the end-product price and recipe unit cost calculations must take the yield percentage into consideration. In our beef tenderloin example, the computation of recipe cost requires the use of the yield percentage ($6.69/pound × 65.5 percent = $10.21/pound). The other recipe items were based on 100 percent for illustration, but the $6.69 as-purchased price is used when computing inventory costs.

Most food products have a predictable and measurable amount of shrinkage or waste. Produce, meat, and seafood are examples of such products. Most inventory items in these groups go through many stages of preparation before they become finished menu items. They might be thawed, trimmed, peeled, cooked, boiled, fried, baked, or made into equal portions. The yield percentage thus reflects the subtraction of waste, by-product, or evaporation to derive your usable yield. Appendix provides a list of tested industry averages for these percentages. However, it is recommended that you conduct your own tests rather than relying completely on industry guides.

actual recipe unit cost
The cost of each ingredient in a menu.

The prep yield percentage is also used to figure your **actual recipe unit cost**. In this way, your recipe costs will automatically factor in the prep yield percentage and raise or lower the recipe unit cost accordingly. This will allow you to compare actual costs between vendors or between products with different yields. This process is ongoing; as you update your yield percentages with new products and vendors, you also need to alter your menu item prices. This will ensure that when you perform potential costing, you get accurate and verifiable costs.

Conducting Food Potential Costing

Use this new item cost information to build your potential recipe costs. We will use vegetable soup and a recipe flowchart to demonstrate the process. For example, suppose you make this vegetable soup in 20-gallon batches and sell it in 12-fluid-ounce (FZ) portions. You need to convert that 20-gallon recipe to a menu recipe for the 12-FZ portion. Here is how this is done:

1. List your ingredients and their units. The chef will list the preprep recipe items (for instance, the zucchini must be sliced or the onion must be diced).

2. Write down the large-batch prep recipe; in this case it is for 20 gallons of vegetable soup.

3. Write down the prep recipes for any accompaniments for the soup, such as the plate garnish, rolls and butter, and so on.

4. Write what are called your sales-mix prep recipes. These are used when the customer is selecting among items such as different soups, salad dressings, or types of potatoes.

These functions are typically performed by the chef and the cost controller in a larger organization. However, in a smaller establishment the chef him- or herself may be responsible for all steps. Now we will go into detail about each of these processes.

List Ingredients and Their Units

Figure 10-5 is an example of a preprep recipe worksheet, listing the ingredients for vegetable soup. The worksheet is used to define and record recipes for menu items. Following the example is an explanation of the terminology for each area on the worksheet. The chef will need one worksheet for each recipe he or she writes.

We talked briefly about the inventory numbering system. A good practice is to use a similar recipe-numbering system that rationally connects the sets of items. This section will use the same format established in the inventory example above. The numbering sequence should be determined by the type of recipe.

1. *Item Number.* In a computerized system, this number will be generated automatically, and you can set categories. For example, the numbering of prep recipes might begin with P100, while menu item recipes might start with M100, for identification and control purposes.

2. *Is the Item Active?* An active item is one that is being used presently. Remove seasonal items from reports when they are not currently being used.

3. *Item Description.* The item description is the name of the recipe for which you are establishing a potential cost. In this case it is vegetable soup.

1. Item number:	100	2. Item active:	YES NO
3. Item description:	Vegetable soup	4. Revenue department:	Food
5. Prep location:	Main kitchen	6. Saleable:	YES NO

7. G.L. account #:	100-125	8. Period tracking:	DAILY MID MAIN
9. Batch size:	20 gallons	10. Recipe group:	Soup

11. Ingredient item number	12. Ingredient Item description	13. Number of recipe units	14. Recipe unit description wz,lb,fz,cup, pint,qt,gal,ct
3245	Carrots baby	12	ct
4024	Celery pascal	4	ct
3223	Onion red	6	oz
3208	Squash yellow	12	oz
3207	Squash zucchini fresh	12	oz
3856	Broccoli florrette iceless	48	oz
3218	Cauliflower florette	32	oz
4220	Base vegetarian	1	fz
4227	Tomato puree	1	oz
4532	Spice thyme ground	16	oz
4688	Spice basil sweet leaf	8	oz
4659	Spice pepper grnd. black	16	oz
4452	Salt bulk	16	oz

Figure 10-5 Prep Recipe Worksheet 1

4. *Revenue Group.* Each item needs to be assigned to a revenue group so you can track actual usage by department. In this case, the revenue group is food.

5. *Prep Location.* This identifies the prep location, or where the recipe is used, for companies with multiple locations. This helps new employees, transferred personnel, and others who might not be familiar with the item.

6. *Is it Salable?* Prep recipes are not salable (able to be sold), while menu item recipes are. Circle YES or NO to correspond with the item's status. This is used to determine whether this item will be counted when you report sales.

7. *GL Account Number.* This space lists a general ledger (GL) account number to which the expenses for this item should be assigned. The **general ledger** is where the accounting department records all the financial accounts for a business. The ledger contains debits and credits. Debits are all the costs and expenses of your business. Credits, on the other hand, consist of all revenue, assets, and other income. Your company will assign several GL account numbers to your department, and you will determine how to charge your purchases to them.

general ledger The formal listing of accounts (ledger) containing all the financial statement accounts of a business. Every transaction flows through it.

8. *Tracking Period.* In many operations, the tracking period is used to state the period of time used when tracking an item's usage. Circle *daily* to indicate that the item is tracked every 24 hours, *mid* if the item is tracked semimonthly, or *main* for a standard

accounting period, usually one month. Typically, items that are most expensive or are used most frequently are tracked more frequently.

9. *Batch Size.* The batch size is the total amount produced by a recipe. In our example it is 20 gallons. You should prepare the item to measure the accuracy of the batch size.

10. *Recipe Group.* Recipe groups are categories of recipes used to control and report what is made and sold. In this case, the category is soup; you might also have categories such as appetizers, entrées, side dishes, and desserts.

11. *Ingredient Item Number.* The ingredient item number is the same code number used in the inventory worksheet above for the purpose of identifying and tracking specific ingredient use.

12. *Ingredient Item Description.* Again as in the inventory worksheet, the ingredient item description is simply the name of the ingredient. It is listed with the generic name first, followed by any specific types: *spice/cinnamon stick* or *berries/raspberries.*

13. *Number of Recipe Units.* Record here the number of units for each item used in the recipe.

14. *Recipe Unit Description.* The recipe unit description will be WZ, FZ, CT, or TS depending on whether the inventory item is measured in weight ounces, fluid ounces, unit counts, or teaspoons. Your establishment may use other measures and designations besides these four.

Write Down the Large Batch Prep Recipe

Our next task is to determine the cost of the 20-gallon batch of vegetable soup. Batch prep recipes are those made in large quantities. Since we are making more than one serving, there may be left-over product that needs to be inventoried. That is one reason batch prep recipes carry inventory numbers—because these inventory items will then be used as "ingredients" in menu item recipes.

To continue with our example, we will extend the table to include costs. Each field of information represents an important function in the process. When filling out these worksheets, you should gather all of the information before you enter it into the computer or manual spreadsheets. You'll see how the unit costs are determined by this equation:

Unit cost = UC

Case cost = c

Yield percentage = y

Unit per case = u

$$UC = \frac{c/y}{u}$$

The same could be express as follows:

$$\frac{\text{case costs } / \text{ yield percentages}}{\text{units per case}}$$

All this data comes from the inventory worksheet (Figure 10-5). If you are using a computer system such as Foodco, this can be automatically calculated by the system. Alternatively, you can complete the computations manually; all of the equations are defined here for your use. Figure 10-6 is an example of how you would derive a vegetable soup recipe.

Items 1 to 14 on this chart are the same as those on the prep recipe worksheet; we are simply adding costs.

15. *Unit Cost.* To determine **unit cost**, take the case cost of an item and divide it by the yield percentage. Then divide that result by the number of recipe units per case

unit cost Cost per item.

1. Item number:	100		2. Item active:		Y/N			
3. Item description:	Vegetable soup		4. Revenue department:		Food			
5. Prep location:	Main kitchen		6. Saleable:		Y/N			

7. G.L. account #:	100-125	8. Period tracking:	DAILY MID MAIN

9. Batch size:	20 gallons	10. Recipe group: soup

11. Ingredient item number	12. Ingredient Item description	13. Number of recipe units	14. Recipe unit description wz,lb,fz,cup, pint,qt,gal,ct	15	16	17
				Unit cost $	Total cost $	Cost %
3245	Carrots baby	12	ct	0.612	7.35	18.96%
4024	Celery pascal	4	ct	0.48	1.918	4.95%
3223	Onion red	6	oz	0.028	0.17	0.44%
3208	Squash yellow	12	oz	0.027	0.323	0.83%
3207	Squash zucchini fresh	12	oz	0.033	0.399	1.03%
3856	Broccoli florrette iceless	48	oz	0.071	3.397	8.76%
3218	Cauliflower florette	32	oz	0.111	3.567	9.20%
4220	Base vegetarian	1	fz	0.431	0.431	1.11%
4227	Tomato puree	1	oz	0.025	0.025	0.06%
4532	Spice thyme ground	16	oz	0.509	8.15	21.02%
4688	Spice basil sweet leaf	8	oz	0.902	7.215	18.61%
4659	Spice pepper grnd. black	16	oz	0.356	5.696	14.69%
4452	Salt bulk	16	oz	0.008	0.134	0.35%
	Potential Cost: for 20 gallons of vegetable soup			$	38.775	100%

Figure 10-6 Batch Inventory Worksheet

(Column 10 on the inventory worksheet). That gives you the cost per teaspoon, count, weight ounce, or fluid ounce. For example, assuming that celery/pascal per our inventory worksheet yields 100 percent, the unit cost of $0.48 is derived as follows:

$$\frac{\$11.51/1}{24} = 48 \text{ cents}$$

16. *Total Cost.* Next, multiply the unit cost (Column 15) by the number of units needed for the recipe (Column 13). For example, 4 counts of celery/pascal are multiplied by the unit cost of $0.48 to derive $1.92. Once you do that for all the ingredients, total all these amounts. The result is the total cost of the 20-gallon batch, or $38.80

17. *Cost Percentage.* The cost percentages are proportions of the cost of each item to the cost of the whole. Divide an item's total cost by the total batch cost to get this percentage (Column 17). If management is considering trimming down the ingredient in the recipe, a review of cost percentage is the first step.

The last step is to divide the total batch cost into individual portion sizes. At 12-ounce portions, there are 213.33 portions in 20 gallons. Here is the equation:

128 wz/gal × 20 gal = 2560 wz/batch

2560 wz/batch/12 wz portions = 213.33 portions/batch.

Then we divide the total cost ($38.775) by 213.33 servings to get our cost, $0.18

Assume the accompaniment price is $0.20 for bread and butter, and we sell this whole meal for $2.00. We will make a one-serving worksheet as our example in Figure 10-7.

1. Item number:	102		2. Item active:		YES	NO
3. Item description:	Vegetable soup		4. Revenue department:		Food	
5. Prep location:	Main kitchen		6. Saleable:		YES	NO

7. G.L. account #:	100-125	8. Period tracking:	DAILY MID MAIN
9. Batch size:	12 ounce/1 serving	10. Recipe group:	Soup

11. Ingredient item number	12. Ingredient Item description	13. Number of recipe units	14. Recipe units wz,lb,fz,cup, pint,qt,gal,ct	15 Unit cost $	16 Total cost $	17 Cost %
L103	Vegetable soup	12	wz	$0.015	$0.182	9.10%
L104	Bread and butter	1	ct	$0.200	$0.200	10.00%

	Potential vegetable soup cost:		$0.382
18	Menu price:		$2.00
19	Potential percentages:		19.10%
20	Target food cost:		20.00%
21	Ideal menu price:		$1.91

Figure 10-7 One-serving Recipe Costing Worksheet

For Numbers 1 to 17, the terms used are the same. Now, however, we are treating a menu item as a recipe and the components of the meal as ingredients. Then we add a new set of steps, Numbers 18 to 21, that will specify the cost of the whole menu item.

18. *Menu Price.* In our example, we set the menu price at $2.00.

potential percentage
Determined by dividing the cost by the selling price.

19. *Potential Percentage.* **Potential percentage** is determined by dividing the cost (in our example, $0.38) by the selling price, $2.00. This percentage may be valuable in comparing your actual cost to this ideal cost. With such comparisons, you can evaluate how well you have been following control procedures.

20. *Targeted Food Cost:* We set 20 percent as our targeted food cost for the soup menu item above. This is the food cost percentage we wanted to achieve for the soup.

21. *Ideal Menu Price.* This is the calculated price goal. Derive the ideal menu price by dividing the cost of ingredients by the targeted cost percentage. In our example, this comes to $1.91—but we are charging $2.00, so the price has a cushion of about 1 percent. Maintaining this cushion is prudent because at this point management is not aware of waste and other negative factors that may influence the actual cost of the menu items.

Write Down Prep Recipes for Any Accompaniments

An accompaniment is something served alongside an entrée. In our example, the soup accompaniments are bread and butter, assumed to cost $0.20. An accompaniment prep recipe looks like other recipe worksheets, except that it contains only the accompanying items and their unit costs. Plate garnishes fall into this category as well.

Many accompaniments go with more than just one meal; for example, bread and butter might also go with a roast beef, meat loaf, chicken, or steak dinner. Thus, you can use this accompaniment prep recipe over and over. Using one set of accompaniments for several menu items will save you time in completing and updating your potential cost recipes. When you change the costs on one sheet, the change will apply to all the meals to which the accompaniment recipe pertains.

In addition to bread and butter, several accompaniments and garnishes (left column, Figure 10-8) can be added to multiple entrées (right column).

In this chart, you can see an important new term: **sales mix**. The quantities of each item you sell will affect your potential costing; these quantities, in relation to one another, are called your sales mix.

sales mix Number of sales of menu items; perhaps patternized. Also, the products and sales packages offered.

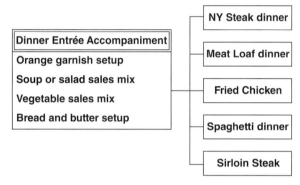

Figure 10-8 Dinner Accompaniment

Sales Mix Prep Recipe

The last type of prep recipe is called the sales mix recipe. This is a special type of prep recipe that allow you to account for cost fluctuations that happen when customers choose from a variety of items in varying quantities. Ideally, your **point of sale**, or **POS, system** will handle this for you; if your system does not have the capacity to do this, however, most menu-analysis systems (such as Foodco) will allow you to make an educated guess. This kind of guessing is adequate for potential-costing tasks.

point-of-sale (POS) system A sales transaction register and processor.

There are several different types of sales mix recipes that you may need to establish. The first type is used for items that are included with a meal but may change on a daily basis. Since soup selections change frequently, for example, you must determine the percentage of sales for each type of soup.

In this type of sales mix recipe, all the ingredients in the sales mix use the same unit of measure. This means that when you set up these recipes for soups or salad dressings, for example, each item will be measured by the fluid ounce (FZ). By setting up sales mix recipes with that measurement, you will have a much easier time determining and comparing the percentages of the products. It will also be easier to adjust the sales mix recipes when needed because the percentage of customer-selected choices will often change. Note, however, that you only need to make sales mix recipes if your POS cannot track which products are used when you offer such choices. Salad dressings might be one example of this situation. Figure 10-9 shows an example of a salad dressing sales mix recipe.

In Figure 10-9, we are using the following percentages as an example: thousand island dressing is used 15 percent of the time, blue cheese 35 percent, French 10 percent, and ranch

1. Item number:	106	2. Item active:	YES NO
3. Item description:	Dressing sales mix	4. Revenue Group:	Food
5. Prep location:	Main kitchen	6. Saleable:	YES NO

7. G.L. account #:	100-125	8. Period tracking:	DAILY MID MAIN
9. Batch size:	1 FZ	10. Recipe group:	Sales mix

11. Ingredient Item number	12. Ingredient Item description	13. Percentage of recipe units	14. Recipe unit wz,lb,fz,cup, pint,qt,gal,ct
200	Dressing Thousand Island	0.15	fz
201	Dressing Bleu Cheese	0.35	fz
202	Dressing French	0.10	fz
203	Dressing Ranch	0.40	fz

Figure 10-9 Prep Recipe Worksheet 2

⑪ Discussion Point

Is it a good idea to build a small percentage of waste into potential costs, since some minor waste is inevitable? Why or why not?

40 percent, for a total of 100 percent. When you use a dressing in a menu item, just enter the number of fluid ounces.

In a perfect world the potential cost will equal the actual cost, but as there is no such thing as a perfect world, there will always be some differences between potential cost and actual cost. It is up to you and management to reduce this difference to acceptable profit-objective levels. It is with this in mind that we discuss the term *actual cost*.

ACTUAL FOOD COST

Actual cost is a fairly self-explanatory term: Actual food cost is how much you actually spend on food. This is the amount that will show up on your profit and loss statement. In Chapter 1 we presented a restaurant industry sales chart prepared by the National Restaurant Association. The chart revealed actual cost percentages from different types of restaurants. As you may remember, the most prominent cost was food cost percentages. As you saw in the chart, there are many expenses in doing business; some are controllable, while others are not. Actual food cost is the most controllable and flexible cost. It consists of the following five areas:

- *Cost of Food Sold to Customers.* This is equal to your potential cost.

- *Cost of Food Lost through Poor Purchasing Practices.* This includes incorrect items ordered or incorrect orders due to poor quality, inappropriate quantity, or other incorrect purchase specification.

- *Cost of Food Lost in Receiving and Storage.* This includes spoilage, theft from the receiving dock, theft from storage, short shipments, and improper receiving procedures.

- *Cost of Food Lost in Production.* This includes inaccurate yield tests, inaccurate recipes, overportioning, overproduction, and waste.

- *Cost of Food Lost by the Front of the House.* This includes incorrect orders, spills, and broken orders.

There are innumerable ways to affect your actual food cost percentage. You may think the process looks complicated, but it is really a combination of common sense and following practical steps. First you calculate the cost of goods used, as follows:

beginning inventory
+ purchases
+/− requisitions and transfers
− ending inventory
= cost of goods used

Let's work through an example. Assume your beginning food inventory is $1,000. You have purchased $600 of goods and transferred $100 between departments. Your ending inventory is $950. Calculate actual food cost according to Figure 10-10. (Note: Some food cost adjustments are a bit more complex; these will be covered in the chapter on monthly inventory and monthly actual food cost, Chapter 11.)

Figure 10-10 Cost of Goods Used

Beginning inventory	1,000
Plus purchases	600
Plus (or minus) net requisitions and transfers	100
Total inventory before ending inventory	1,700
Minus ending inventory	950
Cost of goods consumed or used	**750**

The second step is to determine your food sales. Let us assume that your records show $2,500 in food sales. Now you can calculate your actual cost of goods, as follows:

$$\text{actual food cost} = \frac{\text{cost of goods}}{\text{sales}} = \frac{750}{2,500} = 30\%$$

It is actually quite simple to derive actual food cost percentages. Now we have the challenge of finding out why this actual food cost differs from the potential cost. For instance, assume that the sales figure of $2,500 is equal to selling 100 pounds of prime rib at $25 per pound. But what if you actually used 120 pounds? If you bought the prime rib at $6 per pound, you spent $120 more than necessary, and you lost potential sales of $500. If you do not control this type of loss, the problem will grow and you will be left wondering why. Any one of the forms of loss above could be affecting your loss dramatically; we will now examine each one.

Cost of Food Sold to Customers

This is the only legitimate reason for incurring food cost. The cost of food sold to customers is equal to the potential cost. Anything you spend over and above this is loss. According to the National Restaurant Association, 26 percent of restaurants foreclose each year due to lack of planning and effective cost control. Potential costing gives you an excellent basis against which to measure your success. Then you can analyze where your costs are out of control and fix them. If you account for your sales correctly, and your costing data are accurate, any food cost discrepancies will result from one or more of the factors discussed below.

⑪ **Discussion Points**

1. What are the causes of variances between potential and actual costs?

2. If the actual food cost percentage equals the target food cost percentage set by management, but exceeds the potential food cost percentage, is there a problem? If you were the owner of the operation, what would you suggest?

Cost of Food Lost through Poor Purchasing Practices

Purchasers must follow their own set of specifications in ordering, as discussed in Chapter 4. Loss can occur through this department if purchasers order product that cannot be used, for example. If too much product is ordered, the department loses money in waste and spoilage. If too little is ordered, guest satisfaction can be compromised. It is vital to monitor what and how much is purchased using detailed purchase specifications.

The significance of accurate yield test results cannot be overstated when it comes to food cost controls. If your yield result is not accurate, the information needed for purchasing at the right price and for establishing menu prices is called into question. The primary tenet of cost control is this: *know your cost*. Accurate yield test results will ensure that you are working from the correct cost structure as you plan and implement actions to save money. Take beef tenderloin as an example. Suppose the yield result is actually 40 percent, rather than the recorded 65.5 percent, and assume that the menu price is $30.00. For this example we will also assume that the cost of other ingredients equals $4.00. We already know that the original purchase price was $6.69, and the yield percentage cost was $10.21. We will make the calculation in Figure 10-11.

Figure 10-11 Purchasing Specifications

line		Correct Yield Test at 40%	Incorrect Yield Test at 65.5%
1	Menu Price	$30.00	$30.00
2	Less yield test cost ($6.69 divided by %)	$16.73	$10.21
3	Less other ingredient cost	$4.00	$4.00
4	Total cost (line 2 plus line 3)	$20.73	$14.21
5	Cost percentage (line 4 divided by line 1)	69.10%	47.37%
6	Profit margin (line 1 minus line 4)	$9.27	$15.79

There is a great deal of difference when the yield percentage is distorted even minimally. The company could easily run into financial difficulties if all menu items reflect this kind of inaccuracy.

Cost of Food Lost in Receiving and Storage

You will need to follow all proper receiving procedures from this book to monitor incoming product, to check its value, to extend prices, and to document product movement through the company from the storage dock to the customer's plate. When a company does not adhere to these procedures consistently, unusable or incorrect products slip through—and end up as loss. On the other hand, shipments may not contain everything that was ordered and paid for; this, too, is a loss. Meat cuts, weights, prices, and purchase specifications must be verified for accuracy and compliance with each and every shipment.

The storeroom must be constantly reviewed to see which products need to be used before spoiling. If not kept to a minimum, spoilage can cost a company tremendously. Storeroom personnel must practice proper product rotation to ensure that items are used in a logical and timely manner.

Theft is an industry-wide cost concern. It is alarmingly common and extremely costly to the company. Shipments must be monitored from entry to exit. Even the receiving dock is an unstable location, as are unstaffed storage areas. Every time a product is removed, it must be documented—who took which product, in what quantities, to which outlet or kitchen. Another avenue thieves commonly use is the trash can, in which they might throw whole goods in order to sneak them out of the building. Use clear trash-can liners to make this scheme easier to spot. High-cost meats and seafood are especially vulnerable; in the next sections we will introduce two forms that can help you monitor these items in an organized manner.

Cost of Food Lost in Production

A study conducted by Foodco reveals that between 22 and 25 percent of food cost variance is the result of food lost in kitchen production. In Chapter 1, the Sea Breeze Hotel Food and Beverage Division reported a profit of only 2 percent. The low food and beverage profit was due to high cost: Cost of sales was 38 percent.

When controlling cost, you must set values for your menu items. To be able to do so, you must be sure that each item will be prepared at the same cost each time it is prepared. This calls for great consistency on the part of the kitchen staff. Consistent portion size is critical; put into place measures to standardize portion size. The use of standard portion controls also ensures that the guest receives a consistent product. You will want to display standard portion instructions and photographs in the kitchen and butcher shop areas for constant reference. It is helpful to post exact weights and counts for each item. The restaurant manager needs to enforce consistent presentation; every meal must be prepared to meet your standard specifications. The advantages are twofold; both staff and guests will benefit. Both management and employees will be satisfied for the following reasons:

- Food cost is maintained at a consistent level. A cheeseburger meal will always have the same amount of meat, cheese, and fries per serving, and will therefore cost the same each time.

- Employees will be trained in consistency, so no one feels less qualified for each task. This promotes morale because employees can say, "I know how," and demonstrate it.

- Standard portion control helps management with their documentation efforts. Management can tell the staff why portion control is important and show them some of the data affected by consistency.

- Putting photographs of the meals in the work area facilitates employee referencing and helps to maintain consistent presentation.

- Preparation and serving are easier because they are the same at all times. This translates to faster service, and the staff can be certain that what they promise a guest is what the guest will receive.

Customers will also be more satisfied, for the following reasons:

- They will receive the same portion size for the same menu item each time they come to your restaurant. Even new customers might notice if people at the next table get twice as many fries as they did.

- They will see the restaurant as reliable, uniform, and consistent. They will know what to expect, and they will know what they can afford.

Controlling Entrée Items

It is vital to monitor high-cost entrée items after they have been issued to the outlet kitchens. The purpose of controlling expensive inventory is to monitor the issue and return of such items to and from the butcher shop and through interdepartmental transfers. All high-cost food categories, such as prime cuts of meat, poultry, fish, and seafood, should be tracked in this way. Whole pieces of cooked or raw meat, such as prime rib, tenderloin, and strip loin, should be monitored by weight. Items such as steaks, fish, and seafood that have not yet been portioned should be counted by their units. Items in boxes, such as scampi, are controlled by how many are in each box, or yield per box. One way you can control these items more exactly is by having an independent person perform audits on the process with the chef or the butcher. In a large operation, this person could be the accountant or the cost controller. Figure 10-12 is an example of the form you would use. The chef or butcher and independent auditor should complete this form for each outlet, each day. The following list describes what information goes in each row; the quantities are examples only.

1 CHEF _____   4 OUTLET _____
2 COVER FORECAST _____
3 DATE _____

| 5 ITEM | FILET | FILET | NY STRIP | RIBEYE | PRIME RIB | VEAL CHOP | LOBSTER TAIL |
6	12 OZ	8 OZ	16 OZ	16 OZ	12 OZ	8 OZ	10 OZ
7 BEGINNING INVENTORY	5	3					
8 ORDER AMOUNT	10	15					
9 OPENING INVENTORY	15	18					
10 ADDITIONS	2	3					
11 TOTAL AVAILABLE	17	21					
12 CLOSING INVENTORY	3	5					
13 AMOUNT USED	14	16					
14 POS # SOLD	13	16					
15 VARIANCE	1	0					
16 COMMENTS	One 12 ounce of filet was returned due to over-cooking, and was replaced						

Figure 10-12 Entrée Control Form

1. The name of the person or persons filling out the form.

2. The number of meals, or covers, expected for the meal period.

3. The date.

4. The outlet name, for operations that have more than one.

5. The cut of meat. These can be preprinted, as in our sample, if you have standard offerings.

6. The portion size. These can also be preprinted.

7. The outlet's beginning inventory.

8. The amount that arrived in the day's order or requisition.

9. The amount available when the outlet opens.

10. Any other additions during the meal period.

11. The total available inventory.

12. The inventory after the close of business.

13. Line 11 minus line 12; how much was actually used.

14. The number actually sold during the meal period. Get this information from your POS system, if you have one, or from a manual tally.

15. The difference between lines 13 and 14; this will show any discrepancy that should be investigated.

16. The variance from line 15 should be explained here, if possible.

17. The second form, Figure 10-13, is analogous to the Entrée Control Form. This requisition should include the following data, entered by the butcher or the chef:

1 CHEF _____   **3 OUTLET** _____

2 DATE _____

	ITEM	FILET 12 OZ	FILET 8 OZ	NY STRIP 16 OZ	RIBEYE 16 OZ	PRIME RIB 16 OZ	VEAL CHOP 8 OZ	LOBSTER TAIL 10 OZ
4	ITEM	FILET	FILET	NY STRIP	RIBEYE	PRIME RIB	VEAL CHOP	LOBSTER TAIL
5		12 OZ	8 OZ	16 OZ	16 OZ	16 OZ	8 OZ	10 OZ
6	QUANTITY USED							
7	QUANTITY RETURNED							
	OPENING INVENTORY							
8	TOTAL AVAILABLE							
	CLOSING INVENTORY							
9	AMOUNT USED							
10	ACTUAL SOLD							
11	VARIANCE							
12	COMMENTS							

Figure 10-13 Butcher Requisition

1. The name of the person or persons filling out the form.

2. The date the meat is issued to the outlet.

3. The name of the outlet to which the items were issued (each outlet should have its own sheet).

4. The description of the cut of meat; these can be preprinted.

5. The portion size. These can be preprinted as well.

6. The quantity of each item issued to the outlet throughout the day.

7. The quantity of items returned the next day.

Then the accountant or cost controller enters the following information:

8. The sum of all inventory in a Total Available column.

9. Total available minus closing inventory; the amount used.

10. The actual quantity sold, according to the POS daily sales tape.

11. Quantity used minus actual quantity sold; the variance.

12. Brief descriptive comments, if necessary. The accountant should attempt to reconcile all variances.

From these controls, particularly from the comments, you can get an idea of where to focus your cost control efforts in the area of production losses.

Inaccurate Recipes

Another factor affecting production losses is recipe accuracy. Each recipe must be both tested and standardized. Ingredient specifications and amounts must be exact and must delineate the proper sequence of steps. This also helps to ensure consistency, so that the product comes out of the kitchen the same every time, regardless of who prepares it. You can use the prep and menu item recipe formats from the potential costing worksheets presented earlier in this chapter. Using different ingredients, amounts, or steps can create an excessive cost to the company: consistency and guest satisfaction are compromised, cost calculations are thrown off, and the end result could be completely wasted product. Most operations achieve recipe consistency through the following actions:

- Conducting test recipes for all items

- Placing recipe cards where chefs and servers can always use them

- Displaying photos of what each plate should look like

- Conducting menu tastings on a regular but random basis with all staff members

- Training staff to recognize inconsistencies and to appreciate standard methods

Controlling Waste

Waste is defined as any ill-considered or thoughtless food expenditure without valuable results. It is sometimes an inadvertent or inevitable loss without equivalent gain in food cost. Waste might take the form of spoilage, breakage, or spillage. In addition, production and preparation might not meet your standards. Take the simple case of an onion, for example: The yield factor will be affected by how many layers the cook removes in preparation. What difference will that make? It depends on how many onions you use, and how much of each onion is lost.

Keep an eye on your garbage cans to monitor how much is wasted there. Studies show that waste accounts for 15 percent of total solid trash, and your business has to pay to have that removed—a further loss. It is a worthwhile money-saving endeavor to keep an eye on your trash.

Increasing public concern about the environment lends additional impetus to the issue of waste. Crowded landfills do not need the food and beverage industry's excess. In some cases, waste can be used profitably. For example, residues from frying oil have some market value in the cosmetic industry. Although this does not translate into dramatic food cost savings, at least you can take advantage of an environmentally sound outlet for your otherwise wasteful products.

Waste is a part of production cost, and it should be reported as such. The amount may vary from time to time and from one employee to another, depending on experience with the product. Waste might also be attributable to defects in the products themselves. Though waste cannot be totally eliminated, management control efforts can have a positive impact. Reporting losses will at least show you the areas you need to focus on. Also, you can ask staff members how to control waste problems. This gets them involved and might provide you with innovative solutions. Figure 10-14 is a form commonly used to report products wasted through breakage, spoilage, or spillage. Management should require staff members to use this form or one like it. From this form the manager should determine the unit cost of what was lost, multiply that cost by the lost quantity, and keep records of each loss incident.

As indicated above, waste can also be due to product defects; if so, call it to the attention of the vendor. Depending on how severely the defects affect your food cost, you may wish to consult with vendors by using the questionnaire shown in Figure 10-15. In this way, you can solicit

TO BE USED FOR AUTHORIZING ALL SPILLAGE, BREAKAGE AND SPOILAGE

DATE: _____

AUTHORIZATION: _____

OUTLET: _____

Person Reporting Loss	Item Lost, and Quantity	Brand or Product #	Type: W - Wine L - Liquor F - Food	Value per Unit	Total Value	Reason

Figure 10-14 Waste Control Form

answers and recommendations on food product utilization and avoiding waste. Normally you would accompany this form with a request for a price quotation. We discuss it here because of its relevance to the topic of waste.

Cost of Food Lost by the Front of the House

Restaurant servers and bus personnel can also cause loss. They must be trained to take orders accurately and to be sure that the kitchen knows exactly what the guest wants. In this way you can limit the amount of loss from incorrect orders. Using trays, taking multiple trips, and soliciting help from other staff members can help to minimize dropped-food accidents. There are also proven plate-carrying techniques that help servers keep control of them.

SUMMARY

In this chapter, we discussed controlling the costs of food in a restaurant outlet. In order to help you learn to control these expenses, we showed you the basics of cost establishment. Targeted ideal food cost was defined as the expected percentage of cost that the company wishes to spend, calculated by first defining how much profit the company wants to make. Potential cost is the minimum cost of food products used in preparation; this is the best possible cost amount, based on the items you know you will purchase. Finally, actual cost is what you actually spend. We discussed how to arrive at all of these costs and outlined what they mean to your operation.

Controlling costs involves an amalgam of techniques that minimize your food expenses. You need to look for overspending in the purchasing department, where incorrect ordering and inaccurate yield testing can cost the company money. Receiving and storage personnel must be trained to keep their area free of waste and loss. Incorrect procedures, failing to check each shipment upon receipt, theft, and spoilage are all mistakes to watch for here. Also, the transfers of entrée items must be monitored, as these products are most often stolen and do the most damage to your inventory numbers when they're missing.

Figure 10-15 Waste Price Quote Form

Questions	Yes/No	Brief description of suggestion	Approximate savings if suggestion is approved
Will the quality of the products specified stay consistent throughout the year to eliminate waste and yield variances? If not, why? Which month or period?			
Can you suggest any preparation changes that will lower the cost of the item? Specify products to vendor.			
Can you suggest any product handling difference?			
Are there any finished requirements that could be eliminated or relaxed?			
Have you any other suggestions which might simplify portioning or reduce cost?			
Do you have a standard item that can be satisfactorily substituted for this product? What is it? What does it cost? Is it USDA or qualified? What would a qualification cost?			

In the production area, cooks must test recipes, and each must be measured and recorded accurately, photographed, and displayed to maximize consistency. Kitchen waste is also a loss leader, and it must be monitored daily. Finally, the front-of–the-house staff must be trained to take and deliver orders carefully and with a minimum of mistakes and breakage. With these controls in place, you are well on your way to success with your company's food cost control.

CHAPTER QUESTIONS

Critical Thinking Questions

1. If the actual food cost equals the potential food cost, yet is significantly above the targeted food cost, what is the problem? What should be done?

2. What can cause the actual food cost percentage to drop below the potential food cost percentage?

3. Your favorite purveyor has just approached you with a "great deal." His company received a huge discount on beef by purchasing a massive quantity. Although your specifications call for USDA Prime beef, the price on the USDA Choice is exceptionally low. Given the following information, which should you purchase and why?

	GRADE	AP PRICE per #	YIELD %
Purveyor A	choice	$4.65	85
Purveyor B	prime	$5.98	80

   Never compromise your quality standards.

4. Address this make-or-buy decision: You have made black forest cake at your restaurant for years, but your purveyor just showed you a premade cake that looks and tastes exactly like yours. Given the following information, how much does it cost per portion to make it, and how much does it cost to buy it?

   To make:

       total ingredients: $8.65

       time: 2 hours, 20 minutes

       rate of pay: $12.50 per hour

       yield: 5 cakes (10 slices each)

   To buy:

       cost: $40.00

       yield: 6 cakes (10 slices each)

Objective Questions

1. Although manual cost control systems are typically more time consuming than computerized systems, they can be just as accurate. True or False?

2. Having an actual food cost percentage below the potential food cost percentage demonstrates that the chef is doing an excellent job. True or False?

3. If the total potential food cost for a menu item is $4.57, and the targeted food cost percentage is 30, what is the targeted selling price?

4. If the selling price of an item is $12.95, and the potential food cost is $3.55, what is the potential food cost percentage?

For Question 5: Using the information provided, calculate how many purchase units would be needed to prepare a roast beef dinner serving 600 customers.

Menu Item	Purchase Unit	Portion Size	Edible Yield (Percent)
Beef	1 pound	6 oz.	80
Mashed potatoes	50-pound box	5 oz.	84
Winter squash	1 pound	4 oz.	64
Green beans	10-pound case	4 oz.	76
Wine	1 liter	6 oz.	98

For Question 6: Using the information provided, calculate the number of pounds needed to serve a forecasted weekly customer count of 3,200 covers.

Item	Standard Portion	Edible Yield (Percent)	Menu Mix (Percent)
Steak	12 oz.	75	32
Lamb loin	6 oz.	40	22
Baked ham	6 oz.	65	28
Veal loin	5 oz.	80	18

Multiple Choice and Open Response Questions

1. Assuming the menu contains items with various cost percentages, which of the following can be calculated prior to sales?
   A. Potential cost percentage
   B. Actual cost percentage
   C. Targeted cost percentage
   D. Both A and C

For Questions 2–8: A food inventory taken at the Riverside Inn on January 1, 1998, totaled $3,500. During the month the business purchased $32,000 worth of food products. Prior to business operation on February 1, 1998, the restaurant calculated a food inventory of $4,200. The restaurant brought in $112,000 in food sales during the month of January.

2. What is the cost of food sold for the month of January?
   a. $32,700
   b. $31,300
   c. $39,700
   d. none of the above

3. What is the cost of food sold percentage for the month of January?

   a. 32

   b. 30

   c. 28

   d. 26

4. What should the potential food cost (in dollars and percentage) at the Riverside Inn have been given the following sales mix?

Item	Number Sold	Selling Price	Potential Food Cost (Percent)
Rib-eye steaks	1,000	$23.75	25
Fish	2,000	$28.00	32
Chicken	1,500	$21.50	20

Potential Food Cost: $_____

Potential Food Cost: _____ percent

5. What is the variance between actual and potential food cost? $_____

6. To determine why the variance between the actual and potential food cost occurred, the Riverside Inn's management reviewed the following data:

Item	Portion Size	Yield (Percent)	Beginning Inventory	Purchases Inventory	Ending
Steaks	12 oz	80	#120	#1,000	#182.5
Fish	8 oz	70	#70	#1,600	#130
Chicken	6 oz	90	#85	#650	#110

7. Which item exceeded purchase needs? By how much?

8. Fill in the numbers missing from the income statement below:

Sales

Food	500,000	____
Beverage	200,000	____
Total Sales	_____	
Cost of Sales		
Food	_____	30%

Beverage	_____	20%
Total Cost of Sales	_____	27%
Gross Profit	_____	_____
Controllable Expenses		
Payroll	_____	35%
Utilities	10,000	____
Repairs	2,000	____
Total Controllable Expenses	_____	_____
Profit Before Rent or Occupancy Costs	_____	_____
Rent or Occupancy Cost		
	70,000	____
Net Profit before Income Tax		
	_____	_____

CASE STUDIES

Case Study 1: Cost Control: Dollars and Sense

Michael's Bistro has being losing one cent on the dollar for a number of years, and Joe William, the owner, is tired of writing checks to cover losses. This exercise will show you how to trace where loss is occurring and put a stop to it.

In 2005, Michael's profit and loss statement looked like this:

	Actual Dollars	Percent of Sales
SALES		
Food Sales	$407,774	79
Beverage Sales	$108,396	21
Total Sales	$516,170	100
EXPENSES		
Cost of Food Sales	$152,786	37.5 (percentage by category)
Cost of Beverage Sales	$43,358	40 (percentage by category)
Total Cost of Sales	$196,144	**38 (percentage of total sales)**
LABOR		
Payroll Wages	$144,528	28 (percentage of total sales)
Tax and Benefits	$25,808	18 (as a percentage of wages)

Total Payroll Cost	$170,336	**33 (percentage of total sales)**
OTHER EXPENSES		
All other expenses	$154,851	**30 (percentage of total sales)**
TOTAL REVENUE	$516,170	100
TOTAL EXPENSES	−$521,331	−101
NET PROFIT AND LOSS	−$5,161	−1

According to the annual National Restaurant Association Operating Report, the median cost percentages for full-service restaurants are as follows:

The Restaurant Industry Dollar: Full-Service Restaurants	Percentage
Where it came from:	
Food and Beverage Sales	100
Where it went:	
Cost of Food and Beverage Sales (Note: Beverage is 40 percent of revenue)	33
Salaries and Wages, Including Benefits	33
Operating Expenses	6
Corporate Overhead	3
General and Administrative Expenses	3
Depreciation and Insurance	18
Income Before Income Taxes	4

Your task:

1. Given the situation above, how would you present your concern without creating panic among junior-level staff or revealing figures that would likely find their way into the local paper or a competitor's boardroom?
2. How would you go about identifying cost of sales problems?
3. What corrective steps would you take to address cost of sales problems?

Case Study 2: Loss from Production Waste

"These statements can't be right," said Patrick Matthew, president of Michael's Bistro. "Our sales in the second quarter were up by 25 percent over the first quarter, yet these income statements show a precipitous loss in net income for the second quarter. Those accounting people have fouled something up." Patrick was referring to the following statements:

MICHAEL'S BISTRO Income Statements For the First Two Quarters					
	1st Quarter	Percent	2nd Quarter	Percent	Variance
Food Sales	1,000,000	83.33	1,250,000	83.33	
Beverage Sales	200,000	16.67	250,000	16.67	
Total Food and Beverage Sales	**1,200,000**	**100.00**	**1,500,000**	**100.00**	**25**
Food Cost	320,000	32.00	500,000	40.00	
Beverage Cost	76,000	38.00	95,000	38.00	
Total Cost of Sales	**396,000**	**33.00**	**595,000**	**39.67**	**7**
Salaries and Wages	330,000	27.50	405,000	27.00	
Employee Benefits	35,000	10.61	42,971	10.61	
Tax and Benefits	31,000	9.39	38,030	9.39	
Total Payroll	**396,000**	**33.00**	**486,000**	**32.40**	**−1**
China, Glass, Silverware	10,000	0.83	10,000	0.83	
Credit Card Fee	12,000	1.00	15,000	1.00	
Decorations Expense	4,000	0.33	4,000	0.33	
Equipment Repairs—General	8,000	0.67	8,000	0.67	
General/Office Supplies	2,000	0.17	2,000	0.17	
Janitorial/Cleaning Supplies	5,000	0.42	5,000	0.42	
Laundry and Dry Cleaning	2,500	0.21	4,000	0.21	
Linens—Replacement	1,500	0.13	1,500	0.13	
Operating Supplies	25,000	2.08	30,000	2.08	
	1st Quarter	Percent	2nd Quarter	Percent	Variance
Postage	5,000	0.42	5,000	0.42	
Printing Supplies/Forms	5,000	0.42	5,000	0.42	
Promotion	10,000	0.83	10,000	0.83	
Smallwares/Utensils	10,000	0.83	12,000	0.83	
Telephone	3,000	0.25	3,000	0.25	
Trash Removal	5,000	0.42	5,000	0.42	
Uniforms—Replacement	3,000	0.25	3,000	0.25	
Utilities	15,000	1.25	20,000	1.25	
Controllable Profit	**126,000**	**10.50**	**142,500**	**9.50**	**−1**
Rent	36,000	3.00	36,000	3.00	

Interest Expense	144,000	12.00	144,000	12.00	
Depreciation—Equipment	60,000	5.00	60,000	5.00	
Property & Liability Insurance	60,000	5.00	60,000	5.00	
Total Noncontrollables	**300,000**	**25.00**	**300,000**	**20.00**	**-5**
Profit and Loss Before Tax	**−18,000**	**−1.50**	**−23,500**	**−1.57**	

After studying the statement briefly, Patrick called the controller to see if the mistake in the second quarter could be located before the figures found their way to the press. The controller stated, "I'm sorry to say that those figures are correct, Patrick. I agree that sales went up during the second quarter, but the problem stems from the loading dock, the storeroom, the kitchen, and dining room."

Patrick was confused by the controller's explanation. He replied, "This doesn't make any sense. I ask you to explain why we are losing money, though sales went up, and you talk about the production area. You always tell me that food cost is high because the customer orders high-cost items from the menu. If sales go up, then profit should go up. Shouldn't that be happening? Do you have a better explanation?"

Your answers will be guided by the following information:

	1st Quarter	**Percent**	**2nd Quarter**	**Percent**
Beginning Inventory	100,000		80,000	
Purchases	300,000		490,000	
Ending Inventory	80,000		70,000	

Product Yield	**5.12**	**86**	?	
Average Check	$ 16.00		$ 16.00	
Cover Count	62,500		78,125	

The restaurant consistently uses last-price method for inventory valuation. The restaurant scale is not calibrated.

Your task:

1. Identify and discuss potential problems in receiving.
2. In our case study, the restaurant has a walk-in cooler, and the temperature is very inconsistent, resulting in short product shelf life. Given that, how would you address this problem?
3. What is the percentage for second quarter product yield?
4. Identify and discuss your potential product yield issues.
5. Assuming the yield percentage is correct, what should the cost of sales be?
6. What did the controller mean when he said the problem extended to the dining room?

Case Study 3: Development of Costing and Variance

Colin, the executive chef of the Terrace Restaurant, produces a variety of fruit-flavored frozen sorbets for his dessert menu daily. For many years, frozen sorbets had accounted for 90 percent of restaurant dessert sales, attracting young and old alike. However, other restaurants in the area began featuring similar sorbets on their menu, and price competition has now become increasingly important. Keri, the Terrace Restaurant controller, is planning to implement a potential cost for the fruit-flavored sorbets and has gathered considerable information from Colin on production and ingredient requirements. Keri believes that the use of potential costing will allow the Terrace Restaurant to improve cost control and make better pricing decisions.

The sorbets are produced in 10-gallon batches, with each batch requiring 6 quarts of good strawberries. The fresh strawberries are sorted by hand before they are blended with the other ingredients. Because of imperfection in the strawberries and normal spoilage, 1 quart of berries is discarded for every 4 quarts of acceptable berries. Generally, it takes two minutes of direct labor time to sort berries and to obtain 1 quart of acceptable fruit. These acceptable strawberries are then blended with the other ingredients. Blending requires 18 minutes of direct labor time per batch. After blending, the sorbet is packaged in 12-ounce containers. Packaging takes 30 seconds per container. Keri has gathered the following pricing information:

- The Terrace purchases strawberries at a cost of $10 per flat or case, which is equivalent to 2 quarts of strawberries. All other ingredients cost a total of $2 per gallon.
- Direct labor is paid at the rate of $12 per hour.

We will assume that to produce a 10-gallon batch of sorbet, materials cost was $63.75 and labor cost equaled $24, or two hours at the rate of $12 per hour.

Your task:

1. Calculate the potential cost of material per 12-ounce container based on the information above.

2. Calculate the direct labor cost per dozen 12-ounce containers.

3. Discuss the possible causes of unfavorable materials price variances, and identify the individual(s) who should be held responsible for these variances.

4. Discuss the possible causes of unfavorable labor efficiency variances, and identify the individual(s) who should be held responsible for these variances.

5. How much can the Terrace sell the sorbet for if the target food percentage is 25?

Monthly Physical Inventory and Monthly Food Cost Calculations

Learning Objectives

After reading this chapter, you should be able to:

- perform inventory-taking procedures for food and beverage products;

- use perpetual inventory and periodic inventory, and distinguish between the two;

- calculate inventory value;

- understand and use the various inventory valuation methods;

- assign costs of inventory issues and transfers;

- calculate inventory turnover ratios.

In Practice

Myla Thomas called a meeting with the executive chef, Robert Clark; the purchasing manager, Scott Vincent; and the new beverage manager, Dana Miller, to discuss her concerns regarding the level of inventory on the books and her walk-through observation of inventory conditions.

"Thank you all for coming," Myla said. "I have been reviewing our inventory records. There is a major issue that we need to work on before we do anything else: We have more inventory than similar-sized operations, and we are experiencing waste. And that hurts our bottom line."

"Are you referring to the complexities of our various inventory types and procedures?" asked Robert.

Myla nodded. "Yes. Our procedures seem to be flawed. One part of it is that we are not rotating products consistently," Myla continued.

"Yes, I agree," Scott said. "But things have changed since our last meeting."

"Like a reduction in spoilage?" Myla asked.

"Most definitely. I'd add that we can improve turnover ratios on the inventory," Scott replied confidently.

"I would be very pleased to see that," Myla responded. The new beverage manager, Dana, sat listening quietly and with some satisfaction. She was getting the impression that she had been hired by a group that meant business.

Finally, Dana spoke up. "What method of valuation are we using to determine the value of our inventory?"

Myla replied, "As you know, each of the methods has advantages and disadvantages, but after close examination of the records, we are using the last price method."

INTRODUCTION

As mentioned in Chapter 1, inventory directly affects profit, cash flow, production levels, and customer service. It is a balancing act between not having enough products to satisfy your customer demand, and carrying too much stock, thereby decreasing profitability. Success in inventory management is measured in terms of available cash flow, decreased theft, reduced cost, and reduced waste. **Cash flow** is the total cash available from sales, minus actual cash expenditures required to obtain those sales. The amount of cash invested or tied into inventory on hand could limit the company's ability to operate without cash constraints for other important expenditures like payroll and operating supplies.

There are two kinds of mistakes to avoid regarding inventory: misappropriation (buying too much, too little, or incorrect stock) and incorrect valuation (placing lower or higher value on inventory than is actually the case). For example, a change in menu offerings due to product seasonality (or sales mix) may leave material surpluses because your product needs have changed. As another example, prices may have declined substantially while the inventory values stated on the books remain at the original high prices.

Customer demand changes throughout the year. For example, hot soups are preferred in winter, and salads are more popular during the summer. Restaurants must adjust their inventory levels to take advantage of the seasonal trends in demand. While controlling inventory, the manager or purchaser is responsible for establishing reorder frequencies, economical order quantities, and quantities required to meet desired customer service levels. In this role you will also want to choose vendors that can assure consistent availability of products to meet your demands.

There are three classes of inventories: **raw materials** such as whole, unbutchered tenderloin; **work in progress** such as precut, prepared beef patties; and **finished goods** such as cooked, ready-to-eat patties. In each of these classes, the amount of inventory on hand depends on the type of restaurant and the sales volume. In this chapter, we will discuss proper inventory valuation methods and inventory turnover ratios. A high inventory turnover ratio, which is a figure calculated to show how quickly you are using your products, indicates that you are buying stock at about the right rate.

You will also learn how to value your inventory, which means using one of a number of methods to count what you have and match it to a dollar figure. These values are vital to reporting and comparison, in order to show where the company stands, what costs are being incurred, and where wastes and deficiencies are damaging the company's profit. Improperly valued inventory numbers distort the important data relationships between current inventory and working capital, turnover, and average (inventory) age. This is not something you can do by comparing your values to those at another company; such comparisons may yield invalid numbers because valuation methods are usually different. You have to be able to use the data from your own organization to plan, analyze, and execute inventory controls.

cash flow A stream of receipts (inflows) and payments (outflows) resulting from operational activities or investments.

raw material Uncooked, as-purchased products.

work in progress Partially cooked products that are still in the production process; products that have begun production as raw materials but not yet been completed as finished cooked meal.

finished goods Menu items that have been completely prepared and are ready to serve to customers.

INVENTORY OF FOOD AND BEVERAGE ITEMS

Reporting inventory and unit cost accurately is essential to determining actual costs. Inventory is commonly conducted monthly, but it can be based on any period your company selects. Determining the accurate value of the product inventory is of great importance. Improper valuation of the inventory will cause inaccurate calculations of gross costs and gross profit. Since the ending inventory of one month is the beginning inventory for the next month, any over- or understatement will misrepresent the gross food and beverage cost and the gross divisional profit for the following month. It could also lead to inaccurate ordering because you do not have a true count of your inventory on hand when you place an order. For example, let us assume that the perpetual inventory system is showing four beef patties, but the actual quantity on hand is six. You could easily order more than you need because you do not know what you have. If your perpetual inventory is connected to your POS system, you could actually end up with a negative balance in your perpetual inventory database as you sell your products; the system says you only have four, but you continue to sell more patties and your POS records the sales. It is very easy to lose track of your inventory with these kinds of errors.

Inventory accuracy is a process of continual checking and adherence to your procedures. If you have a large staff, there are many hands in the stockroom to contribute to possible inaccuracies. You will have to set up policies and practices that clarify your methods for your staff, and then ensure that they are carried out. This is important because inventory is an enormous asset to a restaurant. As you attempt to keep costs low and to increase profit, your role is to manage inventory accurately and efficiently.

You can determine the value of your inventory by either physical inventory or perpetual inventory. These numbers are then extended with the correct unit cost—that is, the cost is factored in so that you have a picture of the value of each inventoried item. Both methods are described below so that you will be able to set your own standards and come up with accurate values in your establishment.

Physical Inventory

In a physical inventory process, you should have preprinted lists of all (or the majority of) the items in the inventory, with spaces for entering the correct counts of each item. You should create these sheets for entering the counts in advance. Companies with computerized inventory systems can generate count sheets through the system. The sheets should be organized in the order in which the items sit on the shelves, to facilitate accurate counting and recording. This process occurs once a month. The purchaser also takes a similar but somewhat more extensive inventory before placing an order.

To carry out a physical inventory process, form teams of two staff members. One staff person calls the item counts, while the second records the counts on the sheets. To ensure control, at least one member of each team should not have any connection with the area being inventoried. This encourages integrity and independent verification of the process. It is imperative that the inventory be taken in the order in which the physical stock appears on the shelves. In other words, it is the recorder of the counts who should jump from sheet to sheet if necessary to find the item that has been called. The caller should follow along the shelves to be sure every item is counted. For auditing and verification purposes, both people should sign all of the sheets at the conclusion of the inventory.

It is easiest and most accurate to take a physical inventory during times when the outlet and storeroom are closed. Remember that inventory must also include items that are in the outlets themselves, such as kitchens and bars, so your two-person teams must also call and record what is found there. If you have beverage items used for cooking in the kitchen area, the team counting the kitchen inventory should count them; the beverage team will count any food items in the beverage areas.

When entering inventory counts, you can use whole numbers or decimal values. For example, if you counted 6 gallons of mustard and your case description is four 1-gallon containers, you can enter counts in any of the following formats:

Description	Unit	Case	Parts
Mustard	4/1	1.5	
			6
		1	2

Beverage bottles should be recorded in tenths, which means that one full bottle equals 10/10, while half of a bottle equals 5/10 (expressed on the inventory sheet as 0.5). Great care should be taken that all tenths of a unit are properly noted. Costly errors can be made if tenths of a bottle are recorded as a full bottle.

Various companies handle batch ingredients (processed goods) differently. Some use certain specified amounts to account for the value each month. This is not an entirely correct method because you will likely have different amounts of such items each month, and this could diminish the accuracy of actual versus potential variance depending on how much of the product you actually have.

The correct method is to count exactly what is on hand. Apply the recipe cost or batch cost to what is counted. We will use our vegetable soup example from Chapter 10. From our potential recipe costing data, a batch of 20 gallons of soup costs $38.78. At 1.5 batches in the inventory, our extension is $58.17. It's important to note that the potential costing data must be totally accurate and up to date for this counting method to work.

Figure 11-1 is an example of a limited inventory worksheet that includes a variety of types of items, so that you can see how this might look for your establishment.

Month of:

Outlet: _____	Periods: _____	Date: _____
Signature of who is calling: _____	Signature of who is recording: _____	
	Signature of who extended the count: _____	

Item #	Item Description	Unit Description	Inventory Counts			Unit Price	Extention
			Case	Part	Unit		
	Main storeroom						
565	Mustard	1/4	1	2		$10.00	$15.00
577	Flour all purpose	50#					
555	Rice white	50#					
	Recipe items						
L103	Vegetable soup	20 gal batch	1.5			$38.78	$58.17
L105	Beef roasted entree	10 oz portion					
	Freezer						
212	Beef ground	30#					
215	Beef patties	10#					
210	Beef NY strip	1# (30# avg)					
	Walk-in cooler						
100	Lemons	115 ct					
101	Oranges	88 ct					
110	Tomatoes 5x6	60 ct					

Figure 11-1 Inventory-Taking Worksheet

Perpetual Inventory

A perpetual inventory is a continuous reporting of items on hand. When merchandise is received, sold, issued, or transferred, the system record is adjusted to show the new quantity on hand. In a computerized environment, this is done automatically by the computer system. The perpetual inventory also tells you when you need to reorder, reveals the average monthly use per item, and provides a constant inventory figure. A physical count is taken at month's end to ensure that the real inventory equals the perpetual inventory records. If there are any discrepancies between physical and perpetual inventory records, the inventory will have to be adjusted to reflect the physical count. Some possible reasons for the differences include receiving errors, transfers, items sold with an incorrect inventory number, and theft. These reasons are explained in more detail later in this chapter. Discrepancies should be documented and given to the manager for appropriate resolution. In a larger operation, the cost controller can do the documentation and reporting of discrepancies.

REASONS FOR INVENTORY TAKING AND RECONCILIATION

Determining an accurate value of the product inventory is of great importance. Periodic physical inventory helps to achieve both financial reporting and cost control because it helps you verify your numbers and detect any irregularities. There are no industry standards or benchmarks for measuring actual versus potential variances for food. However, the differences between actual physical inventory and computed inventory should be no more than plus or minus 1 percent. If the difference exceeds the 1 percent variance, the following steps should be taken:

- Verify accuracy of requisitions.

- Verify ending inventory extension methods to ensure consistency. This is discussed more in detail below.

- Verify unit prices on requisitions compared to those on the actual inventory.

- Alert the food and beverage manager of any adjustments to be made.

- Review all the paperwork and calculations related to products that exhibit large variances. Any errors found should be corrected accordingly.

- Review and revise security measures as needed.

Inventory value is recorded as a **current asset** in the company **financial balance sheet**. Owners of a larger company, or their accountants, usually make financial decisions, while control decisions are generally handled by a cost controller. In a more limited, informal, "Mom and Pop" type of business, the owners may handle all these decisions. Many companies use perpetual inventories instead of physical inventories, but such a system may not be as reliable as the operators might wish. Some companies, because of timing and control concerns, may conduct physical inventories in some areas and use perpetual numbers in others. This is a combination inventory approach that uses a rotation system to schedule an area for a physical count one month and to use perpetual figures for that area the following month. At times, the previous month's balance is brought forward to the current month. At a bare minimum, you need to spot-check perpetual inventories periodically and randomly. This is called **circled count**. It is less formal than scheduled physical inventory-taking processes, but if your ability to take physical inventories is limited, it can be an option for at least some oversight of inventories. The objectives are early detection and correction of discrepancies, as well as accurate reporting of inventory value and quantity on hand. The method used for circle count is generally the same as we described above for physical inventory, except that it is done randomly rather than on a set schedule.

INVENTORY VALUATION METHODS

There are several generally accepted accounting practices (GAAPs) for setting inventory values in the industry. The methods are first in, first out (FIFO); last in, first out (LIFO); average method; actual method; and last price method. These methods should be applied only to the raw material inventory; the recipe cost should be used for processed and finished goods.

current assets Assets that are expected to be converted to cash within one year. They include cash, inventory, and accounts receivable.

financial balance sheet A statement reporting on the financial position of a business by presenting its assets, liabilities, and equity on a given date.

circled count A periodic and random spot check of perpetual inventories. The objectives are early detection and correction of discrepancies, and accurate reporting of inventory value and quantity on hand.

Food products are very unstable in price and quality. Because of this, any method used will affect the cost of goods sold. Keep in mind your tax and accounting requirements, and think through any of these methods—with the collaboration of your accounting team, if applicable— before applying them. You must be consistent in which method you use. Below is a brief description of how the methods differ and how each method impacts your cost of goods sold.

First In, First Out (FIFO)

In this method, the cost of goods sold is charged with the latest purchase prices for raw materials, in-process items, and finished items. This method assumes that, as food items are perishable and storeroom space is limited, you will use the oldest inventory before more recent purchases. In other words, products are rotated and used on a strictly first –in, first out basis. To value the products, this method uses recent purchase prices to extend the inventory items' values. In times of rapid inflation FIFO inflates profits, since the least-expensive inventory is charged against the cost of current sales, resulting in inventory profits that may not be accurate. Management could be paying taxes and paying out bonuses to staff members based on reported profit that may not reflect the situation accurately. In Figure 11-2, we use the 6 gallons of mustard from the physical inventory worksheet above to create an example with several possible inventory scenarios.

Figure 11-2 First In, First Out Method 1

	Count	Price	Extension
Beginning inventory	4	$7.80	$31.20
Purchases on 7/7 before inventory	4	$8.50	$34.00
Purchases on 7/14 before inventory	4	$7.95	$31.80
Purchases on 7/21 before inventory	4	$8.95	$35.80
Purchases on 7/28 before inventory	4	$8.00	$32.00

All of different prices in the figure would mean some simple—and possibly inaccurate—inventory calculations. Using FIFO, however, we have a standard for valuation. The ending inventory from our physical count was 6 gallons of mustard; knowing that the older products were rotated and used, these last 6 must be the 4 most recent purchases and 2 of the second-most recent. When we extend the prices of these 6 gallons, we see the result shown in Figure 11-3.

Figure 11-3 First In, First Out Method 2

	Count	Price	Extension
Purchases on 7/21 before inventory	2	$8.95	$17.90
Purchases on 7/28 before inventory	4	$8.00	$32.00
The totals:	**6**		**$49.90**

The price difference between the beginning and ending inventory prices is not very large: $8.00 − $7.80 = $0.20. However, in a highly inflationary period, FIFO is not recommended for inventory valuation.

Last In, First Out (LIFO)

This is not a commonly-used method in the food service industry, but it may be valuable under certain circumstances. In LIFO, the most recent items are considered the first ones used. Items in inventory at the end of the inventory cycle are treated as though they had been in the opening inventory, plus or minus purchases during the period, to make up the correct total. In the United States, the government tends to keep inflation under control. This is not the case, however, in most other countries. Using alternative valuation procedures can help to manage inflationary fluctuations. LIFO offers a lower amount of income than FIFO during a period of rising prices, so there is no overstatement of profits, resulting in income tax and possible incentive payments that are based on results. You still rotate the stock physically by the first in, first out method, and you still rotate stock items on the shelves. However, the value assigned to the inventory is the oldest purchase price. If we were to use LIFO in our mustard example, the ending inventory valuation would be as shown in Figure 11-4.

Figure 11-4 Last In, First Out Method 1

	Count	Price	Extension
Beginning inventory	4	$7.80	$31.20
Purchases on 7/7 before inventory	2	$8.50	$17.00
The result:	**6**		**$48.20**

Average Method

This method is also called the weighted average method; both terms refer to an average of a set of values. This is calculated by adding all of the prices paid, then dividing by the number of different prices. The calculation of this valuation is shown in Figure 11-5.

Figure 11-5 Last In, First Out Method 2

	Count	Price	Extension
Beginning inventory	4	$7.80	$31.20
Purchases on 7/7 before inventory	4	$8.50	$34.00
Purchases on 7/14 before inventory	4	$7.95	$31.80
Purchases on 7/21 before inventory	4	$8.95	$35.80
Purchases on 7/28 before inventory	4	$8.00	$32.00
		$41.20	
Average (divide $41.20 by 5)		**$8.24**	

Our ending inventory value for the mustard is $8.24 × 6 = $49.44. This is a prudent method as it offers a weighted average of inventory value, but it does not represent an accurate assessment of our ending inventory if we are rotating inventory according to FIFO. This method is also quite time consuming if you are using a manual system. If you are using a computer system, the computer can average your entire inventory's items quickly based on any criteria you choose.

Actual Method

This method extends the ending inventory count according to individual purchase prices. This is possible if you write the purchase price on every item. This method is also time consuming if you must read each of the prices. However, there are electronic devices that can read or scan them. Most companies do not have the clerical staff or time to use this method correctly. Also, consider what you're trying to achieve with this method, and then consider how much it costs to achieve it. If this is the method your company uses, you will need to know how to calculate inventory values with it. In the mustard example, assume that the purchase prices recorded on the gallons counted are as shown in Figure 11-6. The purchase prices of the individual gallons are multiplied by the number of gallons purchased at each price and then totaled.

Figure 11-6 Actual Method

	Count	Price	Extension
Purchases on 7/14 before inventory	2	$7.95	$15.90
Purchases on 7/21 before inventory	2	$8.95	$17.90
Purchases on 7/28 before inventory	2	$8.00	$16.00

The result   **$49.80**

Last Price Method

This is similar in concept to the FIFO method except that you use the last purchase price to extend the inventory counted. It is the most commonly used method in the food service industry. It applies the concept of FIFO for product rotation, but the inventory valuation is based on last, or most recent, purchase prices. If you want to compare the actual cost of goods sold to the potential cost, then you must use this method of inventory valuation consistently; otherwise you may have tough time trying to reconcile the difference. The calculation for last price method is shown in Figure 11-7. Now all gallons are extended at the most recent purchase price.

Figure 11-7 Last Price Method 1

	Count	Price	Extension
Purchases on 7/28 before inventory	6	$8.00	$48.00

When we compare all the methods described above, we can see the differences in valuation (Figure 11-8). Although the difference for one item is insignificant, when you apply one method to an entire inventory of hundreds or even thousands of items, the difference will affect the amount that shows up as profit and the amount recorded in your balance sheet.

Figure 11-8 Last Price Method 2

	Value
FIFO method	$49.90
LIFO method	$48.20
Average method	$49.44
Actual price method	$49.80
Summary of Inventory Valuation Method	$48.00

FIFO is the recommended method of product rotation regardless of your method of valuing your inventory because it helps you preserve product quality and reduce waste. However, FIFO is not recommended for inventory valuations based on its poor performance in inflationary times and its lack of consistency with potential costing methods.

LIFO is recommended for inventory valuation during an inflationary period. Average and actual price methods share the disadvantage of taking quite a bit of time to implement, and thereby incurring excessive labor costs. Last price method is the best overall approach because of its sound valuations and because it is also used in potential costing and recipe calculations. Using the same system consistently throughout your entire operation in this way makes accurate reporting easier to attain.

MONTHLY FOOD COST CALCULATION AND CONTROLS

In Chapter 10 we said that the actual cost of goods is determined via the following formula:

(beginning inventory + net purchases +/− transfers) − ending inventory = cost

The result varies depending on which method of valuation you use. Assume that the beginning inventory is $100, purchases total $60, and net requisition and transfers between departments equal $10. Using our example of mustard, the ending inventory will be valued according to each method as shown in Figure 11-9. With just this one item, the differences are small. With the entire inventory, however, the differences can be significant.

Figure 11-9 Monthly Food Cost

	FIFO	LIFO	Average Price	Actual Price	Last Price
Beginning inventory	1000.00	1000.00	1000.00	1000.00	1000.00
Purchases	600.00	600.00	600.00	600.00	600.00
Net requisition	100.00	100.00	100.00	100.00	100.00
Total inventory	1700.00	1700.00	1700.00	1700.00	1700.00
Ending inventory	49.90	48.20	49.44	49.80	48.00
Cost of goods consumed	1650.10	1651.80	1650.56	1650.20	1652.00

From Principles of Food, Beverage and Labor Cost Control, 6th edition, Dittmer and Griffin, Copyright © 1999 by Paul R. Dittmer and Gerald G. Griffin. Reprinted with permission of John Wiley & Sons, Inc.

Other Costs That Contribute to the Monthly Cost Calculation

Before we can calculate the exact monthly cost, we must consider the following extra items that contribute to the figures. We will discuss employee meals, spillage and breakage waste, promotional costs, steward sales, and sales of recyclable products. With the exception of employee meal costs, all of these topics apply to food cost calculations, and most apply to beverage cost calculations as well. Companies generally do not provide alcoholic beverages to employees for employee meals.

Employee Meals

Most companies provide free meals to their employees. How this is accomplished differs from one company to another, and the application of tax is different in each state. Usually, the chef must forecast an expected number of employees each day before preparing employee meals.

Weekly menus are often posted in an employee newsletter or bulletin. This is a fundamentally important area because it requires a balancing act between allowable costs and employee satisfaction. States such as California allow a certain tax-exempt provision for operations that provide complimentary employee meals; these states treat the meals as a form of payment, and so the employee pays the tax.

Figure 11-10 is an example of statutory meal value allowances provided by the State of California. The numbers in this chart are per employee. This money can be collected through the payroll time and attendance records.

Figure 11-10 Statutory Value of Meals

Year	Breakfast	Lunch	Dinner
2009	$2.45	$3.35	$4.50

Based on the number of days an employee works in a given pay period, companies add these meal values to the gross wages for taxation. The meal value is later deducted from net pay. In effect, this all evens out, except that the employee pays the payroll tax. States such as Colorado, however, treat employee meals as an employee benefit rather than as a form of payment. The company pays the sales tax for the reported amount without passing the tax burden to the employee. In both cases, the offset is a food cost credit on the establishment's profit and loss statement.

Whether or not the state provides a tax shelter for an employee meal program, companies try to track portion cost, monitor food quality, calculate waste, and document the difference between allowable and actual costs. The following paragraphs detail the different industry standards used in accounting for employee meals.

The sales credit method charges the employees' departments a retail price for the meals. This is common in a situation in which the employee is allowed to order certain items from the regular customer menu. This method effectively accounts for the labor cost of preparing the meals and for the food cost. Opponents of this method claim that, since there is no actual sale generated, charging retail prices distorts the true sales numbers. The accounting treatment is fairly simple: The departments' meal accounts are charged at retail, and the restaurant keeps the entire recorded sales. The following journal entry can be added to the general ledger:

	Debit	Credit
Employee Meal Expense Account	xxx	
Food Sales Account		xxx

The sales credit is not very popular, due to the fact that it distorts the sales totals on which most companies base their financial reporting. The best alternative is called cost credit. In this method, the menu item is treated not as sales but as cost, and it is charged to the proper department accordingly. The journal entry should then look like this:

	Debit	Credit
Employee Meal Expense Account	xxx	
Food Sales Account		xxx

It is important to note that the government expects use tax to be assessed and paid on self-consumed items such as employee meals. You need to add the use tax amount to the journal entry above. Use tax is a tax that is collectible from the end user by the seller. In this case the end user is the company itself, and it is not exempt from resale certificate status with regards to self-consumed items such as employee meals.

In the requisition method, the cost of employee meals is determined through product requisitions and portion cost control. Many companies use vending machines to control serving sizes. Employee meals are recognized here as a cost center, and all related requisitions and purchases are charged to that center. Companies use this method most often when they have a separate kitchen or area for preparing employee meals. The labor costs of meal preparation can be charged to the cost center by using the payroll time record. Food cost, requisition, and purchase credits and debits are charged, preferably, to the human resources department.

The monthly budget method is most commonly used in the hotel industry. In this method, the controller simply specifies an amount on the books for the chef to use as a food credit. The amount allowed may vary from one accounting period to another, depending on business and staff levels. It is up to the chef to plan and prepare employee meals within the budgeted amount.

Cost of Breakage, Spoilage, and Spillage

The control and reporting of breakage, spoilage, and spillage are important aspects of any food service cost control system. The initial point of control rests with the manager of the outlet, who, when rejecting a particular entrée item from the kitchen, should document the incident. The incident report notes the cause of the spoilage, such as a misordered product, the use of defective recipe items, overcooking, or other errors. Then, at the end of the month, the incident report should be costed to relieve the work-in-progress inventory, and the following journal entry can be added to the general ledger:

	Debit	Credit
Spoiled Inventory	xxx	
Work in Progress Inventory		xxx

This entry is calculated by multiplying the potential cost of the item by the number reported spoiled, spilled, or otherwise wasted. See Chapter 10 for an example of a spoilage form.

Promotional and Entertainment Expenses

Food and beverage used for the purposes of promotion or tasting should be accounted for on a requisition form and ordered through the storeroom. If the promotion is in an outlet, the charge should be processed to the department account of the staff member who is hosting the event. The person who prepares actual food cost numbers should be sent a list of the charges. This person will be responsible for recording the charges in the profit and loss account statement at cost or at retail price, depending on company policies and accounting practices. The accounting entries are as follows: Debit the department (expense account) of the person hosting the entertainment, and credit food or beverage (cost account), depending on the type of menu item ordered.

Generally, most entertainment expenses are tax deductible. For entertainment expenses to be allowed as tax deductions, however, the law requires all pertinent information to be printed on the check, including the following:

- Name of the staff member doing the entertaining

- Name of the person(s) being entertained

- Company affiliation of the person(s) being entertained

- Subject of their discussion

- Signature of the person doing the entertaining

Figure 11-11 provides guidelines for people to whom you may wish to allow this privilege in the example of a hotel setting, either with or without prior approval from management.

Figure 11-11 Food and Beverage Signing Privilege

	Outlets							
	Banquet		**Room Service**		**Cafe**		**Bar**	
Positions	**Promotion**	**Staff**	**Promotion**	**Staff**	**Promotion**	**Staff**	**Promotion**	**Staff**
General Manager	x	x	x	x	x	x	x	x
Resident Manager	x	x	x	x	x	x	x	x
Controller	x	x	x	x	x	x	x	x
Sales Director	x	x	x	x	x	x	x	x
Rooms Director	x	x	x	x	x	x	x	x
Personnel Director	x	x	x	x	x	x	x	x
Food & Beverage Director	x	x	x	x	x	x	x	x
Executive Chef	x	x	x	x	x	x	x	x
Room Service Manager				x				
Cafe Manager						x		
Bar Manager								x

As shown in the chart, staff members might be authorized for promotional spending, staff spending, or both. You can use these categories to delimit your promotional spending—in fact, you will want to base your decisions regarding this authorization on your own operations. Following are descriptions of these two types of spending. They should help you determine who should be allowed to engage in each type.

Spending on Promotions

Persons who are being entertained under the promotional category ought to be potential or current business sources for the company, either for food and beverage outlets or for other aspects of your business. The check should be signed as follows:

- Printed name of staff member

- Printed name of guest(s)

- Printed name of corporation represented by guest(s)

- Discuss: Printed topic of discussion

- Signature of manager

Persons who are being entertained may also be business associates, such as suppliers, associates from other companies, or providers of technical assistance.

Spending on the Staff

If you have an employee cafeteria, insist that managers use it in most cases when they meet with staff. However, there may be occasions, such as a confidential discussion, when it is not practical to use the cafeteria; department heads may use an outlet for such meetings. The check is to be signed as follows:

- Printed name of hosting staff member

- Printed name of staff member(s) attending

- Signature of manager

There are some general rules to observe in any promotional or staff use of your outlets. First, insist upon a check at all times so that it can be signed personally and accounted for. Second, a dollar amount or percentage tip should be added to the check. Third, exercise good judgment; restaurant and lounge entertainment is a significant expense and is a privilege, not a right. Fourth, staff should avoid utilizing the outlets during busy periods, as priority must be given to paying guests.

Steward Sales

Sales of food or beverage products to employees at cost are called steward sales. These should be credited to purchasing to relieve food or beverage cost. For every credit there must be debit. The food or beverage product sold to employee is no longer in inventory. Therefore, the accounting offset is a reduction of inventory. This is a very common practice in the industry. Management should, however, control it to avoid using the purchasing department as the employees' grocery store.

Sales from Recyclable Food Products

This is one instance in which you can make a bit of revenue on your old or used product. Cooking greases or oils can at times be sold to the cosmetics industry as a by-product for making lipstick. The amount of income is relatively small compared to other items, but it is revenue nonetheless. The revenue should be credited to the cost of sales account. In the future, there may be more used products that can be utilized elsewhere. Watch trade journals for this and other ways of saving money by recycling your waste products.

Monthly Food Cost Calculation

After determining all of the other factors that contribute to actual food cost, you will need to adjust the cost of goods sold with respect to each. The net result will look like our example in Figure 11-12. These numbers are just for illustrative purposes; they do not represent any particular establishment. It is important to note that g could also be a negative number, depending on the net results of all the transfers. The final step, after deriving the cost percentage, is to compare the numbers to potential cost and to reconcile any variances. Please see Chapter 10 for a complete discussion of how to determine potential cost and what to do with variances.

				Formula
	Food Sales		220.00	
A	Beginning inventory	100.00		
B	Plus net purchases	60.00		
C	Plus requisitions or transfer from I.e. bar to food	10.00		
D	Total inventory before ending inventory	170.00		
E	Less ending inventory	70.00		
F	Gross cost of food sold	100.00		f = d - e
G	Less transfers food to other outlet I.e. food to bar	10.00		
H	Less steward sales revenue	10.00		
I	Less employees meals credit	10.00		
J	Less promotional food cost credit	10.00		
K	Net cost of food sold	60.00		k = f - g - h - I - j
L	Percentage of cost to sales		27.27%	L = k / food sales

Figure 11-12 Net Result of Food Costs

Accruals

Accrual accounting is an accounting system in which revenues are recognized when they are earned and expenses are recognized when they are incurred. To accrue means to accumulate. In an accrual system, expenses and revenues are recorded at the end of a given period (usually monthly) whether or not cash has been received or paid. The opposite, cash basis accounting, is used in some establishments; however, cash basis accounting may not reflect total cost or total revenue accurately. Most companies practice accrual accounting for their entire operation.

Accrued revenues are revenues that are earned in one month but are posted in another; an example of this might be a New Year's Eve dinner. Because this type of party happens so late at

accrual System of reporting revenue and expenses in the period in which they are considered to have been earned or incurred, regardless of the actual time of collection or payment.

night, any revenue after midnight will probably be recorded by your POS machine as a January sale. When figuring the December revenues, the adjusting entry strategy will be to debit January food receivables for the sales for that night, and to credit the December revenue. Accrued revenues are sometimes referred to as accrual assets; they are shown under current assets in your company's balance sheet.

Accrued expenses are expenses that have been incurred at the end of the reporting period but have not yet been paid. These are also called accrued liabilities, and they are shown under current liabilities on the balance sheet. We will look at a specific situation for an example of how accrued expenses work.

Assume Vendor A sent you $100 of beef tenderloins—15.38 pounds at $6.50 per pound. You used them at your New Year's Eve celebration. At the same time, you received 35 pounds of chicken from Vendor B, though you had ordered only 25 pounds. You rejected the extra 10 pounds, but you must pay the entire invoice and then receive a credit. The chicken costs $2 per pound. Therefore, credit equals $20 and total invoice is equal to $70. On January 1, you've paid neither Vendor A nor Vendor B; nor have you received credit from Vendor B. The accounting treatment is shown in Figure 11-13.

MONTH: DECEMBER Approved by:

ACCRUALS (Expenses)				
VENDOR NAME	**FOOD?**	**BEVERAGE?**	**GL Account No.**	**Amount in $**
A	X		100-1	$100.00
B	X		100-1	$70.00
ACCRUALS (Credits)				
B	X		100-1	($20.00)
Net balance				$150.00

Figure 11-13 Accruals

Net food and beverage accrual is a debit of $150, which is the sum of the numbers in the right-hand column. This amount should be added to the total purchase figure to find the monthly food cost calculation.

Inventory (Asset) or Period Expense: Who Cares?

From Figure 11-13 it is clear that whether a cost is considered an inventory (asset) or a period expense can have an important impact on a restaurant's financial statement. It is important to record revenue and expenses in the proper period. We will discuss four specific considerations.

Period vs. product costs

Period costs are expensed in the time period in which they are incurred. All selling and administrative costs are typically considered to be period costs. The rules of accrual accounting apply to these costs. As previously mentioned, accruals are a system of reporting revenue and expenses in the period in which they are considered to have been earned or incurred, regardless of the actual time of collection or payment. For example, administrative salary costs are "incurred" when they are earned and not necessarily when they are paid to employees.

Product costs, on the other hand, are added to units of product (i.e., "inventoried") as they are incurred and are not treated as expenses until the units are sold. This can result in a delay of one or more periods between the time in which the cost is incurred and when it appears as an expense on the income statement. Product costs are also known as inventoriable costs. Take for example a batch of soup entrée prepared but not sold until the following day—after the end of the period.

Inventory Valuation and Cost of Goods Sold

In a restaurant, raw materials purchased are recorded in a raw materials inventory account. These costs are transferred to a work in progress inventory account when the materials are released to the kitchen departments. Other production costs—direct labor and production overhead—are charged to the work in progress inventory account as incurred. As work in progress is completed, its costs are transferred to the finished goods inventory account. These costs become expenses only when the finished goods are sold. Period expenses are taken directly to the income statement as expenses of the period.

Schedule of Cost of Goods Produced

Because of inventories, the cost of goods sold for a period is not simply the production costs incurred during the period. Some of the cost of goods sold may be for recipe units completed in a previous period, and some of the recipe units completed in the current period may not have been sold and will still be on the balance sheet as assets. The cost of goods sold is computed with the aid of a schedule of costs of goods produced, which takes into account changes in inventories. The schedule of cost of goods produced is not ordinarily included in external financial reports, but must be compiled by the manager within the company in order to arrive at the cost of goods sold.

MANAGEMENT CODE OF ETHICAL CONDUCT

Proper ethical conduct transcends all aspects of our personal and business lives. What happens if management decides not to follow proper accrual principles due to financial pressures? The Institute of Management Accountants (IMA) offers some guidelines to practitioners. The guidelines have two parts. The first part provides general information for ethical behavior. In a nutshell, a manager has ethical responsibilities in four broad areas: maintaining a high level of professional competence; treating sensitive matters with confidentiality; maintaining personal integrity; and being objective in all disclosures. The second part of the guidelines specifies what should be done if an individual finds evidence of ethical misconduct.

Practitioners of management accounting and financial management have an obligation to the public, their profession, the organization they serve, and themselves, to maintain the highest standards of ethical conduct. In recognition of this obligation, the Institute of Management Accountants has promulgated the following standards of ethical conduct for practitioners of management accounting and financial management. Adherence to these standards, both domestically and internationally, is integral to achieving the Objectives of Management Accounting. Practitioners of management accounting and financial management shall not commit acts contrary to these standards nor shall they condone the commission of such acts by others within their organizations.

Competence. Practitioners have a responsibility to:

- Maintain an appropriate level of professional competence by ongoing development of their knowledge and skills.

(continues)

(*continued*)

- Perform their professional duties in accordance with relevant laws, regulations and technical standards.
- Prepare complete and clear reports and recommendations after appropriate analysis of relevant and reliable information.

Confidentiality. Practitioners have responsibility to:

- Refrain from disclosing confidential information acquired in the course of their work except when authorized, unless legally obligated to do so.
- Inform subordinates as appropriate regarding the confidentiality of information acquired in the course of their work and monitor their activities to assure the maintenance of that confidentiality.
- Refrain from using or appearing to use confidential information acquired in the course of their work for unethical or illegal advantage either personally or through third parties.

Integrity. Practitioners have responsibility to:

- Avoid actual or apparent conflicts of interests and advise all appropriate parties of any potential conflict.
- Refrain from engaging in any activity that would prejudice their ability to carry out their duties ethically.
- Refuse any gift, favor, or hospitality that would influence or would appear to influence their actions.
- Refrain from either actively or passively subverting the attainment of the organization's legitimate and ethical objectives.
- Recognize and communicate professional limitations or other constraints that would preclude responsible judgment or successful performance of an activity.
- Communicate unfavorable as well as favorable information and professional judgments or opinions.
- Refrain from engaging in or supporting any activity that would discredit the profession.

Objectivity. Practitioners have responsibility to:

- Communicate information fairly and objectively.
- Disclose fully all relevant information that could reasonably be expected to influence an intended user's understanding of the reports, comments, and recommendations presented.

Resolution of Ethical Conflict. In applying the standards of ethical conduct, practitioners may encounter problems in identifying unethical behavior or in resolving an ethical conflict. When faced with significant ethical issues, practitioners of management accounting and financial management should follow the established policies of the organization bearing on the resolution of such conflict. If these policies do not resolve the ethical conflict, such practitioner should consider the following courses of action:

- Discuss such problems with the immediate superior except when it appears that the superior is involved, in which case the problem should be presented initially to the next higher management level. If a satisfactory resolution cannot be achieved when the problem is initially presented, submit the issues to the next higher managerial level.

(*continues*)

(continued)

- If the immediate superior is the chief executive officer, or equivalent, the acceptable reviewing authority may be a group such as the audit committee, executive committee, board of directors, board of trustees, or owners. Contact with levels above the immediate superior should be initiated only with the superiors' knowledge, assuming the superior is not involved. Except where legally prescribed, communication of such problems to authorities or individual not employed or engaged by the organization is not considered appropriate.

- Clarify relevant ethical issues by confidential discussion with an objective advisor (e.g., IMA Ethics Counseling Service) to obtain a better understanding of possible courses of action.

- Consult your own attorney as to legal obligations and rights concerning the ethical conflict.

- If the ethical conflict still exists after exhausting all levels of internal review, there may be no other recourse on significant matters than to resign from the organization and to submit an informative memorandum to an appropriate representative of the organization. After resignation, depending on the nature of the ethical conflict, it may also be appropriate to notify other parties.

Source: The Institute of Management Accountants, formerly National Association of Accountants, *Statement on Management Accounting: Objectives of Management Accounting.* Statement No. 1B, NY, June 17, 1982, as revised in 1997. NAA PUBLICATION by IMA/NAA. Copyright 1982 by Institute of Management Accountants. Reproduced with permission of Institute of Management Accountants in the format Textbook via Copyright Clearance Center.

The IMA ethical standards provide sound, practical advice for managers. Most of the rules in the ethical standards are motivated by a very practical consideration: If these rules were not followed in business, then the economy and all of us suffer. Consider the following excerpts from a conversation recorded on the IMA Ethics Hot Line:

Caller:	My problem basically is that my boss, the division general manager, wants me to put costs into inventory that I know should be expensed now. . . .
Counselor:	Have you expressed your doubts to your boss?
Caller:	Yes, but he is basically a salesman and claims he knows nothing about Generally Acceptable Accounting Practice (GAAP). He just wants the "numbers" to back up the good news he keeps telling corporate [headquarters], which is what corporate demands. Also, he asks if I am ready to make the entries that I think are improper. It seems he wants to make it look like my idea all along. Our company had legal problems a few years ago with some government contracts, and it was the lower level people who were "hung out to dry" rather than the higher-ups who were really at fault.
Counselor:	. . . what does he say when you tell him these matters need resolution?
Caller:	He just says we need a meeting, but the meetings never solve anything . . .

(continues)

INVENTORY TURNOVER RATIO

Historically, restaurants operated under the assumption that some level of inventory is needed to act as a safety stock to prevent running out of products. Now managers are finding out that the costs of carrying inventory are much greater than were previously supposed—costs such as storage, record-keeping, handling, inspection, and procurement. As a result, some managers prefer that orders be placed more frequently and in smaller amounts. Others are placing fewer but larger orders to avoid high procurement cost. You will have to decide what is best for your restaurant, but the ultimate goal is keeping inventory at a minimum. To monitor progress toward this goal, managers are computing inventory turnover by type of product to reduce these costs, to reduce waste, and to free up capital for other needs.

An inventory turnover ratio indicates how many times the average inventory balance has been used—and thereby replaced—during the period under review (Figure 11-14). The greater the inventory balance in relation to cost of sales, the smaller the number of times that turnover will occur. Therefore, a decrease in the turnover rate is a negative indicator of progress toward reducing the amount of inventory on hand.

It is the responsibility of the manager to maintain storeroom inventory turnover within the company's guidelines to minimize product deterioration, interest on borrowed funds, and the impact on cash flow or other company obligations. Most restaurants adopt one or both of the following methods of reporting: *ratio of inventory to cost of sales* and *turnover ratio by category.* Both are illustrated in Figure 11-14.

Figure 11-14 includes inventory turnover ratios for three categories: food, beer, and wine. It also measures how many times during the course of the year inventory has been sold. Follow the first column and the second column, which are the descriptions and the formulas. You will want to include many months of historical data to judge the effectiveness of inventory management. The formula looks like this:

rate of inventory turnover = Line A (cost of sales) ÷ Line D (average inventory)

In this case, looking at the year-to-date average column, the inventory turnover ratio for food is 2.39 times per month; for beer it is .751 times per month; and for wine it is .266 times per month. Food turnover is generally higher than beverage turnover due to deterioration. Some food service operations do their best to adopt what are called just-in-time (JIT) inventory systems. Under ideal conditions, the manager operating a JIT inventory system would purchase only enough products to meet a given day's needs. This is common in fast-food and catering outlets, in which high volumes of precut or preportioned foods dominate the menu. Hotels that package meals and room rates together are also able to forecast upcoming business for this kind of inventory turnover. In the latter, the meal becomes the chef's choice for the day, and any other meal order is subject to extra charges. This affords the chef or the manager the

Inventory Analysis

JANUARY 2008 DECEMBER 2008

Line #		Jan-08	Feb-08	Mar-08	Apr-08	May-08	Jun-08	Jul-08	Aug-08	Sep-08	Oct-08	Nov-08	Dec-08	YTD AVERAGE
	FOOD													
	Inventory Turnover													
a	Cost Of Sales	69,108	88,752	117,337	123,486	103,812	128,991	124,043	121,138	115,814	96,453	86,882	117,345	107,763.42
b	Beginning Inventory	43,865	41,529	39,357	38,736	51,476	41,866	42,736	40,619	44,439	48,439	45,574	60,621	44,937.90
c	Ending Inventory	41,529	39,357	38,736	51,476	41,866	42,736	40,619	44,439	48,439	45,574	60,621	47,638	45,252.31
d	Average Inventory Balance = (b+c)/2	42,697	40,443	39,046	45,106	46,671	42,301	41,677	42,529	46,439	47,006	53,097	54,129	45,095.11
e	Rate Of Inventory Turnover=a/d	1.619	2.195	3.005	2.738	2.224	3.049	2.976	2.848	2.494	2.052	1.636	2.168	2.390
	Age Of Inventory In Days													
f	Days In Period	31	28	31	30	31	30	30	31	30	31	30	31	30.33
g	Inventory To Cost Of Sales=d/a	0.618	0.456	0.333	0.365	0.450	0.328	0.336	0.351	0.401	0.487	0.611	0.461	0.42
h	Average Age Of Inventory=gxf	19.15	12.76	10.32	10.96	13.94	9.84	10.08	10.88	12.03	15.11	18.33	14.30	12.693
	Sales Efficiency													
i	Revenues	355,325	410,897	537,268	561,119	525,916	638,980	647,114	580,277	615,063	439,707	426,535	459,169	516,447.50
j	Cost Percentages=a/i	19.45%	21.60%	21.84%	22.01%	19.74%	20.19%	19.17%	20.88%	18.83%	21.94%	20.37%	25.56%	21%
k	Sales To Inventory=i/d	8.32	10.16	13.76	12.44	11.27	15.11	15.53	13.64	13.24	9.35	8.03	8.48	11.45
	BEER													
	Inventory Turnover													
a	Cost Of Sales	2,066	987	1,403	4,606	3,121	2,335	2,861	1,463	4,963	2,638	2,113	1,718	2,522.83
b	Beginning Inventory	3,139	2,474	2,813	2,710	8,090	4,914	3,884	2,109	2,063	2,033	2,359	2,930	3,293.22
c	Ending Inventory	2,474	2,813	2,710	8,090	4,914	3,884	2,109	2,063	2,033	2,359	2,930	4,694	3,422.79
d	Average Inventory Balance = (b+c)/2	2,807	2,644	2,762	5,400	6,502	4,399	2,997	2,086	2,048	2,196	2,645	3,812	3,358.01
e	Rate Of Inventory Turnover=a/d	0.736	0.373	0.508	0.853	0.480	0.531	0.955	0.701	2.423	1.201	0.799	0.451	0.751
	Age Of Inventory In Days													
f	Days In Period	31	28	31	30	31	30	30	31	30	31	30	31	30.33
g	Inventory To Cost Of Sales=d/a	1.358	2.678	1.968	1.172	2.083	1.884	1.047	1.426	0.413	0.832	1.252	2.219	1.33
h	Average Age Of Inventory=gxf	42.11	74.99	61.02	35.17	64.58	56.52	31.42	44.19	12.38	25.81	37.55	68.79	40.38
	Sales Efficiency													
i	Revenues	7,208	3,058	5,197	16,165	11,878	7,058	8,624	5,053	16,586	8,085	6,989	5,919	8,485.00
j	Cost Percentages=a/i	28.66%	32.28%	27.00%	28.49%	26.28%	33.08%	33.17%	28.95%	29.92%	32.63%	30.23%	29.03%	30%
k	Sales To Inventory=i/d	2.57	1.16	1.88	2.99	1.83	1.60	2.88	2.42	8.10	3.68	2.64	1.55	2.53
	WINE													
	Inventory Turnover													
a	Cost Of Sales	4,196	3,010	4,827	9,209	8,687	8,461	6,514	4,494	8,237	6,381	4,937	7,530	6,373.58
b	Beginning Inventory	21,389	20,142	18,884	20,800	39,824	28,001	26,803	23,176	22,921	21,017	21,783	20,788	23,793.91
c	Ending Inventory	20,142	18,884	20,800	39,824	28,001	26,803	23,176	22,921	21,017	21,783	20,788	25,299	24,119.77
d	Average Inventory Balance = (b+c)/2	20,766	19,513	19,842	30,312	33,912	27,402	24,989	23,048	21,969	21,400	21,285	23,043	23,956.84
e	Rate Of Inventory Turnover=a/d	0.202	0.154	0.243	0.304	0.256	0.309	0.261	0.195	0.375	0.298	0.232	0.327	0.266
	Age Of Inventory In Days													
f	Days In Period	31	28	31	30	31	30	30	31	30	31	30	31	30.33
g	Inventory To Cost Of Sales=d/a	4.949	6.483	4.111	3.292	3.904	3.239	3.836	5.129	2.667	3.354	4.311	3.060	3.76
h	Average Age Of Inventory=gxf	153.42	181.52	127.43	98.75	121.02	97.16	115.09	158.99	80.01	103.96	129.34	94.87	114.02
	Sales Efficiency													
i	Revenues	9,359	7,274	11,258	21,759	20,772	20,837	18,431	9,968	22,750	15,737	11,206	15,872	15,435.25
j	Cost Percentages=a/i	44.83%	41.38%	42.88%	42.32%	41.82%	40.61%	35.34%	45.08%	36.21%	40.55%	44.06%	47.44%	41%
k	Sales To Inventory=i/d	0.45	0.37	0.57	0.72	0.61	0.76	0.74	0.43	1.04	0.74	0.53	0.69	0.64

Figure 11-14 Food and Beverage Inventory Analysis

flexibility to order what is needed according to the menu of the day. Any leftovers from previous days or catering events are incorporated into the next day's chef's choice menu or made available to employees as employee meals.

As this sequence suggests, JIT means that raw material or semifinished products (such as pre-cut meat or partially prepared dough) are received just in time to be cooked and served to the customers. This requires careful planning of your sales orders, accurate business forecasts, and successful vendor cooperation. The result can be substantial reductions in ordering and ware-housing costs, increases in inventory turnover, and streamlined operations that permit chef creativity and food cost reduction. As Line J in Figure 11-14 suggests:

$$\text{food cost \%} = \text{Line A (cost of sales)} \div \text{Line I (revenue)}$$

There are no industry standards for frequency of inventory replenishment; it depends on sales activity and storage capacity, as well as purchasing factors such as lead time, volume discounts, cash flow constraints, and product shelf lives. For example, produce has a higher turnover than staples, and beer has a higher turnover than wine.

The average age of inventory is a figure used to determine inventory effectiveness in days; with years of reliable average age data and expected sales levels, the manager or controller can predict inventory balances for budgeting purposes. The formula is as follows:

average age of inventory in days = Line G (inventory to cost of sales) × Line F(days in period)

You can see in Figure 11-14 that food is averaging 12.69 days per month, beer is 40.38 days per month, and wine is 114.02 days per month. Fewer days in inventory is better, as we have been discussing. How do you compare to your competitors? You will have to be the judge.

Sales efficiency figures are used to measure the relationship of revenues to average inventory. You can see these results in Line K of Figure 11-14. The result will indicate the adequacy of inventory levels at different sales volumes. The objective is to find that balanced amount of inventory that both meets sales requirements and is quickly utilized. The formula is as follows:

$$\text{sales efficiency} = \text{Line I (revenue)} \div \text{Line D (average inventory balance)}$$

Inventory consumption is more efficient if the decrease in inventory balance does not affect sales efforts or cause inventory shortages, which could affect customer satisfaction negatively. You want to strike a balance between efficiency and customer needs.

What Causes Excessive Inventory?

When a restaurant has excessive inventory on hand, reasons might include the following:

- The manager is depending on a large inventory to avoid running out of stock.

- The purchasing department is not coordinating with the kitchen and the sales department on projected business levels and banquet event orders.

- The kitchen is not coordinating with the front-of-the-house management, and thus is overprepping in anticipation for higher business levels than expected.

- The kitchen may be overprepping to keep everyone busy.

Operating inefficiencies result from circumstances like these. The sheer volume of overinventoried product makes waste and miscounts likely.

You can apply the same chart format used in Figure 11-14 to individual products in order to identify patterns that require improvement. Examples of these patterns include the following:

- Excessive or depleted levels of inventory that may contribute to cash flow constraints or detract from guest satisfaction

- Slow-moving or potentially obsolete inventory, resulting in waste

- Unknown or inaccurate numbers, resulting in the inability to determine production levels relative to sales

Furthermore, to evaluate the performance of the purchasing department, the food and beverage storeroom inventory turnover ratio should be calculated independently of calculating the production inventory. Recommended guidelines for inventory turnover ratios are as follows:

- Food (storeroom only): 4.0 to 2.5 ratio

- Beverage (storeroom only): 2.0 to 1.0 ratio

- Food (storeroom and production): 2.5 to 1.5 ratio

- Beverage (storeroom and production): 1.0 to 0.5 ratio

Dead Stock

The results of the ratio analysis above should also be used to assess the level of dead stock. Dead stock, or stock without significant inventory movement, should be viewed as a waste of company capital. Such items are an expense, and they do not offer any potential revenue generation. A large inventory of dead stock will also lower the inventory turnover ratio. In order to minimize the effect of dead stock, follow these procedures:

- Physically segregate all dead or slow-moving stock into one area of the storeroom.

- Monitor and evaluate inventory levels each month.

- Consult with the purchasing manager; distribute a dead stock inventory list (including on-hand amounts and values) to the manager.

- Discuss the financial impact of these items, and attempt to use them whenever financially feasible (for example, in restaurant specials, the employee cafeteria, steward sales, or catering functions.)

- The catering manager should monitor sales closely in order to make intelligent decisions regarding inventory or specialty purchases, particularly for use in single banquet functions.

Inventory lists and valuation of all stock with or without inventory movement should be updated monthly by the purchasing manager. This gives you a clear picture of the assets in your storeroom and lays out a roadmap for how to use them wisely.

SUMMARY

Reporting inventory and unit cost accurately is essential to determining actual costs. Inventory is commonly conducted monthly, but it can be based on any period your company selects. This helps to achieve both financial reporting and cost control because you verify your numbers and detect any irregularities. Inventory value is recorded as a current asset in the company financial balance sheet.

There are several generally accepted accounting practices (GAAPs) for setting inventory values in the industry. The methods are first in, first out (FIFO); last in, first out (LIFO); average method; actual method; and last price method. These methods should be applied only to the raw material inventory; the recipe cost should be used for processed and finished goods.

It is the responsibility of the manager to maintain storeroom inventory turnover within the company's guidelines to minimize product deterioration, interest on borrowed funds, and the impact on cash flow or other company obligations.

Period costs are expensed in the time period in which they are incurred. All selling and administrative costs are typically considered to be period costs. The rules of accrual accounting apply to these costs. Accruals are a system of reporting revenue and expenses in the period in which they are considered to have been earned or incurred, regardless of the actual time of collection or payment.

CHAPTER QUESTIONS

Discussion Questions

1. Why are accurate inventory counts and valuation critical?

2. What are the advantages and disadvantages of each of the inventory valuation methods?

3. What are the laws governing employee meal benefits in your state?

4. Why is it prudent to audit the inventory function?

Critical Thinking Questions

1. What are the advantages and disadvantages of a perpetual inventory system?

2. What are the advantages and disadvantages of an accrual accounting system?

3. What are the advantages and disadvantages of a high inventory turnover ratio?

Objective Questions

1. Establishing a perpetual inventory eliminates the need to take physical inventory. True or False?

2. Food turnover ratios are typically higher than beverage turnover ratios. True or False?

3. A perpetual inventory records all items purchased and requisitioned, and it should match the physical inventory. True or False?

4. The beginning inventory for February 1998 is equal to the ending inventory for January 1998. True or False?

Multiple Choice Questions

1. Calculate the cost of food consumed, assuming the following:

Beginning inventory	$ 5,890
Net purchases	$22,500
Transfers in	$ 870
Transfers out	$ 490
Ending inventory	$ 5,010

   A. $23,760
   B. $24,250
   C. $29,260
   D. $23,380

2. Assuming the data in Question 1, if employee meals cost $870 and the promotional food costs were $440, what is the actual cost of food sold?

   A. $22,890
   B. $22,450
   C. $23,380
   D. $27,950

3. Assuming the data in Questions 1 and 2, and food sales of $90,000, what is the actual food cost of sales percentage for the month?

   A. 24.94 percent
   B. 26.4 percent
   C. 23.86 percent
   D. 25.43 percent

4. Determine the total value of the inventory based on the FIFO method.

	Count	Price	Extensions
Beginning inventory	6	$5.65	$33.90
Purchases on 2/6 before inventory	6	$6.30	$37.80
Purchases on 2/13 before inventory	12	$6.10	$73.20
Purchases on 2/20 before inventory	6	$6.30	$37.80
Purchases on 2/27 before inventory	4	$5.80	$23.20

Ending inventory: 12 units

   A. $69.60
   B. $73.20
   C. $71.90
   D. $72.67

5. Determine the total value of the inventory based on the average price method.

	Count	Price	Extensions
Beginning inventory	6	$5.65	$33.90
Purchases on 2/6 before inventory	6	$6.30	$37.80
Purchases on 2/13 before inventory	12	$6.10	$73.20
Purchases on 2/20 before inventory	6	$6.30	$37.80
Purchases on 2/27 before inventory	4	$5.80	$23.20

Ending inventory: 12 units

   A. $69.60
   B. $73.20
   C. $71.90
   D. $72.67

6. Determine the total value of the inventory based on the last price method.

	Count	Price	Extensions
Beginning inventory	6	$5.65	$33.90
Purchases on 2/6 before inventory	6	$6.30	$37.80
Purchases on 2/13 before inventory	12	$6.10	$73.20
Purchases on 2/20 before inventory	6	$6.30	$37.80
Purchases on 2/27 before inventory	4	$5.80	$23.20

Ending inventory: 12 units

    A. $69.60

    B. $73.20

    C. $71.90

    D. $72.67

7. Which of the following methods typically generates the greatest credit for employee meals?

    A. Monthly budget

    B. Sales credit

    C. Requisition method

    D. All methods generate credit equally

8. Because no revenue is generated, which of the following should not be recorded?

    A. Spending on the staff

    B. Promotional or entertainment expenses

    C. Employee meals

    D. All of the above should be recorded

9. In an accrual accounting system, if you purchase and receive $50 worth of chicken on January 31, but will not be billed for the chicken until February 6, and the chicken remains in inventory until it is used on February 2, on what date is the expense for the chicken actually accrued?

    A. January 31

    B. February 6

    C. February 2

    D. None of the above

CASE STUDIES

Case Study 1: Business Ethics of Accrual Accounting

Clement Patrick is the controller of a privately held restaurant whose stock is not listed on a national stock exchange. The restaurant has just won a catering contract to supply all food and beverage for a newly built stadium that is expected to yield substantial profits in a year or two. At the moment, however, the restaurant is experiencing financial difficulties, and because of inadequate working capital is on the verge of defaulting on a note held by its bank.

At the end of the most recent fiscal year, the restaurant's president instructed Clement to not record several invoices as accounts payable. Clement objected because the invoices represented bona fide liabilities. However, the president insisted that the invoices not be recorded until after year end, at which time it was expected that additional financing could be obtained. After several very strenuous objections expressed to both the president and another member of senior management, Clement finally complied with the president's instructions.

Your task:

1. Did Clement act in an ethical manner? Explain fully.

2. If the new contract fails to yield substantial profits and the company becomes insolvent, can Clement's actions be justified by the fact that he was following orders from a superior? Explain.

Case Study 2: Missing Data Statement: Inventory Computation

"I was sure that when our menu hit the market it would be an instant success," said Clement Matthew, president of Michael's Bistro. "But just look at the gusher of red ink for the first quarter. It's obvious that we're better cooks than we are businesspeople." Clement is referring to the data shown below:

MICHAEL'S BISTRO, INC. Income Statement For the Quarter Ended March 31, 2005		
	1st Quarter	**Percent**
Food Sales	1,000,000	83.33
Beverage Sales	200,000	16.67
Total Food and Beverage Sales	**1,200,000**	**100.00**
	1st Quarter	**Percent**
Food Cost	320,000	32.00
Beverage Cost	76,000	38.00
Total Cost of Sales	**396,000**	**33.00**
Salaries and Wages	330,000	27.50
Employee Benefits	35,000	10.61
Tax and Benefits	31,000	9.39
Total Payroll	**396,000**	**33.00**
China, Glass, Silverware	10,000	0.83
Credit Card Fee	12,000	1.00
Decorations Expense	4,000	0.33
Equipment Repairs—General	8,000	0.67
General/Office Supplies	2,000	0.17
Janitorial/Cleaning Supplies	5,000	0.42
Laundry and Dry Cleaning	2,500	0.21

(continues)

(continued)

Linens—Replacement	1,500	0.13
Operating Supplies	25,000	2.08
Postage	5,000	0.42
Printing Supplies/Forms	5,000	0.42
Promotion	10,000	0.83
Smallwares/Utensils	10,000	0.83
Telephone	3,000	0.25
Trash Removal	5,000	0.42
Uniforms—Replacement	3,000	0.25
Utilities	15,000	1.25
Controllable Expenses	**126,000**	**10.50**
Rent	36,000	3.00
Interest Expense	144,000	12.00
Depreciation—Equipment	60,000	5.00
Property and Liability Insurance	60,000	5.00
Total Noncontrollables Expenses	**300,000**	**25.00**
Profit and Loss Before Tax	**−18,000**	**−1.50**

"At this rate we'll be out of business within a year," said Keri Patrick, the restaurant's accountant. "But I've double-checked these figures, so I know they're right."

Michael's Bistro introduced a new menu at the beginning of the current year to capture the fast-paced lunch crowd coming from nearby executive suites. Ms. Culver, an experienced accountant who recently left the company to do independent consulting work, set up the restaurant's accounting system. Keri, her assistant, prepared the statement above.

"We won't last a year if the insurance company doesn't pay the $30,000 it owes us for the food inventory lost in the warehouse fire last week," said Clement Matthew. "The insurance adjuster says our claim is inflated, but he's just trying to pressure us into a lower figure. We have the data to back up our claim, and it will stand in any court."

On April 1, just after the end of the first quarter, the restaurant's finished goods storage area was swept by fire, and all $30,000 in food product counted as of March 31 was destroyed. The company's insurance policy states that the company will be reimbursed for the cost of any food inventory destroyed or stolen. Keri has determined this cost as follows:

Total costs for the quarter: $1,218,000

Total meals served for three months: 81,200

Cost per meal served: $1,218,000 ÷ 81,200 = $15

Ending inventory: 2,000 items × $15 = $30,000 insurance claim

The following additional information is available on the company's activities during the quarter ended March 31:

- Inventories at the beginning and end of the quarter were as follows:

	January 1, 2005	March 31, 2005
Purchased Food	$0	$420,000
Raw product counted	$0	$100,000
Ending food inventory counted	$0	2,000 destroyed in the fire

- The restaurant historically uses last price method to value its inventory.

Your task:

1. What conceptual error or errors, if any, were made in preparing the income statement above?

2. Prepare a corrected income statement for the first quarter. Your statement should show in detail how the cost of goods sold is computed.

3. Do you agree that the insurance company owes Michael's Bistro $30,000?

Case Study 3: Cost Allocation

The Water's Edge Resort has three restaurants to serve its guests. The three restaurants have different menu themes, so the guests have a variety of menus from which to choose; however, they share a central purchasing center. About 95 percent of all purchases are requisitioned from the purchasing department, and costs are charged accordingly.

Elizabeth is the controller at the resort. She allocates food cost variances to the three restaurants on the basis of sales dollars each month. All three restaurants adopted standard recipe costing, and menu costs are determined each month. In 2005, the food cost variance was $15,000; this was the difference between the potential cost and the actual cost. These costs were allocated as follows:

	Restaurant			
	A	**B**	**C**	**Total**
Total sales: March 2005	1,000,000	1,200,000	1,500,000	3,700,000
Percentage of total sales	27	32	41	100
Allocation (based on the above percentages)	4,054	4,865	6,081	15,000

During the following month, Restaurant C doubled its sales numbers. This was credited to targeted advertising and to the fact that the executive chef participated in local events, which gave publicity to the restaurant. The sales levels in the other two restaurants remained unchanged. As a result of Restaurant C's sales increase, the resort's sales data appeared as follows:

	Restaurant			
	A	**B**	**C**	**Total**
Total sales: April 2005	1,000,000	1,200,000	3,000,000	5,200,000
Percentage of total sales	19	23	58	100

Food cost variance in the resort remained unchanged at $15,000 during the month of April.

Your task:

1. Using sales dollars as the basis for your allocation, show how food cost variance should be allocated among the three restaurants in the April case.

2. Compare your allocation from March 2005 above to the allocations for April 2005. As the manager of Restaurant C, how would you feel about the allocation that has been charged to you for April 2005?

3. Comment on the usefulness of sales dollars as an allocation base.

Revenue and Cash Handling Control

Learning Objectives

After reading this chapter, you should be able to:

- know about theft in a workplace and develop procedures to prevent it;

- know the economic impact of theft and fraud;

- establish check control and auditing procedures;

- establish cash handling policies and procedures.

In Practice

After observing bar and food service procedures that included serving food and drink that had not been rung into the POS system, Myla wrote a memo to Chef Robert and the new beverage manager, Dana. Part of the memo read as follows:

"Controlling the collection of revenue from all transactions is vital to our success. Although many of the techniques appear to be just common sense, some are not implemented reliably. All of the control techniques are worthless if we do not receive the revenue that goes with production. This requires not only collecting the money from customers, but also, very importantly, assuring by check control procedures that our employees turn over all revenue to the company."

INTRODUCTION

Cases of employee and customer theft have been reported in almost every conceivable phase of the restaurant business, from theft of restaurant meal ticket sales to petty cash purchases. Employee theft can be described as embezzlement, pilferage, inventory shrinkage, and stealing from the cash register or the customer. Whatever name is used to describe this type of theft, the fact is that in over 50 percent of restaurants, crime-related losses are caused by employees. Employee theft is growing to the extent that it is the most critical crime problem facing restaurant owners today. A study indicates that as many as one in three employees admit they have committed some form of theft. Two in ten employees indicate that they have taken food and beverage products or money. Areas that are most vulnerable for employee theft, with examples, are as follows:

- *Cash sales.* A manager is caught pocketing a meal ticket sale for $50. When confronted, she claims it was a customer tip, but the record showed otherwise.

- *Inventory.* Records show very high shrinkage percentage.

- *Receiving.* Storeroom and purchasing product processing invoices are not received and used in the company. Company property is diverted for personal use.

- *Accounts payable.* Accountants pay themselves with fictitious invoices and vendor names.

- *Cash drawer.* Revenue and cash are underreported.

- *Accounts receivable.* Customer payments are diverted to a personal account.

- *Payroll.* A clerk might pay a "ghost" employee and cash the check.

Examples of customer theft include leaving the restaurant after dining without paying, writing bad checks, credit card fraud, disputing a legitimate restaurant charge, and shoplifting in a food court.

Why Employees Steal

There are many reasons why employees steal from their employers. The available research indicates that indirect factors include economic need, a desire to own something, and drug-related problems. Some employees feel that what they are doing is illegal, while others think they deserve whatever they are stealing. In most cases they lack loyalty to the company, are dissatisfied with the job, or feel a lack of job security. This is most prevalent among younger employees who generally have less concern about the permanence of their current positions.

Management Policies and Enforcement

Although the reasons for employee theft may result, in part, from factors beyond your control, the extent of employee theft in any restaurant is also a reflection of management policies and actions. The greater the lack of control and mismanagement, the greater the likelihood of theft.

Where Would You Like to Work?

Nearly all executives claim that their companies maintain high ethical standards; however, not all executives walk the talk. Employees usually know when top executives are saying one thing and doing another, and they also know that these attitudes often spill over into other areas. Working in restaurants whose top managers pay little attention to their own ethical rules can be extremely unpleasant. Several thousand employees in many different food service organizations were asked if they would recommend their restaurants to prospective employees. Overall, 66 percent said that they would. Among those employees who believed that their top management strove to live by the restaurant's stated ethical standards, the number of recommenders jumped to 81 percent. Among those who believed top management did not follow the company's stated ethical standards, however, the number was only 21 percent.

Source: Jeffrey L. Seglin, "Good for Goodness' Sake," *CFO,* October 2002, pp. 75–78.

The answers to the following questions should give some insight into your company's vulnerability to employee theft:

- To what extent are inventory control and accountability procedures enforced?

- What happens if an employee is short or over in cash sales transactions? Is there any disciplinary action?

- Is there any accountability for taking stock items from the stockroom without signing for them?

- Do you screen job applicants thoroughly for past employment offenses before hiring them?

Similarly, if control is not maintained with invoices, purchase orders, shipments, and returned items, there may be an increase in the restaurant's inventory shrinkage as employees notice that accounting and inventory controls are not strict. The idea of strict controls must be reinforced on a regular basis. The use of proper stock controls, security checks, changes of key and combination locks, testing of alarms, and audits of the accounting systems and security procedures will help to show employees that management is not lax.

The use of spontaneous auditing of cash and inventory is another way to keep employees honest. One technique is the use of deliberate errors injected into the system to see what the employee response will be. What will employees do if more cash is delivered as a house bank or in exchange for a large bill? What will happen if more beverage items are delivered to the cash bar than are recorded on the accompanying paperwork? Will the excess cash or beverage items be noted and returned by the employee?

Methods of Stealing

Employees might work alone or with someone else; they might work within the POS system or outside of it; they might steal by misusing products or by taking cash directly. Figure 12-1 lists some possible ways your staff could be costing you money. The second column classifies each way as P, R, or T, which mean *product tricks*, *register tricks*, and *ticket tricks* respectively. It should be noted that this is not an exhaustive list.

Economic Impact of Employee Theft

As Figure 12-1 shows, the potential costs of employee theft are quite considerable. One of the largest direct impacts is the cost of insurance. The increase in today's insurance premiums—added onto the loss of money and merchandise—is one of the prime reasons that restaurants go out of business. Other costs include that of added security personnel and equipment as a deterrent to theft. In today's intensely competitive environment, most restaurant managers are afraid to pass these costs to their customers due to potential loss of customers to competitors.

The indirect costs of employee theft are damage to the company's public image, low employee morale, productivity loss, and compromised quality. How restaurant management considers any particular loss or theft is not the focus of this chapter, but it is important to pay attention to the indirect financial impact resulting from employee theft. Know where your restaurant business is most vulnerable to employee theft. Then devise a cost-effective control mechanism to minimize these areas.

To reduce employee theft, management must hire wisely. This includes pre-employment screening. Human resource experts claim that pre-employment personnel screening is the most important safeguard against employee theft. Types of questions to ask and not to ask an employee before hiring include:

- *Permitted question:* Have you been convicted of any of the following crimes? (The crimes listed must be reasonably related to the job–in this case, theft.)

- *Inappropriate question:* Have you ever been arrested? (This question is too broad; the law bars employers from asking certain questions at employment interviews.)

Details of questions that are permissible are covered in Chapter 14.

Figure 12-1 Employee Theft

Bartender Tricks	
Underpouring drinks, keeping track of the excess, and stealing the sales difference.	**Product Tricks**
Bringing in their own bottle, and keeping the money from selling its contents.	**Product Tricks**
Substituting lower-quality liquor for call brands, charging the guest the higher amount, and keeping the difference.[1]	**Product Tricks**
Watering down the liquor content, and stealing the sales difference.*	**Product Tricks**
Bartender and/or Cashier Tricks	
Applying discounts or coupons to non-discounted checks where cash is paid, and keeping the difference.	**Register Tricks**
Using the "training keys" on a register, which don't ring up real sales; pocketing the cash these tickets bring in.	**Register Tricks**
Real or false register breakdowns, to have manual control of cash coming in.	**Register Tricks**
Overcharging customers, either for more tips or just to pocket the difference.	**Register Tricks**
Underringing or not ringing charges, but charging the guest the full price, and keeping the difference. They may hit "No Sale" on the register to open it and appear to be acting honestly.[2]	**Register Tricks**
"Bunched" sales, or adding charges in their heads. After charging the guest full price, they only enter a partial charge on the register.[3]	**Register Tricks**
Mixing sales income with tips, and putting revenue in the tip jar.[4]	**Register Tricks**
Using another bartender's or cashier's system key to ring up sales, and pocketing the cash.[5]	**Register Tricks**
"Borrowing" from the register.[6]	**Register Tricks**
Misrepresenting sales as spilled, complimentary or returned, and keeping the revenue.[7]	**Product Tricks**
Bartender and/or Server Tricks	
Running a completion report from a POS machine before the shift is over, and only giving the company the sales from a second report.	**Register Tricks**
Reusing a guest check to charge a second guest without turning over the revenue.	**Ticket Tricks**
Giving free food or beverage in hopes of getting an increased tip.	**Product Tricks**
Putting an incorrect amount on a credit card and fooling the customer into signing it.	**Ticket Tricks**
Giving free food or drinks to a fellow employee.	**Product Tricks**
Claiming that the guest left without paying after collecting their cash.[8]	**Ticket Tricks**
Items that don't go through the kitchen, such as desserts, coffee or salads, aren't rung up and the server pockets the difference.	**Product Tricks**
Kitchen and Purchasing Staff Tricks	
Putting a steak in the garbage can, then retrieving it outside after the shift is over.	**Product Tricks**
Splitting vendor "bonuses" with chef or purchaser.	**Product Tricks**
Kickbacks for purchasing with a certain vendor.	**Product Tricks**
Making up their own false invoices, and submitting them to accounting for payment.	**Product Tricks**

---

[1] *Planning and Control for Food and Beverage Operations*, 3d ed., 1991. Jack D. Ninemeier, American Hotel and Motel Association, East Lansing, Michigan.

[2] ibid.

[3] ibid.

[4] ibid.

[5] ibid.

[6] ibid.

[7] ibid.

[8] ibid.

GUEST CHECK CONTROLS

The sections that follow present a series of control techniques to limit employee theft through the proper and monitored use of guest checks, cover reports, and staff controls.

Guest Checks

Guest checks are used to record and collect income due for products and services sold. Some operations use duplicate or triplicate guest checks depending on the level of control desired and particular accounting requirements. One copy may be given to the guest, another copy to the manager or to the person who accounts for revenues, and a third to the kitchen or to the bartender to prepare the meals.

Most modern POS systems use paper receipts that replace traditional guest checks entirely. The printed receipt is placed in a folder and presented to the guest for payment. Restaurants can often get folders free of charge from companies such as American Express, which give them away for promotional purposes. A paper receipt can also be printed in a production area, such as the kitchen or bar, by installing the proper connections and printers. POS systems have a number of advantages over manual systems, including the following:

- Guest checks are eliminated. As you can guess, triplicate checks cost even more than duplicates, so be certain that your control costs are justified.

- Service is faster than with a manual guest check. Automated guest orders are sent immediately to the kitchen or bar for preparation. Such a system is more exact and precise, and therefore can help to avoid overproduction or mistakes.

- Missing revenues are easily identified and accounted for.

- The system produces reports that help identify problem areas, including theft.

- Cashiering functions are faster and more accurate.

- Items can usually be voided only by a manager, which reduces servers' ability to commit fraud.

Disadvantages of POS systems are as follows:

- Modern POS systems are expensive. Review the information provided in the Appendix if you are considering purchasing such a system.

- System failure may mean lost revenues if you do not have adequate contingency plans. See the Appendix under Data Base Information and Computer Systems for information on contingency plans.

No system is perfect, and no system can meet all your needs for protecting your profit. Production staff in the kitchen or bar can still give out products without a legitimate order. Servers can still claim that items were returned and then pocket the money they charge. Still, a good POS system, applied rigorously and consistently, can be very advantageous.

It is often wise to have a manual system in place in case of system failures, and many establishments still use manual guest checks. Thus it is important to understand the manual system procedures discussed here. You will need a verifiable, complete plan that follows these control measures. The check control procedures described below begin from the moment you receive guest checks until you have collected money and recorded them.

Receiving Checks from the Supplier

The manager or person designated to control checks should create a control log, which has spaces to enter the date, the number of checks received from the vendor, their numeric sequence, and an authorizing signature. All checks should remain secured in the storeroom area under the control of the manager or other designated person. Upon receipt, the order should be checked against the purchase order to see that price, quantity, quality, and sequence numbers are correct. Then the total number of checks on hand should be tabulated and entered in the log.

Issuing Checks to the Outlets

All checks issued to a supervisor or outlet manager should be noted in the check control log as well. All checks should be issued in numeric order, and the log entry should consist of the date, the amount issued, the numeric sequence, the outlet's total checks on hand, the outlet representative's signature, and an authorizing signature. Checks should be issued only to an outlet manager or supervisor as designated in your establishment.

The purpose of the check control log is to monitor and account for all guest checks received and issued to outlets. A designated person maintains this log using the procedures outlined in this chapter. This log should be kept in the storeroom at all times. It should be divided into sections by outlet if more than one outlet exists.

The Outlet's Record of Checks Issued

Each outlet will also need a record to control all checks issued. The outlet manager should issue checks, in numeric order and in controlled quantities, to the servers and/or the cashier at the beginning of each shift. The number of checks issued to each staff member should be determined by the outlet manager depending on past usage and forecasted business. The outlet manager should note beginning and ending numbers for the checks issued. Cashiers or servers should sign for all checks issued. Additional checks should be issued as needed and duly noted on the record. The following entries should be noted when issuing checks to a server or cashier:

- Date

- Cashier's or server's name

- Meal period

- Beginning and ending check numbers

- Total number of checks issued

- Cashier's signature

- Outlet manager's signature

Companies with a POS system should prepare such a log in advance and lock it up, with a supply of checks, in a safe area in the restaurant. When the system breaks down, the manager can then quickly retrieve the checks and assign them to servers or cashiers. Such a contingency plan can be crucial to controlling checks and revenue during a system failure—especially when the system goes down during a busy meal period.

All issued checks, including voided and unused checks, should be turned in after the meal period, without exception. Checks should be spot-checked continually by the outlet manager.

A server might use the same check twice, collect double payment, and pocket the difference. Each check should be verified and marked off by the manager at the end of the shift. Unused checks, including any open checks, should be signed over to an incoming cashier or server, or to the closing supervisor, at the end of each shift.

Only a limited reserve supply of checks should be kept by the outlet manager. Boxes of checks should only be ordered as required. Any reserve supply should be kept in a locked compartment controlled by the outlet manager.

Check Control Summary Sheet

This sheet provides a record of all checks issued, breaks down individual checks for review and control, and highlights missing checks. Cashiers, servers, and bartenders should prepare this sheet according to the description below:

Heading	Beginning and ending check numbers, shift time, date, cashier name, meal period, outlet
Column 1	All checks listed in numeric order
Column 2	Number of covers per check
Column 3	Total cash collected for the check, if any
Column 4	Net credit card charge, if any (excluding any tip)
Column 5	Net promotional account charge, if any (excluding any tip)
Column 6	Net room charge, if any (excluding any tip)
Column 7	Total of Columns 3 through 6

From this information the manager can tell how each check was settled, whether by cash, credit card, promotional charge, or room charge. Any check not accounted for should be traced to the production area (kitchen or bar) to determine if any food or beverage was produced. If the duplicate of the missing check is found in the production area with a handwritten order that indicates that the server may have collected payment for the missing check, the company should investigate this anomaly. If necessary, you can then take steps to collect the value of what is written on the duplicate check from the server or cashier, depending on company policies and procedures and the employment law governing your state.

Audit of Check Control

An audit of check control log is prepared to control all checks issued and used by the outlets. It is also used to prepare a missing check report in a timely manner. The manager or the person designated should verify check control using the following information:

- List of check numbers

- Outlet

- Date issued

- Total number of checks issued

- Manager's or designated person's signature

- Outlet manager's signature

You can see how this works in Figure 12-2. The blank column can be used for other methods of payment, such as gift certificates or expense account or tab charges, if these are used at your company. The auditor marks off each check in the right-hand column to indicate that the check has been verified. All missing and voided checks should be accompanied by an explanation, as in our example, or such an explanation can be written by the outlet manager and attached to this sheet.

Figure 12-2 Cover Reporting

Outlet:		Total # of checks:		Date issued:			Audited?
check #		cash	credit card	promo. chg	room chg		
12714	/	$37.50					√
12715	/		$18.71				√
12716	/				$41.02		√
12717	V	(checkfell	in thesoup)				√
12718	0	(server	found check	in pocket)			√
12719	/		$24.18				√
12720	*	(will be	transferred	to next shift)			√
Signatures:							
Auditor:							
Outlet mgr:							

The marks in the second column are standard marks used to denote the following circumstances:

/   *Used:* used by staff and settled by one or more methods of payment

0   *Missing check:* these should be investigated to determine if fraud was committed (see the section on cash handling in this chapter to read about the many ways employees might steal)

*   *Check being held:* applies to unused checks that will be transferred to an incoming server and noted on the check issuing log

V   *Voided check:* might indicate a soiled check or a problem with a guest order; the manager should verify and sign for all voided checks with a written explanation

All checks should be forwarded to the manager or person designated to monitor check control procedures, along with the check control summary sheet discussed earlier. Checks should be reconciled with the audit check control log. All checks not accounted for should be listed on a missing check report.

It is important to stress that no system is totally adequate if the production staff are preparing and giving out food and beverage without guest checks or POS order receipts.

Cover Reporting

Just as the server writes the order for the kitchen to prepare the meal, he or she must also indicate the number of guests to be served on the check. These guest numbers are called covers. When four people sit down to a meal, you often have four covers. The number of covers is not always the same as the number of guests at a table, however. For your reporting data, covers are counted as the number of guests who order a meal, usually including an entrée item.

If these numbers are tallied accurately, they can be used for forecasting, budgeting, and menu analysis. The number of covers multiplied by the average food check gives you total food sales; multiply the number of covers by average beverage sales to get total beverage sales.

You may also count covers in special situations that are less clear-cut than meals or entrées. Use the guidelines below for these situations.

Counting Banquet Reception Covers

Cover counts for banquet receptions should be obtained directly from guest checks or from the catering order. Included in such counts are receptions that immediately precede a meal function, which often have the same host as the meal function and are recorded on a single banquet check.

Counting Snack Bar Covers

All food covers are obtained directly from guest checks or POS systems for the three meal periods (breakfast, lunch, and dinner). Coffee sales alone are not counted in the total food cover count. At points of sale, such as poolside bars, golf or tennis snack stands, or service carts, only the sale of entrée-type items such as sandwiches, hot dogs, or hamburgers are to be counted as covers; each of these items should be counted as one. Snack items, such as candy bars, chips, ice cream cones, and fruit, are not considered entrée items and should not be recognized as covers. Similarly, covers are not counted in connection with in-room minibar sales.

Counting Hospitality Suite Covers

To determine room service hospitality suite average checks, divide sales from the hospitality function by the number of guests expected to be served. For example, if the hospitality order indicates 125 people flowing through and the total sales associated with the suite are $850, then the average check is $6.50. Hospitality covers are to be included in the room service department and total food cover counts.

To illustrate the value of this cover information, Figure 12-3 shows how these counts are used in forecasting.

Following are the uses and meanings of the numbers in Figure 12-3:

- *A. Actual occupied rooms:* The number of guest rooms sold for the reporting period. This only pertains to lodging establishments with food and beverage operations. This information could be used to determine sales per occupied room. If documented consistently and for a long period of time, the manager can use this information to forecast future results.

- *B. Actual occupied room percentage:* This is the number of occupied rooms divided by the total available rooms for the reporting period. In our example in Chapter 1, we assume a hotel with 1,120 rooms, multiplied by 31 days in July; this means we have a room availability of 34,720. Thus, the equation looks like this: $\frac{17,855}{34,720} = 51.4$ percent.

- *C. Number of days in a month.* In our example, it is 31 days.

- *D. Number of days opened per month.* This refers to the number of days each meal period was open for business in the month of July. This may be different from one restaurant to another and from one meal period to another. This information is relevant to determine the actual performance of each meal period in terms of revenue generated per day.

- *E. Number of seats.* This number is usually posted inside the restaurant or bar; it is the legal, certified occupancy number of a restaurant. This information establishes the number of customers the restaurant can hold, and it is part of the calculation for turning over the tables.

| #a Actual occupied rooms 17,855 | #b Actual occupied % 51.4% | #c # of days in a month = 31 |

OUTLET & meal periods	#d Number of days opened per month	#e Number of seats capacity	#f Turnover per seat ($\frac{\#g}{\#e}$)	#g Total covers	#h Covers per day ($\frac{\#g}{\#d}$)	#i Sales per occupied room ($\frac{\#o}{\#a}$)	#j Food sales	#k Food average check ($\frac{\#j}{\#g}$)	#l Beverage sales	#m Beverage average check ($\frac{\#i}{\#g}$)	#n Beverage average per day ($\frac{\#i}{\#d}$)	#o Combined F&B revenues (#j + #l)	#p Combined average check ($\frac{\#o}{\#g}$)
ROOM SERVICE													
Breakfast	31	100	30.00	3,000	97	3.36	40,000	13.33	20,000	6.67	645	60,000	20.00
Lunch	31	100	9.00	900	29	1.40	15,000	16.67	10,000	11.11	323	25,000	27.78
Dinner	31	100	11.00	1,100	35	2.30	26,000	23.64	15,000	13.64	484	41,000	37.27
Nite owl	31	100	5.00	500	16	0.84	10,000	20.00	5,000	10.00	161	15,000	30.00
Hospitality	31	100	6.00	600	19	1.12	15,000	25.00	5,000	8.33	161	20,000	33.33
TOTAL	31	100	61.00	6,100	197	9.02	106,000	17.38	55,000	9.02	1,774	161,000	26.39
FINE DINING													
Dinner	20	100	25.00	2,500	125	13.16	185,000	74.00	50,000	20.00	2,500	235,000	94.00
TOTAL	20	100	25.00	2,500	125	13.16	185,000	74.00	50,000	20.00	2,500	235,000	94.00
CAFÉ													
Breakfast	31	200	32.50	6,500	210	3.16	54,000	8.31	2,500	0.38	81	56,500	8.69
Lunch	31	200	27.50	5,500	177	4.77	74,250	13.50	11,000	2.00	355	85,250	15.50
Dinner	31	200	35.00	7,000	226	7.28	105,000	15.00	25,000	3.57	806	130,000	18.57
TOTAL	31	200	95.00	19,000	613	15.22	233,250	12.28	38,500	2.03	1,242	271,750	14.30
BAR													
Lunch	31	120	5.00	600	19	1.12	5,000	8.33	15,000	25.00	484	20,000	33.33
Dinner	31	120	29.17	3,500	113	7.56	35,000	10.00	100,000	28.57	3,226	135,000	38.57
TOTAL	31	120	34.17	4,100	132	8.68	40,000	9.76	115,000	28.05	3,710	155,000	37.80

Figure 12-3 Monthly Food and Beverage Cover Reporting

- *F. Turnover per seat.* This figure is derived by dividing the number of covers by the number of seats. It refers to the average number of times during a meal period that a given seat is occupied. This information is used to judge the efficiency of seat capacity. You could also use it to compare your establishment with competing restaurants to determine what percentage of the target dining population you are capturing.

- *G. Total covers.* This is a tally of guests who purchased meals. If this information is collected for two or more years, you may be able to use it to forecast future sales levels. In Figure 12-4, we offer an example of how this can be applied, using the information in Columns A, B, and C to represent the cover totals in your restaurant for 2007, 2008, and 2009.

	#a 2007	#b 2008	#c 2009	#d Variance #b - #a	#e Variance #c - #b	#f % difference #d / #a	#g % difference #e / #b
October	2,820	3,000	3,200	180	200	6.38%	6.67%
November	2,750	3,100	3,500	350	400	12.73%	12.90%
December	3,060	3,500	4,000	440	500	14.38%	14.29%
	8,630	9,600	10,700	970	1,100	11.24%	11.46%

Figure 12-4 Fine Dining Covers

Columns D and E show the variance from 2007 to 2008 and from 2008 to 2009, respectively. Columns F and G turn those variances into percentages for comparison purposes. Assuming every indication shows the same trends and you do not foresee any new variables, Figure 12-5 could be your outlook for 2010.

Last quarter Forcast Fine Dining Covers -- 2009

	2009 Covers	% Increase	Cover Increase	2010 Forecast Covers
October	3,200	7.00%	224	3,424
November	3,500	13.00%	455	3,955
December	4,000	14.30%	572	4,572
	10,700		1,251	11,951

Figure 12-5 Last Quarter Fine Dining Covers

- *H. Covers per day.* This is an average calculated by dividing the number of covers by the number of days the restaurant was open for business.

- *I. Sales per occupied room.* This is derived by dividing the combined food and beverage revenues by the actual occupied room total. This figure gives you an indication of average revenue generated per occupied room, and it may also be helpful in future forecasting efforts.

- *J. Food sales.* This is the revenue reported from your guest check summary report. You could also multiply your average check amount by the number of covers, or by forecast data, to derive actual or predicted sales totals.

- *K. Average food check.* This is obtained by dividing the food sales per meal period by the number of food covers during that period. Be sure to subtract voided and promotional covers from period totals to determine this average.

- *L. and M.* Columns L and M are just like Columns J and K, but for beverages.

- *N. Average beverage per day.* This is the average beverage revenue per day. Divide the beverage sales total in Column L by the number of days the outlet was open in Column D.

- *O. Combined food and beverage revenues.* This is the food and beverage revenues added together.

- *P. Combined average check.* The combined food and beverage check for the outlet is obtained by dividing the total food and beverage sales for the outlets by the food and beverage covers for the outlets, or by adding together the average food check and the average beverage check.

Again, it is important to stress that cover reporting must be consistent. If this report is to be meaningful and useful, the server will have to follow the cover guidelines you establish. Once you have maintained a consistent, reliable database on sales and covers, you can use this information to forecast future sales income and cost per cover.

CASH HANDLING CONTROLS

To this point we have been discussing procedures to monitor guest checks and to use the information they provide. The next step is to establish cash handling standards. The development and implementation of these control procedures stems from two types of income-collection systems: server banking and cashier banking. Both concepts originated from the establishment of company policies and procedures of accounting for house bank funds. A **house bank** is the amount of money given to a cashier or server for the purpose of giving out change to customers. The controller should see that this amount is balanced to the company's general ledger.

House banks may be obtained by placing a request at least one to three days prior to the date that the bank is needed. This request should include the amount, outlet and staff member information, and the signature of the person responsible for the bank. All house banks should be approved by the person performing accounting functions or by the manager. House banks should be subject to the cash handling measures detailed below.

A numbered cash vault and key, often using a safety deposit box, should be assigned with each bank. The employee is solely responsible for the safekeeping of the key. If the key is lost, stolen, or broken, it should be reported to the manager immediately so that the money may be removed to prevent further loss. Depending on your company's policies and procedures, the employee may be held accountable for the replacement of the key and the lock. Furthermore, all house banks must be locked securely in the assigned vault when not in use. Failure to secure house funds should result in strict disciplinary action. When stored, all house banks must contain a signed and dated count sheet that shows the total amount in the bank. Currency should be arranged face up, and loose coins should be placed in individual bags by denomination. No personal money or items should ever be stored in the house bank bag or the safety deposit box. Failure to follow these guidelines should be considered negligence.

At the end of each shift, house banks must be counted and balanced to the original issued amount. All checks and traveler's checks must be deposited daily. A house bank should consist only of currency, coin, and due-back slips totaling the amount of funds issued. This requirement should be stated in the signed cash handling acknowledgment or house bank contract.

Every precaution should be taken to secure house funds. Locking the cash drawer, restricting access to the bank, and counting change as it is given to the guest will all help in maintaining the security of the bank. All overages and shortages should result in disciplinary action, as should any violation of the cash handling acknowledgment.

Another commonly used control method is called a floating house bank. This procedure enables a shift manager to audit a server at the end of one shift and then pass the bank to an incoming server. While all control procedures mentioned above apply, variances must be reconciled immediately in order to maintain both a consistent bank amount and the accountability of shift personnel.

house bank The amount of money given to a cashier or server for the purpose of giving out change to customers.

Server Banking

Server banking is a system whereby servers or bartenders are issued a house bank to collect payment and to give out change to guests. They keep these banks until they check out at the end of the shift. The server or bartender actually closes or settles the checks, and he or she is held accountable for each transaction. The server or bartender in this case will fill out a check control summary, as discussed above, which states what amount is due to the company. As previously mentioned, computerized POS systems provide a faster and more efficient manner of conducting these transactions. Each server's POS report will indicate how much is owed and by which method of payment—cash, credit card, gift certificate, or room or promotional charge. It will also list the server's table numbers, outstanding or open checks, voids, taxes, tips, and cover information.

server banking A system wherein the server or bartender also carries out the responsibilities of a cashier.

Cashier Banking

Cashier banking is similar to server banking, except that a cashier actually settles each check by one or more payment methods. The cashier in this case is responsible for each transaction, as well as for the deposit at the end of the shift. The guest may pay the cashier directly, depending on the restaurant setup, or may pay the server or bartender, who then pays the cashier. The bartender may, in some cases, be the cashier. Ultimately, it is the responsibility of the outlet manager to oversee all banking functions with either server or cashier banking systems.

cashier banking A system where a cashier settles each check and is responsible for the transaction.

Responsibilities of Cash Handlers

All cash handlers should be required to sign a statement acknowledging their responsibilities regarding cash and other forms of payment; this form should include your company's policies for when their banks come up short. The original is placed in the employee's personnel file and a copy is given to the employee. This form should include all applicable measures listed below, as well as the server's agreement to follow these rules and a place for him or her to sign and date the document. These responsibilities should include training on detecting and reporting counterfeit bills. Figure 12-6 illustrates some of the key points to look for in a U.S. $100 bill.

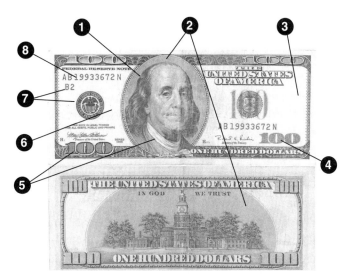

Figure 12-6 Money

Legend

1. *Portrait.* The enlarged portrait of Benjamin Franklin is easier to recognize, while the added detail is harder to duplicate. The portrait is now off-center, providing room for a watermark and reducing wear and tear on the portrait.

2. *Concentric Fine Lines.* The fine lines printed behind both Benjamin Franklin's portrait and Independence Hall are difficult to replicate.

3. *Watermark.* A watermark depicting Benjamin Franklin is visible from both sides when held up to a light.

4. *Color-Shifting Ink.* The number in the lower-right corner on the front of the note looks green when viewed straight on, but it appears black when viewed at an angle.

5. *Microprinting.* Because they're so small, microprinted words are hard to replicate. On the front of the note, USA 100 is within the number in the lower-left corner, and United States of America is on Benjamin Franklin's coat.

6. *Security Thread.* A polymer thread embedded vertically in the paper indicates, by its unique position, the note's denomination. The words USA 100 on the thread can be seen from both sides of the note when held up to a bright light. Additionally, the thread glows red when held under an ultraviolet light.

7. *Federal Reserve Indicators.* A new universal seal represents the entire Federal Reserve System. A letter and number beneath the left serial number identify the issuing Federal Reserve Bank.

8. *Serial Numbers.* An additional letter is added to the serial number. The unique combination of eleven numbers and letters appears twice on the front of the note.

Note: Some of the counterfeit bills in current circulation do not have the security thread mentioned in Number 6. The appearance of a security thread is only a copy.

Deposit of Daily Receipts

Deposits of the day's transactions are to be made daily at the end of each employee's shift. Work should be handled and completed in a designated cash-out area in each department, and the appropriate monies should be "dropped" before the employee leaves the premises. Drops are deposits that are placed in the company safe. These include deposit orders, due backs, money that is reimbursed to the employee's bank, or any transaction affecting the amount in a house bank. The person making the drop is accountable for the balance and content of his or her drop envelope. All drops should be made in the drop safe in a designated area and must be properly witnessed and logged prior to the drop. Failure to make a drop of the day's receipts should be subject to disciplinary action.

Cashier Drop Record

It is the responsibility of the employee who is making the drop to properly fill out a cashier drop record, which includes his or her name, his or her department, the date and time, and the amount of all forms of payment contained in the envelope. All drops must be witnessed. The witness should verify that the amount written on the envelope matches the amount on the drop record. The employee then places the completed and sealed envelope in the drop safe and turns the handle until the deposit drops into the safe. The witness must visually verify this step and then sign the drop record to acknowledge that the drop has been made.

The witness serves to verify only that the drop has been made. This is not a verification of the amount actually in the envelope. It is the responsibility of the cashier to locate a witness who has a moment to verify the drop and to ask for assistance in a professional and pleasant manner. Failure to follow the above procedures should be considered negligence and should be subject to disciplinary action. Whenever the accounting department cannot account for an envelope, the witness who verified the drop should be issued a written warning. The employee responsible for making the drop, whether witnessed or not, may be held accountable for the amount of the drop.

Cash Variances

All cash variances (overages and shortages) must be deposited at the end of each shift. Cash over or short should be reported to the manager to serve as a tracking tool for such variances. When disciplinary action is necessary, a discrepancy report will also be submitted to managers. It is the responsibility of managers to work with the human resources department when handling counseling and disciplinary action. All cash discrepancies should result in disciplinary actions. The server can be disciplined, penalized, or even terminated for improper cash handling procedures.

Personal Check Procedures

All checks, both personal and business, must have check approval prior to being accepted. All information required by the company with regard to personal checks must be included on the front of the check. This includes the name of the department, the type and number of identification card used, and the cashier's initials. All checks must be dropped to the general cashier daily for immediate deposit in the bank. Checks may be dropped as part of a cash drop, or they may be dropped in exchange for cash. Whichever method is used, they must be dropped the day they are received.

Any check that is dropped without the correct approval or that does not clear through the bank will be considered a shortage. Disciplinary action may be taken according to the amount due on an unapproved check. All checks, including traveler's checks, must be made payable to the company, and they must be stamped with a FOR DEPOSIT ONLY stamp on the back of the check at the left-hand end.

The total amount of all checks must be recorded on the front of the deposit envelope under the Vouchers and Checks heading. Traveler's checks also must be totaled and recorded on the front of the envelope on a separate line marked Traveler's Checks. If the total amount of checks being dropped is higher than the total amount due, include a due-back slip equal to the excess amount.

Due-Back Slips

Due-back slips are necessary when the total amount of cash and/or checks in a drop exceeds the amount due. The server should print his or her first and last name, the date, his or her vault or safety deposit box number, and the amount due back on the slip. The server should place the first copy in his or her drop envelope and record the amount due back in brackets (that is, [ ]) on the front of the envelope. He or she should also record the amount in brackets on the drop record. The server should then place the second copy in his or her bank so that all money and due-back slips, when totaled, will equal the issued amount.

When the server needs to exchange checks or large bills for small bills or coins, he or she should fill out the due-back slip in the normal manner and print the word *exchange* on the bottom of the slip. He or she should also print the word *exchange* on the front of the drop envelope and attach a change order form, which specifies what kind of change is requested. To retrieve a due-back slip, servers should go to the accounting or manager's office during business hours to present the second copy of the due-back slip. Servers need to count the amount given to them before leaving the accounting office. In addition, servers must sign the accounting control log to verify that they received the money. Not all companies reimburse due-back slips like this; whatever method you use, be consistent, keep complete records, and follow verifiable procedures.

Credit Card Procedures

All credit card sales must have an approval code, a signature, and an imprint of the credit card. Exceptions in the case of the signature include express checkouts and telephone sales. In addition, the staff member should verify the information while taking the card's imprint or running it through the card system. In a hotel setting, any time the guest's total charges exceed the total amount of their prior approval, an additional approval must be obtained with a written code. The total approved amount must also be written on the voucher at checkout.

Telephone credit card sales must include the following information for credit companies to recognize them as legitimate:

- Credit card number

- Expiration date

- Cardholder's name

- Cardholder's billing address

- Cardholder's daytime phone number

- Total amount of sale

- Approval code

An employee who handles an uncollectable credit card sale may be subject to disciplinary action for any of the following mishandling:

- Lost or illegible imprint

- Credit card approval not obtained

- Credit card approval or guarantee limits not adhered to

- No signature on voucher, excluding hotel express checkouts (an authorized signature should be faxed for telephone sales)

Charges that are deemed not collectable should be considered a shortage and should be treated the same as cash variances—with disciplinary action. Tips paid out on noncollectable credit card sales also should be returned by the servers who received them.

Gift Certificates

Gift certificates are coupons purchased by customers to use in the place of cash at a later date. Many times these certificates are hard plastic gift cards. They can be a good source of revenue, but they require special handling. A gift certificate sold but not yet redeemed is treated as a liability in the general ledger account. The controls are similar to cash, but care must be taken to maintain adequate record-keeping of all transactions, from printing to storing to issuing.

Gift certificates are issued from the accounting office. All certificates issued must be logged and signed for by the employee receiving them. Gift certificates should be handled with the same security procedures as cash. The amount printed on the gift certificate is its value whether it is sold, lost, or stolen. Lost or stolen gift certificates will be recorded as a shortage and should be treated the same as cash variances—with disciplinary action.

When a gift certificate is sold, the amount must be rung through the POS system as "gift certificate sold." The completed stub from the gift certificate, along with a copy of the check or POS report showing that the gift certificate was sold, should be turned in to the accounting office before certificates are replenished. When a gift certificate is redeemed, it must be rung through the POS system as a method of payment. If the gift certificate is higher than the amount due, change should not be given in cash. Gift certificates should also not be redeemable for cash. This policy may vary from one company to another, however.

Failure to process the gift certificate correctly will result in an apparent cash variance. This could be considered negligence on the part of the cashier, who would be subject to disciplinary action. Redeemed gift certificates should be dropped with the cash deposit at the end of the shift. Gift certificates and their totals should be listed on the front of the envelope, but the amount should not be included on the Total Amount Enclosed line.

Be sure to include this information, as well as your entire gift certificate policy, in the cash handling acknowledgment that each server signs. Your staff needs to know that they are responsible for mistakes in this area as in any other.

Petty Cash Receipts

When your outlet needs something in a hurry, you may issue an amount of petty cash. This is a common practice to handle impromptu needs for cash in many establishments. In a busy restaurant environment, however, these monies might not be returned. You will need to establish and uphold the following procedures to ensure that the petty cash privilege is not abused.

A "received of petty cash" voucher must be completed before a request for petty cash is submitted to the accounting office. This petty cash request must include the following:

- Name and department of the individual to receive payment

- Date

- Brief explanation

- Total dollar amount

- Original receipts or other backup attached

- Appropriate approval

- Signature to acknowledge payment received

Approvals for petty cash requests are only valid with an appropriate signature from a manager, or perhaps an executive chef. If the appropriate signature cannot be obtained, the approval of the accountant or the general manager will be accepted. Any petty cash receipts that are turned in without being filled in correctly or without proper receipts and approval should be considered incomplete. This should be subject to disciplinary action if it is not resolved within a reasonable time period, at the discretion of the accounting office manager.

Travel Vouchers

folio An itemized guest-lodging bill.

Travel vouchers from guests are treated as cash. Any questions should be directed to the accounting department. At checkout, settle the **folio**, or itemized guest-lodging bill, with the room and tax balance. Drop all vouchers with a copy of the folio at the accounting office with the daily deposit. Front desk agents should be held responsible for all vouchers lost or settled incorrectly. Lost vouchers will be considered a shortage and should be treated the same as cash variances—with disciplinary action.

NEGLIGENCE

Negligence is defined as failure to perform properly, especially through carelessness. The following should be considered acts of negligence:

- Improper preparation of the deposit envelope, drop record, shift reconciliation, guest checks, vouchers, or other reporting materials used by your company

- Improper endorsement of checks and traveler's checks

- Lack of proper approval on checks and credit cards

- Ringing in any amount under a POS number belonging to someone else and not including that amount in your reconciliation

- Ringing in any amount on your own number after having run the tape for the end of your shift and not including that amount in your reconciliation (deception or intent to deceive are crucial in determining fraud)

- Closing a check to a payment method incorrectly and not correcting it before completing your reconciliation

- Committing mathematical errors resulting in a variance, then leaving the variance until the next scheduled shift

- Failing to perform properly in any other areas of the cash handling procedures referenced in this section

Honesty and controls are the responsibility of everyone at any establishment. The manager should use the "fresh set of eyes" approach any time he or she is observing an outlet's operations. The use of "spotters" or "shoppers" (people hired to observe the bartender and server while posing as guests) can help uncover procedural problems or even theft. In the meantime, you should make sure that controls are in place and are sufficient to minimize these kinds of losses.

SUMMARY

To control checks, the process must include receiving the checks from the supplier, storing them securely, issuing them to outlets and individual servers under strict guidelines, and verifying that all checks are properly accounted for.

There is a plethora of ways that employees can steal from a food service outlet. While it is virtually impossible to eliminate theft, it can be minimized via control procedures. First, all managers should be trained in proper control procedures and randomly checked to verify that they are following these procedures. Collusion between a manager and cash handler can result in significant losses. Second, all cash handlers should be trained in correct cash handling procedures and should sign a form promising that they will adhere to the procedures. In addition, they should be trained to detect and report counterfeit money.

House bank funds must be closely controlled and issued only to authorized personnel who take responsibility for adhering to all control procedures. A floating house bank permits managers to issue the bank to a server for a shift, reconcile any discrepancies, and issue the bank to a new server when the next shift begins. Deposits of all the day's transactions should be made after each shift. Drops must be signed and witnessed. Disciplinary action should be taken for any significant variances. Credit cards, gift certificates, petty cash, and travel vouchers are also subject to strict controls. Because every dollar missing directly affects the bottom line, it is vital that these controls be implemented and closely monitored.

CHAPTER QUESTIONS

Discussion Questions

1. What are the advantages and disadvantages of POS systems relative to manual systems?

2. How are guest checks controlled in the storeroom?

3. How should check controls be monitored at each outlet?

4. Why and how should guest checks be audited?

5. Why and how should cover reports be conducted?

6. How should a check control log be established?

7. What are the responsibilities of cash handlers?

8. How can a counterfeit U.S. $100 bill be identified?

Critical Thinking Questions

1. What information should be recorded in a control log?

2. Which guests should be counted as covers?

3. How might employees steal from a food service operation?

4. If a server is issued checks 1156 through 1178, and returns 20 checks, how many checks are missing?

5. If a restaurant has 200 seats and serves 520 covers during a night, what is the turnover rate per seat?

6. If a restaurant has 150 seats and serves 500 covers at lunch, what is the turnover rate per seat?

7. If 500 covers are served at lunch and food and beverage revenue is $3,000, what is the combined average check?

8. If 400 covers are served at dinner and the combined food and beverage revenue is $6,000, what is the combined average check?

9. If a restaurant is open 31 days during the month, and produced 6,000 covers, what was the average number of covers per day?

10. If a restaurant is open 24 days per month and produced 6,000 covers, what was the average number of covers per day?

Objective Questions

1. Check control procedures begin when checks are issued to servers. True or False?

2. When a server voids a check, he or she should immediately tear it up and dispose of it so that it cannot be reused. True or False?

3. To determine the actual occupied rooms percentage, divide the number of occupied rooms by the number of available rooms. True or False?

4. When calculating average food check, promotional covers should not be included in the cover count. True or False?

5. Drops are deposits that are placed in the company's safe. True or False?

6. Unless dishonest intent can be demonstrated, it is illegal to take disciplinary action against an employee whose drop is short. True or False?

7. Credit card charges that are not collectable should be treated the same as a cash variance—with disciplinary action. True or False?

Multiple Choice Questions

1. Which of the following is NOT an innovation incorporated into the new U.S. currency to deter counterfeiting?
    A. A watermark visible from both sides
    B. A security thread
    C. Color-shifting ink
    D. The signature of the person whose portrait appears on the bill

2. When a manager audits a server at the end of one shift, then passes the bank to an incoming server, it is referred to as a
    A. floating house bank.
    B. house bank.
    C. sequential house bank.
    D. house bank transfer.

3. A witness to a drop should verify which of the following?
    A. The actual amount of money in the drop envelope and the fact that the drop has been made
    B. That the amount of money written on the envelope equals the amount on the drop record, and that the drop has been deposited in the safe

    C.   That all checks are properly accounted for, that the drop equals the amount recorded on the checks and the drop record, and that the drop has been deposited in the safe

    D.   Only that the drop has been deposited in the safe

4. Due-back slips are issued when

    A.   an employee works a split shift and is required to return on the same day.

    B.   the amount of cash and/or checks in a drop exceeds the amount due.

    C.   an employee is disciplined for cash shortages and receives an unpaid leave until the due-back date.

    D.   employees have cash overages.

5. A gift certificate sold but not yet redeemed is treated on the general ledger as a(n)

    A.   asset.

    B.   liability.

    C.   equity.

    D.   income.

CASE STUDY

Case Study: Theft or Not?

Holiday Resort has one restaurant that caters to all guests during three meal periods (breakfast, lunch, and dinner). The restaurant's operating hours are from 7 to 9 A.M. for breakfast, from noon to 2 P.M. for lunch, and from 6 to 9 P.M. for dinner. Breakfast meals are complimentary for in-house guests. Guests visiting from outside can only eat lunch or dinner in the restaurant if they have a prepaid meal ticket, which can only be purchased from the guest registration attendant at the front desk.

One Tuesday afternoon, a guest walks into the front desk area. Mary, the front desk employee, observes Alicia, the manager, handing the guest some meal tickets and receiving money in exchange. Alicia has a reputation of being very friendly with a good sense of humor. Alicia does not ring up the sale, so Mary reports her to a senior manager. When Alicia is confronted, she claims it was a tip given to her by the guest.

Your task:

1. Determine if Alicia can be fired for stealing. If so, what evidence does the company have?

2. Explain how check control can prevent Alicia from defrauding the company.

3. Determine under what circumstances Alicia could be rehired in the future.

4. Describe precautionary steps the company should take to prevent this type of hire.

CHAPTER 3

Menu Analysis and Planning for Sales

Learning Objectives

After reading this chapter, you should be able to:

- apply the concept of menu pricing;
- know what causes menu item demand to falter, and devise a response;
- evaluate menu profitability and popularity;
- implement an appropriate course of action to correct menu deficiencies.

In Practice

Just a few weeks into her job, Myla Thomas was proactive as she reworked the food and beverage cost control methods. She asked Chef Robert what steps he was taking in his menu analysis before introducing new menu items. They spoke on the phone about their next steps.

Myla: Based on guest comments, I can see the need for some revision to the current menu. Have we completed the analysis of the current menu before determining why we need the changes?

Robert: I am working on that now. It's an ongoing process, as you know. I hope to install the new menu in one month. Would you have time this afternoon to do some taste tests with me?

Myla: Certainly. I'd be happy to!

Just as Robert was hanging up the phone, Dana Clark, the new beverage manager, walked into the office. "So, what was it like here before Myla?" asked Dana with a smile.

"Well, our profit margin was just 2 percent. We were barely making it. Myla is exactly the jolt of electricity we all needed!" replied Robert. "We're back on the right track now."

INTRODUCTION

menu analysis The evaluation of menu costs and sales data to identify customers' needs and perceptions and to improve menu performance.

The purpose of this chapter is to show you how to conduct menu analysis as a way to maximize profit. **Menu analysis** is the evaluation of menu cost and sales data to identify customers' needs and perceptions and to improve menu performance. These steps enable you to make better decisions about marketing and operations.

As we saw in Chapter 2, the menu is the number-one sales tool. Figure 13-1 is the same as Figure 2-1, except that now the menu analysis functions are emphasized. These are the functions we will focus on in this chapter.

Just as important as controlling expenses is generating revenue. Increasing revenue has everything to do with your **pricing strategies.** Setting appropriate prices is what menu analysis helps you to accomplish.

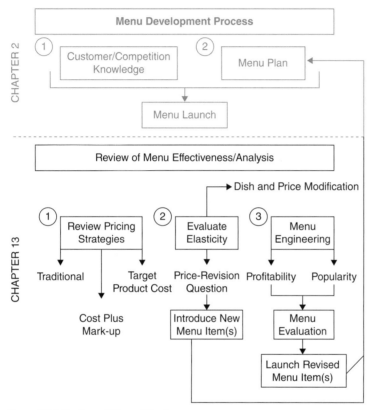

Figure 13-1 Review of Menu Effectiveness

STRATEGIES FOR MENU PRICING

There are three basic methods widely used in the industry to price menu items: traditional approaches, cost plus markup pricing, and product cost percentage pricing.

Traditional Pricing

Traditional menu pricing methods have been based on varied and often unreliable criteria. These pricing methods are not based on actual costs and profits; this uncertainty is dangerous for any restaurant. Some traditional pricing methods include the following:

- *Intuition.* Establishing prices based on intuition or feeling can result in failure to recover full costs, or in an unsatisfactory and unpredictable profit margin.

- *Competitive Pricing.* This simple method of pricing bases prices on what competitors in your market area are charging. In many instances, restaurants price slightly below the competition to capture a greater market share; in others, prices may be slightly elevated to achieve a more upscale image than that of the competition. This is often referred to as market positioning, and it is common in highly competitive areas.

  This may be a satisfactory method of pricing if the product or service is comparable to that of the competition, and if the prices may result in a satisfactory profit. However, this system assumes that both restaurants' costs, target markets, and business volumes are the same or similar. It also assumes that the competitor has established its prices using sound profitability analysis. If the menu was priced on intuition, the competitor may not be profitable, and neither will you. This is common in a buffet situation.

- *Buffet Pricing.* Managers following this method often initially adopt a competitor's pricing structure. This strategy is used because with a new product or new menu, you have no history of sales data to determine costs or average checks. In this case, some restaurants have grand opening sales to attract customers and establish a basis for future pricing and decision-making. The next step, after compiling a few days of sales history, is to determine the average cost per buffet customer. Buffet cost is calculated by subtracting the cost value of ending inventory from beginning inventory plus additions. This is divided by the number of buffet customers to determine the average cost per customer. Then costs are subtracted from sales to determine the profit margin. The final step is to add a desired markup rate to achieve the final price. The prices must be reviewed frequently to ensure that they are in line with customers' perception of what the buffet was worth.

- *"Follow the Leader" Pricing.* A form of competitive pricing, this method implies that there is a leader or dominant operation whose price structure and changes are followed by others in the market. The "follow the leader" method makes the same assumptions as competitive pricing and has the same deficiencies.

- *Psychological Pricing.* This method is based on customers' perceived value. There are two aspects of psychological pricing. The first relates to perception of price. The common practice of pricing an item at $4.95 rather than $5.00 relies upon the customer's perceiving the price as being significantly less than $5.00. This practice is becoming less popular, especially in upscale operations, as the value of a nickel or penny decreases and customers react to $4.95 as though it is $5.00.

  Secondly, management sets the pricing structure based upon a conscious evaluation of what the customer expects to pay for the product or service offered. This pricing method can be used successfully in famous gourmet restaurants, exclusive resorts, or restricted-membership clubs. It is not as effective in most restaurants due to the increased demand for value. Failing to give the customer strong perceived value does not allow for the survival of a restaurant. Each of the above pricing philosophies may be imprudent or incomplete ways of setting prices.

Cost Plus Markup Pricing

This type of method involves adding a markup to the product cost as follows:

$$\text{price} = (\text{item cost percentage} \times \text{markup}) + \text{item cost.}$$

As an example, if we assume that the product cost is $4 and the desired markup for the menu item is 75 percent, the price would be computed as follows: price = $(0.75 \times 4) + 4 = \$7$. It is important to note the distinction between markup rate and percentage margin: Markup rate is a percentage of cost, whereas percentage margin relates the return as a percentage of sales. Based on the example above:

Markup percent = $3 (profit) ÷ $4 (cost) = 75 percent

Margin percent = $3 (profit) ÷ $7 (price) = 43 percent

This method of pricing is very popular in the food-service industry because it is very simple to use and because it is based on hard cost data, helping to reduce the manager's feeling of uncertainty. In many cases, such pricing is practically necessary if the manager is setting prices for dozens of items. In a competitive environment, cost plus markup pricing can be interpreted as a form of tacit collusion or competitive pricing, particularly if the competitors apply conventional industry markup rates for homogenous products.

The logical weakness of cost plus markup pricing is that price is considered a function of cost, whereas the true causal relationship is just the opposite. Cost is determined by volume (production or sales), which, in turn, depends on prices, as you will see later as we discuss sales mix. Cost plus markup pricing also could lead to an irrational pricing policy, if the price is based on total average cost as opposed to direct product cost. Total average cost refers to the sum of allocated fixed cost and direct variable cost. In this instance the restaurant might increase prices when sales decrease because the lower the sales quantity, the higher the fixed cost allocated to a single item—and thus the higher the sales price. As you will see in subsequent sections, a price increase at a time of sales decrease is usually not the best pricing policy. Therefore, markup should be based on menu item cost and not on total cost; in this way, price is not affected by changes in sales quantity. Conventional markup certainly could be the result of the trial and error process by restaurant managers, but basing markup on average variable cost might save you a few errors.

Targeted Product Cost Percentage Pricing

Another form of pricing that is analogous to cost plus markup pricing is known as targeted product cost percentage pricing. Like the costing of food recipes, it can be used with a profit objective in view. The method for calculating product cost percentage is simple. The manager must first determine the **targeted ideal cost** percentage and potential cost of an item. Targeted ideal cost refers to the ideal amount of cost your company hopes to spend for the menu item. Potential costing, discussed in Chapter 4, refers to the calculated expectation of what the cost should be. Let us assume that the manager has set his target cost percentage at 25, and the potential cost of the menu item is $3. The calculation is as follows:

targeted ideal cost The ideal amount your company wants to spend; it is your goal, or what you have budgeted to spend.

price = potential cost / target cost percentage = 3/0.25 = $12.00

Cost-Based or Customer-Based Prices?

Dimitri Zafiris, food and beverage director of Barnabey's Hotel in Los Angeles, says that setting prices used to be easy: "You developed a menu, looked at the costs, and said, 'I need to make X,' and you marked it up accordingly—and people would buy it." Now, he says, the restaurant sets prices based on what customers are willing to pay rather than its own costs. For example, a new four-course menu with wine would have been priced at $180 based on its cost. However, careful analysis revealed that hotel customers would be willing to pay 20 percent more for the menu than the hotel had planned to charge. The hotel settled on a price of $200.

The difficulty with this method is fundamental: Even though your cost is high, if the customer does not perceive value at your price, he or she will not order the item. Likewise, the customer may be willing to pay more than the sales price you calculated. Keep these limitations in mind; you have profit objectives to meet for your establishment, but the customer must also have a positive perception of value.

ELASTICITY OF DEMAND

elasticity of demand The responsiveness of buyers to changes in price, defined as the percentage change in the quantity demanded divided by the percentage change in price.

The most popular measure of the impact of price on sales is demand elasticity. In general, **elasticity of demand** refers to the relationship of a relative change of price to the relative change of demand. The impact of elasticity on demand is mostly felt in a homogeneously competitive environment. For example, if two area restaurants offer a similar item, and one decides to increase its prices, that restaurant may lose sales. The manager must understand the relationship between menu prices and the customer demand for the menu items. The formula for deriving price elasticity of demand is as follows:

$$\text{elasticity} = \text{(relative) percentage change in sales volume} / \text{(relative) percentage change in price}$$

For instance, if reducing a hamburger's price by 2 percent causes a 4 percent increase in hamburger sales, the price elasticity is $4/-2 = -2$; that is, the relative volume change is twice as large as the relative price change. The negative sign is due to the fact that price and sales changes are inversely related. In fact, elasticity is always negative when a drop in price results in an increase in quantity sold. But are you selling enough of these cheaper burgers to make more profit? If you lower the price from $2 to $1.90, for example, and your sales go from 500 to 526 per week, you are still earning the same $1,000 in revenue per week.

Furthermore, the sale of some items (like soups and appetizers) will depend on the prices of other, main-course items. The degree of this dependency is measured by the cross-price elasticity, which is defined as the percentage change in unit sales of one item (such as soup) caused by a percentage change in unit sales of another product (such as a burger). It is important to note that if the main course items are priced too high, customers may not have enough money—or may not want to spend enough money—to buy soup or an appetizer, which often have higher profit percentages than the main-course items.

If two products are competing against each other—say, a mushroom burger versus a chili burger—the cross-price elasticity is positive. If, on the other hand, the products are complementary

---

Elasticity Depends on the Product

The demand for water is much more elastic than the demand for cigarettes. When cities raise the price of water by 10 percent, water usage goes down by as much as 12 percent. When the price of agricultural water goes up 10 percent, usage drops by about 20 percent. Agricultural users of water are much more sensitive to price than city dwellers, but both are much more sensitive to price than smokers. When the price of cigarettes increases by 10 percent, consumption of cigarettes drops by only 3 to 5 percent.

Sources: Terry L. Anderson and Clay J. Landry, "Trickle-Down Economic", *The Wall Street Journal*, August 23, 1999, p. A14; Gene Koretz, "Still Hooked on the Evil Weed," *BusinessWeek*, July 5, 1999, p. 18.

(like pizza and pizza toppings) and the customer must consume them together but buy them separately, the elasticity figure will be negative. In conclusion, the manager must know the price response function to make rational pricing decisions. Note that there may be considerable difference between the value of a meal to a customer and the price he or she is able and willing to pay for it. Pricing should therefore focus on the latter rather than on the former.

PRICE REVISION

The revision of the price of an item may become necessary either because of a change in production costs or because sales fail to reach the expected level. It is reasonable to have an established procedure for examining the problem, in the form of a checklist. Before attempting price revision, the following are some questions the manager should answer:

- Have prices changed recently? If yes, what effects on the volume of sales could be attributable to the price changes?

- Is there a noticeable long-term trend in prices, and if so, what is it?

- What types and amounts of discounts are in place in your restaurant?

- To what extent do your prices, discounts, and terms of sale differ from those of your competitors? Is there any price leadership in operation?

- What volume changes would you need in order to compensate for price changes?

- What information might show the market reaction to price changes of your actual and potential competitors?

- Where is the break-even point? (This is discussed in Chapter 14.) To what extent is the restaurant's target profit attained?

- To what extent does the current contribution per item differ from the potential contribution? (See Chapter 9.)

- What is your market share in the area you serve? Is it increasing, steady, or declining? Does it make sense to change the menu entirely?

- What is the current cost structure of the product? Has there been any departure from the recipes or costing methods?

- Have the cost changes you have experienced also affected your competitors? If not, why not?

- What are the present limits of your productive capacity? To what extent is this capacity currently utilized? If the restaurant is operating at or near capacity, could extra capital be found to increase capacity, and if so, at what cost?

- Have any of the unit factor costs (labor, recipe items, and so on) changed, and if so, to what extent?

Once these questions are answered adequately, the manager should consider eliminating old items and introducing new ones, or conducting menu analysis before deciding.

Introducing New Menu Items

There are several reasons why managers make decisions to eliminate menu items and introduce new ones. Some depend on the answers to the questions above; others could be due to changes in customers' preferences, such as healthy food choices and menu fatigue. Whatever the reason, most decisions are based on both quantitative and qualitative factors.

Quantitative decisions are based on data collection. Some of this data corresponds to the questions asked above. For example, the POS system can provide data on sales of different items.

Qualitative decisions rely on intuition, perception, and professional common sense. These decisions include information from both before and after the menu launch date and involve reevaluating customer trends in product preferences. This is important for continued menu development. As time goes on, your guests' perceived value, tastes, and nutritional wishes will change, as will your available ingredients, and your staff will learn new ways to combine and present recipes. You will need to be able to use these new changes to improve your menu.

MENU ENGINEERING

menu engineering
Techniques used for analyzing menu profitability and popularity.

In this section, we will focus on menu engineering methods to maximize sales. **Menu engineering** is the most conservative and complete approach to maximizing sales. It works on the basis of gross profit and menu item price elasticity, and from that data you can measure the popularity and profitability of each menu item. The gross-profit theory of menu analysis states that profits are maximized through the correct combinations of selling prices, costs, and sales counts. Menu engineering provides a quantitative method of evaluating the success of a new menu as compared to a previous one.

The data required to prepare the menu engineering analysis includes selling prices, sales counts of each menu item, and direct product costs. Non-entrée food items, as well as beverages, should be separated and analyzed by category. Menu engineering includes price elasticity testing. A price is said to be inelastic when the quantity sold does not vary with price increases or reductions. It would be unwise to reduce the price of an inelastic item, since the sales would be unaffected. On the other hand, an item has an elastic price when sales counts can

---

What Did That Salmon Dish Cost?

Restaurants mark up food costs by an average of 300 percent to cover their overhead and to generate a profit, but the markup is not the same for all items on the menu. Some ingredients—especially prime cuts of beef and exotic seafood such as fresh scallops—are so costly that diners would not tolerate a 300 percent markup. So restaurants make it up on the inexpensive items, such as vegetables, pasta, and salmon. Why salmon? The farmed variety is only $2.50 per pound wholesale, much cheaper than prime restaurant-quality beef. At the Docks Restaurant in New York, a 10-ounce salmon dinner garnished with potatoes and coleslaw is priced at $19.50. The actual cost of the ingredients is only $1.90.

To take another example, the ingredients of the best-selling Angus beef tenderloin at the Sunset Grill in Nashville, Tennessee, cost the restaurant $8.42. Applying the average 300 percent markup, the price of the meal would be $33.68. But few diners would order the meal at that price. So instead the restaurant charges just $25. In contrast, the restaurant charges $9 for its Grilled Vegetable Plate whose ingredients cost only $1.55.

Source: Eileen Daspin, "Entrée Economics," *The Wall Street Journal,* March 10, 2000, pp. W1 and W4. Reprinted by permission of The Wall Street Journal, Copyright © 2000 Dow Jones & Company, Inc. All Rights Reserved Worldwide. License number 2103290892213.

be affected dramatically via price increases or reductions. Dropping the price of an elastic item may stimulate sales and increase total profit. On the other hand, increasing the price of a difficult-to-handle, high-cost elastic item that draws in customers may lower the number sold, thus increasing the contribution margin for the item but not the overall restaurant profit percentage.

A menu designed solely from the perspective of achieving the lowest overall food cost percentages will cause the operation to sacrifice total sales revenues. This is because low-food-cost items are usually priced higher in percentages than high-food-cost items. An operation takes dollars, not percentages, to the bank. In many instances, raising food cost percentages to stimulate additional sales may actually increase profitability. As revenue increases, the percentage of fixed costs (such as rent and insurance) is lowered. According to Rick Braa at the 2006 Hospitality Financial and Technology Professional (HFTP) conference: "Opportunities are often lost by focusing solely on percentages, but they are only a good measurement." Take for example the calculations in Figures 13-2. Which item would you rather sell more of: the pasta or the steak?

	Pasta	**Steak**
Price	100.0%	100.0%
Food Cost	25.0%	40.0%
Labor Cost	23.2%	15.0%
Prime Cost	48.2%	55.0%
Gross Profit	51.8%	45.0%

Figure 13-2 Menu Prices 1

Now take a look at Figure 13-3 below. The pasta sells for $12.95 and the steak sells for $19.95.

	Pasta		**Steak**	
Price	$12.95	100.0%	$19.95	100.0%
Food Cost	$3.24	25.0%	$7.98	40.0%
Labor Cost	$3.00	23.2%	$3.00	15.0%
Prime Cost	$6.24	48.2%	$10.98	55.0%
Gross Profit	$6.71	51.8%	$8.97	45.0%

Figure 13-3 Menu Prices 2

What is your answer after seeing Figure 13-3? The answer is obvious; you will take more money to the bank with the steak if both items sell an equal amount.

Menu Profitability Analysis

To determine a menu item's profitability or contribution margin, you need to know two things: the item's selling price and the item's recipe cost. Selling price minus recipe cost is equal to the contribution margin. The contribution margin will be valuable for calculations in this section; you will need to know how to perform it on all of your menu items. Follow this example for an ahi tuna entrée:

Selling price	=	$18.75
Recipe food cost (8-ounce portion of tuna)	=	($0.93)
Garnishes	=	($0.40)
Vegetable, starch, roll, and butter	=	($1.00)
Total cost	=	($2.33)
Contribution margin	=	$16.42

This example shows how to determine the profitability, or total contribution margin, of an item. First, subtract the recipe cost from the sale price. Then multiply that by the number of items sold. For example, if 50 orders of ahi tuna were sold, the total contribution margin for the item would be 50 × ($18.75 − $2.33), or $821. The profitability, then, is the ratio of an item's profit contribution to the total profit contribution of all items sold within one menu category. Here is the formula:

$$\text{profitability} = \text{one item's profit contribution} / \text{total category contribution}$$

Menu Popularity Analysis

Using the selling price and quantity of each item sold, you can determine popularity percentages for each item within a category. A category is a group of like items, such as entrées, appetizers, desserts, or alcoholic beverages. You will also need to know the total number of items sold from the category. Use this formula for each item:

$$\text{popularity percentage} = \text{number of the item sold} / \text{total number of items sold}$$

sales mix Number of sales of menu items; perhaps patternized. Also, the products and sales packages offered.

For the venison in Figure 13-4, the equation would be 54 / 429 = 12.6 percent. These percentages add up to what is called the sales mix. **Sales mix** is the number of individual menu items sold compared to all the items sold in that category.

The popularity of a single menu item could also determine your overall cost, especially when its percentage is very high. Note the example in Figures 13-4 and 13-5, in which item popularity affects cost.

Figure 13-4 Menu Popularity Analysis 1

		#a	#b	#c	#d	#e	#f	#g	#h
# of item	Menu Items	Recipe Cost	Selling Price	January Number Sold	Sales Mix	February Number Sold	Sales Mix	March Number Sold	Sales Mix
1	Tuna Ahi	$2.33	$18.75	48	11.2%	40	9.3%	60	14.0%
2	Pork Chop Grilled	$3.70	$16.95	64	14.9%	64	14.9%	64	14.9%
3	Cod Grilled Atlantic	$4.00	$17.50	26	6.1%	26	6.1%	26	6.1%
4	Tian Of Pepper & Mush.	$4.81	$15.50	51	11.9%	66	15.4%	40	9.3%
5	Huckleberry Glaze Venison	$6.72	$22.50	54	12.6%	60	14.0%	40	9.3%
6	Beef Tenderloin	$4.46	$22.00	95	22.1%	95	22.1%	95	22.1%
7	Chicken Saute with Olive	$3.40	$16.75	37	8.6%	37	8.6%	37	8.6%
8	Monkfish saddle W/lentils	$5.97	$22.00	31	7.2%	31	7.2%	31	7.2%
9	Tomato - Garlic Fettuccin	$2.04	$15.95	23	5.4%	10	2.3%	36	8.4%
Total				429	100.0%	429	100.0%	429	100.0%

Figure 13-5 Menu Popularity Analysis 2

# of item	Menu Items	#i Total Cost January (#a × #c)	#j Total Cost February (#a × #e)	#k Total Cost March (#a × #g)	#l Total Revenue January (#b × #c)	#m Total Revenue February (#b × #e)	#n Total Revenue March (#b × #g)
1	Tuna Ahi	$111.84	$93.20	$139.80	$900.00	$750.00	$1,125.00
2	Pork Chop Grilled	$236.80	$236.80	$236.80	$1,084.80	$1,084.80	$1,084.80
3	Cod Grilled Atlantic	$104.00	$104.00	$104.00	$455.00	$455.00	$455.00
4	Tian Of Pepper & Mush.	$245.31	$317.46	$192.40	$790.50	$1,023.00	$620.00
5	Huckleberry Glaze Venison	$362.88	$403.20	$268.80	$1,215.00	$1,350.00	$900.00
6	Beef Tenderloin	$423.70	$423.70	$423.70	$2,090.00	$2,090.00	$2,090.00
7	Chicken Saute with Olive	$125.80	$125.80	$125.80	$619.75	$619.75	$619.75
8	Monkfish saddle W/lentils	$185.07	$185.07	$185.07	$682.00	$682.00	$682.00
9	Tomato - Garlic Fettuccini	$46.92	$20.40	$73.44	$366.85	$159.50	$574.20
Total		$1,842.32	$1,909.63	$1,749.81	$8,203.90	$8,214.05	$8,150.75

As you can see, the changes in customer demand (popularity) of any item can affect the sales mix percentage of that item in the overall picture. If your least-profitable items are the most popular, for example, your overall cost percentage may be unacceptably high.

The numbers in Figure 13-5 show the revenue and cost totals for each of the months in the example. Each column lists a formula that corresponds to the columns in Figure 13-4. The costs and revenues vary each month solely due to changes in popularity and sales mix.

Although product cost and sales prices remain the same from month to month, the overall cost percentages do not (Figure 13-6). The cost and prices remain the same for January through March, but not the cost percentages in Column Q. The reason that each month varies in total cost percentages is the variation in sales mix, or customer selection. This means the customer, not the manager, has determined the cost percentages. You might do everything—portion control, standard recipes, wise purchasing, and so on—to ensure your control procedures are followed, but it is ultimately customer demand that will determine your actual cost—and the customer's demand is influenced by your pricing strategies.

Evaluating Menu Profitability and Popularity

Figure 13-7 provides the data with which to rank the items in our example by profitability and popularity for the month of January.

Now you have the tools to classify each item in the category into one of four groups (Figure 13-8).

Figure 13-6 Menu Popularity Analysis by Month

Location	#o Total Revenue	#p Total Cost	#q #p #o Cost %
January	$8,203.90	$1,842.32	22.5%
February	$8,214.05	$1,909.63	23.2%
March	$8,150.75	$1,749.81	21.5%
Total	$24,568.70	$5,501.76	22.4%

Figure 13-7 Menu Analysis with Price

Menu Item	Recipe Cost	Selling Price	Difference Between Cost and Price *	Difference Divided by Category Total	Item's Profitability Rank	January Number Sold	Sales Mix	Item's Popularity Rank
Tuna Ahi	$2.33	$18.75	$16.42	12.60%	2	48	11.20%	5
Pork Chop Grilled	$3.70	$16.95	$13.25	10.20%	7	64	14.90%	2
Cod Grilled Atlantic	$4.00	$17.50	$13.50	10.40%	6	26	6.10%	8
Tian Of Pepper & Mush.	$4.81	$15.50	$10.69	8.20%	9	51	11.90%	4
Huckleberry Venison	$6.72	$22.50	$15.72	12.10%	4	54	12.60%	3
Beef Tenderloin	$4.46	$22.00	$17.54	13.50%	1	95	22.10%	1
Chicken Saute with Olive	$3.40	$16.75	$13.35	10.00%	8	37	8.60%	6
Monkfish saddle W/lentils	$5.97	$22.00	$16.03	12.30%	3	31	7.20%	7
Tomato - Garlic Fettuccini	$2.04	$15.95	$13.91	10.70%	5	23	5.40%	9
TOTALS:			$130.41	100.00%		429	100.00%	

* this equals profit contribution

Figure 13-8 Profitability and Popularity

Items	Rank
Highly popular and highly profitable	Star (e.g., beef tenderloin)
Highly popular but less than average profitable	Plow Horse (e.g., pork chop)
Less than average popularity but highly profitable	Puzzle (e.g., monk fish)
Less than average popularity and less than average profitability	Dog (e.g., chicken saute)

Evaluate your items according to their popularity and profitability. All of your menu items will fall into the chart shown in Figure 13-9 below, giving you a picture of how your menu engineering has been in the past and where your energies should be spent in improvement.

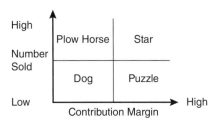

Figure 13-9 Evaluation of Menu Items

It is important to note that, in order to place any value on these calculations, you must prepare your menu items the same way each time. High-profit menu items and house specialties also must be prepared consistently. This is the ideal, but in reality, studies conducted by the company Software Creation show this to be the case only 50 to 75 percent of the time.

In the **star** category, items are both profitable and popular. Give them a highly visible menu location and strictly maintain their quality. Employ the test for elasticity mentioned previously. You want to know if you can raise the price and still sell large numbers of these items.

star A menu engineering classification of items that are both popular and profitable.

Plow horse items are popular but do not attain average profitability. The overall strategy would be to increase the contribution margin of these items. Price increases should be considered. Generally, it is not wise to lower these items' prices due to the already low contribution margin. Furthermore, little money should be spent on promoting these items since they are already popular. However, if the intent is to draw customers' attention to other menu items or to increase total sales volume, this may be a good strategy. Evaluate your recipes to determine whether costs can be reduced without lowering perceived value.

plow horse A menu engineering classification of items which are not very profitable but which are popular with customers.

Puzzle items are profitable but low-sale items. Evaluate the quality of each: Is it a poor product, perhaps with a low standard of presentation? Is it simply an unpopular product that needs some sales promotion? Is it overpriced? These conditions will result in a perception of low value and will reduce customer demand. If the item is elastic and is believed to be a highly popular item, lowering its price could make it a star. If this product is unpopular in your marketplace, perhaps it should be left off the next menu or replaced with another item that has the potential of increasing sales and profitability. Assess its related costs, such as shelf life, waste, spoilage, leftovers, and labor. Remember that it does not matter how much money you make per sale if you have no sales!

puzzle A menu engineering classification of items that are particularly profitable but not very popular with guests.

An item that is neither popular nor profitable, in the **dog** category, should not remain on the menu unless it serves to influence the sales of other menu items or there is hope that it will gain popularity. Increase the price to move it to the puzzle category. Check product quality while promoting the item strongly. Change its image and perceived value to increase sales level significantly, or consider dropping the item.

dog A menu engineering classification of items which are neither profitable nor popular.

The end result of menu analysis or engineering is to minimize the dogs, limit the number of puzzles, and maximize the stars. The remaining items will be plow horses, which will enhance the menu profitability. Note, however, the following caveats to the system: Because menu items are categorized relative to one another, some items must fall into less-desirable categories. Do not put energy into a never-ending battle of adjusting weak items, only to find strong items falling below average. Use common sense to maximize stronger items and profitability.

Loss leaders—items that are less profitable than others—serve a purpose, as do high- and low-ticket items. A weak item may contribute to the overall success of an operation. The operation

loss leader A menu item that is priced low because it is not very profitable and not popular with customers.

may be the only one in the area serving a specialty item. This may attract customers in spite of the item's lack of profitability. These customers are likely to bring in other patrons who will order more profitable items.

There are many ways to use the system outlined above. Consider these variations on the basic menu engineering approach:

- Factor in the variable cost of preparation labor, or prime cost, rather than simply the food cost. How long does it take to prepare this item?

- Factor in butcher costs, and take into consideration differing costs for precut and in-house butchering.

- Rank menu items by a combination of their food cost percentage and their contribution margin.

An Automated Approach to Menu Engineering

Many food-service owners, managers, and accountants use personal computers for accounting functions with the same ease and frequency as they use a telephone. As automated applications for menu engineering increase, so does the need for service operators to become more familiar with computers.

An NRA study titled "The Food Service Manager 2000" rated the need for greater computer proficiency as the most important priority for managers. In fact, managers and food-service operators will continue to move to comprehensive computer-based information systems. In addition to generating menu engineering reports, systems like these can help solve scheduling issues, forecast sales, compile sales reports, and manage inventory.

Because of the wide application of menu engineering in evaluating the performance of the existing menu and in future menu planning and design, we have developed an Excel worksheet, included in this book's companion CD, to aid the student and professional. A complete illustration of how to use this worksheet is provided in Figure 13-10. Please be sure to read the instructions completely before beginning these calculations.

The column descriptions are as follows:

- Column A: The item number within its menu category. This is not a ranking.

- Column B: Names of menu items.

- Column C: Number of menu items sold per guest checks or POS sales reports.

menu mix A proportion of different menu items that make up a complete restaurant menu.

- Column D: Menu mix percentages. The term **menu mix** refers to a proportion of different menu item that make up a complete restaurant menu. Arriving at the correct mix that satisfy the customer and the restaurant profit objective require analysis. The percentage for each item is derived by dividing the number of menu items sold by the total number of all menu items sold. For example, if an outlet sold 48 tuna ahi out of total sales of 429, the menu mix percentage would therefore be 48 / 429, or 11.2 percent.

- Column E: Calculated recipe cost of each item.

- Column F: Selling price of each item.

- Column G: Contribution margin for each menu item. This is the selling price minus the item cost for each item (Column F – Column E).

- Column I: Item cost percentage. The following example shows how this is calculated:

	Tuna ahi	
Price		$18.75 ($a$)
Cost		$2.33 ($b$)
Cost percent =	$\frac{b}{a}$	= 12.43 percent

- Column I: Total cost. This is derived by multiplying Column C (number sold) by Column E (item cost).

- Column J: Total revenue. This is derived by multiplying Column C (number sold) by Column F (selling price).

- Column K: Total contribution margin. This is derived by multiplying Column C (number sold) by Column G (contribution margin).

- Column L: Contribution margin category. The amount that each menu item in Column G contributed to the total menu is compared to the average contribution in Line Q, at the bottom left of the chart. Line Q is derived by dividing the sum of column K by the sum of Column C. The entry (low or high) in Column L is made after comparing Column G and Line Q.

- Column M: Menu mix category. This column evaluates each item's sales performance in the overall menu group category. Each item percentage in Column D is compared to Line P. Each menu mix percentage in Column D is then ranked as high or low in Column M, depending upon its comparison with Line P. Line P is considered the benchmark or average of the entire competing category (although it is really only 70 percent of the real average) and is derived as follows:

  Line P = 1 / number of items $\times$ 0.7

Menu engineering assumes that an item is popular if its sales average 70 percent or more of total average sales. If you lower or increase these average percentages, you will get a different result in terms of what items appear popular.

If there are nine items in a category, the calculation would look like this:

$\frac{1}{9} \times 0.70 = 7.8$ percent

- Column N: Evaluation of the combination of Column L and Column M.

- Line O: Menu category total cost. This is derived by dividing the total of Column I by the total of Column J.

- Line P: See Column M above.

- Line Q: See Column L above.

- Line R: Multiply the total of Column C by Line P to get Line R. In this case, the result is 33.

This chart enables the manager to consider menu changes. The results of these calculations establish a complete picture of the bottom line for the items that are tested. From the calculations, the manager can decide the fate of various items clearly and effectively. In addition, the manager can instruct the service staff on which items to push or to sell as specials, thus making this chart a marketing tool as well.

Menu Engineering Decision Matrix Graph

Having discussed the dynamics of menu analysis, we will now focus on developing a decision matrix for all menu items. This is a useful tool for the manager to evaluate the performance of

Figure 13-10 Menu Dynamics Analysis

(a) No.	(b) FINEDINI.WK1 Menu Item Name	(c) Number Sold	(d) Menu Mix %	(e) Item Cost	(f) Sell Price	(g) Contribution Margin	(h) Item Cost %	(i) Total Cost	(j) Total Revenue	(k) Total C.M.	(l) Total Cat.	(m) M.M. Cat.	(n) Item Class
1	Tuna Ahi	48	11.2%	$2.33	$18.75	$16.42	12.4%	$111.84	$900.00	$788.16	High	High	Star
2	Pork Chop Grilled	64	14.9%	$3.70	$16.95	$13.25	21.8%	$236.80	$1,084.80	$848.00	Low	High	Plowhorse
3	Cod grilled Atlantic	26	6.1%	$4.00	$17.50	$13.50	22.9%	$104.00	$455.00	$351.00	Low	Low	Dog
4	Tian Of Pepper & Mush.	51	11.9%	$4.81	$15.50	$10.69	31.0%	$245.31	$790.50	$545.19	Low	High	Plowhorse
5	Hunkleberry glaze Venison	54	12.6%	$6.72	$22.50	$15.78	29.9%	$362.88	$1,215.00	$852.12	High	High	Star
6	BeefTenderloin	95	22.1%	$4.46	$22.00	$17.54	20.3%	$423.70	$2,090.00	$1,666.30	High	High	Star
7	Chicken Saute with Olive	37	8.6%	$3.40	$16.75	$13.35	20.3%	$125.80	$619.00	$493.95	Low	High	Plowhorse
8	Monkfish saddle W/Lentils	31	7.2%	$5.97	$22.00	$16.03	27.1%	$185.07	$682.00	$496.93	High	Low	Puzzle
9	Tomato - Garlic Fettuccin	23	5.4%	$2.04	$15.95	$13.91	12.8%	$366.92	$366.85	$319.93	Low	Low	Dog
	Totals	429	100%					$1,842.32	$8,203.90	$6,361.58	Report Printed:		19-Jul 09

Date: January09
Outlet: Fine Dinning
Competing Category: Entrees

% Total Item Cost: 22.5% (o)
Menu Mix Percentage: 7.8% (p)
Ave. Contribution: $14.83 (q)
Ave. Achievement # : 33 (r)

each competing menu item within a category. Not all items will share the same characteristics within their groups; therefore, it may be appropriate to conduct this analysis frequently. Further, it is wise to emphasize improving the position of each new item through up-selling, menu design, and reviewing competitors' selling prices.

On the matrix graph shown in Figure 13-11, each menu item is positioned according to its contribution margin and menu mix coordination. The horizontal axis depicts contribution margin, and the vertical axis reflects popularity or menu mix.

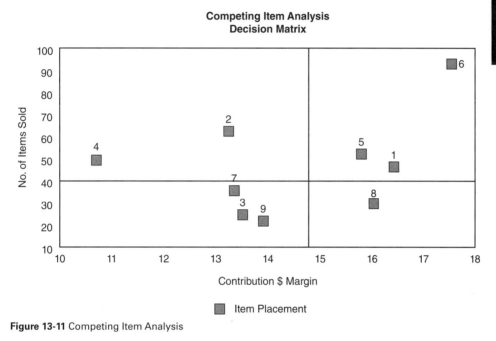

Figure 13-11 Competing Item Analysis

Launching Revised Menu Items

The decision to launch a revised menu item is similar to the decision to launch a new item, as discussed above. The only difference is that management has usually undertaken extensive analysis before making this decision. The menu has been repriced, recosted, and repositioned, and employees' comments considered and documented. For the restaurant to succeed financially, the process of menu development and analysis must start all over again.

SUMMARY

Several methods are used to set menu prices. Menu engineering is the most scientific approach, providing a quantitative method of evaluating a menu. In this approach, both the profitability and popularity of items are evaluated and ranked. Items are categorized as stars, dogs, plow horses, or puzzles, and treated accordingly. To assist in performing this analysis, computers are extremely helpful. A sample spreadsheet has been included in the online companion to this book.

CHAPTER QUESTIONS

Critical Thinking Questions

1. What impact do your potential customers have on the item selections and pricing of the menu?

2. What are the advantages of using menu engineering?

3. What is price elasticity, and why should it be considered when setting menu prices?

4. What is the danger of focusing too heavily on food cost percentages?

Objective Questions

1. As the contribution margin of an item increases, the food cost percentage decreases. True or False?

2. Menu engineering should be used to help determine the placement of items on the menu. True or False?

For Questions 3 and 4: Given the following sales mix, what should the potential food cost (in dollars and percentage) have been?

Item	Number Sold	Selling Price	Potential Food Cost Percent
Rib-eye steaks	1,000	$23.75	25
Fish	2,000	$28.00	32
Chicken	1,500	$21.50	20

3. Potential food cost: $_____

4. Potential food cost: _____ percent

For Questions 5 and 6: Given the following sales mix, what should the potential food cost (in dollars and percentage) have been?

Item	Number Sold	Selling Price	Potential Food Cost Percent
Rib-eye steaks	2,000	$23.75	25
Fish	1,000	$28.00	32
Chicken	1,500	$21.50	20

5. Potential food cost: $_____

6. Potential food cost: _____ percent

Multiple Choice Questions

1. Typical menu pricing strategies include all of the following EXCEPT
    A. Intuition
    B. Competitive pricing
    C. Menu engineering pricing
    D. Quantum analysis pricing

2. Higher contribution margins will generate higher profitability
    A. if the number of items sold does not decrease.
    B. all the time.
    C. under no circumstances.
    D. if price elasticity is great.

3. Which menu category refers to items that are highly popular but less than average in contribution margin?
    A. Star
    B. Plow horse
    C. Puzzle
    D. Dog

4. Which menu category refers to items that are high in both popularly and contribution margin?
    A. Star
    B. Plow horse
    C. Puzzle
    D. Dog

Staff Planning and Labor Cost Control

Learning Objectives

After reading this chapter, you should be able to:

- understand fair hiring practices;
- understand the differences between salary and wages;
- apply FLSA rules to payroll processes;
- calculate overtime pay for hourly employees;
- use governmental and voluntary deductions in payroll processes;
- use staff planning to manage employee morale and labor costs;
- schedule your staff wisely to maximize productivity;
- create a staffing guide and staffing standards;
- forecast business volume for adequate staffing;
- conduct a productivity analysis of sales volume versus labor hours;
- perform a full-time equivalent (FTE) study.

In Practice

Myla Thomas focused on controlling one of the primary costs in the food-service industry: labor costs. With planning and an effective monitoring system, she knew she could keep staff costs within budget and avoid letting these expenses get out of hand.

Myla believed strongly that ability is what you are capable of doing, motivation determines what you actually do, and attitude determines how well you do it. In each of these three areas, she felt that the team could do a better job, which would translate into satisfied customers and improved profits. Myla scheduled a meeting with Sarah Bright, the human resources manager, to discuss challenges facing the company in these areas.

Myla: *There are times when I am not satisfied with the levels of employee performance, and it is at times connected to attitude. What do you think might be contributing to low employee morale?*

Sarah: *It has a lot to do with scheduling and employee recognition. Sometimes we fall short in these two areas.*

(continues)

(continued)

Myla: *Agreed. What about the current standards? Are they contributing to the problem?*

Sarah: *The standards give managers guidelines, so they can encourage staff excellence and efficiency. But I must say that we have never developed reasonable expectations and plans for these costs.*

Myla: *Why not? That should be the foundation for managing labor cost. Wouldn't you agree?*

Sarah: *Yes, of course. I took over payroll responsibilities six months ago to mitigate the challenges we were facing from business and legal reporting requirements. Part of my goal is to provide business and legal support to the team.*

INTRODUCTION

This chapter addresses a basic area of cost control: knowledge about the rules and regulations of labor costs. Then we turn to the laws governing any payroll system, because these affect how labor costs are accumulated and reported. Lastly, we examine labor standards and productivity assessment.

Business success in the food-service industry requires a balancing act among three competing pressures in staff planning and labor cost control:

1. Pressure from the owner or investors to improve productivity and minimize payroll cost

2. Pressure from employees for improved hours and wages

3. Pressure from customers for improved services

The *pressure from the owner* stems from the fact that labor costs represent a significant portion of total operation expenses. Figure 14-1 shows figures reported by the National Restaurant Association (NRA) in 2007.

Figure 14-1 Operating Expenses

	Full service restaurant (with an average check per person under $10)	Full service restaurant (with an average check per person over $10)	Limited service, fast food restaurants
Salaries and wages	28.0% of sales	26.9% of sales	24.2% of sales
Employee benefits	3.9% of sales	4.2% of sales	3.7% of sales
Cost of food sold	32.2% of sales	30.0% of sales	28.4% of sales

In fact, because the combination of labor and food costs typically consumes approximately 60 percent of revenue, it is often called prime cost. In this chapter, we will examine the different components of labor cost.

Employee pressure to improve hours and wages is not limited to the food-service industry. In fact, all employees' happiness and performance are largely influenced by these factors:

*   When are employees available to work, versus when they are scheduled to work?

*   Are employees required to maintain a minimum number of hours in order to be eligible for benefits? What are your company's policies?

- Which position or positions is each employee qualified to fill?

- Do the minimum and maximum shift length conflict with employees' other obligations?

- How many hours do employees want to work per week, versus how many hours they are scheduled?

- Are overtime work requirements an issue?

- Is seniority a factor?

- Do any union rules prevail?

- Is proficiency for a particular task required?

- Can employees get the days off that they want?

- Did the employee receive adequate job training?

- Are the company's hiring practices fair or discriminatory?

Because of the pressure from the owners, many managers often place a much higher emphasis on the bottom line than on employee morale. But the cost of low morale can be enormous: Hiring, training, and motivating staff is not only time-consuming, but also expensive. A recent study of Marriott Hotels, conducted by Schlesinger and Heskett of the Harvard Business Review, revealed that a 10 percent decrease in employee turnover has been found to correlate with a 1 to 3 percent decrease in lost customers and a $50 to $100 million increase in revenue. Because these front-line people are vital to the success of any food-service operation, their morale should be a prime consideration of any manager, even while he or she stays focused on the bottom line.

Discrimination in a work place

One of the key areas in which managers can influence good relations with employees is in fair hiring practices. Using proper hiring practices helps avoid discrimination based on race, gender, or other protected characteristics, and can also set the standards necessary for a non-discriminating, non-harassing environment. To ensure that employers do not discriminate against protected classes in the hiring process, the law bars employers from asking certain questions at the time of an employment interview. The ban applies to all aspects of the hiring process, including the application form, the interview, and questions contained in the testing materials the employer may utilize.

The following are some examples of broad questions that are not allowed, and some narrower, acceptable questions to elicit particular information while not violating interviewees' rights:

Not allowed: *Have you ever been arrested?*

Allowed: *Have you been convicted of any of the following crimes?* (The crimes listed must be reasonably related to the job)

This question might be applicable for jobs for which you need a driver, for example, and wish to check his or her legal driving status. Such a question is legitimate while asking whether someone has ever been arrested could discriminate against someone who was arrested for an unrelated crime or misdemeanor.

Not allowed: *What country are you from?*

Allowed: *Are you authorized to work in the United States?*

While an employer needs to know if a potential employee can legally work, asking "What country are you from?" elicits unnecessary information that could seem discriminatory.

Not allowed: *How many days were you absent from work because of illness last year?*

Allowed: *Are you able to lift 100 pound weight and carry it up to 400 yards, which is required by this job?*

The more specific you are, the better—and the specifics should be exactly those that are required by the position.

Not allowed: *Are you married? Engaged? Divorced?*

Allowed: *Would you be willing to travel as needed for the job?*

An applicant's marital status is personal and does not help the employer understand his or her willingness or availability for travel—remember to stay within the job specifications.

Not allowed: *How old are you?*

Allowed: *Are you over the age of 18?*

Asking someone's age implies that the hiring decision might be made on this basis, but all the hiring manager needs to know is whether or not the applicant is legally able to work in the position.

Not allowed: *What religion do you practice?*

Allowed: *This job requires working weekends and holidays. Is there anything that would prevent you from doing so?*

Again, someone's religion is not a legitimate basis for hiring or not hiring a person. However, you can discern whether or not the person can work the necessary days for the position in question.

Race is one of the grounds on which the relevant statute, called Title VII, outlaws discrimination. The statute's main objective in the beginning was to eliminate discrimination against blacks. Sadly, racism has been a fact in our society, requiring this remedial legislation. Its application, however, is not restricted to any one racial or minority group. In the words of the United States Supreme Court, the prohibition against discrimination in employment on the basis of race bars "discriminatory preference for any racial group, minority or majority." Additional examples of racial groups include Caucasian, Hispanic, Asian, Native American, and Inuit.

The outlawed discrimination includes not only refusal to hire, resistance to promotion, and unjustified firing, but also all other types of discrimination, such as refusal to allow an employee to wear a particular hairstyle or terminating a white employee for associating with a black colleague.

An interesting application of Title VII is found in *Singh v. Shoney's, Inc.*

64 F.3d 217 (5th Cir. 1995). An employer was able to defend against a claim of discriminatory firing by establishing a legitimate, nondiscriminatory reason for the termination. A charge of discrimination made by a Caucasian dining-room supervisor was dismissed because the employer could establish misconduct on the employee's part, thus justifying the termination.

Delores Singh filed a complaint against her former employer, Shoney's, Inc., alleging that she was fired because of her race. The district court granted summary judgment in favor of Shoney's. Singh, a white female, worked for Shoney's for more than ten years. At the time of her termination in January 1993, Singh held the position of Dining Room Supervisor in a Shoney's restaurant in New Orleans, Louisiana. Her duties included hiring, firing, supervising, disciplining, and training the hosts, wait staff, and salad bar attendants who worked in the restaurant.

In January 1993, Shoney's corporate office received a petition signed by 36 workers employed in the same restaurant as Singh. The petition alleged that Singh had been engaging in offensive, racially-discriminating conduct toward subordinate employees. Shoney's responded to the petition by sending its Vice-President of Personnel, John Southerland, and its Equal Employment Opportunity Manager, Juanita Presley (both of whom are black), to New Orleans to investigate the allegations. Southerland and Presley interviewed 44 employees at the restaurant, including Singh. Based on these interviews, Shoney's concluded that Singh had engaged in offensive, inappropriate conduct in the workplace, and terminated her employment.

During the course of the investigation, it came to Shoney's attention that the manager of the restaurant, Terry Dumars, a black male, had also engaged in inappropriate conduct in the workplace, and he was terminated. Dumars was replaced with a white male, and Singh was replaced with another white female. Singh attempted to sue Shoney's for discrimination against her in her firing.

In order to file a *prima facie* case of discrimination, which is a Latin expression meaning "on its first appearance" a plaintiff alleging discriminatory discharge must show (1) that she is a member of a protected group; (2) that she was qualified for the job that she formerly held (and performing her job at a level that met the employer's legitimate expectations); (3) that she was discharged; and (4) that after her discharge, the position she held was filled by someone not within her protected class (or the discharge occurred under circumstances giving rise to an inference of discrimination based on the plaintiff being part of protected class). Once the plaintiff establishes a *prima facie* case of discrimination, the defendant must articulate a legitimate, nondiscriminatory reason for the discharge. If the defendant states a legitimate reason, the plaintiff must show, by a preponderance of the evidence, that the reason provided by the defendant was a pretext for discrimination.

Singh failed to reach the standard of a *prima facie* case of racial discrimination in this case, because she was replaced by a white female. Moreover, Shoney's stated a legitimate nondiscriminatory reason for discharging Singh, backed up by the evidence from the in-person interviews. Shoney's management found reason to believe the allegations contained in the coworkers' petition, and they acted on it in good faith.

A second area of prime concern in hiring and staffing a business is creating a workplace free of sexual harassment or discrimination. This standard is for the benefit of all employees—both women and men have been victims of sexual discrimination and harassment in the workplace, which can destroy productivity and staff morale. Federal guidelines on this issue include the following guiding precepts:

1. Harassment can include *quid pro quo*—such as insinuating that job conditions or assignments will be based on going along with harassment—or simply create a hostile work environment.

2. Employers are responsible for harassment that they knew about or should have known about, unless they immediately act in good faith to correct the problem. This goes for employees and, in some cases, non-employees such as vendors, contractors, or others with whom their employees must come into contact in carrying out their jobs. If the harassment results in promotions or hiring for one person over another, those other persons can also sue the employer.

3. Employers need to act preventatively—ensuring that all staff know about the company's expectations for a harassment-free workplace, and that appropriate sanctions are in place and utilized when necessary.

Sexual harassment in the workplace acts to deteriorate working conditions; what is more, good employees are likely to leave such environments. Each employer should be aware of the threat and take preventive actions to avoid allowing harassment to be part of their workplaces.

Pressure from customers for improved service underlines the business culture of our time. Many companies in the food-service industry have used slogans to market their products and convince potential customers that their service exceeds expectations:

> Burger King: "Have it your way"
>
> Wendy's: "Do what tastes right"
>
> McDonald's: "I'm lovin' it"
>
> DNC: "GuestPath"

Whatever slogan these companies use to distinguish themselves from the competition, the manager must balance the pressure to eliminate overstaffing, which results in wasted labor dollars, and to avoid understaffing, which would mean delivering poor customer service. In most industries, employees can produce in a steady and consistent manner; products that are produced are simply stored until a customer is ready to purchase the product. If product demand exceeds supply, production can be increased after the order has been received.

In the food-service industry, however, an employee's usefulness is more circumscribed by work conditions. If there are no customers present, there is no productivity, but you still must pay the employee. The employee must be paid in order to be ready when the customer does walk in the door. Because food-service demand fluctuates radically with seasons, days of the week, and even hours of the day, maintaining optimal efficiency is difficult. Knowing how to budget for these fluctuating labor costs presents an additional challenge. In essence, the idle hours (unproductive hours) that the employee is on the clock are scheduled by the manager in anticipation for potential business. In most cases, unproductive hours can be greater than the productive hours the employee actually works. Figure 14-2 is an example of what these unproductive versus productive hours might look like. This is a hypothetical example, but disparities like this do exist.

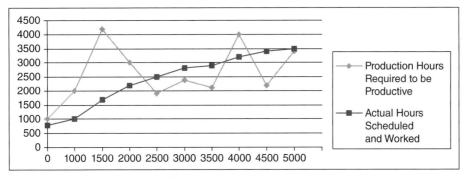

Figure 14-2 Actual Versus Required Hours

Production is inconsistent in this industry. It goes up and down in most businesses, but in food and beverage service, in which peaks and valleys characterize the hours of the day, it is an ongoing challenge. The data points above the line of production hours indicate overstaffing and wasted labor dollars. Conversely, points beneath that line indicate understaffing and jeopardized customer service. These are the challenges facing the manager. This chapter will explore both horns of this labor dilemma and give you techniques to minimize both costs and guest complaints, while getting the most out of your staff.

SALARY AND WAGES

In the beginning of this chapter, Sarah said to Myla, "But I must say that we have never developed reasonable expectations and plans for these costs." Sarah was referring to the two major components of labor-related costs: salaries and wages, and employee benefits and deductions. These costs make up what you saw in Figure 14-1.

The terms *salary* and *wages* are often used interchangeably, but there are important differences. Salary usually applies to managers, supervisors, and executives who receive a fixed amount each pay period regardless of the number of hours worked. They are usually paid monthly or biweekly. These employees are exempt from overtime pay. Wages, on the other hand, apply to payrolls computed on an hourly, weekly, or piecemeal basis. These employees are nonexempt from overtime pay; that means they are eligible to receive overtime whenever they go over a certain number of work hours in a given period.

Gross Pay and Net Pay

Gross pay includes all of an employee's regular pay, overtime pay, commissions, and bonuses—before any payroll deductions. Gross pay may be calculated weekly, biweekly, bimonthly, monthly, daily, or over some other time period. Salaried employees exempt from overtime do not require any special computation for gross pay because they are paid a fixed amount regardless of the actual number of hours worked. Tipped employees, on the other hand, require a special payroll computation, which is addressed in detail later in this chapter.

Net pay is the actual amount of an employee's paycheck. Net pay is the result of subtracting governmental and voluntary deductions from gross pay. Figure 14-3 is an example of how net pay is calculated.

Figure 14-3 Net Pay Calculation

Gross Pay			$500.00
Less:	FICA	(8%)	$40.00
	FIT	(18%)	90.00
	SIT	(5%)	25.00
	TDI	(2%)	10.00
	Union Dues		10.00
	Health Insurance		15.00
	TOTAL DEDUCTIONS		190.00
Net Pay (amount of check)			$310.00

Source: Federal Insurance Contribution Act (FICA), Federal Income Tax (FIT), Federal Unemployment Tax Act (FUTA), Temporary Disability Insurance (TDI), State Income Tax (SIT)

RULES AND REGULATIONS GOVERNING LABOR COSTS

There are many rules and regulations governing the treatment of salary and wages in a workplace. For example, the Fair Labor Standards Act (FLSA) is a federal law adopted in 1938 to eliminate unfair methods of compensation and labor conditions injurious to the health and efficiency of workers. It mandates minimum wages, time-and-a-half pay for overtime work, equal pay for equal work, and restrictions on child labor. The act has been amended and updated numerous times since its original passage.

Minimum Wage

The FLSA requires that, with few exceptions, employers pay employees at least the minimum wage set by the U.S. Congress. As of July 24, 2008, the federal minimum wage is $6.55 per hour. It will increase to $7.25 per hour effective July 24, 2009. For timing purposes, examples will be base on $7.25 per hour rate. States may have legislation that contradicts standards established by the FLSA. In cases where state and federal laws differ, the law offering greater benefits to the employees prevails. For example, the minimum wage in California is $8 per hour. Federal laws require a lower minimum wage. Therefore, employers in California must pay the California rates.

Exceptions to Minimum Wage

There are several exceptions to FLSA rules relating to minimum wage. The low-revenue exception from the minimum-wage requirement applies to employers with less than $500,000 in annual revenue. In the following example, the court had to decide whether a hotel and adjacent restaurant were two separate businesses, each falling below the threshold amount for FLSA coverage (the threshold was then $362,500 in annual revenue), or one business.

Ronald and Beverly Halling appealed the district court's decision that their motel and restaurant business violated the minimum wage provisions of the Fair Labor Standards Act (FLSA). The issue in dispute was whether the Hallings' business was exempt from the provisions of the FLSA as it relates to the low revenue threshold.

Ronald Halling owned the Best Western Sundown Motel, which generated an approximate annual sales volume of $265,000. Beverly Halling owned an adjoining restaurant, Grandmother's House, which generated an approximate annual sales volume of $190,000. If the motel and the restaurant were taken to be separate enterprises, both would be exempt from the FLSA, in that both had an annual sales volume of less than the revenue minimum required for application of the FLSA ($362,500 in this case). The U.S. Secretary of Labor contended that the motel and restaurant formed a single enterprise (with a total income over the $362,500 threshold), because they were related activities performed through a unified operation and common control for a common business purpose.

The district court decided in favor of the secretary. The court found that the motel and restaurant were physically connected; that each business operated without regular payment of rent on property owned jointly by the Hallings; and that the establishments shared a telephone, laundry facilities, and advertising. The court further found that Ronald often did work in the restaurant and once signed the restaurant's income-tax return, while Beverly frequently did work at the motel. The court also found that the Hallings jointly hired a couple to manage the motel and restaurant.

Affirmed. Brock v. Best Western Sundown Motel, Inc. 883 F.2d 51 (8th Cir. 1989)

Another exception to the FLSA rules permits employers to pay a training wage of $4.25 an hour to newly hired employees under the age of 20 for the first 90 days of employment. No specific training is required during this period. Restaurant employers should consult their particular state laws to determine whether this federal training wage is permissible in their states.

Meals and Lodging

Many states put restrictions on employers using employee meals and lodging as part of their calculations of minimum wage. One such state is California, where credit against the minimum wage is not allowed without a voluntary written agreement between the employer and the employee. When credit for meals or lodging is used to meet part of the employer's minimum wage obligation, the amount so credited may not be more than the following:

Meals

- Breakfast, $2.90 effective January 1, 2008

- Lunch, $3.97 effective January 1, 2008

- Dinner, $5.34 effective January 1, 2008

Lodging

- Room occupied alone, $37.63 per week effective January 1, 2008

- Room shared, $31.06 per week effective January 1, 2008

- Apartment, two-thirds of the ordinary rental value, and in no event more than $451.89 per month effective January 1, 2008

- When both members of a couple are employed by the employer, two-thirds of the ordinary rental value, and in no event more than $668.46 per month effective January 1, 2008

Credit for Tipped Employees

Provisions of the FLSA allow employers to apply a tip credit toward the minimum wage of tipped employees. This tip credit effectively lowers the gross wages payable by the employer because tips may be treated as supplemental wages. The FLSA maximum allowable tip credit is $2.13 per hour. This means that an employer may apply a credit of $2.13 toward the hourly rate of tipped employees as long as the actual tips received by the employee are not less than the FLSA maximum allowable tip credit.

Effective July 24, 2009, an employer is in compliance with the FLSA minimum wage and hour standards by paying a tipped employee as follows:

Minimum hourly rate	$7.25
Allowable tip credit	$2.13
Effective hourly payment rate	$5.12

Employee Tip Reporting

IRS Publication 531 provides information on tip income reporting and employers' responsibilities. It also includes sample tip reporting forms.

Employees must report cash, charge, or credit card tips received from customers. An employee may use IRS Form 4070 or a similar statement to report tips to the employer (Figure 14-4). A daily report or card showing the employee's name, cash tips received, and charge tips received is sufficient. Some employers require tipped employees to record their tips daily on the backs of their time cards.

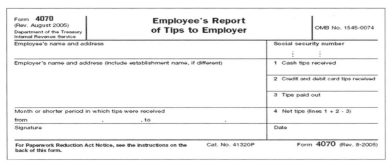

Figure 14-4 Employee Tips Report, IRS Form 4070

Service Charges

Some restaurant operations may add service charges to guests' bills. These service charges are distributed to servers and other customarily tipped employees. A service charge is not considered a tip. Such charges are defined as wages by the IRS and are treated the same as other wages for purposes of tax withholding requirements.

Application of FLSA Rules to Tip Credit

The following example illustrates how the gross wages payable by the employer are calculated when the actual tips received by an employee are greater than the maximum FLSA tip credit. Assume that Employee 1 has worked 40 hours, and the employer has elected to use the allowable tip credit against the minimum wage. The employee reports tips amounting to $98. The maximum FLSA tip credit is $85.20 (40 hours × $2.13 per hour). The gross wages payable by the employer are calculated as follows:

Gross wages (minimum wage: 40 hours × $7.25 per hour)	$290.00
Less the lower of:	
Maximum FLSA tip credit (40 hours × $2.13)	$85.20
Actual tips received	$98.00
Allowable tip credit	85.20
Gross wages payable by the employer	$204.80

Using Actual Tips Received for Tip Credit

Another example illustrates how the gross wages payable by the employer are calculated when the actual tips received by an employee are less than the maximum FLSA tip credit. Assume that Employee 2 has worked 40 hours, and the employer has elected to use the allowable tip credit against the minimum wage. The employee reports tips amounting to $70. The maximum FLSA tip credit is $85.20. The gross wages payable by the employer are calculated as follows:

Gross wages (minimum wage: 40 hours × $7.25 per hour)	$290.00
Less the lower of:	
Maximum FLSA tip credit (40 hours × $2.13)	$85.20
Actual tips received	$70.00
Allowable tip credit	$70.00
Gross wages payable by the employer	$220.00

Tipped Employees' Net Pay

A tipped employee's gross taxable earnings include the gross wages payable by the employer and the actual tips the employee receives from guests. Figures 14-5, 14-6, and 14-7 illustrate how net pay is computed for Employees 1 and 2 from the previous examples. To simplify the illustration, state and local taxes are not considered, a 10 percent federal income tax rate is used, and a $15 voluntary deduction for a group health plan is assumed.

It is possible for the governmental and voluntary deductions of a tipped employee to exceed the gross wages payable by the employer for a payroll period. In this case, available amounts are first applied to FICA taxes, then to federal and state income taxes, and finally to voluntary deductions. However, an employee's paycheck may never be less than zero; if the gross wages payable by the employer are insufficient to cover an employee's governmental and voluntary deductions, the employee may pay the deficiency to the employer.

If the employer is unable to withhold FICA taxes, this fact is reported on the employee's W-2 form and is reported as taxes due on the employee's personal income tax return. It is not necessary to report any deficiency on withheld income taxes because any deficiency will be made up when the employee's total income tax liability is computed on his or her personal income tax return.

Tipped Employees' Overtime Pay

Overtime pay for tipped employees is calculated in exactly the same manner as for nontipped employees. However, in computing the gross wages payable by the employer, the federal or state tip credit is multiplied by the total hours worked (regular hours plus overtime hours) by the employee. For example, assume that Employee 1 and Employee 2 each work 45 hours and report actual tips received of $100 and $80 respectively. Assume further that the employer pays tipped employees $6 per hour and the state's overtime provisions are identical to FLSA provisions. Figures 14-8 and 14-9 illustrate how to calculate the net pay for these employees.

As stressed earlier, the identification of overtime pay varies with different state laws, company policies, and contracts. Federal law requires that overtime be paid for any hours worked in excess of 40 in a payroll week. Thus, an employee who works ten-hour shifts for four days within a payroll week is not entitled to overtime under the FLSA. Some states require that employees receive overtime pay for any hours worked in excess of eight hours in a payroll day. You will need to understand how the laws work in your area.

Figure 14-5 Computing Net Pay For Employee 1: Hourly Rate At Minimum Wage

Gross Wages Payable by Employer		
Gross wages (40 hours x $7.25 per hour)		$290.00
Less the lower of:		
Maximum FLSA tip credit (40 hours x $2.13)	$85.20	
Actual tips received	98.00	
Allowable tip credit		85.20
Gross wages payable by the employer		$204.80
Gross Taxable Earnings		
Gross wages payable by employer	$204.80	
Actual tips received	98.00	
Gross taxable earnings	$302.80	
Less Governmental and Voluntary Deductions		
FICA ($302.80 x 7.65%)		23.16
Income tax withholding ($302.80 x 10%)		30.28
Voluntary deduction (group health plan)		15.00
Net pay (amount of payroll check)		$136.36

Figure 14-6 Computing Net Pay for Employee 2: Hourly Rate at Minimum Wage

Gross Wages Payable by Employer

Gross wages (40 hours x $7.25 per hour)		$290.00
Less the lower of:		
Maximum FLSA tip credit (40 hours x $2.13)	$85.20	
Actual tips received	70.00	
Allowable tip credit		70.00
Gross wages payable by the employer		$220.00

Gross Taxable Earnings

Gross wages payable by employer	$220.00
Actual tips received	70.00
Gross taxable earnings	$290.00

Less Governmental and Voluntary Deductions

FICA ($290.00 x 7.65%)	22.19
Income tax withholding ($290.00 x 10%)	29.00
Voluntary deduction (group health plan)	15.00
Net pay (amount of payroll check)	$153.81

Figure 14-7 Computing Net Pay for Employee 1: Hourly Rate Above Minimum Wage

Gross Wages Payable by Employer

Gross wages (40 hours x $8.00 per hour)		$320.00
Less the lower of:		
Maximum FLSA tip credit (40 hours x $2.13)	$85.20	
Actual tips received	98.00	
Allowable tip credit		85.20
Gross wages payable by the employer		$234.80

Gross Taxable Earnings

Gross wages payable by employer	$234.80
Actual tips received	98.00
Gross taxable earnings	$332.80

Less Governmental and Voluntary Deductions

FICA ($332.80 x 7.65%)	25.46
Income tax withholding ($332.80 x 10%)	33.28
Voluntary deduction (group health plan)	15.00
Net pay (amount of payroll check)	$161.06

The 8 Percent Tip Regulation

The Tax Equity and Fiscal Responsibility Act of 1982 (TEFRA) established regulations affecting food and beverage operations with respect to tip reporting requirements. The intent of the regulation is for all tipped employees to report tips of at least 8 percent of the gross receipts of the hospitality establishment. If tips reported by employees fail to meet this 8 percent requirement for a particular period, the deficiency is called a tip shortfall. This shortfall will require allocation to those employees classified as directly tipped employees.

The 8 percent tip regulation distinguishes between directly tipped employees and indirectly tipped employees. Directly tipped employees are those who receive tips directly from customers.

Figure 14-8 Computing Net Pay for Employee 1: Overtime Pay Calculation

Gross Wages Payable by Employer		
Regular Pay (40 hours × $8.00 per hour)		$ 320.00
Overtime Pay (5 hours × $8.00 × 1.5)		60.00
Gross Wages		$ 380.00
Less the lower of:		
Maximum FLSA tip credit (45 hours × $2.13)	$95.85	
Actual tips received	100.00	
Allowable tip credit		95.85
Gross wages payable by employer		$ 284.15

Gross Taxable Earnings	
Gross wages payable by employer	$ 284.15
Actual tips received	100.00
Gross taxable earnings	$384.15

Less Governmental and Voluntary Deductions	
FICA ($384.15 × 7.65%)	29.39
Income tax withholding ($289.15 × 10%)	38.41
Voluntary deduction (group health plan)	15.00
Net pay (amount of payroll check)	$ 201.35

Figure 14-9 Computing Net Pay for Employee 2: Overtime Pay Calculation

Gross Wages Payable by Employer		
Regular Pay (40 hours × $8.00 per hour)		$ 320.00
Overtime Pay (5 hours × $8.00 × 1.5)		60.00
Gross Wages		$ 380.00
Less the lower of:		
Maximum FLSA tip credit (45 hours × $2.13)	$95.85	
Actual tips received	80.00	
Allowable tip credit		80.00
Gross wages payable by employer		$ 300.00

Gross Taxable Earnings	
Gross wages payable by employer	$ 300.00
Actual tips received	80.00
Gross taxable earnings	$380.00

Less Governmental and Voluntary Deductions	
FICA ($380.00 × 7.65%)	29.07
Income tax withholding ($380.00 × 10%)	38.00
Voluntary deduction (group health plan)	15.00
Net pay (amount of payroll check)	$ 217.93

Examples of directly tipped employees are servers, bartenders, and other employees, such as maîtres d'. Indirectly tipped employees are employees who do not normally receive tips directly from customers. These employees include buspersons, service bartenders, and cooks.

When a shortfall is allocated, the employer is required to provide each directly tipped employee with an informational statement showing the tips reported by the employee and the tips that should have been reported. An employer does not have to provide employees with tip allocation statements when the total tips reported for a period are greater than 8 percent of the gross receipts for that period. For example, assume that the Sea Breeze Hotel Restaurant record shows a gross receipt of $100,000 for a particular period. If the actual tips reported by employees total more than $8,000 ($100,000 × 8 percent), the employer does not have to provide employees with tip allocation statements.

An employee's tip allocation for a calendar year is stated separately from any wages and reported tips appearing on the employee's W-2 form. Employees should maintain adequate records to substantiate the total amount of tips included in income. If possible, the employee should keep a daily record of his or her sales, cash tips, charge tips, and hours worked. To facilitate record-keeping, a business may provide the employee with a multipurpose form similar to the one shown in Figure 14-10.

Figure 14-10 Sample Employee Report of Daily Sales and Tips

	Date	Date	Date	Date	Date	Date	Date	Grand Total
Enter day of the month	Mon.	Tue.	Wed.	Thu.	Fri.	Sat.	Sun.	
SALES 1. Total sales to patrons 2. Charge sales in								
TIPS 1. Total cash and charge tips 2. Total charge tips in								
Total hours worked								

Employee Report of Daily Sales and Tips

Business _____   Week ending __/__/__
                                                    (Month/Day/Year)
Employee _____

Check shift worked: ☐ Days   ☐ Evenings   ☐ Split

Allocation of Tip Shortfall

If, during a particular period, the total tips reported by directly and indirectly tipped employees fall short of 8 percent of the gross receipts of the establishment in the same period, the establishment must do the following: (1) determine the shortfall (the amount by which the total reported tips falls short of 8 percent of the gross receipts), and (2) allocate the shortfall among directly tipped employees. After these computations have been completed, the tip shortfall allocations must be reported to each affected employee. IRS Form 8027 (Figure 14-11) is used to report tip shortfall.

There are several acceptable methods by which to compute tip shortfall allocations for directly tipped employees. One method is through good faith agreement. A good faith agreement is a written agreement between the employer and employees, consented to by two-thirds of the tipped employees at the time of the agreement. This agreement becomes the basis of allocating tip amounts to employees when the actual tips reported are short of the expected 8 percent of gross receipts.

In the absence of a good faith agreement, the 8 percent tip regulation provides tip allocation methods. For purposes of allocating the tip shortfall to directly tipped employees, these regulations permit the use of the *gross receipts method* or, under certain conditions, the *hours worked method*. The following examples explain and illustrate both methods.

The gross receipts method requires that gross receipts (food and beverage sales) and tip records be maintained for each directly tipped employee. Gross receipts are used as a basis for allocating each directly tipped employee's share of the tip shortfall. The tip shortfall allocation may be performed weekly, monthly, quarterly, annually, or at some other designated time period

Form **8027** Department of the Treasury Internal Revenue Service	**Employer's Annual Information Return of** **Tip Income and Allocated Tips** ▶ See separate instructions.	OMB No. 1545-0714 20**08**

	Name of establishment	Employer identification number
	Number and street (see instructions)	Type of establishment (check only one box) ☐ 1 Evening meals only ☐ 2 Evening and other meals ☐ 3 Meals other than evening meals ☐ 4 Alcoholic beverages
	City or town, state, and ZIP code	

Employer's name (same name as on Form 941)		Establishment number (see instructions)
Number and street (P.O. box, if applicable)	Apt. or suite no.	
City, state, and ZIP code (if a foreign address, see instructions)		

Does this establishment accept credit cards, debit cards, or other charges?	☐ Yes (lines 1 and 2 **must** be completed) ☐ No	Check **if:** Amended Return ☐ Final Return ☐

Attributed Tip Income Program (ATIP). See Revenue Procedure 2006-30 . . . . ▶ ☐

1	Total charged tips for calendar year 2008.	**1**
2	Total charge receipts showing charged tips (see instructions)	**2**
3	Total amount of service charges of less than 10% paid as wages to employees. . .	**3**
4a	Total tips reported by indirectly tipped employees	**4a**
b	Total tips reported by directly tipped employees	**4b**
	Note. Complete the **Employer's Optional Worksheet for Tipped Employees** on page 6 of the instructions to determine potential unreported tips of your employees.	
c	Total tips reported (add lines 4a and 4b)	**4c**
5	Gross receipts from food or beverage operations (not less than line 2—see instructions) .	**5**
6	Multiply line 5 by 8% (.08) or the lower rate shown here ▶_____ granted by the IRS. (Attach a copy of the IRS determination letter to this return.)	**6**
	Note. If you have allocated tips using other than the calendar year (semimonthly, biweekly, quarterly, etc.), mark an "**X**" on line 6 and enter the amount of allocated tips from your records on line 7.	
7	Allocation of tips. If line 6 is more than line 4c, enter the excess here	**7**
	▶ This amount must be allocated as tips to tipped employees working in this establishment. Check the box below that shows the method used for the allocation. (Show the portion, if any, attributable to each employee in box 8 of the employee's Form W-2.)	
a	Allocation based on hours-worked method (see instructions for restriction) . .	☐
	Note. If you marked the checkbox in line 7a, enter the average number of employee hours worked per business day during the payroll period. (see instructions) _____	
b	Allocation based on gross receipts method	☐
c	Allocation based on good-faith agreement (Attach a copy of the agreement.). .	☐
8	Enter the total number of directly tipped employees at this establishment during 2008 ▶	

Under penalties of perjury, I declare that I have examined this return, including accompanying schedules and statements, and to the best of my knowledge and belief, it is true, correct, and complete.

Signature ▶	Title ▶	Date ▶

For Privacy Act and Paperwork Reduction Act Notice, see page 6 of the separate instructions.	Cat. No. 49989U	Form **8027** (2008)

Figure 14-11 IRS Form 8027

during the year. The following hypothetical example demonstrates the computations involved when the gross receipts method is used to allocate a tip shortfall among the directly tipped employees of the Sea Breeze Hotel Restaurant.

The Sea Breeze Hotel Restaurant is a food and beverage establishment with an equivalent of more than ten employees and, therefore, is subject to the government's 8 percent tip regulation. The Sea Breeze Hotel Restaurant has food and beverage sales of $100,000 for a particular period. According to the government's 8 percent tip regulation, directly and indirectly tipped employees should have reported a minimum of $8,000 in tips for that period ($100,000 × 8 percent × $8,000); this amount will be referred to as 8 percent gross receipts. The tip records show that all employees reported total tips of only $6,200 for that period. Therefore, a tip shortfall of $1,800 ($8,000 – $6,200) has occurred.

Figure 14-12 presents information compiled by Myla, Sea Breeze's restaurant manager for this particular period, including the gross receipts (food and beverage sales) and tips reported by each directly tipped employee. It also shows that the total shortfall to be allocated is $1,800. This information will be used later in Figures 14-13 and 14-14 to compute tip shortfall allocations for directly tipped employees.

Figure 14-12 Sales and Tips Analysis: Sea Breeze Restaurant

Directly Tipped Employee	Gross Receipts for Period	Tips Reported
1	$18,000	$1,080
2	16,000	880
3	23,000	1,810
4	17,000	800
5	12,000	450
6	14,000	680
Total	$100,000	$5,700
Indirectly tipped employees		500
Total		$6,200

Tips that should have been reported (100,000 × 8%)	=	$8,000
Actual tips reported	=	6,200
Shortfall to be allocated		1,800
Tips that should have been reported	=	8,000
Tips reported by indirectly tipped employees	=	500
Directly tipped employees portion of 8% gross reciepts	=	$7,500

While directly tipped employees are required to account for the tip shortfall, the tips of indirectly tipped employees may be counted toward the 8 percent of gross receipts estimate of total tips that should have been reported. For the Sea Breeze Hotel Restaurant, total tips that should have been reported by all employees are $8,000; the tips reported by indirectly tipped employees total $500. Therefore, the directly tipped employees' portion of 8 percent gross receipts is $7,500.

Figure 14-12 uses the directly tipped employees' portion of 8 percent gross receipts as the basis for calculating shortfall allocation ratios. The shortfall allocation ratios will be used to allocate the $1,800 tip shortfall among directly tipped employees. However, before tip shortfall allocation ratios can be computed, a method must be used to determine each employee's share of the $7,500 portion of tips that should have been reported by directly tipped employees. Each employee's share will be compared to the tips actually reported by the employee in order to determine whether the employee reported tips above or below his or her share of the $7,500 portion of 8 percent gross receipts.

Under the gross receipts method, a gross receipts ratio is used to determine each employee's share of the $7,500. A gross receipts ratio is the proportion of gross receipts attributable to each employee relative to the total gross receipts for the period. This ratio is multiplied by $7,500 (directly tipped employees' portion of 8 percent gross receipts) to determine each directly tipped employee's share of this amount. Figure 14-12 illustrates these calculations for Sea Breeze Hotel Restaurant.

The actual tips reported by each employee are then subtracted from the employee's share of 8 percent gross receipts. The resulting figure is the employee shortfall numerator. For the Sea

Breeze Restaurant, this subtraction process is greater than the share of the tips that should have been reported. From Figure 14-12, Employee 3 declared $1,810, which is above the threshold of $1,725. Therefore, he or she does not have a tip shortfall. The total shortfall ($1,800) must be allocated on a proportional basis among the remaining directly tipped employees.

Figures 14-13 and 14-14 show how the $1,800 tip shortfall is allocated among directly tipped employees whose reported tips did not equal or exceed their share of the 8 percent tip estimate. This proportional allocation is accomplished by the use of a shortfall ratio. The total of the employees' shortfall numerators, or $1,885, is used as the denominator of the shortfall ratio. Each employee's shortfall numerator, together with the shortfall denominator, forms the shortfall ratio used to allocate his or her share of the tip shortfall.

Figure 14-13 Determining Shortfall Ratios: Sea Breeze Restaurant

Directly Tipped Employee	Total Portion of 8% Gross Receipts	Gross Receipts Ratio	Employee's Share of 8% Gross Receipts	Actual Tips Reported	Employee Shortfall Numerator
1	7,500	× 18,000/100,000 =	$1,350 −	$1,080 =	$270
2	7,500	× 16,000/100,000 =	1,200 −	880 =	320
3	7,500	× 23,000/100,000 =	1,725 −	1,810 =	0
4	7,500	× 17,000/100,000 =	1,275 −	800 =	475
5	7,500	× 12,000/100,000 =	900 −	450 =	450
6	7,500	× 14,000/100,000 =	1,050 −	680 =	370
Total			$7,500	$5,700	$1,885

Shortfall Denominator

Figure 14-14 Allocation of the Tip Shortfall: Sea Breeze Restaurant

Directly Tipped Employee	Shortfall Ratio	Shortfall to be Allocated	Tips Allocation
1	270/1,885 ×	$1,800 =	$258
2	320/1,855 ×	1,800 =	306
3	475/1,855 ×	1,800 =	453
4	450/1,855 ×	1,800 =	430
5	370/1,885 ×	1,800 =	353
Total			$1,800

The use of the hours worked method is limited to establishments with fewer than the equivalent of 25 full-time employees during the payroll period. The mathematical procedures in this method are identical to those explained for the gross receipts method. The only difference between the hours worked method and the gross receipts method is that employee hours worked are substituted wherever employee gross receipts were used in the previous method.

Regular Pay and Overtime Pay

The definition of regular pay varies with different state laws, company policies, and contracts. However, under the FLSA, regular pay is based on a 40-hour workweek. The term *regular hourly rate* refers to the rate per hour that is used to compute regular pay.

The definition of overtime pay also varies with different state laws, company policies, and contracts. According to the FLSA, overtime pay is required for any hours worked in excess of 40 hours in a week. The term *overtime hourly rate* refers to the rate per hour used to compute overtime pay. According to FLSA provisions, overtime is paid at the rate of 1.5 times the employee's regular hourly rate. The FLSA prescribes this rate regardless of the number of overtime hours worked and regardless of whether the overtime hours were worked on a weekend or on a legal holiday. In order to calculate the overtime pay for some employees, it may first be necessary to convert either a weekly wage or a monthly salary to an hourly rate.

To qualify for a manager exemption, the employee must pass a duties test and a salary test. To qualify as a manager, the employee's duties must include managing the business (or part of it) and regularly directing the work of two or more employees. In addition, the employee must either (a) be paid a salary (as opposed to an hourly wage) of at least $250 per week, or (b) have the authority to hire, fire, or promote, and be paid a salary of at least $155 per week. If either of these conditions holds, the employee can be considered a manager, and is therefore exempt from overtime.

The issue of whether an employee's job responsibilities satisfy the executive employee test is not strictly a question of how much time is allocated to managerial duties as opposed to other tasks. Rather, a court also would evaluate such factors as the importance of the managerial duties as opposed to other responsibilities, the frequency with which the employee exercises discretion, and his or her relative freedom from supervision, as illustrated in the following example.

A chain restaurant claimed that its lowest-level manager, whose job title was associate manager, was in an executive position and therefore was exempt from overtime pay. The job, an entry-level position, included work that regular crew members do (preparing pizzas, salads, and other food; running the cash register; waiting on customers; and cleaning), tasks described by the company as "learning by doing," and studying company manuals to prepare for management tests. Associate managers perform little or no supervision of other employees, are not in charge of a restaurant, and do not supervise shifts. Not surprisingly, the court held that the position of associate manager was not an executive position.

Dole v. Papa Gino's of America, Inc., 712 F.Supp.1038 (Mass. 1989)

In the case of bonus pay, the U.S. Department of Labor (DOL) now requires employers to add bonuses paid to hourly employees to their gross pay before calculating overtime payment (CFO & Controller Alert. September 1, 2006. Bonuses).

Converting Weekly Wage to Hourly Rate

Some employees are hired at a stated weekly wage. This wage is generally fixed, except for overtime pay and adjustments for absences. For these employees, it is often necessary to convert the weekly wage to a regular hourly rate. These calculations may require rounding. Actual practice varies as to the number of decimal places used in calculating a regular hourly rate. For our purposes, all hourly rates are rounded to the nearest cent.

The regular hourly rate is computed by dividing the weekly wage by the number of hours in a regular 40-hour workweek. For example, assume that an employee is hired at $300 per week for a regular workweek. The regular hourly rate for this employee is calculated as follows:

$$\text{regular hourly rate} = \frac{\text{weekly wage}}{\text{number of hours in a regular workweek}}$$

$$\text{regular hourly rate} = \frac{\$300}{40 \text{ hour}} = \$7.50$$

Once an employee's regular hourly rate is known, an overtime hourly rate can be determined. Following FLSA provisions, overtime is paid at the rate of 1.5 times the employee's regular hourly rate. Therefore, the overtime hourly rate is simply 1.5 times the regular hourly rate:

overtime hourly rate = regular hourly rate × 1.5

overtime hourly rate = $7.5 × 1.5 = $11.25

Converting Monthly Salary to Hourly Rate

As stated previously, some salaried employees may not be exempt from overtime pay. Therefore, it may be necessary to calculate an overtime hourly rate for some salaried employees. Since the number of pay weeks (and, therefore, the number of hours worked) varies from month to month, it is first necessary to annualize the monthly salary and then convert it to a weekly amount. Once the weekly amount is determined, the regular hourly rate and the overtime hourly rate can be computed by following the same procedure as in changing a weekly wage to an hourly rate. For example, assume that an employee is hired at a monthly salary of $1,500 and that the employee is not exempt from overtime pay provisions. First, the monthly salary is annualized by multiplying the monthly salary by 12 months. Then, the weekly regular pay of the employee is calculated by dividing the annual salary figure by 52 weeks. These computations are summarized as follows:

annualized salary = $1,500 × 12 = $18,000 per year

$$\text{weekly rate} = \frac{\$18,000}{52} = \$346.15$$

Calculating Overtime Pay

Two methods by which to compute an employee's overtime pay are the overtime pay method and the overtime premium method. These methods produce identical results with respect to gross pay. The major difference is in the classification of regular pay and overtime pay. According to the overtime pay method, all overtime hours are classified as overtime pay. According to the overtime premium method, overtime hours are separated into regular pay and overtime premium pay.

The overtime pay method computes overtime pay by multiplying the number of overtime hours by the employee's overtime hourly rate. In a state where FLSA provisions prevail, overtime hours are those hours worked in excess of 40 hours in a week. Using the overtime pay method, hours worked up to this 40-hour limit are the basis for computing regular pay. Any hours worked over the 40-hour limit are the basis for computing overtime pay.

Using the overtime pay method and assuming that FLSA provisions prevail, the gross pay for an employee is calculated as follows: (1) computing the employee's regular pay, (2) computing the employee's overtime pay, and (3) totaling the employee's regular and overtime pay. For example, assume that an employee receives a regular hourly rate of $7.50 and reports time worked of 46 hours. Using the overtime pay method, regular pay is computed on a basis not to exceed 40 hours. Multiplying 40 hours by the hourly rate of $7.50 results in $300 regular pay.

The employee's overtime pay is computed by first determining the employee's overtime hourly rate and then multiplying the overtime hourly rate by the number of overtime hours. Under the FLSA provisions used in this example, the employee's overtime hourly rate is $11.25 (1.5 times the regular hourly rate of $7.50). Since the employee worked 6 hours in excess of the 40-hour limit for regular pay, the employee's overtime pay is $67.50 (6 overtime hours multiplied by the $11.25 overtime hourly rate). The employee's gross pay can now be determined as follows:

regular pay (40 hours × $7.50)	$300.00
overtime pay (6 hours × $11.25)	$67.50
gross pay	$367.50

As previously stated, if employers are paying bonuses to hourly employees as a way of motivating and encouraging high performance, those payments should be added to the gross pay before calculating overtime rate. Using the overtime premium example above, and assuming an employee received $100 bonus pay, the calculation will be as follows:

regular pay (40 hours × $7.5)	$300.00
bonus	$100.00
overtime rate ($400 ÷ 40) × 1.5 = $15	
overtime pay (6 hours × $15)	<u>$90.00</u>
gross pay	<u>$490.00</u>

The overtime premium method differs from the overtime pay method in two respects. First, the overtime premium method computes regular pay by multiplying the total hours worked (regular and overtime hours) by the employee's regular hourly rate. Second, the overtime premium method multiplies overtime hours by an overtime premium rate, which is half of the employee's regular hourly rate.

For example, using the overtime premium method and assuming that FLSA provisions prevail, the gross pay for an employee who receives a regular hourly rate of $7.50 and works 46 hours in one week is calculated as follows: (1) computing the employee's regular pay, (2) computing the employee's overtime premium, and (3) totaling the employee's regular pay and overtime premium. The employee's regular pay is computed by multiplying the 46 hours worked by the hourly rate of $7.50. The employee's overtime premium is computed by multiplying the six overtime hours by half the employee's regular hourly rate, or $3.75 (0.5 times the regular hourly rate of $7.50). The employee's gross pay can now be determined as follows:

regular pay (46 hours × $7.50)	$345.00
overtime pay (6 hours × $3.75)	<u>$22.50</u>
gross pay	<u>$367.50</u>

The benefits of using premium and regular methods are the same; both methods are easy to apply.

EMPLOYEE BENEFITS AND DEDUCTIONS

An employee's gross pay is reduced by payroll deductions. Payroll deductions are classified as either governmental deductions or voluntary deductions. It is critically important that deductions be handled correctly to avoid employee frustration, which could affect employee morale and result in poor customer service.

Governmental Deductions

Governmental deductions are mandatory deductions over which an employee has little control. These deductions consist of federal income taxes, FICA taxes, state income taxes, garnishments, disability insurance, and other state taxes on employee earnings. These deductions are not an expense of the business because the employer merely acts as a collection agent for the government. These are considered employee expenses.

government deductions
Mandatory deduction from employees' gross pay, including federal and state income taxes, FICA taxes, garnishments, disability insurance, and other taxes.

Voluntary Deductions

voluntary deductions
Deductions from employees' gross pay that are authorized by the employee, such as insurance premiums, retirement plan contributions, or union dues.

Voluntary deductions may include premiums for health insurance group plans, life insurance group plans, retirement plans, savings plans, stock purchase plans, union dues, and contributions to charities. The employee must approve all voluntary deductions. Employees usually indicate approval by signing authorization forms. When the payroll check is processed, governmental deductions are subtracted before any voluntary deductions are made.

Federal Insurance Contributions Act (FICA)

The Federal Insurance Contributions Act, commonly known as FICA, was enacted to provide workers with retirement and medical benefits. It is also referred to as Social Security and Medicare. The law requires (1) a tax upon the employer, and (2) a tax upon the employee that is deducted from the employee's paycheck. The FICA tax imposed on the employer will be discussed later in this chapter.

The retirement and medical benefits of this act also extend to self-employed persons under provisions of the Self-Employment Contributions Act. The self-employed person pays the FICA tax, which is computed based on the profits of the business. This computation is performed on a special form that is part of the individual's personal income tax return.

The FICA tax consists of two computations, one for the Social Security tax and one for the Medicare tax. Each tax has its own rate, and Social Security has a ceiling—a maximum amount of earnings subject to taxation for a calendar year. Many companies combine these two taxes and show them as one deduction on the paycheck, usually labeled as FICA tax or Social Security tax.

Effective January 1, 2001, the FICA tax rate and ceilings are as follows:

	Tax Rate	Ceiling
Social Security	6.2 percent	$80,400
Medicare	1.4 percent	none

If the Social Security rate is 6.2 percent and the wage ceiling is $80,400, the Social Security deduction for any individual cannot exceed $4,984.80 ($80,400 x 6.2 percent) in a single year. However, the Medicare portion of the FICA tax is unlimited because there is no wage ceiling for this portion.

For example, assume an employee earns $500 gross pay in a given week. The employee's year-to-date (YTD) Social Security deductions total $3,000 prior to this week's earnings.

The current week's FICA deduction is calculated as follows:

Social Security portion: $500.00 $\times$ 6.2 percent   = $31.00

Medicare portion: $500.00 $\times$ 1.45 percent   = $7.25

FICA deduction: $38.25

Note: The employee's new YTD Social Security deduction totals $3,031.00, which is less than the maximum deduction of $4,984.80.

The procedure is different when the current week's calculated Social Security tax causes the YTD amount to exceed the maximum legal deduction. When this happens, the Social Security percentage computation is ignored and the actual deduction is "squeezed." For example, an employee earns $500 gross pay in a given week. The employee's previous YTD Social

Security deductions total \$4,957.40. The first step is to test the Social Security percentage computation:

$500 × 6.2percent = \$31.00
$31.00 + $4,957.40 = $4,988.40 (exceeds maximum of $4,984.80)

The second step is to compute an amount for the current week's Social Security deduction that will bring the YTD deduction to \$4,984.80.

Maximum allowable Social Security deduction:	\$4,984.80
Previous YTD Social Security taxes deducted:	\$4,957.40
Allowable Social Security deduction:	\$27.40

The current week's FICA deduction can then be calculated as follows:

Allowable Social Security deduction	= \$27.40
Medicare portion: $500.00 × 1.45percent	= \$7.25
FICA deduction:	\$34.65

Federal Income Tax (FIT)

The federal government requires an employer to withhold income taxes from the salary and wages of employees and pay these taxes directly to the federal government. This constitutes part of the system under which most people pay their income tax during the year in which income is received or earned. For many employees whose entire income is wages, the amount withheld approximates the total tax due so that the employee will pay little or no additional tax at the end of the year. Circular E of the tax code schedule outlines the requirements for withholding income tax and includes tables showing the amounts to be withheld.

Before a newly-hired employee starts to work, he or she should complete and sign an IRS Form W-4 (Figure 14-15). This form provides the employer with the employee's marital status (for tax withholding purposes), withholding allowances (defined below), and other pertinent data. The employer retains this form, and the information is transferred to the employee's payroll record for future use in preparing the employee's paycheck.

Figure 14-15 W-4 Form

An employee may submit a new W-4 form whenever there is a change in his or her marital status or withholding allowances. For tax withholding purposes, marital status is designated as either single or married. A married employee may claim a single status in order to have larger amounts withheld from his or her paycheck. However, an unmarried employee may not claim a married status in order to have smaller amounts withheld.

Withholding allowances may be claimed by an employee in accordance with the rules provided on the W-4 form. Generally, an employee may claim (1) an allowance, called a personal allowance; (2) an allowance for each dependent the employee is entitled to claim on his or her federal income tax return; and (3) other special withholding allowances and tax credit allowances as described on the W-4 form. An employee does not have to claim all the allowances to which he or she is entitled, but an employee may only claim valid allowances.

The amount to be withheld from an employee's gross pay for federal income taxes is computed by using income tax withholding tables or by using the income tax withholding percentage method. Both of these methods are explained in IRS Circular E, the tax code schedule. Computerized payroll procedures usually involve the income tax withholding percentage method, while employers using manual payroll systems commonly find it more convenient to use the tax-withholding tables. Circular E contains a full set of these tables, which are beyond the scope of this book.

Employers use tax-withholding tables by selecting the proper table and then locating the intersection of the number of withholding allowances claimed and the employee's wages. The following example demonstrates how to use tax-withholding tables to calculate the FIT withholding for an employee who has claimed single marital status and is paid on a weekly basis. Refer to the tax-withholding tables in Appendix. Assuming an employee has claimed zero withholding allowances and receives wages of $245, the FIT withholding is calculated by following a four-step procedure:

1. Select the approximate tax table. Since the employee has claimed single marital status and is paid on a weekly basis, the Single Persons—Weekly Payroll Period table is used.

2. Locate the column that identifies the number of allowances claimed. In our example, the appropriate column is the one labeled 0.

3. Locate the row that identifies the amount of the employee's wages. Since our example employee's wages are $245, the correct row is "at least $240 but less than $250."

4. Locate the figure at the intersection of the allowances claimed column and the wages row. The figure is $47.74. This means that $47.74 will be withheld as FIT from the employee's paycheck.

The same steps can be used to calculate the FIT withholding for an employee who has claimed married status and is paid on a weekly basis. Assuming an employee has claimed two withholding allowances and receives wages of $270, the FIT withholding is calculated as follows:

1. Select the appropriate tax table. Since the employee has claimed married status and is paid on a weekly basis, the Married Persons—Weekly Payroll Period table is used.

2. Locate the column that identifies the number of allowances claimed. In our example, the appropriate column is the one labeled 2.

3. Locate the row that identifies the amount of the employee's wages. Since our example employee's wages are $270, the correct row is "at least $270 but less than $280."

4. Locate the figure at the intersection of the allowances claimed column and the wages row. The figure is $27.04. This means that $27.04 will be withheld as FIT from the employee's paycheck.

State and City Income Tax

Most states have a state income tax. The employer is responsible for withholding these taxes from the employee's gross pay and remitting them to the state as prescribed by law.

Computing the amount to be withheld from an employee's wages for state income taxes is similar to the methods used to compute the withholding of FIT. The state's division of taxation provides employers with the proper tax tables or withholding percentages. In some states, state income taxes are a "piggyback tax" on the FIT. For example, a state may impose its income tax at the rate of 25 percent of the FIT. Therefore, once the FIT is determined, the state income tax may be computed at 25 percent of the FIT.

The methods for computing withholdings for city income taxes are similar to the methods for computing federal and state income tax withholdings.

Employers' Payroll Taxes

The previous sections have discussed payroll taxes imposed on the employee. In these cases, the employer deducts governmental taxes from the employee's gross pay and remits them to the appropriate federal or state agency. Since these payroll taxes are levied on the employee, they are not an expense of the business.

In addition to payroll taxes imposed on employees, there are payroll taxes imposed on the employer. Such taxes are a business expense. This section discusses the following employer's payroll taxes:

- Social Security taxes (FICA)
- Federal unemployment taxes
- State unemployment taxes

Social Security Taxes

The Federal Insurance Contributions Act (FICA) imposes a separate tax on the taxable payroll of a business. Generally, the FICA rate and the FICA taxable ceiling are similar to those specified for employees.

The Social Security tax deducted from an employee's payroll check is not a business expense because the tax is collected from the employee (withheld from his or her wages to arrive at net pay). In addition to the employee Social Security tax, there is an employer Social Security tax that is imposed directly on the employer. A business is responsible for an employer Social Security tax on each employee's wages and tips until the wages (including tips) reach the maximum amount subject to Social Security taxes. This employer's Social Security tax is a business expense.

IRS Form 941 is filed quarterly by an employer. The purpose of this form is to report the amount of employees' FICA and federal income taxes withheld, the FICA tax imposed on the employer, and the remittance of these taxes made by the employer as required by law. Appendix contains a sample of IRS Form 941 and the instructions for completing the form.

Unemployment Taxes

The Federal Unemployment Tax Act (FUTA) imposes a tax on the taxable payroll of a business. Only the employer pays FUTA tax, which is based on the wages of each employee. Like FICA tax, FUTA tax is assessed at a given rate and is subject to a ceiling. The federal government passes the collected taxes on to the state agencies that administer each state's unemployment program.

Similarly, a state may have an unemployment insurance act (commonly referred to as SUTA). Generally, the SUTA tax is imposed on the employer based on the SUTA-taxable portion of each employee's gross pay. However, some states impose this tax on both the employer and the employee.

IRS Form 940[1] is filed annually by an employer. The purpose of this form is to report the employer's liability for FUTA taxes. Appendix contains a sample of IRS Form 940, instructions for completing the form, and a reprint from Circular E. Circular E is the IRS publication that explains the rules for making 940 tax deposits and general information for filing Form 940.

THE PAYROLL SYSTEM

The primary function of a payroll system is to provide information necessary for computing employee payroll. An employee's earnings record is the basis for preparing his or her payroll check. Once the payroll checks have been prepared, they are recorded on a payroll register. From data in the payroll register, journal entries are prepared to record the payroll expense as well as the liability for payroll taxes. The net pay shown on the payroll register represents the cash demand that will be placed on the company's checking account. A payroll system comprises the forms, records, and procedures required to carry out these and other tasks.

Computerized Payroll Applications

Advances in computer technology have made computers affordable, practical, and cost-efficient for most restaurant operations. An operation lacking a sophisticated guest accounting system may still use a computer to prepare payroll checks, to perform general ledger accounting, and to carry out other tasks involving numerical computation and accumulation of data.

However, a small property may not be able to justify an in-house computer system. In this case, banks and computer service companies offer a low-cost alternative. They sell computer services such as payroll preparation and general ledger accounting for modest fees.

In a computerized payroll application, information, such as employee number, pay rate, deductions, and earnings, is not recorded on paper, but rather is stored in a computer file. Computer files are usually maintained on back-up drives, which allow random access of information. In computer terminology, the earnings records for all employees are called the payroll master file or **database**.

database Collection of records or files containing information for users.

The payroll process begins when hours worked are entered into the payroll master file. The computer then processes each employee's hours worked in accordance with information on that employee's file record and instructions in the computer program. This process emulates the manual procedures previously discussed.

The output of a computerized payroll application is similar to that of a manual system—namely, the payroll register and the payroll checks.

LABOR COST STANDARDS

Now that we have discussed the rules and composition of labor costs, in this section we will examine how to control these costs by applying productivity standards and comparing actual payroll results to those standards.

---

[1] U.S. Department of Treasury, Internal Revenue Service, Publication 15, Circular E, Employer's Tax Guide. This publication can be obtained at an Internal Revenue Service office or found online at ww.irs.gov.

Productivity is measured by the production results of an outlet or of a staffing level, and is generally defined as the relationship between output and input. Achieving high productivity in the food-service industry requires minimizing waste and reducing costs per cover. Standard labor costs can be set as a predetermined unit cost for each food and beverage product produced. In determining the standard labor cost, the manager calculates the cost of direct and indirect labor required to produce each unit of a product via its specific recipe processes. For example, producing a tenderloin steak might include the following:

- The receiving clerk's time in receiving, verifying, storing, and extending the price of an order of tenderloin

- The storeroom clerk's time in checking the product for freshness and delivering it to the outlet kitchen

- The butcher's time in trimming, portioning, and packaging the beef

- The prep cook's time in marinating the beef

- The chef's time in preparing the plated item

- The server's time in promoting and presenting the item to the customer

Quantifying the time for each step, and thereby understanding the cost structure of your offerings, gives you a standard against which to compare actual cost data. This system could reveal costs that are out of line, and it permits analysis to locate and deal with trouble spots.

You can establish standard labor costs with one of two basic approaches. You can use a system of performance standards based on historical costs under favorable conditions, or you can use staffing guides based on management's determination of various job cost elements.

productivity A measure of effectiveness in utilizing labor and equipment; the relationship between input and output.

Performance Standards

Determining the precise amount of time needed to perform any specific job function derives what is called a *performance standard*. These specific standards are then categorized into an acceptable standard for each job. There is no universal method of determining specific time standards for all jobs; for example, performance standards of restaurants engaged in fast-food delivery will differ greatly from those in a fine-dining atmosphere. Yet setting performance standards will help you with labor cost budgeting for any type of restaurant, so you should determine your time expectations of service staff. Performance standards are used to do the following:

- Establish labor requirements

- Calculate the anticipated number of hours needed

- Convert estimated hours to direct labor dollars

- Establish direct labor controls and forecasts

- Plan any overtime requirements

- Forecast indirect cost rates

- Evaluate competitors.

The goal of this kind of analysis is to establish a productivity program that will enhance labor control and forecasts without sacrificing service levels. Typically, you'd use the criteria in Figure 14-16 to report performance standards for the departments within a hotel establishment. These are

Figure 14-16 Performance Standard

Department	Criteria
Rooms Division	Occupied rooms and #s of guest (in-house, arrival and departure)
Food and Beverage	Covers (guests) per hour
Laundry and Dry Cleaning	Pounds per hour
Telephone / PBX	Calls per hour
Garage / Valet Service	Cars parked per hour
Maintenance/Facility	# of work orders and special planned projects per hour
Housekeeping room attendant	# of rooms cleaned per hour

based on necessary productivity; that is, the criteria are tied precisely to the work output you are seeking from your employees.

So, how do you set performance standards? The process begins with watching your staff and estimating the time needed to complete a task. Are employees standing around with nothing to do? Are customers receiving inadequate service even though employees are working at top efficiency? Managing in this observant, commonsense manner means managing "from the front door and not the back office," and it has great benefits in evaluating labor standards and productivity. For example, in the kitchen, many staff members typically work on each product by completing multiple steps. You can use your recipes to isolate each step and estimate the time for completion. You will also want to evaluate how volume fluctuates during a shift, and how this affects productivity.

The process of setting performance standards is more valuable for variable and semivariable staffing costs, which are affected by volume, than for fixed labor costs, which are paid regardless of volume. Variable and semivariable labor costs usually involve servers and kitchen personnel, whom you schedule on the basis of volume, while fixed labor costs are often those costs associated with managers, who are working despite volume fluctuations.

Looking at a possible scenario, from your evaluation of productivity, you might say that you expect your dinner servers to handle fourteen covers per hour, or you might decide that your dinner chefs should handle eighteen covers per hour. Then you can evaluate their performance based on your expectations and based on how business fluctuates. If the chefs easily meet the requirement and have time left over for standing around, perhaps your standards need to be set a little higher by including side work or prep work. On the other hand, if your servers are getting complaints about poor service, perhaps fourteen covers per hour is too high a standard to demand. Keep in mind that your standards will be different for a fine-dining restaurant than for a fast-paced lunch spot. Your customers will get an impression of your establishment from your prices, menu, ambience, and image, and they will form expectations of your level of service. These expectations should figure into your calculations of productivity and how your staff should perform. These performance standards may change with the seasons, menu changes, and your own commonsense reassessments.

Although these techniques offer succinct methods for analyzing labor utilization, you must use them with caution; in analyzing labor productivity, there is no substitute for direct observation and common sense. If you can combine management acumen with objective productivity assessment, you will have the tools necessary to keep labor costs as low as possible while satisfying your guests through employees' schedules.

Staffing Guides

The second approach to establishing standard costs involves what is called a **staffing guide**. This is often more practical and easily quantifiable in an environment where there is a continuous flow of product or service with minimal change, such as a restaurant. Once again, common sense and direct observation are vital when setting standards. With a staffing guide, it is not uncommon to alter your standards during the course of a year to meet changing conditions, such as an expansion of the restaurant or a modification of the existing menu. A staffing guide will need to be monitored and updated as your restaurant changes. Figure 14-17 is an example of a simple staffing guide. The number of people needed in each position grows as the number of covers increases. Note, however, that each position has a different rate of increase. How these numbers increase will depend on the potential productivity of the individual and the position requirements.

staffing guide A document establishing labor time standards for productivity evaluation of employees.

Figure 14-17 Sample Staffing Guide

COVERS	WAITSTAFF	COOKS	BUSPERSON
from 0 to 15	1	2	1
from 16 to 35	2	3	2
from 36 to 55	3	3	3
from 56 to 75	4	3	3

To take this guide further and to make it more useful, you will need to convert those personnel numbers to hours that the individuals are needed (Figure 14–18). Then you should relate these numbers to an actual business forecast. You can also include your fixed labor costs, such as managers' salaries, to estimate your total labor costs. Remember that these costs will not vary with volume. It is important to note, however, that most labor costs, while normally classified as either fixed (not related to volume) or variable (directly related to volume), are in reality semivariable (neither fully fixed nor variable).

Figure 14-18 Sample Staffing Guide by Hours. *(Note: the italicized supervisor's time is a fixed amount)*

Date of the month	1	2	3	4	5	6	7	8	9	10	11	12	13	14
Covers forecasted	9	49	50	90	81	37	57	19	83	91	41	65	27	34
HOURS NEEDED:														
Host @ $6.50 / hr	4	4	4	8	8	4	4	4	8	8	4	8	4	4
Server @ $5.25 / hr	4	12	12	20	20	12	16	8	20	20	12	16	8	8
Busser @ $5.75 / hr	4	12	12	16	16	12	12	12	16	16	12	12	8	8
Prep cook @ $6.75 hr	0	5	5	10	10	5	5	0	10	10	5	10	5	5
Line cook @ $8.25 / hr	5	15	15	20	20	15	15	15	20	20	15	15	15	15
Dishwasher @ $7.00 / hr	5	5	10	15	15	5	10	5	15	15	5	10	5	5
Supervisor @ 8.75 / hr	*4*	*4*	*4*	*4*	*4*	*4*	*4*	*4*	*4*	*4*	*4*	*4*	*4*	*4*

This staffing guide in Figure 14-18 uses the hours from Figure 14-17, plus a few additions in terms of positions and greater numbers of covers, and relates this to the forecasted cover information. Remember that this guide is in hours needed, not numbers of people needed. We can make a forecasted labor total from these labor amounts and also be sure to have the correct amount of staff members working at all times. A limited number of the staff members in our example may continue on through the lunch shift; simply repeat this guiding process through the different meal periods of the day, and minimize staffing levels during slow times to keep costs down.

Review of Labor Standards

Management can review the effectiveness of the staffing guide by a method called *revenue per staff-hour*. This is an extension to the staffing guide, and it is often used by top management to measure the effectiveness of the staffing guide or production standards in use. This method takes revenue and divides it by the number of hours spent to generate that revenue. It can be calculated by individual position, as in Figure 14-19, or by department. For the numbers to be relevant, different positions or departments should be measured according to their contributions to the company. Figure 14-19 shows how you would measure these revenue contributions in a hotel operation.

Figure 14-19 Revenue Per Staff Hour

Department	Criteria
Rooms Division	Measurement should be based on room revenue only
Kitchen	Food only
Restaurant (excluding Kitchen)	Total Food and Beverage Revenue
Retail Outlet	Retail revenue only
Spa Outlet	Spa revenue only
Housekeeping	Room revenue only
Administrative departments such as accounting and personnel	Total company revenue

In practice, most restaurants prepare their weekly forecasts and projected revenue figures before posting a schedule on the bulletin board for employees. The next week's revenue projections and your staffing guide set the stage for employee staffing. With accurate forecasting and a workable staffing guide, you should be able to minimize the variance between your standards and the actual hours used. Figure 14-20 provides an example worksheet that would be used to guide staffing decisions for the week ahead.

From the example, the kitchen revenue per labor hour standard is $145, and the projected food revenue for the following week is $116,000. Therefore, the kitchen labor hours schedule is $116,000 ÷ $145 = 800 hours. This is equivalent to 100 8-hour shifts, with an average of 14 employees per day for a week.

The advantage of using revenue per labor hour to determine employees' scheduled hours is that it is very simple to calculate. The main disadvantage is that it fails to take into account possible discounts and complimentary meals, which produce no revenue but require production hours for which the manager must schedule.

Other Labor Costs

Whoever is responsible for preparing employees' schedules must be aware of the circumstances that influence cost fluctuations and, as a result, their appropriate use. Thoroughly assess your company's historical labor expenses and trends. Be sure the data is valid, useful, and complete. As with all control measures, the system used must be cost-effective. It would be counterproductive to spend $1,000 analyzing, planning, and controlling to save just $500 in labor costs.

One cost to consider is restaurant setup time. The cost of setting up the restaurant for operations cannot be related directly to the number of covers. This is one of the many job functions

Figure 14-20 Weekly Labor Control

Labor Control worksheet - weekly

Department	Revenue per labor hour- Standard	Projected revenue	Hours allowed*	8 hour shifts [appx.]	head count average / day
Housekeeping	$95.00	$222,000	2,337	292	42
CSA	$110.00	$55,000	500	63	9
Dining Room	$90.00	$95,000	1,056	132	19
Kitchen	$145.00	$116,000	800	100	14
Retail	$93.00	$14,000	151	19	3
Front Desk	$505.00	$222,000	440	55	8
		$386,000	**5,283**		

*"hours allowed" includes all hourly positions in each department

that are difficult to allocate as either fixed or variable labor expenses. A question often raised is whether the setup costs should be treated as direct labor or as part of other labor costs. In many situations, the restaurant opening period fluctuates widely in relation to covers; the impact of the setup cost in these cases can be more significant than the actual direct labor production time. The cost per cover can vary solely because of the length of the time the restaurant is open, rather than due to the efficiency of the waitstaff.

To establish a consistent cost system, estimate the standard work time that you think is necessary to complete the setup work. Use this figure to compute the standard cover cost. Alternatively, each detail involved in the restaurant setup could be scrutinized using a precise **time and motion study**; then, a total of the required time for all duties can be calculated. Time and motion studies use film to record a continuous operation. One type of time and motion study, micromotion study, can reduce the costs of very fast, very repetitive activities by analyzing the fine motions made. Micromotion studies can help reduce the cost of intermittent operations by using a time-delayed camera to record activities, then using that information to encourage greater efficiency in daily work. Any time you use film, you have a reviewable account of how the process goes, and you can make better decisions based on this fuller knowledge.

One drawback is that this method mixes two different labor elements, each of which is subject to different parameters and cost controls. Where this practice is followed, setup costs should be identified within both the budgeted and the actual labor cost accumulations. In this way, you can measure labor efficiency independently for the productive versus setup time elements.

Another degree of uncertainty exists because the method fails to take into account the unique circumstances of each day's production. For example, if all orders to the kitchen come in early, and then business slows down early, it is desirable for the employees to start on the next day's setup and production while they await the arrival of more customers. A classic adage in the food-service business is "Time to lean, time to clean." Likewise, orders arrive in different sequences or patterns during a shift, and these patterns and sequences affect productivity. For example, it is easier to produce twenty meals if ten orders of the same item come in together than if no two items of the twenty are alike. Some items are easier to prepare than others, so the mix of items affects productivity as well. This is why good managers closely observe the actual production process to assess actual efficiency versus "paper" efficiency. Generally, kitchen hours are regarded as semivariable or fixed labor hours, because as much as they are tied to production, there is much work that must be done whether there is production or not, and menu variety can create an ever-changing efficiency rate.

time and motion study
A systematic observation, analysis, and measurement of the separate steps in the performance of a specific job. This study is done for the purpose of establishing a standard time for each performance, with the goal of improving procedures and increasing productivity.

Scheduling and Labor Forecasting

The schedule is your tool to meet service needs, which you will predict through revenue and labor forecasting. But it is not just your tool; when your employees see the schedule, they feel that they are looking at a map of their livelihood! You will want to be as accurate as you can in forecasting so that you will have enough, but not too much, service staff on hand. But you also need to look at the schedule through your employees' eyes. An employee's happiness and performance are largely influenced by his or her schedule.

To balance the three competing pressures of owners, employees, and guests, you need to understand the task of forecasting business. Expected business levels are crucial in predicting how many employees to schedule. The following information offers a pattern for developing your own solid forecast. To forecast business for next Monday, analyze business volume for the past four Mondays and for this Monday last year. Did you have enough employees for each day? If so, it may be safe to schedule the same number of people for the coming Monday according to the staffing guide.

Extend the forecast, modifying it if necessary, to accommodate economic patterns, upcoming holidays, or special events. For example, research convention business in your area and how it affects your company. If you want to increase scheduling for an event such as a convention, use comparable scheduling data from other such events. If you are new to a company, consult others who have been there during such times. If the company itself is new, you should compile the necessary data yourself and make decisions for the future based on what you learn. You will need to consider the dietary requirements or price elasticity of various convention or event groups, and even watch how weather conditions affect your business volume.

capture ratio The number or percentage of customers a restaurant attracts, depending on set variables such as marketing, convention business or menu offerings.

What you are doing is establishing a capture ratio based on historical trends and management experience. The term **capture ratio** refers to the number or percentage of customers a restaurant attracts, depending on set variables such as marketing, convention business, or menu offerings. If you are forecasting company sales, you should consider the time, the economy, the guest count, and any local conventions or marketing campaigns. If these variables change, so will your results.

Once the forecast is established, calculate how many employees are needed at the varying levels of business volume, and determine each employee's availability. Many businesses schedule each employee a certain number of hours every week, whether or not there is an increase or decrease in volume or sales. This method is easy, and it guarantees that the payroll will not exceed the budget, but it fails to account for changes in demand. A more precise, and likely more profitable, method is to complete a business forecast, affording you the luxury of adding or subtracting labor hours from your schedule based on current conditions.

One prevailing technique for managing schedules with forecasting is to adjust the number of hours for each worker by the increase or decrease in volume of business according to your forecast and staffing standards. Scheduling should be based on the volume of business, not simply on company sales—especially in companies with multiple restaurant outlets, such as hotels. For example, your hotel's occupancy rate may rise due to complimentary or discount packages, but restaurant revenue might not necessarily follow. However, if you do not schedule more workers to accommodate any increase in guests, your customer service standards may suffer. You will have to balance these pressures based on forecasting and then monitoring actual volume fluctuations.

The Difference Between Actual and Standard Labor

Regardless of how labor standards are determined, variances from the standards must be computed and analyzed for control purposes. For direct labor, both wage rate variances and efficiency variances are computed. Typical factors causing wage rate variances include the following:

- Inaccurate or unrealistic wage rate estimates

- Unanticipated overtime hours required to complete work

- A more experienced—and therefore more expensive—grade of labor required than estimated

- Increases in the minimum wage or union pay scale

Efficiency variances generally occur more frequently than variances of wage rate. The following are some common factors that cause a labor efficiency variance:

- Stated labor hour amounts per cover may be accidentally or deliberately set low or high.

- Poor scheduling or materials shortages cause delays or idle time.

- Equipment breakdown causes lost time.

- Inexperienced or apprentice labor needs extra learning time.

- A defective order results in time lost while staff makes corrections.

- More staff may be needed than anticipated in the standards.

- Low morale or motivation to work results in less than 100 percent efficiency.

The causes of any variance should be calculated and explained on a timely basis.

Full-Time-Equivalent Reporting

The full time equivalent, or FTE, technique is a process commonly used to measure performance ratios between departments and companies of similar size. Most companies undertake this step in considering the wisdom of outsourcing a particular function. An FTE study uses special formulas to combine actual regular time, overtime, and double-time hours worked in order to compare them to what would happen if only regular hours were used to produce the same results.

The goal of FTE analysis is to highlight extreme cost of overtime to the company. Restricting overtime hours requires accurate volume and staff predictions. If FTE results are compared against competitors or industry levels, then they must measure against the same benchmarks to ensure relevance. Data collection for the production of FTE reports uses two general classifications: production units and work hours. Nearly all the production unit data required to prepare an FTE report involve familiar business volume units, such as restaurant covers, beverage units, and average unit selling price. These types of figures establish standards that are repeatable and quantifiable, and by which you can judge staff productivity.

To calculate FTE, retrieve work hours from your payroll system. Overtime hours should be reflected in equivalent terms. Thus, four hours of overtime work compensated at time-and-a-half is calculated as six work hours. This means that, for someone who earns $8 an hour, his or her pay, with overtime, was $48. To you, in these FTE calculations, that looks like working six regular hours. Work hours associated with holiday pay should be reflected as straight time. Thus, 8 hours worked on a holiday on which the pay rate is doubled should be calculated as 8 hours, not 16 hours. Vacation hours should not be reflected in the calculation of work hours. Also, some employees may work in more than one department in a larger establishment. While the payroll system often captures their work hours in only one department, it is important to implement a system for identifying interdepartmental transfer of work hours when applicable.

Regardless of the number of days in a month or actual hours worked, the hours reported for salaried employees who have been employed for the entire month are 173.33 per month. Note that salaried work hours are not to be included in work hour calculations for productivity, but only in the calculations of FTEs. If the salaried employee is present regardless of volume, then his or her 173.33 hours are fixed. Some companies include vacation, sick leave, and holiday pay when calculating FTEs, unless the position is filled during these absences. The calculations should exclude work hours reported in connection with disability pay.

The calculation of FTE converts the total number of work hours, both salaried and hourly, to an equivalent number of full-time shifts performed in the relevant period. An FTE workload for hourly employees is equal to 8 hours per day multiplied by the number of workdays available in a month, then multiplied by 5/7. This last fraction is included to account for the 5 days out of 7 worked in an FTE week.

Available work hours are calculated as follows:

$$31\text{-day month} = 31 \times 8 \times 5/7 = 177.14$$
$$30\text{-day month} = 31 \times 8 \times 5/7 = 171.43$$
$$29\text{-day month} = 31 \times 8 \times 5/7 = 165.72$$
$$28\text{-day month} = 31 \times 8 \times 5/7 = 160.00$$

To calculate FTEs for salaried employees, the total number of hours in the particular period is divided by 173.33, regardless of the number of workdays in the specific month. For hourly employees, use the values from the list. The calculation in Figure 14-21 is for a 30-day month.

Figure 14-21 Full Time Equivalent

	Salaried	Hourly
1) Regular hours	450.1 hours	1750 hours
2) Overtime @ 1.5	N/A	32 (actual hours worked = 24; but for FTE purposes, this is expressed at 1.5 times the rate, or 32)
3) Vacation hours	40	N/A
4) Total hours	490.1	1782
5) FTE	490.1 / 173.33 = 2.8	1782 / 171.43 = 10.4
6) Total FTE =	2.8 + 10.4 =	13.2

This calculation results in 13.2 FTE, without overtime. You can compare this to what you actually spent and see where variances are eating into your labor budget. Many food and beverage managers use the results of this calculation to report covers, revenue totals, and payroll amounts per FTE. It is also useful to compare rate of pay and FTE results with competitors once a reliable history has been established, after perhaps one year. A rate-of-pay survey should be done at least once a year to remain competitive.

SUMMARY

Business success depends directly on wise staff planning. Labor costs in the industry typically range from 30 to 40 percent of food and beverage revenue. In conjunction with food cost, labor cost is often referred to as prime cost because it constitutes the vast majority of expenses in most operations.

Staff planning must balance the needs of three groups: management, to minimize costs; employees, for improved hours and pay; and customers, for improved service. Staffing in service industries is extremely challenging because of the widely fluctuating demand from hour to hour, day to day, and season to season. Staffing impulsively, by the needs of the minute, results in wasted money; restaurant production cannot be shelved and resold later. Likewise, understaffing results in dissatisfied guests, which you cannot remedy by overstaffing later.

To control labor costs, the first step is to establish standard labor costs based on historical data or a staffing guide. The second step is to forecast sales. By knowing production needs, and the staff required to meet those needs, scheduling can be done efficiently. Labor costs may be categorized as direct or indirect and scheduled accordingly. Generally, direct labor varies more closely with variations in sales levels than does indirect labor.

Differences between actual and standard labor costs must be analyzed closely and constantly for control purposes. Variances result from either wage rate or efficiency variances, both of which you can monitor and change. Numerous methods are used to analyze labor productivity, but the bottom line is that management must closely observe and control productivity.

CHAPTER QUESTIONS

Discussion Questions

1. Why is staff planning vital to success?

2. What competing interests need to be balanced when scheduling staff?

3. What are labor standards, and why are they critical to proper scheduling?

4. What factors can cause actual labor cost to deviate from standard costs?

5. How can a manager decide what products should be outsourced?

6. What is the purpose of FTE analysis?

Critical Thinking Questions

1. What types of pressure, and from what sources, does operational management receive in attempting to control labor costs? How can management best balance these competing pressures?

2. When are labor costs too low? Too high?

3. What criteria are most pertinent when establishing performance standards?

4. What factors need to be evaluated in forecasting business activity?

5. If a review of labor cost variances indicates that labor costs are below budget standards, what should management do?

6. If the cost of food sold is 30 percent, and labor costs are 32 percent, what is the prime cost?

7. If operating standards indicate the labor cost per cover should be $2, and labor costs for the period were $1,000 with 450 covers served, what is the actual variance in labor cost per cover?

8. If the average nonovertime wage rate is $5 per hour, but hourly employees average 50 hours per week, what is the actual wage average per hour?

9. If staffing guidelines call for 40 hours of hourly labor to produce 100 covers on Monday, and for 60 hours to produce 200 covers on Friday, what is the actual operating efficiency on Monday?

10. If total sales are $12,000 and the cost of labor is $4,200, what is the labor cost percentage?

11. If sales drop to $10,000 and the cost of labor drops to $4,000 what is the labor cost percentage?

12. If the average wage rate increases from $5.00 to $5.50, without an increase in productivity, and labor costs are 35 percent, what will be the new labor cost percentage?

13. In a 30-day month, if 1,000 hours are worked by hourly and/or salaried nonexempt employees, what is the number of FTEs?

14. In a 28-day month, if 1,100 hours are worked by salaried exempt employees, what is the number of FTEs?

Objective Questions

1. In controlling labor costs, direct observation of employees and customer service is superior to accounting analysis. True or False?

2. Because of the high cost of labor, it is essential to control these costs regardless of the time, energy, and expense involved. True or False?

3. Budget standards equal operating standards throughout the fiscal year. True or False?

4. When scheduling staff, a manager focused on maximizing profitability should place more emphasis on performance and operating standards than on any other factor. True or False?

5. The cost of training employees to perform multiple jobs typically increases the cost of labor. True or False?

Multiple Choice Questions

1. According to the NRA, in which food-service category(s) does the cost of wages, salaries, and employee benefits exceed the cost of food sold?
   A. Full service, check average over $10
   B. Full service, check average under $10
   C. Limited service, fast food
   D. All of the above

2. Which of the following is directly related to the precise amount of time needed to perform any job function?
   A. Performance standards
   B. Productivity standards
   C. Staffing guides
   D. Labor standards

3. What two groups would be most likely to find labor costs too low? (select two)

   A. Upper management

   B. Customers

   C. Employees

   D. The IRS

4. Scheduling should be based on

   A. Company sales.

   B. Volume of business.

   C. Occupancy.

   D. Capture ratio.

5. In a flexible budget, what technique can be used to help measure the efficiency of semivariable labor costs such as indirect labor?

   A. Variance factor

   B. Business forecasting

   C. Labor cost percentage

   D. Operating standards

6. Raising wages can lower total labor costs when

   A. labor efficiency increases.

   B. employees have more experience.

   C. a greater number of people apply for jobs at the company.

   D. productivity analysis is performed more often and accurately.

7. FTE reporting is useful for all of the following EXCEPT

   A. comparison of labor efficiency to competitors.

   B. comparison of labor efficiency between departments.

   C. establishing performance standards.

   D. revealing the costs of overtime.

Analyzing Cost-Volume-Profit (CVP) Relationships and Marginal Contribution Break-Even (MCB)

Learning Objectives

After reading this chapter, you should be able to:

- use marginal costing techniques to determine whether to open or close an operation;

- explain and use full-cost accounting;

- use techniques of differential cost, differential revenue, and marginal contribution;

- understand fixed, variable, and stepped cost factors of decision making;

- apply least square analysis to delineate costs.

In Practice

This chapter covers one of the most powerful tools that managers have at their disposal: the relationship between cost, volume, and profit in decision-making. The decisions managers make regularly involve the following:

- *Whether or not to open and close operations*
- *The volume of sales required to break even and generate profit*
- *Menu pricing in relation to cost of sales*
- *Impact of product sales mix on product contribution*

(continues)

(continued)

To understand the meaning of the cost-volume-profit relationship (CVP) and marginal costing break-even (MCB), take the case of Rudy's Restaurant. Rudy and his wife Jackie opened Rudy's Restaurant 20 years ago after their only child turned five. Rudy is thinking about expanding the restaurant seating area to capture the heavy lunch traffic from the new office buildings nearby. Rudy thinks that the current wait time of 15 to 20 minutes before being seated for lunch could be turning customers away to the competition. He is also thinking about lowering menu prices to bring back old customers that the restaurant lost to the competition, but he also has concerns about increasing product costs.

On the other hand, Jackie is thinking about what to do with an open restaurant space about 50 yards from their restaurant, which they acquired in anticipation of expanding their restaurant. They had thought they could use it to cater to military personnel and their families. Unfortunately, the government closed the military base during a base closure and realignment a few months ago. The following discussion took place between them one morning before they opened the restaurant for breakfast:

Rudy: *Jackie, I have more questions than answers for how our restaurant is doing. I don't see many of our old customers, and yet we have more opportunity to serve more people than before.*

Jackie: *I believe that the reason we are losing our old customers to the competition is that our lunch prices are higher. Don't you agree?*

Rudy: *Yes, but what can we do when gas prices and everything else is going up?*

Jackie: *Maybe we should reduce our portion sizes to compensate when we reduce prices. Better yet, why don't we ask Michael to take a look? He is the smart one in the family.*

Michael: *Mom, Dad, I can help answer your questions. We had a good lecture on cost-volume-profit last semester, and my entire dissertation is based on it. Give me few days to review cost, volume, and profit information about the business.*

Rudy: *Good, son. After lunch today you will see what I am talking about. The historical information on cost, volume, and profit are in your mother's office. Your mom would want us to drop prices and maybe advertise in the local newspaper, but how do we pay for all of this and still make money?*

Michael: *Dad, I promise I won't leave any stone unturned. I will even look at the idea of expanding the restaurant as you suggested in light of the growing competition.*

INTRODUCTION TO COST-VOLUME-PROFIT RELATIONSHIPS (CVP)

Before Michael started the analysis of his parents' business, he revisited his books and notes on the subject of CVP. A short story that his teacher told in class came to mind.

With that understanding, Michael studied the relationship between cost, volume (of output), and profit at his parents' restaurant. In your role as cost controller or manager, analyzing this relationship can help you make decisions about many aspects of operations, including menu pricing, budgeting, and capital improvements. The analysis, sometimes abbreviated as CVP (cost-volume-profit), also lends itself to evaluating alternative courses of action. You may decide to open or close a restaurant, or to eliminate, reduce, or add services to an existing operation, based on CVP calculations. CVP analysis applies sales and cost data to reveal the relationships among cost, volume of output, and profit. The decision to invest in any of the above business options depends upon the relationships of these three factors to one another, and on the manager's objectives. Before we explain CVP, we must define certain terms we will be using throughout this chapter.

Know Your Costs

Understanding the difference between fixed and variable costs can be critical. Kennard T. Wing, of OMG Center for Collaborative Learning, reports that a large health care system made the mistake of classifying all of its costs as variable. As a consequence, when volume dropped, managers felt that costs should be cut proportionally, and more than 1,000 people were laid off even though the workload of most of them had no direct relation to patient volume. The result was that morale of the survivors plummeted and within a year the system was scrambling to replace not only those it had let go, but many others who had quit. The point is, the accounting systems we design and implement really do affect management decisions in significant ways. A system built on a bad model of the business will either not be used or, if used, will lead to bad decisions.

Source: Kennard T. Wing, "Using Enhanced Cost Models in Variance Analysis for Better Control and Decision Making" *Management Accounting Quarterly,* Winter 2000, pp. 27–35. MANAGEMENT ACCOUNTING QUARTERLY (PRINT) by Kennard T. Wing. Copyright 2000 by Institute of Management Accountants. Reproduced with permission of Institute of Management Accountants in the format Textbook via Copyright Clearance Center.

Definition of Terms

variable costs (VC) Production cost which changes in direct proportion to sales volume.

fixed costs (FC) Costs that remain constant regardless of sales volume, such as executive salaries.

semivariable costs Costs which vary with, but not in direct proportion to, business volume.

stepped costs Costs that "step up" across specific increases in production volume.

For the purpose of our illustration, we must classify all costs as either variable or fixed. **Variable costs (VC)** are those that increase or decrease in direct proportion to the volume of business, varying upwards or downwards according to and consistent with the level of business. We will use the abbreviation *VC* to refer to variable costs. **Fixed costs (FC),** on the other hand, are nonvariable costs that stay the same no matter how great or small the volume of business. Classifying your expenses into these categories will depend on your specific operation; indeed, it is a matter of judgment.

This seems simple and straightforward. However, in practice, some costs exhibit both nonvariable and variable characteristics. Labor cost is an excellent and important example. This sort of cost behavior pattern is called **semivariable**. For the purpose of our CVP and MCB analyses, any semivariable cost will have to be separated into its fixed and variable elements. Consider that, over long periods, there is the tendency for even fixed costs to display some variability. Within a well-defined volume of the business, the costs are fixed, but once a new volume range is reached, the costs may change. Thus, in Rudy's Restaurant, for example, one manager and a supervisor may be able to deal with a lunch crowd of 350 to 450 covers as normal capacity. On the other hand, from 450 to 550 covers, one manager and two supervisors may be necessary. It is with this in mind that we introduce the term **stepped costs**. Figure 15-1 represents how costs "step up" with certain measures of volume increase.

If you have difficulty finding the amount of variable or fixed elements within the semivariable costs of production, do not worry just yet. We will explain several methods for deriving these figures in this chapter. Consider the following example.

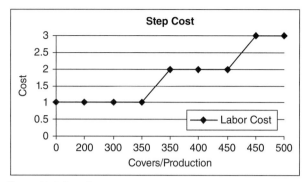

Figure 15-1 Step Cost

Michael uncovered two sets of financial books in his classroom material, one dealing with absorption costing and the other with variable costing. *Absorption costing* is generally used for external financial reports. It treats all costs as product costs regardless of whether they are variable or fixed. The decision to use the open restaurant space between Jackie and Rudy, under the absorption costing method, will consist of direct materials, direct labor, and both variable and fixed overhead. Thus, absorption costing allocates a portion of fixed overhead cost to each entree, along with variable production costs. Because absorption costing includes all costs, it is also referred to as full cost method.

Under *variable costing*, on the other hand, only those costs that vary with output are treated as product costs. This would usually include direct materials, direct labor and the variable portion of overhead. Fixed overhead is not treated as a product cost under this method. Rather, fixed overhead is treated as a period cost and, like selling and administrative expenses, it is charged off in its entirety against revenue each period. Variable costing is sometimes referred to as direct costing or marginal costing.

To complete this summary comparison of absorption and variable costing, we need to briefly consider the handling of selling and administrative expenses. These expenses are never treated as product cost, regardless of the costing method. Thus under either method, both variable and fixed selling and administrative expenses are always treated as period costs and deducted from revenues as incurred.

In the case of Rudy's Restaurant, Michael noted the following data:

Number of covers each month = 6,000
Variable costs per cover:

Direct product	= $2
Direct labor	= $4
Variable overhead	= $1
Variable selling and administrative expenses	= $3

Fixed costs per month:

Fixed overhead	= $30,000
Fixed selling and administrative expenses	= $10,000

Calculations:

1. Compute the entree product cost under absorption costing

2. Compute the entree product cost under variable costing

Solution

Absorption Costing:

Direct materials	=	$2
Direct labor	=	$4
Variable overhead	=	$1
Total variable cost	=	$7
Fixed overhead cost ($30,000 ÷ 6,000 covers)	=	$5
Entree product cost	=	$12

Variable Costing

Direct materials	=	$2
Direct labor	=	$4
Variable overhead	=	$1
Entree product cost	=	$7

(Under variable costing, the $30,000 fixed overhead cost will be charged in total against income as a period expense along with selling and administrative expenses.)

To understand how income statements prepared under the absorption and variable costing approaches are different, Michael applied the financial data from Rudy's Restaurant. See Figures 15-2 and 15-3.

Entrees in beginning inventory	0
Entrees produced	6,000
Entrees sold	5,000
Entrees in ending inventory	1,000
Selling price per entree	$20
Selling and administrative expenses:	
Variable per entree	$3
Fixed per year	$10,000

		Absorption Costing	Variable Costing
Entree product cost:			
Direct materials		$ 2	$ 2
Direct labor		4	4
Variable manufacturing overhead		1	1
Fixed manufacturing overhead ($30,000 / 6,000 entrees)		5	-
Entree product cost		$ 12	$ 7

Figure 15-2 Income Statement

Several facts can be learned by examining the financial statements in Figure 15-3:

1. Under the absorption costing method, if inventories increase, some of the fixed production costs of the current period will not appear on the income statement as part of cost of goods sold. Instead, these costs are deferred to a future period and are carried

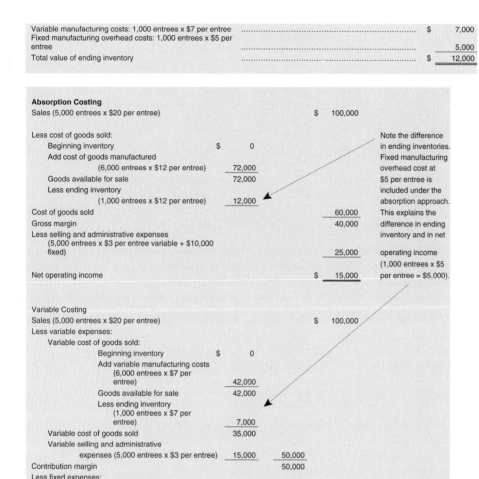

Variable manufacturing costs: 1,000 entrees x $7 per entree		$ 7,000
Fixed manufacturing overhead costs: 1,000 entrees x $5 per entree		5,000
Total value of ending inventory		$ 12,000

Absorption Costing

Sales (5,000 entrees x $20 per entree)		$ 100,000	
Less cost of goods sold:			Note the difference in ending inventories. Fixed manufacturing overhead cost at $5 per entree is included under the absorption approach. This explains the difference in ending inventory and in net operating income (1,000 entrees x $5 per entree = $5,000).
Beginning inventory	$ 0		
Add cost of goods manufactured (6,000 entrees x $12 per entree)	72,000		
Goods available for sale	72,000		
Less ending inventory (1,000 entrees x $12 per entree)	12,000		
Cost of goods sold		60,000	
Gross margin		40,000	
Less selling and administrative expenses (5,000 entrees x $3 per entree variable + $10,000 fixed)		25,000	
Net operating income		$ 15,000	

Variable Costing

Sales (5,000 entrees x $20 per entree)		$ 100,000	
Less variable expenses:			
Variable cost of goods sold:			
Beginning inventory	$ 0		
Add variable manufacturing costs (6,000 entrees x $7 per entree)	42,000		
Goods available for sale	42,000		
Less ending inventory (1,000 entrees x $7 per entree)	7,000		
Variable cost of goods sold	35,000		
Variable selling and administrative expenses (5,000 entrees x $3 per entree)	15,000	50,000	
Contribution margin		50,000	
Less fixed expenses:			
Fixed manufacturing overhead	30,000		
Fixed selling and administrative expenses	10,000	40,000	
Net operating income		$ 10,000	

Figure 15-3 Income Statement

on the balance sheet as part of the inventory account. Such a deferral of costs is known as *fixed production overhead cost deferred in inventory*. The process can be explained by referring to the data from Rudy's Restaurant. During the current period, Rudy's Restaurant produced 6,000 entrees (also called units) but sold only 5,000 entrees, thus leaving 1,000 unsold entrees in the ending inventory.

Under the absorption costing method, each entree produced was assigned $5 of fixed overhead cost (see the entree cost computations above). Therefore, each of the 1,000 entrees going into inventory at the end of the period has $5 in fixed production overhead cost attached to it, or a total of $5,000 for the 1,000 entrees. This fixed production overhead cost of the current period is deferred in the inventory to the next period, when, hopefully, these entrees will be taken out of inventory and sold. The deferral of $5,000 of fixed production overhead costs can be clearly seen by analyzing the ending inventory under the absorption costing method.

In summary, under absorption costing, of the $30,000 in fixed production overhead costs incurred during the period, only $25,000 (5,000 entrees sold × $5 per entree) has been included in cost of goods sold. The remaining $5,000 (1,000 entrees not sold × $5 per entree) has been deferred in inventory to the next period.

2. Under the variable costing method, the entire $30,000 of fixed production overhead costs has been treated as an expense of the current period (see the bottom portion of the variable costing income statement).

3. The ending inventory figure under the variable costing method is $5,000 lower than it is under the absorption costing method. The reason is that under variable costing, only the variable production costs are assigned to entrees of product and therefore included in inventory.

Variable production costs: 1,000 entrees × $7 per entree	$ 7,000

The $5,000 difference in ending inventories explains the difference in net operation income reported between the two costing methods. Net operation income is $5,000 higher under absorption costing since, as explained above, $5,000 of fixed production overhead cost has been deferred in inventory to the next period.

4. The absorption costing income statement makes no distinction between fixed and variable costs; therefore, it is not well suited for CVP computations, which are important for good planning and control. To develop data for CVP analysis, it would be necessary to spend considerable time reworking and reclassifying costs on the absorption income statement.

5. The variable costing approach to costing entrees of product works very well with the contribution approach to the income statement, since both concepts are based on the idea of classifying costs by behavior. The variable costing data in Figure 15-3 could be used immediately in CVP computations.

Essentially, the difference between the absorption and variable costing methods centers on timing. Advocates of variable costing say that fixed production costs should be expensed immediately in total, whereas advocates of absorption costing say that fixed production costs should be charged against revenues gradually as entrees are sold. Any entrees not sold under absorption costing result in fixed production costs being inventoried and carried forward on the balance sheet as assets to the next period.

After one week of compiling and examining data from Rudy's Restaurant, Michael called a meeting with his parents to discuss the approach he would be taking to answer their question regarding the use of the vacant space.

Michael: Mom? Dad? I have some calculations I would like to show you.

Jackie: Will this take long? I only have an hour before lunch starts.

Michael: Well, we can at least get started. The data in Figure 15-3 should help explain why I am going to use the variable costing method instead of the absorption costing method.

Rudy: Wait a minute, son—the absorption method generates higher profit. Isn't that what we want?

Michael: Dad, you and I know that, but the accounting rules view the situation a little differently. If we produce more than we sell, the accounting rules require that we take some of the fixed production cost (depreciation, taxes, insurance, managers salaries, and so on), and assign it to units that end up in inventories at period end.

Jackie: You mean that instead of appearing on the income statement as an expense, some of the fixed production costs—in our batch of soups— winds up on the balance sheet as inventories?

Michael: Precisely, Mom. Therefore, we are showing profits that should not be part of our decision making regarding whether to use the empty space.

Rudy: Why can't we be consistent? I thought accountants were conservative. Since when was it conservative to call an expense an asset?

Michael: Well, I didn't invent these methods. The bank requires that you follow certain accounting rules in preparing these reports. This might come out sounding wrong to you, but we could use different rules for our own internal reports.

Jackie: Rules are rules, especially in accounting.

Michael: Yes and no. For our internal reports, it might be better to use different rules than we use for the report we send to the bank. As you know, fixed production cost is not really the cost of any particular unit of product. These costs are incurred to have the capacity to make products during a particular period and will be incurred even if we did not use the empty restaurant space. Moreover, whether a unit is made or not, the fixed production costs will be exactly the same.

Rudy: Okay son, you've convinced us. Jackie, are you on board?

Jackie: Yes, I think our son is approaching this from a smart perspective.

CVP Relationships

To explain CVP relationships, we will introduce the following scenario: Assume that there was a recession, during which you closed individual restaurants or profit centers within your hotel. Now, all the major business magazines have declared that the recession is over. For your individual restaurants, however, the decision of whether to reopen is yet to be made.

In the above scenario, some restaurants will wait too long in order to be assured of at least breaking even based on their full costs when they do reopen. An undue delay will extend the agony of laid-off employees and will cause the loss of market share as the recovery proceeds. On the other side, another restaurant might rush to reopen and, in the process, book new business at prices that may fail to cover the variable costs of operation. This can do further damage to the financial health of the business. The middle ground is to reopen at the marginal contribution break-even point (MCB), where the incremental revenues that can be generated by reopening equal or exceed the direct and indirect costs of reopening.

In our example above, we mentioned that most restaurants would reopen if they were assured of at least breaking even on their full costs. But this is misleading: It is incorrect to use full-cost accounting to decide when to reopen the restaurant, especially in a hotel situation with multiple outlets.

Full-Cost Accounting

Managers are accustomed to seeing full-cost statements because they are responsible for the long-term perspective, and over the long term, revenues must cover all costs. But there is a danger in using full-cost accounting in decisions that involve the following decisions:

- When to open or close a restaurant

- Whether to buy something from an outside vendor or produce it in-house (the make-or-buy decision)

- When to eliminate one menu and introduce another

The danger of the full-cost trap is that full-cost accounting allocates fixed costs and indirect costs between products or cost centers. The allocation might be prudent and equitable if it is based on direct costs or revenues, but closing a restaurant or eliminating a menu item may not cause those costs to disappear. For example, if you pay rent or a mortgage, those expenses will not disappear just because the business is closed due to economic circumstances.

Another problem with full-cost accounting is that it tends to disguise the relationship between cost and volume by making it appear linear. Costs are depicted as purely variable, rising in a straight line directly proportional to business volume. This is not the case. Nearly every element of cost falls somewhere between purely fixed and purely variable. CVP and MCB techniques

⑪ Discussion Point

What are the relationships among costs, volume, and profit?

depict these cost relationships more accurately. The manager should, when in doubt, employ the techniques of differential analysis, discussed in the next section.

Differential Analysis

Differential analysis is a tool for escaping the rigidity of full-cost accounting and for estimating how costs and revenues actually behave in response to a change in some variable of the business, such as volume, price, or product mix. Differential techniques deliberately exclude costs and revenues, which do not change within the relevant range of operating alternatives. We will use labor cost, which usually exhibits a combination of both variable and fixed tendencies, to explain how this works.

The prerequisites of this technique include eliminating overly broad assumptions. This is important because not every one of your expenses will be relevant to every decision you make. The objective is to include only costs and revenues that will be affected by the changes in the specific operation. Differential analysis, or incremental analysis, is a way of more accurately assessing the situation because it integrates a commonsense evaluation of how each element of cost and revenue will behave in the relevant conditions.

For example, music and entertainment expenses are generally considered a direct and variable cost. However, if entertainment cost is on a "take or pay" basis, it is a fixed cost to be excluded from a differential cost analysis. As another example, a rooms manager's wages are usually considered an indirect and fixed cost. However, if management is contemplating operating without a rooms manager, the savings in wages should be included in a differential cost analysis. Sunk costs should also be exluded.

Sunk Costs

sunk cost A cost that has already been incurred and that cannot be changed by any decision made now or in the future.

Sunk costs are costs that have already been incurred and cannot be changed by any decision made now or in the future. Since sunk costs cannot be changed by any decision, they are not differential costs. Therefore, sunk costs can and should be ignored when making a decision.

To illustrate a sunk cost, assume that a restaurant paid $10,000 for pizza equipment several years ago. The equipment was used to make a pizza that is now obsolete and is no longer being sold. Even though in hindsight the purchase of the equipment may have been unwise, the $10,000 cost has already been incurred and cannot be undone. It would be unwise to continue making the obsolete product in a misguided attempt to recover the original cost of the equipment. In short, the $10,000 originally paid for the equipment is a sunk cost that should be ignored in decision-making.

A Practical View

Hal Arkes, a psychologist at Ohio University, asked 61 college students to assume they had mistakenly purchased tickets for both a $50 and a $100 ski trip for the same weekend. They could go on only one of the ski trips and would have to throw away the unused ticket. He further asked them to assume that they would actually have more fun on the $50 trip. Most of the students reported that they would go on the less-enjoyable $100 trip. The larger cost mattered more to the students than having more fun. However, the sunk cost of the tickets should have been totally irrelevant in this decision. No matter which trip was selected, the actual total cost was $150—the cost of both tickets. Since this cost does not differ between the alternatives, it should be ignored. Like these students, most managers have a great deal of difficulty ignoring sunk costs when making decisions.

Source: John Gourville and Dilip Soman, "Pricing and the Psychology of Consumption," *Harvard Business Review,* September 2002, pp. 92–93.

Now we will use Figure 15-4 to illustrate the relationships of CVP in four restaurants. Restaurant B is Rudy's Restaurant. The first column lists all the costs and denotes them with V for variable cost or F for fixed cost. Please note that most of these costs may in fact be semivariable, and thus dependent on the volume of production.

Looking at the chart, you might assume that higher sales or lower variable cost will automatically yield higher profit. In fact, the food and beverage cost and sales information for Restaurant B looks like a better result compared to Restaurants C and D, yet Restaurant B lags behind all restaurants in terms of income or profit before taxes. Restaurant A is a bit better, but it is still behind C and D.

For Restaurant B, Michael might recommend that his parents lower menu prices to attract more business, thereby increasing variable expenses. Food and beverage costs are variable, so if you reduce your menu price without reducing portion sizes, you get a higher menu cost. Restaurant B could also focus on reducing overall operational cost by providing substandard service, but of course this is likely to turn customers away. However, the key to surviving in a fierce economy is an understanding of your business limitations in terms of cost, volume, and profit objectives. Almost every restaurant experiences different limitations and characteristics of CVP objectives.

As stated earlier, the technique of CVP analysis helps management set prices. Some of the issues surrounding prices were discussed in Chapter 13. It must be remembered, however, that the concept of CVP is not a one-time exercise. You will need to review the system frequently when prices escalate, when labor costs change, or when any other major cost adjustment is made. The CVP technique is based on the assumption of fixed selling prices. When these fixed selling prices change, CVP must be reevaluated. From the above illustration, you can see that a balanced combination of cost, volume, and profit objectives is going to be the key to how management makes the decision about when to reopen. Later in this chapter we will explore the middle ground of MCB analysis.

Restaurants usually use cover amounts to determine an average check amount, which is a standard piece of data you will use often in your work. An average check is the total revenue during a meal period divided by the number of guests served. Assume that Rudy's Restaurant (Restaurant B) is only open for lunch. We know Restaurant B's total food and beverage sales from Figure 15-4: $147,360. If Restaurant B served 17,968 covers for lunch, the average food, beverage, and combined food and beverage checks will emerge as follows:

$$\text{food average check} = \frac{\$120,000}{17,968} = \$6.68$$

$$\text{beverage average check} = \frac{\$27,360}{17,938} = \$1.52$$

$$\text{combined average check} = \frac{\$147,360}{17,968} = \$8.20$$

The same method of calculations used above can also be applied in least square analysis, which is discussed below. In this case, instead of dividing revenue by covers, you will divide costs by covers.

At this point we must ask ourselves this question: If an expense, such as repair and maintenance costs, consists of both variable and fixed costs, what method should we use to untangle the variable and fixed components? Again, we will return to least square analysis, which is a statistical method of deriving the relationship between two or more correlated sets of data. It is used to calculate values of one variable when given values of the others. For each type of semivariable cost, such as maintenance, you can show the correlation between restaurant covers (production volume) and the incurring of expenditure (cost per cover).

THE RESTAURANT INDUSTRY DOLLARS - monthly data

Legend: V = variable
F = fixed

		A Full service restaurant (average check per person under $10)		B Full service restaurant (average check per person over $10)		C Limited service fast food restaurant		D Cafeteria restaurant	
	Sales	**Dollar**	**%**	**Dollar**	**%**	**Dollar**	**%**	**Dollar**	**%**
	Food sales	$150,000.00	86.20	$120,000.00	77.20	$85,000.00	97.50	$80,000.00	98.70
	Beverage sales	$20,700.00	13.80	$27,360.00	22.80	$2,125.00	2.50	$1,040.00	1.30
Characteristic	**Total**	$170,700.00	100.00	$147,360.00	100.00	$87,125.00	100.00	$81,040.00	100.00
	Expenses								
V	Cost of food sold	$49,503.00	29.00	$39,492.48	26.80	$27,095.88	31.10	$25,284.48	31.20
V	Cost of beverage sold	$5,974.50	3.50	$9,283.68	6.30	$609.88	0.70	$405.20	0.50
V	Salaries and wages	$50,527.20	29.60	$41,408.16	28.10	$22,913.88	26.30	$23,339.52	28.80
V	Employees benefits	$8,193.60	4.80	$6,778.56	4.60	$2,178.13	2.50	$4,295.12	5.30
V	Direct operating expenses	$10,754.10	6.30	$10,462.56	7.10	$4,704.75	5.40	$2,269.12	2.80
F	Music and entertainment	$512.10	0.30	$1,031.52	0.70	$87.13	0.10	$0.00	0.00
F	Marketing	$4,779.60	2.80	$4,126.08	2.80	$4,269.13	4.90	$3,484.72	4.30
V	Utility services	$5,291.70	3.10	$3,978.72	2.70	$2,439.50	2.80	$3,727.84	4.60
F	Restaurant occupancy costs	$9,729.90	5.70	$8,399.52	5.70	$5,750.25	6.60	$4,214.08	5.20
V	Repairs and maintenance	$3,072.60	1.80	$3,094.56	2.10	$1,394.00	1.60	$1,539.76	1.90
F	Depreciation	$4,267.50	2.50	$3,094.56	2.10	$1,742.50	2.00	$972.48	1.20
F	Other operating expenses/(income)	($682.80)	(0.40)	($147.36)	(0.10)	$0.00	0.00	$324.16	0.40
F	General and administration	$5,633.10	3.30	$6,336.48	4.30	$3,310.75	3.80	$4,457.20	5.50
F	Corporate overhead	$3,584.70	2.10	$2,947.20	2.00	$1,916.75	2.20	$810.40	1.00
F	Interest	$1,024.20	0.60	$884.16	0.60	$522.75	0.60	$81.04	0.10
F	Other	$512.10	0.30	$736.80	0.50	$348.50	0.40	$0.00	0.00
	Income before income taxes	$8,022.90	4.70	$5,452.32	3.70	$7,841.25	9.00	$5,834.88	7.20
	Total	$170,700.00	100.00	$147,360.00	100.00	$87,125.00	100.00	$81,040.00	100.00

Figure 15-4 Restaurant Industry Dollars Per Month

No method is perfect because factors other than volume of production may influence cost. For example, in one month there may be an exceptionally long run of needed repairs, but in another, there may be very few needed repairs. This could depend on employees' competency levels and training. This and other similar irregular occurrences must clearly temper any conclusions with any methods.

Calculating VC by the Least Squares Approach

The calculations necessary for obtaining an average of variable or fixed cost by least squares are rather involved. However, since they normally are carried out infrequently (probably only once a year), and a quite objective result is obtained, this extra refinement is probably justified.

Below is an outline of the procedures for applying least squares to a calculation of VC. We will use repair and maintenance costs from Rudy's Restaurant (B) to illustrate the calculation. We start from the assumption that the total covers are approximately 1,710 for five weeks. Assume that Figure 15-5 applies to Restaurant B for five weeks. Follow these steps:

Figure 15-5 Calculating VC by Least Square Approach

Column A Repair & maintenance costs (y)	Column B Number of covers (x)	Column C Restaurant cover capacity or # of units (x^2)	Column D Column A x Column B or (xy)
$264	350	122,500	92,400
$300	410	168,100	123,000
$150	100	10,000	15,000
$280	400	160,000	112,000
$400	450	202,500	180,000
Total = $1394	Total = 1,710	Total = 663,100	Total = 522,400

a. Calculate the weekly average output of covers: $\frac{\Sigma x}{n}$

b.   Obtain the weekly average cost: $\frac{\Sigma y}{n}$

c. Square the number of units of production or restaurant cover capacity for each week and find the weekly average: $\frac{\Sigma X^2}{n}$

d.   For each week, multiply the number of covers by costs per cover and find the weekly average: $\frac{\Sigma xy}{n}$

e. Use the results from lines a, b, c, and d in the following formula to find the variable element:

$$VC = \frac{(d) - ((a) \times (b))}{(c) - (a)^2}$$

The following are the answers:

$$\text{Step a} = \frac{1,710}{5} = 342$$

$$\text{Step b} = \frac{1,394}{5} = 278.8$$

$$\text{Step c} = \frac{663,100}{5} = 132,620$$

$$\text{Step d} = \frac{522,400}{5} = 104,480$$

The variable element is found as shown below:

$$VC = \frac{104,480 - (341) \times (278.8)}{(132,620) - (342)^2}$$

$$VC = \frac{9,130.40}{15,656.00} = \$0.583 \text{ cents, approximately}$$

The method of least squares is likely to give the most accurate separation of fixed and variable elements in a semivariable cost. An average cost per cover in our table is approximately \$0.82. This is derived by dividing Column A of Figure 15-5 by Column B. The variable element, the most important part of CVP analysis, is \$0.583.

A Practical View
Soup Nutsy

Pak Melwani and Kumar Hathiramani, former silk merchants from Bombay, opened a soup store in Manhattan after watching a *Seinfeld* episode featuring the Soup Nazi. The episode parodies a real-life soup vendor, Ali Yeganeh, whose loyal customers put up with hour-long lines and "snarling customer service." Melwani and Hathiramani approached Yeganeh about turning his soup kitchen into a chain, but they were rebuffed gruffly. Instead of giving up, the two hired a French chef with a repertoire of 500 soups and opened a store called Soup Nutsy. For \$6 per serving, Soup Nutsy offers 12 homemade soups each day, such as sherry crab bisque and Thai coconut shrimp soup. Melwani and Hathiramani reported that in their first year of operation, they netted a profit of \$210,000 on sales of \$700,000. They reported that it costs about \$2 per serving to make the soup. Thus, their variable expense ratio is one-third (\$2 cost ÷ \$6 selling price). If so, what are their fixed expenses? We can answer that question as follows:

sales = variable expenses + fixed expenses + profits

$700,000 = (\frac{1}{3} \times \$700,000) + \text{fixed expenses} + \$210,000$

fixed expenses = $700,000 = (\frac{1}{3} \times \$700,000) - \$210,000 = \$256,667$

With this information, you can determine that Soup Nutsy's break-even point is about \$385,000 of sales. This gives the store a comfortable margin of safety of 45 percent of sales.

Source: Silva Sansoni, "The Starbucks Soup?" *Forbes,* July 7, 1997, pp. 90–91. Reprinted by Permission of Forbes Magazine © 2008 Forbes LLC.

---

marginal cost The amount of output, at any given volume, by which aggregate costs are changed if the volume of output is increased or decreased by one unit, subject to the condition that fixed cost does not change with the increase in volume.

MARGINAL CONTRIBUTION BREAK-EVEN POINT (MCB)

Now, with an understanding of CVP, we will focus on the marginal contribution break-even point. **Marginal cost** is defined as the amount of output, at any given volume, at which aggregate costs are changed if the volume of output is increased or decreased by one unit. Marginal costing systems are based on the classification of costs into fixed and variable, as shown in our example above. The fixed costs are excluded, and only the marginal, variable costs are considered in determining the cost of products and services. MCB can be more than a simple tool. It can be an approach for dealing with uncertainty intelligently and finding a middle ground. There are always difficulties in estimating uncertain variables, such as customer demand, but by specifying the levels of other variables that affect the revenues of a restaurant, a required or minimum level can be found for the unknown quantity.

In the examples in this section, we will illustrate ways in which MCB analysis can be applied to sales, profit, cost, and selling price problems and how it can be used to help make a sound decision for employing the idle restaurant space Jackie is concerned about—for planning advertising to boost sales and for expanding product offerings. MCB is not a cure-all; it is only one of the many tools available to restaurant managers. However, it is a good tool with which to begin approaching decision-making problems.

Returning to Rudy's Restaurant, imagine that the vacant restaurant Jackie referred to has kitchen equipment sufficient to produce a catering business or a new steak house. Estimated fixed costs for this vacant facility are $5,000 per month. Michael has been given the task of determining the opportunity to open a steak house using this equipment. Michael estimates that menu items will sell for approximately $25 per cover. The variable costs of product and labor combined are estimated at $8 per selling price of $25. At present, Michael feels certain that the market for this steak house menu is 400 covers per day, which translates to 146,000 covers per year. The physical capacity of the vacant space is approximately 600 covers per day.

Simple MCB Analysis

Should the restaurant open a steak house in the vacant space? To begin to answer this question, we need to find the contribution margin (CM) for the steak house menu. CM is simply what is left of revenue to cover fixed costs and profit after variable costs have been subtracted, as follows:

$$CM = revenue - VC$$

When you subtract fixed costs (FC) from the CM, you get gross profit or income before taxes, as in Figure 15-4. You can then calculate the break-even level by dividing fixed costs by the CM. You can express the CM on a per-cover basis or as a percentage of sales. If you express CM on a per-cover basis, the break-even volume will be expressed in covers. If it is expressed as a percentage of sales, the break-even volume will be in dollars. We will look at the steak house project to see how this works.

Figure 15-6 provides preliminary equations.

Note that you can get the break-even dollar total by multiplying the break-even volume in covers by the selling price, or you can get the number of covers by dividing total break-even revenue dollars by price.

What is the answer to the steak house question? The simple answer is that Rudy and Jackie should go ahead with the project. Why? To break even they need to capture approximately 294 covers per day, or only 73.5 percent of the projected market of 400 covers per day. Of course, they need to be sure their projected market is not wishful thinking! Also, they will be operating well under the restaurant's physical capacity of 600 covers per day at break-even. The steak house project ought to be able to make a profit using the vacant facility if it can capture more than 73.5 percent of the projected market. With production and sales at full capacity, the steak house should make a profit of $7,650 per day before taxes (306 covers × $25 = $7,650) since all fixed costs will be covered at the 294 covers level.

Figure 15-6 Simple MCB Analysis

Contribution as percent of revenue	Contribution on a per cover basis
CM = revenue (price) − variable cost (VC)	$\text{CM\%} = \dfrac{\text{price} - \text{VC}}{\text{price}}$
CM = $25 − $8 = $17	$\text{CM\%} = \dfrac{\$25 - \$8}{\$25} = \dfrac{\$17}{\$25} = 68\%$
Break-even volume = $\dfrac{FC}{CM}$	$\text{Break-even} = \dfrac{FC}{CM\%} = \dfrac{\$5,000}{68\%} = \dfrac{\$5,000}{.68}$
Break-even = $\dfrac{\$5,000}{\$17}$ = 294.12 covers	Break-even = $7,352.94 dollars

As an added advantage, if the previous restaurant had a decent reputation, the new operation should attract guests and enjoy quick recognition. Perhaps Michael can take advantage of the previous restaurant's reputation by ensuring that the promotional and public relations campaigns are done correctly.

MCB Applied to Uncertainty

The typical break-even approach develops the volume needed to produce no profit and no loss. But every restaurant is in business to make a profit. Using the steak house example, suppose the owners would like a 5 percent profit margin on the project. The original contribution margin for the menu was 68 percent, but that was at zero profit. In effect, the 5 percent profit acts like a variable cost, so we must adjust the CM percentage accordingly: 68 percent − 5 percent = 63 percent. Now we can calculate the desired 5 percent profit margin using the percent of revenue approach as follows:

$$\text{break-even} = \frac{FC}{CM\%} = \frac{5,000}{63\%} = \$7,936.51 \text{ or } 317 \text{ covers at the } \$25 \text{ price}$$

This is still below the steak house's capacity. Michael should now look at the market and make a judgment based on the probability of selling that many steaks.

Dollar Profit Objective

What happens if Michael wants a fixed dollar profit of $5,000 per month? In this case, we treat the profit as a fixed cost, so we have to add it to the fixed cost established for the steak house: $5,000 + $5,000 = $10,000. We can now calculate the fixed dollar profit volume using the per cover approach as follows:

$$\text{Break-even} = \frac{FC}{CM} = \frac{\$10,000}{\$17} = 588.24 \text{ covers or } \$14,706 \text{ revenue}$$

Again, this is below capacity. Michael must estimate the likelihood of selling this many steaks.

Maximum Out-of-Pocket Cost

Suppose that Michael can forecast sales rather accurately. Michael estimates that the steak house can generate 500 covers per day. What out-of-pocket expenses can it incur and still break even? The formula will be as follows:

$$B(volume) = \frac{FC}{CM}$$

$$B(volume) \times CM = FC$$

$$CM = \frac{FC}{B(volume)}$$

Now we can find the CM for these circumstances:

$$CM = \frac{\$5,000}{500} = \$10$$

Subtracting the CM of $10 from the selling price of $25, we get $15, the variable cost the steak house can incur on each unit and still break even. Similarly, if a $5,500 profit is desired at the proposed volume, we find that the contribution margin equals $10,500 divided by 500 covers, or $21. At this level of desired profit, variable costs must be held to $4 per cover. This example shows how to use break-even to help set product specifications. By isolating the allowable cost structure, you can determine the right menu restrictions and engineer the menu to the cost requirements; this topic was covered at length in Chapter 13.

Selling Price

Assume again that variable costs for producing the steaks are $8 per cover and there are $5,000 in fixed costs. Add to those data the known sales volume of 500 covers and a desire to make a profit of $7,000 per month. What must the selling price be?

$$CM = \frac{FC}{B(volume)} = \frac{\$5,000 + \$7,000}{500} = \frac{\$12,000}{500 \ covers} = \$24$$

The price must equal variable cost plus fixed cost: $8 + $24 = $32. Now you can compare this $32 selling price to the existing local competitors' prices to determine whether the steak house has a good chance of selling at that price or whether the specifications must be altered to get the price down. This approach also works well for vendor bidding. Chapter 5 explores that subject in detail.

Advertising Decisions

Advertising is typically a fixed cost. Any added fixed costs raise a restaurant's break-even point and thus require added revenue (or lowered variable costs) to pay for them. The money for fixed costs comes from the contribution margin. In the steak house example, the CM percentage is 68. Thus, $1.47 additional dollars of revenue are required to cover each additional dollar of fixed cost: $1.00 divided by 68 percent = $1.47. If the steak house project's CM percentage were 50, it would take $2 to cover each additional fixed cost dollar. So, if the restaurant is considering a $500 expenditure for an ad, it will need 1.47 × $500, or $735, in extra sales just to cover the cost of the advertisement. Remember Chapter 2 that when saving money, there is a cost in producing sales. Instead, Michael must know how much the restaurant must take in to be only as well off as they would be without any advertisement. This approach provides a built-in standard for judging the results of advertising. If, after an appropriate period, added sales are not enough to justify the cost of the advertisement, the effort can be abandoned.

Labor Costs

So far the examples have been simple and straightforward. The restaurant business, alas, is not. In the traditional version of break-even analysis, a variable cost generally includes items such as material, labor, and some overhead. In reality, some of these costs may not be variable over the operating range of the restaurant. Figure 15-7 shows the figures from the original steak house example with expanded detail.

Figure 15-7 Labor Costs

Menu price			$25.00
	Variable costs:		
	Recipe or material cost	$4.20 per cover	
	Overhead cost	$.30 cents per cover	
	Labor cost	$3.50 per cover	
Total variable cost			$8.00
Fixed cost per month			$5,000

The labor cost is based on an FTE of a crew of 12 people (front- and back-of-the-house personnel). See the Chapter 14 on staff planning for how FTE should be calculated. For simplicity's sake, assume that each employee makes $116.67 per day. This is determined in Figure 15-8.

Figure 15-8 Pay Per Employee

Total wages	= ($3.50 × 400 covers)	= $1,400
Pay per employee	= $1,400 / 12	= $116.67
Rates per 8 hour shift		= $14.58

We assumed originally that at any level of production, total variable costs were $8 per cover. In reality, however, staff cannot be shifted that smoothly. Thus, in a narrow range of production, some labor costs become fixed. (In Chapter 14 on staff planning you saw a detailed treatment of how this happens.) This fact can change the break-even point of the steak house. It also affects the contribution margin and pricing, promotion, and other decisions.

Using a simple traditional approach, it looked as though the break-even point was 294.12 covers. It also appeared that, if another 200 meals were prepared and sold, the steak house would make a profit of $3,400 (200 covers × $17 contribution margin per cover). In reality, however, the original break-even point represents the effective capacity of the steak house. An extra 200 covers could be produced only if a new crew were put on at an additional cost of $1,400 per day. At the 494.12 cover level we could actually find a new result, shown in Figure 15-9.

The steak house could actually be merely breaking even. Here, the labor could essentially become a fixed cost; overhead, materials, and other employee benefits are the true variable costs. The CM for the steak house has changed dramatically. You need to be aware of volume levels at which these changes would occur for your establishment.

In general, this analysis tells us that the important thing to keep in mind when using break-even is the true nature of the restaurant cost structure, not the academic numbers in a textbook. Some restaurants have a flexible labor force, and standard analysis works well. In many others, such as those with a union workforce, idle labor cannot be manipulated smoothly, and management must treat such costs differently. In many small restaurants, certain skilled

Figure 15-9 Steakhouse Break-Even Point

Sales (494 covers @ $25 per person)	$12,350.00
Less material cost @ $4.20 per cover	$2,074.80
Less overhead cost @ $.30 per cover	$148.20
Less labor cost: (24 crew @ $14.58 per hr.)	$2,799.36
Less employee meals and other costs	$6,994.31
Fixed costs (allocated per # of days opened - 15)	$333.33
Profit	$0.00

workers cannot be laid off without being lost to competitors. The key to success is to increase revenue to help cover costs. Pricing these necessary extra sales and making sound advertising decisions can be greatly aided by using the variations of break-even analysis discussed.

Break-even analysis requires, above all, a realistic calculation of costs, both in amount and in type. If the steak house in the example above were to generate the additional 200 covers for which it has available labor capacity and sell them at a price above the variable cost, it would make profit. As long as new business is added to an existing vacancy capacity, any contribution to cover fixed costs will increase profit, or at least offset losses in other operations. Management must also consider selling the idle equipment or leasing the empty space. Whatever decision is reached, the point is to enhance the financial status of the restaurant owners.

The Advantages and Disadvantages of Break-even Analysis

The major problem is that no restaurant exists in a vacuum. There are alternative uses for the restaurant's funds and resources in almost every case. For example, in the case of the steak house, the vacant space could be leased to another company for some return. It could also be used for a different cuisine. We must, therefore, always consider not only the value of an individual project, but also how it compares to other uses of the funds and facilities.

Break-even analysis does not permit proper examination of cash flows. It is generally accepted in financial theory that the appropriate way to make investment or capital decisions is to consider the value of a proposed project's anticipated cash flows. While a complete discussion of cash flow is beyond the scope of this book, the following comments could help Michael consider the alternatives.

If the discounted value of the cash flows exceeds the required investment outlay in cash, then the project is acceptable. To understand the meaning of discounted value of cash flow, take the following example: A dollar received today is more valuable than a dollar received a year from now because if Rudy and Jackie have a dollar today, they can put it in the bank and have more than a dollar a year from now. Since dollars today are worth more than dollars in the future, Rudy and Jackie must weigh cash flows that are received at different times so that they can be compared. If Rudy and Jackie's bank pays 5 percent interest, then a deposit of $1,000 today will be worth $1,050 one year from now. This can be expressed as follows: $F1 = P(1 + r)$, where $F1$ = the balance at the end of one period, P = the amount invested now, and r = the rate of interest per period. If the investment made now by Rudy and Jackie is $1,000 in a savings account that earns 5 percent interest, then P = $1,000 and r = 0.05. Under these conditions, $F1$ = $1,050, the amount to be received in one year. The $1,000 present outlay is called the present value, or discounted value, of the $1,050 amount to be received in one year. What if the $1,050 is left in the bank for a second year? In that case, by the end of the second year the original $1,000 deposit will have grown to $1,102.50. This can be derived by $Fn = P(1 + r)$, where n = 2 years and the interest rate is 5 percent per year. The balance in two years will be computed as follows: $F2 = \$1,000 (1 + 0.05) = \$1,102.50$.

The reason for the greater interest earned during the second year is that during the second year, interest is paid on the interest. Thus, the $50 interest earned during the first year has been left in the account and added to the original $1,000 deposit when computing interest for the second year. This is known as **compound interest**. In this case, the compounding is annual. The more frequently compounding is done, the more rapidly the balance will grow. Michael can view his parents' investment in two ways. He can view it either in terms of its future value or in terms of its present value. If we know the present value of the sum (such as our $1,000 deposit), the future value in n years can be computed by using the above equation. But what if the tables are reversed, and we know the future value of some amount but we do not know its present value? For example, assume Michael knows that his parents will receive $50,000 two years from now. Rudy and Jackie know that the future value of this sum is $50,000, since this is the amount they will be receiving two years from now. But what is the sum's present value? What is it worth right now? The present value of the sum to be received in the future can be computed as follows:

$$\text{Present value} = \frac{Fn}{(1 + r)^2} = \frac{\$50,000}{(1 + 0.05)^2} = \frac{\$50,000}{1.1025} = \$45,351.47$$

The present value of a $50,000 amount to be received by Rudy and Jackie two years from now is $45,351.47, if the interest rate is 5 percent. In effect, $45,351.47 received right now is equivalent to $50,000 received two years from now if the rate of return is 5 percent. The process of finding the present value of a future cash flow, which Michael just completed, is called discounting. Michael has discounted the $50,000 to its present value of $45,351.47. The 5 percent interest that we have used to find this present value is called the discount rate.

Michael, a student like you, has been able to examine many possible options for his parents. How about you? Can you do the same?

There are other objections to break-even analysis, as noted throughout our discussion. Break-even analysis makes many restrictive assumptions about CVP relationships; in normal use it is basically a negative technique, defining constraints rather than looking at benefits. It is essentially a static tool for analyzing a single short period. What all this theory boils down to is that break-even analysis is too simplistic a technique to be used to make final investment decisions.

What is break-even analysis good for, then? It has its place: It is a simple and cheap screening device. Discounted cash flow techniques require lots of time, and it may be expensive to compile data for them. Break-even analysis can tell you whether or not it is worthwhile to do more intensive and costly analysis.

Break-even analysis provides a basis for designing product specifications. Each menu item has implications for the operations' costs. Costs affect price and marketing feasibility. Break-even analysis permits comparison of different sets of possible specifications before final decisions are made. For example, the steak house project could be tested in terms of portion sizes and steak specifications, and then compared to what the market can bear in terms of selling prices or customers' perceived value. Alternatively, the steak house could be compared to a seafood or Italian restaurant's potential in the area.

Break-even analysis serves as a substitute for estimating an unknown factor in making project decisions. In deciding whether to go ahead on a project or skip it, there are always variables to be considered: demand, costs, price, and other factors such as expertise and space constraints. When most expenses can be determined, only two missing variables remain: profit (or cash flow) and demand. Demand is usually difficult to estimate correctly. By deciding that profit must at least be zero, the break-even point, you can then fairly simply find the demand you must have to make the project a reasonable or worthwhile undertaking. If you can then estimate whether the demand will exceed that break-even point, you are making a more informed decision about how to proceed.

SUMMARY

Marginal cost analysis determines the economic viability of opening or closing an operation, in whole or in part. This technique allows management to project when revenue generated by an outlet will exceed the costs of reopening. This is accomplished by accurately analyzing the behavior of semivariable costs, which are often erroneously designated as either fixed or variable.

The least squares method is presented to differentiate the fixed and variable components of semivariable costs. While the least squares approach is fairly accurate, it requires greater effort. However, this method helps to demonstrate the common fallacy of simply accepting fixed and variable cost assumptions without closely examining the accuracy of these assumptions.

Managers are accustomed to seeing full-cost statements because they are responsible for the long-term perspective, and over the long term, revenues must cover all costs. But there is a danger in using full-cost accounting in decisions that involve CVP.

To avoid the rigidity of using full-cost accounting, managers generally apply the concept of sunk cost and Marginal cost analysis. Sunk costs are costs that have already been incurred and cannot be changed by any decision made now or in the future. And marginal cost is the amount of output, at any given volume, at which aggregate costs are changed if the volume of output is increased or decreased by one unit.

Both sunk and marginal cost approach can be more than a simple tool. It can be an approach for dealing with uncertainty intelligently and finding a middle ground in setting selling price, making advertising decisions, and deciding on affordable labor rate.

There are always difficulties in estimating uncertain variables, such as customer demand, but by specifying the levels of other variables that affect the revenues of a restaurant, a required or minimum level can be found for the unknown quantity.

The major problem is that no restaurant exists in a vacuum. There are alternative uses for the restaurant's funds and resources in almost every case. Break-even analysis does not permit proper examination of cash flows. It is generally accepted in financial theory that the appropriate way to make investment or capital decisions is to consider the value of a proposed project's anticipated cash flows. If the discounted value of the cash flows exceeds the required investment outlay in cash, then the project should be acceptable.

CHAPTER QUESTIONS

Discussion Questions

1. When is it beneficial to lower sales prices?

2. How can labor be viewed as both a fixed and a variable expense?

3. What are the advantages of using differential analysis?

4. What is marginal costing?

5. What is meant by *the full-cost trap*?

6. Define differential analysis.

7. Define fixed, variable, and semivariable costs.

Critical Thinking Questions

1. What is the potential problem with using full-cost accounting to determine when to open or close an operation?

2. Why is it valuable to differentiate fixed from variable expenses?

3. When might it be advantageous to keep an operation open when full-cost accounting analysis indicates it will not be profitable?

4. How do stepped costs affect break-even analysis?

5. If the fixed costs of an operation are $7,000, and the contribution margin is 35 percent, what is the level of sales required to break even?

6. If the check average could be increased to $15, how many covers will be required to break even?

7. Using MCB analysis, and assuming that a profit margin of 6 percent is desired to justify opening or reopening the facility, what is the dollar volume required?

8. If a fixed profit of at least $3,000 is required to justify opening the facility, what is the dollar volume required to meet this objective?

9. If fixed costs are $4,000, desired profit is $5,000, check average is $10, and the estimated number of covers is 1,500, what is the variable cost percentage that must be maintained to reach this objective?

Objective Questions

1. All cost categories may be properly designated as fixed or variable. True or False?

2. Fixed costs are fixed in direct proportion to sales. True or False?

3. It is desirable to use full-cost accounting in deciding when to reopen a restaurant in a hotel. True or False?

4. The results achieved through the least squares approach can be taken at face value. True or False?

5. True variable costs will retain the same cost percentage regardless of fluctuations in business. True or False?

Multiple Choice Questions

1. Which of the following accounting methods excludes costs and revenues that do not change within the relevant range of operating alternatives?

   A. Accrual accounting

   B. Full-cost accounting

C. Cash-flow accounting

D. Differential analysis

2. The amount of output, at any given volume, at which the aggregate costs are changed if the volume of output is increased or decreased by one unit is called

A. Marginal costs.

B. Regression analysis.

C. Variable costs.

D. Fixed costs.

3. Contribution margin percentage equals

A. Fixed costs / variable costs.

B. 1 – variable cost percentage.

C. Sales / expenses.

D. None of the above.

4. Determine the break-even point given the following information: Fixed costs: $400,000; variable cost percentage: 70

A. $1,000,000

B. $571,428.57

C. $680,000

D. $1,333,333.33

5. Determine the number of covers required to break even given the following information: Fixed costs: $300,000; CM percentage: 40; check average: $20

A. 37,500

B. 39,862

C. 75,000

D. 35,500

6. If the check average in Question 5 is raised to $25, how many covers are needed to break even?

A. 37,500

B. 39,862

C. 35,500

D. 30,000

7. Determine the break-even point given the following information: Fixed costs: $300,000; CM percentage: 40; desired profit margin: 6 percent

A. $882,353

B. $856,853

C. $652,174

D. $783,762

8. Given the following information, determine the break-even selling price: Fixed costs: $10,000; number of covers: 1,000; variable cost: $7 per cover

A. $20

B. $17

C. $15

D. $18

9. How much additional revenue must be generated to justify an advertisement costing $500, given a variable cost percentage of 55?

A. More than $2,000

B. More than $1,000

C. More than $1,111

D. More than $1,222

10. Break-even analysis does not factor in

A. Profit for the owner.

B. All labor costs.

C. Cash flows.

D. All of the above.

CASE STUDIES

Case Study 1:   Cost Classification

The following is a list of typical cost categories in the food-service industry:

Expenses
Cost of food sold
Cost of beverage sold
Salaries and wages
Employees benefits
Direct operating expenses
Music and entertainment
Marketing/advertising
Utility services—gas, others
Trash removal
Repairs and maintenance
Depreciation
China and glassware
General and administrative costs
Rent
Interest expenses

Your task:

Prepare an answer sheet as shown below. For each cost item, indicate whether that cost would be variable or fixed in behavior (that is, would it fluctuate substantially or not over a fairly wide range of volume of production?), and then whether it would be a selling cost or an administrative cost. If it is an administrative cost, indicate whether it would be direct or indirect with respect to units of product for pricing purposes. Two sample answers are provided for illustration.

Cost Item	Variable or Fixed	Selling Cost	Administrative Cost	Production Cost	
				Direct	Indirect
Cost of Food Sold	V	Yes	No	Yes	No
Depreciation	F	No	Yes	No	Yes

Case Study 2: Making the Business Decision (Breaking Even)

Tracy Chen began dabbling in pastry making several years ago as a hobby. Her pastry is quite creative, and it has been so popular with friends and others that she has decided to quit her job with a travel agency and prepare pastry full-time. She will be giving up her salary from the travel agency, a steady $2,000 per month.

Ms. Chen has found a small building near her former employer to rent for her pastry shop at $400 per month. She estimates that for all her specially selected pastries, the ingredient cost will be $0.50 per finished piece. She plans to hire workers to produce the pastries at a labor rate of $7.50 per hour, and it will take 8 hours to produce 12 dozen sets of ten assorted pastries. The retail selling price for each pastry is $2.50. To sell her pastries, Ms. Chen is of the opinion that she must advertise heavily in the local area. An advertising agency states that it will handle advertising for a fee of $200 per month. Her brother will sell the pastries at the counter and to local businesses for a commission of $5 per dozen pastries.

Ms. Chen already owns the production equipment, which she purchased several years ago. This equipment will depreciate at a rate of $50 per month. A phone installed in the shop for taking orders will cost $20 per month. In addition, a recording device will be attached to the phone for taking after-hours messages. The phone company will charge Ms. Chen $0.40 for each message recorded.

Ms. Chen has some money in savings that is earning interest of $5,000 per year. These savings will be withdrawn and used to get the business going. For the time being, Ms. Chen does not intend to draw any salary for herself.

Your task:

1. Do you think that Ms. Chen should open the pastry shop, and what advice would you give her?

2. What is her break-even point?

Case Study 3: The Decision to Shut Down or Continue to Operate

The Seafood Restaurant is a popular restaurant in the Monterey area, with an average of 1,000 covers daily and an average food check of $20 per cover. During the winter months from December until March, the restaurant can hardly pay its bills because tourism is very low. This downturn affects the whole Monterey area. Mr. Jacob, the owner, has tried to attract the local community to eat at the restaurant during the winter months by writing a new menu, offering discounts, and increasing advertisement. Unfortunately, his efforts have not worked.

Mr. Jacob's variable expenses are $8 per menu item; fixed overhead costs total $5,000 per month. Due to the current low level of sales, Mr. Jacob is thinking about closing down the restaurant during the four months that he is losing money. If Mr. Jacob does close down the restaurant, it is estimated that fixed overhead costs can be reduced to $1,000 per month. Start-up costs at the end of the shutdown period would total $2,000. Since the Seafood Restaurant uses just-in-time purchasing, product waste or spoilage would only be $1,000, and no inventories on hand are expected.

Your task:

1. Calculate the break-even point.

2. Would you advise Mr. Jacob to close the restaurant or continue to operate?

Case Study 4:   Cost and Pricing Decisions

Mary and Elizabeth own a catering business called M and E Catering Services. Their core business is catering parties. The catering business is very seasonal, with a heavy schedule during the summer months and holidays and a lighter schedule at other times. One of the major events M and E's customers request is a cocktail party. The standard cocktail party lasts three hours, and M and E hires one worker for every six guests, which works out to one-half hour of labor per guest. These workers are hired only as needed and are paid only for the hours they actually work. Mary and Elizabeth offer a standard cocktail party with an estimated cost per guest as follows:

Food and beverage   = $20
Labor at $12 per hour for 0.5 hours   = $6
Overhead at $14 per hour for 0.5 hours   = $7
Total cost   = $33

When bidding on cocktail parties, M and E adds a 15 percent markup to yield a price of $37.95 per guest. They are confident about their estimates of the costs of food, beverages, and labor but not as comfortable with their estimate of overhead cost. The $14 overhead cost per labor hour was determined by dividing total overhead expenses for the last 12 months by total labor hours for the same period. Monthly data concerning overhead costs and labor hours follow:

MONTH	LABOR HOURS	OVERHEAD EXPENSES
January	2,500	$55,000
February	2,800	59,000
March	3,000	60,000
April	4,200	64,000
May	4,500	67,000
June	5,500	71,000
July	6,500	74,000
August	7,500	77,000
September	7,000	75,000
October	4,500	68,000
November	3,100	62,000
December	6,500	74,400
Total	**57,600**	**806,400**

M and E has received a request to bid on a 180-guest fundraising cocktail party to be given next month by an important local charity. The party would last the usual three hours. They would like to win this contract because the guest list for this charity event includes many prominent individuals whom they would like to land as future clients. M and E is confident that these potential customers would be favorably impressed by their company service standard at the event.

Your task:

1. Estimate the contribution to profit of a standard 180-guest cocktail party if M and E charges the usual price of $37.95 per guest. In other words, by how much would their overall profit increase?

2. How low could M and E bid for the charity event in terms of a price per guest and still not lose money on the event itself?

3. The individual who is organizing the event has indicated that he has already received a bid of under $30 per guest from another catering company. Do you think M and E should bid below its normal $37.95 per guest for the event? Why or why not?

Learning Objectives

After reading this chapter, you should be able to:

- understand both forecasting and budgeting in depth and utilize their techniques;

- apply the techniques used for budgeting operational expenses and capital expenditures;

- explain and utilize the terms *assets* and *liabilities*;

- apply current ratio and working capital tests to financial results;

- know how to measure how well the company is doing financially through return on investment (ROI).

In Practice

Myla Thomas received a note from the owner, Eric Breeze. Part of the note read, "I like what you and your team have accomplished so far. I would like to meet with you to discuss incentive packages and the challenges for next year's budget." Myla took this as an endorsement of what she was doing—and rightly so.

When they met later, Eric extended his hand for a handshake with Myla and said, "Please, have a seat. I will not take too much of your time."

"Thank you for the note," Myla remarked.

"That's quite all right. You've made some positive changes to this place, and it shows in the employees, the customers, and the bottom line. Now, do you have any thoughts on the incentive package I sent to you last month?" Eric asked.

"Well, to begin with, it's quite reasonable given the circumstances surrounding the business climate. I do have one exception to note: I don't believe Scott Vincent deserves an incentive at this time," Myla answered.

"Why?" asked Eric unemotionally.

"To put it simply, Scott failed on every benchmark we set for him to achieve the budgeted guidelines—both in purchasing and in labor cost control," replied Myla.

"Very well then," Eric replied, pensively. "There have to be consequences for not achieving departmental goals. Please work out budget numbers for next year that include sales and marketing, as well as your capital plan, for my review."

INTRODUCTION

Without a reasonably accurate sales forecast, which we covered in Chapter 1, planning and budgeting are questionable at best and harmful at worst. In the role of manager, you will use past performance data to lay groundwork for a forecast. A business's past performance is guided by two sets of effects on your operations: those due to external business conditions—such as levels of tourism, natural disasters, terrorism, and local events—and those caused by internal management policies and procedures, such as system and product changes. Compiling this information will reveal trends. In the case of uncontrollable events like natural disasters or economic downturns, you can only collect data to analyze how these events affected your business. But in the case of internal management policies and procedures, your data will tell you which of your own company policies are most helpful and harmful. All of this data is what you will be analyzing in order to create a forecast.

The analysis requires general data on economic conditions, along with detailed information about past menus, customers, employees, and salespeople. By analyzing past performance, the controller can identify weak areas. Analyses of purchasing, storage and movement of inventory, hiring and use of labor, and the purchase and use of facilities will help pinpoint the factors that can be improved in the next budget year. Outside consultants can also contribute somewhat less subjective perspectives to this analytical process.

THE FRAMEWORK FOR FORECASTING AND BUDGET PREPARATION

Detailing what the sales department does in forecasting is beyond the scope of this book; however, the order in which elements are brought together to produce the forecast is important. First, management must establish the basic assumptions to be used in developing the forecast. These include assumptions about overall economic trends, product and service changes, and contemplated marketing actions such as sales initiatives and promotional campaigns. For these changes, you can assist in your role as controller by providing market research studies. Individual guest and group needs must be surveyed, and the data must be collected and analyzed. The basic assumptions may then be refined, and statistical projections can be made. These steps must precede creating the budget, since the sales forecast and sales plan usually serve as the basis for other budget computations. This illustrates how forecasting differs from budgeting: The forecasting process includes studies to determine which budgeting course of action will ultimately be taken.

The sales plan should then be compared to prior years' figures. Remember to consider the costs that are necessary to carry out this plan, including the costs of marketing, depreciation from capital improvements, and training. Other sales-related costs must be estimated. These are the costs of finding and bringing in both old and new business to the company. These costs should be factored into the budget. Each company will have different methods and costs, but the budget needs to include funds for your marketing, whatever form it takes. Some food-service operations use a factored sales value plan to control sales-force costs. This plan recognizes that different factors affect field sales performance—for example, customer density and quantity, product popularity and profitability, and economic conditions. Once the sales numbers are finalized into a budget and approved, management can evaluate sales costs and predict their usefulness for the future.

The Difference Between Forecasts and Budgets

The meanings of the terms *forecast* and *budget* should not be confused. They differ both in content and in intent. A food and beverage forecast is a quantitative report that attempts to predict the outcome of a series of events, with little or no effort made to control the results of those events. Forecasts are often produced on a "what-if" basis in order to determine what would happen to guest count, income, and/or expenses if various conditions occur. A food and beverage budget, on the other hand, is a strategic plan that calls for a series of actions to produce certain outcomes, with effective controls incorporated into these actions. For example, management may include budget funds to invest in a POS system to increase employee productivity and facilitate guest service. These controls maximize the chances of achieving the desired income and expenses and ultimately return on investment—what is known in the business as ROI.

Nearly everyone budgets to some extent, even though many of the people who use budgets do not recognize what they are doing as budgeting. People spend and save according to what their income levels dictates; that in itself is budgeting. For example, most people make estimates of their income and plan expenditures for food and other necessities accordingly. As a result of this planning, people restrict their spending to some predetermined, allowable amount. These budgets may exist only in the mind of the individual, but they are budgets nevertheless.

The budgets of a restaurant serve much the same functions as the budget prepared informally by an individual, but they are more detailed and involve more work to prepare. Like a personal budget, they assist in planning and controlling expenditures; they also assist in predicting operating results and financial conditions in the future period. By definition, budgets are quantitative expressions of management's short- and long-range strategic goals. They help management establish its most profitable course of action. In this way, budgets help to connect distinct departments into one entity, at least financially. For example, the maintenance department budgets expenditures for repairing items in the food and beverage department.

The controller and management must choose the budgetary policies to follow and the standards to use. They must ask the following questions:

- Which products and services should be offered?

- How shall marketing and sales be conducted?

- What price levels should be set?

- What distribution methods should be used?

- At what payroll levels should employees be?

- How should reporting be managed from each department?

If this planning process is conceived intelligently and administered effectively, the budget will likely be a creative and indispensable tool for accomplishing management goals.

The controller is responsible for establishing control mechanisms used by management to safeguard its resources and investments. Therefore, in that role you will also take the lead in developing the annual budget. The budget should include measuring and reporting techniques that act as an early warning system. This system alerts the people directly responsible for taking corrective action. You should also be alerted, because you must ultimately keep the entire department on the charted budgetary course.

A budget must deal with the following basic functions: planning, execution, and control. Successful budgeting benefits the company by doing the following:

- Forcing the formulation of goals, strategies, and tactics

- Encouraging management's participation and strengthening its commitment to proper implementation

- Developing coordination and cooperation between and among departments and programs

- Encouraging more effective and efficient use of material, labor, facilities, and capital

- Encouraging the development of a sound organizational structure with clear lines of authority and descriptions of positions

- Demanding the development of a valid accounting system that generates current, accurate data

- Forcing management to determine its capital requirements and to consider optimum means for obtaining the capital

---

Using Budgeting to Head Off a Potential Crisis

A government facility managed by a concessionaire in Ohio faced a potential financial crisis. The concessionaire paid the government a certain percentage of fees based on the gross income generated from the operation (food and beverage sales, hotel guest rooms, and other services). Financially, the resort appeared to be doing well. However, a five-year budget revealed that within a few years, expenses would exceed revenues and the resort would be facing a financial crisis. Realistically, cutting costs would not work because of the resort's already lean operations; cutting costs even more would jeopardize the quality of the resort's operations. Raising prices was ruled out due to competitive pressures and the belief that this would be unpopular with many guests. The government would not reduce its fees as stipulated in the contract for fear of a lawsuit charging preferential treatment in the prior year's bidding process.

Several solutions were considered, and forecasts were made based on the costs of the different options. The solution was to build more guest rooms and expand the existing restaurant space to capture the overflow during the busy summer season. By developing a long-range budget, the management of the resort was able to identify in advance a looming financial crisis and to develop a solution that would avert the crisis in time.

APPROACHES TO BUDGETING

There are several approaches to budgeting. At times, corporate headquarters may set all budgeting guidelines that the subsidiaries will follow. This is done in order to maintain consistency in projected revenue and profit expectations. In other cases, individual restaurants or branches can present their own plans. This approach tends to work well with branch managers; however, in practice, if the corporate office oversees expenditures in marketing, payroll, and advertising dollars, then corporate control is both more warranted and more likely. The drawback is that corporate managers often do not recognize the importance of the human aspect in budgeting. It is easy to become preoccupied with the technical aspects of the budget, excluding consideration of the various human aspects—managers must be included in the budgeting process.

Indeed, the use of budget data in a rigid and inflexible manner is often the greatest single complaint of people whose performance is judged based on how well they meet their budgets.

Management should remember that the purposes of the budget include motivating employees and coordinating their efforts. Preoccupation with the dollars and cents in the budget, or being rigid and inflexible, is usually counterproductive.

Corporate Management Defense?

Towers Perrin, a consulting firm, reports that the bonuses of more than two out of three managers are based on meeting targets set in annual budgets. "Under this arrangement, managers at the beginning of a year all too often argue that their targets should be lowered because of the tough business conditions, when in fact conditions are better than projected. If their arguments are successful, they can easily surpass the targets."

Source: Ronald Fink and Towers Perrin, "Riding the Bull: The 2000 Compensation Survey," *CFO,* June 2000.

In the case of independent operations, managers and controllers must devise their own strategies and budgets, and they will certainly find the methods used here instructive. You might even find it worthwhile to combine the corporate and local approaches to make the budget work best for you.

Capital Budget

capital budget A budget of capital expenditures, such as equipment, building and other fixed assets.

The next step is to review which capital expenditures you will undertake, such as the purchase of equipment, construction, and leasehold improvements. This is sometimes referred to as a **capital budget**. The economic approach to such an investment decision rests on a comparison of the marginal cost of an item and the possible rate of return from that investment. Marginal costing is defined as the amount of output, at any given volume, by which aggregate costs are changed if the volume of output is increased or decreased by one unit. This is, however, subject to the condition that fixed cost does not change with the increase in volume. Chapter 14 details marginal costing procedures, and you can use them in analyzing a variety of purchasing decisions.

When the rate of return exceeds the marginal cost, then it is in the restaurant's financial interest to invest the additional capital. A capital expenditure proposal should be classified by the type of project—whether it is an actual capital expenditure or an operational expense that could be charged to the budgets of one or more departments. Proposals should be recorded in the general ledger under these classifications. Whether or not management approves these requests will depend on their cost effectiveness, growth options, and affect on operations. You will learn how to assess these criteria in the section on return on investment, or ROI.

The Budget Period

fiscal year Any continuous 12-month period used by a company as its accounting period.

Budgets generally cover a one-year period corresponding to the restaurant's **fiscal year**. The planning phase includes preparatory work to provide the framework of the budget. The actual preparation of the budget typically starts four months before the next budgeted fiscal year. However, some food-service operations use a continuous or perpetual budget cycle. A continuous or perpetual budget is a twelve-month budget that rolls forward one month (or quarter) as the current month (or quarter) is completed. In other words, one month (or quarter) is added to the end of the budget as each month (or quarter) comes to a close. This approach keeps managers focused on the future at least one year ahead. Advocates of continuous budgets argue that with this approach there is less danger that managers will become too narrowly focused on the short-term results.

It is important to note that hotels use this method for forecasting but not for budgeting. In this chapter, we will look at a one-year operating budget. However, using the same techniques, operating budgets can be prepared for periods that extend over many years. Even though it may be difficult to forecast sales and required data accurately, rough estimates can be very valuable in uncovering potential problems and opportunities that would be overlooked otherwise. Whatever method your company adopts, you should be accumulating pertinent data about the current economy and predictions made about its direction in the following year. These predictions provide a basis for considering the company's objectives and its strategies for achieving them. You will want to undertake a reasoned critique of the current year's budgeting experience as well, to provide additional information for revising or reformulating budget process procedures.

Whatever budget you adopt should reflect the following planned positions:

Internal factors

- A particular budget method (zero-based, simple markup, or percentage)

- Anticipated growth of payroll percentages and fixed cost

- Staff training costs to be incurred

- Capital improvements

- Market conditions

External factors

- Anticipated percentage of inflation

- Old and new competition

After determining this outline, the plan must be translated into responsibility reports from each department. To do so, the food and beverage controller creates budget forms, which list expense categories such as labor, supplies, food cost, uniforms, and others. These categories will correspond to those of the *chart of accounts*, to which the department manager charges expenses for accounting purposes. Budget forms like the one in Figure 16-1 can help you determine the effect of each outlet's departmental budget.

Figure 16-1 Examples of Assets, Liabilities, and Owner's Equity

Assets	Liabilities	Owners equity
Investments	Current liabilities (account payable, accrued liabilities, salary and wages payable	Retained earnings
Property, plants, and equipment	Long term liabilities	Capital stock
Current assets (cash, account receivable, inventory, prepaid expenses		Paid in capital in excess of current or par value
Intangible assets such as patents and goodwill		

Next, the controller incorporates revenue and cost projections into the budgeted figures. The individual department budgets are then consolidated into a company-wide budget operating statement or income statement, a position statement or balance sheet, and a cash flow projection. These reports are similar, except that the content and company reporting requirements may differ. They are usually presented in comparative form, including the current year's budget statement and statements of one or more preceding accounting years. Comparative statements are useful in evaluating and analyzing trends. They show the financial position of the company at a particular moment in time, including the company's economic resources (assets), economic obligations (liabilities), and the residual claims of owners (owner's equity). Assets are usually shown in the order of their liquidity (nearness to cash), and liabilities are usually in the order of their maturity date (payment date).

The budgeted balance sheet is usually presented in one of the following formats:

- Account format: assets = liabilities plus owner's equity

- Report format: assets less liability = owner's equity

current ratio The relationship between current assets and liabilities; measures the liquidity of a company.

The relationship between current assets and current liabilities is referred to as the **current ratio** and is a measure of the liquidity of the company. It is derived as follows:

current ratio = current assets / current liabilities

This ratio is used to determine the ability of the company to finance or pay for current operations and to meet obligations as they mature. Most companies use a ratio of 2:1 as a benchmark. This means the company should have $2 of current assets or cash for every $1 of current liabilities or short-term debt. Another indicator is the excess of current assets over current liabilities (current assets minus current liabilities). This is called **working capital**. A high balance of current assets over current liabilities may indicate that you are not investing your excess cash wisely. On the other hand, a low balance may reveal a potential problem with debt services or cash flow constraints. You will need to generate your own report to judge where you stand.

working capital Current assets less current liabilities. This measure serves as an indication of the amount of readily available funds that can be used in operation of the business. Also called *net current assets*.

Too Much Cash?

Microsoft has accumulated an unprecedented hoard of cash and cash equivalents—over $49 billion at the end of fiscal year 2003—and this cash hoard is growing at the rate of about $1 billion per month. This cash hoard is large enough to give every household in the United States a check for $471. What does Microsoft need all this money for? Why doesn't it pay more dividends? Microsoft executives say the cash is needed for antitrust lawsuits. Critics of the company's power, including some of its competitors, claim that the cash gives the company a huge competitive advantage. Because of this huge reserve of cash, the company can afford to lose money by entering risky new markets like the Xbox game console.

Sources: Jay Greene, "Microsoft's $49 Billion Problem," *BusinessWeek,* August 11, 2003, p. 36, and the Microsoft Annual Report for the year 2003.

All of these statements are then compiled in the same format as the historical financial statements. In the absence of historical data, compile these forms in a logical fashion so that they can be accessed by anyone who reads them. You need details in order to be effective; the degree of detail presented in each of these forms should be sufficient for good accountancy. These budget summaries and projected financial statements are presented to top management, together with comments and recommendations from the controller. If the budget is unsatisfactory because desired goals or returns on investments are not met, or because planning assumptions have changed, revisions can be made. Either management or the outlet managers who submit the original budgets can make these revisions. After revisions, the department budgets are resubmitted to management. The compilation and review process is then repeated until, ultimately, a satisfactory operating budget is approved.

In the role of controller, you are responsible for the following:

- Compiling the research on which budgetary planning assumptions are made, and submitting this research to the outlet manager

- Determining and monitoring the forms' design and paperwork flow (Figure 16-2)

- Issuing instructions to the various department heads, such as what tax and inflation rates to consider when calculating the budget numbers, including pay rate (wage) increases

- Specifying the type of budget to adopt (zero-based, fixed, or variable; described below)

- Assisting managers in preparing initial operating plans and budgets, or, in some cases, actually preparing the budgets after discussions with the managers

- Consolidating the operating budgets of the various departments and compiling them into management summaries and financial statements

- Revising unsatisfactory budgets and discussing them with the responsible managers

- Distributing the approved budgets to the department managers

- Monitoring each department's actual performance compared with the budgets

- Preparing periodic reports on variances, which are submitted to management

---

Suspicious Budgeting

Restaurant management compensation is often tied to the budget. Typically, no bonus is paid unless a minimum performance hurdle, such as 90 percent of the budget target, is attained. Once that hurdle is passed, the manager's bonus increases until a cap is reached. The cap varies with different levels of managers, but it could be up to 110 percent of the budget target. This common method of tying a manager's compensation to the budget has some serious negative side effects. For example, a general manager of a chain restaurant intentionally grossly understated demand of the restaurant's main beef entrée, so that the budget target for revenues would be low and easy to beat. Unfortunately, the corporate supply management team based "meat hedging" on this biased forecast and missed an opportunity to maximize purchasing power that could have resulted in $150,000 savings for the corporation during the holidays when the price was high.

As another example, six months before the end of the fiscal calendar year, repair and maintenance's budgeted expenses were cut in half, and the preventive maintenance budget (that is, elevator and fire sprinkler systems) was frozen. The manager claimed that these expenses would be in next year's budget and that the current market conditions could not sustain these expenses. The manager was taking an unnecessary risk in this case. There are laws governing elevator inspections and permits. The manager might make such bad decisions simply in order to meet budget numbers and thus earn a bonus.

A resort in California suspended a marketing campaign three months before the end of the year so as to achieve current year budgeted goals. Sales in the following year dropped. This started a negative cycle: What trick might managers pull to meet their sales targets next year in the face of this decision to hold back on sales initiatives?

TWELVE MONTHS BUDGET FORM

	JAN	FEB	MAR	APRIL	MAY	JUNE	JULY	AUG	SEPT	OCT	NOV	DEC	Total
	Budget	Budget	Budget	Budget	Budget	Budget	Budget	Budget	Budget	Budget	Budget	Budget	Budget
FOOD SALES													
BEVERAGE SALES													
PUBLIC ROOM SALES													
COVER CHARGES													
GIFT SHOP													
OTHER													
TOTAL GROSS SALES													
COST OF FOOD SOLD													
COST OF BEVERAGE SOLD													
COST OF GIFT SHOP SALES													
OTHER DIRECT EXPENSE													
CHINA, GLASSWARE AND UTENSILS													
CLEANING AND CLEANING SUPPLIES													
DONATIONS													
FUEL AND ICE													
LAUNDRY AND DRY CLEANING													
LICENSES AND PERMITS													
LINENS													
MENUS AND BEVERAGE LISTS													
MUSIC AND ENTERTAINMENT													
PRINTING AND STATIONERY													
PROMOTION													
SILVERWARE AND HOLLOWARE													
SUPERVISION													
SUPPLLIES AND OTHER													
TELEPHONE, TELEGRAMS & POSTAGE													
TRAVEL AND RELATED													
UNIFORMS													
MISCELLANEOUS													
TOTAL LABOR COST (FROM BELOW)													
TOTAL EXPENSES													
GROSS PROFIT													
% OF PROFIT TO GROSS SALES													
% OF COST OF FOOD TO FOOD SALES													
% OF COST OF BEVERAGE TO BEV. SALES													
% OF COST OF GIFT SHOP SALES													
LABOR COST													
GENERAL													
MANAGERS													
PREPARATION													
'MAINTENANCE & CLEANING													
SERVICE													
STEWARDS													
MISCELLANEOUS													
SUB-TOTAL													
VACATIONS													
RECOVERED SALARIES													
TOTAL SALARIES AND WAGES													
PAYROLL TAXES AND EMPLOYEE RELATION													
EMPLOYEE MEALS													
CONTRACT LABOR SERVICES													
TOTAL LABOR COST													
% OF SALARIES AND WAGES TO GR. SALES													
% OF LABOR COST TO GROSS SALES													
TOTAL FOOD COVERS													
AVERAGE FOOD CHECK													
COMB. FOOD AND BEV. CHECK													

Figure 16-2 12-Month Budget

Note that the food and beverage controller does not have direct decision-making responsibilities in the budgeting process. The controller's position here is one of liaison and clarifier of issues such as inflation rate and cost of contract—not one of dictating revenue or expenditure amounts. The department heads are responsible for coming up with a budget. The idea underlying the notion of a department head is that this person is responsible for the items that that he or she can actually control. Each line item—revenue or cost in the budget—is made the responsibility of a manager, and that manager is held responsible for subsequent deviations between the budget and the actual results. Bonuses based on meeting and exceeding budgets are often a key element of compensation for the department head. Typically, no bonus is paid unless the budgeted goals are met.

Post-Completion Procedures

Periodic reports comparing actual performance with budgeted performance are essential for effective management control. The controller is responsible for designing these **variance reports** in order to provide timely danger signals. Analyses of variances should be more than just recitations of the quantities of dollar differences. The controller should talk to the outlet managers to determine the causes of any variances, and such causes should be verified with the company records and documented in the variance report for management's review. When variances occur, operating decisions must be made. A newly hired outlet manager may decide to change the operating plan to achieve the results anticipated in the budget, for example, or the budget may be modified to reflect changed conditions and more realistic objectives. In the latter case, operating deviations may be approved, and the resulting variance deemed acceptable if it falls within company standards.

variance report A report comparing actual performance with budgeted performance.

Some operations and expenditures, such as dining room expansion, sales promotion, or benefit plans, are subject to precise control. On the other hand, some operations or expenditures may be affected by external factors, such as market conditions, guest demand, natural disasters, terrorism, or the level of economic activity affecting the restaurant's results. If changes occur in external conditions beyond management's control, the budget program must be revised promptly, or other corrective measures taken, before the impact is felt. This gives outlet managers the chance to change their predictions. The idea is to make the most of positive changes and to minimize the effect of negative changes.

CHOOSING A BUDGET TYPE

Just as management determines the timing of its budget periods, it must also consider whether to prepare a fixed (static), variable, flexible, or zero-based budget.

Fixed-Cost Budgets

Fixed costs, by definition, do not vary proportionally with volume, but rarely are they completely fixed in a real sense. They might fluctuate for other reasons.

Food-service operations often start with a fixed-cost budget. It is the simplest to construct because it counts on one level of business activity. The company assumes a certain level of operations, measured as a certain level of cover units, sales, services, or other relevant volume measures. The percentage of revenues and costs that are expected at that volume then constitute the budget. A fixed-cost budget is an adequate tool if the food-service establishment can reasonably predict sales volume, if the actual sales approximate the budgeted level, and if the comparisons are meaningful. With fixed-cost budgets, variances are easily calculated and explained.

On the other hand, a fixed-cost budget is an ineffective planning and control tool if actual volume differs substantially from budgeted volume. The larger the variance, the less meaningful the budget is, and the budget becomes merely a benchmark for determining a difference.

How to Treat Labor in Fixed Budgets

Fixed or static labor budgeting means that you establish both a given level of operations and a corresponding amount of required labor. The number of covers required to reach the targeted sales can be multiplied by the labor cost per cover to find the expected labor rate. Then, as the year progresses, actual labor costs are compared to this expected labor cost. A simple example serves to demonstrate the process of analyzing variances:

estimated labor rate   = $4.25 per hour
estimated labor usage = 1.5 hours per cover

Therefore, to produce 5,000 covers, the manager should plan for 7,500 labor hours with a total labor cost of $31,875. Now, assume these are the actual labor costs from a restaurant:

covers served   = 5000
labor hours used = 7600
total labor cost   = $33,000

Dividing the total labor cost by the number of hours, the rate implied in this data is $4.34 per hour. An excess of actual cost over budget could be caused either by a wage rate that is higher than your estimate, or by using more hours of labor than you estimated. The amount attributed to each can be determined by computing the following variances:

(actual rate − estimated rate) × actual hours = variance
    $4.34 per hour − $4.25 × 7,600 hours = $684

labor efficiency = (actual hours − estimated hours) × standard rate = variance
    7,600 hours − 7,500 hours = 100 hours × $4.25 per hour = $425

With these calculations in hand, management can understand how the variance happened and work to avoid repeating mistakes, perhaps with extra coaching or training for staff members. Furthermore, a variance can be analyzed to determine whether it resulted from inefficiencies, an unusual occurrence, or inadequate estimates. In some instances, actual labor costs may be lower than the established standards. In this case, it is vital that management know if the service levels were adequate. The labor standards should be reviewed and, when appropriate, changed to reflect actual efficiency.

On the other hand, a variance may not require a change to your standards, but it definitely bears noting. The actual hours worked may, in fact, correctly reflect the most efficient possible labor under the given circumstances. Say, for example, that the mix of menu items ordered one night includes all of the most complicated meals to prepare. This certainly explains some variance. Or perhaps your restaurant caters to tourists who generally relax over their meals for a long while, but in a week filled with conventioneers on tight schedules, you serve more covers in less time. That, too, would explain a variance. Whatever your unique circumstances, you will often see variances that are justifiable and explainable.

Variable Budgets

Variable budgets are also called flexible budgets as it relates to direct cost. Both methods treat indirect expenses differently. These are plans that are made to change with the actual level of business activity. They are based on the premise that a budget can be derived from whatever volume level is attained. In order to derive a budget based on volume level, you must first separate costs into fixed and variable categories. Figure 16-3 provides examples of fixed, variable, and semivariable costs.

Each variable cost can then be related to revenues as a percentage. This is a simple mathematical process: Divide the cost amount by the total revenue amount. Suppose we want to know the percentage of a $327,000 labor cost in an operation with $771,000 in gross sales. Dividing the former by the latter, we get 42.4 percent. This can be done for each cost category as well

Figure 16-3 Different Costs

Fixed Cost	Variable Cost	Semi or Mixed Cost
Definition: These costs do nor vary with changes in the level of output or sales, over a relevant range of production or sales.	**Definition:** These are cost associated with the variable factors of production. They fluctuate in direct proportion to the fluctuation of the volume of production or sales.	**Definition:** These are costs that fluctuate with production or sales, but not in direct proportion. They contain elements of fixed and variable costs.
Example: rent	**Example:** direct hourly labor and food and beverage cost	**Example:** costs of supervision.

as for total costs. Fixed costs should not change with volume levels, so they are added in separately to determine total costs. A budget formula for a typical restaurant might be as follows:

$$\text{total costs} = (\text{variable cost percentage} \times \text{revenue level}) + \text{fixed costs}$$

Assume that the information in Figure 16-4 represents the Sea Breeze Hotel Restaurant with Myla Thomas as the controller. Applying the above equation, the budget total equals ($10.56 × anticipated guest covers) + $8,750. If the anticipated guest cover volume is 9,000 for January and 10,000 for February, then using the formula above we find the following:

January: ($10.56 × 9000) + $8,750 = $103,790
February: (10.56 × 10,000) + $8,750 = $114,350

The formula is valid as long as actual production volume is within the normal or relevant range. However, in some cases production levels outside this range may require different fixed costs, and variable costs will assume different levels as well.

The fixed and variable budgets costs are not merely cost forecasts. They reflect management's expected standards—that is, goals to be achieved. As the controller of Sea Breeze Hotel, Myla Thomas will measure actual results against these standards, and she will account for significant variances. She must then inform management why the company's expectations were not achieved.

Figure 16-4 Fixed and Variable Costs

Fixed and variable costs			
Fixed Costs Per Month		**Variable Cost Per Cover** Assume Average Food Check = $15 and Beverage Average Check = $5	
	Cost		**Cost**
Licenses and Beverage Permit	$500.00	Food Cost per cover	$4.50
Management Salary	$5,000.00	Beverage Cost per cover	$1.10
Music And Entertainment$	1,750.00	Employees Wages per hour	$4.50
Depreciation - Equipment	$500.00	Laundry And Dry Cleaning per 10 lb. Load	$0.40
Property Tax	$500.00	Utilities such as water and electricity	$0.01
Education And Training	$500.00	Other Supplies	$0.05
Total fixed cost	$8,750.00	Total variable cost	$10.56

The information in Figure 16-5 is an example of a comparative 12-month food and beverage budget statement form that Myla will use to review actual performance against budgeted numbers. This form is just an extension of Figure 16-4. It enables the managers and Myla to identify, correct, and reevaluate problem areas.

TWELVE MONTHS BUDGET STATEMENT

	JAN	JAN	JAN	FEB	FEB	FEB	MAR	MAR	MAR	APR	APR	APR	MAY	MAY	MAY	JUN	JUN	JUN	JUL	JUL	JUL	AUG	AUG	AUG	SEP	SEP	SEP	OCT	OCT	OCT	NOV	NOV	NOV	DEC	DEC	DEC	Total	Total	Total
		Current	Last year		Current	Last year		Current	Last year		Current	Last year		Current	Last year		Current	Last year		Current	Last year		Current	Last year		Current	Last year		Current	Last year		Current	Last year		Current	Last year		Current	Last year
	Actaul	Budget	Actaul	Actaul	Budget	Actaul	Actaul	Budget	Actaul	Actaul	Budget	Actaul	Actaul	Budget	Actaul	Actaul	Budget	Actaul	Actaul	Budget	Actaul	Actaul	Budget	Actaul	Actaul	Budget	Actaul	Actaul	Budget	Actaul	Actaul	Budget	Actaul	Actaul	Budget	Actaul	Actaul	Budget	Actaul
FOOD SALES																																							
BEVERAGE SALES																																							
PUBLIC ROOM SALES																																							
COVER CHARGES																																							
GIFT SHOP																																							
OTHER																																							
TOTAL GROSS SALES																																							
COST OF FOOD SOLD																																							
COST OF BEVERAGE SOLD																																							
COST OF GIFT SHOP SALES																																							
OTHER DIRECT EXPENSE																																							
CHINA, GLASSWARE AND UTENSILS																																							
CLEANING AND CLEANING SUPPLIES																																							
DONATIONS																																							
FUEL AND ICE																																							
LAUNDRY AND DRY CLEANING																																							
LICENSES AND PERMITS																																							
LINENS																																							
MENUS AND BEVERAGE LISTS																																							
MUSIC AND ENTERTAINMENT																																							
PRINTING AND STATIONERY																																							
PROMOTION																																							
SILVERWARE AND HOLLOWARE																																							
SUPERVISION																																							
SUPPLIES AND OTHER																																							
TELEPHONE, TELEGRAMS & POSTAGE																																							
TRAVEL AND RELATED																																							
UNIFORMS																																							
MISCELLANEOUS																																							
TOTAL LABOR COST (FROM BELOW)																																							
TOTAL EXPENSES																																							
GROSS PROFIT																																							
% OF PROFIT TO GROSS SALES																																							
% OF COST OF FOOD TO FOOD SALES																																							
% OF COST OF BEVERAGE TO BEV. SAI																																							
% OF COST OF GIFT SHOP SALES																																							
LABOR COST																																							
GENERAL																																							
MANAGERS																																							
PREPARATION																																							
'MAINTENANCE & CLEANING																																							
SERVICE																																							
STEWARDS																																							
MISCELLANEOUS																																							
SUB-TOTAL																																							
VACATIONS																																							
RECOVERED SALARIES																																							
TOTAL SALARIES AND WAGES																																							
PAYROLL TAXES AND EMPLOYEE RELA																																							
EMPLOYEE MEALS																																							
CONTRACT LABOR SERVICES																																							
TOTAL LABOR COST																																							
% OF SALARIES AND WAGES TO GR. SA																																							
% OF LABOR COST TO GROSS SALES																																							
TOTAL FOOD COVERS																																							
AVERAGE FOOD CHECK																																							
COMB. FOOD AND BEV. CHECK																																							

Figure 16-5 12-Month Budget Sheet

How to Treat Labor in Variable Budgets

Variable budgeting relates actual costs to expense budgets at a given activity level. Such a relative system works well for labor that is directly involved in production, such as in the kitchen, but does not work as well for labor employed in support activities. For instance, how can expenditures for the kitchen cleaning crew be controlled? It is unlikely that usage and costs of these services will vary in direct proportion to output.

A simple solution is to set a target level of output and determine the amount of indirect labor, like that of the kitchen cleaning crew, that will be needed to produce that output. After the budget period has ended, you can compare actual expenditures to budgeted expenditures. This technique is the same as for fixed budgeting, but in this case, you use it only for the indirect labor. But suppose that the target output is not reached, or is exceeded. Can we compare expenditures that should have been made at one level of output with those that actually were made at a different level of output? Imagine the situation in Figure 16–6.

Figure 16-6 Return on Investment to cover

	Actual	Budgeted	Variance
Covers Produced	5500	6000	500
Indirect Labor Costs	$1250	$1300	$50
Percentage of Cost / Covers	22.7%	21.7%	

Take a look at the first two lines. Even though production goals were not met, there appears to be a favorable variance for indirect labor, without computing the percentage difference. But when you calculate the percentages in the third line, you can see that indirect labor makes up a larger percentage of cost; less indirect labor should have been necessary to produce that smaller number of covers. You need a method to determine how much less labor should be necessary in order to evaluate the efficiency of indirect labor personnel.

Flexible Budgeting

Flexible budgeting provides a solution to the problems found in both fixed and variable budgets. With flexible budgeting, a formula is developed for the target amount of indirect labor that should be used for a given range of outputs. For instance, the target may be $1 of indirect labor for each 1.5 hours of direct labor.

An obvious problem with flexible budgeting is that indirect labor costs, such as cleaning, may not vary directly with activity measures. Frequently in the food-service industry direct labor hours can double without a commensurate increase in indirect labor costs. As a result, to make flexible budgeting work precisely, you will develop a variance factor that expresses the response of semivariable costs, such as indirect labor, to changes in activity.

This technique requires that a budget be prepared for a target level of output and indirect costs be budgeted for that level. Then, for each different indirect expense, measure and record how closely the expense fluctuates compared to the direct labor costs. If the expense varies with the direct labor costs, you can plot that variance factor. This factor sets the variance at a percentage that you can apply to that cost any time. If sales and direct labor change, use the variance factor to determine how much additional money you will have to spend on that indirect labor expense. Here is an example to show how the process works:

1. Determine the indirect labor cost at the target volume. (For this example, we're assuming that these costs are $1,000 for a direct labor expenditure of $5,000.)

2. For the variance at another business level, determine how much the direct labor activity differs from the targeted level. (Now assume that an additional $2,000 of direct labor will be necessary.)

3. Identify the variance as a function of change in indirect labor cost for every $1 change in direct labor costs. That is, if you historically must spend $40 more in indirect cost to accommodate $100 more in direct labor, the variance factor per direct labor dollar is $0.40. The $0.40 was derived by dividing indirect labor cost ($40) by direct labor cost ($100).

4. Compute the budgeted amount of indirect labor using this formula:

$$\frac{\text{targeted indirect labor}}{\text{targeted direct labor}} \times (\text{actual sales} - \text{targeted sales}) \times \text{variance factor}$$

or, in our example, $\dfrac{1000}{5000} \times 2000 \times \$0.40 = \$160$

$160 is the additional amount of indirect labor cost that should be budgeted as a result of the increased direct labor cost. The indirect labor budget should be $1,160 when the direct labor budget is $7,000.

Zero-Based Budgeting

zero-based budgeting A budget which starts at zero in preparation and in which the writer must justify every expense line.

Another approach to budgeting is **zero-based budgeting**. Zero-based budgeting is a very different approach from other methods, and starts with determining which functions are necessary to achieve your goals. The controller and manager divide expenses based on their functions, similar to an organizational chart that divides hierarchy based on job descriptions. Then they examine the goals of each function to determine what specific programs are necessary to accomplish them. The programs are further subdivided into specific activities; the costs for these are justified by matching their identified benefits with the costs necessary to achieve them.

In preparing a budget for the coming year using standard budget approaches (fixed, variable, or flexible), the current year's budget is taken as the starting point. Management determines a percentage increase or decrease from the current year's sales and expenses to be used in preparing next year's budget. In the case of zero-based budgeting, the process comes from the idea of "building up from zero" the benefits and expenses associated with each proposed program in the budget. The manager's decision to fund each activity is based on how it is expected to contribute to achieving the outlet's goals. Each item in the budget is not based on the current year's revenue or expenses, but must be justified for the coming year; thus, the department head starts each year from zero. Once an item is in the budget, the controller does not question its presence and magnitude; only variances from the budgeted numbers are questioned.

The final step in the zero-based budget process is allocating available resources to each activity based on that activity's contribution to revenue. For operations that must work with a budget mandated by headquarters, zero-based budgeting will be appealing as a tool for effective and efficient trade-offs with corporate management. Zero-based budgeting allows and even requires that the manager preplan revised budgeted numbers. As a matter of company policy, the food and beverage controller should encourage the use of zero-based budgeting while noting the benefits to both outlet managers and the operation. In other words, this type of budgeting must be sold to managers as both an operational concept and an effective tool for meeting their responsibilities.

The following are definitive strengths of zero-based budgeting that can help to encourage its use:

- Good planning and the establishment of goals are required to approve or deny costs or to pay for new or old items or programs.

- Management must systematically review and evaluate activities and rank them in order of importance.

- Follow-up evaluation of approved expenses or activities is heavily encouraged.

- The controller and management have more control over the operation because they must monitor more closely the ongoing expense activities and their results.

- There is improved communication among managers within the functions and throughout the organization's management levels.

One disadvantage of zero-based budgeting is that it requires a commitment of time to plan, coordinate, communicate, delegate, and execute the strategies that will make it successful. If this time is deemed cost-effective, zero-based budgeting can have extraordinary effects on budgetary goal setting and achievement.

When Improvement Is Not Better

A good friend of mine, Vieden Zahariev with Delaware North Companies, once said, "Whatever you manage, you measure." He advised managers to focus on the right metrics when measuring performance. He relates the following story: "A fast-food chain gave lip service to many objectives, but what senior managers watched most rigorously is how much chicken the chef had to throw away. What happened? As one restaurant operator explained, it was easy to hit your . . . targets: the chef would simply not cook any chicken until the customer ordered it. Customers might have to wait twenty minutes for their meal, and would probably never come back—but you'd sure make your numbers. The Moral is: a measurement may look good on paper, but you need to ask what behavior it will drive."

Source: "Using Measurement to Boost Your Unit's Performance," by John Case, *Harvard Management Update,* October 1998.

How to Treat Labor in Zero-Based Budgets

Zero-based budgeting techniques define expenses as discretionary or nondiscretionary. Such costs as direct labor are considered nondiscretionary because they are determined largely by the type of POS system, restaurant, and menu you have. Management cannot significantly alter the amount of labor required to produce a given amount of output without first making changes in the recipes, POS system, or service level required. The primary impact of zero-based budgeting, on the other hand, is on discretionary costs, such as wages for maintenance personnel and supervisory staff.

For indirect labor, management must first define alternative ways to perform the necessary functions, and then select the most cost-effective method. Next, the outlet manager defines various levels of business activity for performing the function and the cost of each successive level. These levels will include a minimal level of activity below which it is no longer wise to operate the restaurant, and any number of additional levels up to and exceeding the current level of activity and the forecast. This leveling technique resembles the approach used to develop the restaurant staffing guide, and it is called a **decision package**. A decision package is a document that describes the level of effort required to meet outlet objectives.

decision package A document that describes the level of effort required to meet objectives.

In preparing a decision package, rank the various activities by priority. Then define a cutoff point on this listing, and all activity packages deemed vital (above the cutoff) receive a budget allotment. You may see that you need an additional person to avoid poor service, or that your staff should be able to handle a higher sales volume. This technique allows the manager to evaluate discretionary costs, such as indirect labor, as packages of activities instead of as dollar value allotments.

MANAGEMENT PERFORMANCE REVIEW USING ROI

Thus far, this chapter has focused on how to prepare a company budget. This section presents methods for evaluating management performance on key decisions needed for arriving at budget goals and actual results in dollars and cents. We said at the beginning of the chapter that a food and beverage budget is a strategic plan that calls for a series of actions to produce certain outcomes, with effective controls incorporated into these actions. For example, management may budget funds to invest in a POS system to increase employee productivity and facilitate guest service. This is a decision that could maximize the chances of achieving the desired income and expenses and, ultimately, the operation's **return on investment (ROI)**.

ROI is defined as net operating income divided by average operating assets:

$$\text{ROI} = \text{net operating income} / \text{average operating assets}$$

The higher the return on investment of a restaurant, the greater the profit earned per dollar invested in the restaurant's operating assets (i.e., POS systems).

Net operating income is income before interest and taxes. It is sometimes referred to as *earnings before interest and taxes* (EBIT). Net operating income is used in the formula because the base (that is, the denominator) consists of operating assets. Thus, to be consistent, we use net operating income in the numerator.

return on investment (ROI) Net operating income divided by average operating assets. A measure of profitability of the business expressed in percentages.

> ## Quiz
> If you were measuring ROI on a new POS system, would the correct figure be the increase in net operating income divided by the cost of the POS system?

In the food-service industry, operating assets are assets you will use to run the day-to-day business of the restaurant (including cash, accounts receivable, physical plant and equipment, and inventory). Assets that would not be included in the average operating asset definition are buildings rented to someone else, investments in another company, and land held for future use. These are considered nonoperating assets because they are not held in order to operate the restaurant. The operating assets base used in the formula is typically computed as the average of the operating assets between the beginning and the end of the fiscal year.

Most restaurants use the net book value (the acquisition cost less accumulated depreciation) of depreciable assets to calculate average operating assets. This approach has drawbacks. An asset's net book value decreases over time as the accumulated depreciation increases. This decreases the denominator in the ROI calculation, thus increasing ROI. Consequently, ROI mechanically increases over time. Moreover, replacing old depreciated operating equipment with new equipment increases the book value of depreciable assets and decreases ROI. Hence it is argued that using net book value in the calculation of average operating assets results in a predictable pattern of increasing ROI over time as accumulated depreciation grows and discourages replacing old equipment with new, updated equipment. An alternative to the net book value is the gross cost of the asset, which ignores accumulated depreciation. Gross cost stays constant over time because depreciation is ignored; therefore, ROI does not grow automatically over time, and replacing a fully depreciated asset with a comparably-priced new asset will not adversely affect ROI. Others may argue that it does adversely affect ROI because of inflation, unless technology becomes cheaper, causing replacement to have the opposite effect. Nevertheless, in the restaurant industry, net book value is widely used to compute average operating assets because it is consistent with the format of financial reporting—recording the net book value of assets on the balance sheet and including depreciation as an operating expense on the profit and loss statement.

Application of ROI to Sea Breeze Hotel (SBH) Food and Beverage Operation

The equation for ROI—net operating income divided by average operating assets—does not provide much help to controller Myla Thomas at SBH, who is interested in taking actions to improve ROI. It only offers two options for improving performance: net operating income and average operating assets. Fortunately, ROI can also be expressed as follows:

ROI　　= margin x turnover
margin　= net operating income / sales
turnover = sales / average operating assets

This formula provides additional insights. Figure 16-7 provides a useful diagram from Myla's perspective, margin and turnover are very important concepts that she can use to measure how well SBH is doing financially. From Chapter 13, we know that increasing sales or reducing cost of sales improves margin. The lower the operating expenses (or cost of sales) per dollar of sales, the higher the margin earned. Some managers tend to focus too much on margin and ignore turnover, and it is this that has created the cash crunch at SBH discussed in Chapter 1.

Turnover incorporates a crucial area of a manager's responsibility—the investment in operating assets—and Myla Thomas understands that. Excessive funds tied up in operating assets (such as cash, inventory, accounts receivable, plant and equipment, and other assets) depresses turnover and lowers ROI. In fact, inefficient use of operating assets can be just as much of a drag on profitability as excessive operating expenses, which depress margin.

Delaware North Companies (known as DNC), a world-class food-service company, pioneered the use of ROI and recognized the importance of looking at both margin and turnover in assessing the performance of a manager. Figure 16-7 is a graphic interpretation of ROI, and it is communicated to all unit managers at DNC.

A memorandum by Chuck Moran, president and chief operating officer of DNC, to all subsidiary managers on April 10, 2006, said it in a nutshell in this extract, titled "The Power of Focus":

> "We have invested significantly in new business, both in capital and human resources. Many of these investments have not met financial expectations. Needless to say, these trends are in conflict with our strategic imperative of financial growth. We need to invest our capital wisely in order to achieve sustainable growth in revenues and profitability."

So, just how do you measure revenue and profitability growth? You will find out from the exercises below. ROI is now widely used as the key measure of investment center performance, and it reflects in a single figure many aspects of the manager's responsibilities. Myla Thomas uses it to compare the returns of all restaurant investments at SBH, past, present, and future.

Any increase in ROI must involve at least one of the following:

- Increased sales
- Reduced operating expenses
- Reduced operating assets

Many actions involve combinations of changes in sales, expenses, and operating assets. For example, a manager may make an investment in (that is, increase) operating assets in order

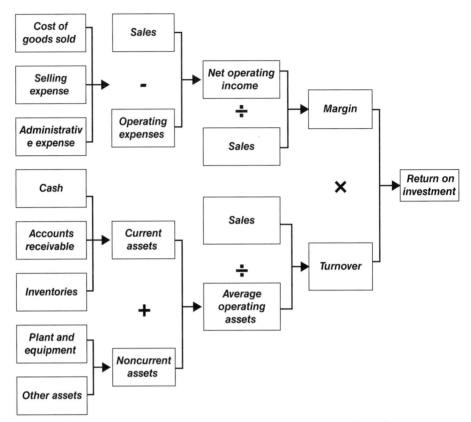

Figure 16-7 Return on Investment. Courtesy of Ray Garrison, Eric Noreen and Peter Brewer, *Managerial Accounting* (11th edition), © 2006. Published by McGraw-Hill/Irwin. Reproduced with permission of The McGraw-Hill Companies.

to reduce operating expenses or to increase sales. Whether the net effect is favorable or not is judged in terms of its general impact on ROI, and that is the general theme of Chuck Moran's message to the DNC management team.

To illustrate how ROI is affected by various actions, we will go back to our Sea Breeze Hotel Restaurant example. The Sea Breeze operates a full-service restaurant in its Monterey hotel. Myla Thomas's evaluation is largely based on the ROI of the food and beverage division's performance.

The following 12 months' data represent the results of operations before Myla joined the management team of SBH:

Sales	500,000
Operating expenses	450,000
Net operating income	50,000
Average operating assets	300,000

The ROI is computed as follows:

$$\text{ROI} = \frac{\text{net operating income}}{\text{sales}} \times \frac{\text{sales}}{\text{net operating assets}}$$

$$\text{ROI} = \frac{50,000}{500,000} \times \frac{500,000}{300,000}$$

$$= 10.00\% \times 1.67$$

$$= 16.67\%$$

First Scenario

One year after Myla Thomas joined SBH, sales increase by 10 percent without any increase in operating assets, due to using the menu engineering techniques covered in Chapter 13. The increase in sales requires additional operating expenses such as cleaning cost and food cost, but as long as fixed costs are not affected by the increase in sales and Myla exercises effective control over costs, operating expenses will increase by less than 10 percent, and therefore the increase in net operating income will be greater than 10 percent. If we assume that the increase in operating expenses is 8 percent of the prior year's $450,000, rather than 10 percent, the new net operating income would therefore be $64,000.

$$
\begin{aligned}
\text{Sales } (1.10 \times 500,000) &= 550,000 \\
\text{Operating expenses } (1.08 \times 450,000) &= \underline{486,000} \\
& \ \ 64,000
\end{aligned}
$$

In this case, Myla's new ROI will be as follows:

$$
\text{ROI} = \frac{\text{net operating income}}{\text{sales}} \times \frac{\text{sales}}{\text{net operating assets}}
$$

$$
\text{ROI} = \frac{64,000}{550,000} \times \frac{550,000}{300,000}
$$

$$
= 11.64 \text{ percent} \times 1.83
$$

$$
= 21.33 \text{ percent (compared to 16.67 percent originally)}
$$

This is the type of result Myla should be proud of, and it should ideally be tied to some form of incentive payment.

Second Scenario: Decrease Operating Expenses with No Change in Sales or Operating Assets

For another example, suppose that Myla Thomas saves $5,000 by applying effective purchasing techniques or cost control (See Chapter Three). When Myla saves on expenses by implementing cost control, she increases SBH's bottom-line profit by that entire dollar—that is, $5,000 saved is equal to $5,000 more in profit. When added to $50,000, the new profit is now $55,000. Therefore, Myla's new ROI calculation will be as follows:

$$
\text{ROI} = \frac{\text{net operating income}}{\text{sales}} \times \frac{\text{sales}}{\text{net operating assets}}
$$

$$
= \frac{55,000}{550,000} \times \frac{550,000}{300,000}
$$

$$
= 11.00 \text{ percent} \times 1.67
$$

$$
= 18.33 \text{ percent (compared to 16.67 percent originally)}
$$

From the onset, there was no effect on turnover, which remained at 1.67 (as is common), so there had to be an increase in margin in order to improve the ROI. It is important to note that when margins are being squeezed, cutting expenses is often the first line of attack by managers. In this case, Myla has done it wisely through effective cost control techniques in purchasing. However, in many instances discretionary fixed expenses (such as preventive maintenance) come under scrutiny first, and various programs are either curtailed or eliminated in an effort to cut costs. Food and beverage managers must be careful not to cut too much or cut something in the wrong place. This may have the effect of decreasing sales or indirectly incurring costs elsewhere. Also, managers must remember that indiscriminate cost-cutting can destroy employee morale.

Third Scenario: Decrease Operating Assets with No Change in Sales or Operating Expenses

Assume that Myla Thomas is able to reduce inventories by $25,000 using just-in-time or consignment purchasing and pricing techniques. This might actually have a positive effect on sales (through fresher ingredients) and on operating expenses (through reduced inventory spoilage), but for the sake of illustration, suppose the reduction in inventories has no effect on sales or operating expenses. The reduction in inventories will reduce average operating assets by $25,000, from $300,000 down to $275,000. The new ROI will be as follows:

$$\text{ROI} = \frac{\text{net operating income}}{\text{sales}} \times \frac{\text{sales}}{\text{net operating assets}}$$

$$= \frac{50,000}{500,000} \times \frac{500,000}{275,000}$$

$$= 10.00 \text{ percent} \times 1.81$$

$$= 18.18 \text{ percent (compared to 16.67 percent originally)}$$

In this example, Myla used JIT or consignment and pricing techniques to reduce operating assets. Another common tactic for reducing operating assets is to speed up the collection of accounts receivable. For example, many hotels and food-service companies now encourage customers to pay electronically rather than using the much slower method of sending checks by mail.

Fourth Scenario: Invest in Operating Assets to Increase Sales

Assume that Myla Thomas is able to convince the owner of SBH to purchase a pizza oven for $1,500, and the oven is capable of making a number-one seller: pizza. This new equipment results in additional sales of $15,000 and additional product and labor costs of $4,000. Thus, net operating income increase by $11,000 to $61,000 from the original $50,000. The new ROI is as follows:

$$\text{ROI} = \frac{\text{net operating income}}{\text{sales}} \times \frac{\text{sales}}{\text{net operating assets}}$$

$$= \frac{61,000}{515,000} \times \frac{515,000}{275,000}$$

$$= 11.84 \text{ percent} \times 1.71$$

$$= 20.23 \text{ percent (compared to 16.67 percent originally)}$$

In this example, the investment has effects on both margin and turnover, which were originally 10 percent and 1.67, respectively. In some cases, the impact will only be noticeable in one factor or the other.

So what can you learn from the four scenarios above? Simply exhorting managers to increase ROI is insufficient. In the food-service industry, managers who are told to increase ROI will naturally wonder how this is to be accomplished. A clear directive must come from top management, as you have seen from Chuck Moran's statement and from Figure 16-6, to provide manager with some guidance. Generally speaking, ROI can be increased by increasing sales, decreasing costs, and/or decreasing investments in operating assets. However, it may not be obvious to many managers in the food-service industry how they are supposed to increase sales, decrease costs, and decrease investments in a way that is consistent with the company's short- and long-term strategies. For example, a manager who is given inadequate guidance may cut back on investments that are critical to implementing the company's strategy. For that reason, a constant review of unit performance is recommended with participation from headquarters management. A well-constructed review, without corporate intimidation, should answer questions such as the following: What internal business processes should be improved? Which customers should be targeted, and how will they be attracted and retained at a profit? In short, a well-constructed review can provide managers with a road map that indicates how the company intends to increase its ROI. In the absence of such a road map of the company's strategy, managers may have difficulty understanding what they are supposed to do to increase ROI, and they may work at cross purposes rather than in harmony with the overall strategy of the company.

SUMMARY

For purposes of evaluating company performance and for future investment decisions, companies generally prepare annual budgets that represent the financial goals of the company. Several approaches to developing a budget are possible: fixed budgets, variable budgets, flexible budgets, and zero-based budgets. Only by setting clear financial goals and implementing controls to monitor performance is a company likely to achieve maximum profitability. Returns on investment (ROI) are widely used to evaluate the performance of investment decisions. ROI suffers from an underinvestment problem: Managers may be reluctant to invest in projects that would drag down their ROI but whose returns exceed that unit's specific required rate of return.

CHAPTER QUESTIONS

Critical Thinking Questions

1. Differentiate a forecast from a budget.

2. Why is zero-based budgeting used?

3. How does successful budgeting benefit the company?

4. Why is it important, especially in writing a variable budget, to differentiate fixed from variable costs?

5. What is the formula used to calculate gross profit?

6. When performing variable budgeting, if total fixed costs for the month are $10,000, food cost per cover is $2.35, beverage cost per cover is $0.85, labor cost per cover is $1.85, and other costs per cover are $0.65, what is the total budgeted expense if 3,000 covers are forecast?

7. Given the data above, what is the total budgeted expense if 15,000 covers are forecast?

8. Describe the treatment of labor in fixed budgeting.

9. Describe the treatment of labor in variable budgeting.

10. Describe the treatment of labor in zero-based budgeting.

Objective Questions

1. One example of an internal factor affecting the budget is staff training costs. True or False?

2. A high balance of current assets over current liabilities may indicate that you are not investing excess cash wisely. True or False?

3. In a large operation, the food and beverage controller has direct responsibilities for operational decision making. True or False?

4. Fixed costs are fixed in dollars, and thus the fixed cost percentage decreases as sales increase. True or False?

Multiple Choice Questions

1. A plan that calls for a series of actions to produce certain outcomes, with effective controls incorporated into these actions, is a
   A. budget.
   B. forecast.
   C. feasibility analysis.
   D. corporate policy.

2. On a balance sheet, assets equal
   A. owner's equity minus liabilities.
   B. liabilities plus owner's equity.
   C. liabilities.
   D. owners' equity.

3. The type of budget that is simplest to construct and refers to a single level of business activity is the
   A. variable budget.
   B. zero-based budget.
   C. fixed budget.
   D. cash-flow budget.

CASE STUDIES

Case Study 1: Budgeting or Planning

One element necessary to the success of an organization is strategic planning. Strategic planning establishes an organization's long-range goals or objectives and the means to achieve them. Even before a company can begin operations, decision-makers must answer the following questions: What products or services will the company provide? How will the company be financed and structured? Where will the company and its distributors be located? How will the company's products or services be marketed?

Line and staff management play specific roles in strategic planning. They have different responsibilities and functions in an organization. In addition, the activities of these two management groups must be coordinated.

Your task:

1. In the formulation of an organization's strategic plans, describe the contribution to be made by:

    A. The line managers

    B. The staff groups and departments

    In your answer, identify the types of decisions that these two groups of managers would probably make as they participate in the formulation of strategic plans.

2. In the implementation of an organization's strategic plans:

    A. State how the responsibilities of line management differ from those of staff management.

    B. Describe how line and staff responsibilities interrelate in the implementation of strategic planning.

Case Study 2: Approach to Budgeting

An effective budget converts the objectives and goals of management into data. The budget can then serve as a blueprint that represents management's plan for operating the organization. Moreover, the budget is frequently a basis for controlling management performance, which can be evaluated by comparing actual results with the budget.

Creating an effective budget is essential for a successful operation. There are several ways in which budget data can be generated, and all involve extensive contacts with people at various operating levels. The manner in which the involved people perceive their roles in the budget process is important to the successful use of the budget as a management tool.

Your task:

1. Discuss the behavioral implications associated with preparing the budget and with using the budget as a method to control activities when a restaurant employs:

    A. A budgetary approach in which budget data are imposed from above.

    B. A budgetary approach in which budget data are prepared at various levels in a self-imposed, participatory manner.

2. Communication plays an important part in the budget process regardless of whether the budget is imposed from above or a participative budget approach is used. Describe the differences in communication flows between these two approaches to budget preparation.

Case Study 3: Approach to Budgeting

Fish King Restaurants, a well-known restaurant chain in the Midwest, is in the initial stages of preparing the annual budget for 2008. Kevin Vieden recently joined Fish King's accounting staff and wants to learn as much as possible about the company's budgeting process. During a recent lunch with Scott Bruce, restaurant manager, and Brenda Nolan, sales manager, Kevin initiated the following conversation:

Kevin: Since I'm new around here and am going to be involved with the preparation of the annual budget, I'd be interested to learn how the two of you estimate sales and production numbers.

Brenda: We start out very methodically by looking at recent history, discussing what we know about current accounts, potential customers, and the general state of consumer spending. Then, we add that usual dose of intuition to come up with the best forecast we can.

Scott: I usually take the sales projections as the basis for my projections. Of course, we have to make an estimate of what this year's closing inventories will be, which is sometimes difficult.

Kevin: Why does that present a problem? There must have been an estimate of closing inventories in the budget for the current year.

Scott: Those numbers aren't always reliable since Brenda makes some adjustments to the sales numbers before passing them on to me.

Kevin: What kinds of adjustments?

Brenda: Well, we don't want to fall short of the sales projections, so we generally give ourselves a little breathing room by lowering the initial sales projection anywhere from 2 to 5 percent.

Scott: So, you can see why this year's budget is not a very reliable starting point. We always have to adjust the projected production rates as the year progresses and, of course, this changes the ending inventory estimates. By the way, we make similar adjustments to expenses by adding at least 10 percent to the estimates; I think everyone around here does the same thing.

Your task:

1. Kevin, Brenda, and Scott have described the use of what is sometimes called budgetary slack.

    A. Explain why Brenda and Scott behave in this manner, and describe the benefits they expect to realize from the use of budgetary slack.

    B. Explain how the use of budgetary slack can adversely affect Brenda and Scott.

2. As a management accountant, Kevin Vieden believes that the behavior described by Brenda and Scott may be unethical. Explain why the use budgetary slack may be unethical.

Case Study 4: Evaluating a Company's Budget Procedures

Colin Patrick and Al Johnson strolled back to their offices from the company headquarters. Colin is the director of food and beverage; Al is the director of engineering. The men had just attended the monthly performance evaluation meeting for the Shoshone Hotel food and beverage division. These meetings had been held on the third Tuesday of each month since Carlton Drakes Jr., the chairman's son, had become the managing director a year earlier.

As they were walking, Colin spoke. "Boy, I hate those meetings! I never know whether my department's accounting reports will show good or bad performance. I'm beginning to expect the worst. If the accountants say I save the company a dollar, I'm called 'Sir,' but if I spend even a little too much—boy, do I get in trouble. I don't know if I can hold on until I retire."

Colin had just been given the worst evaluation he had ever received in his long career with Shoshone Hotel. He had been the most respected of the experienced food and beverage managers in the company. When Carlton Drake Jr. became the managing director, he directed that monthly performance comparisons be made between actual and budgeted costs for each department. The departmental budgets were intended to encourage the supervisors to reduce inefficiencies and to seek cost reduction opportunities. The company controller was instructed to have his staff "tighten" the budget slightly whenever a department attained its budget in a given month; this was done to reinforce the hotel supervisor's desire to reduce costs. The managing director often stressed the importance of continued progress toward attaining the budget; he also made it known that he kept a file of these performance reports for future reference when he succeeded his father.

Colin Patrick's conversation with Al Johnson continued as follows:

Colin: I really don't understand. We've worked hard to get up to budget, and the minute we make it they tighten the budget on us. We can't work faster and still maintain quality. I think my staff is ready to quit trying. Besides, those reports don't tell the whole story. We always seem to be interrupting the big job for all those small rush orders. All that setup and equipment breakdown time is killing us. And quite frankly, Al, you were no help. When our baking oven broke down last month, your people were nowhere to be found. We had to take it apart ourselves and got stuck with all that idle time.

Al: I'm sorry about that, Colin, but you know my department has had trouble making budget too. We were running well behind at the time of that problem, and if we'd spent a day on that old machine, we never would have made it up. Instead we made the scheduled inspections of the elevators because we knew we could do those in less than the budgeted time.

Colin: Well, Al, at least you have some options. I'm locked into what the catering department assigns to me, and you know they're being harassed by sales for those special orders. Incidentally, why didn't your report show all the supplies you guys wasted last month when you were working in Kevin's department?

Al: We're not out of the woods on that deal yet. We charged the maximum we could to our other work and haven't even reported some of it yet.

Colin: Well, I'm glad you have a way of getting out of the pressure. The accountants seem to know everything that's happening in my department, sometimes even before I do. I thought all that budget and accounting stuff was supposed to help, but it just gets me into trouble. It's all a big pain. I'm trying to put out quality work; they're trying to save pennies.

Your task:

1. Identify the problems that exist in the Shoshone Hotel's budgetary control system, and explain how the problems are likely to reduce the effectiveness of the system.

2. Explain how Shoshone Hotel's budgetary control system could be revised to improve its effectiveness.

Case Study 5: Behavioral Impact of Budget Costs and Variances

Alison Snyder is the restaurant and kitchen manager of Briscoe Gourmet Restaurant. Each month, Alison receives a performance report showing the budget for the month, the actual activity, and the variance between budgeted and actual costs. Part of Alison's annual performance evaluation is based on her department's performance against budget. Briscoe's purchasing manager, Kevin Scott, also receives monthly performance reports, and he, too, is evaluated in part on the basis of these reports.

Kevin: I got the same treatment. All I ever hear about are the things I haven't done right. Now I have to spend a lot of time reviewing the report and preparing explanations. The worst part is that it's now the 16th of March, so the information is almost a month old, and we have to spend all this time on history.

Alison: My biggest gripe is that our production activity varies a lot from month to month, but we're given an annual budget that's written in stone. Last month we were shut down for three days when a strike delayed delivery of fish. You know about that problem, though, because we asked you to call all over the city to find an alternative source. When we got what we needed on a rush basis from the local supermarket, we had to pay more than we normally do.

Kevin: I expect problems like that to pop up from time to time—that's part of my job—but now we'll both have to take a careful look at our reports to see where the charges are reflected for that rush order. Every month I spend more time making sure I should be charged for each item reported than I do making plans for my department's daily work. It's really frustrating to see charges for things I have no control over.

Alison: The way we get information doesn't help, either. I don't get copies of the reports you get, yet your department affects a lot of what I do. Why do the budget and accounting people assume that I should only be told about my operations despite these effects? And the general manager regularly gives us pep talks about how we all need to work together as a team—how ironic.

Kevin: I seem to get more reports than I need, and I am never asked to comment on them until top management calls me on the carpet about my department's shortcomings. Do you ever hear comments when your department shines?

Alison: I guess they don't have time to review the good news. One of my problems is that all the reports are in dollars and cents. I work with people, machines, and material. I need information to help me this month to solve *this* month's problems—not another report of the dollars expended last month or the month before.

Your task:

1. Based on the conversation between Alison and Kevin, describe the likely motivation and behavior of these two employees resulting from Briscoe Gourmet's variances reporting.

2. When properly implemented, both employees and companies should benefit from a system involving timely actual costs versus potential cost reporting.

    A. Describe the benefits that can be realized from a potential cost system.

    B. Describe how the gripes above can be addressed.

FOR FURTHER READING

Michael C. Jensen, "Corporate Budgeting Is Broken—Let's Fix It," *Harvard Business Review*, November 2001; Michael Jensen, "Why Pay People to Lie?" *The Wall Street Journal*, January 8, 2001, p. A32.

Glossary

A

A la carte Menu items that are priced individually or separately.

Access control A system that authorizes or denies access to a restricted area.

Accounting period Financial period of time based on a company's established policies. Could be monthly, yearly, or another measure of time.

Accrual System of reporting revenue and expenses in the period in which they are considered to have been earned or incurred, regardless of the actual time of collection or payment.

Actual cost The product cost that appears on the profit and loss statement as expenditures.

Actual recipe unit cost The cost of each ingredient in a menu.

Ambience The atmosphere of an operation, including (but not limited to) its sounds, sights, smells and team attitude.

As-purchased price (AP) The original price paid for a product.

Available guests The percentage of the total registered guests that may come to dine in a hotel restaurant.

Average (inventory) age A figure used to determine inventory effectiveness in days; with years of reliable average age data, and expected sales levels, the manager can predict inventory balances for budgeting purposes.

Average check The average sale value of food, beverages, or food and beverage combined revenue. Derived by dividing total or categorical revenue by number of customers served in a period.

B

Bartering Trading goods and services without the exchange of money.

Base price The actual unit price excluding discounts, shipping, taxes and other services.

Beginning inventory The quantity and value of food and beverage products on hand at the beginning of an accounting period.

Bid sheet A sheet used to record and compare item prices of different vendors in order to select the best-priced items.

Bin cards A manual system for keeping track of inventory items.

Bin number A specific reference number assigned to an inventory item.

Bottle mark A label or ink stamp with company information, to identify bottled products as company property.

Bottom line Used synonymously with profit.

Break-even point The relationship between volume of business produced and the resulting sales income, expenditures, and profits or losses.

Budget A company's plan of operation for a specified period of time that forecasts activity and income, sets limits on expenditures, and establishes any other disposition of company funds.

Butcher test A yield test used to determine the actual portion cost of meat, poultry, fish, or seafood after accounting for waste, trim, and cooking losses.

C

Capital budget A budget of capital expenditures, such as equipment, building and other fixed assets.

Capture ratio The number or percentage of customers a restaurant attracts, depending on set variables such as marketing, convention business or menu offerings.

Cash bar Opposite of **host bar;** individual customers are required to pay for drinks.

Cash budget Management's plan for cash received and cash disbursement.

Cash flow A stream of receipts (inflows) and payments (outflows) resulting from operational activities or investments.

Cashier banking A system where a cashier settles each check and is responsible for the transaction.

Circled count A periodic and random spot check of perpetual inventories. The objectives are early detection and correction of discrepancies, and accurate reporting of inventory value and quantity on hand.

Communication The ongoing process of exchanging information between different departments and people in an organization.

Compound interest Interest calculated based not only on the original principle but also on any of the unpaid interest.

Consignment purchasing A merchandising technique in which payment for the goods is deferred until they are resold by the buyer.

Consistency In purchasing, means that the products purchased remain the same at all times..

Contract price A commitment to buy a group of items at a certain price.

Contribution margin (CM) Contribution to profit and overhead costs; or, the excess of an item's revenue after subtracting product cost.

Controllable expenses Expenses over which management may exercise control.

Costs The sum of all money paid out during a given period of time.

Cost allocation The process of distributing costs among departments.

Cost factor The ratio of the cost per servable pound to the purchase price per pound.

Cost of sales Food and beverage cost for menu items during an accounting period.

Cost per purchased pound Purchase price of a cut of meat divided by the weight in pounds.

Cost per servable pound The cost derived from butcher test results. Calculated by subtracting secondary costs from the purchase price, and dividing by the weight of the primary cut.

Cost-plus Pricing method which involves paying the vendor's actual product cost plus a certain, fixed percentage.

Covers The number of meals served.

Credit memo Used to record a credit due from a supplier when the merchandise received does not conform to what was ordered. The discrepancy could be in terms of quality, quantity, specification, and/or price.

Current assets Assets that are expected to be converted to cash within one year. They include cash, inventory, and accounts receivable.

Current ratio The relationship between current assets and liabilities; measures the liquidity of a company.

D

Database Collection of records or files containing information for users.

Dead stock Stock without significant inventory movement in sales due to menu or service changes.

Decision package A document that describes the level of effort required to meet objectives.

Depreciable assets Assets such as computers, vehicles, or equipment that will depreciate in value.

Direct competition refers to the homogeneous environment; for example, all the restaurants nearby that offer the same type of menu that you want to offer.

Direct issue A purchase charged directly to a receiving outlet.

Direct cost Costs related to direct purchase or transfer.

Dog A menu engineering classification of items which are neither profitable nor popular.

Dram shop law A law requiring that not only must the consumer take responsibility for his or her actions while intoxicated; so too must the provider of the alcohol.

E

Economical order quantity (EOQ) Inventory decision model which calculates the optimal amount to order based on fixed costs of placing and receiving an order, carrying costs of inventory, and sales. EOQ is used extensively in the purchasing department.

Elasticity of demand The responsiveness of buyers to changes in price, defined as the percentage change in the quantity demanded divided by the percentage change in price.

Elasticity of supply Responsiveness of output to changes in price, defined as the percentage change in the quantity supplied divided by the percentage change in the price.

Ending inventory The quantity and value of inventory on hand at the end of an accounting period.

End-of-month Transaction period, such as the due date for receivables or the date of a closing inventory.

End product (EP) refers to final yield after processing.

End-product price refers to the price of usable product, including the price of wastage.

Ethanol is alcohol.

Expense control refers to managing expenses according to budget.

F

Financial balance sheet A statement reporting on the financial position of a business by presenting its assets, liabilities, and equity on a given date.

Financial position An account or status of a company's assets, liabilities, and equity as of a certain time, as shown on its financial statement.

Financial statement A written record of the financial status or position of a company. This includes a balance sheet and income statement.

Finished goods Menu items that have been completely prepared and are ready to serve to customers.

Firm price A price the purchaser and the vendor agree to that will not change until the material is delivered and the transaction is completed.

First in, first out (FIFO) Method of inventory valuation and management in which cost of goods sold is charged with the cost of raw materials, in-process goods and finished goods purchased first and in which inventory contains the most recently purchased materials.
Fiscal year Any continuous 12-month period used by a company as its accounting period.

Fixed costs (FC) Costs that remains constant regardless of sales volume, such as executive salaries.

Flexible budget A statement of projected revenue and expenditure based on various kinds of production.

Folio An itemized guest-lodging bill.

Food cost refers to the cost of food items and ingredients.

Forecasting Estimating future revenue and expense trends.

Full time equivalent (FTE) A way to measure worker productivity in a work schedule.

Full-cost accounting A tool to identify, quantify, and allocate the direct and indirect total cost of an operation.

G

General ledger The formal listing of accounts (ledger) containing all the financial statement accounts of a business. Every transaction flows through it.

Government deductions Mandatory deduction from employees' gross pay, including federal and state income taxes, FICA taxes, garnishments, disability insurance, and other taxes.

Gross The highest amount, often referring to sales or income.

Gross profit The difference between revenue and the cost of goods sold.

Guest check A printed form and system for ordering and recording food and beverage.

Guest check audit A system of controlling the difference between guest checks issued and those actually used.

H

Hedging is a contract on a future price, entered into to maintain a fixed price for a product or commodity you will need.

House bank The amount of money given to a cashier or server for the purpose of giving out change to customers.

I

Indirect competition comes from those restaurants that do not share the same cuisine but do share a customer base.

Indirect labor refers to labor hours and costs that are not directly related to producing the output. An example is cleaning crew hours and wages.

Internal controls An accounting method, procedure, or system designed to promote efficiency, ensure the implementation of company policies, safeguard assets, and discover and avoid fraud or errors.

Inventory control Accounting systems for maintaining inventories to prevent items from being out –of-stock, to reduce holding cost, and to permit theft detection.

Inventory issues Food and beverage products requisitioned and supplied to outlets to service the needs of the customers.

Inventory on hand The quantity and value of inventory currently present.

Inventory target Refers to the desired level of inventory.

Inventory turnover ratio A ratio of sales to inventory, which shows how many times the inventory of a company is sold and replaced during an accounting period.

J

Jigger A measuring device used to serve predetermined quantities of a beverage.

Job classification A method of categorizing jobs into ranks or classes for the purposes of work and wage comparison.

Job description A formal documentation of the tasks and duties of a given position.

K

Key performance indicators (KPI) Defined benchmarks by which to measure a company's progress.

L

Labor cost The dollar amount paid to employees.

Last in, first out (LIFO) An inventory costing method that assumes the most recent units purchased are the first units used. The result is that ending inventory consists of the oldest costs and the most recent costs are in the cost of sales.

Lead time The time between the receipt of a purchase order and the receipt of the goods from the vendor.

Least square analysis is an accounting and financial model for calculating and investigating the value of the unknown. The unknown could be revenue, costs, production, and other relevant data for decision making.

Loss leader A menu item that is priced low because it is not very profitable and not popular with customers.

M

Make or buy decision A decision regarding whether to buy prepared products to save labor cost, or to purchase less expensive raw products and prepare them on-site.

Marginal cost The amount of output, at any given volume, by which aggregate costs are changed if the volume of output is increased or decreased by one unit, subject to the condition that fixed cost does not change with the increase in volume.

Market basket analysis compares purchase prices over time and across vendors to build reveal patterns in price fluctuations.

Market reports Reports written by vendors to inform businesses of present and future product conditions, particularly with farm and seafood products.

Meat tag A system for controlling meat by tagging, used for identification and verification of actual use.

Memo invoice A list of all items received.

Menu analysis The evaluation of menu costs and sales data to identify customers' needs and perceptions and to improve menu performance.

Menu design Refers to menu layout, physical characteristics, and content.

Menu engineering Techniques used for analyzing menu profitability and popularity.

Menu mix A proportion of different menu items that make up a complete restaurant menu.

Menu pricing How much a customer is charged for an item.

N

Net income The excess of revenue earned over expenses for the accounting period.

Net revenue Sometimes referred to as net sales, this term represents revenue realized

Net profit Net revenue less all operating costs and expenses.

Non-revenue departments Support and service departments that generally do not generate revenue. Examples include Security, Facility, Personnel, Accounting, and Sales.

O

Open bar A bar used in a banquet function in which customers are not charged individually for the drinks consumed during the function. The host pays for this consumption.

Operating budget Detailed revenue and expense plan for an accounting period.

P

Par level Set inventory amounts that maintain enough stock, but not more than is necessary for the business volume.

Par stock Stock levels established by management for individual inventory items in varying outlets.

Perceived value The customer's perception of value as it relates to his or her restaurant experience.

Perishable products Food and beverage products that need attention and appropriate handling to avoid spoilage. An example is seafood.

Perpetual inventory A system of accounting for inventory changes, in which beginning and ending inventories are noted along with any sales or purchases.

Physical inventory A count of actual inventory items, in order to note quantities and values.

Plow horse A menu engineering classification of items which are not very profitable but which are popular with customers.

Point-of-sale (POS) system A sales transaction register and processor.

Popularity The number of a specific item sold. To derive the percentage of a single item sold, take the number of the item sold and divide it by the total number of items sold.

Potential cost The expectation of what the cost should be, if you comply with all cost control procedures. It is the standard whereby you measure the cost efficiency of your operation.

Potential percentage Determined by dividing the cost by the selling price.

Preventive maintenance Measures taken to maintain efficient corking of operational equipment and facility without affecting the operation.

Price elasticity The change in the rate of sales due to change in the price.

Price index A set of numbers generated via market basket analysisto indicate changes in product prices.

Prime cost The labor, material, and overhead costs identified in product preparation.

Productivity A measure of effectiveness in utilizing labor and equipment; the relationship between input and output.

Profit A positive sum after expenses are deducted from revenue or income of a business as shown in an income statement. The opposite of a loss.

Profit and loss statement A written document of net revenue and expenses showing the financial gain (profit) or failure (loss) for a particular time period.

Profit margin is determined by subtracting your cost from your sales.

Proof is the measure of the alcoholic content of a spirit, each degree of proof being ½percent alcohol by volume; often written with the degree symbol, as 100°.

Purchase order (PO) An order which includes vendors' prices, products, and agreed arrangements for delivery and payment.

Purchase price Refers to the original price paid to receive the product

Purchase specifications Detailed, precise descriptions of items desired to be purchased and under what conditions.

Puzzle A menu engineering classification of items that are particularly profitable but not very popular with guests.

Q

Quality control Maintenance of quality standards; carrying out assigned responsibilities according to established standards.

R

Raw material Uncooked, as-purchased products

Requisition Request for food, beverage, supplies, or personnel.

Restaurant minimum standards Refers to service, food and beverage offerings, and the entire operation—for instance, cleanliness.

Return on investment (ROI) Net operating incovme divided by average operating assets. A measure of profitability of the business expressed in percentages.

Revenue is the same as income or sales.

Revenue center Revenue-producing outlet or department.

Receiving report A report or form that indicates value and quantity of items received from a vendor.

S

Safety stock Extra inventory kept on hand to ensure that you will have time to order more before running out.

Sales mix Number of sales of menu items; perhaps patternized. Also, the products and sales packages offered.

Sales The sum of more than one sale. It is often used interchangeably with income or revenue.

Seat turnover The number of times a seat is occupied during a meal period. This is calculated by dividing the number of guests served by the number of available seats.

Semivariable costs Costs which vary with, but not in direct proportion to, business volume.

Server banking A system wherein the server or bartender also carries out the responsibilities of a cashier.

Staffing guide A document establishing labor time standards for productivity evaluation of employees.

Standard issue A repeated restocking of banquet beverage products to par levels, just as in a regular outlet. Every item issued, minus the ending inventory, should be charged to the function.

Standing order An arrangement made with a vendor to deliver specific goods on a regularly scheduled basis.

Star A menu engineering classification of items that are both popular and profitable.

Stepped costs Costs that "step up" across specific increases in production volume.

Steward Sales. Sales of food or beverage products to employees at cost are called steward sales.

Storeroom issue Purchases sent to the storeroom to be stored and issued to the outlet when they are requisitioned.

Sunk cost A cost that has already been incurred and that cannot be changed by any decision made now or in the future.

T

Tare weight The weight of various empty containers used to determine the net weight of perishables in these containers.

Targeted ideal cost The ideal amount your company wants to spend; it is your goal, or what you have budgeted to spend.

Theoretical cost The calculated expectation of what the cost should be, assuming you comply with all cost control procedures.

Time and motion study A systematic observation, analysis, and measurement of the separate steps in the performance of a specific job. This study is done for the purpose of establishing a standard time for each performance, with the goal of improving procedures and increasing productivity

Inventory turnover How many times the average inventory balance has been used and replaced during the period under review.

U

Unit cost Cost per item.

Up-selling A sales technique whereby an attempt is made to have the customer purchase more expensive items, or upgrade and order, to increase revenue.

V

Variable costs (VC) Production cost which changes in direct proportion to sales volume.

Variance report A report comparing actual performance with budgeted performance.

Vendor minimum order quantity Required minimum amounts for orders from a vendor.

Vintage means the yield of wine or grapes from a vineyard or district during one season. Wine is usually identified as to year and vineyard or district of origin.

Volume pricing Lower prices when products are purchased in larger quantities.

Voluntary deductions Deductions from employees' gross pay that are authorized by the employee, such as insurance premiums, retirement plan contributions, or union dues.

W

Work in progress Partially cooked products that are still in the production process; products that have begun production as raw materials but have not yet been completed as a finished cooked meal.

Working capital Current sssets less current liabilities. This measure serves as an indication of the amount of readily available funds that can be used in operation of the business. Also called *net current assets*.

Y

Yield The net weight or volume of a food item after it has been processed from raw materials and made ready to eat.

Yield percentage is the amount of usable product available from raw materials. To find this, divide the usable weight by the original weight.

Yield price Refers to the end-product cost of the product after yield testing or cleaning.

Yield tests determine the amount of usable product available after processing raw items.

Z

Zero-based budgeting A budget which starts at zero in preparation and in which the writer must justify every expense line.

Appendix

Weights and Measurements

This section has been written to give you instant access to a table of weights and measurements when you are entering your recipes. You should understand that the table of weights and measurements is only approximate. You can never be precise for many reasons:

- The moisture contents of products vary constantly.

- The sizes of individual pieces or particles will vary from container to container.

- The exact weight of a gallon or a pound of product is seldom a convenient, round number.

- It is impractical to say that a pint of water is 1 9/10 cups. It is simpler 2 cups.

- Products containing moisture become lighter as they dry out.

- Wet products containing sugar become heavier when the moisture evaporates and they become thicker.

- A cup of flour could weigh 4 ounces. If you sift it, it may weigh less.

- Any measurement such as a level teaspoon or level cupful is seldom exactly accurate.

The most accurate measurements are fluid ounce (FZ), weight ounce (WZ), count (CT), or portion of a recipe (PR). These are the measurements that we use in this book and in this section, adopted from the Software Creation. Accuracy is essential in food and beverage cost control.

Practical Weights

The following products are used so frequently in recipes that it is simpler to use the practical weights and measures rather than the actual figures. In the case of hydrogenated shortening and whipped butter, in which air is incorporated into the product, the exact weight should be used when using recipes for more than 25 servings. You make the decision according to your experience and record it in weight ounces (WZ), fluid ounces (FZ), or count (CT) (Figure A-1).

Figure A-1

Product	Pound	Cup	Ounce	Tablespoon
PRACTICAL MEASURE	2 cups	8 WZ	2 tbl	1/2 WZ
Salts	2 1/8 cups	9 3/4 WZ	1 5/8 tbl	2/3 WZ
Fats/lard/butter	2 cups	8 WZ	2 tbl	1/2 WZ
Sugar granulated	2 1/2 cups	7 1/2 WZ	2 1/8 tbl	1/2 WZ
Whipped butter	2 2/3 cups	6 WZ	2 2/3 tbl	1/3 WZ

Examples of Typical Weight Difference

Water weighs 8.14 pounds per gallon (WZ). Milk weighs 8.59 pounds per gallon (WZ). Light syrup weighs 10 pounds per gallon (WZ). Honey weighs 11.75 pounds per gallon (WZ). (1 gallon = 128 fluid ounces (FZ)) (Figure A-2).

Figure A-2

Group Characteristics	Example	Cup	Fluid Ounce	Tablespoon
Very dry, light, weight	Oregano, whole	1 WZ	16 TBSP	WZ = 0.063 (1/16)
Dry light leaves, ground	Thyme leaf	2 WZ	8 TBSP	WZ = 0.125 (1/8)
Moist product, ground	Curry powder	4 WZ	4.5 TBSP	WZ = 0.250 (1/4)
Wet products like meat	Peaches, sliced	9 WZ	2 TBSP	WZ = 0.500 (1/2)
Ordinary liquids	Water	8 WZ	2 TBSP	WZ = 0.500 (1/2)
Thick liquids	Molasses	11.2 WZ	1.3 TBSP	WZ = 0.750 (3/4)

The following charts are for reference purposes.

Water Conversion from Fluid to Weight

Cups	Pints	Quarts	Fluid Ounces	Pounds and Ounces	
0.5	0.25	0.125	4	0	4.00
1.0	0.5	0.250	8	0	8.25
1.5	0.75	0.375	12	0	12.50
2.0	1.00	0.500	16	1	0.50
2.5	1.25	0.625	20	1	4.75
3.0	1.50	0.750	24	1	9.00
3.5	1.75	0.875	28	1	13.00
4.0	2.00	1.000	32	2	1.25
4.5	2.25	1.125	36	2	5.25
5.0	2.50	1.250	40	2	9.50
5.5	2.75	1.375	44	2	13.75
6.0	3.00	1.500	48	3	1.75
6.5	3.25	1.625	52	3	6.00
7.0	3.50	1.750	56	3	10.25
7.5	3.75	1.875	60	3	14.25
8.0	4.00	2.000	64	4	2.50

Figure A-3 (*continued*)

Water Conversion from Fluid to Weight (*concluded*)

Cups	Pints	Quarts	Fluid Ounces	Pounds and Ounces	
8.5	4.25	2.125	68	4	6.50
9.0	4.50	2.250	72	4	10.75
9.5	4.75	2.375	76	4	15.00
10.0	5.00	2.500	80	5	3.25
10.5	5.25	2.625	84	5	7.25
11.0	5.50	2.750	88	5	11.50
11.5	5.75	2.875	92	5	15.50
12.0	6.00	3.000	96	6	3.75
12.5	6.25	3.125	100	6	8.00
13.0	6.50	3.250	104	6	12.00
13.5	6.75	3.375	108	7	0.25
14.0	7.00	3.500	112	7	4.25
14.5	7.25	3.625	116	7	8.25
15.0	7.50	3.750	120	7	12.50
15.5	7.75	3.875	124	8	1.00
16.0	8.00	4.000	128	8	5.00

Figure A-3 (*concluded*)

Abbreviations for Recipes (Unit Measure)

Unit of Measure	Abbreviation	Unit of Measure	Abbreviation
milliliter	ml	large	lge
demiliter	dm	medium	Med
Liter	L	small	Sm
package	pkg	inch	In
Weight	wt	minute	Min
volume	vol	gram	G
Gram	Gm	ounce	Oz.
Pound	Lb. or #	cup	Cup or C.
pint	pt.	quart	Qt.
Gallon	Gal.	each	Ea.
Fluid ounce	Fz	weight ounce	Wz
Count	Ct	Bunch	Bch.
Batch	B	Dozen	Doz.
teaspoon	Tsp. or t.	tablespoon	Tblsp., Tbl., or TBL.

Figure A-4

Abbreviations for Inventory

Abbreviation	Unit of Measure	Abbreviation	Unit of Measure
*	weight not available	bchd.	bunched
bskt.	basket	bu.	bushel
crt.	crate	ctn.	carton
contr.	container	hmpr.	hamper
lb.	pound	lyr.	layer
oz.	ounce	pk.	pack
pkg.	package	pt.	pint
sk.	sack	std.	standard
var.	various	wbd.	wirebound
wrpd.	wrapped		

Figure A-5

Other Abbreviations

Abbreviations	Unit of Measure
°F	degree Fahrenheit
°C	degree Celsius
psi	pressure per square inch
cm	centimeter
in.	inch
A.P.	as purchased
E.P.	edible portion (less preparation waste)

Figure A-6

Common Abbreviations and Descriptions

Abbreviation	Ingredient Description	Abbreviation	Ingredient Description
AMR	american	CRSNT	crescent
AST	assorted	CUBD	cubed
BLNCHD	blanched	DCD	diced
BM	bilmar	DETR	detergent

Figure A-7 (*continued*)

Common Abbreviations (*continued*)

Abbreviation	Ingredient Description	Abbreviation	Ingredient Description
BNLS	boneless	DRND	drained
BRDED	breaded	DRSG	dressing
BRKN	broken	DVL`S	devil`s
BRSKT	brisket	EA	each
BRST	breast	ENR	enriched
BTRSCH	butterscotch	FD	food
BUTR	butter	FLKD	flaked
BX	box	FRNCH STYL	french style
CAFF FREE	caffeine free	FRSH	fresh
CANADN	canadian	FRZ-DRY	freeze-dried
CAULFLWR	cauliflower	FURN	furniture
CHED	cheddar	GB	goldberger
CHIN	chinese	GERSTYL	german style
CHIPD	chipped	GM	general mills
CHLLD	chilled	GRHM	graham
CHOC	chocolate	GRN	green
CHOPD	chopped	GRND	ground
CKD	cooked	GRTD	grated
CLEAND	cleaned	HLF	half
CLEND & HULD	cleaned and hulled	HLVD	halved
COARSLY	coarsely	HLVS	halves
COTT	cottage	ICBRG	iceberg
CRMBLD	crumbled	IND	individual
CRNBRY	cranberry	INST	instant
CRND	corned	ITAL	italian
CRSHD	crushed	JUL	julienne

Figure A-7 (*continued*)

Common Abbreviations (*concluded*)

Abbreviation	Ingredient Description	Abbreviation	Ingredient Description
KELGS	Kellog's	PROV	provolone
LNTHWSE	lengthwise	PRTNS	portions
LO FT	low fat	PS	paper supplies
LO SOD	low sodium	PUR	purpose
LRG	large	QTRS	quarters
LT SYR	light syrup	RCH	Rich's
LVS	leaves	RGH	rough
MAND	Mandarin	RND	round
MARA	maraschino	RNSD	rinsed
MEX	Mexican	RSTD	roasted
MNCD	minced	S LEE	Sara Lee
MOZZ	mozzarella	SAND	sandwich
MSHD	mashed	SAUT	sauteed
MTLS	meatless	SCRD	scored
ND	nondairy	SDLS	seedless
NTRL	natural	SECT	sections
OZ	ounce	SED	seeded
PCKD	precooked	SEMISWT	semisweet
PCKLD	pickled	SOFTND	softened
PCS	pieces	SHRED	shredded
PELD	peeled	SHVD	shaved
PIZA	pizza	SIRLN	sirloin
PK	packet	SL	slices
PLD	pulled	SLCD	sliced
PLN	plain	SLCS	slices
PLSTC	plastic	SLD	solid
PNUT	peanut	SMKD	smoked
PR	pair	SNKA	Sanka
PRECKD	precooked	SP	spice
PREM	premium	SPLT	split

Figure A-7 (*concluded*)

Gram Weight Conversion Table

NOTE: When you know the weight ounces, multiply by 28.35 to find the grams. Divide the grams by 453.6 to find the pounds.

Ounces	Grams	Pounds	Grams
1	28.35	1	453.6
2	56.70	2	907.2
3	85.05	2.5	1134.0
4	113.40	3	1136.8
5	141.75	4	1814.4
6	170.10	5	2268.0
7	198.45	6	2721.6
8	226.80	7	3175.2
9	255.15	8	3628.8
10	283.50	9	4082.4
11	311.85	10	4536.0
12	340.20	15	6804.0
13	368.55	20	9072.0
14	396.90	25	11340.0
15	425.25	30	13608.0
16	453.60	35	15876.0
17	481.95		
18	510.30		
19	538.65		
20	567.00		
21	595.35		
22	623.70		
23	652.05		
24	680.40		

Figure A-8

Metric Size Fluids

Metric	U.S. FL. OZ.	3/4 Oz.	1 Oz.	1 −1/8 Oz.	1 −1/4 Oz.	1 −1/2 Oz.	Closest Previous Container (U.S. Oz.)
1.75 Liter	59.2	78.9	59.2	52.6	47.4	39.5	1/2 Gal. = 64 oz.
1.0 Liter	33.8	45.1	33.8	30.0	27.0	22.5	Qt. = 32 oz.
750 Milliliters	25.4	33.9	25.4	22.6	20.3	16.9	5th = 25.6 oz.
500 Milliliters	16.9	22.5	16.9	15.0	13.5	11.3	Pt. = 16 oz.
200 Milliliters	6.8	9.1	6.8	6.0	5.4	4.5	1/2 Pt. = 8 oz.
50 Milliliters	1.7						Miniature = 1.6 oz.

Figure A-9

Standard Measures References

Beverage Yield Chart: U.S. Measurement System

Size per Bottle	Quart	Yield per 1 −1/8 oz Drink	Yield per 1 −1/4 oz Drink	Yield per 1 −1/2 oz Drink
10/10	32.0 oz	28.3	25.6	21.3
9/10	28.8 oz	25.5	23.0	19.2
8/10	25.6 oz	22.7	20.5	17.1
7/10	22.4 oz	19.8	17.9	14.9
6/10	19.2 oz	17.0	15.4	12.8
5/10	16.0 oz	14.2	12.8	10.6
4/10	12.8 oz	11.3	10.2	8.5
3/10	9.6 oz	8.5	7.7	6.4
2/10	6.4 oz	5.7	5.1	4.3
1/10	3.2 oz	2.8	2.6	2.1

Size per Bottle	Fifth	Yield per 1 −1/8 oz Drink	Yield per 1 −1/4 oz Drink	Yield per 1 −1/2 oz Drink
10/10	25.6 oz	22.7	20.5	17.1
9/10	23.04 oz	20.4	18.4	15.4
8/10	20.48 oz	18.1	16.4	13.6
7/10	17.96 oz	15.9	14.4	12.0
6/10	15.36 oz	13.6	12.3	10.2
5/10	12.80 oz	11.3	10.2	8.5
4/10	10.24 oz	9.1	8.2	6.8
3/10	7.68 oz	6.8	6.2	5.1
2/10	5.12 oz	4.5	4.1	3.4
1/10	2.56 oz	2.3	2.1	1.7

Figure A-10 (*continued*)

Beverage Yield Chart: U.S. Measurement System (*continued*)

Size per Bottle	1/2 Gallon	Yield per 1 –1/8 oz Drink	Yield per 1 –1/4 oz Drink	Yield per 1 –1/2 oz Drink
10/10	64 oz	56.6	51.2	42.7
9/10	57.6 oz	51.0	46.1	38.4
8/10	51.2 oz	45.3	41.0	34.1
7/10	44.8 oz	39.6	35.8	29.9
6/10	38.4 oz	34.0	30.7	25.6
5/10	32.0 oz	28.3	25.6	21.3
4/10	25.6 oz	22.7	20.5	17.1
3/10	19.2 oz	17.0	15.4	12.8
2/10	12.8 oz	11.3	10.2	8.5
1/10	6.4 oz	5.7	5.1	4.3

Size per Bottle	Liter Ounces	Yield per 1 –1/8 oz Drink	Yield per 1 –1/4 oz Drink	Yield per 1 –1/2 oz Drink
10/10	33.8	29.9	27.0	22.5
9/10	30.4	26.9	24.3	20.3
8/10	27.04	23.9	21.6	18.0
7/10	23.66	20.9	18.9	15.8
6/10	20.28	18.0	16.2	13.5
5/10	16.90	15.0	13.5	11.3
4/10	13.52	12.0	10.8	9.0
3/10	10.14	9.0	8.1	6.8
2/10	6.76	6.0	5.4	4.5
1/10	3.38	3.0	2.7	2.3

Size per Bottle	750 ml Ounces	Yield per 1 –1/8 oz Drink	Yield per 1 –1/4 oz Drink	Yield per 1 –1/2 oz Drink
10/10	25.4	22.4	20.3	16.9
9/10	22.86	20.2	18.3	15.2
8/10	20.32	18.0	16.2	13.5
7/10	17.78	15.7	14.2	11.9
6/10	15.24	13.5	12.2	10.2
5/10	12.70	11.2	10.1	8.5
4/10	10.16	9.0	8.1	6.8
3/10	7.62	6.7	6.1	5.1
2/10	5.08	4.5	4.1	3.4
1/10	2.54	2.3	2.0	1.7

Figure A-10 (*continued on next page*)

Beverage Yield Chart: U.S. Measurement System (*concluded*)

Size per Bottle	1.75 liters Ounces	Yield per 1 −1/8 oz Drink	Yield per 1 −1/4 oz Drink	Yield per 1 −1/2 oz Drink
10/10	59.2	52.3	47.3	39.5
9/10	53.28	47.1	42.6	35.5
8/10	47.36	41.9	37.9	31.6
7/10	41.44	36.6	33.1	27.6
6/10	35.52	31.4	28.4	23.7
5/10	29.6	26.2	23.7	19.7
4/10	23.68	20.9	18.9	15.8
3/10	17.76	15.7	14.2	11.8
2/10	11.84	10.5	9.5	7.95
1/10	5.92	5.2	4.7	3.9

Figure A-10

Approximate Equivalents in Metric and U.S. Measures of Weight

Grams	Ounces	Pounds	Kilograms	Ounces	Pounds
1	0.035		0.756	26.67	1 2/3
5	0.175		0.793	28	1 3/4
15	0.525		0.832	29.33	1 5/6
28.35	1	1/16	0.850	30	
43	1.5		0.907	32	2
57	2	1/8	0.964	34	2 1/8
71	2.5		1.000	35.28	2 1/5
76	2.67	1/6	1.020	36	2 1/4
85	3		1.135	40	2 1/2
114	4	1/4	1.25	44	2 3/4
128	4.5		1.36	48	3
142	5		1.59	56	3 1/2
151	5.33	1/3	1.81	64	4
170	6		2.04	72	4 1/2
198	7		2.27	80	5
227	8	1/2	2.50	88	5 1/2

Figure A-11 (*continued*)

Approximate Equivalents (*concluded*)

Grams	Ounces	Pounds	Kilograms	Ounces	Pounds
255	9		2.72	96	6
283	10		2.95	104	6 1/2
302	10.67	2/3	3.18	112	7
312	11		3.63	128	8
340	12	3/4	4.08	144	9
368	13		4.54	160	10
378	13.33	5/6	5.44	192	12
397	14		5.90	208	13
425	15		6.35	224	14
454	16	1	7.26	256	16
510	18	1 1/8	8.17	288	18
529	18.67	1 1/6	9.07	320	20
567	20	1 1/4	10.89	384	24
605	21.33	1 1/3	12.70	448	28
623	22		13.60	480	30
681	24	1 1/2	14.51	512	32
737	26		18.14	640	40

Figure A-11 (*concluded*)

Equivalent Measures for Fluids

NOTE: This table gives measurement/weight equivalencies for water. Other liquids may vary.

3 Teaspoons	=	1 Tablespoon
16 Tablespoons	=	1 Cup
28.35 Grams	=	1 Ounce
1 Cup	=	1/2 Pint
2 Cups	=	1 Pint
2 Pints	=	1 Quart
4 Quarts	=	1 Gallon
768 Teaspoons	=	1 Gallon
1 lb (water)*	=	16 Fluid Ounces
1 lb (water)*	=	1 Fluid Pint
2 lb (water)*	=	1 Fluid Quart

Figure A-12

Volume Conversions for Recipe Writing

	Teaspoon	Tablespoon	Quart	Cup
1 Teaspoon	1.0	0.333333	0.0052083	0.020833
1 Tablespoon	3.0	1.0	0.015625	0.062500
1 Cup	48.0	16.0	.25	1.0
1 Pint	96.0	32.0	.50	2.0
1 Quart	192.0	64.0	1.0	4.0
1 Gallon	768.0	256.0	4.0	16.0

Figure A-13

Common Measurements and Conversions

Weight	Volume (Fz)	Count (Ct)
grams	teaspoons	each
ounces	cups	slices
pounds	pints	can
	quarts	bottle
	gallons	leaves

Figure A-14

Pounds and Ounces to Grams

Ounces	To	Grams	Pounds	To	Grams
1		28.35	1		453.60
5		141.75	5		2268
10		283.50	10		4536
12		340.20	25		11340
16		453.60	50		22680

Figure A-15

Teaspoon and Tablespoon

Teaspoons			Tablespoons		
3 Teaspoons	=	0.5 Ounce	1 Tablespoon	=	3 Teaspoons
6 Teaspoons	=	1 Ounce	2 Tablespoons	=	1 Ounce
48 Teaspoons	=	1 Cup	4 Tablespoons	=	.25 Cup
96 Teaspoons	=	1 Pint	8 Tablespoons	=	.5 Cup
192 Teaspoons	=	1 Quart	16 Tablespoons	=	1 Cup
960 Teaspoons	=	5 Quarts	128 Tablespoons	=	.5 Gallon
768 Teaspoons	=	1 Gallon	256 Tablespoons	=	1 Gallon

Figure A-16

Metric Equivalents: Weights

1 Gram	0.3547 Wz	1 Wz	28.35 Grams
1 Kilogram	2.2046 Pounds	1 Pound	0.454 Kilograms
1 Metric Ton	1.1023 English	1 English Ton	0.9072 Tons
1 Kilogram	1000 Grams		

Figure A-17

Dry Measures

2 pints	1 quart	4 pecks	1 bushel
8 quarts	1 peck	36 bushels	1 chaldron
28.35 grams	1 WZ	8 WZ	.5 pound
226.80 grams	8 WZ	16 WZ	1 pound
453.60 grams	16 WZ		

Figure A-18

Liquid Measures

3 teaspoons	1 tablespoon	2 pints	1 quart
16 tablespoons	1 cup	4 quarts	1 gallon
2 cups	1 pint	31 ½ gallons	1 barrel
4 gills	1 pint	2 barrels	1 hogshed

Figure A-19

Other Equivalencies

1 pound	16 WZ
1 cup	8 FZ
1 pint	2 cups (16 FZ)
1 quart	2 pints (32 FZ)
1/2 gallon	2 quarts (64 FZ)
1 gallon	4 quarts (128 FZ)

Figure A-20

Avoirdupois

16 drams	1 WZ	112 pounds	1 long hundredweight (CWT)
16 ounces	1 pound	4 quarters	1 hundredweight
25 pounds	1 quarter	2000 pounds	1 short ton
100 pounds	1 short hundredweight (CWT)	2240 pounds	1 long ton

Figure A-21

Measure of Volume

1 Cu. Centimeter = 0.061 Cu. Inch	1 Cu. Inch = 16.39 Cu. Centimeters
1 Cu. Decimeter = 0.353 Cu. Foot	1 Cu. Foot = 28.317 Cu. Decimeters
1 Cu. Meter = 1.308 Cu. Yard	1 Cu. Yard = 0.7646 Cu. Meter
1 Ster = 0.2759 Cord	1 Cord = 3.642 Steres
1 Liter = 0.908 QuartDry	1 Quart Dry = 1.101 Liters
1 Liter = 1.0567 Quarts Liquid	1 Quart Liquid = 0.3785 Liter
1 Dekaliter = 2.6417 Gallons	1 Gallon = 0.3785 Dekaliter
1 Dekaliter = 0.135 Peck	1 Peck = 0.881 Dekaliter
1 Hektoliter = 2.8375 Bushels	1 Bushel = 3.524 Hektoliters

Figure A-22

Linear Measure

1 Centimeter = 0.3937 Inch	1 Inch = 2.54 Centimeters
1 Decimeter = 0.328 Feet	1 Foot = 3.048 Decimeters
1 Meter = 1.0936 Yards	1 Yard = 0.9144 Meter
1 Dekameter = 1.9884 Rods	1 Rod = 0.5029 Dekameter
1 Kilometer = 0.62137 Mile	1 Mile = 1.6093 Kilometers

Figure A-23

Square Measure

1 Sq. Centimeter = 0.1550 Sq. Inch	1 Sq. Inch = 6.452 Sq. Centimeters
1 Sq. Decimter = 0.1076 Sq. Inch	1 Sq. Foot = 9.2903 Sq. Decimeters
1 Sq. Meter = 1.196 Sq. Yards	1 Sq. Yard = 0.8361 Sq. Meter
1 Acre = 3.954 Sq. Rods	1sq. Rod = 0.2529 Acres
1 Hectare = 2.47 Acres	1 Acre = 0.4047 Hectare
1 Sq. Kilometer = 0.386 Sq. Mile	1 Sq. Mile = 2.59 Sq. Kilometers

Figure A-24

Fractional Equivalents for Use in Converting Recipes

The following chart is designed to help you change fractional parts of pounds, gallons, cups, etc., to accurate weights or measures. For example, reading from left to right, the table shows that 7/8 of a pound is 14 ounces, 1/3 of a gallon is 1 quart plus 1 1/3 cups, 1/16 of a cup is 1 tablespoon, and so on.

	1 Tablespoon	1 cup	1 pint	1 quart	1 gallon	1 pound
1	3 tsp.	16 TBL.	2 cups	2 pints	4 quarts	16 WZ
7/8	2 1/2 tsp.	1 cup less 2 TBL	1 2/3 cups	3 1/2 cups	3 quarts + 1 pint	14 WZ
3/4	2 1/4 tsp.	12 TBL.	1 1/2 cups	3 cups	3 quarts	12 WZ
2/3	2 tsp.	10 TBL. + 2 tsp.	1 1/3 cups	2 2/3 cups	2 quarts + 2 2/3 cups	10 2/3 WZ
5/8	2 tsp. (scant)	10 TBL.	1 1/4 cups	2 1/2 cups	2quarts + 1 pint	10 WZ
1/2	1 1/2 tsp.	8 TBL.	1 cup	2 cups	2 quarts	8 WZ
3/8	1 1/8 tsp.	6 TBL.	3/4 cup	1 1/2 cups	1 quart + 1 pint	6 WZ
1/3	1 tsp.	5 TBL. + 1 tsp.	2/3 cup	1 1/3 cups	1 quart + 1 1/3 cups	5 1/3 WZ
1/4	3/4 tsp.	4 TBL.	1/2 cup	1 cup	1 quart	4 WZ
1/8	1/2 tsp. (scant)	2 TBL.	1/4 cup	1/2 cup	1 pint	2 WZ
1/16	1/4 tsp. (scant)	1 TBL.	2 TBL.	4 TBL.	1 cup	1 WZ

Figure A-25

Food Portioning Aids

Hint: A pastry bag with tip may be used for portioning meringue for shells, filling cream puffs, stuffing eggs, and adding dressing to salads.

Item	Size	Use	Gram	Oz.	Tsp.	Tbsp.	Cup
Scoop	No. 100	Dainty cookies	10	0.35	2	2/3	1/48
	No. 70	Small drop cookies	11	1/8	2	2/3	1/48
	No. 60	Small drop cookies	15	1/2	3	1	1/16
	No. 40	Medium drop cookies	23	2/5	5	1 3/5	
	No. 30	Large drop cookies	28.35	1	6	2	1/8
	No. 24	Sandwich or cream puff pudding	38	1 1/2	8	2 2/3	
	No. 20	Sandwich fillings, salads, muffins, desserts	42	1 1/2	10	3 1/3	
	No. 16	Entrees, muffins, desserts	57	2	12	4	1/4
	No. 12	Entrees, salads, croquettes, vegetables	76	2 2/3	14	4 2/3	1/3
	No. 10	Meat patties, cereals, croquettes, vegetables	92	3 1/4	19 1/2	6 1/2	3/8
	No. 8	Meat patties and casserole dishes	114	4	24	8	1/2
	No. 6	Main dish salads	170	6	36	12	3/4

Figure A-26 (*continued on next page*)

Food Portioning Aids (*concluded*)

Item	Size	Use	Gram	Oz.	Tsp.	Tbsp.	Cup
Ladles	1FZ	Sauces, relishes	228.35	1	6	2	1/8
	2FZ	Gravy, sauces	57	2	12	4	1/4
	4 FZ	Creamed dishes and vegetables	114	4	24	8	1/2
	6 FZ	Stews, baked dishes, chili, creamed dishes, vegetables, soups, chili, stews	170	6	36	12	3/4
	8 WZ	Soups, chili, stews	227	8	48	16	1
	12 WZ	Large soups, goulash	340	12	72	24	1 1/2
	24 WZ	Kitchen dipper	681	24	144	48	3
	32 WZ	Quart dipper	907	32	192	64	4
Demiliter			496	17 1/2	105	35	2 1/16
Liter			1000	35.28	210	70	4 1/8
2 Quart			1990	64	384	128	8

Figure A-26

Critical Temperatures for Quality Control

Degrees Fahrenheit	Produces
212°	Water boils at sea level. Most resistant bacteria killed within 2 minutes.
195°	Water above this point sprayed from dish washing machine rinse nozzles vaporizes so readily that rinse action is reduced.
180°	Water at this temperature in rinse line of the dishwasher will give 170 F°—killing temperature—at utensil.
170°	Practically all common disease-producing bacteria killed at this temperature.
160°	Some foods start to cook on utensils here.
140°	Bacterial growth practically stopped. May die.
98.6°	Body temperature. Bacteria`s most rapid growth.
70°	Room temperature. Bacteria grow fast.
50°	Bacterial growth slowed greatly; almost stopped below this point.
45°–40°	Store fruits and vegetables.
37°–33°	Store dairy products.
36°–33°	Store meat and poultry.
32°	Freezing point of water. Practically no bacterial growth.
30°–23°	Store fish and shellfish.
10°–6°	Store ice cream.
0°–10°	Store frozen foods.

Figure A-27

Canned Goods Information

Canned Goods Overview

Some excellent reasons for using canned fruits and vegetables include the following:

- less expensive than fresh produce
- easy storage—no refrigeration required
- wide variety available all year
- no waste—everything in the can is edible
- little or no preparation required
- quantities needed easily calculated
- portion cost easily calculated
- immediately available in emergency

Are Canned Goods Less Nutritious Than Fresh?

The attention given to "freshness" by some gourmets and food writers have made many of us feel that we are doing something wrong when we use canned or frozen foods. Fresh local products certainly taste better and are nutritionally superior to preserved foods. But when the so-called "fresh" foods have actually been plucked before they are ripe, trucked thousands of miles to market, and perhaps stored for a time before you buy them, the advantage of "freshness" is extremely low. The fact is that canning and freezing, when done properly, preserve most of the vitamins, minerals, and flavor of the original. In addition, canning and freezing make it possible for you to have year-round variety in your daily diet, with plenty of fruits and vegetables, even in midwinter, at less cost than fresh ones flown in out of season from faraway places. We would face far greater troubles in feeding this nation and the world if it were not for modern methods of preserving foods.

Grades

The most important factor in considering canned goods is the grade, or quality. The different qualities of a product are the top qualities, the next-to-the-top qualities, and the lower qualities. The grade names used for expressing these qualities are the letters A, B, and C. The corresponding canning industry grade names are Fancy, Choice, Extra Standard, and Standard.

For some products, only two grades, A and B, have been developed. Peas and carrots are an example. Some products, such as asparagus and apples, do not have a B grade. Mostly, the grades run from A through C.

Grade A or Fancy: Excellent high-quality foods. Practically uniform in size, color, and texture. Practically free from defects. Grade A products are carefully selected as to size, color, texture, uniformity, and other qualities.

Grade B or Choice (for fruits) and Extra Standard (for vegetables): High-quality foods. Reasonably uniform in size, color, and texture. Reasonably free from defects. Vegetables are more mature, fruits less uniform.

Packing Media

Densities of syrups differ according to the fruit being canned. Some fruits, such as berries, can carry a very heavy syrup, while others, such as pears, would break down in a very heavy syrup. The density is measured by Brix instruments known as the Brix Hydrometer and/or refractometer, and is expressed in terms of degrees. For example: the cut-out density of syrup in choice peaches is expressed as "brix cut-out" 18 degrees or more but less than 22 degrees; 1 degree brix equals approximately 1 percent sugar by weight. The difference between in-going and cut out densities is due to the natural blending or equalization of the juice of the fruit and the syrup and also to the absorption of the sugar by the fruit after canning. An in-going syrup of 50 degrees will cut out 22 degrees or more. Such tests are always made 15 days or more after the product is canned. The following packing media are used:

- *Brine solution* is added to most vegetables. Brine solution may be water and small amounts of salt; or the solution may be water and small amounts of sugar and salt and be used for flavoring such products as peas and corn.

- *Natural juices* from the product are sometimes added. Pineapple and tomatoes are examples of foods to which natural juices from the product are added. Other natural fruit juices are added to special packs of fruit. These have lower sugar and sweetness than light syrup, but slightly more than water pack, and have far better palatability and are still acceptable for most sugar-controlled diets. "Solid pack" (SP) products have no liquid added, such as, preheated SP pie, peaches, or apricots. (These are regulated by federal law.)

- *Plain water* is used for "salt-controlled" dietetic packs of vegetables, for "reduced" or "low caloric" dietetic fruits, and for pie pack fruits.

Syrups are used almost entirely for fruits and/or sweet potatoes. Usually, the syrup density varies according to the grade; that is, the syrup with the greatest amount of sugar is used for the best grades and sugar content decreases with the grade. However, higher costs and a trend toward less sugar in the diet is leading to an ever-increasing amount of choice in light syrup or choice in juice fruits. Typically, the following applies:

Extra Heavy Syrup	Fancy Grade Fruit
Heavy Syrup	Choice Grade Fruit
Light Syrup	Standard Grade Fruit
Water	Dietetic Fruits and Vegetables; Pie Fruit

What Is "Drained Weight"?

Simply speaking, drained weight is the net weight of a portion of fruit or vegetable after the syrup, juice, or water is drained off for two minutes through a colander-like sieve. It is important to know the drained weight of a product packed in a liquid medium. Recommended minimum drained weights are included in the federal standards and are published in other sections of this guide.

How to Determine Drained Weights

For a No. 10 can of fruit or vegetables, use a circular sieve with vertical sides, 12 inches in diameter, with 8 meshes to the inch. For a No. 2 1/2 can (and smaller), use a sieve 8 inches in diameter, with 8 meshes to the inch. For tomatoes only use similar sieves, with 2 meshes to the inch. For all products, record the weight of the sieve. Set the sieve over the pan in an inclined position. Empty the contents of the can in the screen so as to distribute the contents evenly. Promptly weigh the screen with the contents inside. Subtract the weight of the empty screen; the difference is the drained weight of the product. If a screen of the foregoing type is not available, use a colander.

Containers

Containers normally are variously-sized cans that may be plain or enamel-lined on the inside. Tin cans are made of steel that has been coated inside and out with tin. Enamel linings may be yellow or gray in color and are used for foods that can cause an unfavorable reaction with tin. There are many types of enamel linings. One type is used for red-colored foods, such as beets and berries, in which the color tends to bleed out when in contact with tin; another type is used for foods containing sulphur, such as corn. These foods could discolor the inside of a plain can, and sometimes the food itself is discolored. A third type of can has an enamel liner inside with a strip of tin (approximately 1/16 inch) along the inside seam. This is called an HTF can (high tin fillet). This type is now used in canning asparagus.

Can Equivalents		
One #10 can	equals approximately	7/#300 cans
One #10 can	equals approximately	6/#303 cans
One #10 can	equals approximately	5/#2 cans
One #10 can	equals approximately	4/#2 1/2 cans
One #10 can	equals approximately	2 1/4/#3 Cyl. cans

Sizes: Counts

Size refers to sieve size, or girth of an item. Range of count refers to number of pieces in a can. The sizes of fruit are designated by the numerical count, according to the size of the can, for instance, 6/#10 Peaches, 30/35 count; or 6/#10 apricots, 86/108 count.

Sieve sizes and actual sizes are used to designate the sizes of vegetables: 5 Sv. peas; 4 Sv. beans; medium slices carrots; tiny whole beets; mammoth asparagus; medium olives, and so forth. In fruits, usually the larger the size, the higher the grade. In vegetables, the reverse is usually true: The larger the size, the lower the grade.

Fill of Container

Unless defined by Food and Drug regulations, the USDA grades recommend generally that cans be filled as full as practicable without impairment of quality, and that the product and packing medium occupy not less than 90 percent of the capacity of the can. For all practical purposes, this is determined by measuring the head space inside the can. Head space is measured from the top of the double seam down to the surface of the product in the can.

FDA regulations have defined the fill of container for only a few canned fruits and vegetables. Containers that fail to meet those requirements must be labeled "below standard in fill."

Maximum Gross Head-space Permitted to Avoid a Charge of Slack Filling

Can Size	Maximum Gross Headspace in Thirty-seconds of an Inch
No. 300	19
No. 303	19
No. 2	19
No. 2 1/2	20
No. 3 Cylinder	27
No. 10	27

Figure A-28

Common Can Sizes and Their Appropriate Contents

Can Size	Principal Products
No. 5 squat	
75 oz. Squat	
No. 10	Institution size-fruits, vegetables, and some other foods
No. 3 Cyl	Institution size-condensed soups, some vegetables; meat and poultry products; economy family-size fruit and vegetable juices
No. 2 1/2	Family size-fruits, some vegetables
No. 2	Family size-juices, ready-to-serve soups, and some fruits
No. 303	Small cans-fruits, vegetables, some meat and poultry products, and ready-to-serve soups
No. 300	Small cans-some fruits and meat products
No. 2 (vacuum)	Principally for vacuum pack corn
No. 1 (picnic)	Small cans-condensed soups, some fruits, vegetables, meat, and fish
8 oz.	Small cans-ready-to-serve soups, fruits, and vegetables
6 oz.	

Figure A-29

Common Can Sizes and Their Appropriate Weights and Volumes

*Volumes represent total water capacity of the can. Actual volume of the pack would depend upon the contents and the head space from the fluid level to the top of the can.

Can Size	Volume (WZ)	Average Fluid (FZ)	Average Cups	Cans per Case	Approx. Weight
75 Squat				6	4 LB 11 WZ
No. 5	56			6	4 LB 2 WZ
No. 10	105.1	99 to 117	12 to 13	6	6 LB 9 WZ
No. 3 Cyl.	49.6	51 or 46	5 3/4	12	46 FL. WZ
No. 2 1/2	28.55	27 to 29	3 1/2	24	12 WZ
No. 2	19.7	20 or 18	2 1/2	24	1 LB 13 WZ
No. 303	16.2	16 or 17	2	24 or 36	1 LB
No. 300	14.6	14 or 16	1 3/4	24	15 1/2 WZ
No. 2 (vacuum)		12	1 1/2	24	
No. 1		10 1/2 to 12	1 1/4	48	
8 oz.	8.3	8	1	48 or 72	8 WZ
6 oz.	5.8	6	3/4	48	6 WZ

Figure A-30

Can Equivalencies

Can Size	Equivalent
1 #10 Can	2 1/4 #3 Cyl.
	4 #2.5 Cans
	5 #2 Cans
	6 #303 Cans
	7 #300 Cans

Figure A-31

Spices/Seasoning Conversion
Measuring Equivalents

Teaspoons	Tablespoons	Fluid Ounces	Cups	Scoops	Fluid Measure
3	1	1/2			
6	2	1	1/8	30	
12	4	2	1/4	16	
15	5	2 1/2	1/3	12	
	6 2/3	3 1/2 to 4	2/5	10	
	8	4	1/2	8	
	10	5	2/3		
	12	6	3/4		
	14	7	7/8		
	16	8	1		1/2 pint
	18	9	1 1/8		
		12	1 1/2		3/4 pint
		16	2		
		24	3		1 1/2 pint
		32	4		1 quart
		64	8		2 quarts
		128	16		1 gallon

Figure A-32

Spice/Seasoning Conversions for Recipe Writing Ingredient Weights

Ingredient	Weight of 1 Teaspoon in a Decimal Part of a Pound
Allspice (ground)	0.0039164
Baking powder	0.0078085
Baking soda	0.0078085
Basil leaves	0.0013020
Bay leaves (whole—approx. 1361 leaves/pound)	0.0013020
Caraway seeds	0.0053232
Cayenne pepper	0.0035215
Celery seeds (whole)	0.0052083
Chili powder	0.0054766
Cinnamon (ground)	0.0047608
Cloves (ground)	0.0033952
Cloves (whole)	0.0044363
Cream of tartar	0.0083060
Cumin (ground)	0.0035216
Curry powder	0.0044363
Dill seed	0.0054659
Garlic powder	0.0032491
Ginger (ground)	0.0035213
Mace (ground)	0.0039160
Marjoram (ground)	0.0026041
MSG	0.0078085
Mustard (dry)	0.0032491
Nutmeg (ground)	0.0113928

Figure A-33 (*continued*)

Ingredient Weights (*concluded*)

Ingredient	Weight of 1 Teaspoon in a Decimal Part of a Pound
Onions (dehydrated)	0.0031243
Oregano (ground)	0.0031243
Paprika	0.0043767
Parsley Flakes (dehydrated)	0.0008680
Pepper, Black (ground)	0.0051772
Pepper, Black (whole)	0.0078085
Pepper, Red (crushed)	0.0047091
Pepper, White (ground)	0.0051162
Pickling Spices (whole)	0.0033952
Poppy Seed	0.0054659
Poultry Seasoning	0.0026041
Rosemary Leaves (whole)	0.0026041
Sage, Rubbed	0.0019580
Salt, Celery	0.0091214
Salt, Garlic	0.0092510
Salt, Onion	0.0087241
Salt, Table	0.0104166
Seafood Seasoning	0.0098085
Sesame Seeds (whole)	0.0052083
Sugar, Brown	0.0091214
Sugar, Confectionery (6x)	0.0047608
Sugar, Granulated	0.0091214
Tarragon Leaves (whole)	0.0013020
Thyme Leaf (whole)	0.0019580

Figure A-33 (*concluded*)

Spices and Their Conversions

Ingredient	Weight Ounce	Tablespoon	Teaspoon	Count
Allspice ground	1 WZ	4.725 TBSP	14.77 TSP	
Allspice whole	1 WZ	6 TBSP	18 TSP	
Anise Seed	1 WZ	4.231	12.69 TSP	
Arrowroot	1 WZ	4 TBSP	12 TSP	
Baking Powder	1 WZ	2.667 TBSP	8 TSP	
Baking Soda	1 WZ	2.667 TBSP	8 TSP	
Basil Leaves	1 WZ	15.873 TBSP	47.619 TSP	
Basil grd	1WZ	6.3 TBSP	18.9 TSP	
Bay Leaves crm	1 WZ	15.75 TBSP	47.25 TSP	
Bay Leaf whl	1 WZ	142.85 EA		
Capers whl	1 WZ	2.667 TBSP	8.001 TSP	10–15 TSP
Caraway Seed grd	1 WZ	5.319 TBSP	15.957 TSP	
Caraway Seed whl	1 WZ	4.232 TBSP	12.696 TSP	
Cardamom Seed grd	1 WZ	4.890 TBSP	14.67 TSP	
Cassia Buds	1 WZ	4 TBSP	12.048 TSP	
Celery Flakes drd	1 WZ	21.33 TBSP	64 TSP	
Celery Salt	1 WZ	3 TBSP	9 TSP	
Celery Seed grd	1 WZ	7 TBSP	21 TSP	
Celery Seed whl	1 WZ	4.363 TBSP	13.089 TSP	
Chervil drd	1 WZ	15.873 TBSP	47.619 TSP	
Chili Powder	1 WZ	4.016 TBSP	12.048 TSP	
Chinese 5 Spice				
Chives freeze drd	1 WZ	6.4 TBSP	19.2 TSP	
Cinnamon grd	1 WZ	4.169 TBSP	12.50 TSP	
Cinnamon sticks	1 WZ	5 sticks		
Cloves grd	1 WZ	4.296 TBSP	12.885 TSP	
Cloves whl	1 WZ	90 CT		
Cocoa	1 WZ	4 TBSP	12 TSP	

Figure A-34 (*continued*)

Spices and Their Conversions (*continued*)

Ingredient	Weight Ounce	Tablespoon	Teaspoon	Count
Coriander Seed	1 WZ	5.670 TBSP	17.01 TSP	
Corn Meal	1 WZ	3 TBSP	9 TSP	
Cornstarch	1 WZ	13.545 TSP		
Cream of Tartar	1 WZ	3.003 TBSP	9.009 TSP	
Cumin grd	1 WZ	4 TBSP	12 TSP	
Cumin seed	1 WZ	4.975 TBSP	14.925 TSP	
Curry Powder	1 WZ	4.566 TBSP	13.698 TSP	
Dill seed	1 WZ	4.295 TBSP	12.885 TSP	
Dill Weed	1 WZ	9.146 TBSP	27.438 TSP	
Fennel Seed	1 WZ	4.89 TBSP	14.67 TSP	
Fenugreek Seed	1 WZ	2.554 TBSP	7.662 TSP	
Gumbo File	1 WZ	7 TBSP	21 TSP	
Garlic Granulated	1 WZ	2.5 TBSP	7.5 TSP	
Garlic Powder	1 WZ	3.375 TBSP	10.125 TSP	8 Cloves
Garlic Powder	1 WZ	2.5 TBSP	7.5 TSP	
Ginger, candied	1 WZ	2 TBSP	6 TSP	
Ginger crystals	1 WZ	2.667 TBSP	8.001 TSP	
Ginger grd	1 WZ	5.250 TBSP	15.75 TSP	
Horseradish	1 WZ	2 TBSP	6 TSP	
Italian Seasoning	1 WZ			
Leeks fr drd	1 WZ	142.86 TBSP	428.58 TSP	
Mace grd	1 WZ	5.349 TBSP	16.047 TSP	
Marjoram drd	1 WZ	16.677 TBSP	50.031 TSP	
Monosodium Glut.	1 WZ	1.89 TBSP	5.67 TSP	
Mustard creole	1 WZ	2 TBSP	6 TSP	
Mustard grd	1 WZ	4.050 TBSP	12.15 TSP	
Mustard seed	1 WZ	2.532 TBSP	7.596 TSP	

Figure A-34 (*continued on next page*)

Spices and Their Conversions (*continued*)

Ingredient	Weight Ounce	Tablespoon	Teaspoon	Count
Mustard prepared	1 WZ	2 TBSP	6 TSP	
Nutmeg grd	1 WZ	4.050 TBSP	12.15 TSP	
Onions Dehydrated	1 WZ	5.672 TBSP	17.016 TSP	
Onion Salt	1 WZ	2 TBSP	6 TSP	
Onion Powder	1 WZ	4.362 TBSP	13.086 TSP	
Oregano grd	1 WZ	6.300 TBSP	18.9 TSP	
Oregano whl	1 WZ	16 TBSP	48 TSP	
Paprika	1 WZ	4.109 TBSP	12.327 TSP	
Parsley Flakes drd	1 WZ	21.810 TBSP	65.43 TSP	
Parsley Flakes fr drd	1 WZ	70.921 TBSP	212.763 TSP	
Pepper black	1 WZ	4.430 TBSP	13.29 TSP	
Pepper grd	1 WZ	3.20 TBSP	9.6 TSP	
Pepper whl	1 WZ	5.349 TBSP	16.047 TSP	
Pepper cayenne grd	1 WZ	4.83 TBSP	14.49 TSP	
Pepper green	1 WZ	12 TBSP	36 TSP	
Pepper green glks	1 WZ	60 Per Portion		
Pepper lemon	1 WZ	6 TBSP	18 TSP	
Pepper red cruched	1 WZ	4.667 TBSP	14 TSP	
Pepper white	1 WZ	3.993 TBSP	11.979 TSP	
Pepper white grd	1 WZ	3.20 TBSP	9.60 TSP	
Peppercorns whl blk	1 WZ	6 TBSP	18 TSP	90
Peppercorns green	1 WZ			
Poppy Seed	1 WZ	3.222 TBSP	9.666 TSP	
Poultry Seasoning grd	1 WZ	7.662 TBSP	22.986 TSP	
Poultry Seasoning whl	1 WZ	8 TBSP	24 TSP	

Figure A-34 (*continued*)

Spices and Their Conversions (*concluded*)

Ingredient	Weight Ounce	Tablespoon	Teaspoon	Count
Pumpkin Pie	1 WZ	5.062 TBSP	15.186 TSP	
Rosemary dried	1 WZ	8.591 TBSP	25.707 TSP	
Saffron	1 WZ	13.514 TBSP	9.6 TSP	
Sage grd	1 WZ	14.184 TBSP	42.5 TSP	
Sage grd fine	1 WZ	8 TBSP	24 TSP	
Sage rubbed	1 WZ	12 TBSP	36 TSP	
Sage rubbed pkd	1 WZ	8 TBSP	24 TSP	
Sage whl	1 WZ	16 TBSP	48 TSP	
Salad Herbs	1 WZ	12 TBSP	36 TSP	
Salt	1 WZ	2 TBSP	6 TSP	
Salt Seasoned	1 WZ	1.667 TBSP	5.001 TSP	
Salt and Pepper Mix	1 WZ	1.667 TBSP	5.001 TSP	
Sausage Seasoning	1 WZ	5 TBSP	15 TSP	
Savory grd	1 WZ	6.443 TBSP	19.329 TSP	
Savory whl	1 WZ	12 TBSP	36 TSP	
Sesame Seeds	1 WZ	3.544 TBSP	10.63 TSP	
Tarragon leaf	1 WZ	16 TBSP	48 TSP	
Tarragon grd	1 WZ	5.907 TBSP	17.721 TSP	
Thyme leaf	1 WZ	8 TBSP	24 TSP	
Thyme grd	1 WZ	6.593 TBSP	19.779 TSP	
Tumeric	1 WZ	3.334 TBSP	10.002 TSP	

Figure A-34 (*concluded*)

Meat/Seafood Prep Yields

Meat Prep Yields: Raw, Trimmed, and Cooked

Description in Pounds	Best Weight Raw Trimmed	Prep Yield Cooked (%)	Prep Yield (%)
PORK			
Ham boneless (skin removed)	7	98	71
Ham shank (half bone in)	10 to 14	60	57
Loin (bone in whole)	14 to 17	70	54
Loin (boneless whole)	8	95	74
Ham butt (half bone in)	5 to 8	63	42
Shoulder picnic (bone in)	12	77	39
Sausage	10	48	
Spareribs	58	48	
Liver	92	66	
Heart	93	57	
Tongue	65	50	
CHICKEN			
Chicken (whole)	78	51	
Breast (skin on)	74	63	
Breast (skinless)	65	46	
Drumsticks	42		
Tights	45		
Heart	58		
Liver	57		
TURKEY			
Turkey (whole)	84	61	
Neck and Giblets	77	50	
Breast (quarters)	75	48	
Breast (whole)	87	55	
Leg (quarters)	75	45	
BEEF			
Flank steak	2 to 2 1/2	94.5	75
Gooseneck bottom round	26 to 29	78	65

Figure A-35 (*continued*)

Meat Prep Yields: Raw, Trimmed, and Cooked (*concluded*)

Description in Pounds	Best Weight Raw Trimmed	Prep Yield Cooked (%)	Prep Yield (%)
Hamburger	10	80	
Blade meat	2 1/2	95	
Brisket	10 to 12	71	52
Chuck roll	13 to 15	85	68
Chuck shoulder clod	16	70	53.5
Eye round	5 to 6	88	84
Fillet tips	6 to 7	90	76
Knuckle	80	58	
Rib eye roll	96	81	
Rib (oven ready boneless)	98	56	
Rib (oven ready bone in)	96	81	
Sirloin butt top	65		
Strip lean boneless	87.5	75	
Tenderloin fillet	83	80	
Top round	93	77	
Tongue	78	56	
Liver	93	89	
Heart	72	54	
LAMB			
Ground	68		
Leg (bone in)	45		
Leg (boneless)	70		
Shoulder (bone in)	57		
Shoulder (boneless)	73		
VEAL			
Ground	65		
Leg (cutlets boneless)	70		
Leg (bone in)	49		
Leg (boneless)	60		

Figure A-35 (*concluded*)

Seafood Prep Yields

Description	Prep Yield (%)	Description	Prep Yield (%)
Bass	40	Lobster (New England-American)	25
Bluefish	52	Lobster (spiny-tails only)	46
Catfish	95.4	Mackerel	54
Corvina	94	Mahi	94
Calms (breaded fried)	85	Mahi (head on)	55–60
Clams (hard)	14	Mahi (head off)	78.5
Clams (soft)	29	Monk	85
Clams (sucked)	48	N-T King	65–68
Cod	31	Ohi	92
Crab (blue)	10–18	Ono	95
Crabcakes (fried)	95	Opaka (whole)	92.5
Crab (dungeness)	22–26	Oysters	40
Crabmeat	97	Oysters (breaded raw)	88
Fish fillets (species variation)	64	Oysters (whole)	100
Flounder	40	Petrale	98
Gulf (fillet)	88	Perch	36
Gulf (whole)	46	Sole	72
Haddock	48	Pinobass	93.5
Halibut (fillet)	97	Pollock	45
Halibut (small 40–60 lbs)	50–60	Pompario	52
Halibut (large 80–120 lbs)	65–67	Redfillet	93.5
Halibut (whole)	59	Red (whole)	61
Ling Cod	96	Roughy	92.5
Lobster (cooked in shell)	25	Salmon	65–75
Salmon (fillet)	94–96	Spear	92.5
Salmon (large king whole)	61–64	Steel Head Salmon	52–60
Scallops (breaded fried)	90	Sword	94.2
Scallops (raw)	81	Trout	90
Scrod	94	White Sea Bass	96
Shark	96	Y-Tail (fillet)	95.2
Shark (skin on)	91	Y-Tail (whole)	62
Snapper	94		

Figure A-36

Produce Prep Yields

Description	Packing Size	Prep Yield	Avg. Weight per Case	Avg. Counts per Pound
Apples (peeled & cored)	Box 113	70–76	37–40	3
Asparagus	Pound	49–56	1	10–20
Avocados	1 lyr ctrn tray pack	60–75	13–14	2 med
Avocados	36–40 ct	60–75	19	2 med
Banana	Ctns	68	40	3
Beans (green or wax)	bu wbd crts	86	26–36	
Beans (in pod)	39			
Beets	wbd crt 24 bchs	76	36–40	
Berries	12 1/2 pts	93	5 1/2–7 1/2	
Blueberries	12 pt trays	84–92	11–12	
Broccoli	18 bunches	42–62	40–42	1 = 1.25 lbs
Broccoli	14 bunches	42–62	20–23	1 = 1.25 lbs
Brussel Sprouts	ctns wax treated loose pk	74–77	25	
Cabbage (green)	24 heads	79	50–55	1 = 1.25 lbs
Cantaloupe	9, 12, 18, 23 ct	50–60	38–41	1 med
Cantaloupe	18, 24, 30 ct	50–60	53–55	
Carrot (stick 3")	100	150/#		
Carrot (w/o tops)	50 bag	75–92	50	
Carrot (bchd)	ctn 2 doz bchs	82	23–27	
Cauliflower (trimmed)	12–16 head film wrpd	95	23	
Cauliflower (untrimmed)	Long Island type crt	31–45	45–50	1 med
Celery (stick 3")	100	150/#		
Celery (whole)	24 stacks	71–75	55–65	1 = 2 lbs
Celery (bchd)	flat wbd crt	70	55–60	
Celery hearts	12 film bagt in crt	95	24–28	
Chard	77			
Cherries (pitted)	cnts	79–89	16–20	
Coconuts	burlap bag 40–50	45	75–80	
Corn (sweet on the cob)	wbd crt 54–66 ct	40	40–60	
Crenshaw	flat crt	35–50		
Cucumber (pared)	ctns place pk or LA lug 24 ct	92	30	
Cucumber (unpared)	72–73	30	1.5 med	
Dates (fresh)	45			

Figure A-37 (*continued on next page*)

Produce Prep Yields (*continued*)

Description	Packing Size	Prep Yield	Avg. Weight per Case	Avg. Counts per Pound
Eggplant	bu bskt or ctn	75	30–34	
Endive	ctns 8 wbd crt 24 pk	74–75	35–40	1 = 1.6 lbs
Garlic	telescope ctns loose pk	81	30	15 pods
Grapefruit (sectioned)	cs = 36 ct	47–48	34–36	1
Grapes (red seedless)	lug or ctn	96	24–28	91
Grapes (white seedless)	lug 16,22,24 wrpd bchs	96	22	85
Honeydew	flat crt 12 ct	56–60	28–32	1 = 2.5 lbs
Kale	18–25 lb bchs p/ct	74–81	20.5	
Leeks	12 bch p/ct	50	25–30	12–25 p/bch
Lemon (115 ct slices)	37–40 lb ctn	80	38	3–4
Lemon (115 ct wedges)	37–40 lb ctn	98	38	3–4
Lemon (juiced)	37–40 lb ctn	43		
Lettuce (boston)	eastern ctr 1 1/9 bu wbd	74	20–25	
Lettuce (iceberg)	cs = 24 heads	69–74	40–45	1
Lettuce (romaine)	cs = 24 heads	74	23	
Lime (wedges)	cs = 200 ct	98	40–41	
Lime (juice)	box or ctn	43	40–41	
Mushrooms (large whl)	cs = 10	97	10	25
Nectarines	slanger lug 22 lyr ctn	76	19–22	
Okra	ctn or LA lug loose pk	78–96	18	
Onion (green)	ctns 4 dy bchs	60	15–18	11/bch
Onion (mature)	cs = 5 0 lbs	76–89	50	2 med
Orange (sectioned)	80, 88, 100, 113	56–57	45	
Orange (juice)	50	45		
Parsley	ctn 5 doz	76	21–25	30/bu
Parsnip	1/2 bu or ctns	84–85	25	
Peaches	LA lug 2 layer	76	22–29	
Pears	LA lug	67–78	25	
Peas (green in shell)	bu bskt hmpr or wbd bu	27–38	28–30	
Pepper (green)	ctns from Calif	78–82	30	
Peppers (chili)	LA lug or ctn is pk	16–25		
Peppers (sweet)	ctn	80	28–34	
Pineapple	1 lyr flt 4, 5, 6	48–52	18–20	

Figure A-37 (*continued*)

Produce Prep Yields (*concluded*)

Description	Packing Size	Prep Yield	Avg. Weight per Case	Avg. Counts per Pound
Plums	93–94			
Potatoes	sack or ctn	76–85	100/50	
Potatoes (sweet)	bu bskt or ctn	75–81	50	
Radish (bchd)	ctn or crt 4–5 doz bags	63	30–40	
Radish (topped)	film bag bulk	90	20	
Rhubarb (leaf off)	ctns place pack	86	20	
Rutabagas	film bags Calif	82	25	
Spinach (untrimmed)	bu bskt or crt	72	18–25	
Spinach (cello pkd)	film bag 12/10 dz	92	7.5–8	
Squash (acorn peeled)	66			
Squash (acorn seeded)	88			
Squash (hubbard)	62			
Squash (small)	1–1/9 bu wbd ctn	83	44	
Squash (summer)	bu bskt or ctn	83–98	40–45	
Squash (Zucchini)	83–98			
Strawberries	12/1 pint	84–87	11–14	24
Tangerines	Calif ctn and lug	23–30		
Tangerines	fla 4–5 bu wbd ct	45		
Tomatoes	ctn or wbd ct	86–91	24–33	3
Tomatoes (5X6)	flats ctns 2 lyr	86–91	30–33	3
Tomatoes	LA lug	86–91	30–34	3
Tomatoes (cherry)	12 basket or crt	100	12–17	400 p/cs
Turnips		81		
Watermelon		36–46		

Abbreviations

bchd	=	bunched	oz	=	ounce
bskt	=	basket	pk	=	pack
bu	=	bushel	pkg	=	package
crt	=	crate	pt	=	pint
ctn	=	carton	sk	=	sack
contr	=	container	std	=	standard
hmpr	=	hamper	var	=	various
lb(s)	=	pound(s)	wbd	=	wirebound
lyr	=	layer	wrpd	=	wrapped

Figure A-37 (*concluded*)

Internal Audit Checklist: Minimum Cost Control

REVIEWED and APPROVED: DATE:

	COST CONTROL FUNCTIONS	YES	NO	COMMENTS
1	CONTROL 1 MARKET BASKET SURVEY ANALYSIS. 1. Are market basket analyses on file? For how many months?			
	2. Are copies of related invoices on file? For how many months?			
	3. Is overall weighted average percentage increase in price computed? Over what period of time?			
	4. How many items have been surveyed each month?			
	5. How many of the total items are high-cost entree or specialty items? What percent of total?			
	6. Are the controller, food and beverage director, and chef on the distribution list?			
2	CONTROL 2 WEEKLY AUDIT OF RECEIVING PROCEDURES. 1. Are audits of receiving dock procedures on file? For how many months?			

	2. Are they performed:
	  a. Weekly?
	  b. Biweekly?
	  c. Monthly?			

	3. Is there evidence that discrepancies are reconciled?			
	4. Are the controller, food and beverage director, and chef on the distribution list?			
3	CONTROL 3 MEAT TAG SYSTEM and WEEKLY AUDIT. 1. Is a meat tag system in place? 2. Are there duplicate or triplicate tags?			

	3. Are tags audited and reconciled?
	  a. Weekly?
	  b. Biweekly?
	  c. Monthly?			

	4. Is there evidence that discrepancies are reconciled?			
	5. Are the controller and chef on the distribution list?			

Figure A-38 (*continued*)

Internal Audit Checklist: Minimum Cost Control (*continued*)

	COST CONTROL FUNCTIONS	YES	NO	COMMENTS
4	CONTROL 4 MENU ENTREE ITEMS INVENTORY CONTROL. 1. Are menu entrée items inventory control sheets being used?			

	2. Are results reconciled to sales tallies per
	  a. POS?
	  b. Guest checks?			

	3. Is there evidence that discrepancies are reconciled?			
	4. Are the chef and food and beverage director on the distribution list?			

5	CONTROL 5
	BANQUET BEVERAGE CONTROL AUDITS
	1. Are banquet beverage control sheets being completed?
	  a. All?
	  b. Using 80/20 methods?			

	2. Sample three for material accuracy of all calculations:
	    Function # of Errors:
	    Banquet # Date + or − 5%
	--- 	
	--- 	
	--- 				

	3. Are they consolidated at month-end to compute banquet beverage cost percentages?			

	4. Is there evidence that on-site audits of large functions are being done? How often?
	  a. Three times weekly?
	  b. Weekly?
	  c. Biweekly?
	  d. Monthly?			

	5. Are the chef and food and beverage director on the distribution list?			
6	CONTROL 6 BEVERAGE OUTLET AUDITS 1. Are beverage outlet audits being done?			

	2. For which outlets?
	OUTLET Most Recent Date
	  a.
	  b.
	  c.
	  d.
	  e.			

Figure A-38 (*continued on next page*)

Internal Audit Checklist: Minimum Cost Control (*continued*)

	COST CONTROL FUNCTIONS	YES	NO	COMMENTS
	3. How often are they done? a. Twice weekly? b. Weekly? c. Biweekly? d. Monthly?			
	4. Is there evidence that discrepancies are being reconciled?			
7	CONTROL 7a FOOD POTENTIAL COSTS 1. Are butcher / yield tests on file?			
	2. How many different tests?			
	3. Are they current? What are oldest and most recent dates?			
	4. Are written food recipes on file? Are they current ?/Date a. b. c. d. e.			
	5. Are food potential costs on file? For which outlets / meal periods? Meal Period Date? All? a. b. c. d. e. f.			
	6. Is there a master food item cost list? Has it been updated recently? When?			
	7. Are food recipes costed with current cost data from the master item list?			
	8. How recently? Sample three recipes for consistency. Recipe's Name Costed Correctly Updated a. b. c.			
	9. Do appropriate entree item recipes reflect impact of butcher/yield test factors on their costs? Sample three: Recipes Cost Cost per name per recipe Yield Test a. b. c.			

Figure A-38 (*continued*)

Internal Audit Checklist: Minimum Cost Control (*concluded*)

COST CONTROL FUNCTIONS	YES	NO	COMMENTS
10. Have individual food menu item cost calculations been consolidated to compute meal period and overall outlets food cost potential percentages?			
11. Are overall potential food cost percentages within 1.5 points of actual? Sample last three months: Month Potential Actual a: b: c: d: e:			
CONTROL 7b. BEVERAGE POTENTIAL COSTS 1. What liquor pour size is being used? 1 1/8 oz?			
2. Are written beverage recipes on file?			
3. Do these recipes reflect the liquor pour size *actually* used by all the outlets? Yes No a. _____ _____ b. _____ _____ c. _____ _____			
4. Is there a master beverage items cost list?			
5. Is it updated daily by purchasing department? Inventory Item Cost			
6. Have individual menu item beverage cost calculations been consolidated with the actual cost data for bottle wine sales to compute the overall outlet beverage cost potential percentages?			
7. Is overall beverage cost potential percentages within 1.0 points of actual? Sample last three months month potential actual a. b. c.			
8. Are popularity analyses being done?			
9. Are profitability analyses being done?			
10. Is profit margin being calculated for each item before and after the cost of preparation labor			
11. Is there a staffing guide in place?			

Figure A-38 Internal Audit Checklist: Minimum Cost Control (*concluded*)

Self-Inspection Checklist

This is a sample self-inspection checklist. A potential customer, an income auditor, or any person with a vested interest may ask these questions. The cornerstone of any successful business is to anticipate problems and address them. Certainly you can design these questions differently to meet your company's needs. Regular inspection with checklist in hand is the best way to ensure maintenance of your company quality standards. Remember, if there are deficiencies in any of these areas, they may translate to negative responses on your Guest Survey. See Figure A-39 for an example.

Loading Dock

Loading Dock, General			
Yes	**No**	**Inspected**	**Frequency**
☐	☐	Is grease container and surrounding area free from spills and particles of food? Comments:	daily
☐	☐	Is trash compactor free of food particles and litter outside dumpster? Comments:	daily
☐	☐	Are dock walls clear of trash or garbage which is due to the dumpster being full? Comments:	daily
☐	☐	Are lights in proper working order? Comments:	daily
☐	☐	Are wooden pallets stacked neatly? Comments:	daily
☐	☐	Is dock floor swept, on both upper and lower levels? Comments:	daily
☐	☐	Are storage facilities for supplies and equipment clean, dry and free of trash, debris, wrappings, and cartons, which might provide nesting for rodents? Comments:	weekly

Figure A-39 Self-Inspection Checklist (*continued*)

		Loading Dock, General (*continued*)	
Yes	**No**	**Inspected**	**Frequency**
☐	☐	Are supplies stored in a neat and orderly manner? Comments:	as needed
☐	☐	Are supplies stored off the floor and away from walls to permit access for cleaning and to prevent harboring ofrodents and roaches? Comments:	daily
☐	☐	Are containers of pesticides in a marked cabinet and apart from detergents and other chemicals? Comments:	daily

		Loading Dock, Safety	
Yes	**No**	**Inspected**	**Frequency**
☐	☐	Are emergency exits marked by illuminated signs? Comments:	daily
☐	☐	Is there a first-aid kit present or nearby, with an adequate supply of materials? Comments:	weekly
☐	☐	Have employees been instructed to report all slips, cuts, burns, and falls to their supervisor immediately? Comments:	daily
☐	☐	Is the edge of dock floor clearly marked or painted in a bright, prominent color to prevent falls? Comments:	daily
☐	☐	Are stairs leading down marked with non-slip tape to prevent falls? Comments:	daily

Figure A-39 Self-Inspection Checklist (*continued on next page*)

Yes	No	Inspected	Frequency
	**Loading Dock, Safety (*continued*)**		
☐	☐	Is the loading dock bell working and used for all receiving? Comments:	
☐	☐	Are loading-dock areas hazardous in other ways? Suggest safety improvements. Comments:	as needed

General Comments: _____

_____

_____

_____

_____

_____

Inspected By: _____

Date: _____

Food and Beverage Outlets

Yes	No	Inspected	Frequency
	**Employee Cafeteria, General**		
☐	☐	Is there adequate stock of CO_2 gas for soda machines? Comments:	daily
☐	☐	Are hot-line vent hood and walls clean and dust-free? Comments:	weekly
☐	☐	Are ceiling vents in dining area clean and dust-free? Comments:	monthly

Figure A-39 Self-Inspection Checklist (*continued*)

Employee Cafeteria, General (*continued*)			
Yes	No	Inspected	Frequency
☐	☐	Are light fixtures, bulbs, tubes, etc., protected with screen guards? Comments:	as needed
☐	☐	Are hot-line counter top and shelves clean and free of dust? Comments:	daily
☐	☐	Are hot-line floor mats clean? Comments:	daily
☐	☐	Is microwave clean and in good working condition? Comments:	daily
☐	☐	Is soda machine in good working condition? Comments:	daily/as needed
☐	☐	Are there adequate supplies of sodas? Comments:	daily
☐	☐	Are cutting boards cleaned and sanitized between uses? Comments:	as needed
☐	☐	Are coolers and freezers equipped with accurate thermometers? Comments:	weekly
☐	☐	Are refrigerators clean and free from mold and objectionable odors? Comments:	daily
☐	☐	Are potentially hazardous foods maintained by refrigerators at temperatures of 45° F or lower? Comments:	daily

Figure A-39 Self-Inspection Checklist (*continued on next page*)

		Employee Cafeteria, General (*continued*)	
Yes	**No**	**Inspected**	**Frequency**
☐	☐	Are foods stored in a manner to permit First-in, First-out rotation? Comments:	daily
☐	☐	Is salad bar properly used (plug in drain, ice and water in contact with bottom of pans) to maintain 38–40° F product temperature? Comments:	daily
☐	☐	Is ice-machine vent hood free of dust and dirt? Comments:	monthly
☐	☐	Are tea and coffee machines sanitized on a regular basis? Comments:	daily
☐	☐	Are coffee-counter top and shelves clean and free of dust and debris? Comments:	daily
☐	☐	Are food handlers wearing hats, caps or hairnets effective hair restraints? Comments:	daily
☐	☐	Do any food servers have infected burns, cuts, or boils? Comments:	daily
☐	☐	Are food servers issuing proper food portions? Comments:	daily
☐	☐	Is tray-counter underside clean and free of grease? Comments:	weekly

Figure A-39 Self-Inspection Checklist (*continued*)

		Employee Cafeteria, General (*continued*)	
Yes	**No**	**Inspected**	**Frequency**
☐	☐	Are silverware and serving utensils stored and presented in a manner which both prevents contamination and ensures their being picked up by the handles? Comments:	daily
☐	☐	Are clean and sanitary cloths used for wiping dining-table tops and for no other purpose? Are cloths stored in sanitizing solution between uses? Comments:	daily
☐	☐	Are facilities for supplies and equipment clean, dry and free of trash and debris? Comments:	daily
☐	☐	Is trash container clean outside and inside with liner in place? Is it washed down regularly? Comments:	as needed
☐	☐	Is dining-room hand sink supplied with soap, paper towels, hot and cold running water, and trash can? Comments:	daily
☐	☐	Are drains clean and odor-free? Comments:	bi-monthly
☐	☐	Are all food products maintained at proper temperatures (such as soup, tuna salad, potato salad)? Comments:	daily
☐	☐	Have all employees been instructed on minimum sanitation and food-protection requirements? Comments:	as needed

Figure A-39 Self-Inspection Checklist (*continued on next page*)

		Employees Cafeteria, Safety	
Yes	**No**	**Inspected**	**Frequency**
☐	☐	Are smoking and non-smoking signs posted in dining area? Comments:	daily
☐	☐	Are emergency-exit doors marked by illuminated signs? Comments:	daily
☐	☐	Is there a fire extinguisher present, properly mounted and in view? Comments:	daily
☐	☐	Do employees know how to use fire extinguisher in case of emergency? Comments:	as needed
☐	☐	Is there an evacuation map posted in case of emergency? Comments:	daily
☐	☐	Is all electrical food-preparation equipment in good repair and performing satisfactorily? Comments:	daily
☐	☐	Do employees know how to use equipment that is required in their positions? Comments:	as needed
☐	☐	Do employees unplug equipment before removing parts or before cleaning? Comments:	daily
☐	☐	In case of choking or heart trouble, has the supervisor been instructed in CPR and first aid? Comments:	as needed

Figure A-39 Self-Inspection Checklist (*continued*)

		Employees Cafeteria, Safety (*continued*)	
Yes	**No**	**Inspected**	**Frequency**
☐	☐	Is the cafeteria otherwise potentially hazardous? Suggest improvements. Comments:	daily

General Comments: _____

_____

_____

_____

_____

_____

Inspected By: _____

Date: _____

		Dish Washing Area	
Yes	**No**	**Inspected**	**Frequency**
☐	☐	Are dishes and utensils being pre-scraped and flushed prior to washing? Comments:	daily
☐	☐	Is rinse temperature of at least 170–180° F being maintained for tableware and utensils? Comments:	daily
☐	☐	Are floor and walls free of spills and particles of food? Comments:	daily
☐	☐	Are soaps and detergents stored away from clean china, glass and utensils? Comments:	as needed
☐	☐	Is spray hose free of leaks to prevent back-flow? Comments:	daily

Figure A-39 Self-Inspection Checklist (*continued on next page*)

Dish Washing Area (*continued*)			
Yes	**No**	**Inspected**	**Frequency**
☐	☐	Is garbage disposal in satisfactory working order? Comments:	daily
☐	☐	Are undersides of drain board clean and free of food particles? Comments:	weekly
☐	☐	Is trash can odor-free, provided with a liner, and clean? You may wish to use a clear liner to see what has been wasted. Comments:	daily
☐	☐	Are ceiling tiles and vents free of food and dust particles? Comments:	quarterly
☐	☐	Are ceiling lights in proper working condition? Comments:	as needed
☐	☐	Is there sufficient supply of soap, towels, garbage bins and hot and cold running water for hand sink? Comments:	as needed
☐	☐	Are there bins provided for dirty and clean rags? Comments:	daily
☐	☐	Is silver-burnishing machine in proper working condition? Comments:	daily

Figure A-39 Self-Inspection Checklist (*continued*)

		Dish Washing Area (*continued*)	
Yes	**No**	**Inspected**	**Frequency**
☐	☐	Is silver-sink electric water heater in proper working condition? Comments:	daily
☐	☐	Is silver room clean and organized and equipment off floor? Comments:	daily
☐	☐	Is storage-room mop sink clean, odor-free and organized? Comments:	daily/as needed
☐	☐	Is counter, top and bottom, clear of food and spills? Comments:	daily
☐	☐	Are jets and nozzles cleaned of food particles and de-limed? Comments:	daily/ monthly
☐	☐	Are pots stored upside down and utensil handles stored facing one direction? Comments:	daily
☐	☐	Are glass racks stored at least 6 inches off floor? Comments:	daily
☐	☐	Is hand sink supplied with soap, paper towels, hot and cold running water, and trash can? Comments:	daily/as needed
☐	☐	Is reach-in cooler clean and neat? Comments:	weekly/as needed

Figure A-39 Self-Inspection Checklist (*continued on next page*)

Dish Washing Area (*continued*)			
Yes	**No**	**Inspected**	**Frequency**
☐	☐	Are espresso, coffee and tea machines operational and clean? Comments:	daily

General Comments: _____
_____
_____
_____
_____
_____

Inspected By: _____
Date: _____

Outlets, General			
Yes	**No**	**Inspected**	**Frequency**
☐	☐	Is top of ice machine free of objects and door rim free of mold, and is there an ice scoop present? Comments:	daily/ as needed
☐	☐	Is floor underneath ice machine clean? Are vent hood above and side and back walls next to machine also clean? Comments:	daily
☐	☐	Are all trash cans clean inside and out with clear plastic liners? Comments:	daily

Figure A-39 Self-Inspection Checklist (*continued*)

		Walk-in Coolers	
Yes	**No**	**Inspected**	**Frequency**
☐	☐	Is temperature in cooler at or below 45° F (check outside thermometer and compare with thermometer inside)? Comments:	daily
☐	☐	Is all food being stored off the floor of walk-in cooler? Comments:	daily
☐	☐	Is cooler clean and free from mold and objectionable odors? Comments:	daily
☐	☐	Is proper cleaning and maintenance of walls and floors being conducted? Comments:	daily/as needed
☐	☐	Are foods stored in a manner to permit "First-in, First-out" rotation? Comments:	daily
☐	☐	Are any spoiled foods present? Is the "spoilage sheet" being used for documentation? Comments:	daily
☐	☐	Are raw foods stored separately from cooked foods? Comments:	daily
☐	☐	Are dairy products stored separately from strong-odor foods? Comments:	daily
☐	☐	Are cooked foods or other products removed from original containers, stored in clean, sanitized, covered containers and identified? Comments:	daily

Figure A-39 Self-Inspection Checklist (*continued on next page*)

		Walk-in Coolers (*continued*)	
Yes	**No**	**Inspected**	**Frequency**
☐	☐	Is there sufficient space in the cooler to permit good air circulation around the stored food? Comments:	daily

General Comments: _____

_____

_____

_____

_____

_____

Inspected By: _____

Date: _____

		Bar Area	
Yes	**No**	**Inspected**	**Frequency**
☐	☐	Are liquor dispensers free of leaks and dust? Comments:	daily
☐	☐	Are floor lights and ceiling tile OK? Comments:	daily
☐	☐	Is storage of liquor bottles proper? Are automatic pours free of dust? Comments:	daily
☐	☐	Are cooler and freezer free of broken glass and spills? Comments:	daily

Figure A-39 Self-Inspection Checklist (*continued*)

Bar Area (*continued*)			
Yes	**No**	**Inspected**	**Frequency**
☐	☐	Are all glasses stored on bar mats, rim down? Are insides of nozzles free of mold? Comments:	daily
☐	☐	Is underneath the counter free of spills and debris? Comments:	daily
☐	☐	Are drains clean and sanitized? Comments:	daily
☐	☐	Are floor and mats clean? Comments:	daily
☐	☐	Is bar area free of boxes and other litter? Comments:	daily

General Comments: _____

_____

_____

_____

_____

_____

Inspected By: _____

Date: _____

Figure A-39 Self-Inspection Checklist (*continued on next page*)

		All Restaurants, Safety	
Yes	**No**	**Inspected**	**Frequency**
☐	☐	Are smoking and non-smoking sections provided in dining area? Comments:	daily
☐	☐	Is there a sign posted restricting smoking in the back –of the house? Comments:	daily
☐	☐	Are there extinguishers present, properly mounted, and in view? Comments:	daily
☐	☐	Is the manager provided with a high-power flashlight in case of blackout? Comments:	daily
☐	☐	Are routes to exits, and the exits themselves, clearly marked? Comments:	daily
☐	☐	Is there a well-stocked first-aid kit nearby? Comments:	daily
☐	☐	Are employees instructed to report all slips, cuts, burns and falls immediately? Comments:	daily
☐	☐	Are employees trained in safe use of cleaning compounds? Comments:	daily
☐	☐	Are hand trucks, carts, and dollies used for receiving food and supplies in good repair? Comments:	daily

Figure A-39 Self-Inspection Checklist (*continued*)

Yes	No	Inspected	Frequency
		All Restaurants, Safety (*continued*)	
☐	☐	Are racks, hooks, and gloves provided so that dishwashers do not have to put their hands into sanitizing baths of hot water or chemicals? Comments:	daily
☐	☐	Is all food-preparation equipment in good repair and performing satisfactorily? Comments:	daily
☐	☐	Do employees know how to use equipment (steamers, dish machine, broiler, ovens, fryers) that their position requires them to use? Comments:	daily
☐	☐	Are the kitchen area and dining room potentially hazardous? Suggest improvements. Comments:	daily
☐	☐	Has dining-room manager received training in CPR and first aid? Does he or she know what to do if a guest is choking? Comments:	daily

General Comments: _____

_____

_____

_____

_____

_____

Inspected By: _____

Date: _____

Figure A-39 Self-Inspection Checklist (*continued on next page*)

		Room Service/In-Room Dining, General	
Yes	**No**	**Inspected**	**Frequency**
☐	☐	Is food stored properly? Comments:	daily
☐	☐	Are silver urn and utensils clean and polished? Comments:	weekly/as needed
☐	☐	Is flatware on tables clean and polished? Comments:	quarterly
☐	☐	Is linen stored properly on shelves? Comments:	daily
☐	☐	Are portable warmers clean? Comments:	monthly
☐	☐	Are table legs and wheels clean? Comments:	weekly/as needed
☐	☐	Are condiments clean and arranged for "first-in, first-out" rotation? Comments:	daily
☐	☐	Are food-storage shelves clean and free of dust and debris? Comments:	weekly
☐	☐	Is the floor clean and free from spilled food? Comments:	bi-weekly
☐	☐	Is trash receptacle cleaned and lined? Comments:	weekly

Figure A-39 Self-Inspection Checklist (*continued*)

		Room Service/In-Room Dining, General (*continued*)	
Yes	**No**	**Inspected**	**Frequency**
☐	☐	Is bun warmer clean? Comments:	daily
☐	☐	Is counter, top and bottom, clean and free of grease? Comments:	daily
☐	☐	Is coffee machine cleaned and sanitized regularly? Comments:	bi-weekly
☐	☐	Is water-glass storage area (wall, floor) clean? Comments:	weekly
☐	☐	Is refrigerator clean inside and outside? Comments:	weekly
☐	☐	Are products being stored and wrapped properly? Comments:	daily
☐	☐	Is hand sink supplied with soap, paper towels, hot and cold running water, and trash can? Comments:	daily
☐	☐	Are Queen Mary and Cres-Cors removed and cleaned periodically? Comments:	monthly
☐	☐	Is storage closet clean and organized? Comments:	weekly
☐	☐	Is there a bucket for soiled rags and sanitizer present? Comments:	daily

Figure A-39 Self-Inspection Checklist (*continued on next page*)

Room Service/In-Room Dining, General (*continued*)			
Yes	No	Inspected	Frequency
☐	☐	Is there a no-smoking sign posted in plain view? Comments:	daily
☐	☐	Is there a well-stocked first-aid kit nearby? Comments:	daily
☐	☐	Are all staff instructed to report all cuts, slips, burns and falls immediately? Comments:	daily
☐	☐	Are all electrical boxes accessible? Comments:	daily
☐	☐	Is there an evacuation map posted next to the elevator? Comments:	daily
☐	☐	Are routes to exits and the exits themselves clearly marked? Comments:	daily
☐	☐	Is there an extinguisher present, properly mounted and in view? Comments:	daily
☐	☐	Are flammable chemicals such as Sternos stored in a safe location away from other equipment? Comments:	daily
☐	☐	Are all flammable items kept clear of heating chemicals in food warmer? Comments:	daily

Figure A-39 Self-Inspection Checklist (*continued*)

		Room Service/In-Room Dining, General (*continued*)	
Yes	**No**	**Inspected**	**Frequency**
☐	☐	Do staff members know the hazards associated with their duties and related equipment? Comments:	daily
☐	☐	Is all food-preparation equipment in good repair and performing satisfactorily? Comments:	daily
☐	☐	Has supervisor received training in CPR, first aid, and the Heimlich maneuver? Comments:	as needed

General Comments: _____

_____

_____

_____

_____

_____

Inspected By: _____

Date: _____

Main Kitchen

		Kitchen General Area	
Yes	**No**	**Inspected**	**Frequency**
☐	☐	Is top of ice machine free of objects and door rim free of mold, and is there an ice scoop present? Comments:	daily
☐	☐	Is floor underneath ice machine clean? Are vent hood and side and back walls next to machine also clean? Comments:	daily

Figure A-39 Self-Inspection Checklist (*continued on next page*)

		Kitchen General Area (*continued*)	
Yes	**No**	**Inspected**	**Frequency**
☐	☐	Is time clock accessible? Comments:	daily
☐	☐	Are all trash cans clean inside and outside with clear plastic liners? Comments:	daily
☐	☐	Are all china and silverware shelves and area beneath shelves clean, organized and sanitary? Comments:	daily
☐	☐	Are walls next to dish machine area clean? Comments:	monthly
☐	☐	Is stained china being checked, removed from circulation and put in a chemical solution? Comments:	daily
☐	☐	Is spray hose free of leaks to prevent back-flow? Comments:	daily
☐	☐	Is glass-rack shelf clean and neat? Comments:	daily
☐	☐	Is silverware placed in bus tub with foil and soil loosening chemical solution? Comments:	daily
☐	☐	Are all chemicals stored in one central location away from clean china, glass and silverware? Comments:	daily

Figure A-39 Self-Inspection Checklist (*continued*)

Kitchen General Area (*continued*)			
Yes	**No**	**Inspected**	**Frequency**
☐	☐	Is the rinse temperature between 180 and190° F? Comments:	daily
☐	☐	Is the wash water at the proper temperature of 150–160° F? Comments:	daily
☐	☐	Are jets and nozzles cleaned of food particles and other obstructions and contaminants? Comments:	twice daily
☐	☐	Are dish dollies clean and soil-free? Comments:	monthly
☐	☐	Is dish machine free of lime and crust? Comments:	monthly
☐	☐	Are all kitchen staff wearing clean uniforms and effective hair restraints? Comments:	daily
☐	☐	Is hand sink supplied with soap, paper towels, hot and cold running water and trash can? Comments:	daily
☐	☐	Is the floor clean beneath glass racks? Are glass racks stored at least 6 inches off the floor? Comments:	daily

Figure A-39 Self-Inspection Checklist (*continued on next page*)

Kitchen General Area (*continued*)
General Comments: _____ _____ _____ _____ _____ _____ Inspected By: _____ Date: _____

Server Station Area			
Yes	**No**	**Inspected**	**Frequency**
☐	☐	Is espresso machine in proper working condition? Comments:	daily
☐	☐	Is toaster operating properly? Comments:	daily
☐	☐	Is milk machine clean, odorless, and free of ice buildup? Is there a thermometer inside? Compare with unit thermometer. Comments:	daily
☐	☐	Is hand sink clean and supplied with soap, towels, and hot and cold running water? Comments:	daily
☐	☐	Are wall and ceiling above counter clean and stain-free? Comments:	daily

Figure A-39 Self-Inspection Checklist (*continued*)

		Server Station Area (*continued*)	
Yes	**No**	**Inspected**	**Frequency**
☐	☐	Is storage of supplies clean, organized, and 6 inches above floor? Comments:	daily
☐	☐	Is ice-cream cooler clean and equipped with a thermometer? Comments:	daily

General Comments: _____
_____
_____
_____
_____
_____

Inspected By: _____

Date: _____

		Cold Line	
Yes	**No**	**Inspected**	**Frequency**
☐	☐	Is reach-in cooler clean and free from mold and debris? Comments:	daily
☐	☐	Are mats clean and floor swept twice daily? Comments:	daily
☐	☐	Are bottoms of refrigerators clean and free from mold and objectionable odors? Comments:	daily
☐	☐	Are refrigerators maintaining potentially hazardous foods at temperatures of 45° F or lower? Comments:	daily

Figure A-39 Self-Inspection Checklist (*continued on next page*)

		Cold Line (*continued*)	
Yes	No	Inspected	Frequency
☐	☐	Are refrigerators equipped with accurate thermometers? Comments:	daily
☐	☐	Are refrigerator shelves showing signs of rust? Comments:	weekly
☐	☐	Are foods stored in a manner to permit "first in, first" out rotation? Comments:	daily
☐	☐	Check the temperatures of at least three foods. Comments:	daily
☐	☐	Are display window and shelf clean and dust-free? Comments:	daily
☐	☐	Is salad bar properly maintaining 38–40° F product temperature? Comments:	daily
☐	☐	Are food handlers wearing hats or other effective hair restraints? Comments:	daily
☐	☐	Is hand sink supplied with soap, paper towels, hot and cold running water, and trash can? Comments:	daily
☐	☐	Is salad bar supplied with protective shields? Comments:	daily
☐	☐	Is ice-cream freezer clean and odor-free? Comments:	monthly

Figure A-39 Self-Inspection Checklist (*continued*)

		Cold Line (*continued*)	
Yes	No	Inspected	Frequency
☐	☐	Is wall clean and wiped down? Comments:	monthly
☐	☐	Is yogurt machine clean and wiped down with sanitizing solution? Comments:	daily
☐	☐	Is counter clean and wiped down with sanitizing solution? Comments:	daily
☐	☐	Are bottom shelves free of food and debris? Comments:	daily
☐	☐	Has dining-room manager been certified through a sanitation food-service course? Comments:	as needed

General Comments: _____
_____
_____
_____
_____
_____

Inspected By: _____
Date: _____

Figure A-39 Self-Inspection Checklist (*continued on next page*)

Pastry Kitchen

		Pastry Kitchen, General	
Yes	**No**	**Inspected**	**Frequency**
☐	☐	Are clean pots and pans stored upside down? Comments:	daily
☐	☐	Are floors underneath shelves clean? Comments:	daily
☐	☐	Is ice-cream freezer clean and equipped with thermometer? Comments:	weekly
☐	☐	Are all products wrapped? Comments:	daily
☐	☐	Is floor drain next to freezer clean? Comments:	bi-monthly
☐	☐	Is floor clean? Comments:	daily
☐	☐	Is dough machine clean? Comments:	daily
☐	☐	Is roll clean? Comments:	daily
☐	☐	Is sorbet machine clean? Comments:	daily

Figure A-39 Self-Inspection Checklist (*continued*)

Pastry Kitchen, General (*continued*)			
Yes	**No**	**Inspected**	**Frequency**
☐	☐	Is table mixer clean? Comments:	daily
☐	☐	Is cookie Cres-Cor clean? Comments:	monthly
☐	☐	Is floor mixer clean? Comments:	daily
☐	☐	Is wooden countertop clean and sanitized? Comments:	daily
☐	☐	Are stainless tables, top and underside, clean and sanitized? Comments:	daily
☐	☐	Is floor clean and free of food particles? Comments:	daily
☐	☐	Is reach-in cooler equipped with thermometer? Compare with thermometer on outside of unit. Comments:	daily
☐	☐	Is reach-in cooler free from mold and objectionable odors? Comments:	daily
☐	☐	Is food wrapped and stored properly? Comments:	daily
☐	☐	Is marble top clean and sanitized? Comments:	daily

Figure A-39 Self-Inspection Checklist (*continued on next page*)

		Pastry Kitchen, General (*continued*)	
Yes	**No**	**Inspected**	**Frequency**
☐	☐	Is food stored underneath counter wrapped and labeled? Comments:	daily
☐	☐	Are walls clean and free of dust? Comments:	monthly
☐	☐	Is grill top clean? Comments:	daily
☐	☐	Is large kettle clean? Comments:	daily
☐	☐	Is wall behind cooking units clean and free of odor? Comments:	daily

		Pastry Kitchen, Cooler	
Yes	**No**	**Inspected**	**Frequency**
☐	☐	Is cooker working properly and maintaining a temperature of between 38–45° F?	daily
		Comments:	
☐	☐	Are walls clean?	monthly
		Comments:	
☐	☐	Are lights in working order?	daily
		Comments:	
☐	☐	Are Cres-Cors being removed periodically for cleaning?	monthly
		Comments:	
☐	☐	Is food wrapped or covered properly?	daily
		Comments:	

Figure A-39 Self-Inspection Checklist (*continued*)

		Pastry Kitchen, Cooler (*continued*)	
Yes	**No**	**Inspected**	**Frequency**
☐	☐	Is freezer working properly and maintaining a temperature of 0° F or lower? Comments:	daily
☐	☐	Are walls clean? Comments:	monthly
☐	☐	Are lights in working order? Comments:	daily
☐	☐	Are carts being removed periodically for cleaning? Comments:	monthly
☐	☐	Is food wrapped or covered properly? Comments:	daily
☐	☐	Is floor clean? Comments:	daily

		Pastry Kitchen, Safety	
Yes	**No**	**Inspected**	**Frequency**
☐	☐	Is there a fire extinguisher present, properly mounted, and in clear view? Comments:	daily
☐	☐	Is there a well-stocked first-aid kit nearby? Comments:	daily
☐	☐	Are all staff instructed to report all cuts, slips burns, and falls to Security immediately? Comments:	daily
☐	☐	Is all food-preparation equipment in good repair and performing satisfactorily? Comments:	daily

Figure A-39 Self-Inspection Checklist (*continued on next page*)

		Pastry Kitchen, Safety (*continued*)	
Yes	**No**	**Inspected**	**Frequency**
☐	☐	Do associates know how to use equipment which their position requires them to use? Comments:	daily
☐	☐	Do employees unplug equipment before removing or before cleaning? Comments:	daily
☐	☐	Are spills and debris removed from the floor immediately? Comments:	daily
☐	☐	Are all electrical boxes clear of carts and debris? Comments:	daily
☐	☐	Has chef or supervisor received training in CPR and first aid? Comments:	daily

General Comments: _____
_____
_____
_____
_____
_____

Inspected By: _____
Date: _____

Figure A-39 Self-Inspection Checklist (*concluded*)

DATABASE INFORMATION AND COMPUTER SYSTEMS

After reading this section of the appendix, you should be able to:

- Make decisions concerning the purchase or upgrading of POS, purchasing, inventory, and menu analysis systems

- Evaluate computer system contracts and lease agreements

- Maintain database information and assign security access to users

- Develop computer systems contingency plans

Overview

A wide array of increasingly important issues pertaining to the functions and operations of computerized information systems are covered in this chapter. Issues covered include selection and procurement options, maintenance and security, and especially contingency planning for disaster recovery.

Buying or Upgrading of Point-of-Sales and Purchasing Systems

Considering upgrading or purchasing a new computer system often means that your current system is inadequate. Downtime may be affecting guest service. Perhaps the system is too expensive to maintain. The current system may negatively affect employee morale and productivity, often increasing overtime costs. Any of a number of problems can affect the decision to purchase or to upgrade. It is important not to compromise on an inadequate system that does not meet all of your needs. It may cost you more money in the long run if you settle for an inadequate system.

If your role is to assist your company with respect to the functionality of computer systems, first ascertain the transaction functionality of the current system. Conduct a thorough research of the current system by asking the system users to list in writing the advantages and disadvantages that they encounter in the current system. Their answers become the benchmark for new systems evaluation and testing. This survey will aid in the selection of a computer system that confronts all the problems addressed by the staff.

Contract and Lease Agreements

Many businesses prefer contracts and leasing agreements for their computer systems, often to avoid the initial capital outlay for a new system or to avoid inevitable obsolescence. In appraising the merits of the various contracts and lease agreements available, evaluate the following:

- Which equipment is offered through leasing agreements, and with which companies?

- Is the equipment already part of the company's inventory, and, if so, at what location?

- Is equipment properly tagged for identification?

- Is the working condition of the equipment acceptable?

- Review the maintenance agreements of the equipment, if any, to establish dates, clauses, and maintenance schedules.

- Establish the last date the equipment was inventoried.

- Check the equipment against fixed asset accounts reports.

- Consider other companies before signing an agreement.

- Establish written contingency or disaster recovery plans.

Reviewing the reliability and integrity of lease and contract documents could have a significant impact on control procedures. Furthermore, this review should include an inventory listing of all equipment with date of purchase or lease, date received, cost, location, and working condition.

Database Maintenance and Security Access

Though often ignored, questions of database maintenance have the potential to create serious and long-lasting problems for the financial and operational reporting of any company. At times, employees have greater levels of computer access than necessary to perform their duties. Physical access to the computer room is often unrestricted. Employees responsible for processing invoices into the purchasing database need to be trained on the physical layout of the storeroom and given a working knowledge of the products. Item classification as food versus beverage, for example, becomes vital for true cost reporting. Item descriptions must be verified for consistency, absence of duplication, and easy referencing.

These kinds of deficiencies often plague a system endlessly. It may be necessary to start from scratch in setting your system to higher standards. On a base level, it is crucial to establish a checks and balances system with more than one person verifying data. One person, for example, will enter the invoices into the purchasing system, and another person will post the invoice after verifying that the items have been entered properly with the correct quantity, price, and description. This checks-and-balances system is also extended to POS price look-up numbers (PLUs). If the general ledger classification of an item is as a beverage, then the invoice for that item should be classified into the beverage group for inventory extension and costing.

Computer Contingency Plan

Every company's financial health is dependent upon its computer data-processing systems. In varying degrees, these systems are vulnerable to partial or total violation and breakdown. Whether it is from a disgruntled employee, a fire, malicious outsiders, or operator error, company management must be aware of the possibility of a system loss.

Many businesses are unprepared for any computer system-related disaster; often companies have no contingency planning whatsoever. Companies who do have recovery plans often fall short in addressing the full range of possible disasters. Not all disaster recovery plans are inadequate, but for the most part, the issues and questions raised here do not fall into the standard disaster recovery risk scenarios, so they are often not planned upon. During an actual disaster is an inopportune time to encounter an overlooked issue. Some of the issues are not significant in themselves, but when merged with the problems arising from the process of disaster recovery, these issues can cause confusion and irritation to both the organization's staff and its executives. Most of these overlooked components can be categorized into two general groups: people issues and communication issues.

As part of any adequate disaster recovery plan, certain key staff members need to be available to enact the recovery plan. The first step in establishing a plan, therefore, is to determine which staff members need to be involved to recover individual systems. This recovery team will normally be composed of the information services staff, and, according to the system being addressed, the appropriate department head.

People Issues

During a disaster, whether the entire organization or just the information services department staff face relocation, people issues arise that ought to be addressed in a disaster recovery plan. These issues center on the ability of employees to actually get work done, and involve mainly the ability of the recovery team or the user departments to access computer systems. The information systems administrator needs to plan for access to current records in order to reconstruct damaged data. In addition, those who will be involved in recovery must be available for that task. A step-by-step recovery plan, delineating responsibilities, tasks, and requirements, must be in place and understood before disaster occurs. Running through the plan before a disaster will embed these needs and responsibilities in the minds of all concerned.

Communications Issues

For a recovery process to be successful, people must be able to perform their usual job responsibilities. For the user, business recovery requires communication with the recovery team and requires that the following situations occur:

- reestablishment of the information services department systems and telecommunications capabilities

- reestablishment of customer service applications

- reestablishment of the ability to perform the order entry, purchasing, payroll, general ledger, and/or other essential information processing applications

- assurance that logged transactions are carried forward to the point of the disaster or processing failure

- balancing to such known values of total transactions

- closing the applications safely

- reopening for a new business day (this step is the true test of a disaster recovery plan).

If your hotel or business tests the disaster plan, at least one test should include end-user participation. An end user is one whose work relies regularly on the information systems. In addition, selected customers should be included in a test to determine whether the hotel can actually conduct business in a normal fashion after a catastrophe. Management, end users, and customers get a better feeling about the continuity of business when they are involved at this level of recovery testing. Figure A-40 profiles communications needs and a process for reestablishing readiness.

Essential Service or Application	Covered Section in Your Manual	Affected Areas	Contingency Coordinator
Accounts Payable	*Example:* Enter the page in your manual for accounts payable	Accounting Cost Control Purchasing System	Cost Controller Purchasing Manager Assistant Controller
Inventory, Purchasing, and Menu Analysis		Accounts Payable General Ledger Purchasing Storeroom Cost Control	Assistant Controller Assistant Controller Dir. of Purchasing Cost Controller
Payroll System		All Departments	Department Heads
POS/Posting Systems		Restaurants Front Desk	Cost Controller Front Desk Manager Restaurant Manager

Figure A-40

Several hours of downtime for the online reservations, POS, front office, and financial records systems, to mention but a few, would constitute a disaster. Identify these critical areas of vulnerability in order to focus recovery planning on the areas most affected by actual disaster. View the information that you accumulate here as a resource that merits protection. Planning for disaster recovery is valuable because it provides an opportunity for the following:

- improved protection of your organization's assets
- reduced insurance costs
- enhanced site and information security
- improved information management

The extent of resources allocated to the development of a disaster recovery plan should be directly related to the value that management places on the information the plan is intended to protect. No organization is perfectly prepared for disaster and recovery preparedness, yet it is prudent to acknowledge the inevitability of disaster. Business must include the unthinkable as an integral part of management strategic planning.

Identify critical areas of vulnerability. Identify critical operations that could be affected by a disaster in order to improve the focus of the planning and the actual disaster recovery efforts. For example, for the safety of financial records, backup disks should be stored in a fireproof area outside the computer room. There should be no water sprinkler device in the computer room. All workstations or terminals should have some type of anti-virus program to detect and prevent contamination. And there should be a blueprint of all the cable lines connecting the computer systems.

Identify and classify potential types of disaster events. For each critical area of operational vulnerability, determine potential crises due to technological breakdown, confrontational issues, malevolent behavior, or management failure. Each type of crisis should be classified according to its potential severity, and resources allocated per the classification. Each operational area will have unique concerns. Consider asking staff opinion on what functions are critical, and how to maintain them in the event of a crisis. If you have never had disaster recovery plans before, chances are your staff will know from experience what is most crucial and what avenues of backup already exist. They probably developed current contingency measures.

Use disaster recovery technologies for everyday situations as a way to maintain the reliability of a disaster recovery plan. To do this, review your disaster contingency manual, and utilize it in every unforeseen situation relating to computer systems. Establishing open lines of communication through these recovery channels will assist when an actual disaster does occur. This will also help disaster recovery team members to maintain confidence in the plan.

Determine the critical timeliness associated with the effort to recover from a disaster. Set standards: When must the computer system or information processing application be sufficiently operational? Which operations are critical to return the organization to business? Which functions can be superseded in initial recovery attempts, and which will cost the company less money in the waiting?

Answer each question in the following impact analysis questionnaire by department; identify the risks of loss and clarify exposures resulting from a computer or other disaster in dollars and cents terms. Your management team should review the approach and results. An impact analysis is essential for numerous reasons. By definition, an impact analysis identifies the nature of an organization's business in detail. How and what does the business use to accomplish specific operational objectives? Which computer resources and functions are critical to the achievement of those objectives? What loss can the organization expect to incur from such disasters?

Performing a Risk Analysis

- Review the existing data center environment.
- Identify the critical information processing applications.

- Estimate the value of the assets used by these applications that must be protected.

- Quantify the estimated loss associated with the occurrence of a disaster in dollar terms.

- Use the questionnaire below to assess your business's vulnerability and to estimate resources necessary for disaster recovery.

Impact Analysis Questionnaire

Impact analysis consist of the user department and department manager describing and documenting the effects of system failure as it relates to applications, financial, controls, operation, and post-recovery issues.

Application Systems

1. List the application processing systems used in the department, including any outside computer services.

2. Write a brief description of each application, including its general purpose, the number of users, and the type of functions performed by the application (e.g., data entry, inquiry, and report generation).

3. For each type of function performed, specify the volume of the transactions processed and their dollar value for the following time periods: 8 hours, 24 hours, 48 hours, 72 hours, 5 days, 10 days, 30 days.

4. Describe the frequency of this application's use (e.g., daily, weekly, or monthly) and the variations in that use, including peak loads.

5. Provide detailed information about the application's regular hours of operation and any variations in that operation (e.g., those caused by seasonal conditions such as the year's end).

6. Provide detailed information on any reports or transaction listing generated for each application.

7. If the application passes information from one system to another, provide detailed information on the following:

   - the name of the system and/or any outside computer service

   - the types of transactions

   - the volume of transactions

   - the dollar value of transactions

   - how these transactions are linked to other systems

Financial Impact

1. Describe in dollar terms the likely impact of a computer disaster (e.g., the unavailability of each application system) on the regular operations of the department in terms of each of the following: 12 hours, 24 hours, 48 hours, 72 hours, 5 days, 10 days, and 30 days.

2. Describe the contractual obligations that would be affected by a computer disaster and qualify the exposure in dollars, including such issues as contracts with clients and responsibilities to customers.

3. Describe how a computer disaster within the department would affect your company image in the marketplace and the general community.

Management Information and Control

1. List the management controls that would be affected by a disaster that has made the computer unavailable to the department.

2. List the department's daily operational activities or functions that would be affected by a computer disaster. (Substantiate this answer with examples).

3. List the management reports that would be affected by the unavailability of the computer after the occurrence of a disaster.

4. Describe the impact of a computer disaster on management decision-making in the department.

Operational Impact

1. Detail the impact of a computer disaster on the level of service provided to other departments within your company or to its clients and guests.

2. Describe the impact of a computer disaster on the department's management reporting functions.

3. Estimate the department's productivity loss that would be caused by a computer disaster in business days and in dollars: 12 hours, 24 hours, 48 hours, 72 hours, 5 days, 10 days, and 30 days.

4. Estimate the number of hours, days, or weeks that could pass before the unavailability of the application system following a computer disaster would affect the regular operation of the department.

Post-recovery

1. Provide detailed information on how the backlog of data that would accrue during a period of downtime would be collected and processed following a disaster, and by whom, and at what cost.

2. Estimate the impact on the ongoing operations of the department of not recovering the backlog of information following a computer disaster.

3. Estimate the minimum processing period needed to support the department's operations if certain information processing applications were available for a minimum number of hours per day, week, or month during the disaster recovery period.

Summary

As described in the various chapters, computers can provide valuable assistance in performing many calculations in a timely fashion. The expense and quick obsolescence of computers make the process of purchasing and upgrading computers critical. After needs are determined, a decision must be made to purchase or lease a system.

Maintenance and security of databases are also critical. Access to the system should be restricted to only people with need and authorization. Checks and balances should be implemented. Likewise, a contingency plan needs to be designed in case of system failure or compromise. This should specify, step by step, processes and responsibilities for system recovery, as well as how business will be conducted in the interim. As with any emergency planning, the plan should be tested on a regular basis prior to actual need. While this may be costly, the cost incurred by failure to develop contingency and recovery plans may be even more expensive. Determine the potential cost of system failure and create a cost-effective alternative. By having users complete a questionnaire similar to the one described in the chapter, costs and cost-effective solutions may be analyzed.

Computer Systems Surveys

Transaction Functionality	Minimum Function of any system	Additional Feature (nice to have)	Not required by users	Do not Understand Function	TOTAL Responses	System 1	System 2	System 3
System Design								
Purchasing, Inventory, Recipe modules are integrated								
Purchasing, Inventory, Recipe modules can operate independently								
User controls and defines:								
System set-up tables for products, product groups, storerooms, departments, etc.								
System control tables for record retention, processing date, batch reports, etc.								
Data entry can be performed from various locations (storerooms, outlets)								
Item number and quantity only data required for defined item entries								
Help screens, data search and inquiry functions are accessible form data entry screens								
Automatic updating of inventory and recipe item costs as items are purchased								
Ability to reference capital project or work order numbers								
Tracking by lot or serial number supported								
Report writer available								
Inventory costing methods:								
First-In, First-Out								

Figure A-41 Computer Systems Surveys (*continued on next page*)

Transaction Functionality	Minimum Function of any system	Additional Feature (nice to have)	Not required by users	Do not Understand Function	TOTAL Responses	System 1	System 2	System 3
			User				System	
Weighted Average								
Last-In, First-Out								
Last Price Paid								
Audit Trail								
Complete audit trail of inventory and purchasing transactions								
Online inquiry of transactions by item, department, and document type								
Transaction records contain user name, workstation, date, and time of inquiry								
Interfaces								
Vendor invoices to accounts payable								
Inventory to general ledger asset control accounts								
Purchasing and inventory to job costing/project tracking system								
Point of Sale system sales data to Menu item module								
Point of Sale System sales data interfaced to produce outlet Menu Item Control variances								
Bar code reader/printer systems for ordering, receiving, issuing inventory								
Purchasing to and from vendor systems via electronic data transfer (e.g. Kraft-Link)								

Figure A-41 Computer Systems Surveys (*continued*)

Transaction Functionality	Minimum Function of any system	Additional Feature (nice to have)	User		TOTAL Responses	System		
			Not required by users	Do not Understand Function		System 1	System 2	System 3
Purchasing to vendors via automatic facsimile								
Recipe/menu items and cost updates to MIRACLE Catering Book								
Interface from MIRACLE catering orders to determine purchasing quantity requirements								
System Security								
Vendor purchase requisition dollar limits defined per user								
Hotel requisitions dollar limits defined per user								
Purchase order approval dollar limits defined per buyer								
Group user profiles for categories of users								
Users see all menus								
Users see only the menus to which they are authorized to access								
Level of security determined by:								
Function (Inventory, Purchasing, or Menu Analysis)								
Product Groups								
Other (please specify)___ USER NAME/PROFILE___								
Other (please specify)___ SYSTEM ADMINISTRATOR___								

Figure A-41 Computer Systems Surveys (*continued on next page*)

Transaction Functionality	Minimum Function of any system	Additional Feature (nice to have)	User		TOTAL Responses	System		
			Not required by users	Do not Understand Function		System 1	System 2	System 3
						1	2	3
Users defined by department and $ amount for automatic approval notification of documents								
Daily System Maintenance								
Automatic purge (based on user definition) of:								
Closed or deleted purchase / requisition records								
Transaction records and Audit Log **								
Incomplete purchase / requisition records								
Automatic generation and printing of:								
Purchase requisitions using reorder / par quantities								
Re-order reports								
Automatic print of scheduled reports								
Perform month end updates and report functions								
Automatic data back-up								
Product Description Parameters								
Product name screen display:								
30 characters								
Other (please specify)___64 Characters___								
Purchase order product description:								
1 line, 60 characters								
Other (please specify)___30–45 characters___								

Figure A-41 Computer Systems Surveys (*continued*)

Transaction Functionality	Minimum Function of any system	Additional Feature (nice to have)	Not required by users	Do not Understand Function	TOTAL Responses	System 1	System 2	System 3
			User				System	
Other (please specify)____64 Characters____								
Specification sheet product description:								
3 lines, 60 characters each								
Pre-formatted industry standard specification screens for product type								
1 line, 40 characters								
Purchase and Inventory Stock Control Factors: Product Description								
User defined units of measure and ratios for purchasing, inventory, and recipes								
Allowable percent variances from ordering price to invoiced price								
Allowable percent quantity variances from amounts ordered to received								
Preferred vendor								
Assigned vendor								
Low bid vendor								
Manufacturer name or code								
Bar code number								
Default tax code								
Alternate product number								
Last purchase vendor, date, and price—updated automatically								

Figure A-41 Computer Systems Surveys (*continued on next page*)

Transaction Functionality	User				TOTAL Responses	System		
	Minimum Function of any system	Additional Feature (nice to have)	Not required by users	Do not Understand Function		1 System 1	2 System 2	3 System 3
Inventory usage history								
Unlimited stock location definitions								
User defined:								
Product par quantity								
Product order points								
Product safety stock quantity								
System generated product order points based on historical usage								
Department and primary physical stock locations defined for each product								
User defined physical inventory period								
Order review period factors are user defined								
Products can be flagged for automatic vendor purchase requisition								
Products can be flagged for automatic departmental stock transfer								
Storeroom shelf or bin locations specified								
Product Inquiry and Catalog Functions								
Inquiry by:								
Product number								
Product name								
Storeroom reference								

Figure A-41 Computer Systems Surveys (*continued*)

Transaction Functionality	Minimum Function of any system	User — Additional Feature (nice to have)	User — Not required by users	User — Do not Understand Function	TOTAL Responses	System 1	System 2	System 3
Product group								
Vendor (distributor)								
Manufacturer name								
Product catalogs listed:								
Numerically								
Alphabetically by name								
Storeroom reference								
Product group								
Vendor (distributor)								
Manufacturer name								
Support Issues								
24 hour, 7 days a week support system								
Dial-up accessibility for trouble shooting and program download								
TOTAL RESPONSES:								
PERCENTAGE OF RESPONSES:								
General Vendor Information								
System support available 5 days per week								
Telephone support available								
Vendor completed a detailed system review in seattle								

Figure A-41 Computer Systems Surveys (*continued on next page*)

Transaction Functionality	Minimum Function of any system	Additional Feature (nice to have)	Not required by users	Do not Understand Function	TOTAL Responses	System 1	System 2	System 3
			User			System 1	System 2	System 3
Age of the software package								
Last update of software								
Number of current software systems installed								
The vendor maintains international installation and support services								
How long has the company been in business?								
System Cost Information								
Vendor-discountable software (5–10 Users)								
Other software requirements								
SUBTOTAL								
DISCOUNT RATE								
DISCOUNT VALUE								
TOTAL SOFTWARE								
Installation and Training								
Installation and Training: Number of Man Days								
TOTAL SYSTEM INVESTMENT								
AVERAGE SYSTEM PRICING								
Percent Variance to Average System Pricing								
Annual System Maintenance								

Figure A-41 Computer Systems Surveys (*continued*)

Transaction Functionality	User				TOTAL Responses	System		
	Minimum Function of any system	Additional Feature (nice to have)	Not required by users	Do not Understand Function		1 System 1	2 System 2	3 System 3
Storeroom Inventory Control								
Food and beverage items inventory control								
Non-food and beverage items inventory control								
Item quantity updates and adjustments are controlled by:								
Centralized inventory control department or person								
Issuing storeroom								
Outlet cost transfers automatically updated by issues from storeroom inventory								
Inventory adjustments require an explanation and the appropriate security level								
Inventory Management								
System automatically computes:								
Reorder points based upon user definition								
Safety stock based upon user definition								
Economic order quantities based on usage histories								
Order review reports generated daily based upon item specification								
Stock order review worksheets generated on demand by product group								
Zero balance inventory reports produced daily								

Figure A-41 Computer Systems Surveys (*continued on next page*)

Transaction Functionality	Minimum Function of any system	User			TOTAL Responses	System		
		Additional Feature (nice to have)	Not required by users	Do not Understand Function		System 1	System 2	System 3
Zero balance inventory reports produced on demand								
Automatic purchase requisitions generated for selected products that have reached order point								
Inventory Requisitions								
Issues from storerooms to cost centers								
Automatic back order requisitions for stock-outs								
Transfers between departments								
Returns to stock								
Requisitions entered interactively from cost centers								
Requisitions printed in the issuing storeroom stock location sequence for use as picking lists								
Frequently used products defined on a profile requisition for:								
Recall for requisition generation								
Automatic generation by day of week or specific date								
System generated Outlet Liquor Bottle Stickers per daily requisitions								
Physical Inventory								
Inventory periods controlled / defined by individual storeroom								

Figure A-41 Computer Systems Surveys (*continued*)

Transaction Functionality	User				TOTAL Responses	System		
	Minimum Function of any system	Additional Feature (nice to have)	Not required by users	Do not Understand Function		System 1	System 2	System 3
May be taken any number of time within an inventory period								
Items may be selected for counting by:								
Product class								
Stock location								
Item number								
Alphabetical listing								
Items that are selected for counting are "frozen" to prevent updates								
Count sheets are printed "blind" without perpetual or on-hand quantities noted								
Count sheets are printed with perpetual or on hand quantities noted								
Variance between physical and computed counts:								
Listed in descending order								
Listed in descending order with user defined filter								
Physical inventories by pen based system								
Physical inventories by bar code scanner								
Inventory Inquiry								
Display of individual requisitions								
Open line item inquiry (ability to view all period activity for item or product)								

Figure A-41 Computer Systems Surveys (*continued on next page*)

Transaction Functionality	Minimum Function of any system	Additional Feature (nice to have)	Not required by users	Do not Understand Function	TOTAL Responses	System 1	System 2	System 3
			User				System	
Requisition item summary display by department and item								
Current period and year to date balance display by item								
Inventory transactions displayed by:								
Product								
Department								
Document type (requisition, purchase order, purchase request)								
Inventory Report Options								
Inventory requisition transaction summary by product								
Inventory requisition summary by product groups								
MTD summary of requisitions by product groups								
Inventory items with zero balance								
Item usage analysis - flexible time frames, prior year comparison								
Inventory on-hand balance adjustments								
Inventory balance report								
Physical inventory variance report								
General Ledger distribution report								
Inventory stock status review worksheet								

Figure A-41 Computer Systems Surveys (*continued*)

Transaction Functionality	Minimum Function of any system	Additional Feature (nice to have)	Not required by users	Do not Understand Function	TOTAL Responses	System 1	System 2	System 3
			User			System 1	System 2 System	System 3
Merchandise received								
Re-Order report								
Inventory summary by location								
Inventory variance by location								
Inventory usage by location								
Slow moving / dead stock products								
Daily Record of Purchases and Issues (And B Forms) with MTD figures								
Month end summary: Daily Record of Purchases and Issues with YTD figures								
TOTAL RESPONSES								
PERCENTAGE RESPONSE BY CATEGORY								

Figure A-41 Computer Systems Surveys (*continued on next page*)

Hotel and Restaurant

INVENTORY FEATURES: Inventory, Purchasing, Recipe, Menu Analysis System

Transaction Functionality	Minimum Function of any system	Additional Feature (nice to have)	Not required by users	Do not Understand Function	TOTAL Responses	System 1	System 2	System 3
			User			System 1	System 2	System 3
Base Recipe Items (Items that are not directly priced or sold)								
Non-food and beverage items may be defined in recipes								
Created using any inventory stock, direct purchase, and other recipe items as ingredients								
Base recipe definition includes:								
Recipe name and category								
Number of servings								
Listing of ingredients								
Preparation method								
Cost updated automatically when recipe items are purchased								
May be linked to multiple outlets or storerooms for costing								
System tracks cost by storeroom and calculates average recipe cost								
Recipe types:								
Ingredient Recipe (used to establish credits and common units)								
Base Recipes (bulk preparation, butcher tests, items used in other recipes)								
Finished Recipes (menu items resolved to a per unit/serving cost)								

Figure A-41 Computer Systems Surveys (*continued*)

Transaction Functionality	User				TOTAL Responses	System		
	Minimum Function of any system	Additional Feature (nice to have)	Not required by users	Do not Understand Function		System 1	System 2	System 3
System supports nested recipes (recipes within recipes)								
May define in inventory locations for requisitions and transfers								
Capable of producing shopping lists of inventory items based upon recipe yield								
Capability for experimenting with quantities, yields, and costs								
Recipe retrieval for:								
Recipe editing								
Recipe printing								
Scaling quantities up or down								
Determination of food cost								
Cross referencing								
Conversion of units measured								
Basic Recipe Inquiry Functions								
Ingredient to recipe item cross reference display								
Recipe item inquiry listing defined ingredients								
Expanded ingredient listing of lower level ingredients (full recipe explosion)								
View or print multiple recipes:								
By type or category								
By date of last change								

Figure A-41 Computer Systems Surveys (*continued on next page*)

Transaction Functionality	Minimum Function of any system	Additional Feature (nice to have)	User			TOTAL Responses	System		
			Not required by users	Do not Understand Function			1 System 1	2 System 2	3 System 3
By cost percentage									
By dollar cost									
Menu Recipe Items (Items that are Directly Priced and Sold)									
Menu items are referenced by:									
Menu name									
Category									
System recipe number									
Point of Sale system or Price Look Up code									
Typing first few characters of recipe name activates a selection window									
May be defined with effective and expiration dates for inclusion in sales analysis									
May be defined by meal period									
Current and future sales prices defined with effective dates for sales analysis									
Daily sales updating options:									
Through workstation entry									
Automated interface to POS									
Sales pricing may be updated globally:									
Using a percentage increase or decrease									
Using a dollar value									
Experimental test sales and cost updates available for pro forma profit analysis									

Figure A-41 Computer Systems Surveys (*continued*)

Transaction Functionality	Minimum Function of any system	Additional Feature (nice to have)	User		TOTAL Responses	System		
			Not required by users	Do not Understand Function		1 System 1	2 System 2	3 System 3
Menu modeling allows changes in prices, ingredients, and portions:								
To indicate food cost dollars and percents								
To show variance from targets								
Menu Item Inquiry								
Sales analysis display by menu item category for:								
Daily item sales summaries								
MTD item sales summaries								
YTD items sales summaries								
Recipe and inventory item to item cross reference display								
Menu item reference display by cost center								
Recipe Menu Reports								
Menu item sales detail ranked by:								
Dollar sales								
Gross margin								
Units sold								
Menu engineering classifications (star, plow horse, puzzle, dog, etc.)								
Pro forma sales update analysis								
Test recipe expanded ingredient listing								

Figure A-41 Computer Systems Surveys (*continued on next page*)

Transaction Functionality	Minimum Function of any system	User			TOTAL Responses	System		
		Additional Feature (nice to have)	Not required by users	Do not Understand Function		System 1	System 2	System 3
Profile recipe options:								
Expanded ingredient listing								
Average cost ingredient listing								
Costs by selected department								
Item ingredient report (for kitchen use) to include:								
Item description								
Item type								
Unit of measure								
Count								
Preparation instruction								
Recipe cards to include ingredients, amounts, and instructions								
Recipe item descriptions report available by kitchen or outlet								
Menu item ingredients report available by kitchen or outlet								
Sales item description report available by outlet								
Ingredient search report by outlet								
Monthly / Weekly sales report by outlet to include:								
Description								
Price								

Figure A-41 Computer Systems Surveys (*continued*)

Transaction Functionality	Minimum Function of any system	Additional Feature (nice to have)	Not required by users	Do not Understand Function	TOTAL Responses	System 1	System 2	System 3
Count								
Total dollars in sales								
Percent of total revenue								
Gross margins								
Other (please specify) ___ Food Cost___								
Other (please specify) ___ Comparative Date Ranges___								
Comparative sales reports by outlet by day of the week:								
Description								
Count								
Total dollars in sales								
Percent of total revenue								
Other (please specify) ___ Percentage comparisons for each item___								
Theoretical profit from sales report by outlet:								
Description								
Price								
Theoretical cost (dollars and percent)								
Count								
Total dollars								
Cost of sales (dollars and percent)								

Figure A-41 Computer Systems Surveys (*continued on next page*)

Transaction Functionality	User				TOTAL Responses	System		
	Minimum Function of any system	Additional Feature (nice to have)	Not required by users	Do not Understand Function		System 1	System 2	System 3
Sales report by menu item:								
Units sold								
Total dollars								
Cost								
Gross margin								
Percent cost								
Contribution margin by category for each menu item								
Sales summary showing MTD and YTD sales								
Sale summaries by user defined market groups								
Exception report, identifying menu items over cost percentage target								
System generated Standard Portion Control Sheets for kitchens and butcher shop								
System format available for Banquet Beverage Control Form entry								
TOTAL RESPONSES:								
PERCENTAGE OF RESPONSES:								

Figure A-41 Computer Systems Surveys (*continued*)

Transaction Functionality	Minimum Function of any system	Additional Feature (nice to have)	User			TOTAL Responses	System		
			Not required by users	Do not Understand Function			System 1	System 2	System 3
							1	2	3
Cashier Open and Sign-In Functions									
Server open									
Server sign-in									
Cashiers allowed to service checks									
Compulsory sign-in for reorders									
Prevent servers from transaction settlement									
Time-In and Time-Out									
Banked server operation									
Operator Sign-In Functions									
Multiple server / bartender sign-in									
Compulsory closed drawer									
Magnetic stripe or ID badge reader sign-in capabilities									
Training mode									
Operator Sign-Out Functions									
Automatic sign-out									
Manual sign-out									

Figure A-41 Computer Systems Surveys (*continued on next page*)

Transaction Functionality	Minimum Function of any system	Additional Feature (nice to have)	Not required by users	Do not Understand Function	TOTAL Responses	System 1	System 2	System 3
Basic Guest Check Functions								
Opening check								
Process reorders								
Change table number								
Change number of persons								
Ability to settle check								
Settlement correction noted by revenue center								
Multiple checks per table								
Ability to split check after it is open								
Ability to combine electronic (soft) checks								
Electronic guest check retention and storage in system:								
Until End of Day								
Until End of Day, for the day after the transaction								
One Week								
Automatic soft check number generation (versus the table number plus transaction number)								
Tip reporting functions:								
Transfer partial revenues to different servers from one check								
Ability to transfer checks between servers								

Figure A-41 Computer Systems Surveys (*continued*)

Transaction Functionality	Minimum Function of any system	Additional Feature (nice to have)	Not required by users	Do not Understand Function	TOTAL Responses	System 1	System 2	System 3
Guest Check Format								
Electronic (soft) check								
Paper check without bar code								
Paper check with bar code								
Sales Transaction Order Entry								
Price look up function and preset keys								
Open departments								
Price modifiers								
Print modifiers								
Promotional pricing								
Menu item quantity up to 999								
Menu item quantity up to 9,999								
Cover count quantities up to 999								
Cover count quantities up to 9,999								
Mnemonics up to 12 characters								
Mnemonics up to 18 characters								

Figure A-41 Computer Systems Surveys (*continued on next page*)

Transaction Functionality	Minimum Function of any system	Additional Feature (nice to have)	Not required by users	Do not Understand Function	TOTAL Responses	System 1	System 2	System 3
Correction Keys								
Error correct on the last item entered								
Void capability for items previously entered								
Void transaction after item totaled								
Cancel transaction before items are totaled								
Discounts								
Transaction level:								
Fixed dollar								
Fixed percentage								
Open dollar								
Open percent								
Item level:								
Food Discounts								
Food and Liquor Discounts								
Liquor Discounts								
Coupons								
Fixed dollar (Premier, Special Packages, Tours)								

Figure A-41 Computer Systems Surveys (*continued*)

Transaction Functionality	Minimum Function of any system	User			TOTAL Responses	System		
		Additional Feature (nice to have)	Not required by users	Do not Understand Function		1 System 1	2 System 2	3 System 3
Fixed percent								
Open dollar coupon								
Tax								
Tax exempt								
Manual tax								
Tax percentage								
Value added tax								
Canadian taxing								
Other (please note)								
Transaction Total								
Depressing "Total" will initiate automatic tax calculation								
Fast Finalize (Cash bars, No guest check opened)								
Initiate printing								
Depressing will initiate customer viewing of rear total display								
Menu item sorting (combine like items)								
Automatic service charge posting (Room Service)								

Figure A-41 Computer Systems Surveys (*continued on next page*)

Transaction Functionality	User				TOTAL Responses	System		
	Minimum Function of any system	Additional Feature (nice to have)	Not required by users	Do not Understand Function		1 System 1	2 System 2	3 System 3
Running subtotal								
Prompt for number of persons								
Transaction Settlement / Tracking								
Numeric entry tendered								
Exact amount tendered								
Preset tendereds ($5, $10, $20, etc.)								
Paid outs								
Currency conversion								
Complimentary tendereds								
Tendered Key Options:								
Depressing key will initiate change dispenser								
Depressing key will initiate drawer opening								
Account number entry check digit verification for city ledger accounts								
Ability to depress tender key for exact change								
Stub receipt with compulsory gift certificate								
Multiple tenders will print 1 check per settlement type								
Charge posting capabilities								

Figure A-41 Computer Systems Surveys (*continued*)

Transaction Functionality	Minimum Function of any system	Additional Feature (nice to have)	User			TOTAL Responses	System		
			Not required by users	Do not Understand Function			1 System 1	2 System 2	3 System 3
Coupon settlement									
Integrated credit card authorizations capabilities									
Function Keys									
Keyboard positioning of function keys is variable									
Screen display key									
Repeat last item key									
Print a receipt key									
Change location key									
No sale key									
Help keys									
Menu shift key									
Terminal mode switch key (guest check versus cash bar receipt mode)									
Preset supervisor function keys									
Charge tip key									
Cash bar key									
Tips paid out key									
List function keys:									
Price Modifier numbers									

Figure A-41 Computer Systems Surveys (*continued on next page*)

Transaction Functionality	User					System		
	Minimum Function of any system	Additional Feature (nice to have)	Not required by users	Do not Understand Function	TOTAL Responses	System 1	System 2	System 3
Print Modifier numbers								
Price Look Up numbers								
Departmental specific numbers								
Void by transaction key								
Audit Journal								
Journal printer								
Electronic data capture								
Employee Time Keeping								
Time-in function								
Time-out function								
Ability of time keeping functions to interface to Payroll system								
Miscellaneous								
Customer display screens (so customer can view transaction)								
Up to two cash drawers per terminal								
Track activity data by location								
Touchscreen terminals								
Hand held terminals								

Figure A-41 Computer Systems Surveys (*continued*)

Transaction Functionality	Minimum Function of any system	Additional Feature (nice to have)	Not required by users	Do not Understand Function	TOTAL Responses	System 1	System 2	System 3
Hand held touchscreen terminals								
Pen-based handheld device								
Integrated magnetic stripe readers								
Integrated signature capture capability								
Minimum of 300 server numbers per system								
Minimum of 400 server numbers per system								
Minimum of 30 meal periods								
Minimum of 50 meal periods								
Minimum of 3,000 menu items with pricing								
Minimum of 5,000 menu items with pricing								
Room Service Functions								
Server assignment when order is ready for delivery								
Automatic gratuity, service charge posting								
Ability to batch enter Door Knob orders after pick-up								
Batched (entered) door knob order report formats:								
Orders are grouped by like item								

Figure A-41 Computer Systems Surveys (*continued on next page*)

Transaction Functionality	User						System		
	Minimum Function of any system	Additional Feature (nice to have)	Not required by users	Do not Understand Function	TOTAL Responses		1 System 1	2 System 2	3 System 3
Orders are grouped by delivery location and time									
Batched orders are sent to kitchen remote printers at appropriate time									
Kitchen printer automatically sorts orders with similar delivery time to facilitate preparation									
Other Applications									
"Hot Key" from PC to POS for Service Express (network compatible)									
Banquets									
Portable stand alone terminals that will down load information to host									
Team Service Applications									
Automatic separation of tips and revenue between team members									
Point of Sale Interfaces									
Interface to in-room (TV) service ordering system									
Front Office guest room billing									
Back Office journal posting									
Server tip reporting data to the payroll system									

Figure A-41 Computer Systems Surveys (*continued*)

Transaction Functionality	Minimum Function of any system	Additional Feature (nice to have)	User		TOTAL Responses	System		
			Not required by users	Do not Understand Function		1 System 1	2 System 2	3 System 3
Inventory, Purchasing, Menu Analysis System								
Private Bar systems								
Banquet Sales systems								
Bar code hand held devices								
Retail operation applications								
System Reports								
Easy report customization by "low-tech" staff								
Cashier Financial								
Server Financial with average check								
Outlet Financial with average check computation by meal period								
Outlet Financial with average check (minus staff and promo sales)								
Hourly activity by outlet								
Automatic timed printing of server open checks (to monitor buffet and brunch)								
Sales activity analysis period reports for:								
Daily								
Weekly								
Monthly								

Figure A-41 Computer Systems Surveys (*continued on next page*)

Transaction Functionality	Minimum Function of any system	Additional Feature (nice to have)	Not required by users	Do not Understand Function	TOTAL Responses	System 1	System 2	System 3
			User			System 1	System 2	System 3
Yearly								
Sales analysis must break out covers by meal periods								
Maximum system End of Day down time not to exceed 30 minutes								
Automated Back Office Food and Beverage Journals to include server / cashier settlements								
Customized automated employee tip reporting formats								
Support Issues								
24 hour, 7 days a week support system								
Dial-up accessibility for trouble shooting and program download								
TOTAL RESPONSES:								
PERCENTAGE RESPONSES:								
General Vendor Information								
System support available 7 days a week								
Telephone support available 24 hours per day								
Vendor completed a detailed system review								

Figure A-41 Computer Systems Surveys (*continued*)

Transaction Functionality	Minimum Function of any system	Additional Feature (nice to have)	User		TOTAL Responses	System		
			Not required by users	Do not Understand Function		System 1	System 2	System 3
						1	2	3
Age of software package								
Last update of software								
Number of current software systems installed								
Vendor maintains international installation and support services								
How long has the company been in business?								
System Cost Information								
Hardware								
Software								
Software, Labor Module								
SUBTOTAL								
DISCOUNT RATES								
DOLLAR DISCOUNT								
Installation and Training Expense								
Installation and Training Number of Man Days								
TOTAL SYSTEM INVESTMENT								

Figure A-41 Computer Systems Surveys (*continued on next page*)

Transaction Functionality	Minimum Function of any system	Additional Feature (nice to have)	Not required by users	Do not Understand Function	TOTAL Responses	System 1 System 1	System 2 System 2	System 3 System 3
				User			**System**	
AVERAGE SYSTEM PRICING								
Percent variance to average system pricing								
Annual Maintenance Information								
Extended Program								
Basic Program								
Depot Program								
Purchasing Request Records								
Ability to process food and beverage item purchasing								
Ability to process non food and beverage item purchasing								
Allow purchase of products not defined in system								
Typing first few characters of product name activates a selection window								
Permit specification of generic products								
Automatic line numbering								
Multiple sort options for item sequencing								
Defaults programmed for:								
Item description								

Figure A-41 Computer Systems Surveys (*continued*)

Transaction Functionality	Minimum Function of any system	Additional Feature (nice to have)	User			TOTAL Responses	System		
			Not required by users	Do not Understand Function			System 1	System 2	System 3
							1	2	3
Unit of measure									
Variance percent									
Account numbers									
Vendor									
Low bid prices used as default for purchase order entry of defined products									
Last purchase price used as default for purchase order entry of defined products									
Allow comments in body of purchase requests									
Tax, discounts, freight charges prorated over product items									
Ability for authorized person to approve purchase requests on-line									
User assigned:									
Requisition numbers									
Purchase order numbers									
Market list numbers									
System assigned:									
Requisition numbers									
Purchase order numbers									
Market list numbers									
Printing of Receiving Worksheet in the Receiving area:									

Figure A-41 Computer Systems Surveys (*continued on next page*)

Transaction Functionality	Minimum Function of any system	Additional Feature (nice to have)	User Not required by users	Do not Understand Function	TOTAL Responses	System 1 System 1	System 2 System 2	System 3 System 3
when purchase order is generated								
on date item is due to be delivered								
Unlimited number of lines on purchase request								
Departmental Purchasing Requests								
Distributed entry by departments								
Centralized entry by authorized users								
The following areas / numbers are identified:								
Charge department								
Ship department								
Capital project number								
Job cost number								
Fast line entry support for defined products								
Credit memo record entered as a control feature for stock returns								
Types of departmental purchase request supported by the system:								
Standard blank format								
Pre-defined profiles used to generate standard orders								
Standard blanket releases (multi-shipment, annual orders, i.e. drop ship)								

Figure A-41 Computer Systems Surveys (*continued*)

Transaction Functionality	Minimum Function of any system	Additional Feature (nice to have)	User		TOTAL Responses	System		
			Not required by users	Do not Understand Function		1 System 1	2 System 2	3 System 3
Purchase Orders, Market Lists, etc.								
Centralized entry by authorized purchasing users								
Departmental entry by authorized purchasing users								
Items grouped by buyer, vendor, and requesting department for selection								
Items may be entered directly								
Items may be selected from multiple or partial departmental requests								
Departmental purchase requests closed by selection to purchase orders								
Capital project orders that exceed budget are rejected by system								
Exceeding buyer approval limit requires separate entry for approval								
Purchase orders may be closed with partial receipts								
Purchase orders are retained in the system until all items are received								
Interactive automatic suggested order amounts based upon on-hand inventories and banquet events								

Figure A-41 Computer Systems Surveys (*continued on next page*)

Transaction Functionality	User				TOTAL Responses	System		
	Minimum Function of any system	Additional Feature (nice to have)	Not required by users	Do not Understand Function		1 System 1	2 System 2	3 System 3
Blanket Purchase Orders: Multi-Shipment, Annual Orders, Drop Ship, etc.								
May be defined with or without product items								
Dollar limits defined per blanket contract and per release								
Automatic review based on review date and percentage of $ amount released								
May be authorized for release by specific departments								
System maintains number and dollar amount of releases by department								
System maintains detail history of item purchases by blanket purchase orders								
Receiving								
Purchase order or market lists updated by entry of invoice or packing list								
Receiving confirmation log (record of packing list) maintained as separate record								
Receiving confirmation log created directly from user selected P.O. items								
Received status updated in P.O. item by receiving confirmation log								
Worksheets printed with remaining open items during receiving logging								
Receiving confirmation log may be modified or deleted until selected for invoicing								

Figure A-41 Computer Systems Surveys (*continued*)

Transaction Functionality	Minimum Function of any system	Additional Feature (nice to have)	User		TOTAL Responses	System		
			Not required by users	Do not Understand Function		1	2	3
						System 1	System 2	System 3
Inventory (perpetual) stock records updated at P.O. prices by receiving log entry								
Bar code reader support for receiving								
Automatic printing of bar code labels for expected deliveries								
Vendor Invoices								
Items may be entered directly or selected from open P.O. and receiving logs								
May be created from multiple or partial P.O.s								
P.O.s and receiving logs automatically closed by selection to invoices								
Regular and credit adjustment invoices supported								
Computed extensions verified against invoice totals								
Price, quantity, vendor, and extension variances displayed for resolution								
Payment due date specified by vendor for transfer to Accounts Payable								
Ability to track invoices by batch ID number entries for Accounts Payable interface								
Vendor Bid Specifications								
Defined by buyer and product group								

Figure A-41 Computer Systems Surveys (*continued on next page*)

Transaction Functionality	User				TOTAL Responses	System		
	Minimum Function of any system	Additional Feature (nice to have)	Not required by users	Do not Understand Function		System 1	System 2	System 3
Automatic printing of vendor bid specifications								
On demand printing of vendor bid specifications								
Items entered with different maximum quantities for price bids with quantity breaks								
Bid prices may be entered with future effective dates								
Purchasing Reports								
Purchase history reports								
Merchandise received								
Monthly purchase summary								
Item, product group, location purchases								
Cost changes / variance reports								
Cost by product category reports								
Reconciliation of General Ledger accrual expense accounts (C.G. and U., etc.)								
Distributor / Manufacturer Purchase history by dollars and products								
Total Responses:								
Percentage of Responses:								

Figure A-41 Computer Systems Surveys (*concluded*)

Cost Controller Checklist

DAILY ACTIVITIES AND REPORTING RESPONSIBILITIES			
	Key Officers' Names		
Assignments	**Completed by**	**Dead Line**	**Completed**
Review F&B requisitions—			
Note extensions, unit prices and any discrepancies			
Butcher sales reconciliation to POS			
Review issues, including returns			
Reconcile requisitions to Inventory			
A bid sheet comparison to invoices			
Review Food to Bar and Bar to food			
Prepare average F&B check report			
Banquet Beverage Controls as needed			
Reconciliation of host and cash bar			
Review daily Flash Report			
Weekly Activities and Reporting Responsibilities			
Review inter-bar Transfers			
Review and summarize credits to cost			
Spot-check portion control			
Spot-check storeroom stock rotation and controls			
Spot-check weekly bid sheets			
Review buying procedures			
Observe banquet serving control			
Spot-check bar pars, rotating bars			
Review Cafeteria food requisition			
Walk through all kitchen storage			
Check MOD Key log for after-hours			
Observe storeroom issuing and receiving procedures			
Compare F&B purchase prices to reveal increases			
Review cost for special functions, e.g. special brunches, advertised events, etc			
Monthly Activities and Reporting			
Prepare inventory memo			

Figure A-42 Cost Controller Checklist (*continued on next page*)

Cost Controller Checklist (*concluded*)

Prepare outlets for inventory			
Review Unit/Case prices before inventories			
Complete inventories procedures			
Prepare Cost Controller Checklist			
Do outlets P&L pages			
Cover Analyses Report			
Analyze menu for popularity and popularity			
Review F&B dead stock list			
Review potentials - rotating basis			
Conduct butcher potential variances			
Market basket survey			
Annual Activities and Reporting			
Third quarter, prepare business plan			

Figure A-42

Forms

Beverage Pour Cost Sheet

Product Number	Item Name	Size of Item	# of Units per Bottle	Cost Pour in Ounces	Mixers	Total Cost	Selling Price in dollars	Selling Price in Percent

Figure A-43

Weekly Food Bid Form

Date Received: BID IN EFFECT FROM: TO:

Prepared By:

Product Number	Item Description	Pack Size	Brand Name	Unit of Measure	Vendor	Vendor	Vendor	Vendor

Figure A-44

Standard Recipes Cost Sheet

RECIPES COST SHEET

DATE:_____

ITEM:_____

OUTLET:_____

PORTION YIELD:_____

MEAL PERIOD:_____

PORTION SIZE:_____

Item #	Ingredient	Quantity	U/M	Cost Data		
				Unit	Cost	Total Cost
			TOTAL COST =			

PORTION COST : _____

SALES PRICE : _____

COST PERCENT: _____

Figure A-45

To Be Used for Authorizing all Spillage, Breakage, and Spoilage

DATE:_____

AUTHORIZATION:_____

OUTLET:_____

Name of Server, Chef, or Bartender	Number of Drink, Food, or Items Lost	Brand or Product #	Type:W -Wine L - Liquor F - Food	Value per Unit	Total Value	Reason

Figure A-46

Interdepartmental Transfers

Note: Send a copy to the Accountant

Date:

To – Outlet: From – Outlet:

Manager Approval: Manager Approval:

Item Number	Item	Quantity	Item Cost	Total Cost

Figure A-47

Guidelines on Discrimination based on Gender (From the Code of Federal Regulations, Vol. 29, § 1604.11). Sexual Harassment

a) Harassment on the basis of sex is a violation of Sec. 703 of Title VII. Unwelcome sexual advances, requests for sexual favors, and other verbal or physical conduct of a sexual nature constitute sexual harassment when (1) submission to such conduct is made either explicitly or implicitly a term or condition of an individual's employment, (2) submission to or rejection of such conduct by an individual is used as a basis for employment decisions affecting such individual, or (3) such conduct has the purpose or effect of unreasonable interfering with an individual's work performance or creating an intimidating, hostile or offensive working environment.

b) In determining whether alleged conduct constitutes sexual harassment, the Commission will look at the record as a whole and at the totality of the circumstances, such as the nature of the sexual advances and the context in which the alleged incidents occurred. The determination of the legality of a particular action will be made from the facts, on a case by case basis.

c) With respect to conduct between fellow employees, an employer is responsible for acts of sexual harassment in the workplace where the employer (or its agents or supervisory employees) knows or should have known of the conduct, unless it can show that it took immediate and appropriate corrective action.

d) An employer may also be responsible for the acts of nonemployees, with respect to sexual harassment of employees in the workplace, where the employer (or its agents or supervisory employees) knows or should have known of the conduct and fails to take immediate and appropriate corrective action. In reviewing these cases the commission will consider the extent of the employer's control and any other legal responsibility which the employer may have with respect to the conduct of such nonemployees.

e) Prevention is the best tool for the elimination of sexual harassment. An employer should take all steps necessary to prevent sexual harassment from occurring, such as affirmatively raising the subject, expressing strong disapproval, developing appropriate sanctions, informing employees of their right to raise and how to raise the issue of harassment under Title VII, and developing methods to sensitize all concerned.

Other related practices: Where employment opportunities or benefits are granted because of an individual's submission to the employer's sexual advances or requests for sexual favors, the employer may be held liable for unlawful sex discrimination against other persons who were qualified for but denied that employment opportunity or benefit.

Index

Note: Page numbers followed by *f* refers to figures.